Beautiful Theories

Elizabeth W. Bruss (1944–1981) was associate
professor of English at Amherst College. She is the
author of *Autobiographical Acts: The Changing
Situation of a Literary Genre,* also published by Johns
Hopkins.

ELIZABETH W. BRUSS

Beautiful Theories .

THE SPECTACLE OF DISCOURSE
IN CONTEMPORARY CRITICISM

The Johns Hopkins University Press
Baltimore & London

This book has been brought to publication with the generous
assistance of the Andrew W. Mellon Foundation.

The Johns Hopkins University Press, Baltimore, Maryland 21218
The Johns Hopkins Press Ltd., London

Library of Congress Cataloging in Publication Data

Bruss, Elizabeth W.
  Beautiful theories.

  Includes bibliographical references and index.
  1. Criticism—United States. I. Title.
PN99.U5B77   801'.95'0973   81-48178
ISBN 0-8018-2670-5   AACR2

Contents

Publisher's Note

At the time of her death, in May 1981, Elizabeth W. Bruss was completing final revisions of *Beautiful Theories*. Her husband and literary executor, Neal H. Bruss, prepared a final text for the publisher and read the proofs for the work.

Research for this volume was generously assisted with grants from the John Simon Guggenheim Foundation and the trustees of Amherst College.

I
Suddenly, an Age of Theory

> ... philosophers, bound by theoretical or logical con-
> siderations, have lacked a sensibility to the concreteness
> and individuality of works of art. . . . To specify is to
> limit, to create a well defined, but much narrower re-
> lation to literature.
>
> WILLIAM RIGHTER, *Logic and Criticism*

It was late in the 1960s when the symptoms, heretofore fugitive and for the most part manageable, could no longer be ignored. The Anglo-American literary community, which had been erected on the rock of Johnsonian empiricism and Arnoldian sensibility, found itself suddenly possessed by an alien spirit of speculation, infected by an unspeakable cant of theoretical abstractions. The signs were everywhere (as, indeed, everything seemed destined to become yet another sign): Professional meetings that might once have spent their sessions in admiring the visionary system of a Blake or a Yeats turned instead to the great system-building critics and the deconstructive subverters of those systems; graduate programs in "poetics" began to displace the more familiar period specializations; and the annual bibliography of the Modern Language Association (which had made no official mention of "literary theory" until 1960, and then continued to group it together, indifferently, with "aesthetics" and "literary criticism" until 1967) was reorganized to create a separate subdivision devoted exclusively to "Literary Criticism and Literary Theory"—and the number of entries immediately began to swell from a scant two hundred in 1967 to over six hundred in 1975.[1] All at once the books that were most honored, most frequently cited or condemned, were no longer scholarly monographs on the roots of Restoration comedy or readings of the later Eliot but were instead the collected papers of the latest international symposium (e.g., *The Languages of Criticism and the Sciences of Man*)—books in which one set of critics offered introductions to another, complete with histories and arduous appraisals of the structure of their arguments, their ideological positions, even their characteristic rhetorical modes (Culler's *Structuralist Poetics*, Jameson's *Prison-House of Language* and *Marxism and Form*, de Man's *Blindness and Insight*, Said's *Beginnings*, to name but a few key examples).

Even more dramatic perhaps was the massive outpouring of new journals—*Critical Inquiry, Diacritics, New Literary History, Glyph, Semiotexte, Sub-stance, Ideology and Literature*, the *Oxford Literary Review, Praxis, Poetics,*

Boundary = 2, *Salamagundi*, *Clio*, *New German Critique*, *Telos*, *Semiotica*—that reserved substantial portions or even the whole of each issue for broad speculative debates and minute studies of individual critical texts.[2] But as significant as the sheer quantity was the quality of these new journals— self-consciously interdisciplinary, often deliberately blurring the bound- aries of the political and the aesthetic, and (most notable, against the background of a "perennial English disinclination to use a specialist vocabulary")[3] almost aggressively extraordinary in their language. The breadth of reference might suggest the rebirth of the encyclopedist or the man of letters, but these new letters were obdurately, forbiddingly opaque. The old dream of a common language had shrunk, in the cooler light of the morning after, to (at best) an antique curiosity or (at worst) a piece of malevolent sophistry—"The terrorism of plain language, that mythical weapon of those who prefer the comforting repetition of the ideological caress," as Stephen Heath put it.[4] With no language capable of claiming the loyalty of all classes and professions, and with the academy itself divided into contending and mutually unintelligible research tra- ditions, the only hope seemed to lie in strenuous invention and artifice. Hence the distinctively synthetic cast to this new theoretical writing, its penchant for the chemical and the mechanical, for terms derived from cybernetics, economics, or topology rather than from the homelier idioms of horticulture and handicraft. Look where one would, it was becoming increasingly difficult to find anything that seemed scaled to fit the indi- vidual, any mirror that gave back the image of a coherent, separate self. Instead, only plurals and collective nouns (*agencies, intensities, the symbolic,* and *the text*) abstract nominal processes (*figuration, emplotment,* and of course *writing/écriture*), and a kind of jaded familiarity that took what had once seemed complex, unpredictable exercises of judgment and casually compressed them into predictable single verbs (*valorize* or *thematize*). Little food remained for narcissism in this discourse where positions were more stable than their occupants, which saw, behind the veil of superficial variation, the same essential operations repeated endlessly.

Traditional literary humanism thus found itself bereft of both its object and its end, but not yet vanquished as long as the older and more well-established journals remained immune. It was one thing for a par- venu to trouble itself about the *cogito* but quite another for a publication like *MLN*, with its long and honorable history of patient philological accumulation, to suddenly forego such rigor for the sharp stochastic pleasures of epistemological controversy. When even the standard pub- lications were involved, those that were by definition "normal" and, indeed, responsible for defining what normality might be, it was impos- sible to dismiss the new tendencies as merely transient aberrations. A change in the intellectual and discursive manners of the articles that made their way into *PMLA* was (and is) a reliable indication of some broader force for change affecting the Anglo-American literary establishment as a whole. Consider the language of a study of Kafka published in 1968:

> One of the salient stylistic features in Kafka's first-person stories is his tendency to use the grammatical present as a narrative tense. . .
>
> [This] gives the illusion of capturing the speaker's situation at the moment of experience, and does so in the only way available to fiction written in the first person. . . . In contrast to a third-person narrative, a first-person narrative cannot eliminate the temporal distance between the moment of narration and the narrated moment while remaining within the past tense. . . . Only if these two selves become fused, if the moment of narration coincides with the moment of experience, can a first-person narrative achieve absolute immediacy. By using the present tense, the act of narration is itself shortcircuited and therefore becomes unreal; the result is an interior monologue. . . .
>
> The grammatical present at the end of "Ein Landarzt," then, signifies the present moment of narration from which the first-person narrator views his past experiences in retrospect. We would therefore expect him to describe these experiences in the past tense. And the fact is that he uses this tense in the beginning of his account, and again at its end, where it serves as a necessary reminder of the essential temporal relationship within the story. The long, intervening, present-tense passage, however, seems to confound this logical arrangement. It is interesting to note that Willa and Edwin Muir, Kafka's English translators, have either not noticed this use of the present, or have found it too puzzling for literal translation. . . . I would suggest, however, that the incongruity and complexity that have generally been sensed in this story, and that have most usually been attributed to the multivalence of its meanings and to the contradictory quality of its images, are compounded by the difficulties arising from its tense structure. . . .
>
> The same is not true for the past tense within the third-person form. If the author limits his angle of vision entirely to the perspective of one of his characters, the fictional world is seen through the latter's thoughts and sensations. This character's vantage point in time and space becomes the reader's own, and the past tense of narration loses its past meaning. Moreover, the impersonated viewpoint enables a novelist to weave in and out of a fictional consciousness by using the narrated monologue (or *erlebte Rede*) technique, without interrupting the flow of narration and without changing either tense or person. The internal angle of vision within a third-person idiom thus offered Kafka the advantages he seems to have sought by shifting to the present tense in "Ein Landarzt," without the incongruities we pointed to in its narrative structure.[5]

The terms of discourse have changed radically in a study published in 1977:

> Though vivid in violence, the whipping scene in Kafka's *Der Prozeß* seems at first almost contrived, for it adds neither logically nor structurally to the story of K.'s confrontation with the law that describes the novel's progress. . . .

The whipping scene represents the first moment in the novel when the circle of collusion, deviation, and retribution linking the characters comes fully to a close and when, consequently, the delineations separating accused, accuser, and the arm of the law fall away . . . . K. is now as much the accuser as the accused, as corrupt as the officials of the Court and as hostile to openness as those officials' work requires them to be. Implicit in these reversals is an extreme threat to the coherence of the novel, for its categories have undergone but one in a series of violent interpretive shifts that will characterize, more than any character or theme, the movement of Kafka's novels . . . . No less than K. must the reader labor to extract coherence . . . .

Although insufficient to sustain K. in his attempts to translate the textuality of the law into existentially coherent terms, the anaerobic atmosphere of the Court does serve as a medium for an endless exchange of interpretations, each crystallization demonstrating partial but limited validity. Early in the novel, Kafka places this movement of succession, as he often does, in a sexual context. . . . With the verbal stem *tauschen* (literally, "to exchange") Leni describes how she and K. have come to possess each other sexually. Implicit in the term is the priority of the movement of replacement spanning past and future encounters over any particular relation at hand. The novel's concept of exchange is further enriched by Kafka's carefully planted confusion of the economic and sexual *tauschen* with the evaluative *tauschen*, "to deceive," a verb that will figure prominently in the novel's final theater of interpretation, the recounting and exegesis of the parable of the doorkeeper. . . . By the time the priest makes repeated use of *tauschen* to designate the parable of the doorkeeper as a whole and to characterize the misinterpretations to which it has given rise on the part of both its character and its commentators, the play between almost identical verbs has long been established, so that in their multiplicity alone the various explanations invoked by the priest also appear as deceptions. . . . The play between *tauschen* and *tauschen* in the background of the parable implies that in the novel's successive explanations of the law are its most authentic exchanges, but that these, like their verbal stem, are hardly to be distinguished from deceptions. . . . If the parable of the doorkeeper provides no more authoritative a commentary on the novel than appears in the story of K.'s confrontation with the law, it is also characterized no less than the rest of the narrative by a relentless movement of hermeneutic supplanting. More important than the parable's few thematic parallels with the story of K. is the prevalence of its movement of disqualification. In the light of this continuity, the canonical origin and imputed venerability setting the parable in relief are to be viewed ironically. The setting off of the parable from the remainder of the novel does, however, provide the reader with an opportunity to observe an isolated episode of this interpretative supplanting, one which must be acknowledged to be, however, neither more nor less privileged than any other instance of the replacement epitomizing the novel's textuality.

The metaphor of the Court has served, throughout the novel, as a context to which all developments in the narrative could be referred. . . .

Rather than imposing unity or hermeneutic uniformity, the ubiquitousness of the Court frames the stage upon which the movement of the uncontained supplanting is played out. In the succession of interpretations that it accommodates, the metaphoric centrism dominating the narrative disqualifies itself. This is the theater in which Kafka surveys the limit of metaphor both from the outside and from the inside, a vocation encompassing the corpus of his writing.[6]

Even so limited a sample gives striking evidence of difference.[7] Both critics begin with an anomaly, something unexpected or illogical in the way Kafka constructs his text, but whereas for Cohn (example one) the task is to explain the incoherence and ultimately to transcend it by incorporating it as a passing stage in Kafka's overall development, for Sussman (example two) it has become instead a matter to explore, a mystery that deepens even as its necessity becomes more absolute. Not only does Sussman fail or refuse to use a narrative framework to give order to Kafka's career, there is a similar fluidity and lack of a priori stages to his own argument. The proof is meandering, elements circulate and overlap; it is ultimately the density of the web thus produced on which the case must rest. Cohn's work is situated in a well-defined polemical space, between the axes of antecedents and adversaries whose opinions are explicitly acknowledged and set off from Cohn's own argument. Concepts are either attributed to particular "owners" or designated as the shared property of the scholarly community at large. There is little or no attribution machinery in Sussman's work, however, which relies on the reader's familiarity with key terms like *textuality* and *exchange* to establish its relationship to the work of other critics. Glancing blows and playful allusions replace official footnotes, making Sussman's text seem more porous than Cohn's, full of minute fissures through which concepts seep in and leak out, impossible either to claim or entirely disclaim. The opponents and/or audience are at once more generalized and less communal—anyone and everyone may function as "the reader" whose solitary struggles for coherence Sussman equates with Kafka's own. Indeed, *The Trial* has become an adventure in and of interpretation, thus eroding the "privileges" of both protagonist and author and merging criticism, creation, and the frantic gestures of K. himself into a single hermeneutic quest. The consequences of this are ambivalent, at once an elevation and a contamination of the critic's powers, whose disinterest is challenged precisely to the extent that his or her trial is aggrandized.

Cohn's critic has nothing in common with the character, functioning as a purely transcendental subjectivity whose only operations are professional analyses. An array of technical terms acts as a barrier between critic, text, and naive reader, terms for cataloging the various devices that the craftsmanlike author may employ. The devices—first-person narration, third-person narration—seem to function automatically, compelling the appropriate responses from any attentive reader and providing a sure guide for the activities of the critic, who need only locate and label what has triggered these responses. Beyond their role in establishing the genre, the position of the speaker, and the intimacy of the reader's involvement with the story, the devices have no further significance. While Sussman also locates certain textual devices, they are incapable of producing mechanical effects; at best they can "provide an opportunity for the reader to observe." But though this makes Kafka's writing in some respects less potent, the implications of that same writing have become immeasurably broader; discourse matters more—sexually, economically, intellectually—even as it determines less. The writing has also become indeterminate in another sense, no longer identified with a set of isolated stylistic features. Instead it is the dynamism of the text, the process of exchange, succession, supplantings, and displacements that we are asked to notice, a pattern that disappears the moment we try to localize it in a particular turn of phrase. Because this is precisely what escapes our vision, what cannot be arrested in an image, Sussman's criticism seems peculiarly abstract in comparison with Cohn's despite the fact that it is no less "closely read." The verbal play between *tauschen* and *täuschen*—which the critic both identifies and indulges in—is certainly as minute as one could wish, yet the slipperiness of his sentences, which may begin with one subject and end with another, is such that there is no rest for contemplation and accumulation of the sort that Cohn provides.

Paying such exclusive attention to a single piece of fiction may appear to diminish the pretensions of Sussman's essay to represent the recently altered status of literary theory, yet even here it is apparent that the reading of *The Trial* functions more (in Sussman's words) as a "theater of interpretation" than as an end in itself. The novel becomes a site for demonstrating a certain set of problems: of the nature of textuality, of validity and disqualification, of the limits of metaphor. (In fact, one of the peculiar features of contemporary literary theory is that, while attacking or inverting much of what New Criticism held most dear, it has not abandoned the habit of close reading; great speculations typically from the smallest parapraxes grow.)[8] Moreover, it is the relationship between the two essays that is most significant and that most faithfully replicates the developments we are pursuing: the markedly different status of the reader ca. 1968 and 1977; the new unleashing of powers of analogy (or—better—"homology," since it is no longer intrinsic properties but intervals and structures that justify comparison); the tendency to treat works of literature as if they were themselves theoretical efforts—the "most complex account of signification we possess"[9]—and literary theory as a tacit drama, narrative, or poem; the discovery and (in place of remedy) the willful exacerbation of difficulty and the fragmentation and reconstruction of familiar texts in such a way as to "make the text a little harder to understand and the visible a little harder to see."[10] Although Sussman is, if anything, even less willing, in 1977, to speak of imitation and reference, his essay illustrates a paradoxical implosion of the tenets of formalism, whereby the long banished "extrinsic" problems of belief and history and economic necessity return in the guise of strictly formal problems. And if the autonomy of art seems less certain as a result, the neutrality of criticism seems even more insecure as the received notions of how to write criticism give way.

This last is perhaps the subtlest and the easiest to dismiss, but it is (or should be) an event of major proportions in any literary history when habits of discourse change. In fact, most of those who attack the new theoretical tendencies make specific reference to the license and "bad manners" of the writing it has produced.[11] Nor are such outcries simply an evasion of the "real" issues; they indicate an implicit awareness of altered strategies and affiliations that have deep institutional implications but that find their clearest expression in a new kind of prose. It is chiefly in discourse, on the page or in the classroom, that criticism exists and when that discourse changes, a whole profession is ultimately involved. Thus, the labored puns, the neologisms, the sudden internationalism of knowledge, the intellectual and aesthetic pretensions of his new critical writing, and even the way it organizes a page are important for its proponents and opponents alike. "Not annotating the idea" (according to an adherent like Geoffrey Hartman) is an expression of "a hope for the naturalization of the idea, for the appreciation of its figurative power apart from its appearance in technical and special contexts."[12] The equally sympathetic Edward Said cites the "need to reorient and distort the meaning of words and phrases whose use as a *means* for thought has been so habit-ridden and so literally debasing as to have become completely unthinkable."[13]

But how has it come about that, in little more than a decade, the practices and the very subject matter of Anglo-American literary studies have shifted so profoundly? Pointing to the unprecedented influence of French structuralist and poststructuralist thought is tempting but ultimately circular, since one must then explain why such "foreign" influences (once so easily resisted) should all at once become overpowering. The simple fact remains that it is easier to name the various schools of critical thought—whether domestic or imported—that have achieved prominence during the last decade and a half than it is to name any comparable movements among writers of fiction and poetry. Against the "new contextualism," the new literary histories, the renewed Freud and the revitalized Marx, the rediscovery of the Frankfurt School, the studies of reader response and *rezeptionästhetik,* the stylistics, narratology, deconstruction, archeology, semiotics, speech act theory, schizoanalysis, entropology, etc., what else can one oppose than an amorphous and singularly uncompelling postmodernism? When Randall Jarrell complained, in 1951, that "it will probably seem one more absurdity of our age that as the volume of criticism increased, the actual writing of literature—poems, stories, plays, novels—declined,"[14] the asymmetry was far less striking than it is today.

Jarrell's "Age of Criticism" at least presented itself as a modest servant of literary art—scrupulous, methodical, but as far as possible free from any constructions of its own. How unlike the current situation, in which, in Murray Krieger's words, "not only has theory come into its own, but it seems to be nourishing itself as a separate institution, to which literature sometimes seems almost totally irrelevant."[15] The practical criticism of the past purported to exhaust itself in a single act of exegesis and evaluation, an act that arose ex nihilo (or at most from an exposure to other literary works and a handful of widely shared beliefs about art and human nature) and then vanished without residue. But the theoretical criticism of today—however well it meets the usual requirements placed on theory in other ways—has at least an acknowledged existence of its own beyond the moment of interpretation. In fact, where once it was roundly assumed that the only purpose (or perhaps the sole excuse) for literary theory was to facilitate such individual acts of judgment and interpretation, agreement about the role of theory is now far less clear.[16] The prominence and energy of recent theoretical writing is no doubt partly due to just this failure of consensus and the need to make a given program—investigating the nature of literary semiosis, say, or the relationship of literary production and/or reception to political economy—more attractive and convincing than its rivals. And the new respect for the power of "speculative instruments,"[17] for the way one's premises and governing metaphors, typologies and permissible associations, shape critical practice—and for the "object" upon which it is brought to bear, is in direct proportion to the lack of consensus as well. No single program has such universal support that its instruments appear inevitable and its speculation takes on the look of simple common sense.

One plausible, but not wholly sufficient, explanation of what has occurred is to say that the hegemony of the New Criticism, a dominion that began in the late 1920s and reached its height in the period following the end of the Second World War, is finally at an end.[18] But such a statement in itself says too little about the specific nature of the break and how or why it had to happen, beyond mere enervation and the wearing down of all things New. A more promising tactic would be to try to trace the source of recent changes back to inconsistencies within New Criticism itself that became progressively more apparent, exclusions that were increasingly more difficult to enforce, and even certain tendencies that were already present but were either left undeveloped or prevented from reaching their logical conclusion.

New Criticism was not, of course, a unified effort; the label designating it as a single movement was already something of a retrospective fiction when John Crowe Ransom applied it in 1941.[19] But despite differences of time and temperament and nationality, one can still point to a core of common values and shared antipathies, along with a small number of progenitors—Eliot, Richards, Empson—whose authority was uniformly acknowledged. Then too, the fact that the principles of New Criticism remain dispersed and more or less implicit, or when they did become explicit were so often negative—a series of prohibited "fallacies" and "heresies"—is itself characteristic. The suspicion that explicit procedures might impede the range and the acuity of spontaneous perception ("discrimination that directs, without stifling, an alert sensibility and a full responsiveness," is the ideal proposed by John Wain in 1955)[20] was deeply ingrained, as was the fear that intellectual self-consciousness would lead to spiritual and emotional paralysis.[21] According to Jonathan Culler, New Criticism made theory a "negative activity, designed to rule out of court, by labelling as fallacies, approaches that might prevent an innocent and direct contact with 'the words on the page.' "[22]

The chief theoretical concern of New Criticism was to define the nature of the literary object, which would in turn determine which critical activities were appropriate and which were not and would illustrate as well the sources of a naive reader's response to literature. It stressed the peculiarity of literature, especially its difference from other kinds of language, defending it on several fronts from those who might want to test it for verifiability or to treat it as data for historical and linguistic speculations or simply to probe it for autobiographical revelations on the part of the author. Such activities as these threatened to trivialize the effort and the satisfactions of aesthetic experience (attacking the last refuge for certain human capacities—imaginative freedom, disinterested contemplation—allowed no other outlet in modern life) by ignoring the specificity and integrity of literary constructions. The defense rested on the putatively unique ontological status of literary works; their "autonomy" or independence from the context in which they originated; their ability to stand alone, apart from whatever private intentions the author may have had for them; and their autotelic nature, which gave words meaning according to their structural role rather than their referential value. The correlative of this was a notion of the sort of experience art must induce—a "rapt, intransitive attention" blocking all desire to test or categorize and dominating the will to act (a notion owing something to Kant's discrimination between aesthetic judgement on the one hand and both pure and practical reasoning on the other)—and hence, the qualities a work must have to induce that experience.[23] Certain literary devices—irony, paradox, ambiguity, tension, and closure—became the focus of analysis because of their "natural affinity" for autonomy, their purported ability to cause crude referential urges to misfire or, on the contrary, to emerge with especial clarity for those engaged in the aesthetic contemplation of language. (The arguments often moved uneasily in both directions.)

By taking its stand on ontological grounds, New Criticism was pushed progressively toward treating literature as an object—an urn, an icon, a spatial form—and framing its discussion in terms of the essential and the accidental properties of that object. The literary object was appealing on other grounds as well, as the final stay of critical "objectivity"—some publicly observable check on private fantasies (which became more menacing when interpretation could no longer appeal to a determining intention).[24] Moreover, the repudiation of wayward impressionism on the part of critics mirrored Eliot's search for the "objective correlative" of otherwise incommunicable subjective experiences, that which would allow poetry to embody emotion and yet remain impersonal.

The insistence on "close reading," then, arose from a desire for greater proximity (and presumably greater fidelity) to the object, with less chance of distraction from extrinsic associations or irrelevant questions about its history or its veracity or its practical value. The "dignity" of literary criticism lay in this effort to "preserve its autonomy from domination by the methods of historical studies or science."[25] Such exclusions necessarily restricted the explanatory power of criticism to demonstrating the connections between elements within a single text, to showing "how the interaction of the poem's parts produces a complex and ontologically privileged statement about human experience."[26]

At times, however, fidelity to the method of analysis threatened to supplant whatever premises had originally justified it—obscuring for example, Richard's arguments about the ordering of impulses; or the pedagogical goal of making literature less exclusively the province of specialized philological scholarship and more immediately available to the general reader; or the desire to display literary work in opposition to a pervasive modern alienation of labor and to pit aesthetic value against the profit motive.

> The critics sought to re-establish communication between reader and poem by demanding attention to formal features, to the poem as poem—not as biography, sociology, or history; and they found the human values of literature in the attention to concrete particulars of the individual work. It was assumed that the discovery of these particulars made readers cognizant of the varieties of literary individuality—and in so doing made them capable of understanding their own greater potentialities for fulfillment.[27]

But, paradoxically, this preoccupation with preserving the literariness of literature—what Edward Wasiolek has called New Criticism's constant movement "in the direction of excluding more and more on the grounds of some irrelevance to the unattainable purity of poetic texture"[28]—threatened to render literature ever more vacuous as it became more precious. In the words of Hayden White:

> ...artworks "did" things that no other cultural artifact (and very few human beings) could ever do. . . . this suggested that the literary world was self-contained and self-generating, hovered above other departments of culture and bore little responsibility to them and finally existed for itself alone—like a Platonic idea or an Aristotelian autotelic form. . . .
>
> It would not do to say, without qualification, that the Inflationary mode fetishized the artwork and turned criticism into a priestly service to the object thus fetishized. But for the critics who worked within this mode, the basis for such fetishism was potentially present. . . . In this tendency to endow "art" with a value which mere life itself could never lay claim to, the Inflationary critics seemed to be saying that if a choice between them had to be made, they would choose art over life every time.[29]

With a subject matter thus rarified and the prohibition on "talk about ideas, psychology, social relations, and other extrinsic disciplines"[30] thus extended and made nearly absolute, literary studies became increasingly parochial and isolated from the very cultural developments they had once promised to scrutinize and combat. According to Ralph Cohen, the upshot was that: "The subtlety of literary analysis of individual poems was surely increased, but the insistence on the purely literary function of the analysis served to heighten rather than control the crisis it was meant to solve."[31]

The situation provided the ideal polemical context for the reassertion of all those interests that had been tenuously held in check: Hence the explosion of self-proclaimed "antithetical" studies—psychological, sociological, historical—in recent years. But it simultaneously made patent the need for some new *literary* theory capable of encompassing these hitherto excluded interests and able to match sophisticated developments in other disciplines with an equal sophistication of its own. Nor can all blame be put on the return of the repressed; tensions and even contradictions within the New Critical project were equally responsible for its collapse. The uneasy synthesis between an Arnoldian piety for poetry and a critical technique valued chiefly for its scrupulous objectivity and "scientific" empiricism is one such tension. Another was that while espousing an official faith in unmediated perception and the powers of plain talk, New Criticism had also begun as a revolt against musty institutions and had offered its own refinements of the casual, impressionistic vocabulary of its predecessors.[32] The fascination with rigor it sometimes tacitly and sometimes openly exhibited is not so very far removed, in spirit, from the current hunger for theoretical coherence. There is even some continuity in the issues that preoccupied Richards and those preoccupying contemporary theorists who also wish to understand the "reservoir of language"—without, however, preserving Richards's desire to keep language strictly subservient to the will of its individual user.[33] Even in its most vehement defenses of the autonomy of art, New Criticism could not imagine a text that did not erect its own ghostly persona and speak with the recognizable "tone" of a single human voice. In fact, a great deal of effort was expended precisely to the end of keeping language in its place, particularly by introducing additional constraints (consistency, "plenitude," the "intolerability of incompatibles") to contain the polysemy released when the text became autonomous.[34]

Such forcefully articulated principles would appear to exercise control over the practice of criticism, yet there remains a strong resistance among New Critics to admitting that any independent rules govern either critics or casual readers, that anything mediates the response to the stimulus the work itself provides. In the words of René Wellek: "What the formalist wants to maintain is that the poem is not only a cause, or a potential cause, of the reader's 'poetic experience' but a specific, highly organized control of the reader's experience, so that the experience is most fittingly described as an experience of the poem."[35] This assimilation of literary works to perceptual objects and the attempt to make meaning a matter of ontology were a desperate (and misguided) attempt to give criticism the certainty of a natural science. Yet the discrepancy between a doctrine of ideal passivity and a practice that was in fact both aggressive and highly regulated remained, down to the very metaphors of "attack" and "descent" used to describe the relationship between the critic and a chosen text.[36] Then too, there was the problem of explaining the persistent need to educate responses that should, if no more than responses, be nearly automatic. Indeed, would not interpretation itself, the endless series of highly accomplished individual "readings" that New Criticism produced, be more or less superfluous if the literary object exercised so absolute a control over the reader's experience?[37] One sees here an inconsistency into which current notions that reading is a rule-governed activity that *produces* meaning might eventually insinuate themselves. One also sees how the long buried questions of authorial intention and historical context might be resurrected when the formalist premise no longer seemed sufficient as either an account of meaning or a guide to interpretation.

> The alteration, even the supersession, of the formalist premises occurs in at least three ways. With regard to language, the analyses of meaning in Wimsatt's or Brower's sense are found to be inadequate because such analyses no longer confirm how words mean. With regard to the reader's relation to a work, the subjective (or affective or Freudian) responses become primary because the reader is the valued being in the relationship. Finally, with regard to contemporary affairs or history, the premises cease to be appropriate to literary activities because they lack the values such activities are supposed to have.[38]

When form at last begins to appear neither determining nor determinant but itself dependent for its completion upon social and semiotic conventions, the way is opened for an assault on the dichotomy between intrinsic and extrinsic approaches to literature. Not only is reading freed from reverent responsiveness, but it may even turn openly irreverent, suspicious, or subversive, practicing "a new violence never before associated with reading."[39] If reading is an activity or a strategy, then it is no longer will-less or entirely disinterested, thus raising unprecedented questions about the motives (especially those psychological and ideological motives that remain unconscious) that propel it. But the ultimate consequence of the "decline of the object" is the liberation of literary theory to determine its own proper ends, no longer ruled by what the object itself seems to demand—a demand, let it be said, that had always smacked of circularity, since that object was actually a product of theoretically imposed definitions in the first place.

Interestingly, the rise of theory and the correlative decline of faith in the self-sufficient literary object and unmediated empirical observation was not confined to literary studies alone. Both the natural and the social sciences experienced much the same crisis of epistemology, the same challenge to the dominion of a model of knowledge based almost exclusively on perception.[40] In sociology and linguistics, for example, the belief that significant results could be achieved through methodology and technique alone gradually gave way to a wary recognition that there must be some preliminary grounds for using one method rather than another, and that, in the absence of an explicit theory, the presuppositions and consequences that no method can avoid will continue to operate covertly, untested and unchecked.[41] Paradoxically, researchers in the so-called hard sciences were actually much quicker to acknowledge the limits of methodological observation and purely inductive reasoning than their imitators in other fields, recognizing the impossibility of inferring laws unequivocally from facts and challenging the myth that scientific knowledge consists solely of the "accumulation of separate truths by the addition of one fact to another fact, each independently verified by experience."[42] According to Werner Heisenberg, "Natural science does not simply explain and describe nature; . . . it describes nature as exposed to our method of questioning."[43]

Although logical priority of theory and the indispensable role of deductive inferences had been a commonplace of the philosophy of science for some time, the critique of the neutrality of observation and description gained broad acceptance only in the 1960s, along with a fresh appreciation that the suggestiveness or fertility of a theory might be as important a consideration in evaluating rival theories as logical coherence. Characteristic of the new thrust were statements like Harré's "There are no modes of description which remain invariant under all changes of theory. . . the accepted way of explaining phenomena enters into the very meaning of the terms used to describe them"[44] and Hesse's claim that science depends more on open-minded models than on general laws.[45] Once dominated by an exclusive regard for internal consistency and logical structure (not unlike the New Critical concern for form) and by a distaste for the psychology of discovery and the effect of history on scientific development, the philosophy of science underwent a shift of attention (again with striking literary parallels) to the dynamics of change and the economic and political contexts in which scientific priorities are established. And here too, as the questions began to outstrip the self-imposed boundaries of the discipline, interdisciplinary work gained a sudden respectability.[46]

When changes in longstanding intellectual commitments are so widespread and when, in addition, the same direction of change recurs from case to case, it is worth asking whether forces beyond the individual disciplines themselves are involved. And the decade in which these changes occurred was certainly one in which knowledge and the institutions responsible for gathering and disseminating it were faced with unwonted skepticism and even open attack, both for the uses to which research had been put and for those to which it had not. Charges of irrelevance, on the one hand, and of ideological contamination or even wholesale appropriation for corrupt and inhuman ends, on the other, were hardly to be met by the usual appeal to disciplinary purity and technical efficiency. At issue were not the means but the ends of knowledge, its founding assumptions, its institutional and material supports, and the consequences of using it.

One can pick out easily enough the factors that promoted this condition of unrest and suspicion: cooperation between the academy and the military in covert political operations and an overtly unpopular war; a burgeoning of the school population (both students and teachers), especially at the upper levels; and beyond the problem of sheer mass, the problem of a new heterogeneity of ethnic heritage and race and class erupting into what had been the small and traditionally restricted world of higher education.[47] Schools were increasingly subject to contradictory demands, made responsible for more and more of the primary socialization of children, for certifying students ready for professional training and contributing to the upward mobility of the poor, for simply keeping a certain percentage of the population off the job market, above and beyond their responsibility for imparting basic intellectual skills and the polish of a liberal education.[48] The conflict among these demands on education could be ignored—at the price of a feeling of bad faith—or an attempt could be mounted to meet them—at the price of institutional incoherence. Coherence was also threatened by a student body that lacked the common preparatory training, the shared experience of the world, and even the uniform language upon which teachers had formerly been able to draw. Such a setting made notions like "ordinary language" and "common sense" increasingly problematic, and the tacit interests and assumptions that had always governed classroom procedures and curricula were suddenly exposed to view. At the same time a subsidized and expanded faculty was producing scholarship at an unprecedented rate and achieving an equally unprecedented degree of specialization, making a "community of scholars"—with access to the same information—all but impossible. And the fact of subsidy, underwriting all this expansion, made the academy's traditional claim that it was acting as the gadfly of the state ring rather hollow.

But this situation within the academy was only part of a larger breaking up of the appearance of consensus in the culture as a whole, where the same sudden revelation of contending interests and the same suspicion of the biases of inherited institutions was repeated on another level. Here the fear of "rationalization as technocratic violence" and the "quarrel with an industrial society's uses of objectivity" became the basis for outright social struggle.[49] The long romance with humanism, the delight in the masterful imposition of human form on the chaos of nature, had turned sour, and there was increasing public talk about the need instead to preserve nature from human impositions.[50] Indeed, the means of mastery seemed to have outstripped human desire, and a menacing gap opened between "a realm of fact without subjective commitment and a new subjectivity without authority to rule it."[51] This dichotomy was not only intellectual but political and economic as well. Adorno had called it the "administered world" where institutions seemed possessed of a "senseless autonomy" of their own, their workings too massive and complex for individual control or even comprehension. Yet the gradual merger between state and society, the growing dependence of private life on these same institutions to assure "a sphere of freedom, free time, and freedom of movement," made complete disassociation impossible.[52] This confused sense of personal impotence mingled with responsibility was exacerbated by a greatly expanded network of mass communication that ceaselessly informed one about events that seemed remote and intimate at once, where action was impossible and reaction impossible to avoid. Television was perhaps the sole remaining universal, the only thing that every member of this complex and divided society could share, yet through it, social relations were turned into spectacle and reality was defined as an object of consumption.[53] Thus it is understandable that against this pervasive sense of personal isolation and passivity, of social structures aloof, mysterious, and unwieldy, of an intellectual and technological pursuit of mastery that had become dangerously self-contained and capable of manufacturing its own ends, the characteristic demand of the various political and student movements that took shape during the sixties should be for greater participation in all phases of collective life. And that fixed hierarchies, received traditions, covert understandings of all types should be anathema.

While this is far from a full account of the conditions preceding and accompanying the rise of literary theory, it does provide a necessary background against which that rise may appear less artificial, less a work of self-promotion on the part of a few ambitious scholars (as some of its severest critics claim). The study of literature—even literature itself—could hardly be untouched by pressures so severe and bearing so directly on the educational establishment and the life of the mind. However adequate or successful it might be, the recourse to theory must be recognized as a response to a situation of extreme challenge and discontent, one in which traditional approaches were on the verge of losing all authority. If literary works continued to be treated as sacred and ineffable objects, there would be little place for them in an atmosphere where skepticism and iconoclasm were the reigning modes of thought:

> The loss of the reader's interest in the study of literature can be partially seen as a consequence of inadequate questions. The readers were constantly exposed to an unsound rhetoric, a language that concealed meanings, that had first to be mastered in order to be understood. The need to provide different questions arose, then, from the reader's awareness of how language was used in a society in contrast to how it was being taught in the classroom.[54]

The more literature was isolated from other kinds of discourse and the more high culture was elevated over low, the greater the antipathy of the newly militant egalitarian mood. (Not by accident did the ascendancy of theory come at the same time that English departments began offering courses in film, popular culture, and minority literatures.) At this cultural moment, the defense of art as a superior reality had lost its former social meaning as an attack upon utilitarian values and had become instead a plea for quietism and social withdrawal—by implication tolerant of any world, no matter how ugly or unjust, so long as it allowed some small protected space where art could function.[55] Although acknowledging the pain of a dissociated sensibility, New Criticism was content to leave the mending of the gap to poetry, while its own writing (and the writing it demanded of its students) maintained a strict dichotomy between reputable critical objectivity and mere self-expression. Both in its mechanistic treatment of reading as a response and in its obeisance to the ideal of autonomy, New Criticism embodied (whether accidentally or through some genuine continuity between textual and social politics) precisely those constraints on praxis that had become the most noxious element in modern life.

All of this helps to explain why there might develop a felt need for some alternative, for other programs that would not wear this face of complicity and would at the same time refresh the flagging interest in literature and the study of literature. An uneasy recognition that "too little criticism arises to meet a genuine demand, to answer questions that are really worth asking" is apparent even to those critics like Gerald Graff who find the effort of the Yale school to inject "fear and trembling" into their work otherwise preposterous.[56] A sense of the moment also makes it easier to understand why the proposed alternatives take the shape they do: repudiating native common sense for Continental conjecture; avoiding (if not openly attacking) the traditional claims of humanism; emphasizing subjectivity and/or the "praxis" of reading; demystifying literature—probing it for symptoms of insufficiency and ideological blindness; searching for principles common to all discourse (and not just literature alone); attempting to reconstruct governing "codes" and histories; and seeking the ways in which context interacts with text to produce meaning and value. And to understand also why, common to all these alternatives, should be the same wary sense of estrangement, of remoteness from literature, whether it was viewed as an insurmountable distance and "otherness" that authentic criticism should struggle to retain,[57] or as a call "to re-establish response in depth through conceptual mediation,"[58] or as a mission to rediscover and reassert "the subversive/ Utopian features of art."[59]

Yet a further step in the argument is needed to explain why, if prompted only by a desire for alternatives, a simple change of approach was not enough—why bother with elaborate systems, formal categories, definitions, and all the rest that theory-building entails? The answer appears in the very terms in which the question is framed: The "bother" of elaborating and formalizing and defining is part of the reform, part of the effort to distinguish the new mode of literary study from the old genteel tradition where implicitness and informality were so highly esteemed. Like other institutions, scholarship is subject to its own legitimation crisis: "At a certain point in the life of these activities, the simple fact that they *are* conducted no longer suffices; the existent sanction must be replaced by a rational one."[60] That point (which doubtless occurs more than once in any activity that is sufficiently long-lived) was reached for the study of literature in the later sixties, for all the reasons I have outlined above. Criticism had become largely self-justifying, a matter of fulfilling professional requirements.[61] Indeed, the sheer bulk of professional output could supply another motive for taking refuge in theory "to cope with the multiplying burden of texts and interpretations and disburden us by allowing the mind to generalize from a sample."[62] And no doubt the rivalry of other, more highly formalized disciplines played a role as well, especially when those disciplines were fast encroaching on the domain of language and symbolic form that once had been the exclusive province of departments of literature. Whereas one may read New Criticism as an attempt to overcome the so-called human sciences by a process of exclusion, now the process was inverted and an attempt was made to gain the authority of linguistics or anthropology by adopting their style.[63]

But a deeper motive arises from the history of the discipline *as* a discipline: a course of development that seems nearly inevitable, as Nicholas Rescher portrays it:

> One does not just explain something, one explains it *to someone* (perhaps only to oneself), so that the explanatory enterprise proceeds within a concrete framework of common inquiry. . . . With time and professionalization, however, one can imagine (or postulate) an abstract impersonal framework, rather than a concrete dialectical setting. . . . assume a range of questions marked off by abstracted boundaries of a *discipline* rather than by a personalized range of interests.[64]

Thus, when the discipline itself is challenged, as the whole of the academic establishment was being challenged during the period in question, the enterprise loses its justification, both its sense of an audience to whom the explanation is addressed and its confidence in providing an interesting or even a necessary response. To continue its work of explanation, it must have a new set of acceptable questions. After the long silence of disciplinary habit, the terms of inquiry will necessarily seem crudely outspoken, but only by placing the entire framework in view can one begin again, establishing by act of will the common framework that has vanished. Thus it becomes the function of theory to make articulate a range of fundamental questions that will enable the inquiry to go on and—just as important—will give those investigations the appearance of responding to legitimate needs.

There were other reasons for trying to uncover fundamental premises as well. The general climate of suspicion and contending points of view made any claim to naked truth and innocent observation seem like a piece of hopeless naïveté, if not deliberate deception. The voices claiming that there could be no relationship to literature at all without some guiding set of expectations, no matter how vague or unsystematic, were growing more insistent[65]—especially as the problems of teaching literature to a less homogeneous range of students (whose primary allegiance, as a group, was more likely to be to the mass media than to books) became more vexing. Something that could previously be taken for granted was gone and had to be reconstructed artificially, from scratch. Moreover resentment was also mounting against the arbitrariness inherent in "la tranquille circularité du code innommé" that ruled the classroom, which simply blamed failures to learn on insensitivity or a lack of natural gift.[66] Here then was another role for theory, to uncover those assumptions and operations that had for so long "gone without saying," perhaps to establish new ones, and to try to formalize them as rules or strategies capable of being taught. Literary theory might then serve as the missing common background for a divided student body and, being an artificial language with no identification with any particular group, might prove more palatable to all. At the same time, theory could perhaps provide a stay against relativism, a principled way of making educational distinctions and weighing artistic merits, without recourse either to arbitrary authority (at a moment when students were nothing if not antiauthoritarian) or to the now tarnished standard of the Great Tradition.

Arnold (and later, Trilling) had perhaps hoped that by avoiding the intoxication of general systems and great ideas, literary studies could escape ideological rigidity and attain the ideal of a cultivated play of mind. But now there were charges that eclecticism was actually an "instrument of conservatism," a means of avoiding engagement.[67] Rather than escaping from ideology, "only through a lucid awareness of our own situation within ideology. . .can we begin. . .to move away from its domination."[68] Even the most thoroughly practical of criticisms could not help but rest on some assumptions about the nature of literature and of knowledge itself, which tacit commitments (according to Hayden White): "predetermine the *kinds* of generalization one can make,. . .the kinds of knowledge one can have,. . .and hence the kinds of projects one can legitimately conceive for changing the present [situation] or for maintaining it in its present form indefinitely."[69] Through theory, one might at least become less susceptible to accidental commitments and unintended alliances. And (pace Arnold) ad hoc and a priori assumptions, far from freeing one from error, seemed actually *less* corrigible, since less open to opposing arguments and counterevidence.

Thus, for a literary establishment made (at times with pain) acutely sensitive to possibilities of bias and ideological entanglements, theory had two functions. First, it was a means of flushing out expectations and ends, exposing hidden motives, and probing for inconsistencies and equivocations. But theory was also attractive for its capacity—as an extraordinary and invented language—to go beyond the range of the familiar and the usual that are the province of ordinary language and that never even appear problematic as long as terms derived from ordinary language seem inevitable. The unconscious and the ideological are precisely what are hidden to habitual perception. Not unexpectedly, then, literary theory gradually became the vehicle for all manner of forbidden extradisciplinary speculations, even for disciplines other than its own, such as Continental psychology and philosophy, whose concerns could find no room amid the dominantly empirical and descriptive emphasis of their Anglo-American counterparts.[70]

Taking a broader view of the changing fate of theory, one begins to discern a subtle pattern touching ultimately on our most profound beliefs about the foundations of our knowledge and our capacity to present that knowledge in discursive form. It was not the advent of structuralism that altered our relationship to language, or even the translations of Wittgenstein's *Philosophic Investigations* some years earlier, although both are symptomatic of that alteration and a declining trust that the meaning of words was determined by the objects that they named. Naming itself had slipped from its long-established position as the paradigm and source of language, to become just one among a number of other practices that depend on the institution of language itself for their force and meaning. Generalized, this becomes a doubt about the status of all representations, whether purporting to be fictional or strictly factual. The tendency toward auto-commentary and "meta-fictions" in literature is actually another version of the theoretical tendency in scholarship; both appear when innocent representation is no longer possible and when, at the same time, pure formalism or methodology-for-its-own-sake have proved equally unsatisfactory. The theoretical impulse is a move to save (or to reinstate) the transitivity of discourse at a higher level, to preserve its claim to be "about" (or to operate on) something without at the same time succumbing to the myth of transparency—of knowledge achieved without mediation or of words that merely reflect a pre-established world. It does so by baring the device, showing the labor that goes into the construction of any object of knowledge and the vantage point that gives it the appearance it has.

The myth of transparency will survive as long as everyone is willing to accept the same descriptions, as long as there exist substantial areas where vocabularies overlap and express a mutually presupposed background of expectation and conceptual commitment. Even then it is not actually a case of transparent language but of "a language whose theoretical assumptions are not at issue."[71] But when, especially as in recent years, convergence is less frequent and consensus much less easy to achieve, the assumptions will, of course, be very much at issue, and representations will quickly lose their air of unconstructed neutrality.

In their own way, aestheticism, formalism, and New Criticism were earlier attempts to oppose this already dated myth, to demonstrate the specific powers of symbolic fabrication. But the opposition went awry in stressing the peculiarity of art and establishing an exclusively literary sanctuary where "texture," "ambiguity," and the rest were acknowledged to be part of the language. Moreover, the proposed dichotomy between literary and normal discourse, between pseudoassertion and assertion, actually enhanced the epistemology and theory of meaning to which formalism and the rest were officially opposed.

"Where science stops," it is said, "there art begins." . . . The most striking aspect of this debate is that both parties share the definition of rationality, the same divisions between means and ends, facts and opinions, and objectivity and subjectivity. Both accept similar assumptions about the separation of science and rationality (the objective, cognitive) as against feeling and art (the subjective, sensual). The difference between the two camps is that positivists take facts and objectivity to be the grounding of their work while their opponents believe that ideas and subjectivity constitute a "higher science."[72]

There was further comfort for the "enemy" in the fact that the methods of argumentation and research that the critics themselves were using often bore a far closer resemblance to positivism than to poetry.

The defense of poetry had ceded far too much in the interest of establishing autonomy; the liberation of the constructive powers of literary language had been attained only by robbing it of most of its efficacy and conceptual value. In the rapt, intransitive attention of aesthetic contemplation, literature was isolated from the sort of colloquy and interchange enjoyed by other discourse. Here, then, is a final function for literary theory, to effect a change in the status and function of literature itself (redeeming it from the impoverished situation to which a previous critical program had confined it). But why should literature require this assistance? What prevented it from altering its own situation, as it had done so many times before? Some of these questions must await a more detailed treatment in chapters yet to come; here it is enough to say that the moment when literary theory began its remarkable ascendancy was also a moment of flagging inspiration and apparent confusion among writers of fiction and poetry, and that this inverse correlation is probably more than a coincidence. One contributing factor has already been mentioned, the problem posed when both mimesis and formalism seem to offer little scope for either fresh invention or further refinement. Of course, one could simply hold to the familiar formulas with redoubled force, as in the spate of neorealistic novels, for example. But no act of will could prevent the value of the old formulas from changing precisely because of their familiarity or because of an altered cultural milieu—developments in other arts, mass-produced entertainment, and economic and educational changes influencing the range of available readers.

The plotting and the characterization traditionally associated with realism are, arguably, ill-adapted to the task of representing the complex social organization and the forms that personal identity take in the contemporary world—even if the traditional claims of representation were still in force. It is far more likely that the "return of realism" is based, not on its credibility, but on its sheer desirability: the sense of intense security it offers to those who wish to remain within its limited and well-known parameters. No literary form is free from assumptions about the nature of the psyche, the extent of social and political possibility, even a rudimentary metaphysics of its own. Thus, there are limits to what can be done to alter the status of literature by working within existing modes, or even by remaining within the existing range of literature as defined by the twin poles of formalism and mimesis. Literary theory could help to undo or "disestablish" the extant categories in a more sustained and systematic way than parodies or antinovels were capable of doing and could propose other frameworks that—at this moment in cultural history—might prove more fruitful.

But it would appear, in some instances, that contemporary literary theory has arrogated to itself an even less equivocal role. No longer behaving as a servant or even a prophet of literary development, it attempts to embody the renovations directly and to itself become the literature that it foretells. Reactions, both friendly and unfriendly, to this tendency were not long in coming, from Lionel Abel's despair that now "critics are expected to be more original than the works themselves" to Geoffrey Hartman's celebration that critical essays have become "more demanding" than poetry,[73] since, to Hartman, "both criticism and fiction are institutions of the human mind, one cannot foretell where the creative spirit may show itself."[74] But while champions and detractors are plentiful enough, few writers go beyond simply acknowledging it as a "cultural phenomenon...a mode of mental behávior rooted in our time and plight"[75] to grant it the kind of sustained attention such a phenomenon should warrant, both for itself and for what it might tell us about the state of contemporary "letters" as a whole. As Hayden White remarks:

> ...significant periods of literary change will...be signalled by *changes in the linguistic code*: changes in the code will in turn be signalled by changes in both the cognitive content of literary works (the messages) and the modes of contact (genres) in which messages are transmitted and received. Changes in the codes, finally, can be conceived to be reflective of changes in the historico-natural context in which a given language game is being played.[76]

The effort to make theory a kind of literary writing indicates that just such a change in "modes of contact" and "messages" is now underway. Hence, when theory asserts itself as a candidate for aesthetic appreciation, it should not be treated as an accidental accumulation of individual arrogance or genius but rather as a sign that the available literary genres—principally the novel, lyric poetry, and the drama—are not fulfilling some set of intellectual and aesthetic needs that theoretical writing promises to fulfill. What those needs are and why literary theory should offer itself as a plausible alternative is the burden of the study to follow, which will consider too how well theoretical writing actually fulfills its promises and what range of possibilities—as demonstrated in the work of particular writers—it may afford.

By recognizing the literary pretensions of recent literary theory, the final pieces of the puzzle fall into place: Certain features that might otherwise have seemed anomalous or intrusive in Henry Sussman's circling prose are less surprising when that prose is no longer measured exclusively against the solidity and professional dispatch of Dorrit Cohn.

Its tenuousness becomes that of a writing that must struggle, self-consciously, to beget itself, that "needs to reorient and distort the meaning of words and phrases whose use as a *means* of thought has been so habit-ridden and so literally debasing as to have become unthinkable."[77] These are qualities that one associates readily enough with literature, but not (until now) with writing about literature. Certainly they are a far cry from the restrained, analytic effort "to make an intellectual situation of which the creative power can profitably avail itself" that Matthew Arnold called the supreme function of criticism—even during those "epochs of concentration" when it achieved a temporary ascendancy over literature.[78] The role Arnold allocates to criticism and the alternation of mutually exclusive historical epochs appear logical enough if one accepts his original premises about the nature of the creative ("[which] does not principally show itself in discovering new ideas. . . [but in] synthesis and exposition. . . dealing divinely with these ideas, presenting them in the most effective and attractive combinations") and of the critical ("analysis and discovery. . . to establish an order of ideas if not absolutely true, yet true by comparison with that which it displaces")—and accepts as well the absolute cleavage between them.[79] Arnold's melancholy vision of periods of sober intellectual retrenchment brought on by "poor, starved, frag-mentary, inadequate creation," of criticism struggling (unsuccessfully) to fill the resulting void "since at some epochs no other creation is possible," has more than once been invoked to explain the recent prominence of literary theory. Although hardly sufficient to account for the extrava-gance of the current situation, Arnold's cyclic version of literary history undoubtedly retains its rhetorical power. In his summary of "The Way We Think Now," for example, Warner Berthoff seems to take for granted that the rise of literary theory must constitute a "metaphysical counter-attack on the creative imagination":

> . . . at the heart of the newest "new criticism" [is] a reflection of a very different primary situation. . . no steady succession of books reconstituting, by their fresh power, our conceptions and general valuation of the literary enterprise itself and consequently of the basic purpose of criticism. Feeling no comparable pull of major invention whose overruling authority must somehow be accommodated, it turns to generalized system-monitoring and to the search for some methodological key to all possible problems of explanation.[80]

To be sure, there is something attractive in the stoicism and moody strength with which Arnold resigns himself to inevitable decadence, but the plausibility of such a stance finally depends on the soundness of his premises. If one does not hold (as Krieger presents one side of Arnold's thought) that the critical power is of lower rank than the creative[81] or, more to the point, if one disputes the neat dichotomy between invention and analysis, unadorned intellect and mindless ornament, then it becomes possible to envision a subtler interplay between criticism and creation and to arrive at less melancholy functions for the present spate of theoretical criticism.

In fact, neither history nor logic compels us to believe that the role that criticism plays must always be the same, just as the form it takes may vary according to need, from casual eclecticism to polished formal systems. Trying to account even for the present outburst of literary theory forces one to speak of several, overlapping functions: to supply alternative programs of reading; to give a new legitimacy to criticism; to oppose the tacit definitions of the genteel tradition; to meet the challenge of rival disciplines; to avoid hidden ideological entanglements; to overcome the problems of teaching students with disparate backgrounds and a deep suspicion of traditional authority; to face the impasse of mimesis and formalism, in literature and scholarship alike; to change the status and the function of literature; to meet new needs that familiar literary genres seem unable to meet. In his studies of the development of Western criticism, Jean Starobinski traces a continuous revision of its primary functions, from selecting the works that are to survive, to restoring and reinterpreting now-classic works, to an ever more irascible drive to universalize its premises and eventually supplant the very traditions and texts it had begun by fostering.

> Initially the ambition of a critical scholarship was that of restoring the full force of authority to the revealed word or the great literary models of the past. But the difficulty of the task, the obstacles, the irreducible uncertainty of the sources, the conflicts among commentators, as well as the growing doubt as to the legitimacy of the authority thus served, forced critical reasoning to retreat. This retreat was turned into a victory when the critical mind discovered in itself the authority, the sovereign reason, which it had refused to consider as imposed from the outside by the infallible text of some revelation . . . the variations of critical thought far transcend the scope of what is commonly known as "literary theory" or "aesthetic concept," these variations involve every explicit conscious *relationship* which man can entertain with literary works, from respectful submission to an attitude of rejection, from spontaneous participation to "scientific curiosity," and so on.[82]

Many other versions of the roles and characteristic stages of critical activity have been proposed, including Watson's familiar distinction between "legislative" and "descriptive" criticism or Jauss's chronicle of the movement from a classic period built upon exemplary texts, to the more abstract arguments of "historico-positivism," to "aesthetic formalism."[83] But perhaps a better gauge of how diverse the functions of criticism are comes when one examines each of its separate dimensions more closely: its relationship to writers and literary production; its relationship to other scholarship and other criticism; its relationship to the public and to the reception of literature. There is a marked difference, for example, between a criticism that takes its chief impetus from rival commentators and criticism that instead directs itself to chastising would-be authors for their faults. There are differences too in how broadly or how narrowly criticism construes its range—a perennial point of dispute and still very much at issue, as one can see from Robert Weimann's complaint that "academic critics have largely abandoned the broadly civilizing function of criticism."[84] The proportion of criticism to work may range as well from scant marginalia and footnotes to an exhaustive explication de texte. Indeed, one of the distinctive features of theoretical, as opposed to practical, criticism is in how it treats individual texts, not necessarily ignoring their peculiarities but generalizing from them, using them as representative instances or as a point of departure.[85] Indeed, for Edward Said, the way each age depicts the text is actually the chief determinant of criticism; the different intellectual / discursive operations it uses to frame and "secure" the text (as illustrated by the kind of metaphors—spatial, material, military—it favors), and where it establishes the limits of relevant association will shape what the critic may then go on to say about it.[86] Certainly much of the consternation and bitterness over the abstractness of recent literary theory is really a response to shifting the boundaries between text and context and to the "dissolving of the work as a concrete particular."[87] But, then, treating literary texts as concrete particulars was itself the result of theory: The apparently autonomous text was an object that derived its shape from habitual practices and institutional sanctions.[88]

Whatever the primary affiliation of criticism, that relationship itself may still be more or less oblique. It may be a polemic or a verdict that attempts to control critical or creative practice directly by addressing the practitioners. Or it may instead content itself with more distant assessments, with interpretations and explanations that treat only the fact of production and not the producers, with little apparent desire to control or redirect it. The latter is especially common when the canon is already closed and criticism becomes largely retrospective, an act of preservation and a mediation between the present and the great works of the past. (This stance is not, of course, entirely without implications for contemporary writers, who are either tacitly enjoined to repeat the lessons of tradition or written off, as though true literature could no longer be produced.) At such times criticism is much less likely to be openly evaluative, relying instead on the implicit standards that have already been incorporated in the canon itself, and is more likely to limit itself to description, classification, and interpretation.[89]

Normally, the greater the distance between criticism and literary production, the more strongly it will ally itself to reception and the more the fate of art will seem to rest in the hands of an alert and demanding audience. The function of criticism then becomes the cultivation and correction of public taste, or the training of readers, or simply the study of the tacit competence readers already seem to possess. As before, the criticism may address itself *to* readers or simply speak *about* them; it may exhort and persuade—as is most often the case when "taste" is at issue—or may offer logical or practical demonstrations of what a good reading consists of.[90] And, although such criticism does require that there be some distance between the critic and the more general audience, that critic may as easily function as the representative of public opinion as its leader or chastizer, or may—(and did,) in recent years—forego all of these for the role of ethnographer or chronicler of literary response. Thus, the familiar stance of "look at what I see that you don't see," that Stephen Spector finds at the base of so much critical discourse, is not a critical universal but only a particular historical development—one that is, moreover, subject to further historical changes.[91] Criticism will also change markedly according to the kind of literary public it imagines, a few selected patrons or an entire populace, an audience devoted to the careful study of literature or one interested only in deciding which new book to buy.

Critical intervention may have originally been based on an historical or cultural gap that prevented works from reaching their potential audience, a gap that only specialized scholarship or philological expertise could hope to close. But once established, that function becomes the foundation for a discipline and the characteristic apologia for a profession. The intervention need not always be restorative, however; it may (in Paul Ricoeur's useful distinction) change from a "positive" to a "negative" hermeneutic, from restoring a lost original to demystifying false appearances:

> The task of hermeneutics...has always been to read a text and distinguish the true sense from the apparent sense, to search for the sense under the sense, to search for the intelligible text under the unintelligible text.
> ...a *general exegesis* of false-consciousness... belongs by this fact in a *hermeneutics*, in a theory of interpretation, under the negative form of demystification,...demystification is characterized in the first place as the exercise of *suspicion*,...the act of dispute exactly proportional to the expressions of false consciousness.[92]

It is not that critics set out to invent difficulties, hidden meanings, and deceptive appearances or to create incapacities in their audience, but rather that their specialization presupposes such activity. Indeed, the machinery of culture itself—writing, publishing houses, educational institutions—has gradually come to reserve a place for interpreters and arbiters of public taste. Even contemporary authors can come to depend on critics willing to "immerse themselves in the work."[93] Literature—the ancient works and the most sophisticated modern experiments—has become a thing associated chiefly with the schools that both preserve the distance between high culture and low and work to overcome it. Mass education is, of course, but one of many institutions that exist to order and disseminate knowledge in the modern world, giving the general reading public a loose social coherence while at the same time allowing it to disband into a collection of separate "interest groups." Indeed, a split has developed in the ranks of professional criticism itself between those who speak of the "popular" arts and address a mass audience through the press magazines, and television (offering publicity to the entertainment industries and a form of consumer protection to the public) and those who, having acquired the requisite credentials, are allowed to address an audience of pupils and fellow scholars on the subject of "serious" literature. Hardly surprising, then, that this situation should make criticism more and more an academic matter or that the relationship between experimental literature and criticism should become close enough to allow criticism to "cross over" into creative writing.[94]

Thus, while criticism is certainly an act of reflection on discourse—analyzing it, evaluating it, helping to define and circumscribe the official limits of the literary—it is also made of discourse, a reflective operation on language that can only be carried out in language. As with other discursive institutions, criticism follows its own laws of formation, preservation, and transmission; it occupies a particular cultural "space" to which different speakers and writers will have access at different times, thus affecting the nature and the function of critical knowledge. In the well-known formulation of Michel Foucault:

> Knowledge is that of which one can speak in a discursive practice, and which is specified by that fact: the domain constituted by the different objects that will or will not acquire a scientific status (the knowledge of psychiatry in the nineteenth century is not the sum of what was thought to be true, but the whole set of practices, singularities, and deviations of which one could speak in psychiatric discourse); knowledge is also the space in which the subject may take up a position and speak of the objects with which he deals in his discourse (in this sense, the knowledge of clinical medicine is the whole group of functions of observation, interrogation, decipherment, recording, and decision that may be exercised by the subject of medical discourse); knowledge is also the field of coordination and subordination of statements in which concepts appear, and are defined, applied and transformed (at this level, the knowledge of Natural History, in the eighteenth century, is not the sum of what was said, but the whole set of modes and sites in accordance with which one can integrate each new statement with the already said); lastly, knowledge is defined by the possibilities of use and appropriation offered by discourse (thus, the knowledge of political economy, in the Classical period, is not the sum of the different theses sustained, but the totality of its points of articulation on other discourses or on other practices that are not discursive). There are bodies of knowledge that are independent of the sciences, . . . but there is no knowledge without a particular discursive practice; and any discursive practice may be defined by the knowledge that it forms.[95]

Hence, the body of critical knowledge will alter if, as has been the case for perhaps the last two centuries, it is a professional rather than an amateur activity, and if it develops in consort with the other professions—poetry, pedagogy, philosophy, social science—with which it is chiefly allied. The training that prepares one to become a critic, the accepted channels of critical communication and the discursive manners they uphold, exert a decided influence on the methods and the doctrines that constitute the criticism of any given epoch. Not only will such things as the putative difficulty or mystery of the reading process be affected, but the fundamental stance of criticism, whether it is basically retrospective or prospective, an avant-garde or a force of social and cultural conservatism.

To be sure, the popular impression is that criticism, especially in its theoretical form, must always lag behind or resist literary innovation, hence Lionel Abel's surprise at the current "effort to produce a new movement in literary criticism, one not based on new works of literary art."[96] Starobinski notes that the earliest forms of criticism arose only after poetry was already an institution with sufficient diversity to allow comparison and selection. Criticism—as a system of argument in the abstract, without reference to particular works—was a much later development.[97] Yet once it has become a discipline in its own right, there is nothing to prevent criticism from establishing an ever more independent position for itself. And while classicism and restorative criticism are, by definition, conservative, there are instances enough—Wordsworth's "Preface to the Lyrical Ballads," the various surrealist manifestos—where the role of criticism is just the opposite, to promote the new rather than to prevent deviations from the old.

Thus, there is no a priori reason for taking the prominence of literary theory as either a sign of decadence or a diversion from the proper path of literary development. Moreover, if one looks more deeply into the history of criticism, one can even uncover precedents for treating criticism as a form of art—Dryden's dialogues, the apologies of Sydney and Shelley, the elegant paradoxes of Oscar Wilde, who himself argued that criticism "works with materials, and puts them into a form that is at once new and delightful. What more can one say of poetry?"[98]

For our purposes, a more revealing history of Anglo-American criticism comes when one examines it from the perspective of how changing conditions and affiliations have changed the nature and the meaning of the critical act. Beginning, say, with Samuel Johnson, one recognizes in his sharply judgmental criticism that his is a period when the canon is (once again) in formation, yet because his judgments can still appeal to general principles and common public standards, there is nothing veiled or mysterious about Johnson's authority and no need for recondite faculties or peculiar expertise to justify his inclusions and exclusions. Indeed, there is a strong sense of public fellowship in Johnson's criticism and an interestingly balanced mode of address that suggests that, as yet, there is little recognized difference between those who write (either poetry or criticism) and those who read. But his outspoken resistance to specialization of any kind, the occasional strenuousness of his efforts to connect moral, psychological, scientific and aesthetic norms, suggests that the balance is extremely precarious and already threatened.

Johnson's balance was in fact never to be attained again: For critics writing after him the lines between artist and audience are clearly drawn, and a choice must be made between a criticism directed to the problems of writing, a criticism concerned with the problems of reading, and (increasingly) a criticism caught up in the problems of relevance, the heresies and fallacies of criticism itself. Even when the critic is himself a poet, as Coleridge, Arnold, Eliot, and Pound clearly were, the distinction is preserved between a creative and a critical poetics, between promulgating a certain artistic program on the one hand and establishing standards for analysis and appreciation on the other. (Frequently, even the work of promulgation takes as its audience, not prospective writers, but prospective readers who require assistance to enter fully into an unfamiliar literary mode.) The Romantic repugnance at any mechanical constraints on genius is certainly one reason why criticism from the nineteenth century onward is so seldom framed as a guide to poets; another is the insistence on "organic" works of art able to live independently of their makers. But what finally cemented the tie between criticism and reception was the role that critics came to play in the spread of mass literacy and mass education. Arnold is a case in point, a pioneer of "education by poetry," and a cultural impresario fighting the parochialism and self-satisfaction of the British middle classes by exposing them to "the best that has been known and thought."[99] It was now no longer a question of forming the canon but of preserving it from the eroding forces of carelessness and mediocrity. Arnold's is a criticism in which the act of writing of literature becomes progressively more remote, occult, at times all but impossible—less, perhaps, in his explicit pronouncements than in his persistent air of reservation and stricture and his almost superstitious handling of sacred poetic touchstones, those passages that appear as if from nowhere and exist only as monumental fragments on the page before us. Arnold's rhetoric is far more mobile than Johnson's, his premises more often covert, his persuasive power more often the result of the grandeur of his attitudes than of the cogency of his arguments. All of this bespeaks a greater isolation, a wary elevation of critic over audience. Standards must be introduced rather than invoked, and achieving this introduction requires no little strategy and tact. But the introduction alone is apparently sufficient; no further training is required beyond exposure to specimens of poetry of the very highest quality.

Arnold's confidence stands in sharp contrast to I. A. Richards and the shock of disappointment with which his *Practical Criticism* opens, a disappointment that fuels his entire program and much of criticism in general for several decades to follow. For Richards, true appreciation does *not* occur automatically; readers need a guidance more sustained than Arnold's evocative introductions can possibly provide. Critics, accordingly, must become teachers rather than occasional essayists or impressarios. The critical apparatus is enriched (although not yet as rich as it would eventually become) in proportion to the new pedagogical tasks assigned to it—greatly reducing the need for personal authority on the critic's part. The work of explication and instruction proceeds with, for the most part, well-established texts and displaces the more quarrelsome effort of selecting and defending works worthy of aesthetic appreciation. As a result, critical writing takes on a more subdued and deliberative quality.

The sobriety of its immediate predecessor no doubt contributes to the apparent upheaval of the present moment, when many of the most prominent critics are not only quarrelsome again but florid, almost gaudy. The shock of this writing often seems calculated, as if aware of its own place in the history of criticism. Indeed, this awareness by critics of their making of history must be recognized as an increasingly potent force in shaping new critical activity in this century. The emphasis on theoretical rather than practical criticism is partly the result of such self-conscious interplay; criticism of criticism necessarily promotes greater abstraction and greater specialization. But an increase of theoretical activity also arises whenever the function of criticism itself is in doubt. Theory then emerges to renew, with its formality, operations that have grown confused and vague, or to provide fresh justifications for methods that have lost their sense of purpose. It may even prescribe entirely new activities or sketch possibilities yet to be realized. Such would seem to be its major function now.

Today, the relationship between criticism and its reception is, if anything, more intimate than it has ever been before, but the wheel has come full circle and reception has become itself productive; when reading is a way of *making* meaning, critical theory, as the following pages hope to show, easily becomes an act of extravagant invention.

1
Theory of Literature
Becomes Theory as Literature

What therefore is truth? A mobile army of metaphors,
metonymies, anthropomorphisms: in short a sum of human relations which became poetically and rhetorically
intensified, metamorphosed, adorned, and after long usage seems to a nation fixed, canonic, and binding; truths
are illusions of which one has forgotten that they *are* illusions; worn-out metaphors which have become powerless
to affect the senses,... For between two utterly different
spheres, as between subject and object, there is no causality, no accuracy, no expression, but at the utmost an *aes-
thetical* relation, I mean a suggestive metamorphosis, a
stammering translation into quite a distinct foreign language, for which purpose, however, there is needed at
any rate an intermediate sphere, an intermediate force,
freely composing and freely inventing
FRIEDRICH NIETZSCHE, *The Dawn of Day*, No. 507

i.

If the sudden glamour of literary theory is the product of a number of
distinct but overlapping factors, the routes by which theory passes from
writing *about* literature to literary writing are equally many, and often
devious. Yet such "glamour" is telling, as are the hyperbolic and occasionally disfunctional displays of rigor that are so common in contemporary
literary theory—the spectacle it makes of its estrangements and its skep-
ticisms. Together they suggest that (for us) the theoretical impulse and
the aesthetic are closely intertwined. Nor would this convergence seem
particularly surprising were it not for certain deeply rooted antagonisms,
both ideological and institutional, that have for so long kept imagination
and investigation separate, dividing knowledge from desire and truth
from beauty.

In its extreme form, this segregation produces polemic and self-
deception: crude positivism and mystified aestheticism, mechanical objec-

33

tivity and wayward inspiration. Theory itself has never fit comfortably into either category, hence the discomfiture it provokes among purists on either side and the pronounced changes of evaluation to which it is subject. The entry under *theory* in the *Oxford English Dictionary* is a tissue of contradictions and ambivalence, beginning with antique controversies over whether it is contemplative "deepe studie" or only "sick mens phrensies" and continuing right up through our own more subtly equiv- ocal uses of the term.

> 3. A conception or mental scheme of something to be done, or the method of doing it; a systematic statement of rules or principles to be followed,....4. A scheme or system of ideas or statements held as an explanation or account of a group of facts or phenomena; a hypothesis that has been confirmed or established by observation or experiment, and is propounded or accepted as accounting for the known facts; a statement of what are held to be general laws, principles, or causes of something known or observed,....5. In the abstract (without article): Systematic conception or statement of the principles of something; abstract knowledge, or the form- ulation of it: often used as implying more or less unsupported hypothesis: distinguished from or opposed to *practice. In theory*...opp. to *in practice* or *in fact*,....6. In loose or general sense: A hypothesis proposed as an ex- planation; hence a mere hypothesis, speculation, conjecture;...an indi- vidual view or notion.[1]

From principles that underlie and guarantee a given practice to principles opposed to any practice, from well-established hypotheses to unsupported speculations, from a repository of shared knowledge to idiosyncratic notions—so goes the pendular sweep of the definition. *Theory* is evidently another one of Derrida's *pharmakons*, those pivot words that turn so easily into their opposites, and in their rotations reveal, for just a moment, the machinery of thought as it struggles to produce and maintain the key distinctions upon which all subsequent operations will depend.[2] In the play of inconsistencies surrounding the term *theory* is an unresolved dispute about the grounds of certainty and the very possibility of establishing general principles of knowledge or behavior. On one side stands the intelligible and the conceivable, on the other stands the "real"—both necessary to knowledge, yet somehow seeming to exclude each other. The deeper the attempt to probe the fundamental order of things, the keener the fear (or perhaps the hope) that one is chasing chimeras, that "things can't work that way." The more steps taken to assure validity, the more truth seems to escape us; the more elaborate our intellectual schemes become, the less confident we are about the status of our knowledge.

Resistance to theory usually takes the shape of casual irritation: What need for all those abstractions and systematic programs? How can one possibly preserve them in the face of "raw" experience? But this impatience springs from a set of deeper, if often inarticulate, commitments: trust in certain modes of reasoning; loyalty to certain standards that distinguish genuine "knowledge" from mere "belief" (and hence determine those things that, for methodological reasons or because they fail to meet the required standards, must remain unknowable); allegiance to a framework of basic categories and relationships, to certain modes of being, that seem irreducible.[3] The fate of theory is therefore a fairly accurate index of individual and even cultural credulity, not only what will prove believable, but when it will and with what degree of confidence or reservation. If, for example, it is the correspondence between a given statement and a state of affairs that is the standard of truth, the status of theory is likely to be lower than when truth is a matter of the coherence, the logical agreement between statements. "To report the facts objectively, the voice of science ideally must correspond to its objects in this one-to-one fashion. . . . The part of communication that cannot be reduced to pointer readings or mathematics is declared to be subjective and hence epistemologically invalid—a kind of symbol cloak beneath which "reality" remains hidden."[4]

When only seeing is believing and perceptual knowledge is esteemed more certain than inferential, theoretical discourse (indeed discourse of all kinds) is devalued, reduced to an ancillary device for summarizing past observations and calculating the likely outcome of future observations. Significantly, these same epistemological, logical, and metaphysical commitments influence the arts as well as the sciences, affecting both the subject matter and the status of representation: now favoring formalism and now imitation, now the representation of appearance and now of essence, focusing on entities or on processes according to whichever seems more central or more knowable and communicable.[5] Of course, the arts need not parallel the sciences; there may instead be a division of intellectual labor that relegates certain "unknowables" to the arts or attempts to preserve certain subjects from the scrutiny of science.[6]

Because these commitments are so broad in their implications, it is not surprising to find the status of theory changing radically and in many different fields at once. But a sudden swing from opprobrium to praise, a quick elevation of theory over ad hoc practical solutions and/or the careful collection of data, is not just an inversion. Clearly it is not a matter of our admiring the very features that were only recently condemned or of turning the clock back from materialism to idealism or substituting realism for operationalism, but instead of construing the role of theory in another way. The new respect for theory comes from recognizing that one cannot extract a framework directly from the data, but must already have some framework to establish which data are relevant and which are not. This does not require, as some would have it, abandoning all pursuit of fact, but it does mean reconceiving what we mean by *fact*. As Quine remarks: ". . . man has no evidence for the existence of bodies beyond the fact that their assumption helps him organize experience, . . . instead of disclaiming evidence for the existence of bodies. . . [we should recognize that] such, then, at bottom is what evidence is."[7]

Similarly, it now appears that no compilation of separately confirmed statements will ever add up to an explanation or produce a satisfactory configuration; for this, there must be what Hayden White calls "an enabling and generically fictional matrix."[8] The matrix must, of course, be justified in some way and consistent with experience, but it remains the work of a "disciplined theoretical imagination" and not a simple accumulation of data.[9] One cannot, in fact, set about gathering data and attempting to verify hypotheses without presupposing the adequacy of the general theory that provides the terms for describing and classifying what one has observed. The line between observation and speculation, theory and fact, is not as sharp as it was once supposed. "There are no modes of description which remain invariant under all changes of theory. . . . The accepted way of explaining phenomena enters into the very meaning of the terms used to describe them."[10] While there is still a distinction between a description that any observer would be willing to accept and a theory-laden description in which terms are unfamiliar or still at issue, the interplay between the two poles is constant and complex: "Expectations and conceptual commitments influence perception. . . . The predicates we use in describing the world and the categories with which we classify events depend on the regularities we anticipate. . . ."[11]

It is reflections such as these that have produced a change in the relative status of fact and theory, making strict empiricism a more and more difficult position to maintain. Interest in theory must run high, if only for defensive reasons: "If the assumptions are known, they can be changed systematically, explicitly, controllably. No amount of experimental work alone can determine what concepts are best to use, because to make an experiment already requires some formulation of a problem, and this requires the use of some concepts."[12]

But esteem for theory may be widespread without there being any equally widespread agreement about what a theory must be or do. Discussions of theory show marked discrepancies about the structure, the degree and kind of internal cohesion theoretical discourse is expected to possess. Positions range from the claim that any theory worthy of the name should comprise a mathematical axiom system, a closed corpus of fully specifiable laws together with the predictions these entail, to the opposite claim that "a theory would still be a theory if its laws did not fit easily or at all into a logical system: the laws might only hang together because they were laws of the same subject matter."[13] Opinions differ too about the necessary core of any theory, what propels it and gives it efficacy. Must every theory have a model, or "symbolic representation devised to account for observed phenomena,"[14] which thereby makes the phenomena more intelligible, or is it enough to have a set of laws that facilitate prediction and control, without attempting to characterize the mechanism responsible for those laws?[15] Or can one get by simply by assembling all the relevant factors and their associated probability values so as to know "what degree of expectation is rational?"[16] Such distinctions are related to quite different notions of how theoretical discourse establishes its case, illuminates its subject, how it manages to be persuasive—the standards of logic or of plausibility or of iconography to which it ultimately appeals. Thus, for some writers, a theory is a convenient device for making calculations, while for others it is a mode of argument that works by demonstrating the logical fit between predictions and initial premises, while still others feel that what theory offers is less a proof than a display, "an exhibition of the way in which regularities fit into the causal structure of the world."[17]

Some of this disagreement is of relatively recent date, part of a general disenchantment with the deductive-nomological model of theory that had held almost unquestioned sway for several previous decades. Against this view, which is based on a concern for precision and validity and which likens the construction of a theory to a geometric proof, it is now argued that few if any theories actually achieve this ideal condition or even aspire to it. Mathematics need not provide the only pattern for building successful theories (nor, for that matter, need literary theory take the form of theories in the physical sciences). Insisting that nothing short of deductive certainty will do seems both too stringent and too lax, since the criterion does nothing to exclude irrelevant or unilluminating syllogisms like: "Either all crows are black or all crows are white / No crow is white / Therefore all crows are black." Finally, the deductive-nomological ideal threatens to limit our understanding to what can be subsumed under already established generalizations, with no room for theoretical innovation or extension.[18] The model did provide a powerful critique of the inductive method and a striking demonstration of the primacy of theory, and it still retains many adherents who admire its purity and rigor. But the current scene is one in which many views contend, and to embrace this definition of theory is really to express a preference for one among a number of reputable alternatives.

All are agreed that a theory must be *general* both in its terminology and in the conditions under which it is said to hold, and that it must be *hypothetical* and/or prospective in relation to whatever documentation or embodiment it will eventually receive. Indeed, no amount of evidence, no accumulation of enactments can ever logically exhaust it, since the theory applies to "all actual and even hypothetical cases of the relevant sort."[19] It should also be as *formal* (that is, well regulated and explicit) and as *coherent* as possible—so much all writers would agree. Every theory also has its own *domain*, that set of objects, processes, and so forth, to which it applies; the larger the domain, the more "powerful" the theory—a point frequently cited when the value of rival theories is being weighed or when doubts arise about whether two theories really do contend or simply complement each other or fail to overlap at all.

One can also distinguish, in the case of every theory, between its *justification* and its *vindication*, the principles that validate or confirm it as opposed to the pragmatic and aesthetic considerations that contribute to its acceptance.[20] No theory—as Gödel and Tarski both have pointed out—can justify itself, and when a defense is necessary, it must appeal to other principles, to standards of confirmation and/or rules of logic that all parties recognize. Yet such justifications can only demonstrate that a given theory has no hidden inconsistencies or makes no incorrect predictions; they cannot determine which of two equally consistent and equally well-confirmed theories is the better one. Since even incompatible premises can have the same consequences and the same state of affairs may receive a number of equally accurate explanations, there must be further grounds of appeal—vindications that differ both in the level at which they are invoked (only after minimum standards of confirmation and logic have already been met) and in the precision and completeness with which they can establish their case. There are no fixed rules, comparable to the rules of validity, for usefulness or elegance of a theory. This lack makes vindication of a theory a far more slippery process than its justification. But a vital one nonetheless, when all theories are underdetermined by their evidence and must at some point resort to criteria like power, simplicity, or ease of handling. Some writers even subdivide theory approximately along these lines into testable and untestable portions, the latter being the framework of conceptual organization that regulates research but remains immune to empirical falsification (though not to complaints of awkwardness, inefficiency, etc.).[21] As Grover Maxwell portrays the situation:

> Mr. A.... introduces the class term... "multicolored surface" to designate his "new kind of entities." Suppose that Mr. B. demurs, insisting on locutions such as "chartreuse," "reddish-green," and so forth. Then the frameworks of A and B would differ in that they would embody, respectively, slightly different meaning of words such as "colored surface";... in B's framework, the sentence "No surface can be simultaneously red and green all over" would be A-true, while in A's it would be *contingently* false. And since in principle both A and B can, each in his respective framework, express and explain all the "facts" concerning *colored surfaces* (in either sense), "the facts" can never compel either to accept the other's framework.[22]

In practice, the distinction between the conceptual or metaphysical framework and the remainder of the theory is extremely difficult to preserve, since the boundary between what is true by definition and what requires confirmation continually shifts and most theories have a "belt of auxiliary hypotheses" that can be altered or abandoned in order to preserve more central commitments.[23] Thus, if one keeps altering one's notions of the properties of atoms, one may never have to relinquish the claim that there are elementary units of matter.[24] Moreover, although the defense of a theory may move from justification to vindication, "invention" seems to move in the opposite direction, with conceptual categories and pragmatic and aesthetic preferences eliminating certain possibilities before they can even become "candidates for reality."[25] As the deductive-nomological model recedes and philosophers of theory turn from an exclusive focus on validity to questions of composition and heuristic value—probing what makes a conceptual structure vivid, memorable, interesting enough to arouse interest in its initial stages and loyalty in its later stages—the aesthetic and pragmatic considerations that have always played a-part in theory have gained steadily in significance.[26] It is still possible to distinguish between logical structure and the psychology of belief—to know the difference between innovation and intelligibility, on the one hand, and validity, on the other, without denigrating one at the expense of the other.

Beyond this point however, consensus disappears and theory becomes an essentially contested concept, subject to stipulative definitions and veiled recommendations designed to favor models over axioms, or assimilation over prediction, or exhibition over argument. And even when one eliminates differences of attitude from the *O.E.D.* account of theory, a fundamental ambiguity remains respecting its function—does theory carry the force of an explanation, or a prediction, or does it instead count as a directive or a program? In one case, theory is an attempt to "fit words to the world" (in John Searle's language), although it may at the same time alter eternally what we take the world to be. In the other, it is an effort to make "the world fit to the words," to shape and define an activity, to bring something about that might not otherwise exist. To be sure, the prestige of science and the outright attacks by Popper and Chomsky on so-called discovery procedures (methodological recommendations that control the collection of information but have no proven explanatory value) would make it seem that unless a theory does explain, it cannot be justified and therefore should not count as a theory at all. But reasons can be offered to justify a program, and, although vindication—with all its vagaries—is likely to weigh more heavily in regard to a program than in the case of explanation, there are no a priori grounds for restricting theory to explanation alone.[27]

One does, of course, need to discriminate between rules of procedure and hypotheses—only the latter can be true or false, as opposed to simply feasible or infeasible. Because the structure of inference is different in each case—from recommended ends to proposed means in the case of programs, rather than from inferrred causes to observed effects—and because it is possible to reach incompatible conclusions about which inferential strategies are best, the reasoning associated with programs is often called "practical" and set off from "theoretical," or "pure," reason.[28] The relationship between means and ends lacks the clarity and necessity of the deductive relationship between premises and conclusion, yet there is ample historical precedent for calling programs "theories." (Explanatory theories occasionally resort to means-ends reasoning as well—especially to account for biological processes—despite the long hegemony of mechanical causation.)[29]

Thus, neither the style of reasoning nor the need for pragmatic vindication is peculiar to programmatic theories. The distinctions between program and explanation are real but not absolute, and there are differences almost as great in the range of what philosophers of science accept as theoretical—between laws and statistical regularities, say, or between models that aid comprehension and calculating devices that merely produce correct predictions. This suggests that *theory* can embrace programs as well without losing its integrity. The real danger is not in calling both explanations and programs *theory*, but in confusing one kind of theory with another: allowing procedural recommendations to mask themselves as explanations or failing to provide sufficient reasons for their use.

Depending on how one defines *theory*, a theory of literature may turn out to be either impossible or unavoidable. If, for example, one accepts Harré's reasoning that "in learning to apply descriptive terms we are also learning theories,"[30] then almost any talk about literature becomes, indirectly at least, theoretical. It is in this spirit that M. H. Abrams answers the challenge that theorizing about the arts is useless.

> Granted the use of "presuppose" to include relations [like "generate" or "suggest"], we can say with assurance that yes, all criticism presupposes theory, and in at least two ways. First any discourse about works of art that is sufficiently sustained and ordered to count as criticism has attributes—for example, the kinds of features in the work it discriminates or ignores, the kinds of terms it uses or fails to use, the relations it specifies, the literal or analogical mode of reasoning it exhibits—which serve as indices of the type of theoretical perspective to which the critic is committed, whether explicitly or implicitly, and whether deliberately or as a matter of habit. Second, any sustained critical discourse is likely to use some aesthetic theorists, and will inescapably use other terms, taken from ordinary language, but applied in accordance with specialized rules of usage which, historical investigation shows, have been developed by earlier aesthetic theorists.[31]

Abram's reminder that even the least speculative criticism rests on a store of habitual assumptions about the properties of literature, the goal of criticism, and how one constructs a convincing case is well taken; he is perfectly correct to question the purity of descriptive terms and to use the de facto constraints on what critics find it relevant or irrelevant to talk about as evidence that a wholly spontaneous and unmediated criticism is a delusion. But it is one thing to argue this and quite another to claim that all criticism therefore presupposes a theory. In the first place, this would undermine a valuable distinction between criticism that attempts to be theoretical and criticism that makes no such attempt. It violates our intuitive sense that the difference between a Coleridge and an Arnold or a Leavis and a Richards is more than a matter of degree, or what one man chooses to make public and the other keeps to himself. Plainly it *is* possible to conduct a sustained criticism that employs a mixed terminology, relies on muddy or inconsistent premises, and stops short of making any fundamental commitments. There are even cases where deliberate mystification functions as part of a rhetorical strategy of persuasion-by-intimidation. Presuppositions of some sort may be unavoidable, but they need not add up to a single, coherent theory. Responding to Abrams, Arthur Moore has argued that the presuppositions of most criticism are too vague to provide a clear warrant for any particular method of observation, although they may and often do rule *out* some approaches and act as "barriers to alien modes of inquiry."[32]

If, then, theory is not necessary to criticism, is it at least useful? Is a theory of literature even possible? Those who entirely deny or reject literary theory typically fall into one of two groups, holding either that theory is indeed possible but pernicious, or that it is logically impossible and that whatever now goes by the name is mistaken, self-deluded, counterfeit. The first position is usually put forward to defend the fluidity and ineffability of art and to preserve the breadth and subtlety of the critical performance. How can one—the question goes—hope to construct generalizations or laws of literature, without at the same time destroying the very uniqueness and difference for which it is so highly prized? How issue predictions or prescriptions without foreclosing opportunities for innovation and confining literary discourse within the familiar limits of hackneyed formulas and clichés? "It is as though the laws—the syntax—of nature were variable. . . . the idiosyncratic actualization of art calls for a flexible strategy, ad hoc reasons which no rules determine. Criticism is pedantic, can only explain the routine cases without these."[33]

An assumption that seems to run through this passage and others like it is that natural phenomena, unlike works of art, display no variation and that the laws proposed in scientific theories are meant to exhaust their subject matter rather than simply to isolate certain aspects of it for study.

Yet all events are in themselves unique, and generalizations are designed to apply to events only insofar as they are typical.[34] It is the parameters of research, not the nature of the object, that establish the ideal lack of variation; the failure to appreciate whatever escapes typification is not the fault of the theory but of its users. Indeed, it is only against a background of the typical that we are able to pick out idiosyncratic features and to recognize innovation. It is difficult to imagine a criticism that makes no generalizations at all, that does not at least "consume" laws—the laws of nature, the rules of grammar, the norms of social behavior—in reaching its interpretations and assessments, even if it invents none of its own. Writers as well as critics tacitly acknowledge certain regularities by adhering to generic categories and traditional metrical schemes; neither parody nor allusion would be possible if every work were truly to be read *ab novo*. And since even the laws of physics have their boundary conditions (delimiting the scope of their operation), there is nothing to prevent our proposing further constraints to arrive at the far more flexible and limited generalizations we will need to account for socially and historically conditioned phenomena like literature. More flexible, in fact, than the commonplaces—that art must always innovate, that originality is more valuable than, say, refinement or cultural continuity—from which the attack on theory gains its sense of urgency. Although not formulated as laws, such generalizations (as Abrams notes) are no less "highly specialized, employed exclusively by a class of intellectuals who share a current climate of opinion, and are a heritage from quite recent developments in aesthetic theory."[35]

The objection that theory artificially restricts the critic's own resources and narrows the focus and function of criticism is more sophisticated. "In what ways," asks William Righter, "could regularity, precision, internal coherence be brought about in the performance of such a mixed variety of tasks [as those performed by traditional criticism]?"[36] Yet Righter must still have his own determinant, if complex, model of what criticism should be in order to ask this question—a model that he simply assumes, without defending, and without wondering whether a change in the circumstances or purposes of criticism might not make the depth of theory better than the breadth of ad hoc methods. Nor is there any reason to suppose that without a theory to constrain it, criticism would naturally become more resourceful, more fluid and imaginative. The force of habit may make criticism as narrow, or narrower, than any limits theory consciously imposes—with the added disadvantage that, with habit, one may not even know that the constraints exist or why one is obeying them. Such criticism becomes extremely vulnerable to crises of confidence and, when challenged, all too easily gives way to cynicism or utter obscurantism. Theory, then, may actually arouse long-dulled senses to the potential breadth of literary concerns, while giving critical reasoning a dignity it cannot have when it is strictly instrumental, performing an evangelical task in any way it can.

To the extent that theory strives to make procedures and results replicable, it is, of course, the enemy of criticism as an inspired individual performance. And there are peculiarities to the study of literature that suggest that the performance factor may be harder to eradicate here than it is when procedures are simple, more or less mechanical, and when all that needs to be achieved is the same measurements and observations. There is a quality to literary experience that the act of criticsm itself embodies, and communicates to readers without being able to guarantee that they will have it too. If this indeterminacy does not do away with literary theory, it does suggest how it is apt to differ from other theories and why its expressive qualities might bring it to the verge of literature itself.

The second sort of objection that literary theory faces focuses on the logic of theory, a logic that—putatively—literary criticism not only should not but cannot emulate. Literature, like art itself, is an open concept, whereas theory is a quest for essences, and hence "an illegitimate procedure of criticism in that it tries to define what is indefinable."[37] The criteria for calling something a piece of literature are mixed and frequently subject to debate; it would be impossible to cite a set of necessary and sufficient conditions that all uses of the term *literature* must meet, since the term must be flexible enough to extend to new and unforeseen situations and especially since it is an evaluative as well as a descriptive term. Not only need there be no set of features that all acknowledged works of literature have in common, but even experts may disagree about when it is appropriate to call something a piece of literature in the first place, to make it—whatever its properties—a "candidate for appreciation."[38] They may not even agree about what appreciation, in the case of literature, amounts to. Literary theory errs by trying to reduce an irreducibly protean concept. (Apparently the challengers assume that theories of literature must always employ essentialist definitions or that they must always strain to embrace the whole of literature, rather than some more determinant subset. The possibility that prescriptive or stipulative definitions might have a legitimate place in literary theory is never entertained at all.)

Most of these efforts to dismiss literary theory follow the lead of Wittgenstein's later writings, where he attempts to demonstrate that many language "games" are capable of functioning smoothly and rationally without necessary and sufficient conditions. Hence, there is no disrespect for literary studies, only an insistence that they adopt the looser framework appropriate to them. Strangely though, while championing open concepts and repudiating essences in the case of art, such arguments continue to treat *theory* as a closed concept, a term whose application is forever fixed. Yet (as we have seen) a closer examination of the writings devoted to theory reveals no such calm consensus, but instead a range of heterogeneous and disjunctive criteria, and even outright squabbles over what should be allowed to count as theory—much as in the case of art. Thus, while it is possible that many literary theories do mistake the nature of aesthetic concepts, it is also possible that dismissive attitudes are the result of mistaken ideas about the nature of theory, a too hasty effort to force literary theory to conform to alien standards and a too ready despair when it does not.

As a category, literature differs from the categories that characteristically figure in scientific theories. One of the great problems with New Criticism, for example, was its attempt to put on the objectivity of science by actually treating literature as if it were an object, despite the fact that one cannot determine meaning or value in the same way—or with quite the same assurance—with which one determines the properties of an object. (Of course even perceptual judgments involve some interpretation, but interpretations that are far more entrenched and uniform.) Whatever one believes meaning to be—a value conferred by convention, or by intention, or both—it is not a property of the text in the sense that the width of its margins or its typeface is. It takes an effort, then, an additional layer of argument and/or persuasion, even to achieve agreement on what the "data" for a theory of literature are. And when one then attempts to account for these data, the likeness to the scientific study of "entities and causes" becomes even weaker.[39] Most attempts at causal explanation turn out to be circular: e.g., only "significant form" is capable of inspiring "aesthetic emotion," but aesthetic emotion can only be identified as the emotion produced by contemplating significant form.[40] The relationship between a text and its appreciation is not to be assimilated to mechanical causation; understanding and enjoyment are not effects that the text produces mechanically, but demand the active cooperation of the reader.[41]

As a rule, the logical relation between a literary interpretation or assessment and the arguments supporting it is neither inductive nor deductive but "criterial." What we offer are reasons for accepting a claim—reasons that may require a fair amount of training even to appreciate—rather than a mass of indisputable evidence or premises that directly entail a conclusion.[42] Indeed, some (following another of Wittgenstein's cryptic remarks, that reasons in aesthetics are of the nature of further descriptions) would deny that reasons really *support* critical judgments at all:

> Rather they explain them; make it clear what it is that we mean . . . . we are not moving from hypothesis to conclusion or in any other formally logical way, but we show, point, compare, draw attention to, and generally try to make others see what it is that we mean by offering alternative

descriptions or suggesting different ways of looking at a particular work. Our judgments are not supported by arguments, but rather are elucidated by a variety of remarks of many possible linguistic types.[43]

Again, this may overestimate the peculiarity of literary arguments by underestimating the important role elucidation plays even in scientific explanations—which, according to Mary Hesse, are frequently not deductive either but consist of a "metaphoric redescription of the domain of the explanandum."[44] Still the caveat against expecting all explanations to work in exactly the same way is well taken, especially when this becomes a superstition that only certain "fundamental processes" have any real "explanatory efficacy."[45] Whatever the prestige of a process like mechanical causation, however fundamental it may have been to the rise of modern science, it could still be completely inappropriate to literary study. Indeed, the recent surge in literary theory would seem to be connected to the appearance of an entirely new explanatory framework, rooted in linguistics rather than in physics, which stresses the "explanatory efficacy" of structure and rules—agencies far better suited to the study of literature than of mechanical force.

If there are those who still feel that literary theory is impossible, it is not for any lack of practitioners. But the very welter of these and the difficulty of deciding between their competing claims makes skeptics even more skeptical. The so-called pluralism of literary studies, the fact that so many theories can coexist without necessarily excluding one another, seems to strengthen the case against true literary theory. Often enough there is no actual contradiction between theories, since the domains are not at all the same: One theory applies to all novels, another only to "great" novels, while a third attempts to account for historical changes in the novel. Yet there is no consensus as to what the proper domain for a theory of literature is—form alone or form relative to some purpose or social setting? Authorship or readership? Synchrony or diachrony? One function of those restrictive definitions of art and the beautiful that are so often the target of detractors is to limit the domain of literary theory (as it were) by force. An illegitimate procedure no doubt, yet no question of domain can be resolved empirically. Even if there were a perfect popular consensus about what matters most in literary matters, it would not follow that providing an account of this consensus is the most interesting or most useful thing for a literary theory to do. One could, for instance, construct a forceful argument that the role of literary theory is to reform and redefine commonplace assumptions. Demanding that literary theory cover all the currently accepted view of literature and only those might at least help to narrow the field, however, and with fewer competing theories, literary studies might eventually achieve the steady refinement and progress one associates with science. But the desire for progress is, logically, only a way of vindicating a certain class of theories. Depending on the circumstances, linear development and the fewest possible contending theories might no longer seem so desirable; contention itself might be esteemed for the excitement it produces, and diffuse inventiveness prized more than progress.

Yet the wealth of literary theories involves more than disparate domains, since tolerance apparently extends even to cases of outright incompatibility. While there are many equally correct and compatible ways to explain the same phenomena—an apple falls because of gravity; an apple falls because the stem is loose—it is impossible for both of two contradictory hypotheses to be true. What occurs in the case of literary theory seems to be more consistent with programs than with explanations; incompatible means for reaching the same end are neither illogical nor uncommon. Thus, if the goal of literary theory is (as Abrams puts it) "knowledge how to experience and enjoy works of art...by providing terms and analytic devices which enable us to experience them in a discriminating rather than a crude way,"[46] it is surely not hard to conceive of a number of incompatible proposals for accomplishing this.

Proponents of theory are hesitant to admit any prescriptive element, fearful that they will thereby endorse willfulness and relativism, while sacrificing whatever claim to rigor or validity literary theory may now enjoy. Thus, while insisting that "literary theory is not a science" in his article on theory in the *Princeton Encyclopedia of Poetry and Poetics*, Abrams still maintains that "a valid poetic theory is empirical in that it begins and ends in an appeal to the facts of existing poems."[47] Though his preferred domain is different, Jonathan Culler is even more adamant that literary theory function strictly as an explanation, "a mode of knowledge" and not a "tool" for producing interpretations.[48] Culler's ideal theory would be a model of literary competence, capable of accounting for the intuitions and abilities readers of literature actually display, a theory that could be falsified if its predictions fail to tally with what we otherwise observe. Even if we disregard the difficulty of gaining access to these intuitions (which are considerably more complex than the judgments of grammaticality and ambiguity that guide the linguistic theory Culler emulates), there is still the fact that Culler himself appears to waver between explanation and program at several crucial points. For example, he defends Lévi Strauss's study of myth, not for its accuracy, but for its ability to make "these myths become interesting and intelligible when read against one another" (p. 51); he praises the New Rhetoric as a "method for reading" that illustrates how to "naturalize" and "integrate the deviant" (p. 179); and in his conclusion, he states that the major task of criticism is "making the text interesting" (p. 262).

Culler recognizes perfectly that if what literary theory offers are hypotheses rather than regulative principles, then there must be some way to test for truth and falsehood; yet the tests he actually proposes don't really do this. "One's proposals will be sufficiently tested by one's readers' acceptance or rejection of them"—an acceptance that need not be immediate or spontaneous, but may extend to what readers are "willing to accept as plausible when explained" because of the "justice" of the critic's "operations" (p. 124). Hence, as the passage goes on, verification gradually gives way to something closer to persuasion, and the critic's success is no longer measured by what readers saw or felt independently but by what they can—with reason—be induced to see or feel.

As Culler himself admits, the problem is, at bottom, that "the institution of literature is fostered and maintained by literary education" (p. 51); literary competence may exploit innate capacities of mind, but it is also partly acquired, and literary theory plays an important part in that process of acquisition. This paradox has been formulated as follows by Leonard Meyer: "because works of art (the phenomena) are created by men, they can be affected by explanatory theories"—a problem that does not exist in the sciences, where no such interaction between theory and phenomena is possible.[49] Human actions differ from natural processes in being carried out under descriptions that help to constitute their value; the postulates of literary theory are capable of altering our understanding of what the text is doing and what we ourselves should do when we study or respond to it. Thus, though a theory may set out only to answer "why" some aspect of literature is the way it is, circumstances make it very difficult to avoid at the same time demonstrating "how" to read or write—showing where to focus attention, which connections to deem relevant, what experiences to expect.

The true test of an explanatory theory would therefore not be "one's readers' acceptance or rejection" but a controlled comparison between what the theory says and what is said by readers who have never read the theory. A theory that is addressed directly to those who are to test it is hopelessly compromised; prediction mingles inextricably with invitation or challenge. This does not mean that such a theory goes untested, only that the testing is altogether different than in the case of prediction and verification. There are indeed strictures on programmatic theories. A program must be plausible and feasible, for example; if a theory invites one to find certain features in a poem, it must be possible to find them—although they need not be the features one might otherwise have noticed. And the procedures for finding them, especially if they are unusual or unfamiliar, must be somehow specified and must in addition prove themselves adequate to the task. A literary theory that could not meet these minimal "performance" tests would fail as surely as a theory that made false predictions.

This is not to minimize the difference between explanation and program nor to deny that literary theory may aspire to both. The relative weight of these aspirations and the degree of success in attaining them must be judged case by case. For in practice (pardon the paradox) literary theory turns out to do many things—explain, instruct, regulate, even occasionally constitute its object of study—and it may take careful scrutiny to tell whether a proposal is being offered as a definition, a hypothesis, or an enabling postulate. Yet amid this diversity, there remains for members of the literary community a clear and persistent opposition between something called literary theory and something that is not theory—including textual emendation, explication de texte, practical criticism, and the act of composition. There are also two discursive features that literary theories characteristically share: a tendency to invent new terminologies, a common fondness for abstraction and for "posits," be they hypothetical or purely ideal types. These departures from a genteel, concrete, and understated prose are the traces of the pursuit of greater generality, precision, and explicitness one usually expects from theory. But a more important aim of literary theory is to erect a comprehensive schema, to make knowledge (whether it is "knowledge-how" or "knowledge-why") principled and whole: "bringing together" by an intellectual operation "what can only be experienced seriatum."[50] It is this above all that binds literary theory, in all its various forms, to theoretical work in other disciplines.

ii

There is reason to believe in literary theory, then, even beyond Mencken's practical nostrum "believe in it—I've seen it." What matters is not just the features it shares with other theories but the functions it is able to perform—the fundamental clarification, renewal, and reform it can provide, the fresh foundation for broad movements of research and / or creative writing. And now, in addition, there are those theoretical writings that also serve as literature—a function for which theory is admirably suited in several ways. First there is the fact, noted earlier, that too many theories are consistent with the same data or the same goals; if a theory is to win adherents, it must do so for reasons over and above its accuracy or feasibility. The reasons can include *vraisemblance*—the greater credibility of theories that are consistent with other, more well-established truths—pragmatic factors like "ease of handling" and, to a surprising extent, aesthetic preferences. Take the criterion of "simplicity" that is so often invoked to defend the choice of a given theoretical framework. "Certainly there are no purely logical reasons," according to Grover Maxwell, "for supposing that a simpler hypothesis is more likely to be true."[51] Simplicity, "the construction of systems having the fewest independent elements, in the simplest structure,"[52] is therefore best understood as a quest for beautiful proportions, for something fit for contemplation. Indeed, as often happens in the arts as well, the demand for aesthetic satisfaction may outstrip the bounds of verisimilitude, and lead to what Quine has named as one of his favorite "ironies": "It is the quest for system and simplicity that has kept driving the scientist to posit further entities as values of his variables. . . . By positing molecules, [Boyle's] law could be assimilated into a general theory of bodies in motion. . . . Man's drive for system and simplicity, leads, it seems, to ever new complexities."[53]

We may at first be hesitant to call this drive for system and simplicity aesthetic, so accustomed have we become to a different set of aesthetic values—stressing tension, difficulty, and surprise over classical harmony. But our hesitation is also fueled by the Kantian claim that aesthetic judgments must be indifferent to truth—a claim enlarged in post-Romantic art to make the two forms of judgment seem mutually exclusive, the "presentational" values of art apparently emerging only when all questions of "propositional" value have been suspended.[54] But these seemingly separate values achieve an astonishing intimacy in the construction of theories, reminding us that even logic involves a certain amount of sheer exhibition and that a valid syllogism "yields an experience of consummation" and an appreciation of "mutually relating" elements not unlike the experience usually reserved for art.[55]

Indeed, it is hard to separate the "drive for system and simplicity" from the theoretical enterprise itself; neither explanation nor prescription actually require it. In some contexts, as Peter Achinstein points out, the best explanation might be the most immediate one: "An explanation of a blow-out in an automobile tyre that makes reference to kinetic theory is deeper than one appealing only to the expansion of the air as a result of temperature increase. But it is not necessarily better. Here we do have to consider the knowledge and concerns of those in [the situation]. . . . Similar remarks apply to completeness and unification."[56] If, then, theoretical explanations and prescriptions strive for greater scope, for depth, completeness, unification, and the rest, they are reaching for an ideal, exceeding what is strictly necessary. The drive for system and simplicity is a drive indeed, touched by the gratuitousness, the hyperbole of all desire. Theory pursues knowledge past usefulness, past even power, since one can achieve rudimentary control without really caring to know how or why. It is here, in its extremity, that the theoretical and the artistic enterprises overlap, which may explain why our terms of praise—*elegant, symmetrical, powerful, interesting, bold*—are so often the same.

"Speculative Knowledge contemplates Truth for itself, and accordingly stops and rests in the Contemplation of it, which is what we commonly call Theory"—according to an obsolete (1710) citation in the *O.E.D.* Yet the definition may not be entirely out of date; to render contemplable, arresting, assimilable, the scattered and fragmentary experiences that would otherwise elude our concentration, the significance of which might otherwise escape us—such is the very raison d'être of theorizing. As Norbert Hanson describes it: ". . . there are moments when I find myself confronting a cluster of symbols, or observed anomalies, that, after having come to view through the appropriate *scientific theory*, configure, cohere, and collapse into meaningful patterns within a unified intellectual experience."[57] Confusion and insentience give way to an intense, focused awareness; emergent orderings of this sort are part of all that we acknowledge by the name of art. To theorize is to make coherence sharper, deeper, and more palpable. It therefore need not render theory useless to find it beautiful—in fact, the usefulness of theory may depend (at least in part) on that very thing.

Of course there are strictures on theory that do not exist in the case of novels and poems. The rush of sudden illumination is not enough; a theory must expose itself not only to immediate criticism and experimental tests, but to the test of time as well, to repeated applications, and to the steady incursions of its rivals.[58] To propose a theory is to risk—in fact to court—failure, to stand forever ready to alter and discard. This is true even of programmatic theories, where failure is apt to be less dramatic, since prescriptions and recommendations are not (as Kermode has said of fictions) "subject, like hypotheses, to proof or disconfirmation; only, if they come to lose their operational effectiveness, to neglect."[59] This brings literary theory, to the extent that it is programmatic, even closer to literature, to all conceptual frameworks where commitment depends less on demonstrable truth than on intellectual pleasure, the satisfaction of social and psychological need, "width of appeal, ability to withstand certain kinds of rational criticism, . . . feasibility, ideality, and of course . . . how it actually feels to live by them."[60] Yet because theory risks rejection more openly, it also brings something new to literature when it becomes a recognized form of art. An emphasis on simplicity may make theory's aesthetic richer and more complicated, refusing as it does to isolate our pleasure in the "presentational" aspects of discourse from our curiosity, our speculation, and if need be, our skepticism.

The literariness of recent literary theory is therefore an extension (although no doubt a hyperbolic one) of something that has always been implicitly part of theorizing. Not only do aesthetic considerations weigh heavily in the construction of theories, but there are striking parallels between the entities and forces that a theory posits and the fictitious characters and events that appear in literature. Compare, for example, R. B. Braithewaite's remarks below on "the 'reality' of theoretical concepts" to his remarks that follow, on the status of fictions:

> "Do electrons really exist?" . . . Instead of answering the question directly, an answer is given which refers not to the concept of electrons, . . . but to the word "electron" . . . and the use of these symbols in the

initial formulae of the calculus. . . . be satisfied with an explanation of how the symbol is used, combined with a recognition of the fact that symbols can have meaning in the context of a calculus without having any meaning outside such a context. . . .

Once the status within a calculus of a theoretical term has been expounded, there is no further question as to the ontological status of the theoretical concept.[61]

. . . there is no "universe of discourse" outside the real world in which imaginary objects exist. . . .

We can use [names] significantly without knowing whether. . . they are designations or only pseudo-designations. . . .

. . . the criterion by which I should judge whether the proposition expressed by "Mr. Pickwick visited Bath" is. . . nothing to do with the records of Bath, but solely something to do with words in a book.[62]

Theory obviously raises for Braithewaite many of the same logical, epistemological, and metaphysical problems that attach to fiction, and the method he has devised for handling (or rather disposing of) them is much the same in either case. There are differences between theoretical concepts and fictitious characters that Braithewaite's treatment fails to capture, but it is enough for the moment to note that both electrons and Pickwicks stand in opposition to what Quine has called "the gross bodies of common sense,"[63] those entities that are discernible by our unaided senses. When a name (especially a proper name)—the "paradigm referring expression"[64]—is used as it is in theory or fiction, hypothetically or playfully, with no such body ready at hand to function as the referent, a gradual discomfiture sets in. Is there some special mode of being that only fictions and theoretical constructs possess, some set of intentional objects that complement mental and verbal acts as extentional objects complement perceptual ones? Braithewaite would fiercely oppose any multiplication of the modes of being, decrying, as Russell before him, the "failure of that feeling for reality" that produces special heraldic universes where unicorns "exist."[65] But there is another tradition, here voiced by Harré, which would insist just as firmly on the need for a more flexible metaphysical standard. "Each kind of existence—in the world, in the imagination, as an after-image, etc.—is distinguished by the different sets of *stable expectations* that are fulfilled by instances of these kinds. . . . Pepper's Ghost isn't a real man: on the other hand it is a real illusion, because when we punch its nose we encounter no resistance, just as we should have expected."[66]

The advantages of the latter, "reconstructed realist" position is that it at least allows one to distinguish beliefs about and emotional attachments to a character from beliefs about words on a page; one cries or laughs over the death of Little Nell as one does not over "the death of Little Nell."[67] The disadvantage, however, is that it preserves the sense that language is only and always referential and that the meaning of a term somehow derives from the objects that it names. Wittgenstein labored too long and too hard to separate "grammar" from ontology, and to demonstrate that the meaning of a term is not what (if anything) it names but how it is used, to make this a truly attractive position. Yet Wittgenstein's salutory insight has been too often wielded selectively, to dismiss ontological considerations only in the case of "deviant" fictional or theoretical discourse, while tacitly·preserving ordinary language as a place where the correspondence between words and things is perfectly secure.

Often the antipathy to theoretical and fictional discourse is fueled by hidden metaphysical and epistemological preferences. A determined faith that individual objects and events are the only realities leads to the belief that only concrete nouns are able to express reality adequately.[68] Even events and objects may become suspect, leaving only our knowledge of immediate sensations—patches of color, eruptions of sound, the sting of cold and heat.[69] Obviously, the greater the distrust for memory, expectation, and all the abstracting and extrapolating powers of language, the more unreal theoretical and fictional constructions will become and the more it will be necessary to invent ornamental, psychological, or instrumental explanations for their continued appeal. Thus, for positivists like Bridgman and Carnap, theoretical categories are no more than "uninterpreted" ciphers that, given an appropriately limited operational definition, help to correlate observations. Slightly less severe than this view, which allows theory to make no independent contribution to our knowledge of the world, is the "instrumentalist" position, which grants theory some heuristic and organizational value and does not insist on translating theoretical concepts entirely into observations and physical operations. A close neighbor is "fictionalism," which allows theories a certain plausibility, depending on their internal coherence and their ability to exploit "known laws of nature,"[70] but emphasizes the psychological convenience and "vividness" of theories rather than their heuristic value. Both instrumentalism and fictionalism stop far short of calling theoretical discourse "true."[71] Yet ironically, as Quine points out, the same skepticism could as easily by turned against ordinary language and eventually undermine the most commonplace ontological judgments:

> If we have evidence for the existence of bodies in common sense, we have it only in the way in which we may be said to have evidence for the existence of molecules. The positing of either sort of body is good science insofar merely as it helps us to formulate our laws. . . . The positing of molecules differs mainly in degree of sophistication. In whatever sense the molecules in my desk are unreal and a figment of the imagination of the scientist, in that sense the desk itself is unreal and a figment in the imagination of the race.[72]

By attacking theory and fiction, then, one attempts a ritual purgation of discourse itself, a dramatic but largely futile effort to rid language of its freedom and to confine knowledge to sensation. If truth is limited to isolated descriptive sentences capable of direct observational verification, then a theory can at most have true consequences, and fiction must despair of any degree of truthfulness. Classical two-valued logic would second this opinion. Traditionally, truth requires that a proposition identify or refer to something that the predicate then characterizes; to verify the proposition, we simply locate that thing and determine whether it has the properties in question. Thus, sentences that apparently refer to "quarks" or "Mrs. Dalloway" force one either to declare them false—and preserve the law of the excluded middle at the price of lumping theories and fictions indiscriminately with lies and errors—or to invent another category, neither true nor false, but thereby lose the reassuring clarity of an absolute dichotomy. Yet the history of science shows us that what a theory posits is followed by persistent efforts to locate it. New instruments are devised expressly for this purpose, for example—an incongruous activity if theories were actually deemed "false" from the outset or were valued only for their vividness or success in making predictions: "There is a certain style of experiment which can only be understood as the attempt to prove or disprove the reality of a model. . . . Sometimes an experiment or series of experiments convinces us of the unreality or purely hypothetical character of a model. Then we can either invent another or, in certain circumstances, go on using our original conception with our attitude to do it alone unchanged."[73]

This, of course, distinguishes the later stages in the life of a theoretical posit, like an electron, from the history of a fictitious charcter, since no one who knew how to read fiction would then go out and seek confirmation of Mr. Pickwick's existence, either by consulting the records of Bath or by constructing the novelistic equivalent of a cloud chamber. And yet would we not feel some doubt about the abilities of any reader who was unable or unwilling to recognize "a Pickwick" when s/he saw one?[74] "A great artist invents a type," says Oscar Wilde, and goes on (only half in jest):

> and life tries to copy it, to reproduce it in a popular form like an enterprising publisher. . . .
> The nihilist, that strange martyr who has no faith, who goes to the stake without enthusiasm, and dies for what he does not believe in, is a purely literary product. He was invented by Turgenev, and completed by Dostoevski. . . .
> Things are because we see them, and what we see, and how we see it, depends on the arts that have influenced us.[75]

If a fiction helps us to "organize our responses to stimulation" successfully, as a theoretical posit does, then one would like to claim for it something akin to truth or at least a heuristic value that goes beyond Braithewaite's symbols that "have meaning in the context of a calculus without having any meaning outside such a context." This is not to return to art-as-imitation; in fact, if one pursues the analogy to theoretical posits far enough, it suggests a way of evaluating fictions that is the inverse of imitation: "the positing of physical objects must be seen not as an *ex post facto* systematization of data, but as a move prior to which no appreciable data would be available to systematize."[76] A theory may illuminate reality without being a transcription of reality; instead of copying, "theory is always *extending* our conception of phenomena and what there is in the world."[77] In a more diffuse fashion, these remarks would seem to apply to fiction as well.

Together, theoretical and fictional discourse expose the limits of two-valued logic. Unconditional truth and falsehood take no account of time or change or alternative "possible worlds," and therefore they cannot cope with nomic necessity, what could not fail to be the case, or what might hypothetically be the case, or what is believably the case. In the absence of a logic able to confront the provisional, the potential, the desired, and the feigned, theory and fiction must both stand beyond the pale. Instrumentalism and fictionalism, like Richards's doctrine of pseudostatements, are surely preferable to outright rejection, but all they really win is a temporary exemption; the standards of truth remain unchanged, and the stress placed on the formal and psychological values of theory and fiction may make it appear that our attraction to other modes of discourse is entirely free of those values. Only when one begins to complicate traditional logic by taking time and place and propositional attitude into account, or by redefining truth as conformity to one of several possible worlds, does it become possible to grant theories and fictions a less anomalous status. For the peculiarity of such discourse is not a matter of *failed* reference or *unverifiable* assertions, but of another use of language altogether, where different canons of criticism apply and new rules alter the conditions on reference.

Of course at a certain point theory and fiction will themselves part ways, according to the nature and the rigor of expectations each must fulfill. Fiction (by most modern conventions) frees its author of the responsibility to supply evidence or arguments for what is said. Indeed, fiction frequently introduces an intervening voice, a "dramatic speaker" to whom the fictitious narrative is attributed, whose mannerisms and peculiar vantage point not only screen the actual author but often saturate and even supplant our interest in the tale itself.[78] Readers of fiction, for their part undergo a similar doubling, at one level playing the credulous *narrataire* [reader] to the author's narrator, while at another level deliberately refraining from the kind of responses to these words that would be appropriate in other contexts and indulging those particular patterns of inference that do apply to fiction.[79] Fiction is therefore not discourse that lacks something that other discourse has, but a higher-order operation on discourse that follows rules of its own.[80]

Theory—at least until it becomes a form of literature—is usually less devious; one can, after all, attribute the theory of relativity directly to Einstein. And yet theories typically enjoy a greater anonymity. The proposer is less important than the proposal itself, which, ostensibly, belongs to no one, demands no idiosyncratic perspective and indeed only lives as long as it is able to pass indifferently from hand to hand. Theory therefore reduces the distance between writer and reader and muddies the distinction between origin and repetition, making itself thereby more amenable to summary and paraphrase.[81] At a time when the privileges of the author and the value of originality are being questioned in literary circles, theory has its own distinct appeal.

If the ability to dismantle and diminish the usual privileges of reference brings theory close to literature, it is brought closer still by its power to transform our habits of description, to alter how we characterize and hence how we interpret phenomena. Here the literary analogy is no longer fiction, but figures of speech, particularly metaphor. What a theory does when it models molecules after billiard balls in motion to explain the characteristic behavior of gases or when it speaks of "waves" of electrical energy is very like what a poem does when it figures forth the rosy fingers of dawn or a sea torn by dolphins and tormented by gongs. Both situations certainly seem to provoke the same kind of uneasiness, with the same effort to expel or segregate the disruptive element by establishing two separate classes of language: literal vs. figurative and observational vs. theoretical, respectively. Literal or observational language is by reputation stable, its range of application fixed by bonds of natural affinity (at best) or at the very least by clear and invariant conventions that allow for no indeterminacy; its values are predictability, accuracy, and universal accessibility. By contrast, theoretical or figurative language is mobile, unpredictable, tendentious; it violates or oversteps established patterns of usage, pushing terms where they have never yet applied. Its values are surprise, intensity, and a haze of suggestive associations. Such distinctions as these are not implausible initially, but when pressed, they begin to break down. First to disappear is the notion of two isolated and mutually exclusive languages, for it turns out to be almost impossible to determine, out of context, whether an expression is literal / observational or not: 'Spherical' is observable of baseballs . . . but not of protons; 'charged' is observable of at least some of these senses of pitched balls but not of ions, and so on."[82]

The words do not change at all (such is the insidiousness of the figurative-theoretical), only the circumstances of their use. Meaning itself is more or less constant, although in the process of construing a metaphor or a theoretical model, certain additional associations—not strictly part of the sense of an expression—will be called upon, and certain standard but irrelevant implications will be weeded out.

. . . metaphor belongs exclusively to the domain of use. It is something brought off by the imaginative employment of words and sentences and depends entirely on the ordinary meanings of those words and hence on the ordinary meanings of the sentences they comprise. It is no help in explaining how words work in metaphor to posit metaphorical or figurative meanings, or special kinds of poetic or metaphorical truth. These ideas don't explain metaphor, metaphor explains them.[83]

Eventually, of course, the spontaneous efforts to extend and revise our expectations as required by a given metaphor may recur so often that the revisions are incorporated into the standard definition of the term, altering or supplanting the original sense or establishing a second meaning. Thus, the paradox—and the threat to those who would prefer their implements of thought less slippery and less often double-edged—of figures is that they can die into a perfectly literal afterlife. So too can matters of theory, with age, turn into matters of fact: "If one is studying the early stages of the history of science during which the phenomena of magnetism are not yet understood, then it makes sense to take "magnet" as a theoretical term. If one is considering some more advanced stage at which the basic magnetic phenomena are understood and some other theory is being developed, then it makes sense to treat "magnet" as an observational term. . . ."[84]

The opposition between theoretical and observational (alternately, "descriptive") language actually brings a new clarity to the traditional distinction between figurative and literal expression. Comparing them, one sees the persistent dream of an entirely neutral language, one that does nothing more than point and that cannot misinform or misinterpret because it makes no interpretation at all, but simply records experience scrupulously and unselectively. Unfortunately, no perfect "pointer language" ever did or ever could exist; even the most familiar words imply as well as indicate because of the relationships (like synonymy and antonymy) that they contract with the other words that make up the language system as a whole. It is this subtle and fairly fragile network, the sediment of our daily linguistic practices, that determines how widely or narrowly a term may be applied; words indicate *through* their implications and not in spite of them. "Understanding a language," according to Grandy, "is not a matter of correlating individual terms with specific kinds of experiences but rather of confronting the totality of experience with the total conceptual structure of the language."[85]

Therefore the best (or worst) that one can hope for is a language that does not *appear* to have intrusive implications or to place interpretations on events because its implications are so commonplace and its readings so clichéd that they are unexceptionable. The more entrenched an expression, the less it is "subject to change of function in ordinary discourse," then the less "revelatory" it will be "of the speaker's commitments to a system of laws or of his relative ignorance of such systems."[86] It is this background of entrenched expectations that makes theoretical and figurative language stand out as highly colored, expressive, perhaps idiosyncratic: all because they reveal commitments that hackneyed turns of phrase cannot. Not surprisingly, for every voice that therefore takes expressiveness as the end of metaphor, and claims that figures represent a noncognitive, subjective, or stylistic use of language, there is an echo that applies the same sentiments to theory. "There are exactly parallel views of scientific models that have been held by many contemporary philosophers of science, namely that models are purely subjective, psychological and adopted by individuals for private heuristic purposes.... But models, like metaphors, are intended to communicate."[87]

In fact, it is precisely by veering from the well-worn path that theories and figures make their distinctive "cognitive" contribution. Without such attempts to redeploy descriptions, such invitations to reexamine gases through the model of scattered balls in motion or to reconceive autumnal trees as bare, ruined choirs, we should—in the words of Mary Hesse—"be imprisoned forever inside the range of our existing experiences."[88] There are, then, two simultaneous but logically distinct functions that theoretical models and literary metaphors perform: first, to shatter, or at least temporarily dispel, more familiar characterizations (and the implications and inferences that go along with them), and second, to offer a new characterization, which implies a new classification and inspires a fresh series of inferences. The two are usually of equal importance, but one can imagine situations in which the principal aim and the most lasting effect would be simply to show that a reexamination is possible and so break the conceptual hold of an old model and open the subject up to a freer play of mind.

The relative emphasis on defamiliarization may be greater in the arts than in the sciences, as may the type of redescription preferred. Scientific theories generally choose as their models objects or processes that are more completely and more precisely understood than the objects or processes under study here. By selecting a model one already knows how to deploy, one has a richer set of implications to work with and something more than blind conjecture to guide the invention of hypotheses.[89] But well-known models, especially if they are associated with a particular research tradition (as balls in motion are with classical mechanics), also provide a limit for invention; one usually knows with a scientific model, as one does not with most metaphors, which features are most likely to prove relevant and when the effort of construal should stop. But when Wallace Stevens looks at blackbirds, it is the difficulty, the incongruity, and most of all the mystery of the various identifications that we find compelling. In poetry we often know *less* about the metaphoric lens through which we are asked to look than we do about the subject matter itself. Nor do we have the same well-defined research traditions to tell us which aspects of the metaphor to count and which to discount. Stevens's metaphors are no doubt as fruitful, as richly suggestive and replete with potential lines of speculation, as any scientific model, but because the suggestions are so many and so diffuse, they are far less likely to produce a coherent system of hypotheses.

Models and metaphors both begin by taking words and phrases beyond their normal range of application, using them in situations where we are not entirely certain about how they should apply. This initiates a process of trial and error, which leads to a reorientation of our own approach and a reorganization in how we see a given subject matter. What guides us in our search is, classically, an analogy or homology, something in the new situation that corresponds to features found in the original and tells us how the term could apply here as well. But it is an emergent correspondence, part discovery, part creation; many of the features thus exposed (in both the original and the derived application) might easily have been dismissed as marginal or have gone entirely undetected.[90] As one would expect, the balance between discovery and creation is not the same in poetry as it is in theory. Theories generally draw upon recognized similarities—the so-called positive analogy—to construct a model that will then project a set of further points of correspondence, a provisional area of the so-called neutral analogy.[91] Metaphors are more likely to arise ex nihilo, trailing unsuspected similarities in their wake. Although there is always tension between the new and the derived use of an expression, metaphors typically involve greater actual anomaly or logical incompatibility and thus cannot be pursued as far nor function in as many different contexts as a model can.[92] Indeed, in metaphors the negative analogy is frequently as valuable as the positive (and becomes ever more significant as one moves to other figures like irony). Of course the power of the illumination increases as the ease of the analogy decreases, as does the sheer excitement of the construing of it and the poignancy of the (transient) recognition scene when it is finally achieved.[93]

Metaphors as well as models may be deemed "true" to the extent that we can find compelling grounds for applying them to their new situations, but usually they have the force of an invitation rather than an assertion.[94] They therefore do not provoke the sort of guarded scrutiny and scrupulous experimental tests that theoretical models do, however tentatively and conditionally they are proposed. A model is elaborated until it will produce predictions that can be falsified; according to its record, it will eventually be accepted, modified, or cast utterly aside. Success for a theoretical model is therefore almost the reverse of what success means for a metaphor: ". . . a successful scientific theory tends to become so much a part of our ordinary way of perceiving of relations in the world that it loses its aura of strangeness and novelty."[95] Should this happen to a metaphor, we would call it dead, not successful. For a metaphor to remain vital, it must constantly retain the power to startle, to provoke curiosity without ever completely satisfying it and initiate speculations that will never be exhausted. A metaphor invites us to *do* more, but it is an invitation we can take up briefly and then put down; a model asks less of us, but commands a more sustained effort and may therefore penetrate further into the whole of our intellectual life.

iii

Theory always borders on literature, but it might have forever remained just there, on the borderline, if circumstances had not been ripe for making the metamorphosis complete. The transformation of theory of literature into theory as literature was clearly overdetermined, bred both by forces in literature itself and by the kind of questions that literary criticism was asking. Whatever the source of these questions and however disparate the answers, the cumulative effect was to make it increasingly difficult to dissociate the writing used in poems and novels from the writing used to subject them to critical analysis. It grew harder and harder to keep theoretical discourse from falling prey to its own operations and revealing, under reflexive scrutiny, the same rhetorical cunning, the same crucial indeterminacies, the same multiplicity, as literature itself. For convenience I shall treat these critical issues (language and writing; the displaced subject; reading practices and the labor of producing meanings; acts, performances, pulsions; intertextuality; context and ideology; the question of "literariness" and borderline genres) separately, although in fact they form a dense and overlapping network of concerns that one might enter at almost any point, from which to proceed to almost any other.

The preoccupation with language and with the written text is coeval with criticism itself, and certainly one could hardly complain that New Criticism ignored the problem—quite the opposite, as the frequent neo-humanist and Neo-Aristotelian attacks will testify. But with the advent of structuralism and poststructuralism, the linguistic turn became at once more systematic and more sinister, no longer confined to occasional remarks about diction and style but requiring fundamental changes in one's whole critical orientation and opening out eventually upon a whole unknown terrain of epistemology and psychology, cultural formations and metaphysical foundations. First came the recognition of language as an institution in its own right—a total system of phonetic and conceptual categories regulated by its own distinctive laws, and not a group of random sounds and sentences whose sole regularity and only measure came from corresponding to observable states of affairs. This discovery obviated most of the New Critical linguistic speculations, centered as they were on the problem of reference, and also made it possible to introduce many of the conceptual and philosophic questions that had been banished when the peculiar antireferential nature of poetic language made it seem that it could not bear the same intellectual scrutiny as scientific language. Thus, there could emerge a more generalized mode of criticism, with literature joining other discourse as one more instance "among the many which make up the human capacity to create, manipulate, and consume signs."[96] For some observers this meant a denigration of literature, for others an elevation that promised to endow it with more intellectual weight. But in either case the power of literary theory itself was enormously enhanced, its pretentions growing apace with the imperialism of the linguistic model.

Yet, as mentioned earlier, the spread of this new model was due in no small part to the relief it offered from the equally imperious mechanistic model that had dominated so many disciplines and for so long seemed the only form that rigorous inquiry could take. What the example of Saussure (and later Chomsky) offered was a framework built for social rather than natural phenomena, a way of accounting for significance and value rather than brute facts, without a loss of rigor. "To explain social phenomena is not to discover temporal antecedents and to link them in a causal chain," as Jonathan Culler glosses it, "but to specify the place and function of phenomena in a system."[97]

In fact "function in a system," the relationship between elements, totally supplanted substance, further distinguishing the study of the meaningful from the study of the physical. This also made it that much easier to transpose the structural model from one discipline to another, without regard for the material differences between languages and narratives or consanguinity and money. For literary criticism, it was no longer form that mattered but the system underlying form, the codes and mechanisms propelling it and making it intelligible. And soon even these relatively localized and discrete systems were under attack; the purely differential nature of the sign became part of a massive epistemological and metaphysical critique, beginning with a modest attack on any naive empirical claims to know reality directly, without linguistic or cultural contamination, and ending with an assault on the very notion of "being" itself. Lacan's psychoanalytic study of the sign as the mark of an absence, able to function only when the object of desire is lost, was one source of this radical metaphysical skepticism, followed quickly by Derrida's even more elaborate critique of the nostalgia for simple "presences"—even the presence of an absence, upon which Lacan's analysis depended.

The upshot of this was to make literary representation even more problematic, although in another way than it had been for New Critics. "Voice," for example, remained one of Richard's premier categories in the analysis of poetry, an integral subjective presence that one was invited to seek behind the words even as objective presences of any kind were being officially proscribed. But appealing to an antecedent voice is really just another way of evading the implications of the sign, trying to reduce language to an instrument that conveys or copies an already formulated meaning and preserves it faithfully until someone can decode it and recover the original intact. "The voice is *heard*," according to Derrida, "closest to the self as the absolute effacement of the signifier: pure auto-affection . . . which does not borrow from outside of itself, in the world or in 'reality,' any accessory signifier, any substance of expression foreign to its own spontaneity."[98] A concern for voice suggests a desire to turn meaning back into an immanence, a presence, rather than a relationship that cannot inhere in any element or substance. The value of the sign if forever "poised between," an eternal process of deferring and differentiating that has neither origin nor end—since each sign defers and presupposes something yet to come for which it will be exchanged and by which it will be differentiated, a sign becomes itself only with respect to something it is not. Even Saussure was not quite equal to the task of facing the full implications of the sign: "that ill-named thing, the only one, that escapes the instituting question of philosophy: 'what is . . . ?' "[99] By treating written signs as mere representations of language "itself," he violated his own insight into the diacritical nature of the sign and covertly restored to verbal signs the power to embody meaning.

This attack on representation in the name of the unlimitable "free play" of the signifier was also what divided structuralism—a science of fixed inventories and limited combinations—from the various versions of poststructuralism that eventually supplanted it. Henceforth writing must no longer be viewed as derivative, the expression or the representation of some more fundamental mode of being, but as a "radical and inaugural act" that inscribes rather than transcribes its objects and conceptions.[100] Voices, objects, and events lost their density and their centrality; no longer treated as the source of writing but as its products, they were not even necessarily the most interesting ones. Writing itself, the depthless script repudiating its origins and resisting any full or final recuperation, took on a terrible new and vaguely hieratic beauty. Sudden bursts of typographic play were insinuated into the midst of study and academic prose.

The mobility and fragility of the written word became so engrossing that meditations on the nature of textuality threatened to displace interpretation entirely. A criticism that aspires "to make one read the signifying of things rather than their meaning"[101] or that constitutes itself as a prolonged inquiry into the possibility or impossibility of representation must of necessity operate at a more abstract level and must more frequently broach theoretical questions. But at this level of abstraction, theoretical discourse also loses its own immunity: It too is writing. If literary representation has become problematic, then the way theoretical texts represent other texts can be no less so. It is not entirely with glee, then, (as has been sometimes intimated) that criticism, "increasingly aware of its situation,. . .finds its own predicament as interesting as— sometimes more interesting than—poetry itself."[102]

When language—long deemed the one uniquely human capacity— ceases to have the reputation of a simple instrument or a simulacrum, it must perforce profoundly alter our notions of what it means to be human. Instead of being added to man as a special kind of acquisition or tool, it becomes constitutive of man, not the exercise of an already extant human will but that without which humanity and all its projects would be inconceivable. This in itself would be enough to shake the foundations of traditional humanism, with its man-centered, man-dominated world, but the implications of the linguistic model can be pressed even futher. Not only does humanity appear to be as much a construct as a constructor, but we cannot even fully know the nature of our own position, since that position conditions all our perceptions and our knowledge of ourselves. We cannot examine where we are without ceasing to be there. Here the "discovery" or rediscovery of language converges with the discoveries of Freud and Marx, to open:

> a new space of explanation which has come to be called the unconscious. . . .
> . . .something not immediately given to consciousness yet deemed to be always present, always at work in the behavior it structures and makes possible.
> . . .the whole enterprise of the human sciences becomes one of deconstructing the subject, of explaining meanings in terms of systems of convention which escape the subject's conscious grasp. The speaker of a language is not consciously aware of its phonological and grammatical systems, in which terms his judgments and perceptions can be explained. Nor is the subject necessarily aware of its own psychic economy or of the elaborate system of social norms which governs its behavior. The subject is broken down into its constituents, which turn out to be interpersonal systems of convention. It is "dissolved" as its functions are attributed to a variety of systems which operate through it.[103]

As a single sentence that depends for its intelligibility upon a vast invisible grammar, so the self—the image that presents itself to me and that I come to acknowledge as my own—is but a single lucid point in the larger, darker web out of which it is woven. Yet it is the bright images, the instances of focused self-awareness, of which literature is classically composed. Hence the frequent abrasiveness and the sense of almost willful dislocation in recent literary criticism, which must so often read against the grain. Hence too the need for a thorough theoretical grounding to guard against the temptations of a more comfortable collaboration with the text. Subjectivity and character within the text, authorship without—those places where criticism had been wont to find its rest now splinter under the determined pressure of archeological and deconstructive analyses bent on goading us to greater restlessness instead. This attack on authorship goes deeper than the familiar rejections of biography and the intentional fallacy, penetrating to the very principles of ownership and closure that New Criticism left entirely intact, or even strengthened. For Foucault, however, these are precisely the most problematic aspects of authorship: "The author is he who implants, into the troublesome language of fiction, its unities, its coherences, its links with realities. . . . The author principle limits this same chance element the hazards of discourse through the action of an identity whose form is that of *individuality* and the *I*."[104]

In Foucault's treatment, authorship is at once an artifact of history, a rule of formation (which controls and distributes access to discourse and keeps the construal process within a certain, arbitrary limit), and a carefully preserved delusion. The fact is that discursive practices precede and exceed individual writers, who are born and educated into possibilities and procedures that they may exploit in different ways but that they neither originate nor control. Thus, *author* turns out to be a misnomer: not a divine creator, not even a divine creation, but a secular invention and an economic convenience. Of course, criticism has its own conventions of authorship, which conventions Foucault and others struggle to subvert through a studiously anonymous style—deliberately remote, impersonal, "inhuman"—and by using a terminology and entire arguments that transport themselves with surprising ease and only the most cursory attributions from one writer to another. Obviously this too creates a climate hospitable to theory, with its greater tolerance for paraphrase, its relative indifference to origins (especially "personal" ones), and its esteem for the replicable and repeatable.

Throughout this recent writing there is a visible and as yet unresolved quest for a new critical vocabulary that will be free from the "theological" and phenomenological assumptions that have heretofore dominated discussions of literature. There has appeared a new and unstable language of "performances" and "self-consuming artifacts," of "processes" and "drives," of "acts," "events," and "institutions" that is full of internal inconsistencies. But where full accord is lacking, it is compensated for by shared antipathies: for individualism, for inert substance, for permanence, Nature, and unaccommodated man. "Acts," "performances," and "practices," for example, have in common their skepticism about seemingly spontaneous behavior, although they differ sharply in the weight that they accord to the action or the actor, in the sort of artificial constraints they imagine, and in the amount of willfulness, foreknowledge, and mastery they attribute to the individual who enters into them. "Performances," "events," and "pulsions," so unalike in other ways, at least share the same emphatic transciency and mobility, the same distrust of fixed essences.[105] Unbound energy has been a particular preoccupation of French poststructuralism.

Fueled by such things as the translation of Bakhtin's comparison of the restricted "monologic" world (limited to only one version of truth and falsehood) to the happy "polyphony" of contradictory voices of the medieval carnival, and by the recovery of Saussure's long suppressed study of Latin anagrams (again construed as support for multiple, conflicting meanings), poststructuralism became identified with the effort to overthrow repressive codes of every sort. This mean undoing the strictures of convention and exceeding Lacan's symbolic order where psychic energies were trapped within preexisting channels. It also meant liberating the signifier from the weary cycle of consumption and exchange that forced it to behave in predictable ways—in short constructing an "a-signifying semiotics" where signs might be allowed to follow ludic or erotic impulses and behave as sheer "intensities"—"qui vous conviennent ou non, qui passent ou ne passent pas" ("which suit you or do not, which satisfy or do not").[106] Although generally confined to demonstrating how restrictions are enforced or where gaps or flaws appear beneath the superficial closure of a text, such a doctrine is ultimately an act of radical enfranchisement. It grants readers the right to ring endless changes on a text—indeed, only a process of interminable analysis (or total abstinence from analysis) could meet the extraordinarily exacting standards of the liberated signifier. Not surprisingly, then, the Anglo-American reception of this doctrine has been tempered by an equally eager interest in a renovated hermeneutics—in Gadamer and Ricoeur, in Hirsch, and in the Constance school—where there is the promise of a way to bring exegesis to a halt.

But even under the earlier and more modest accounts of the differential nature of the sign, there was always the implicit thrust (or promise) of unending interpretation. Since meaning is not a matter of a single sign—or single text—but rather a relationship between them, reading must move from one work to another and another, passing through the "intertextual" space that defines, develops, and in general serves as the only "medium" where meaning can unfold. "Every text takes shape," according to Julia Kristeva, "as a mosaic of citations, every text is the absorption and transformation of other texts. The notion of intertextuality comes to take the place of intersubjectivity."[107] It comes to take the place as well of representation, making it possible once again to grant that a text does have its antecedents (and consequents). But these are to be seen no longer as sources that are mechanically copied, but as a set of prior texts—some quite distinct, others vague and widely diffused cultural commonplaces—that have been selectively assimilated. The process of attending to and ignoring, dismembering and restoring, forms another text that cannot be confidently pronounced either derivative or new. The angle of relationship and the kind of operation linking one text to another may produce anything from seamless ingestion to violent purgation to petty thievery, parody, or overt controversy. Intertextuality may include anticipation as well, a dialogue with posterity or the omnipresent Other. But a relationship of some sort there must always be; a word outside the grammatical system is only senseless sound, a text in isolation is no text at all, but only a curiously figured and black white object.

This is a blow, of course, to the once sacred law of textual autonomy, and to all its critical consequences—the fallacies, heresies, and standards of relevance, the various constraints on legitimate associations and reputable sources of aesthetic pleasure. The operations that replace these will be as stridently inclusive as the others were exclusive, even to the point of inserting "alien" materials into a given text to demonstrate its constitutive evasions, the alternatives that it scrupulously suppresses. Gradually the surface of the text becomes a mass of hauntingly suggestive fragments, each with its own itinerary and history, its own potential field of play that need no longer be limited to the text at hand. It becomes impossible, in fact, to establish a "natural" limit, since each time a word appears it is already and necessarily the trace of another appearance, always part of a spreading network from which it cannot extricate itself without lapsing into insignificance. Originality therefore loses something of its former luster, seeming now less Promethean than just ungrateful or self-deceived. To allow oneself to be trapped in the "simplistic opposition between originality and repetition" may well be, as Edward Said puts it, "hopelessly paralyzing,"[108] but to escape it means muddying the distinction between primary and secondary texts and the traditional subordination of criticism to literature. It is hard to disdain the former as a parasitic text, if the latter is equally involved in commenting on other works. And if meaning is not and cannot be immanent, then no text can ever be complete in itself. It must give rise to other texts, lest its meaning never be put into play. This elevates the status of criticism from parasite to partner, and makes the goal of isolating the spark of pure creation recede even further. From another point of view, however, it could also be a loss of status for criticism, since the "metalanguage" of commentary and theory is reduced to just another language, no more final or self-contained than the "object language" that it treats. Commentary thus spawns further commentary. Not by accident have so many of the most influential works in recent years turned out to be doubled; Lévi-Strauss on Mauss, Althusser's Marx, Freud as rendered by Lacan, or Derrida's deconstructions of Heidegger, Plato, Hegel, and Husserl. At the same time, with the barrier between literary and theoretical discourse down, the latter begins to change its intertextual manners, taking on more of the allusive and absorptive qualities usually reserved for poetry.[109]

By replacing the relationship between text and source with an infinite intertextual circuit, literary theory has, in effect, enormously expanded the powers and responsibilities of the reader. The analogy between literature and language is again in evidence here, since one of the defining features of language is the reversibility of production and reception, without which communication would be impossible. In fact, literary speculations have outstripped contemporary Chomskyan linguistics (which still retains a markedly "Cartesian," speaker-centered model) by paying more attention to the productivity and labor of reception. Since the words in any text must interact with other words, the reader must supply them, acting as the "repository of codes which account for the intelligibility of the text."[110] Certainly the emphasis on reading is related to the professional affiliations of contemporary critics. But the newly impolite and skeptical tack that it has recently taken makes reading palpably more potent, able to turn a familiar narrative passage into a metaphysical disquisition or to unearth in antique lyrics a sophisticated meditation on the vanities of reference. No doubt such strenuous efforts to reread are indicative as well of something that is missing in contemporary literature, an incapacity or disinclination to pursue the topics that are of greatest critical interest, leaving it to readers to produce—if only indirectly—what they cannot seem to find.

As there are different modes of intertextuality that a literary work may exploit, so too there are different reading strategies—conservative, revisionist, marginal, and insurgent[111]—which differ less in their pace and proximity to the text than in their basic posture of aggression or defense, their rage for order or their delight in introducing new disorder, the different guiding interests that they bring to bear. Yet no reading is really passive. There is action even where there seems to be no struggle at all, only the soothing contemplation of regularity and harmony. In fact, the greater the apparent harmony, the greater the suspicion that secondary revision has been at work, to repair, censor, and otherwise erase any trace of labor from the text itself or the reading process. For now writing and reading are both construed as "specific production processes . . . comparable to other processes of human work." It was the medieval dichotomy between the active and the contemplative life and the later genteel repudiation of labor as vulgar, material, and demeaning that kept the analogy concealed. The lesson of the linguistic model is that literature, like language, is an institution shaped by its own rules and practices, no less "real" or efficacious than other social and economic forces. The operations that produce meaning may be less physically evident, but they are no less powerful for all that. It simply requires better methods to make them evident—ideally through theoretical models that reproduce the operations in a form that we can see, but failing this, at least helping to locate the likely symptoms of strain in any given text. [112] Yet as this goes on, theoretical prose must itself become more quizzical and unfinished, in accord with the desire to display its own operating principles at work. Presentational value, which is never a negligible factor in our appreciation of theory, becomes even more pronounced, but the values being exhibited have changed from fitness, ease, and clarity to difficulty, indeterminacy, and open-ended process.

But if writing and reading are rule-governed practices, the rules are notoriously subject to change and not always for purely semiotic reasons. Obviously psychological and social forces do enter in, as literary history is touched by and touches in turn the history of the culture as a whole. The revived interest in context did not have to await new definitions of the text but was itself a major force in the decline of New Criticism and was frequently at odds with what appeared to be the ahistorical and determinist implications of early structuralism. Certainly "the methodological suspicion that data are not given but produced, that phenomenal forms are mystifying," was not inspired by the example of linguistics alone, and it is this "suspicion," according to Jean Franco, that one should really regard as "the basic ingredient of modern criticism."[113]

Critical speculations have aroused needs that can be filled only by further speculation—warning us that we are without sufficient skepticism and prey to endless misconception, while teaching us how and when to be more skeptical. Distrust of "the given" can take a variety of forms, depending on what initiates it. In some cases it is merely that the given seems somehow incomplete and requires further historical or biographical or bibliographical context to restore it to its native fullness. In other cases it is not simply a remediable gap in documentation that provokes doubt, but deeper problems of human comprehension that admit of only partial solutions through hermeneutic rigor, a developed philosophy of understanding, and a final leap of empathetic faith. Finally, there are those cases where one suspects outright distortion (as often as not unconscious) designed to conceal the actual conditions and desires that underlie the text. Criticism must then seek out a repressed or censored "antitext," identified by certain excesses and inconsistencies, rather than a contingently missing context.

Whether hermeneutic or historical or ideological, however, this new contextual research is far more sensitive than its predecessors to the problems of reduction: the futility of reaching for more basic facts that require no interpretation and the indignity done to literature when it is only deemed to reflect, and is denied all shaping powers of its own. A writer like Foucault even reverses the terms and makes it the power of discourse to shape what can be known, and hence, be subjected to social control. In the same spirit but less dramatically, Fredric Jameson suggests that literature is not a reflection of, but an operation on the "real":

> If we try to accustom ourselves to thinking of the narrative text as a process whereby something is done to the "real," whereby operations are performed on it and it is in one way or another "managed" (Norman Holland) or indeed "neutralized," or under other circumstances articulated and brought to heightened consciousness, then clearly we will begin to think of the "real," not as something outside the work, of which the latter stands as an image or makes a representation, but rather something borne within and vehiculated by the text itself, interiorized in its very fabric in order to provide the stuff and the raw material on which the textual operation must work.[114]

At the very least, there is a growing willingness to credit literary form with a history, an economy, a politics of its own.

But like so many of the other topics that literary theory now broaches, the questions of historical situation and political function cannot be contained. Whatever darknesses surround and whatever doubts therefore attend the literary text, the same obscurities and suspicion must attach to critical and theoretical texts as well. Thus, the study of literary history has its own recognizable epochs, and forms of ideological analysis their own distinctive ideologies. The way is opened for a potentially infinite autocritical regress, but even short of this, the innocence of literary scholarship is surely lost when its every gesture, doctrinal or practical, becomes vulnerable to a symptomatic reading. To advocate or just adhere to a critical program is all at once fraught with unprecedented difficulties. The range of alliances and consequences for which one can be held responsible is now greatly expanded and the reigning analogies for the critical act are ever more tendentious. Interpretation shows a sudden kinship with other and ranker modes of appropriation, turning rapacious, tyrannous, obsessed with a desire to dominate in the name of truth. In some circles this vision gives rise to a form of renunciation; criticism avoids "mastery" by forbearing to interpret at all; "se laisser traversée par le flux du discours . . . ne pas chercher à intérpréter, ni même à discuter, mais écouter et prendre au passage ce qui nous convient" (to allow ourselves to be traversed by the flux of discourse . . . not to seek to interpret, or even to inquire, but to attend and take from a passage what suits us").[115]

But in other cases it makes interpretation more aggressive, eager to press its now acknowledged interests to their limit. If analytic practices are not neutral, then offering an account of literature may not seem to be enough; one may feel compelled to intervene more directly: to alter by violating rather than by explaining the accepted codes and so to release a given piece of discourse to mean in other ways. Paradoxically, at the very moment when the issue of context is most alive, when fears of extrinsic criticism have been largely assuaged and talk about the history or the politics or the libidinal economy of literature should come most easily, it cannot—because that talk must scrutinize its own context as well. There is not transcendental discourse, no escape into harmless "ideas." One can (many do) try to write equivocally and noncommittally, or to write subversively, or even threateningly, as a sort of theoretical terrorist. But one cannot write away the problem of writing itself.

An exacerbated historical and social sensitivity means that the very notion of literature will not go unexamined, given the relatively late (eighteenth century) emergence of what we now know as literature and its strongly marked regional and class affiliations. When one is made to look at the category long enough and hard enough, it begins to come apart, with no attributes that are always and only literary, and few, if any, that are absolutely debarred.[116] Neither a timeless nor a universal category, literature is also closely intertwined with those "extraliterary" orders that it opposes but that nonetheless help to define it and to give it its prestige.

The introduction of new categories—text, *écriture*, discourse, signifying practice—that are indifferent to the usual literary/extraliterary distinctions is a product of this same historical and social urgency. Such terms represent a piece of knowing provocation, and are not just evidence of theoretical excess or a massive failure of taste. The fact that many of the most admired and most influential writers are not "literary men" at all but philosophers, anthropologists, and intellectual historians is another instance of this deliberate indifference. If literature no longer seems to be a viable category, it may not be the result but the instigator of new theories, less an accidental loss than a liberation longed-for and deliberately sought out.

But what does one hope to gain from the abolition of literature? First, *freedom from* a heritage of now questionable elitism, from "taste" wielded as a mystifying social weapon, from the encumbrances of a prolonged association with mimesis, expressionism, and formalism. And, second, *freedom to* explore interests long proscribed and motives cast aside as unworthy or irrelevant. The very features that an earlier generation of critics had been wont to praise turn into terms of condemnation; literature becomes "a secondary elaboration, a unifying, repetitive, fantasmatic activity which contrives to inhibit the textual process."[117] Yet we need the concept of literature if we are to explain the animus of such attacks. If it were truly moribund or nonexistent, there would be no need to subvert it and no possibility of being provocative or insulting. Thus, as Paul de Man has remarked, "at the moment that they claim to do away with literature, literature is everywhere."[118]

And indeed one could say that, not the absence, but the omnipresence of literature is the real issue; that what has eroded is the pride of all those other writings that once opposed themselves to literature as more serious, more immediate, more true. " 'Literature' can no longer be called such when the relationship to truth and reality that allegedly distinguished literary, scientific, and philosophical texts from each other breaks down."[119] If language always mediates, if rhetoric is inescapable, if the perfect literal language is a primal scene that never really happened, then the distinctiveness of literature is lost—but not quite for the reasons outlined above. One would now be tempted to read the incursions of anthropologists, philosophers, and historians as a symptom of their own neediness and not of ours. And on closer examination, it does appear that the exchange of theoretical assumptions and key words has gone both ways, with as many tropes exported as codes and economies imported. But rather than trying to assign priority to one discipline or another, Stephen Melville suggests that we simply acknowledge that "we are witness to and participants in a redistribution in the business of knowing" in general.[120]

However permanent or pervasive this redistribution actually turns out to be, it has certainly had a pronounced effect on literary theory itself. The more theory ambiguates the boundary between the literary and the extraliterary, the more interest it shows in extending the canon to include such borderline genres as new journalism or documentary fiction, the more joy it takes in finding parallels between apparently discrepant texts (novels and political tracts, grammars and fables)—then the more it must endanger its own position. This precariousness, however, has its own distinctive beauty, an "imbalancing act" that can be read and savored as perhaps the most characteristic achievement of the very literary culture it means to undermine.

Thus, by zealously pursuing each of these favorite questions, literary theory is led inexorably back to its own initial premises—in particular to its presumption to be permanently other and outside of the discourse it examines. Add to this the sheer accumulation of theoretical writings and the confusion of competing claims, accidental convergences, and rumors of distant excommunications, and one has a situation ripe for ubiquitous irony. Hence, yet another reason why theory should become more sportive, more duplicitous, more evanescent and intent on its own elegance. Interestingly, Harré notes that in the history of scientific theories, there is the same increased emphasis on aesthetic considerations whenever "there is some kind of crisis . . . where current theories are many and there seems to be no way of resolving the issue between them."[121] Thus, when literary theories collect, as they do now, in almost overwhelming number and make so many incommensurable promises, there is a natural tendency to defer attempts to test or apply them and to simply contemplate them as conceptual structures. And when there are, in addition, cases of outright contradiction (still without the necessary means for deciding which is right) the appeal of "fictionalism" is likely to be even greater. The standards of truth that traditionally apply to fiction are, after all, far less severe and there are even sanctions for incompatible points of view and intersecting worlds. What better recourse could one have, then, for confronting a highly contentious critical scene, and for entertaining a number of inconsistent possibilities at once? Consider the conflicting claims: the militant textuality and the new contextualism; the her-meneutic search for intentions that determine meaning while the struc-turalist decentered subject dissolves into a mere position in language; signs vs. symbolic practices vs. an uncoded a-signifying flow; exhaustive structural analysis on the one hand and oblique deconstructive insin-uations on the other; readings ever more microscopic and arguments ever more macroscopic in their scope.

The fact that so many of these issues have been imported into Anglo-American criticism, arriving in an anachronistic heap from dis-parate and frequently inimical national traditions—Soviet information theory, French and German phenomenology, French and Italian struc-turalism, and all the subtle shades of Marxism à la Frankfurt, à la Berlin, à la Paris—further distances them. And translation adds its own alienating touch, rendering the now polyglot language of literary theory tan-talizingly opaque and unfamiliar. The result is something exotic, the native tongue of no one—not unlike what once fascinated Pound in (mis)translations of Chinese poetry.[122]

iv

The beauties that theory brings to literature, then, are not entirely unprecedented, yet theoretical writing has certain effects that seem peculiarly in tune with our own moment and condition, which other genres may attempt but theory alone fully achieves. "For ours is an age of theory," according to Frank Kermode: "It might even be argued that we have a more honest understanding of our intellectual plight than our predecessors, and that this accounts for our mistrust of simple rules and remedies. We are bound to be skeptical, of renovation as well as deca-dence. But one thing we do know: there is no going back."[123]

Still the continuities with a certain segment of contemporary litera-ture are worth noting; doubtless theory would not have seemed so plausible a literary form without them. One can, with more or less effort, find almost the entire range of contemporary critical preoccupations— with signs and reading, with textuality and intertextuality, with praxis and performance—at work in contemporary "creative writing" as well. The opacity and autotelic play of language has certainly figured prominently in literature since the earliest modernist experiments, so much so that

French theorists often seem more indebted to Mallarmé than to Saussure. For Anglo-Americans, it is the example of Joyce and especially the *Wake*, where one seems to catch the signifier in the act of making meanings (although with an all-too-prominent vocal timber and little if any sense of underlying codes). In Joyce, it is the effort of the artist and not impersonal structures and rules to which we are referred. One can trace a steady movement from the Promethean modernists who impose personal meanings on a meaningless world to the growing postmodernist concern for the impersonal mechanisms whereby meanings are imposed—most prominently in works by Calvino, Roche, Sollers, Ricardou, and the *Ou-li-Po* group founded by Queneau. Many of these same writers (especially where there is an association with *Tel Quel* or another theoretical journal) also effect a certain "voicelessness" through deliberate fragmentation, collage, and the insertion of graphic symbols, drawings, and a general concentration on the surface of the page itself. But even when they stop short of this (as Anglo-American experiments usually do) the writers' mistrust of reference and subversion of representation is still patent. These are works that openly project or "fabulate" imaginary worlds rather than imitating the real one, and take obvious delight in exposing their own invention. This literary "use of the fabulous to probe beyond the phenomenological" parallels the more elaborate critique of presence and representation in literary theory.[124] There is even something that approaches the abstraction of a theory in the general elevation of conception over realization—the quick proleptic hints and extraordinarily foreshortened narratives of Borges and the *"littérature potentielle"* of Queneau's exercises. But, paradoxically, the process has gone much further in the visual arts—where phenomenological "presence" would seem to be not only indispensable but literally unavoidable. Hence the air of reticence and even grim restriction in minimalist canvases and the comic incongruity of the documents and recipes that make up "conceptual" art. Theory would seem to stand in the same relation, and to perform much the same function, vis-à-vis narrative and lyric in the verbal arts, as abstraction does vis-à-vis figuration, hue, and texture in the visual arts. "The formalization of this discourse is something analogous on the skin of words to what so-called abstract painting is on that of colors," according to Lyotard, who also reminds us that even such formalization and abstraction are "material for the libido."[125]

Postmodern art seems to rely on differential values, upsetting prior expectations or formulating projects yet to be enacted—in every way, trading the sticky pleasures of immanence for bright spasms of significance. As striking as the parallel to current theory is, however, one hesitates to claim that one has "influenced" the other; more likely both are products of something larger; perhaps the "age of mechanical reproduction" is making itself felt. Long ago, in "The Work of Art in the Age of

Mechanical Reproduction," Benjamin had prophesied that the capacity to produce representations by machine automatically, and in unlimited supply, would eventually replace art based on aura, on uniqueness and substance, with a new art of indefinite multiplication. The new art would be inimical at once to individualism, to questions of originality, and to all attempts to lay hold of it as if it were a piece of property. Photographs and films were Benjamin's inspiration, but since then the mechanization of culture has gone far enough to serve as a model for other and older arts. Writing can be seen as a sort of machine as well, a device with its own capacity to produce sense automatically, a human artifice and yet independent of any particular human will. But theory is particularly consonant with an age of mechanical reproduction, since it is the one mode of discourse that actually presupposes replication and reenactment.

Something else that literature and literary theory now have in common is an openly acknowledged relationship to other texts. Parody, quotation, and even "self-citation" (in the form of internal reduplication) have become almost the whole condition of some contemporary texts—no longer on the margins, in the form of an occasional allusion or an initial premise that frames what is central and original to the work, but as an antagonism at its very core, an internalized otherness that mocks the very notion of originality. It is noteworthy, however, how few of the writers who write this way seem to relish it, how much more often it is the occasion for bitterness and ennui (à la John Barth) than for Nabokov's dazzling cosmopolitan counterpoint, or for the quiet plenitude of Borges's labyrinthine speculation. But criticism, long schooled to regard itself as derivative, would seem far better prepared to accept the "radical intertextuality" expected of postmodern writing. And the same applies to the new appreciation for the reading process, an appreciation that seems to come more easily to critics and literary theorists, although it is certainly a profound concern of postmodern literature as well, and one of the features that distinguishes it from modernism proper. No longer are readers expected to stand back in awe before the accomplishments of a remote and godlike author; instead they must enter in, fully and responsibly, to render intelligible a text that remains deliberately unfinished. As Maurice Roche says of his own *Circus*, the work is "reduced to notation so that the reader can add details of his own. I think we should try to write 'do-it-yourself' books."[126] At times the only meaning of a work may be the reader's own forced recognition of disappointed expectations.[127]

Clearly these experiments are most successful where the act of reading overlaps conspicuously with the act of writing. Borges is especially notable for writings—one hesitates to call them "stories"—that operate as mischievous readings of another text, whether an extant masterwork like *Don Quixote* or the spectral *Cyclopedia* article on "Uqbar" (where both the book and the place it names are the products of the reading). It is only a slight step from such fictitious criticism to the "critical fictions" and constructs of a theorist, which in their most extreme form may themselves be only ideal types—extrapolations and projections that have never actually been observed but that nonetheless help to classify and measure the real. But in taking this additional step, and granting that theoretical constructs have a literary value too, one grants to reading that much more artfulness, acknowledging its power and its burden to transform. Still, because theory normally operates in the realm of the potential and the hypothetical, and not the fictional, the unheard music of its constructs is less likely to be wistful or elegiac: What it treats are not possibilities foreclosed, but what might still, with time and effort, prove to be the case. Thus, in times of dearth, uncertainty, and flagging inspiration, theory can resist compromise and at least hold out in conception what cannot *yet* be fact, granting us what Terrence Des Pres calls its "provisional grace."[128]

Finally, for their part, creative writers seem to be quite as eager as contemporary critics to test the limits of the literary, by experimenting with forms once deemed wholly extra-literary and by developing new hybrids—part essay (or history or anthropology) and part fiction—that fall conspicuously between the literary and the extraliterary. This is one way in which art, like theory—and in the same spirit of reform—may address the very possibility or impossibility of art. Another way is to leap directly into meta-fiction, to write fiction about fiction or to insert within each text its own autocommentary. But when art "explicitly points to the principles of its own generation and structure," it has already crossed over into criticism—albeit a criticism with a dangerous potential for self-absorption and tautology, since it need have no focus beyond the revelation of its own devices.[129] Should these devices become less arresting and the revelations more obvious, the trick of baring the device could lose its ability to startle us into reflection or to arouse us from the stupor of consumption. At most, it would provide a rather tepid entertainment, the satisfaction of a foregone and rather banal conclusion. The problem for self-reflexive literature, then, is that having abandoned naive imitation and "aboutness," it will be tempted to remain arrested at this stage, or even to substitute self-reference for the referent it has lost, becoming obsessively "about itself . . . about the impossibility of its own existence."[130] Even if it refers only to itself, such works are ultimately no freer of the belief that they are copying a preexistent meaning than are conventional representations.[131] Not bothering to construct rich or convincing illusions, its disillusionments will be petty and will therefore offer little insight into the nature of our faith and fantasies, however discourse manages to pique our curiosity and to arouse our credulity. Thus the impasse of contemporary art: on one side, a curiously falsehearted attempt to return to realistic representation (curious because what results is an "imitation" of traditional representation), and on the other an equally phlegmatic avant-garde that has, in the words of Robert Scholes, "failed to find viable, continuing solutions to the problem of linguistic limitations."[132]

To the extent, then, that theory does not become wholly absorbed in the scrutiny and exposure of its own devices (which in any case would mean that it had ceased to be theory, since it would lack the requisite generality and replicability), it appears to offer the most promising way out of the current literary impasse..Theory preserves all that is best and most authentic in contemporary skepticism, our "lost capacity for naive response,"[133] but—because it must focus at least some of this analytic scrutiny on the operations of another set of texts—it manages to avoid its most debilitating consequences. This is the advantage of what I earlier referred to as the "radical intertextuality" of theory: the fact that it necessarily invests its energies in several texts at once, allowing illusions to well up in one place while it dispels them in another. The literary devices that literary theory exposes are thus allowed to do their own work and to achieve their own most characteristic effects, rather than being made futile from the start. The resulting analysis is bound to be more interesting, capable of greater depth and subtler illumination. As one piece of writing penetrates the different native figures of another, it strikes sparks in all directions rather than the steadily increasing pallor of images that mirror one another. In addition, theory avoids the bad faith of pretending to do the impossible, to catch itself in the act when in fact the act of scrutiny can never be the same as the act it scrutinizes, leaving an eternal blind spot that no discourse can overcome. Contemporary theory also moves beyond naive representation by acknowledging more openly its own interventions, by recognizing that its gestures are never neutral, always productive or destructive. Yet it retains at the same time a sense of transitivity and an awareness of the potential efficacy of discourse that sheer autocommentary can never have.

But it is not just the logic of representation that troubles contemporary literature. The question of the appropriate *units* of representation (or rather, of discursive production) is equally vexed. Character and situation, plot and point of view—these staples of mimetic art, which have for so long shaped our novels, poems, dramas, and even films—no longer have the same unquestioned credibility and authority. It is not that they are, strictly speaking, untrue—in the sense that we do not live our daily lives by them or that almost all our knowledge of self and others does not rely on them. Indeed, a quick glance at mass entertainment and the press would suggest that they have gained an increasingly unyielding hold over the popular imagination—as uncertainty and fear of the complications, and immense technological sophistications of the modern world increase as well. Such commercial representations themselves provide another impetus for art to escape the competing din and the entropy that sets in when any mode is used too freely and too cynically. Coherent narrative and cohesive characters have ceased to be achievements wrung from the stubborn contingencies of life and have become instead a manufactured form of instant gratification. The very ease of their production and consumption, the immediate and widespread recognition they win, seems to have less to do with their truth than with the audience's carelessness or evasions and the maker's cool manipulations. At such a cultural moment, the desires to delay gratification, to disrupt the cycle of production and consumption, and to expose the machinery of representation before it has a chance to do its work is both reasonable and creditable. But it does risk being unintelligible and unpleasant for readers who are not yet prepared to undertake their new responsibilities. Habituation in itself is not the whole problem: It is an addiction to devices that are useful and pleasant enough to live by (or else they would not be so addictive), which are even accurate enough as far as they go, but are incapable of going any farther. Traditional characterization and plot will not fail to illuminate some portion of our lives, but they will obscure others, and preserve that obscurity in ways that could weaken and imprison us. Ours seems to be a world which, as Fredric Jameson puts it, "makes the old-fashioned subject a mere location in a mechanism, yet victim of the illusion of its own centrality."[134]

Given our present suspicions about society and the psyche, the notion of an individual who knows him or herself fully and creates his or her own destiny out of whole cloth seems dangerously superficial, yet it remains stubbornly at the core of our public fictions and our private fantasies. It is the only notion we at present know "how it feels to live by" and perhaps the only one that will allow us to have these particular feelings of authority about our life. Theory, however, pushes us to move beyond the "illusion of centrality"—which is the truth of our own condition insofar as we can directly sense it—to those other forces whose activities we can only know by inference. We could, of course, try to alter our notions of character, subjectivity, time, and place in order to take these forces into account, but the result would be unrecognizable. The fact that certain pieces are missing—the unconscious, the war of class against class, and so forth—is not a contingent part of our condition, but constitutes it. Their absence is what gives our experience its characteristic flavor. Some would go even farther and condemn character and plot as devices actively involved in repressing energies and foreclosing human possibilities, as Leo Bersani does:

> The realistic novel, for all its apparent looseness, is an extremely tight and coherent structure: it encourages us to believe in the temporal myth of real beginnings and definitive endings, it portrays a world in which events

always have a significance which can be articulated, and it encourages a view of the self as organized (if also ravaged) by dominant passions or faculties. These ordered significances of realistic fiction are presented as immanent to society, whereas in fact they are the mythical denial of that society's destructively fragmented nature. The straining toward coherent, enclosing sense in literature is a power tactic consonant with a larger cultural strategy which elevates a certain type of intelligibility into the very criterion by which we are expected to recognize or to legitimize "experiences." And an implicit agreement about the natural shape of human experience is of course far from politically neutral: it creates a field of irreducible "truth" to which all new versions of social organization must conform, and which insures that any criticism of existing social arrangements will not transgress restrictive notions of possibility. . . . [135]

But whether one seeks, as Jameson does, to construct a new order that acknowledges what traditional, bourgeois literature excludes, some new way of imagining the position of the individual and the forces that intersect in her/him, the relationships into which s/he enters, or endeavors, like Bersani, to decompose all categories whatsoever and plunge into a more fertile disorder—are the traditional literary genres elastic enough to undergo such a transformation? Is the association between a given social or psychological order and a given literary form too close, are forms too intimately bound to the task of articulating a certain sense of possibility to allow for reform? Or must we seek other forms of discourse—with literary theory prominently among them?

Certainly one can (both Jameson and Bersani do) discover in traditional literary works the telling symptoms or luminous anticipations of what they wish had been expressed. But the discovery takes place because of another act of writing, their own theoretical re- or de-constructions. It is not "in" the literary work itself nor even in the commentary, but is generated between them by the work of one upon the other. The fruits of this interaction compare favorably—in the understanding and pleasure they make possible—with the awkward attempts at extended characterization, plotless novels, insurrectionary *écriture*, et al. that one finds in unaccommodated postmodern literature. Consider the uneven seriocomedy, the distended caricatures and paranoiac systems of a Pynchon, for instance, or the calculated oneiric excesses and almost predictable subversions of grammar and diagetic continuity in a Hélène Cixous or Phillipe Sollers. In this respect, two discourses seem better than one; theory provides the abstract or absent categories, the logic for extended inferences and a redistribution of elements that may seem distant or irrelevant to one another at the level of more recognizable identities and familiar events.

There is, in fact, a peculiar tendency among writers otherwise obsessed with the power of expectation, to underestimate the gap between traditional literary experience and the new sophistication of taste and intellectual training a reader must suddenly put on to read experimental texts. Of course, ever since the advent of so-called avant-garde literature there has been a silent army of interpreters and exegetes ready to fill that gap and to mediate between the latest literary experiments and the unreadiness of the audience. As Linda Hutcheon has noted, simply being exposed to extravagant postmodern texts has done nothing, on the Continent, to change "the reading habits of a public whose tastes are rooted in the sentimental, realistic fiction of the past." Most of this writing secretly "needs the author's intentions, his explanations in order to be read. . . . When this stage is reached, we require the extratextual aid of the author—from *Comment j'ai écrit certains de mes livres* to those crucially important back-cover comments of the *Tel Quel* literary collection in order to understand the functioning of the texts."[136]

It is easy enough to create an avant-garde art of violation. But how can one then get beyond the first crude shock and the abrupt pain of nonrecognition, how avoid the (all too quick) setting in of numbness and indifference—or worse, the simple readjustment that makes the unexpected precisely what is expected? Exhaustion is built into the very premises of modernism, its effort to "challenge the art of which it is the inheritor . . . drawing itself to its limits, purging itself of elements which can be foregone and which therefore seem arbitrary or extraneous."[137] Postmodernism is left with the appetite for challenge and purgation undiminished, but the opportunities for satisfying it, in ways that will not become immediately tedious, are all too rare. The period of challenge and the satisfaction it affords may be drawing to an end, and yet—one must admit—the new age still shows itself powerless to be born.

It is this void that literary theory finds so inviting, that has made it for so many readers the most interesting of contemporary discursive forms. Often enough, theory has been condemned for its schematic or reductive qualities, but now these very qualities seem liberating, allowing imagination to be suggestive when it cannot be concrete, to sketch with broad strokes what cannot yet be rendered in any great detail, and to open a conceptual space where we might someday learn to dwell. Theory is also free, as fictions and lyrics usually are not, to mount extended explanations and to engage in elaborate argumentation without provoking charges of digression. Such leisure for development, so much more room for exposition and defense relative to what is actually posited or claimed, are precisely what the present situation, with all of its uncertainties, its diffidences, its necessary hesitations, calls for. This is no more than the work of mediation and instruction that criticism has been tacitly expected to perform for half a century and more, but with less of the old servility and willing self-effacement. There is less assurance now that literary theory *is* strictly ancillary to the real business of literature, or that argument and explication must be mechanical and artless, with no compelling interest or exhiliration of its own.

An unprecedented crisis of audience confronts contemporary literature—from the competition of other, more immediately accessible, more profitable and broadly distributed mass media and films to the increasingly esoteric levels to which its own accumulated experiments and avant-garde impatience has brought it. The tendency of these experiments, moreover, is to ridicule or just remove almost all of the incentives—the pleasures of recognition, of identifying with a character, of being able to follow and occasionally foresee the sequence that events must take—which readers formerly enjoyed, at the very moment when the task of reading has become more arduous. Thus, it falls to literary theory to illustrate and perhaps to devise the fresh incentives for reading and to train, even to invent, a fit audience for contemporary literature. Yet while explaining the potential satisfactions of reading against the grain of habit and of exchanging the narcissistic pleasures of identification for the austere and largely fleeting joys of reflexive awareness,[138] theory is simultaneously presenting its own case as a candidate for aesthetic appreciation. And if the reading public as a whole is shrinking, if literature is increasingly relegated to the schools as something to "be studied"[139]—if, in a word, the majority of readers now are scholars (whether students or professional academics)—then the claims of literary theory to be our representative literary genre become stronger still. What better inspiration could a literature of theory have than an audience composed of theorists and critics?

2
Entrances to the Theoretical Text

Reading criticism, otherwise than in the presence, or with
direct recollection, of the objects discussed is a blank and
senseless employment.
ARNOLD ISENBERG, *"Critical Communication"*

Although both logic and circumstance have conspired to plunge literary
theory all at once into competition with its own subject matter, this does
not mean that we will find ourselves immediately possessed of the proper
style of reading and the most appropriate ways to talk about this new
genre. Indeed, if my description of the situation in which theoretical
discourse has emerged as a literary form is at all accurate—if theory does
"come of age" as part of a general break with old reading habits and
familiar assumptions about the nature of literature—it would be surprising if there were no problems of adjustment at all. And despite the
fact that theory is a more openly didactic form and able therefore to
instruct its would-be readers more explicitly and at greater length in the
mysteries required of them, it remains a hybrid, and like all hybrids is apt
to provoke misunderstanding and discontentment on every side. Nor is
the problem confined to the expectations imposed from without; the
weight of its own internal contradictions also makes it a highly unstable
form. Even Geoffrey Hartman—one of its most sympathetic readers—
has noted how this "uneasy coexistence" of different functions, this
struggle to maintain a "strong weight of ratiocination" without sacrificing
"intellectual poetry," can produce an ill-mixed "medley of insight and
idiosyncratic self-assertion."[1]

Using the comparison developed in the last chapter between the
devices conventionally associated with literature and the parallel devices
in theoretical discourse, we may be in a better position to see where the
signs of strain are most likely to occur. Theory resembles literature in
placing great weight on aesthetic satisfaction, although other
considerations—plausibility, logical consistency, applicability, and

falsifiability—count even more, unlike literary discourse, where these considerations enter in only marginally, if at all. The entities and processes that a theory posits have, at the outset, almost precisely the same problematic ontological status as literary fictions do, and the modality of theory—its imaginative flights into the realms of necessity and possibility—is troublesome in just the same way that the modality of fiction is troublesome to those who prefer a simple, binary choice between what is absolutely true and real and what is absolutely not the case. The fictional and the theoretical are a powerful blow to the belief that language derives its meaning from the antecedent states of affairs to which it refers, and the corollary belief that when language does not so refer or make immediately verifiable assertions, it is meaningless.

Yet though both challenge the primacy of perceptual knowledge and question the privileges accorded to assertion and description, their fate is not ultimately the same. As one goes beyond the moment of inception to examine each of them in their full temporal and pragmatic extension, the differences become quickly apparent. We pursue theoretical claims further and test them by different standards than we use for fictions. Where fiction *can* have a diffuse heuristic value and prove itself fitfully useful in organizing our other experiences, theory *must* do so and within far more precisely defined parameters. Where fiction invites, theory exhorts and/or predicts—the one we may decline or indulge as the mood strikes us, but the other commands our commitment and thus our efforts to refute or repudiate it. This is true too of whatever features literary and theoretical discourse ascribe to the world by redescribing it and of the new objects they summon into (virtual) being. Both metaphors and models are efforts to transform our habits of interpretation, but a model must withstand a wider range of logical and empirical tests, must serve on all occasions and not just in one, highly charged situation. As a result, they tend to be far less flamboyant, their edges are worn down by a process of continual modification, and they are proposed with far more caution—rooting themselves in regions that are already well and widely known. In contrast, metaphors are issued with as much care for their vibrancy as for their accuracy: for their power to arrest, stimulate, and startle, to make strange what is only too familiar. They can, at times, be more obscure than the subjects they set out to illuminate, dazzling us with the sheer difficulty of applying them and forcing us to search for (or to invent) something to justify this sudden and incongruous departure. Models are more likely to build upon a set of similarities that have already been established. Moreover, metaphors resist—to the death—the full assimilation of tenor to vehicle, the complete identity of characterization and subject matter that is the ultimate goal of models[2]—suggesting that in literature we savor the fact of conflict and the process of transformation as much or more than we do any final resolution.

Thus, while theory shares many of the features that we find in literature, it does not grant them the same importance or make quite the same use of them. One may, for example, speak of "presentational value" in connection with theory—the way a model exemplifies complex relationships at a glance or an argument displays the rectitude of its logical form—but the presentation is, by literary standards, strangely sparse and diagrammatic, in accordance with the greater generality of theory. Not only is a theory general in its scope, but the very formulation is "generic and repeatable,"[3] tolerating a wider range of synonyms, summaries, and paraphrases than are conventionally allowed to literature. We more easily accept that the thrust of a theory may be cumulative, gaining in power as it passes from one treatment to another, entering at last into a common pool of concepts and operations that C. P. Snow has called "the most beautiful and wonderful collective work of the mind of man."[4] Hence, we expect theories to take more scrupulous account of alternative interpretations— to weigh what rivals or predecessors or posterity has said or will say—than we do poetry and novels. If recent literary theory has called the principle of authorship into question and has tried to demonstrate that literature too is concerned, indeed obsessed, with its predecessors, it is perhaps turning its own condition into doctrine, or at least proposing a doctrine amenable to treating theory as a literary form.

When the theoretical and the literary impulses converge, there is no telling in advance which—if either—will be dominant, nor any assurance that the result will be invigorating rather than stultifying. The burden of literary responsibilities might breed theoretical irresponsibility, an indifference to the need to justify a chosen framework as long as it is elegant or has glamorous associations or affords the necessary shock of incongruity. The aesthetic appeal of simplicity and scope is inextricably and irreducibly a part of theorizing, not just as a covert motive for our fascination but also as a perfectly reputable reason for choosing one theory over its rivals. But no matter how appealing, a theory still "must be subjected to rigorous criticism and experimental testing."[5] There is a danger, then, that the sudden illumination may prove too intoxicating, that theoretical literature will be too intent on its own internal symmetries and will neglect such criticism. Already there are instances of theories that make no provision for testing or application at all, that are too inexplicit, imprecise, and equivocal to allow one to probe their assumptions and derive their consequences.[6] Readers and writers may rest content with the apparatus and the technical vocabulary of theory, enjoying the alien sound, the foreign graphic contours, and may lose all interest in what these instruments were originally designed to do. And even short of this, it is almost certain that with its new literary function, theory will stress the novelty, the boldness, of its hypotheses, and the fruitfulness of the categories it proposes, and will pay proportionately less attention to the evidence or arguments that count for and against them. It could fall from fictionalism into fiction, and treat competing hypotheses as just so many provocative variations, interesting as different points of view but requiring no real commitment or energy of investigation.[7] And this could become in turn a surrender to the "severance of literary culture from knowledge and power,"[8] or an excuse for shirking the work of developing a "coherent field or practice of literary criticism."[9]

Yet the obverse of every threat is a promise. If, as William Rueckert contends, theory in the end becomes "an act of intellectual and critical closure," a rigid and self-justifying system that prohibits any thought that is not "an application of the coordinates of the system,"[10] then the playfulness of literature becomes a boon and not a bane. It could throw questions open once again, make the claims of theory humbler, suppler, less insistent on exhaustiveness and total control. The irony of stance that is so prevalent in modern literature acts as a constraint (as Nietzsche himself well knew) on the simple will to power, teaching one to respect the loss that accompanies each gain, the many possibilities shut off for every one pursued, and especially the distortion that attempted mastery inevitably imposes on whatever it would enslave. To equivocate is at least to be attended by a vision of alternatives. Thus though it may be true (in the words of Richard Brown) that "to take a metaphor as purely fiction is to miss a possible occasion to elaborate it," it is equally true that "to take models as literal is to overlook their possible rivals."[11] Even the incongruity of metaphor can be a theoretical gain:

> ...when the highest degree of incongruity is combined with the greatest degree of inevitability, there results a statement of the greatest theoretical value....
>
> Where isomorphism is perfect, it is unlikely that *new* information will be yielded. Conversely, where metaphors yield the greatest insight, they are unlikely to be very isomorphic.[12]

The disjunction that literature traditionally effects between writer (or reader) and text, displacing the responsibility for belief downward unto a mediating narrator and *narrataire*,[13] also has its advantages. In such a situation one might be willing to undertake conceptual risks, to sample, if only tentatively and with an eye for avenues of escape, claims that might in any other circumstances seem too costly or too offensive or too terrifying to entertain at all. From literature, as Hillary Putnam puts it, "one learns to see what it would be like if it were true, how someone could possibly think that it is true."[14]

Theoretical generalization, especially in the case of literary theory, may give rise to a peculiar form of dogmatism that expresses itself in efforts to *force* the subject matter to conform to its own predictions and edicts. From the start, according to Starobinski, literary theory and poetics have been plagued with the problem of "ritualizing," using the achievements of the past as a rigid guide for every future effort.[15] This not only narrows the range of the possible experiments that writers feel themselves sanctioned to perform but also reinforces a hunger for crude repetition on the part of the audience, an unwillingness to face anything that departs from prior expectations. Thus, the healthy doubts about the value of originality that theory provokes must be weighed against a pathological compulsion to repeat—with the hybrid form of theoretical literature promising a more successful balance than either form taken singly.

Oddly enough, because aesthetic considerations play a less important role in theory, the standards of beauty it uses tend to be precisely that: standardized and unadventurous. "There is, of course, a difference between aesthetic valuation in the arts and outside of art. In the arts, aesthetic valuation necessarily stands highest in the hierarchy. . . . Outside of art, the various components of the phenomenon to be evaluated are not integrated into an aesthetic structure and the yardstick becomes the established norm that applies to the component in question."[16] But when theory becomes a literary genre, it need not go on endlessly proliferating symmetries and may instead put on a beauty that is far more unexpected or disturbing. And with this more demanding aesthetic, there also comes a heightened appreciation for the manner in which theoretical writing screens and shapes its subject; a more unobtrusive and normal beauty would not confront us as forcefully with the labor by which knowledge is produced.

Then too, as aesthetic value becomes more prominent, it reminds us that our attachment to a system of thought or conduct is rarely a response to its truth or feasibility alone. True and false are relatively easy distinctions; by using them, we reduce the welter of vague and exceedingly delicate criteria that we might bring to bear to a single, clearly demarcated scale. But there are harder questions we can and should pose to any "scheme of things" that we are asked to believe in and to use—questions that go beyond economy, congruence, and consistency, beyond even elegance, originality, and scope.[17] Why, for example, seek to establish predictability or control, what other interests might this knowledge serve? Regardless of how much evidence supports it, a schema may also prove attractive because it "fulfills social and psychological needs," because it fosters the unity of a group or the integration of a personality, because it gives direction and helps to allay anxieties, because it motivates a preferred course of action.[18] Truth is only one criterion of appropriateness, albeit an important one, but as Nelson Goodman remarks, "truth and its aesthetic counterpart amount to appropriateness under different names."[19] And this becomes the opening through which appropriateness of all kinds can be considered.

Finally, theory as literature drops all pretense to transcendence, confesses that it is capable of being object as well as subject, and gives itself over to the gaze of other readers who will, doubtless, recognize its limitations and its characteristic blind spots. Theoretical discourse usually tries to exist "on a plane that would be absent from that of which it speaks." By descending into literature, theory loses this ideality, but it gains a capacity to "stage" what it cannot yet render as proposition, to enact those process for which there are not ready names.[20]

Beyond these inherent attributes of theory are those things that theory could contribute to literature, along with the dangers it might pose—the temptation to make art out of what is only method and to level all efforts as if they were all equally creative. The peril is real, but so is the potential profit. As noted earlier, literature is already a peculiarly mobile category; to be literary, a piece need have no particular properties, form no special relationships, evoke no one set of emotions. We may argue over what deserves to be called literature and why or decline to argue because the criteria are irreparably vague or simply adopt whatever norms seem to govern the literary community at any given epoch. But even under the broadest and most flexible definition that claims only that literature is "a candidate for appreciation,"[21] theory would still constitute a departure. It is not the features that we are asked to appreciate—after we have been through automatic writing and the outpouring of drugged expletives and tape recorders talking to themselves, it is hardly likely that theory could wrench our finer sensibilities—but the altered nature of appreciation itself. If in the past the aesthetic has been detached from all questions of belief or action, from "any desire to possess or use the object of attention" or any concern for its real existence apart from the phenomenal impression that it makes,[22] then the emergence of theory signals the advent of a new age, one where the faculties are not so easily dichotomized, and it is harder to believe that contemplation is ever wholly disinterested. But by the same token, it is also an age in which "interest" has become a richer and more complex category, no longer the crude and instrumental passion it was of old. This opposition between a motiveless and inconsequential realm of contemplation and a world of practical concerns forms part of the tissue of distinctions that surrounds and conditions our response to literature: the old antipathies between thought and pleasure, reason and emotion, the fear (expressed most cogently by Arnold) that ratiocination will inevitably kill intuition and lead to spiritual and imaginative paralysis. To the extent, then, that it succeeds in uniting sensuousness with abstraction, theory poses a paradox the resolution of which will require that we abandon, one by one, each of these seminal definitions, until literary experience as we have known it has been quite transformed. Or, viewing it in less apocalyptic terms, one could say instead that the effort to assimilate theory represents another stage in a long history of literary change, which has seen the core formal values shift from harmony to sublimity, to grotesquery and decadence, to absurdity—with correlative changes in the nature of aesthetic experience from contemplative calm, to awe, to shock, to sardonic or bemused resignation. What theory seems to feed is a new appetite for difficulty (the inverse, perhaps, of the increasingly facile entertainment industry), a new appreciation for the problematic and the speculative as aesthetic categories. It provides a new quality of satisfaction—when an explanation suddenly realigns the elements of a familiar scene or a series of questions slowly reveals to us the precariousness of the ground on which we stand—which we lamely try to express with words like *interesting, engrossing, illuminating,* and *intriguing.*

In place of the monuments of modernism, so crippling for those who followed after, theory offers an art that one can contend with and discard, which stands ready to be assimilated or even superceded by its posterity. (This owes something, perhaps, to the myth of scientific progress but tempered by, and tempering, the myth of artistic decline.) Theory does not, conventionally, express a peculiar sensibility; the feats of association it performs must be open to other minds as well, which will add to them, correct them, put them to the trial. Because theory is not deemed to be a particular speaker's declaration of idiosyncratic beliefs, it is easier to paraphrase a theory; since we are not quoting words that "belong" to some one individual, we need not take the same precautions against misquoting.[23] Theory does not need, as postmodern novels do, to seek artificial ways of dispelling representational illusion or construct extra pieces of textual machinery to arouse greater self-awareness and a more aggressive role in readers; contentious reading is traditional to theory, and trompe l'oeil, with its erasure of all signs of spectatorship, has never been so. Theory is always and openly dialogic, always actively related to proposals that precede and follow it, and literary theory adds to this polyphony by taking other discourse as its subject matter. Thus (as mentioned earlier), literary theory promises to manage the difficult move beyond representation without lapsing into solipsism. It maintains a salubrious balance between pride in its own powers of construction (or deconstruction),—recognizing the role that our own intellectual operations play in producing the objects of our knowledge—and humility at its own powerlessness to stand alone. Without pretending to be a mere reflection or hiding its own labors, it retains a necessary relationship to things beyond itself—other writings, future readings, the entire array of practices, observations, and experiments it both presupposes and enjoins.

How hard it is, though, in light of the internal tensions of a hybrid text and the ingrained assumptions with which we ourselves arrive, to keep from slipping back into familiar reading habits, from seeking the same effects and pressing the same critical vocabulary that served us for novels, plays, and poems. But to pick up a piece of literary theory looking for suspense, for personality, for a densely rendered mise en scène, is to court disappointment and at the same time to miss those peculiar pleasures that the theoretical text can afford. For example, in his pioneering studies of criticism as a literary form, Cary Nelson still feels compelled to find a voice, "a special way of projecting individual experience," to justify his claim that these texts have aesthetic value.[24] As a result, the absence of a readily identifiable persona becomes for Nelson a symptom of "depersonalization," if not a deliberate disguise. Yet voicelessness—or at most the uninflected voice of reason—is the native tendency of theoretical discourse. Thus, what is most striking, as Lionel Abel characterizes it, is the "twilight tone" of Maurice Blanchot,[25] or—as in certain of Borges's more speculative fragments—the power to "make us feel the approach of a strange, neuter and impersonal power."[26] The more interesting question, then, is whether and how a given theoretical text manages to project a personality or—since authorship is still very much a "live" category for most readers of literature—how it manages to deflect efforts to humanize it, to hear in it a characteristic voice.

If we persist in hearing voices, it is because we are not yet ready to give up the satisfactions of recognition, of reading as a process of identifying and identifying with. But theory begins where recognition ends; if our prior experience and our usual classifications were sufficient, there would be no need for theory. It does not present us with an image of ourselves (although the texts it studies may); properly speaking, it presents no images at all, but introduces us instead to the apparatus—the elements and conditions—out of which such images are made. Theory is an art not of the imaginary but of the symbolic, and in this respect it comes even closer to the chaste and taxing standard that Adorno sets for art in general—to break "the spell of stupid self-preservation" and become a "model of state of consciousness in which the ego no longer derives happiness....from self-reproduction."[27] But the power of theory need not be simply nugatory. If it does deny the usual scenic values, there is still the excitement of being taken behind the scenes, into the exchange zone where constructions first take shape and fantastic metamorphoses occur.[28]

Taken in isolation from its subject matter, theoretical discourse presents us with a grid of abstractions, a set of conditions, operations, strategic recommendations, key distinctions, and favorite conceptual categories that together provide the basis for an explanation or a program. The basis is not always the same, however, as we shall see more fully below, for a theory may offer a full metaphoric reconstruction or only a convenient framework for sorting and storing information. But whatever schema it does provide must be a solvent for our initial assumptions, since it is this dissolution, reordering, and renaming that gives rise to the fresh sense of possibility on which explanation and prescription depend. This power to "refigure" is one locus for our interest in theory; there can be surprise or strain or subtle grace in the way a theory seizes on and juxtaposes the elements of a literary work—rather like the effect of a more or less daring montage.

But equally important is how a theory wins (or fails to win) our assent for its operations: through the closeness of its "fit" or through the intrinsic appeal of the conceptual framework itself or through whatever additional arguments it mounts to justify or vindicate its chosen framework. Just as the usual standards of literary criticism fall short in such a case, so the customary criteria for assessing the appeal of a theory—simplicity, consistency, elegance, scope, congruence with evidence, compatibility with other accepted theories—are insufficient to explain what makes a theory winning when it functions as a piece of literature. We may, for instance, be expected to savor the *in*congruity, the stunning partiality, of its fit, and certainly our appreciation for the conceptual framework itself will hardly be content with bland respectability or coherence. We are already well beyond this when Nelson speaks of the "delicate crises, these terminological ballets" in Kenneth Burke, or when Richard Klein tries to "characterize the poetry of Said's thinking, the sensual pleasure of his dialectic . . . . an argument constructed by metonymy—as in a dream," or when Leo Bersani notes "a certain form of even excessive intelligibility" in Foucault that "masters an adversary power by reducing it (and elevating it) to one's own superior version of its sense."[29] These remarks illustrate not only that the structure and internal economy of theoretical discourse is capable of exciting rapt attention but also how words like *simplicity* or *scope* do little to illuminate the quality of that attention—hence the recourse to a renovated rhetoric, to dream-work, dance, and power politics. (It is perhaps no accident that the interest in tropes, in semiotics, and in social and psychic structures surfaced in literary studies at about the same time that the study of prose—theoretical and otherwise—came into vogue as well.)[30]

How a theory articulates its conceptual space—the kind of categories that it considers basic, the relationships (of likeness and difference, of subordination and domination) that these categories contract with one another, the range and delicacy of the distinctions it can mount, and with what mobility or rigidity it maintains them—all of these may sound dauntingly remote from the usual sources of aesthetic satisfaction, yet they are to theory what dramatis personae or cardinal images or master tropes are to other literary genres. Although they may repel our efforts to visualize or embody them, theoretical categories share the capacity of characters and images to "endure and absorb detail,"[31] to propel the discourse forward and collect its scattered energies into a momentary intensity. (The staying power of any verbal construct, no matter how abstract or purely terminological in nature, is doubtless the reason that an arch-deconstructionist like Derrida is so chary of preserving any of his own key terms from one writing to the next, although whether he can as easily abandon his basic method is another question.) Then too, the elements that comprise the framework of a theory have their own distinctive epistemological and metaphysical implications that we must confront as well. They are, after all, the compass within which the phenomenal world will be made to fit, if only by a process of hypothetically extending "our conception of what there is in the world."[32] Our fascination with theory, therefore, draws upon our sense of fundamental possibility—what we take to be or wish to be or can (for the nonce) imagine to be basic and irreducible. And since in reading theory we must eventually assume the position of the "subject," must be ready to see and operate through these categories (rather than taking them as the marks of another subjectivity whose character we are studying), this position must have its own compensations for us, its own comforts or tantalizing discomforts.

Our difficulty is not, then, that theory affords no pleasures of its own, or that writing is more or less superfluous here, subordinate to the ideas it conveys. Indeed, one could argue just the reverse, that in the absence of well-defined generic conventions, the writing sprawls before us as never before, in all its strangeness.[33] Theoretical literature must struggle to establish through its writing alone the nature of its subject, its space of operation, its principal devices, even its ideal audience, as more familiar modes of literature need not.[34] It is a writing that we cannot take as natural since we do not know in advance where to place it and we lack "the terms in which to classify the things we encounter."[35] Thus, it is with no small trepidation that I offer the following, highly tentative proposals for the reading of theory, recognizing that its power as a literary form may depend in large part on its intractability and its resistance to definition. Yet it seems better, in the end, to seek out terms that will be appropriate to theory than to risk having other, distorting terms imposed on it by accident or habit.

The Elements of Theory

The Problem

There can be no theory unless something has first been rendered problematic. Until we sense a lack or we doubt the sufficiency of appearances or we wonder how or why things happen to come about as they do, there is no energy, no urgency to invest in theorizing. Prescriptions can be elegant and efficient, but we must first feel the need for renovating our usual practices; explanations can increase our understanding—whether by removing our perplexity, or by banishing or diminishing our surprise, or by clearing up an obscurity—but only if we feel a need to understand.[36] The great theories are great not only because they answer questions successfully but because they initiate them, because they have the capacity to "bring a problem to life . . . and make it seem formidable."[37] Frequently the doubt outstrips the attempted resolution, passing from theory to theory and surviving long after the original hypotheses have been abandoned. It is a tricky business this, to insinuate a need even as one tries to fill it, yet this is what theory as a literary form must accomplish—particularly so because it lacks the calm assurance of responding to a set of "official" questions and to an audience that is already curious.

There are no problems, however, that are guaranteed to be "lively," not even a sure method for demonstrating that a problem does indeed exist. Much of the potential interest of reading theoretical literature is in how it finally manages to strip familiar objects and commonplace practices of their obviousness, and making them stand before us in all their irritating unaccountability. The strategies may vary from a mock Cartesian meditation, where an ambitious and would-be universal doubt is presented under the guise of a purely personal dilemma, to the opposite extreme of simply and boldly assuming that such doubts already exist. A single resonant question may be enough. But in one way or another, the subject matter must be isolated from its old surroundings—where it fit only too well—and readied for insertion into a new theoretical context, where it will become the effect of a putative cause, the end of a proposed means, a position in a hypothetical pattern, or an instantiation of an apparent rule. "There must be a feeling of doubt, a sense that the situation somehow does not allow us to respond to it in terms of our normal expectations. . . . And this feeling of having lost our way is complemented by a need to fill out the situation, to imagine a new hypothesis by introducing new terms which might synthesize the disparate elements."[38]

Equally significant is where a theory situates its problem. The principal sites are three: within the object of study itself; or in the casual assumptions, attitudes, and opinions which usually attach to that object; or in the claims that other theorists have made about it.

In the first instance, the conventional context that is reversed is a widespread, complacently held belief. In the second case, the conventional context is a theoretical one, a taken-for-granted paradigm of normal science. In the first, the audience is the larger community and its idealogues; in the second, it is the community of scholars.[39] Doubt can operate at different levels, the phenomenological as opposed to the epistemological, the professional as opposed to the lay context. This will in turn alter the range and the quality of experience, the very language that enters into the theory. Theory has a different force, a different kind of strenuousness or aggressiveness when the problem is simply an accident of time and place than when it arises because of human error. Typically, when the problem is located in the phenomena themselves (a text or set of texts, in the case of literary theory), the theory will be more explicit about the extent of its domain and the nature of its own operations. When it begins as a response to another theory, however, it may put all its energy into correction and / or subversion, with none left for defining its own operations or determining how the changes it has introduced might affect the old theory, altering its domain or scope of application. Of late, literary theory has drawn its impetus more and more from other theories, and such problems have proliferated. Take, for instance, *Anti-Oedipus*,[40] a book that is all but unintelligible to those who have no knowledge of its predecessors. An unsympathetic reader could dismiss it as hopelessly imprecise and unworkable, if s/he failed to appreciate that its real work is corrective, that it constitutes an attempt to overcome the political and psychological implications of preceding theories by altering or inverting their categories.

The site of the problem need not preexist the theory, however. Conjuring up misleading appearances, shallow opinions, and wrong headed theoretical claims is an ideal way to introduce and develop a problem. And by going further, projecting the figure of an actual opponent (whether the victim of false impressions or the propagator of errors), theory can create its own atmosphere of urgency.[41] Then too, theories do not just raise issues that their predecessors and rivals have ignored; they also act to forestall or evade problems, even problems that no one else may have noticed. The impulse to shut off an unprofitable line of inquiry is probably as strong as the impulse to open one up, and there are numerous instances of theories that deflect attention onto new, less fearsome objects of investigation—as Max Weber does when he exchanges Marx's inflammatory economics for the more neutral and rational study of politics.[42] When a theory has erected itself in opposition to another theory—actual or imagined—it is interesting to see how or whether it then tries to keep itself from eventually being circumscribed in precisely the same way. Maneuvers range from an effort to construct an impregnable wall of justifications and evidence, to anticipatory counterattacks, to equivocations and defensive ironies. The latter defense, particularly popular in literary circles, can become so extreme that theorizing eventually gives way to the pursuit of an ideal (and doubtless impossible) mobility. Hassan's "paracriticism" has something of this deliberately disarming quality, but it reaches its most extreme form in the orphic asseverations of "schizoanalysis" recommended in *Anti-Oedipus*. At a certain level, theory seems to be the death of theory (a point to which I will return in subsequent chapters).

Often the underlying problem is posed so inchoately or obliquely that we ourselves as readers must reconstruct it. This can be done by examining the inaugural and especially the terminal points of whatever explanation or prescription the theory offers, since the nature of the question will determine when an answer is complete.[43] Of course it is always possible for a theory to stop short of its projected completion. Theories are often more provocative, from a reader's point of view, when they do so—provoking our curiosity about the source of the blockage and what Jameson calls the "strategy of containment," which arrests and conceals its original trajectory.[44] But even when it is not premature, the terminus is still a place of quickened engagement with a theoretical text, showing us the edge of an imagination, the point beyond which doubt or desire cannot even be conceived. To read a theory is to feel these edges, these moments of flagging interest or resplendent consummation, as one might feel the rhythms of a poem or the episodes of a narrative.

A theory's domain—where it applies and the scope of that application—the shape and the extent of the claims it makes, and even the type of theory it is—(explanatory or programmatic)—are all a function of the kind of problem faced. Some doubts can be laid to rest with a suitable explanation, but others—uncertainties about how best to accomplish what we want to do or what we should want to do in the first place—require an entirely different response: recommendations, plans, stipulations, and stimulation. Theories may share the same domain and the same explanatory or prescriptive force and still differ in the ends that they are designed to achieve—whether, that is, they contribute to our understanding, on the one hand, or our ability to exercise control, on the other. Then too, a theory may aim less at solving an initial problem than at exposing it as a false problem, an issue that is the result of misleading first impressions or even other theories. A good deal of current literary theory (or anti-theory) is devoted to the task of perpetuating doubt, of making it insoluble. To render something forever problematic, however, means maintaining its power to tease or annoy or tempt us, and thus requires some silent hope of resolution, however often and however resolutely the hope is dashed.

When a number of theories isolate the same subject, in response to separate but overlapping questions, a "field of knowledge" is projected. There emerges a set of apparently autonomous entities or processes that seem to be the source of our preoccupation, rather than the product of it. It is interesting to ask, with Foucault, why such new spaces of operation should suddenly open up, under what conditions doubts would erupt and collect just there. What is to be gained by having this subject matter to contemplate, manipulate, and discourse upon? What interest, institutional and personal, might it serve? But to answer such "meta-theoretical" questions, one must first be able to read a theory and recognize its characteristic operations.

The Conceptual Design

The heart of any theory is its so-called "conceptual machinery,"[45] the principled response—in the form of a model, a law, a taxonomic scheme—with which it confronts a given problem and that then becomes the source of its explanatory power. Such conceptual designs are, of course, drawn with extremely broad and generalized strokes, made as they are for constant extension and continual reapplication, but they are no less distinctive than the densely textured descriptive passages we usually admire in literature.

Theories have their own characteristic logic, depending upon the internal disposition of their categories and how these categories are deployed (e.g., to subsume, to redefine, to designate, and so forth). But this logic invites further and deeper responses when we read a theory for its literary value. Thus, as a reader, Louis Marin notes "the epistemological optimism of the modelling power of linguistics," and Fredric Jameson sees that the "naive linearity" of vulgar Marxism might have been enough to provoke Weber's rejection of it and his own subsequent attempt to construct a more satisfying account of the relationship between religious ideologies and social structure. Theories fail for reasons of design as well as for reasons of insufficient evidence or imprecision. As Brown states of sociological theories, "only when sociology fails to be dramatic, only when it does not reveal unexpected relationships that have an ironic necessity, does it become banal."[46] And if there is a potential for irony, optimism, linearity, and banality even in theories that have no overt aesthetic intentions, it becomes actual when theory openly embarks upon a literary career.

Typically, the conceptual design of a theory is not localized in a single passage but dispersed throughout the text, and it may take the form of charts, diagrams, or mathematical formulae as well as of sentences and paragraphs. In fact, the points of exchange between discursive and graphic presentation, how one supplements or complements the other and the place each occupies in the gradual emergence of the full design, is one of the more curious and alluring features of theoretical literature—particularly now, when interest in general semiotics and antipathy to logocentrism runs so high. Thus, what I have called the design—the conceptual machine and the constituent categories and relations that make it up—is something we must abstract from the text itself, as we might (with greater reservations) extract the "story" from a novel. It is a level of textual operation that we locate by the transformations it undergoes over the course of the theory's history or during periods of controversy—the compressions, the expansions, substitutions, and exclusions that together indicate the principal elements of the theoretical framework. The conceptual design is usually the most memorable part of a theory because it is largely the product of memory, what survives the translation and accumulation, the ever renewed applications that are the fate of theory. Yet as with stories, one can learn to count on certain recurrent features or types that will allow one to process a theory and to sound its conceptual core even on the first encounter.

The most common devices are: models, methodologies, metalanguages, laws and generalizations, narratives and / or emblematic patterns, taxonomies, definitions and enabling postulates, translation functions, and the strategems of deconstruction. The order reflects the relative power and integration of each device, and especially how principled its operations are. A good deal has already been said about *theoretical models* and the new authority they have gained in the eyes of philosophers of science in the past decade or two. Indeed, the prestige is so great that *model* and *theory* are often treated as if they were synonymous, although theories need not employ a model, and many so-called literary models are not really models at all but emblems, classifications systems, or simply suggestions for generating more interesting readings. The difference is in the model's explanatory powers and its pretentions to reality. A theoretical model is a mechanism or process postulated (usually by analogy to a more familiar mechanism or process) to account for a set of observations.[47] It should replicate in all relevant respects the behavior of the object under investigation and, at the same time, should allow us to make further inferences about that behavior and to extend our understanding of why it takes the form it does.[48] Models are usually causal, but teleological and structural models are possible as well and may prove more compelling, depending on the situation and the subject matter. And while models are usually used for explanation, there is no reason why they could not be used prescriptively as well, as something to which our subsequent behavior should conform rather than something that explains what we already do.

The popularity of models in recent years is no doubt a function of their epistemic value; models provide a foundation for laws and generalizations and make us feel that we know why and how something is the case. They give us access to regions we cannot directly observe, transfer new hypothetical features to whatever subject we are studying, and by describing that subject in unfamiliar terms, "shift the relative emphasis attached to details, in short, help us to see new connections."[49] But this revisionary power means that a true model must be subject to severe scrutiny and test, in proportion to the seriousness of its claims. It must be more than a convenient framework; if discrepancies appear, the properties of the model must be changed. And if such changes introduce inconsistencies in the model itself, we must either discard it or recognize it as no more than a useful fiction.[50] It is the integrity of its design that makes a model so illuminating, since we can follow its internal logic to arrive at new hypotheses about the structure, the history, the inherent capacities of the object of investigation, and can initiate new lines of research accordingly. But this same integrity makes the model extremely fragile and leads to such paradoxes as complementary distribution, where two different models must be invoked to explain the behavior of subatomic particles, since the internal logic of each model prevents our combining them into a single framework: half-particle, half-wave.[51]

While models may be founded on a tentative analogy or homology, the initial resemblances may gradually disappear in the course of time and with further adjustments. It may have begun with billiard balls, but the model of gas molecules has undergone enough refinements to become almost a new thing. It is particularly interesting for literary readers to consider how important the role of resemblance is in any given theoretical model and, in addition, what kind of resemblance is being claimed— material, formal, structural, behavioral, and so forth. Although theory is that mode of literature least bound by the strictures of perception and experience, it may resort to substances, to imagery and the familiar world of the visible and the palpable, to construct its models—although it may also manage to refine them out of sight again along the way. Thus, of any piece of theoretical literature, we may ask whether it employs a model and what the function of that model is. We may ask further whether it is an arbitrary construction or is derived from another source, and what basis the derivation had. How great is the tension between the model and the subject matter? What faculties and memories does the model appeal to? As theories become more literary, however, modeling is apt to become a far more complicated matter, with rapid shifts in function and perspective that make strict testing and straightforward application very difficult. But should it ever become impossible, the perilous and exhilarating balance of theoretical literature—a genre where illumination should never be terminal, which should occupy without entirely satisfying our attention—will be lost.

A *metalanguage* is a language or logical system rich enough to analyze, explain, or justify the workings of another language or logical system. As Gödel pointed out long ago, no logic can ever demonstrate its own consistency, since to do so it would have to make use of the very operations that are at issue. The first metalanguages were constructed to test the soundness of certain mathematical systems (especially Euclidean geometry) by uncovering the basic calculations they allow and reformulating these in terms of formal axioms whose accuracy and consistency one could then assess. In time, however, the notion of a metalanguage was transferred to natural languages, with the goal changed from one of testing and rectifying the underlying system to simply baring it and explicating it.[52] If the metalanguage does purport to explain a language, then it becomes a specialized type of theoretical model, one devoted exclusively to the study of languages from the point of view of their internal organization, their components, and their rules of combination.

Recently, metalanguages have become models in a second sense as well, appropriated from their original domains to apply to new objects—narratives and myths, clothing and architecture, economic and psychological behavior—that are not, literally, languages or systems of logic. The transfer to a new domain results in a reinterpretation, turning the object under study into a kind of language at the same moment that its "syntax" is being cataloged and explained. The popularity of these models twice-removed is due partly to the aptness of the categories and explanatory framework they offer, and partly to the very considerations that they exclude—the traditional literary concern for representational fidelity, moral assessment, relative aesthetic merit. Thus, metalanguage often "represents a revolt against the belief in the humane value of literary criticism."[53] (This may not be an inherent property of metalanguages; it is just that the most familiar and most highly developed linguistic models focus almost exclusively on syntax, at the expense of semantic or pragmatic value.)

Not all metalanguages are explanatory, however. Often the categories and structures they propose have an uncertain status, useful enough as a preliminary framework for parsing or decoding, but perhaps inadequate as a model of how the language system really works. Even if the metalanguage seems to be isomorphic in all respects with its object language, it can still lack real explanatory force; a simulacrum is not necessarily a model, although it can clarify certain patterns by presenting them in a more concentrated form, stripped of accidental details. Only when the metalanguage ceases to be a simple inventory and affords us insight into the processes underlying language, making it possible to infer and predict what we have not yet observed, does it become a model.[54] This does not mean that inventories serve no useful purposes, however, only that the purposes are different, as are the standards of criticism that apply to them. It is not always easy to distinguish one sort of metalanguage from another, for analyses and catalogs never fail to introduce some new features of their own and cannot help but alter our appreciation of the nature of language, if only by collecting together in one place what is usually too scattered to strike us with full force. One must look carefully at any metalanguage, therefore, and ask precisely what its pretentions are: whether it purports to be an explanation or an inventory, and whether, in addition, it effects a metaphoric transformation, making language out of what was initially something else.

Like models, metalanguages are highly integrated and tend therefore to treat their object language as if it too were all of one piece, a closed and coherent system.[55] More recently linguistics has attempted to introduce such notions as variable rules, structures that are sensitvie to context, and "fuzzy logics" to allow for some of the play and change and indeterminacy characteristic of natural languages. But perhaps because its roots are in artificial languages, metalanguage generally seeks strict recurrences, categories and relations that are constant and discrete, principles of distinction that are absolute and unremitting—like the famous and much maligned binary oppositions. It punctuates and immobilizes its subject more patently—if not more deeply and more lastingly—than other models do. Perhaps this is a function of its austere and finely articulated surface, which offers us no visualizable billiard balls, no waves or particles, but only diagrams and *combinatoires* and sequences of rules. Yet even these austerities have their own distinctive qualities, their own particular vision of how a system works and at what price. Different metalanguages have different predilections for hierarchy or for networks, their taste for certain modes of alternation, even a kind of latent numerology. In most literary theories that use metalanguages, there is the faint whiff of the immense distances that the borrowed categories have come, the delicious estrangements, introduced by all those imported topologies, chemistries, algebraic hieroglyphs. Some metalanguages are built around the joy of stripping down, of purging all excess, while others take the opposite delight in intricacy and sheer compilation. Within this admittedly compressed and rarefied range, the differences of aesthetic possibility are still as great, in their own way, as those that separate a Frost from a Shelley, or a Beckett from a Tolstoy.

Literary studies, like history, are more apt to "consume" *laws and generalizations* than they are to construct them, to apply them to the illumination of particular cases rather than to the accumulation of particular cases in order to establish the existence of a law.[56] It will often prove more profitable to read literary theory for the laws it chooses to import than for the laws it makes. One could look, for example, for the place from whence they came, or for the kind of correlations (laws of succession, laws of coexistence, etc.)[57] they establish; or for the strength (universal or statistical) or the grounds of the purported correlation (natural necessity or social convention), as well as for how the theory exploits them. There are marked degrees in how much a theory is willing to sacrifice for the sake of establishing a universal; regularities themselves are not difficult to find, but significant or interesting ones are, and a given theory may prefer a daring probability to a tepid law that brooks no exceptions.

Indeed, a taste for laws, for generalizations as the source and goal of knowledge, is distinctive in itself and takes a different set of sympathies and tolerances than either models or metalanguages do. To embrace laws, one must hunger after proximate certainties, must prefer predictable and rigorously formulated regularities to more remote causes and hypothetical entities that can be verified only indirectly. Of course, laws too must be taken partly on trust, since logical necessity is not something one can see or demonstrate empirically. Yet the leap of faith is less extreme, asking of us only that we extend our credulity, not that we alter it. To accept a law or generalization as a sufficient explanation (or prescription) is to stop short of knowing *why* something should happen and to be satisfied with knowing simply that it has always happened so. We are comforted by the normality of the event in question and by the firm connective tissue that seems to tie together what might otherwise dissolve into the loose contingencies of life—even if we will never entirely understand why these regularities and no others should occur.

Often the value of theoretical laws is more logical or pragmatic than epistemic, allowing us to reach valid or at least plausible conclusions. But perhaps the biggest difference between a theory based on law and one based on a model, from a literary point of view, is the distinctly different appeal of exhibition and metaphoric transformation on the one hand and of exposition and argument on the other. The mode of demonstration need not be the same in every case, of course; the finality of deduction is reserved for true laws, while generalization, resting on a convergent network of evidence, demands, hedges, qualifications, and an occasional bout of speculative overreaching. Within the same discipline or tradition, it is desirable that laws should be consistent with each other, but this is a far less stringent standard than the perfect integration expected of a model or a metalanguage, allowing greater potential mobility to explanations and prescriptions, a wider range of strategies and terminologies. Yet just because laws lack the continuity and wholeness of a model, they are unable to direct our inferences toward new connections and fresh lines of investigation. Their applications are well defined but forever fixed, pure but static, opening only on a future of eternal recurrence.

Theoretical discourse cannot be reduced to a story, but it can make use of *narratives* (of a highly truncated sort) as part of its conceptual machinery. Actually, one should not stop at narrative but should include all manner of *emblematic patterns*, those based on spatial as well as temporal contiguity. Such narratives and emblems resemble models in their sheer force of exhibition, their ability to display complex relationships directly, but they are far more limited in their logical implications and usually far less abstract in their formulation. In fact, theories resort to fable or emblem when they must exemplify a rule that they cannot yet state in more formal terms, one that seems to change too greatly with each new circumstance or is perhaps not even a rule at all, but only a particular and transient correlation.[58] No doubt if the exemplum becomes too local or too idiosyncratic, it risks reducing theory to mere description, with little or no explanatory or prescriptive power for other cases. Yet it is a risk worth taking when the subject is something as mutable as literature or literary history, which might otherwise, for lack of simple causes or uniform laws, entirely escape our effort to comprehend it. And when, as now, theory must confront and somehow overcome an imaginative impasse, such emblematic gestures, parables, and allegories may be the most suitable forms available. As Louis Marin describes the service utopian fables perform in much the same impasse:

> Utopia is a social theory, the discourse of which has not yet attained theoretical status. . . . On the one hand, it expresses what is absolutely new, the "possible as such," what is unthinkable in the common categories of thought used by the peoples of a given time . . . . On the other hand, utopia cannot transcend the common and ordinary language of a period and of a place. It cannot transgress completely the codes by which people make reality significant, by which they interpret reality, that is the systems of representation, of signs, symbols, and values which recreate, as significant for them, the real condition of their existence.[59]

The explanatory and prescriptive force of narratives and emblems is (or should be) tempered, in proportion to their relatively weak theoretical status. They cannot prove, but only arouse a sense of "fit," of "rightness," of a reasonable—but not the only reasonable—account.[60] Yet they differ from fictions and images per se in the obligation they bear to the alternative frameworks that might be placed around the same subject matter.[61] We accept and employ them not only because they make a subject intelligible but also because they do so more successfully than other accounts do. In the case of programmatic theories, using an exemplum may alter the very grounds on which we accept it, by awakening in us a desire to emulate rather than by compelling us to obey the rules.[62]

Emblems and narratives work by filling in the gaps around what we have actually observed or recommend—introducing a continuity and context that makes them seem less anomalous or less like a naked imposition. (In much the same way, a model introduces hypothetical entities and processes or a law interjects an element of universal necessity.) But whereas one can test a law by seeking further instances, or seek independent motivation for hypothetical entities, stories are normally built around a fixed body of evidence and can only be validated against the same evidence again—for accuracy, coverage, and so forth. This is the old problem of the hermeneutic circle that has dogged literary theory for so long, and will continue to dog any theory that works with a closed corpus of materials.[63] Without access to new evidence, all one can do is consult rival accounts of the same material and, ultimately, whatever standards of "good design" currently govern emblems and narratives. In the case of narrative, these may include everything from very general beliefs about the nature of human action and of time to changing predilections for closed or open forms, a rising trajectory or a dying fall, expectations fulfilled or slyly overturned.[64] (Even among narrative analysts, arguments are many and rife about what the fundamental design of narrative actually is. Is sequence essential, or is it only an accidental medium for expressing deeper relationships?[65] Is the logic of narrative inherently causal [with each episode giving rise to the next], or teleological [with every episode mutually oriented to the same conclusion][66] or structural [with each episode functioning retrospectively and prospectively at once]?[67] And how are we to identify the fundamental elements of a story—with reference to literary or cultural codes, by a painstaking comparison of a body of texts, or by ad hoc strategies?)[68]

The relationship between elements in a narrative (or in an emblem, for that matter) is not one of strict entailment; elements condition the appearance of other elements without precisely causing them. Given one part of a pattern, we may expect another, but not deduce it or predict it.[69] Narratives and emblems can shed light on why something is the case, but not on why it could not have been otherwise.[70] Post hoc, ergo propter hoc is, after all, a fallacy, even if it is one that narrative occasionally exploits, as emblems exploit the related fallacies of composition and division.[71]

Since they are limited to providing a suggestive framework, stories and configurations need not have the tautness and uniformity of a model. Science characteristically isolates a single factor—one element in a complex situation that is allowed to vary while the rest stay constant—that is then dubbed "the cause."[72] But this simplicity is obviously an artifact of the experimental method. Though narratives cannot be tested like scientific laws, they do allow more room for overdetermination and a tangled web of incommensurable associations. They are more open to changes of explanatory strategy along the way. This fluidity, or even logical laxity, makes them a particularly apposite device for exploring subjects that do not conform to the strictures of classical rationality—the workings of the unconscious, for example, or of textuality itself. Not by accident did Freud seize on the Oedipus myth[73] or Hegel resort to the story of a master and a slave; Lacan's need for emblematic mirrors is just as great, in this respect, as Borges's.

Without trying to resolve the perhaps insoluble problem of what a narrative "really" is, one can at least distinguish story-types that are superficially unlike: those that seem to be primarily sequential (whether that sequence is temporal, causal, teleological, or dialectical) and those that seem to follow a structural imperative instead (working toward or away from a particular configuration of forces, passing through a series of mediations, displacements, and homological substitutions). Either of these narrative patterns is capable of exhibiting a change of state, but they differ in what they consider most important—the process of transition or its roots and consequences. Emblems, of course, tend to be more static, but may—if they show signs of internal strain or imbalance—suggest a state of suspended animation and a capacity for change.

In addition to the underlying story, there is also the plot—or the exposition, in the case of emblems—which reorders it and gives its own selective emphasis to different elements.[74] Hayden White suggests (following Frye) four basic modes of "emplotment" that alter "the hierarchy of significance" and turn mere chronicles into tales of romantic transcendence, satiric decay, comic reconciliation, or tragic epiphany.[75] Nor does White-Frye topology exhaust all the possibilities: One thinks immediately of etiologies and eschatologies, or of plots that neutralize or dissolve apparent contradictions rather than transcending or temporarily reconciling them. By stressing parallelisms or brutal incongruities, plotting too has its contribution to make to the conceptual design of a theory, suggesting (although not demonstrating) unsuspected likenesses and relevancies, breaking the continuum of the story into moments that seem to have the power to stand alone, and suffusing the whole with a delicate (and doubtless unverifiable) glow of terror or delight.

Taxonomy, or classification, is no longer a highly respected form of conceptual machinery, yet it remains among the most common devices of literary theory. The low esteem of taxonomy in scientific circles is a reflection of the fact that it can organize information without otherwise illuminating or explaining it. The chosen categories, and the criteria used to assign items to one or another category, may have not further application beyond the task at hand, and most taxonomies provide no way to test the accuracy or desirability of the groupings they propose. Worse yet, they can promote a false satisfaction with merely arranging and storing information that diverts attention from the more serious business of seeking after laws and underlying causes.[76] Yet classification is not always or solely factitious. As Louis Mink describes it: "The relation of theory to its objects is that it enables us to infer and coordinate a body of true statements about that kind of object; the relation of categories to their objects is that they determine of what kind those objects may be. Thus a set of categories . . . [gives] form to otherwise inchoate experience."[77] Some such preliminary categorization and classification scheme is part of every theory, although a part that can be neither verified nor falsified. Without it we could never locate the items to which the theory putatively applies or identify the recurrences upon which laws, predictions, and inferences of all kinds depend. The value of a taxonomic framework thus depends on how and why it is devised, on the cardinal distinctions it recognizes and how cleanly it deploys them, and especially on its capacity to stay within the limits appropriate to taxonomy.

According Fredric Jameson, the best taxonomies are veiled narratives; the connective tissue may be gone, but the relationship between the categories is implicitly the same. It is this that gives the system its appeal: "each category is understood as a *moment* within the intelligibility of some larger ongoing process in which it is subsumed." But Jameson also warns that such a taxonomy can easily degenerate, lose sight of its founding assumptions, and "attempt to convert its insights into eternal . . . essences."[78] Jameson's is far from the only account of why and how taxonomies succeed, however. White, De Man, and Culler—following the lead of Burke's seminal *Rhetoric of Motives* and Jakobson's "grammar of poetry"—insist instead that the underlying logic of taxonomic systems is the relationship between part and whole.[79] They are less concerned than Jameson with the *array* of categories than with how membership in a category is determined. According to these writers, we construe rhetorical figures according to a logic of "container and contained," which makes the different basic tropes an ideal way to establish the different basic styles of ordering phenomena into classes. Thus, *metaphor* (the trope of substitution based on resemblance) designates those systems that rely on inherent similarities to establish what "goes together" to form a class; *synechdoche* (the figure in which a part stands for the whole because it partakes of the quality of the whole) names those methods that group together members that are organically a part of the same whole; *metonymy* (where the relationship is merely associative and no longer based on shared qualities or organic ties) names those taxonomies that stress that class inclusion is conventional; and *irony* (which dissolves even conventional relationships and allows us to say one thing and mean the opposite) stands for those instances where classifications are whimsically imposed or overturned.[80] A slightly less ornate version of the fundamental modes of classification appears in Foucault's *Les Mots el les choses*, where classification systems are distinguished by whether they base themselves upon visible or invisible properties: that is, whether class membership (and the application of the appropriate name) can be determined by observation alone or requires some additional knowledge of structure or function.

One can appreciate taxonomies, then, on at least two levels—reading them both horizontally and vertically, for the relationship between the array of categories making up the framework and for the relationship between the items that are classed together under the same heading. Does, for example, the array of classes aim to be exhaustive, covering all logical possibilities, or does it include only those types that have already been observed? Does it make us of ideal types—categories that have no actual instances but help to dramatize tendencies that do not, perhaps cannot, reach their fullest imaginable development in reality? How are the categories generated: does one give rise to all the others, or does one category function as an amorphous catchall for what the other categories leave out? Is there indeed a hidden narrative, a concealed emblem, even a formal (if implicit) logic that connects them all? Is there any continuity between them, or only absolute discontinuity?

How, on the other hand, are the classes themselves composed—and how strictly? Must all members share the same feature, or is there room for a looser network of family resemblances? How much reduction, how extreme a process of elimination, must any item undergo to become a member of a given class? And is this reduction, this elimination, the secret goal of the taxonomy—to suppress those features upon which more familiar classification systems depend and thus populate a strange new world with its own fantastic creatures?

Of course to say *world* here is hyperbolic and even misleading since taxonomy is the sparest of all conceptual designs, with litte evident integration and little to invite our more domestic associations. Indeed, taxonomy might be read as a willed violence practiced on the density of the world as we experience it, an exercise in controlled and strictly parsed responsiveness.

At the nether end of this hypothetical scale we have been drawing is a loose collection of informal devices—*enabling postulates, definitions, methodologies, and translation functions* that are too casual, too eclectic, too serendipitous to rank with models, metalanguages, laws, or even emblems and taxonomies. Generally there is little effort to ground or to justify them beyond the pragmatic argument that they do work—do produce operations that can be applied to literary texts to produce more or less exciting, more or less convincing, readings. The status of the categories that such "machines for reading" propose is typically ambiguous; we may have no way of telling whether they are prescriptive or hypothetical, ideal or real. And frequently the uses to which the machinery is put are equally uncertain; what begins as an explanation may suddenly turn into a classification, and an inference about the cause of an aesthetic effect change by degrees into an invocation. In a rigorous treatment of theory, such imprecise conceptual instruments would have no place at all, but they are included here because they are so often the last court of appeal, the "meta-" level, to which criticism refers. In common parlance, the bulk of literary theory is here, and when theoretical writing becomes a literary form, such dramatic and self-justifying frameworks are all but irresistible. The most popular devices are definition (that bête noire of aesthetic philosophy), manifesto, and methodological recommendations (often taking the form of a target language and a procedure for translating whatever text we read into its privileged terms).

Definitions may be stipulative or descriptive or heuristic, and may accompany and introduce a neologism or refine the accepted usage of an old word, expanding or contracting it, elevating or degrading its usual-normative force. More telling is what a writer chooses to treat as the core and what the periphery of the definition—which features seem necessary to distinguish the term from others and which are merely clarifying or edifying.[81] The balance between core and periphery gives some indication of the underlying problem that the definition is designed to confront. This effort to erect distinctions makes definition kin to taxonomy, although the whole of the classification scheme remains tacit, more or less taken for granted. Abrams actually suggests that to define is ". . .an indispensable heuristic device for blocking out an area of investigation; . . . [serving as a] starting point for reasoning about poetry and for developing a coherent set of terms and categories to be used in classifying, describing, and appraising particular poems."[82] Yet in many cases definition is the end and not the beginning of an investigation, an isolated distinction that may presuppose a classification system but does not explore it or defend it. It is just as useful to ask why a writer works only with discrete definitions, rather than developing a full taxonomy, as it is to ask why the theoretical impulse stops at taxonomy rather than developing a set of laws, a model, or at least a narrative.

Definitions are not, of course, the only way to block out an area of investigation; outright methodological *directives* and *enabling postulates* will do as well, although these generally require more bravura than claims or programs that have the official imprimatur of a founding definition. To cover their nakedness, as it were, such proposals often make their procedures extraordinarily elaborate or take self-conscious pains to develop an immaculate vocabulary, "a cohering and self-sufficient set of terms,"[83] capable of repelling any doubts about the adequacy or purpose of that vocabulary. In defining, as in every other aspect of theory-building, one must place all those efforts to put on the glamour of a science by adopting everything from a few key words to an entire model, without considering the original motivation for those devices or how well they suit the new subject matter.[84] But since even theoretical models, when they are first proposed, belong "not to the logic of justification or proof but to the logic of discovery," these lower-level conceptual instruments at least share the same desire for discovery—although the "logic" is apt to be quirky, impulsive, even deliberately counterintuitive. The hope of "breaking down an inadequate interpretation" is often far greater than the hope of "laying groundwork for a new interpretation."[85]

The operation that these rudimentary instruments most often enjoin is a kind of loose *translation*, providing a bridge between a given text and a second discourse constructed in terms of the various structural, thematic, and evaluative categories that the theory supplies.[86] In some cases we are given little more than the bare target categories, with perhaps a "master reading" to demonstrate their proper use. In others we are presented with exhaustive instructions about how to effect the desired transformation, where to make the appropriate equations and substitutions. Whatever difference these two strategies make for would-be disciples, for more detached readers the effect is like moving from alchemy to chemistry, or from a ritual transubstantiation to a mundane and comfortable recipe. Then too, there is the interest of the translation function itself—its weight, its scale and scope, its apparent goals. There is the humble pedantry of trying to provide "simpler equivalences. . . to bridge the distance from reader to work,"[87] and there is the opposite extreme, the effort to wring agreement or support from a text, like Mallarmé struggling to find among "les mots Anglais," "a place where his poetry could occur."[88] And there is every shade between.

A separate word should be reserved for those *strategic* interventions and interpolations that figure in most deconstructive operations. Although using categories that are deliberately ephemeral and eschewing any and all efforts to master the subject matter, the operations are still based upon a set of deep and (surprisingly) coherent commitments to a particular philosophy of meaning and (non)being. By definition antipathetic to construction, and by polemical stance adamantly opposed to theory—indeed bent on pushing every system (even its own) to "an awareness of its limits. . . of the possibility of producing a coherent and comprehensive theory"[89]—deconstruction establishes the boundary of conceptual design. It establishes a paradox as well, since at the moment it abandons and subverts the theoretical impulse, it does so hoping to achieve a more principled procedure and a scheme of comprehension that will be more fitting in its very lack of comprehensiveness—in a word, to accomplish precisely what theory itself sets out to do.

There are other ways to approach the question of theoretical design. One could, for instance, concentrate on basic means of explanation rather than on the conceptual design—explanation by efficient cause, by geneology or teleology or analogy, by structural formalism or conformity to a rule. Or one could examine the characteristic uses to which explanations are put: symptomatology, therapy, demystification, and the rest. (These modes are, for the most part, indifferent to the kind of conceptual machinery a theory actually employs, with the possible exception of taxonomy.) One could also focus on the nature of the constituents that enter into the design, the sort of entities and qualities and relations that the theory treats as irreducible. These form the ultimate stratum of explanation, the level at which no further causes or components can or need be sought.[90] According to Harré, the ruling styles of scientific explanation are a combination of a favored explanatory mode *and* a set of irreducible entities and relations.[91] (Thus, classical physics favored not only efficient causes but causes that operate by direct contact; any other influence, any action at a distance, being in this system inconceivable.) Theories not only explain or recommend change but make assumptions about what change itself is—the production of an entirely new state of affairs or simply a rearrangement of the old.

The character of a theory is entirely altered by the kind of entities and relationships it recognizes, how it distinguishes between them, and which roles they are allowed to play—as means or end, cause or effect, agent, act or scene (to use Kenneth Burke's designations). But it seems fruitless, if tempting, to try to name all of the possible, or even all of the extant, permutations that result when these different aspects of theoretical design—conceptual machinery, explanatory mode, basic categories, and metaphysical assumptions—combine. It is far better to appreciate the independent force of each and to assess the full significance of different combinations as they arise than to begin enumerating fixed world views and to constrict theories by espousing one or another of them.

Before leaving the subject of design, however, it is necessary to say a few words about how that design is grounded, the justifications and vindications that are offered in its defense. There may, of course, be no explicit apologia at all, no supporting arguments and only the most casual documentation. The greater the bellelettrism, the more rapt theory becomes in the contemplation of its own designs, the less likely that such provisions will be made. Beauty is its own excuse for being, even among theories; appealing to aesthetic criteria is certainly one legitimate way to vindicate a conceptual design, and it would be odd, perhaps, for a piece of literature to pause to point out its own attractiveness. Nor is it necessary for a text to tell, when it can show, how provocative it is, how boldly it departs from accepted authorities, how fecund and fresh are its suggestions. To do this might ruin the surprise, turn the discourse damp and clumsy as a joke that has to be explained.

But other virtues are less immediate and less easy to display. Scope, power, exhaustiveness, the consequences and side effects that might follow on the adoption of a certain framework are equally important grounds for choosing between theories. They may easily outweigh elegance of formulation or freshness of approach. But it takes additional labor to make these comparative and inferred values evident, and even then the defense remains entirely pragmatic. To justify as well as to vindicate itself, a theory must demonstrate that it obeys the rules of logic, that it is consistent with all known evidence, or—if it is prescriptive—that its recommendations are feasible, reasonable, and able to produce the promised end. Literary theory, whether it functions as a literary form or not, has always tended to favor vindication over justification, defending itself as effective and enlivening, "something to enable and refine perception,"[92] rather than as true in the narrow sense of the word. The quotations that seem to be offered as evidence of a claim usually turn out to illustrate it rather than to demonstrate it.[93] Rarely is there a solid search for contravening evidence—or much effort expended on defining what would count as such. And in the heat of presentation, even the most scrupulous theoreticians are apt to make inferential leaps that go well beyond what their premises allow.[94]

In sum, the test of a literary theory is public exposure rather than accumulations of evidence or logical cogency; a claim is "to be confirmed or falsified by . . . other competent readers"[95]—with all the confusion over who should be considered competent and where proof leaves off and persuasion begins that this trial by public exposure necessarily entails. It is, therefore, no surprise to find this tendency exacerbated in theories that are out-and-out literary. Yet there are often traces of some residual shame that shows itself in compensatory strategies to divert us from the failure to amass evidence or to test the logical grounds on which the theory rests. But just as arresting, for readers, are those cases when the effort to defend or document a theory instead produces subtle inconsistencies and exposes minute cracks in the seemingly smooth surface of the conceptual design. For example, as Paul de Man remarks, in Rousseau's political theory, "the model disintegrates as soon as it is put in motion . . . produces more or less than the theoretical input," thus turning the text as a whole into an "allegory" of the inability to achieve a perfect science of politics.[96] This discrepancy between what the theoretical machinery promises and what it then proves able to do becomes, for readers like de Man, less a theoretical failure than a literary figure, a symptom of unspeakable and perhaps unalleviable doubts that could not otherwise be expressed. Discrepancies likewise appear when efforts to put a theory on firmer ground, by probing "the space in which the model is produced,"[97] lead instead to contradictions that undermine the theory's otherwise untroubled mastery of its subject. The machinery functions smoothly and produces what it should, but the foundations on which it is built seem suddenly dubious. Thus, by seeking to supplement its own authority with the authority of biblical revelation, the Port-Royal grammar was (according to Louis Marin) forced to introduce something "that did not derive from the model, that the model did not account for, but that on the other hand, did account for the operation of the model."[98] Like de Man's reading of Rousseau, Marin's *Critique du discours* is, not a complaint about inept theorizing, but a study of how theoretical discourse may, at given points, reveal what it could never say outright: the pessimism and doubt that is the nether side of its confidence and optimism, the blind spots that must remain blind if the theory is to continue operating at all. To recognize the governing assumptions on which the conceptual machinery rests, to be forced to see—especially in literary theory—that the discursive operations employed are the very ones the theory has not taken into account, or has even denigrated, could be paralyzing. Thus, these aporias are to theory what parapraxes are to the psychopathology of everyday life, the ventings of a theoretical unconscious that relieve the pressure of deep misgivings without obstructing the theory's normal operations. While these "slips" may damage the validity and integrity of the machine, they enrich the veracity of the discourse as a whole.

The conceptual design is compounded of all these elements: the structure and the operations of the core appáratus; the individual categories that enter into it, the kind of explanations and prescriptions that issue from it, the grounds that support it. The compound may be more or less unstable, more or less truncated or asymmetrical. One finds cases where everything is sacrificed to the perfection of the framework, where the pull of its internal logic is irresistible, multiplying (or eliminating) entities with a fine disdain for evidence or even usefulness. Each design has its own characteristic trade-offs: its willingness to posit unseen entities, and to accept the ontological complexity that ensues, for the sake of uniform laws—or the reverse, to forego logical simplicity in exchange for a less ghost-ridden world. One notes where a distinction (e.g., "form / content") seems to be drawn in the hope of cleansing one category of the evil or the excesses of the other, to elevate it over the other or to demonstrate that the other is simply a degenerate version of the same thing. One discovers in the conceptual design a surreptitious or tendentious yearning for some other semiotic system, one more abstract and well regulated than words or, on the contrary, more languorous and less hard-edged. And one measures how taut or slack the design as a whole is, its points of rigidity and its lapses into informality, seeking what governs this particular distribution of intellectual energy. One probes it for symptoms of self-deception or willful mystification, armed (as often as not) with the very instruments the theory itself supplies. "In a 'discourse of knowledge'. . . power is consummated—and exploded—at the (perhaps inconceivable) moment when its diagrams survive its frictional diagramming activity . . . It defeats its own objective by always producing in excess of the calculable requirements of a strategy of domination."[99]

One reads a conceptual design asking whether there is an effort to erase the places of enunciation, to conceal not only the grounds but also the interests that set this particular machine in motion. Do we have an apparatus that purports to be entirely independent of any act of consciousness or one that is saturated with the subjectivity (always anonymous and interchangeable in this kind of discourse) that constructs and operates it?[100] Where must we stand to appreciate this design, what kind of subjects must we ourselves become to occupy it, what faculties must we learn to exercise or to ignore?[101] What ends must we implicitly or explicitly be willing to pursue—does the theory appeal to our desire to comprehend or merely that to control, to live safe from the unforeseen or to act with clarity and alacrity and a sense of rectitude even when certainty is impossible? If there is indeed no "value neutral mode" of theory,[102] if to explain or prescribe is always to indulge some "set of prescriptions for taking a position in the present world of social praxis and acting upon it (either to change the world or to maintain it in its current state),"[103] then what possibilities of action and of change does one thereby entertain or refuse?

The choice of conceptual design determines the power of the theory to reverse received opinion and to invert phenomenal appearance; it also determines how many and how heterogeneous are the causes, reasons, rules, associations, and analogies it can weave around its chosen subject matter. Models and metalanguages effect the most dramatic transformations, offering the greatest possibility for subversion and redefinition. Narratives, laws, and taxonomies are less potent in this respect, able to alter our assumptions about the place the subject occupies or what it is an instance of, but usually working with normal appearances rather than against them. Yet they are also freer, (particularly in the case of narratives and taxonomies) to range more widely in search of illuminating conditions and associations, providing more numerous, if more eclectic, insights even if those insights remain largely on the surface.

Finally—something that probably cannot be ascertained from the design alone, but that still profoundly affects its value—there is the questions of just how literally we are to take this whole imposing apparatus. All this machinery, all these categories—how tentatively or heuristically or playfully are they proposed? Are they, after all, ephemeral, disposable, apt to vanish like Wittgenstein's proverbial ladder when we have got where we were going? Do they in fact lead us anywhere, or only remove us long enough to let us see where we have always been, the limits we have lived without knowing them as such? How much realism or instrumentalism or aestheticism (or even cynicism), and in what proportions, informs this design? Gradually such considerations lead us to ask what "*capacity* of appropriation and identification"[104] the theory allows to its own language and diagrams. It is a capacity that literary theory, theory as literature, can afford to take neither too seriously nor too lightly: The ludic impulse to treat every construct as a fiction, to qualify and undercut every possible act of appropriation, can make theory much more wily or simply incapacitate it, can make our science gay or condemn us to the gaiety of ignorance.

Intertextual Relations

Literary theory is by nature plural; its conceptual machinery is designed to process, directly or indirectly, another set of texts—projecting them as ideal or hypothetical objects, citing them as illustration or support, defining in and through its handling of them the nature of its own conceptual instruments. The intertextual space that a theory constructs for itself is, in fact, one clue to how seriously one is expected to take the proposed categories. A capacity of appropriation and identification is embodied in the way the theoretical text transforms, subsumes, and places other texts, the relationship it manages to establish between the language it encounters and the language that it must itself employ to talk about that language. Even the most radical skepticism is apt to falter here; discrepancies between what a theory preaches about the characteristic power or impotency of language and what it then practices are among the chief aporias or figures of disruption that engage us when we read these theoretical texts. Having disdained the vanity of synechdoche, for instance, a theorist will then calmly choose a "representative" passage in which that error is displayed. Or, while zealously condemning the delusions of representation, and proclaiming the utter intransitivity or total productivity of discourse, a theory will point out the delusions of other texts, trusting fully in its own capacity to reproduce without unfair distortion. Not all theories are so patly or so poignantly contradictory, of course. But how a theory tries to hold and assimilate its objects, the ties between word and object—of natural affinity, logical necessity, or artificially enforced convention—it must take for granted in order to go about its business, along with how clearly it recognizes the force of its own phantasmic interventions in the texts it scrutinizes, are rich sites for reading.

The polyphony of theory, the interpenetration of texts, is one of the ways in which we are diverted from our usual preoccupation with the source, the single authoritative voice. If there are many voices, it becomes difficult to reduce that text to an expression of a single personality where our "models of plausible human attitudes" apply.[105] The result may be a contentious babble or a new kind of choral music, or it may be a space that gradually opens into a magisterial and inhuman silence. Even if it produces only inconsistency and tension, however, this plural text says, by definition, "what *I* cannot say,"[106] what is beyond a single consciousness and the carefully managed coherence of a self. For a period as suspicious of individualism and unconflicted individuality as our own—as wary of single truths and as uncertain, in some circles, of the capacity of language to tell any truth at all—the opportunity to inhabit such intertextual spaces, where different voices and different versions of the truth may meet, compete, or just annihilate each other, must hold a peculiar fascination.[107]

As mentioned earlier in connection with the theory's underlying problem, there are different levels of intertextual relationship. The most intimate interchange may be between theory and rival theory, between theory and audience, or between the theoretical text and the texts it studies. Occasionally the most interesting exchanges may actually be "autotextual," with qualifications and self-citations, prefaces and epilogues, creating a texture of "allusiveness and vertiginous echo."[108] To cite oneself is to become (provisionally) another, one's own double, and to fracture the single speaking subject and the single listener into so many separate sites of speech that the words are pulled in different directions rather than swept along in a triumphant linear flow.[109] Of course this same effect may be achieved with intertextual as well as intratextual colloquy, if it is rich enough. Much will depend on the permeability of the theoretical discourse, how strictly it polices its own borders and how clearly it delimits

its various importations and citations. But even deliberately imposed barriers may do little to stop one discourse from infecting another. The theory may gradually come to mimic the movements of the texts it studies or citations may begin to mirror the prevailing tone and interests of the theory itself. The degree of stylistic variation, discord, or dissension it allows is one index of a theory's rage for order and even of its epistemology—how many "truths" it can conceive of. Many are the celebrations of polymorphic perversity in which everything sounds strangely, wearily, alike.

One should add that intertextuality is not limited to verbal exchanges. Some of the most compelling are intersemiotic; indeed, silent underlinings, ellipses, marks of punctuation, even page position may be more expressive than explicit commentaries or rebuttals.[110] Then too, there is more than one level of verbal language at which intertextual relations can operate. Parody, for example (a prime example of intertextuality), may base itself on phonology or graphology, on syntactic mannerisms or abstract propositions, on extended themes or whole generic patterns.[111] Another subtle but important difference involves whose position is taken up—the writer's or the reader's. Is the intertextual operation essentially hermeneutical, seeking to recapture the values of the sender? Or is it dialogic, responding to the text with the separate interests of a receiver? Perhaps it is neither one of these, but a third thing—taking up the estranged stance of a nonparticipant, studying the formal properties and the functioning of the text as a philologist or semiologist. To side with the writer or the reader is an intersubjective stance, even when the subjectivities are at war, but the latter is also the stance of an ironist, circumscribing the efforts of a slightly alien being.[112]

Thus, though there are a range of ways in which one text can encounter another, the most important distinction remains that between *compartmentalization* and *confrontation*—between discourse "about" and discourse "with" or "to" or even "through" another text.[113] There is a correlation between this distinction and the aforementioned permeability of the theoretical text, since the less one text acts as the interlocutor of another, the more remote and object-like that other text becomes. "The cited text no longer speaks, it is spoken."[114] To stress the distance between the discourse that it actually uses and the discourse that it only quotes or mentions, a theory will hold itself aloof, indulge only in "a certain usury of limited duration," pay strict attention (through quotation marks, footnotes, direct attribution) to the "limits of propriety, the rights of ownership, and the duties of the nonowner."[115] Obeying the laws of ownership is another way of disowning something, confining it to another context that is not the context in which "we" operate. Of course the function of such isolation may be, not mastery, but just the opposite: to preserve the independence and priority of an authority upon whom one hopes to lean.

The proportion of citation to commentary may not, incidentally, be a sure guide to the power that one text exercises over another. Marginalia may dominate as effectively as total encapsulation. The constant here is not dominion but distinction, the gap that keeps one text forever other.

Careful allocation of ownership and graphic isolation have become the norm in scholarly discourse, although it was not always so, according to Bakhtin: "In the Middle Ages . . . boundaries between the other's words and one's own discourse were flexible, ambiguous, often intentionally devious and tangled. Certain types of works were constructed like mosaics, from the texts of others."[116] Even now, the texts a theory cites most openly may not be the ones from which it draws its real impetus, those it defines itself against or absorbs into itself. The more intimate and full the interchange, the more profoundly a text responds to or even enters into another, and the less compartmentalization and objectification there is likely to be. Styles of compartmentalization are relatively limited, a simple alternation of direct and indirect quotation—with some freedom in the latter case for adjusting how much distance and what kind of filtering one imposes. Confrontation, however, is far more variable, ranging from almost imperceptible allusions to fully staged dialogues, from minor plagiarisms to elaborate counteroffensives, and from uniform parody to multiform collage. Then too, citations are generally—if not exclusively—restricted to antecedent texts, whereas confrontations may more easily be hypothetical; a text may presuppose or even build its own anti-text.[117] Because, in confrontation, the work of assimilating and transforming is so patent—because it is so clear (as it need not be in the case of citation) that our glimpses of another text are produced and not just reproduced—flexible and ambiguous boundaries have become especially popular of late. It is not only for the sake of a more literary and less scholarly surface that footnotes, bibliographies, and indented blocks of print have disappeared from the work of many contemporary theorists, but also to avoid the greater sin of naive representation.

Obviously the mere fact of merging words and structures from one text into another is no guarantee of affinity or fellow feeling between the two. Nor is volume; a parody is almost wholly given over to the mannerisms of another text, but its disenchantment is as great as the rapture that usually accompanies a passing allusion. There are degrees and kinds of empathy as well, and different directions of absorption, from the sympathetic but controlled interrogation of a Heidegger to the ideal of total self-surrender in Poulet.[118] One text may shrink into the merest shadow of the other or both may stand as equals—and all the while maintain the same unmarred interchange.

The basic intertextual operations are *selection, intervention*, and *incorporation*. *Selection* means not only the choice of certain crucial fragments but, in the case of literary theory, establishing the boundaries of the text as a whole, distinguishing it from the nontext—the false inter-polations, accidental features, and irrelevant associations that are to be excluded from our engagement with and assessment of it as literature. Thus, how the text is "bound" will determine the other kinds of discourse—biographical or psychological categories, the terms of history or politics or ethics—that can legitimately enter into the exchange. At its most stringent, the only allowable discourse will come from other literary works, or other works by the same author, or even (pristinely) only what appears elsewhere in the same text.

Once the limits of the text itself have been defined, selection then picks out those points where the theoretical machinery may be brought to bear and the key passages that will later serve as citations, illustrations, evidence, allusions. There is often a characteristic scale to the choices made, a tendency to dilate or compress,[119] to garner up snippets or to swallow chapters whole, as well as favored sites (openings and closings, for example) and levels of attention. Equally important is whether the atten-tion turned upon the text is fixated or mobile, concerned with isolated passages and their properties or with the relationship between passages and the movement from one passage to another. Yet another aspect of the selection process is the representative value each passage bears: A text may delve into another text for purposes of its own or may, on the other hand, try to choose passages that are typical of the work in question. In the latter case, then, one must know how or why the passage is considered typical—is it an arresting part or a microcosm of the whole? And by what standards was it determined to be representative—the theorist's own or those that are imputed to the writer?

The operation of selection shows what one text "makes of" (in a double sense) another—object or action, substance or structure, a suc-cession or a copresent pattern,[120] a changeless monument or something mutable that alters with each reading. The degree of finish a theory attributes to the other text is particularly significant. By treating the text in question as complete, already full of meanings ready to spill forth, it casts itself in the role of a mere conveyer of that meaning. If instead it holds that the text is incomplete, perhaps a pastiche of the other texts it has appropriated and repudiated, then its own pose as a simple transmit-ter of information need no longer be maintained.[121]

Of course, the dream of a perfectly transparent transcription is precisely that, a dream, but it does suggest one ideal pole of intertextual work, the other pole of which is a total transformation and rewriting by the critic.[122] What actually varies is the relative discretion of the *intervention* and the ability to acknowledge it as intervention. The alterations range from truncation and ellipsis to full decomposition, recombination, and rewording.[123] Some have compared the changes thus introduced to the syntactic transformations of generative grammar—deletion, substitution, permutation, adjunction, embedding, and even negation, comparison, and passive retopicalization. These alterations have in turn been supplemented by other writers who stress the likeness to the more extreme and irrational interventions of dreamwork and the more extravagant gestures of rhetoric—paronomasia, amplification, hyperbole, chiasmus, inversion, and the rest.[124] But in truth, there are as many styles of intervention as there are relationships between one text and another.

But intervention is only half the story, the other half being *incorporation*, how a text then assimilates this alien material—changing both its own value and the value of whatever it imports. The patterns range from the predictable, if soothing, rhythms of simple alternation to more jarring interpolations and dense, hallucinatory superimpositions. Sometimes it will be the absence, and not the presence, of the other text that one notices, betrayed by such things as abrupt changes of topic or tone, sudden bursts of energy, disproportionate insistence or denial. Often the theoretical text will strive to efface itself for the sake of the other, holding its own powers of language scrupulously in check in order to invest the fragment with the brilliance of a jewel in a matte setting.[125] One may experience a palpable descent, an agony of ruptured intimacy when the fascinated gaze is forced to leave the glowing object behind and return to its own, "sensible" prose.[126] But commentary can just as well be a jubilant continuation, even an embellishment, englobing the borrowed fragments all around with its own more luminous ruminations, its polished points and trenchant epigrams. Yet to the extent that the commentary merely extends and ornaments, drawing its energy and trajectory from the imported material, there is still a peculiar form of self-denial. As Richard Klein describes the essays of Edward Said, one of the most "citational" of contemporary literary theorists:

> The ornamental performance, . . . celebrates the superiority of another by vanishing. . . . It wraps itself around its object like a circlet, enhancing and glorifying it. . . . What is only a mere ornament flatters what it decorates with *being*. By designating itself as merely cosmetic it designates the other as the authentic, substantial thing. It rejoices in the humility of being a fiction so that another may appear to be real. . . .
> The critic's nominal presence vanishes in the impersonality of a text that says another text: Said Said. Its only trace is the mark of the difference that gives us to read the sudden brilliant emergence of what acquires visibility for the first time by the fact of being displaced and reset.[127]

And even more impalpable is the sort of wordless assemblage and sly montage that Derrida delights in constructing, proving how potent a voiceless commentary can be.

Of course commentary is not the sole mode of incorporation. One text may speak of another, but it may also speak against, to, or through the other. It may try to answer it, to annihilate or inhabit it, as well as to surround and ornament it. Even commentary can attach itself to its object by different means, through parallelism, for example, or brute contiguity. (Herein one catches a glimpse of what implicit philosophy or mythology of language it follows.)

The meanings one can attribute to intertextuality are many. Literary theory begins as an effort to do something to or about another set of texts, although in the process it alters its own text as well. When theory intervenes in another text, it is to trace a configuration or to introduce a disfiguration or to effect a renovation—reconfiguring a new text out of selected elements of the old.[128] The disparity between those intertextual operations meant to demonstrate how a work achieves (a perhaps hidden) coherence and closure and those meant instead to expose its inconsistencies and gaps is disconcerting for readers bred to the doctrine of organic unity. But while the difference between "normalizing" and "problematizing" the text is probably more dramatic, there are additional ways to render a text problematic. Some theories lift the veil of familiarity largely to explain how it was lowered in the first place, dismantling the text "to move through it toward an understanding of the systems and semiotic [or phenomenological, psychological, or historical] processes which make it possible.[129] There are others that decompose a text in order to recompose it, in a different form, on another level. The goal is no longer to discover what makes it readable, but to find what can't be read in it at all—because of a contradictory ideology, a stage of historical or psychological development that must repress certain conceptions or is incapable of formulating them at all. To do this, one must presume the full text that might have been, but others have no such "ur-text" to offer, no truth of which the present text is a degenerate distortion. The motive for this final kind of intertextual operation is not to determine an otherwise indeterminant surface, but to deepen that indeterminacy, to show something "disseminated in texts which refuses re-assembly." The goal may be "a multiplication of relations, a sense of liberty and proliferation of possibilities,"[130] or to dispel the specter of meaning entirely, in favor of hydraulic "flows" and electrical "intensities."

To fix meanings or free them; to conserve, reform, or overthrow the text; to punctuate it or meld it; to bring something into the foreground or force it into the background, to make strange, banal, transparent, or opaque: These are the effects the theoretical text can have on the text that it incorporates. But what effects does it, in turn, achieve for itself? According to the nature of its intertextual relations, theory styles itself as a voyeur or a narcissist, a parasite or a tyrant. It may choose to live in borrowed glory, dissimulate any art of its own, and become "the art of wearing the disguises of literature."[131] Or it may instead elevate its own peculiar art of explication and promulgation, deploying other texts only as evidence or illustrations. Solidarity and total parity are in fact extremely rare and tenuous achievements in literary theory;[132] the balance seems always to swing between reverence and mastery, with only the most determined self-irony to prevent it from freezing into one or the other of these attitudes. The simplifying desire is to have one text circumscribe and control the other, either by aggressive inquisition or by idyllic admiration. But the most enriching intertextuality is more ambiguous. Literary theory more easily attains this when it has become a form of literature itself, and therefore has less need to demonstrate its alien superiority or inferiority.

The Writing

Talk about the prose of current literary theory—which typically emphasizes its crabbed or circuitous exposition, its fugitive impersonations and impersonalizations, its wandering paragraphs, jointless sentences and the abstract, undercooked, "translationese" that haunts its diction—is mostly about how bad it is. If it is "good," then the talk shifts to the modesty of its theoretical pretensions. Obviously, some buried dualism between the prosaic flesh and the disincarnate ideas that must sink into it still influences readers and may occasionally affect theoretical writing itself. The fallacy goes something like this—Theory is difficult to understand / This prose is difficuly to understand / Ergo, it must be theory.

Not, of course, that there are no legitimate reasons why theoretical writing might appear strained or bizarre given only the decorums of polite scholarship and the familiar essay to go on. The literature of theory falls comfortably into neither camp, being too stylish (or stylized) and insouciant for one and too obscure and barren of anecdote for the other. Moreover, a good deal of contemporary theory holds that "the writing is all"—that the succession of words and sentences must invent itself, having nothing to imitate and no contextual ties to supply it with an extrinsic sense of necessity or direction.[133] Wary of reification of any sort, chastened by the poststructural assault on the analytic glance that "freezes" discourse into regimented rules and thus induces conformity, many writers engage in a kind of deliberately randomized and disorderly prose. But even those who are wholly unscathed by Continental controversies, and espouse no particular doctrine of écriture, must still struggle with the problem of writing in an unfamiliar and, indeed, unestablished genre. There are no patterns to follow or even violate, and only the strangest sort of claims, commendations, and hypothetical posits into which to channel one's discursive energies.

While conceptual design and intertextual relationships do exercise some control over the writing—an argument would, for instance, seem the most appropriate way to present a law, and the more one text merges into another, the more difficult it will be to stage their confrontation as a dialogue—the control is weak at best. In writing, the bare machinery of the theory is "given depth, substance, and a 'thickness' aimed to persuade and keep a reader following an arduous chain of discourse."[134] Slight discrepancies, an unexpected or incongruous presentation, can increase this depth, give the text cunning and a power to surprise. Then too, the struggle to construct a theoretical distinction need not—perhaps cannot—employ that same distinction. Developing a conceptual instrument, exhibiting it all around, playing with it until one knows its heft and how to handle it—none of this can really be controlled by the nature of the instrument itself, and the more foreign the conception, the more difficult and labored the introduction will necessarily be.

Hence, it is no surprise that in its writing, a theory may violate some of its own most cherished premises. It may even need to do so, to show why those premises are necessary. Socrates had, after all, his benighted interlocutors, Wittgenstein his myriad false starts. But the tension may go deeper than this. The writing may never catch up to the design at all; it may commend, describe, support, an ideal framework that it never can employ, may lust impotently after clarity and efficiency with sprawling paragraphs and muddy diction or may promote ideal dichotomies in sentences that are inherently and persistently triadic in their structure. These discrepancies, however, are not the stuff of which logical contradictions are made. The sequencing of a paragraph is not an assertion; a passing figure of speech is not on the same level as a theoretical model. Misalliances and misalignments between the microscopic and the macroscopic levels of the text are just enough to shade and qualify the impact of the theory—perhaps winning our adherence illicitly or breeding in us an inarticulate uneasiness. When we sense that a literary theory is too extreme or too tentative to be taken at face value, it is usually the writing and not the conceptual design that makes us hold our fire and decide that we will play with it first, and interrogate or test it later.

In reading theory, one often notes where the energy of the writing seems to have been expended—in lush diction or well-turned phrases, in the juxtaposition between sentences or the organization of larger episodes. From this, one receives a first (if not always a lasting) impression of the power or delicacy of mind that informs the theory. Writing too determines whether that general and anonymous capacity of mind shall be invested in a personality and provided intellectual history or shall retain its neutral and purely operational value. First, there is the overall *mode* into which the writing falls: meditation, polemic, apology, reverie, chronicle of discovery, instruction manual, allegory, aphorisms, book review, or geometric proof—one could go on and on, since theoretical literature is part of a larger prose "revival." The renewed fascination with general discourse is especially strong for those modes that were abandoned when literature became largely a purveyor of fictions and ceded to other disciplines the responsibility for prosaic truth. At a moment of willful experimentation and hybridization, it would be too unwieldy to enumerate the modes of writing that theory might adopt. Better to examine the dimension of "symbolic action" that recur from text to text. For instance (as mentioned earlier), most theoretical writing is either central or marginal, the latter including both what is literally situated in the margins of another text and what simply occupies a position of discipleship, producing its own theory as a commentary on or a correction of another work. Marginality extends to those deliberately provisional forms (anecdotes, aperçus, gnomic fragments) that are forever partial and anticipatory, never quite (officially) adding up to a finished system.[135] Another distinction involves whether or not a theory uses a borrowed mode—as Newton borrowed from Euclid or Dryden borrowed from the stage. Then there are the parameters of symbolic action named by Burke himself: the way a text responds to and organizes a situation; the various ratios of agent, agency, act, scene, and purpose that—according to the mix—produce either a prayer or a caress.[136] Both the putative relationship to an audience (Burke's "rhetoric") and the relationship to a scene in which or on which the text operates (Burke's "grammar") enter into what we commonly call mode. (The conditions governing "speech acts" that Searle proposes—the interests and the relative positions of speaker and hearer, the appropriate emotions and the degree of commitment expected, the different propositional contents—may be useful as an amplification of Burke.)[137] But two caveats are necessary. First, the presentation of a theory can rarely be reduced to a single or a uniform act, and with literary license comes even greater complexity, since a literary text can secrete additional layers of symbolic action, the exact status of which may be impossible to decide.[138] Second, both Burke's dramaturgy (with its emphasis on agent and motive) and Searle's speech act (with its stress on the speaker and his / her psychological state) demand precisely what theoretical discourse puts at issue—a single and idiosyncratic speaker. As part of its rhetorical strategy, a theoretical text may indeed establish a persona or "ethos." But as Aristotle himself noted, ethos is only one part of rhetoric; one could forego the development of a personal character and could play instead upon the audience's own emotions (pathos) or could appeal to an impersonal standard of logic.[139] Even today we can recognize the difference between a text that offers reasons for belief and a text that offers only motives long after the classical division between "demonstration" and "exhortation" has fallen away.[140]

It is a matter of *rhetorical strategy*, then, whether or not discourse will place a vivid subjectivity at its center, and whether it will identify that subjectivity with the writer or with the reader or as the common property of both. When the chief means of persuasion is the ethos of the narrator, who becomes "the agent of truth to his auditors and the validator of their emotions,"[141] then, of course, there must be a persona—even an unpersuasive one, whose function it is to make certain views unpalatable.[142] The same obviously holds for the reader, or *narrataire*, as well, who will be more or less boldly drawn and endowed with different powers for the sake of producing favorable conviction or reducing an unfavorable one. But whatever mode and rhetorical strategy it adopts, theoretical discourse—unlike most other forms of contemporary literature—is usually designed to make its own claims plausible (or rival claims implausible) and hence must establish concord with its audience. The concord may be mediated through unreliable narrators and weakminded *narrataires*;[143] there may be many layers of antagonism and vituperation to penetrate, but some saving remnant, some select band of convincibles, however small, must remain. (Often enough, this very selectivity helps to arouse conviction by offering an escape from irony only to an elect few.) Thus, theoretical discourse is less likely to be "overheard," less likely to place its audience in the position of a voyeur or an eavesdropper—meaning as it does to win a more active and a more critical engagement. And yet, because of the ideal of replication that it involves, theory need not image its audience in any great detail at all. The intensely public nature of theoretical discourse brings it, strangely, to the verge of the most intense privacy—the point, that is, where identifiable voices and interlocutors disappear.[144]

At its most extreme, theoretical writing moves toward an almost superhuman symbolic, struggling to lift itself above even the dross of ordinary verbiage and to lose itself in artificial language. Because audience and author are ideally interchangeable, they become featureless to one another and fuse into a single "logical subject" without idiosyncratic mannerisms and emotions: "The *subject* involved in scientific utterance is not the individual person—whether the scientist or the ordinary man. . . . The subject is actually a *logical subject*, a sentence, a sign, a proposition. . . the critical fact is the relationship between a sentence and some state of affairs."[145]

This characterization of the logical subject as a bare propositional function is, perhaps, too naive with respect to its disinterested and dispassionate nature—as Lyotard derides: "what gives you a rise, theoreticians. . . is the coldness of the clear and distinct."[146] Yet the drive, the passion itself, remains impersonal, a compulsion without fixed location or private identity. Thus, the theoretical text may more closely approximate the sort of pure discursive force, exceeding any particular authorizing subject and irreducible to any individual personality, a force has been so lionized and vilified in recent years. Undoubtedly this kind of rhetoric could be used to evade responsibility, to disguise private obsessions as

sheer technique, yet ethos and pathos have their own perverse employ-
ments too—intimidation, demagoguery, the satisfactions of sensationalism and sentimentality. Moreover, Nelson's remark that in supreme critical achievements, "the persistence and consistency of their
individual methods gives their work the very quality of personality they
seek to avoid"[147] is still at least half true—true, that is, if it applies to the
fascinating specificity (and not the personality) that theoretical works are
capable of achieving. Personality remains simply one (and not the most
characteristic one, at that) of the rhetorical strategies that theoretical
discourse may adopt.

With different rhetorical strategies come different possible ways of
laying out the text. A text with a personified source may use that personality to control the direction and the pace of its *exposition*. Intuitive
leaps and associative logic will be more intelligible, seem more legitimate,
if we can read them as musings and self-amusements. Similarly, a dramatized audience allows exposition to follow the course of their fascination
and disgust, or to turn into a colloquy and move with the give and take of a
conversational or an argumentative exchange. In the absence of personality, exposition may take on any number of other familiar semiotic
shapes—genealogical, anatomical, temporal, topological, syllogistic,
mythic. In fact, "any cultural convention can end up in a text as a rule to
arrange discourse."[148] Minimally, one can at least trace ascending and
descending order; can separate inductive from deductive logic (with its
various classical subdivisions—modus ponens, modus tollens, reductio ad
absurdum) or from the various patterns of informal argument (the most
familiar being the movement from statement to support to summary).
Temporal order has its own traditional devices: entrance in medias res,
flashbacks, zero endings, frame tales.[149] The strategies of classical
rhetoric: amplification, asyndeton, polysyndeton, antithesis, periphrasis,
alloiosis (which breaks down a subject into alternatives), antanagoge
(which balances an unfavorable aspect with a favorable one)[150] are perhaps
too remote now to win immediate recognition. Eventually these names
fade into namelessness, and each exposition proceeds according to a
mysterious rhythm all its own. Discovering these episodic intensities,
these sudden points of accumulation and digression, expansion and
condensation, closeup and panorama, becomes one of the chief excitements in reading theoretical prose. In the absence of a form that is
inherited or imitated, writing must invent its own imperatives, and we
must learn to read "in terms of expansions, the detours it allows, not in
terms of the totality it achieves."[151]

Exposition "deforms," delays, and qualifies our apprehension of a
theory's conceptual design. Berel Lang has suggested that rhetorical
strategy and expository style, in fact, make "a claim about the character of
philosophy [we might say theory] as a project"—with some expositions

intimating that the subject matter is utterly independent of anything that is said about it, while others hint that the writing performance "affects and is affected by the assertion made."[152] Exposition establishes—especially through its proportions, its repetitions, and its summaries—which aspects of the conceptual design shall be focal or thematic and which shall shrink into the background of dispensable or obvious or unimportant detail. Expository appearances may, however, be deceiving. The merely "by the way" may not be so easy to dispense with, after all. Exposition can provide a dynamic surface for a framework that is essentially static or can obscure the dynamism of a conceptual design by presenting it in a series of tableaux. An ascending order, from evidence or argument to claim, may invert the actual force of the reasoning, asyndeton may conceal it, and polysyndeton may distort it by introducing factitious connections. The choice of a melodramatic rhetorical strategy may belie a theoretical proposal that is itself quite tame or may mislead readers into thinking that the theory has no solider foundation—that ethos and pathos are all—when this is not the case. For readers of a theoretical text, then, it is a live question whether the mode, the rhetorical strategy, or the order and the pace and the space allotted to the gradual exposure of the conceptual design is really concordant with that design.

Of course, the *diction* of the text—whether or not it is channeled through a narrative persona—may also move subtly athwart of the theory's major categories. This is a matter not only of the kind of terms deployed but of how variable they are and whether formulations stay fixed or keep changing, with new terms constantly displacing the old. If the terminology is slippery, so shall the categories seem, giving the theory an appearance of fluidity or an unresolved quality that suggests that all this finely wrought machinery may collapse at any moment.

Even in its most confined form, within the boundaries of each separate sentence, the *style* of theoretical discourse gives an impression of energies and interests to convey. It is also that portion of theorizing that is least translatable, least transferable from one occasion to another and least subject to summary—making its conceptual weight the most difficult to measure. Yet the tendency to subordinate or coordinate at the level of individual phrases may show arresting parallels to the way the text arranges itself into expository episodes or with the arrangement of the conceptual design itself. It may be, however, that the balance between nouns and adjectives, verbs and adverbs, suggests a division of the world into essence and accident that does not in all respects bear out the more self-conscious distinctions of the conceptual framework. The theory may, for instance, favor the view that we can have no certainty beyond our present sensations, and yet speak constantly in terms of things that persist even when they are unobserved.[153] Especially interesting in this regard is the relationship between a preferred explanatory mode (by efficient cause or final cause or structure) and the semantic framework of individual sentences. One may find a tendency to construct sentences in terms of agents and their goals despite the most adamant rejection of intentionalism and teleology at another level.

The most adventurous or even chilling effects of theoretical discourse often arise from the manipulation of syntax; it is here that the ultramundane can make itself felt along our pulses, here that we receive our first and most disturbing sense of disorientation. Yet the grip of grammar is also the hardest to break; even neologisms tend to follow familiar morphological patterns. Moreover, if the rules of syntax and morphology are too seriously disrupted, the theory as a whole may become unintelligible. Thus, the most radical theorist must strike a balance between impatience with old conceptual habits and the need to give that impatience a comprehensible and convincing form. The result is usually a cunning compromise—legible phrases that cluster in unpredictable and unnerving ways, or syntax that forms a solid and respectably sane frame around a verbal lunacy of dismembered syllables and awkward neologisms.

We receive our first impression of how literal-minded a theory is from the giddiness or austerity of its style. Certainly we sense how highly *figured* a stretch of prose is, and we are perhaps sensitive as well to the kind of figure that dominates. One might expect a theory based on models to be more tolerant of metaphors in general, or at least to show a predilection for analogies, but this is not always the case. At times the imaginative effort seems to be expended by that single conceptual leap, leaving the individual sentences entirely untouched; the very fact of the core analogy might breed a cautious desire to use only the most entrenched and incontestable language in every other respect. Moreover, there are delicacies of interpretation that can be brought to bear on individual tropes as they cannot on broad conceptual schemes, which must apply so generally and systematically. The difference between a metaphor, a simile, and a pun, for example, is glossed over by theoretical models, and though a theory reverses all our expectations, it lacks the nuances of irony, which can shade from wry qualification all the way to bald sarcasm.

Beyond the figures that stand out because of their "deviance" or stylization are the "normal" syntactic operators: quantification and negation, modal, interrogative, imperative, and conditional constructions. These quite ordinary devices can plunge an entire theory into a thick haze of denial or uncertainty, making it seems merely wishful or barely credible. And even the most unmarked indicative sentence can still perform the subtle trick of presupposing certain propositions in order to assert another. "Presuppositions are what must be true in order that a proposition be either true or false . . . . It is of considerable importance which propositions a work chooses to assert directly and which it chooses to relegate to the intertext or pre-text, to identify them as a part of the *déjà lu*, as a set of sentences already in place."[154] To presuppose in this way may be an evasion, or it may be part of a strategy to wring from unwary readers concessions they might not otherwise make. But it may only reflect the traditions that the text takes for granted, the background of common knowledge that (from this point of view) goes without saying. Thus, when there are no other, blatant signs of intertextual exchange—no obvious citations or allusions, no denunciations or obeisances—such small moments throw a mild sardonic light on the seeming self-sufficiency of every text.

Of punctuation and pagination, diagramming and graphic display, one hardly knows at present how to speak—which may be part of their contemporary appeal. Some of these devices have a fairly long history. Parenthetic asides have been with us for some time, although seldom in such profusion and rarely used, as they are now, to interrupt the unfolding of a single word. The result of massive parentheses is a layering of the prose, as if it moved on several intersecting planes at once. The greater the multiplication, the greater the difficulty in saying which discourse is dominant and which is the aside. The same effect is produced by erratic spacing, which forces one to move among scattered points of orientation and to experience the gaps between the printed passages as a teasing but inaudible commentary, a plastic void for which there are no ready synonyms.[155] The use of graphic symbols—diagonal lines, asterisks, diacritical markers—is for certain writers an attempt to avoid or to undermine the speaking subject with signs that cannot be spoken. For others, graphic display seems to be a way of transcending language. Diagrams achieve an ideal simultaneity that language cannot and supplant with their incised and volumeless lines the amorphousness of words. Theoretical discourse resorts to graphics when it grows impatient with or suspicious of language. Indeed, there is a certain pathos in the trust with which it reaches out to these other symbols, as if they were somehow less subject to the vagaries and misreadings to which verbal discourse is heir. When, for example, Derrida writes under erasure, crossing out words on his page, it is almost as if the meaning of the graphic slash that cancels out a word were unequivocal in a way that words themselves are not.

In many (perhaps most) cases, theoretical discourse makes no obvious use of nonverbal symbols or typography or page design. Yet read against the newly expanded repertoire of graphic possibility, even "normal appearances" take on a piquancy of their own. To establish and remain within a regular margin, to mark the endings of one's sentences, to provide convenient footholds (in the shape of a table of contents or an index) for readers suddenly has a different meaning—pehaps more than one. One reads in these a concern for proper etiquette, a nascent classicism, a desire to guide or control the entrances to the text.[156] Violating the graphic norms of scholarly prose is frequently a sign of a text's pretentions, its will to overcome the limits of a staid and self-effacing informative writing. But it is not the only sign of such pretentions, and is perhaps a better signal of the *kind* of art to which the text aspires. Dadaist incongruity and surprise are but one form that the aesthetic impulse can take; there is also an art of chastity and decorum and an art that stresses functional design. Thus, in certain cases, the iconography of a theoretical text may be the most sensitive measure of its tastes and tacit ambitions, its inarticulate assumptions about the necessary drudgery or the potential purity of language. Here one may see the theory of literature that is actually embraced, even if it is not precisely the one that is being promulgated.

The Economy

Economy is of course a metaphor for the overall system of exchange that seems to operate internally, among elements of the same text, and externally, between one text and the various other texts and contexts with which it interacts. It is not even an original metaphor, but one that has gradually become more general in recent years, along with the changes in literary theory and literature that I have been tracing.[157] It can be a tendentious term, and part of its popularity is no doubt due to that. To speak in economic terms is to avoid the assumptions buried in the older critical vocabulary of *imaginary worlds* and *vision* and *sensibility*. It lacks the substantiality we associate with *texture* and the history of formalism that attaches to words like *structure* and *architecture*. It is a word with an aura of productivity and transactions, of labor, use, and power. Above all, it allows one to grant discourse a value, but on an abstract level where the standards may be epistemological or political or libidinal or architectonic, according to the need.

The economy of theoretical discourse is, then, a system for the production and distribution of attention; it establishes what we usually think of as the "themes" of the text, which are made up of the interplay of its own various levels and what passes from this text to others. Each economy has its own peculiar character and quality, depending on the foci it establishes, the equivalences it honors, the standards of value it recognizes. Just as characteristic are those things that the economy ignores or devalues—what it deems uneconomical, excessive, wasteful, or fruitless. Each economy establishes its own "correlates" as well—those other systems of value that can be translated or inscribed within it. According to its economy, a theory will adapt itself more easily to some uses than to others, will perform certain functions more efficiently, will absorb certain kinds of energy and interest more naturally. The economy of discourse thus leads one ultimately to the kind of release and / or control a theory promises, the outlets it opens up or blocks, the alliances it most easily accepts, the power over other situations and other people it affords to those who will employ it.

First, there is the "medium of exchange"—the way each level of the text, from conceptual design to graphic devices, is divided into units of value. The manner of articulation will determine whether values will be discrete (wholly distinct from one another) or continuous (overlapping with one another). The latter can allow for intermediate stages—for development, growth, and even indeterminacy—as the former cannot. When values are discrete, things must be either one thing or another, and changes will be abrupt, without transition or degree. Of course continuums can have occasional gaps, just as discrete terms can be further divided to make room for partial or incomplete instances.

But just as important as the manner of articulation is its scale—how delicate or gross the distinctions are. The greater the delicacy, the less reductive or abstract the theory is apt to seem. *Abstract* and *reductive*, however, are really relative terms that depend on how well a theory compares to its available alternatives; if they are to provide fresh insights, all theories must inevitably reduce or multiply the number of distinctions that go into more commonplace descriptions. Articulation may be more or less exhaustive as well, clustering on one end of a projected scale or trying to cover every possibllity—with all that this reveals about the ambition and the scope of the imagination governing the theory. Even so simple a thing as the number of basic units a theory recognizes can be significant. Dyads, for example, facilitate such operations as comparison and contrast, subordination, reversal, and the positing of such relations as cause-and-effect, before-and-after. Triads permit mediation, concatenation, the discovery of a common denominator; with triads one can unfold a series or establish a sense of repetition or violation. Fourfold divisions are often allegorical or iconic—figuring forth the seasons, the social classes, and the four ages of man. Because of the symmetry they afford, they are useful for offsetting, negating, or inverting simple dyadic relationships.

The value of any unit comes, in part, from its position relative to its fellows, the "rate of exchange" that makes them commensurable or even incommensurable with each other. When exchange is difficult—the units heterogenous or the relationship between them vague—the system will be more open to expansion or to frictions that may eventually tear it apart. A closed, homogenous system is more efficient (more "economical," in one sense of the word), but there will also be no way to expand the range or the value of any particular unit except at the expense of all the others. One can thus speak of "comic" or "tragic" economies—those that, because they have only "a restricted available quantum of energy"[158] must inevitably run down and must then trade off one value against another, as opposed to those economies that begin with no such restrictions and hence give rise to no such competition and entropy. Economies can also be divided into the fundamentally conservative, which aim only to preserve a certain equilibrium, and those that are more liberal or radical in their implications.

But value is also a function of exchanges that operate outside the theoretical text itself: the "purchase power" (as it were) these categories and distinctions have when they are applied. Obviously, since theories are composed of language—a generalized medium of exchange—they are debarred from the sort of barter, good for good, use-value for use-value, of which idyllic exchanges are said to be made.[159] Words in themselves are without substance, useful only for exchanging. Their value is a matter of long-standing conventions—although in the process of turning language into discourse some labor is expended, and the value of any given word may undergo more or less dramatic change. Perhaps this can, in turn, transform the entire circuit of exchange, "deautomatize" perception and conception as the Russian formalists contend, so that the altered range and power of words leads us to make unforeseen connections. Clearly, different theories vary greatly in the amount of labor they expend on devising new conceptual designs, expository forms, and styles. They differ too in the status they accord to these discursive labors, often concealing them by treating the categories they devise as if they were already present in the subject matter and ignoring what their own interpretive and editorial interventions do to the texts they treat.

Literary theory is unusual in that it not only has its own economy but also helps to determine the economy of the literature it studies. It does this by establishing the boundaries within which exchanges are appropriate (with a single text, an oeuvre, a genre, a historical period) and whether such exchanges shall remain within or go athwart of the lines the text seems to establish for itself.[160] It also stipulates where and when the process of exchange must come to an end, which interpretations (if any) should be considered final.[161] In its relationship to these other texts, and to whatever other data it considers, a theory will usually strive either for depth and saturation or for the greatest possible scope and breadth of application. It may attempt both, of course, or refrain from doing either, preferring fragile, episodic illuminations and representative anecdotes. In recent years, literary theory has even come to take some pride in demonstrating how partial its mastery of the subject is, how delicately it refrains from domination.

The meeting between the various levels at which a theory operates from the problem that it presupposes and within which it situates itself, to the solution that it proposes and how it presents itself, to the domain where it applies and the future that it projects for itself—is a complicated juncture. The tensions between one level and another produce various economic figures as elements reduplicate or dominate or mesh with each other, or instead qualify, resist, and undermine each other—or simply act in isolation from each other.[162] It is here that one seeks evidence of obsessiveness or blindness or blockage and discovers that excess that is the sign of uneconomical longings, that "incoherence [that] expresses the force of desire."[163] The theory may, of course, resist all such efforts to see through or around it. But just as often it will supply us with the very instruments for doing so, leaving it to us to uncover a "truth that does not speak, but works"—less in the efficiency of the system than in its lapses and transgressions.[164]

By their terminology, literary theories embrace certain immediate systems of value; by their economies, they invite or repel other, "correlative" values. An epistemological claim may have an erotic parallel; formal analyses may have political or ethical correlates—whether these are deliberately invoked or not. Some literary theories have been designed chiefly to *prevent* the use of an "alien" terminology in literary study. The goal of such theories would be a system so intricate and idiosyncratic that it could have no other, extraliterary applications,[165] and no analogues or collateral values into which the theory might be translated. This ideal purity is probably impossible to achieve, however, for while certain parallels are evaded, others unconsciously insinuate themselves.

Ultimately, the economy of a theory facilitates certain "possibilities of use and appropriation."[166] It allows it to perform some functions more easily than others and relates it, as well, to broader social practices and beliefs that the theory may not directly endorse but that it nonetheless relies upon in going about its own business. A theory of literature must, for example, embody some general notions about language, culture, social relations, and "human nature." These will enter, if not into its treatment of writers and readers, then into its handling of collective codes and of literary history. At the very least, they will figure in the text's own elected rhetorical strategies. To write at all, one must come to terms with the laws that currently govern discourse—specifying what can be said, how it can be said, and from what position of observation and enunciation. This position, the "subject" of theoretical discourse, may be constructed in a number of different ways; personal or impersonal, generalized or particularized, communal or isolated, coherent or conflicted. It may be a subjectivity that produces knowledge or one that consumes it instead; it may be no more than "a place within a complex system more fundamental than itself" or a potentiality that exceeds the system of the text.[167] Whichever of these options it elects, theoretical discourse will take on implications that extend beyond the overt claims it makes and are no longer subject to its own control, exposing it to all manner of symptomatic readings—historical, ideological, and psychological. However cautious, however rarified, however disinterested or devious a theory tries to be, this much extratextual value it cannot avoid.

Thus, the economy of theoretical discourse does not end where the text itself ends. In the words of Michel Foucault: "Discursive practices are not purely and simply ways of producing discourse. They are embodied in technical processes, in institutions, in patterns for general behavior, in forms for transmission and diffusion, and in pedagogical forms which, at once, impose and maintain them."[168] Theory can function to create or to maintain a class of experts, the sole initiates to its mysteries and the only legitimate transmitters of its specialized procedures. It can establish or invoke authority, create rights of ownership, according to how it treats the literature it studies and how it governs itself, by circumscribing the range of those who shall be deemed capable or worthy of employing it or even of objecting to it. The power it exercises may take the shape of naked coercion, or of a more or less internalized "discipline," a regimen it both introduces and itself obeys.[169] It can allow lay readers to become disciples and students as well or can turn them into objects of study. It can even have more curious consequences, as when a preference for "closed corpuses" breeds an unconscious (and rather morbid) interest in dead or silenced authors.

These are the immediate institutional antecedents and alliances of theoretical discourse, but there are also the changing forms of the "will to knowledge" itself, of which theory is one of the chief expressions.

> . . . few conceptual tools have been elaborated for analyzing the will to knowledge. The notions on hand are, at best, imprecise: "anthropological" or psychological notions like those of curiosity, the need for mastery or appropriation through knowledge, distress before the unknown, reactions to the threat of the undifferentiated; historical generalities such as the spirit of the period, its sensibility, its types of interests, its conception of the world, its system of values, its essential needs; philosophical themes such as a horizon of rationality. . . . We are faced with the unavoidable fact that the tools that permit the analysis of the will to knowledge must be constructed and defined as we proceed, according to the needs and possibilities that arise from a series of concrete studies.[170]

And hence the series of concrete studies—case histories, as it were—to follow, in which we trace the interests and investments, the various economies, of the theoretical enterprise as close range.

The Pleasures of the Theoretical Text

One cannot end these general notes on reading theory without some indication of the excitement it affords. And plainly it does do this for the increasing number of readers who turn to it with obvious relish; who debate its merits with more passion than they do all but a few novels, poems, plays, and films; and who feel impelled to keep up with the latest developments in theory as they do not with other aspects of contemporary culture. At one level, the thrill of reading theory is rather like being confronted with an exotic language or a blueprint drawn to an unknown scale—an overwhelming and undifferentiated confusion that will gradually (for the patient inquirer) resolve itself into perceptible lines and a usable order. There is an intoxication even in this simple passage from obscurity to sense, from helplessness to mastery—or to (increasingly) a mastery just out of reach, always promised but forever postponed. The first encounter with a theory differs from the preliminary brush with other literary forms, however—where one concentrates on establishing sympathies and antipathies, reading for a sense of the situation, and for the tenor and the associated character of the narrative voice or the perspective of an implied author. Instead, the anonymity and transitivity of theoretical discourse invite one to learn to manipulate its terms for oneself, to see not only what sense a theory makes but how it makes it; one must discover how to perform its recommended operations before one can truly appreciate or criticize it. To read a literary theory is to acquire, along with its framework and its categories, a new space of operations, to alter what one can imagine doing to and with other literary texts— perhaps significantly, perhaps only superficially. Perhaps every text projects some such loose epistemology and praxis, but theory insists that the mode of apprehension it introduces applies beyond the limits of the text at hand, crossing out of that universe of discourse and into our own. It may well be true that every text also rests on a hidden problem, some discrepancy or doubt or need it must resolve, but the problem is much more palpable in theoretical discourse, and the initial premises are much more exposed. Moreover, with theory it is not the act of writing itself that solves the problem, as it usually is in other literary works. The theoretical text simply initiates or proposes a solution, the full force of which remains to be tested, tried, and demonstrated. It is not a finished composition that readers then consume, but a process into which they are introduced—a program for them to carry out or a hypothesis for them to test on other objects and other occasions.

But there is a special quality as well to theoretical solutions, the peculiar allure of intelligibility in a highly concentrated form—a pattern so refined, so intense, so generally or even infinitely deployable, that it seems to verge on intellectual apotheosis. Notice how often appreciations of theory are cast in terms of mountainous heights and an air too thin to quite support our mundane breathing, as in Jameson's description of the experience of reading Adorno: "...it seems to afford the reader a sudden release, a sudden sense of overflight, instantaneous intellectual inter-relationship and liberation from things."[171]

In defense of his own highly idealized theoretical categories, Max Weber once remarked: "In its conceptual purity, this mental construct cannot be found anywhere in reality. It is utopia."[172] No doubt Weber is speaking in extremity of the theoretical impulse in one of its most extreme forms; not all theoretical constructs are so resolutely unreal and deliberately utopian as Weber's. Yet the drive for system and simplicity, the desire to reduce, purge, and purify the stubborn material of experience is inseparable from theorizing itself. But reduction and abstraction are no less capacities of the imagination (as Dennis Donoghue reminds us in his study of that "sovereign ghost") than the celebration of particularity and plenitude.[173] The mind feels itself equally alive in its power to dissolve phenomena, to (in Blanchot's phrase) "destroy the world in order to create it again on the level of meaning."[174] Moreover, this struggle to make reality conform to its own design, to illumine with the same singular light every darkened corner, to leave nothing inexplicable or ineffable behind, is a prime source of the drama of theoretical discourse. We know a theory by how it confronts recalcitrance, by the manner in which it comes to terms with the excessive or the unexpected—meeting it with compromise, bemusement, vainglory, pathos, or pathology.

The romance of transcendental intelligibility need not reach consummation, however, and doubtless will not as theories become more playful. Yet because theory must be hypothetical by its very nature, it will never come entirely down to earth. Even when it stops short of Weber's pure idealizations and aspires only to limited generalizations, theory cannot be confined to particular instances or occasions; it must project, extrapolate beyond actual experience to date. In this it accords well with certain tendencies in postmodern fiction, the fascination with the potential in "conceptual art," the Borgesian predilection for "the possibility of a story always postponed."[175] The abstraction of theoretical discourse is a product of this eternal anticipation as much as it is of the drive to eliminate whatever might stand in the way of a comprehensive system.

There are two ways (at least) to interpret this fascination with abstraction. One might construe it as a natural outgrowth of the complex and distended organization of contemporary life. The dizzying social and economic and technological interdependencies that implicate each of us in systems that we cannot localize or even directly experience do make concrete descriptions seem somehow anachronistic or naive. Or one could interpret it as a protest to our present situation—the survival of a last instinct for fantasy and imaginative projection that is neither escapist nor simply coy or droll, just when "it had come to seem increasingly futile and childish for people with a strong and particularly repressive reality-and-performance-principle to imagine tinkering with what exists."[176] The precise shadings will probably vary with each individual theory, but the rootless or schematic quality of the prose itself is inevitable so long as it remains theoretical and does not lapse into mere description.

The hypothetical is theory's answer to the dilemma of representation, its own way of acknowledging that writing is indeed productive (rather than imitative) without accepting either formalism or solipsism as its fate. Not the light that never was on land nor sea, and yet not a reflected light either—what it presents to us could not have been recognized prior to the theory and no set of actual sightings will ever exhaust it. There are individual differences in how the hypothetical mode is handled: Some theories promise truth (or falsifiability), others just utility, but none rests solely on its beauty or its plausibility or its desirability. Yet at the same time, theory makes truth and utility much more complicated matters. A hundred other systems are just as verifiable and just as useful, and there is no real need for the sophistication of theory if verifiability and utility are all that one desires. Theories are never absolutely true or absolutely useful, since future failures can always dispel the present appearance of success. This inverts the usual literary emphasis on originality and priority and in fact means that the "authenticating moment" is eternally deferred.

Delay is part of literary theory in another sense as well, since theory has as its core, not imagery and imaginary worlds, but a conceptual machine—a set of operations, rules, categorical frameworks, and tentative constructs that lack the fullness, the repleteness, the immediate assimilability of imagery. One comes to know the nature of this machinery through watching how it functions and using it for oneself, rather than by visualizing or possessing it as a set of properties. "Ideally," according to Geoffrey Hartman, "nothing would remain, except in the form of a self-consuming labor of thought."[177] This barred possession, pitted against our usual literary appetites, breeds a tantalizing prolongation of desire, a pain of anticipation so quietly acute and so indefinable that it is quite akin to pleasure.

Suspension and prolongation also arise from the intertextual relations in literary theory. All criticism, of course, involves a certain degree of arrested apprehension, a temporary hesitation over quoted passages while the reader anticipates the gathering force of an interpretation yet to come. In theory, a general impression of the cited text is even more lightly sketched. It awaits the interventions of the second, theoretical text to repunctuate and redistribute attention, to reclassify ad recirculate meanings as any truly interesting theory is expected.[178] The closer the intertextual mesh between the two texts, the more they will ambiguate one another and forestall the assignment of a final meaning. In some cases, the moment of arrest and the process of transformation will entirely supplant interpretation and will instead become the main source of our satisfaction as readers.[179] In general, the more theoretical the criticism, the longer particular interpretations will be postponed.

> . . . the vain or naive critic claims permanence for this illusory [final interpretation], thus blinding himself both to the bivalency and instability of

his own text and to the capacity of the original. . . to exceed upon further readings any permanent constraints he might hope to impose upon its positional/referential play. Of course, within the realm of practical criticism, where the critic is expected to generate specific meanings for specific texts, . . . this displacement of a permanent ambivalence by resolution is almost inevitable. . . . [which] suggests that the move from practice to theory may not be so easily inverted: having sacrificed example for rule and the particular for the general, the theorizing literary critic may have to relinquish the thought of return—and its necessity.[180]

At this point, it is hard to say whether postponement is the by-product of a desire to delay and forestall the end of the game.

Ours is said to be an age dogged by skepticism. If we have indeed been pushed by our very accumulations of knowledge that much deeper into the nightmare of history (or anthropology or psychology or ideology), if we now stand haunted by the forces that mysteriously condition all our gestures and the complicities we do not yet know how to break, then this theoretical deferral serves another purpose as well. It gives vent to our inchoate suspicions and allows us to escape the paralyzing burden of critical self-consciousness by incorporating those suspicions and that self-consciousness as its organizing premise. In this way suspicion heals itself—by reconstructing a new grounds for belief and action or by explaining the mechanisms that make appearances misleading. Either way, "theory is the reorganization of that which criticism destroys,"[181] the means for going on when (as Becket says) it is impossible to go on. Already much of contemporary literature seems divided against itself—"new, reflective in nature, and casting upon itself a glance filled with suspicion and the charge of treason."[182] The formal break between theory and its object therefore comes almost as a relief; a clearly divided nature need no longer be so strenuously at war within itself. At the same time, the split makes it possible for suspicion to become more penetrating and precise.

The task of criticism, then, is not to situate itself within the same space as the text, allowing it to speak or completing what it necessarily leaves unsaid. On the contrary, its function is to install itself in the very incompleteness of the work in order to *theorize* it—to explain the ideological necessity of those "not-saids" that constitute the very principle of its identity. Its object is the *unconsciousness* of the work—that of which it is not, and cannot be, aware.[183]

Theory represents, no doubt, an "interruption of pre-reflexive enjoyment,"[184] spoiling the aforementioned pleasures of simple recognition, identification, absorption, and appropriation. But have these pleasures not become more guilt-ridden of late, more hysterical or forced? And are there not compensatory pleasures in the jolt of interruption: the sharp but interesting pangs of estrangement and disorientation, the receding of comfortable acquaintance and the approach of an entirely different mode and magnitude of apprehension—oblique, denatured, yet thrillingly pellucid? The precise quality of this pleasure will depend upon what balance each text strikes between the traditional virtues of literary and of theoretical discourse. And the balance will determine as well whether the dominant effect of theoretical literature is one of chill remoteness or arduous struggle, crisp containment or stunning audacity.

Because the potential range of effects is so great, there is a need for closer study and especially for the study of distinctly different theorists. The four who follow by no means exhaust that range, but they do give some suggestion of its extent. They were selected, first, for their status as "hybrid" writers who have proved somehow disturbing, difficult to place, and who in this respect illustrate some of the problems and ambivalences that attend theoretical literature. None of them are (at least at the moment) "high theorists"—the element of play, of pure conjecture and suggestion, of sheer theatricality, is too prominent; the rigor and proof too weak. Yet in several cases—most prominently in that of Roland Barthes—there has actually been a palpable development *away* from strict construction and would-be scientism. Harold Bloom, in so many ways the antipode of Barthes, shows a slightly different pattern of development, from a literal-minded if ambitious program of practical criticism to an equally ambitious but highly colored and extravagant theoretical enterprise. These are, then, careers in which one can see at close hand the changing status of theoretical writing and the pressures that have helped to bring that change about.

Two of the writers to be considered—Susan Sontag and William Gass—have also worked in more traditional artistic forms: in fiction and in film. And the discrepancies, the greater imaginative success they each seem to achieve when they are writing about art rather than writing what is reputed to be art is illustrative as well. The cases of Gass and Sontag expose certain impasses in contemporary literature and the egress from them that theory seems to afford.

The four writers differ even in their adopted forms. Sontag is almost exclusively an essayist, while Bloom can hardly contain himself within those narrow limits and requires the epic scope of several volumes. Barthes and Gass (with Bloom in their wake) have produced texts that are so deliberately and ambiguously mixed as to take the merger of literature and theory almost to its limit. Yet all four retain some final faith (perhaps just barely in the case of Barthes) in the possibility of building theories and in the power of theoretical constructs. None has passed entirely over into the camp of deconstruction and pronouncements against theory.

Because it is the emergence of theory on the Anglo-American scene, so sudden and so stunning, that provides the impetus for this study, the range of writers I have chosen is largely American—with one notable exception, and Barthes's early and wide acceptance in England and the

United States raises interesting questions of its own about the meaning of such imported criticism. Moreover, each of the other writers displays subtle and shifting ties to alien traditions, from Sontag's role as a harbinger of Continental trends to the lasting impress made on William Gass by the philosophy of a displaced Austrian, Ludwig Wittgenstein.

I have focused on four authors rather than a set of separate texts because their careers seem to me exemplary, because their names have a certain cultural and academic currency, and because their writings have been organized—by others, if not by themselves—around these names and as parts of these individual careers. But how well their texts accept the principle of authorship and where they actually subvert it are questions that I shall raise as I go on.

There is method to my choice, but there is also taste. Each writer has, in my eyes, made something different of the burden of critical consciousness that is so central to the theoretical enterprises, whether by turning it into a cause for suffering or for rejoicing. And each has given a characteristic force (not always the same from text to text) to the aesthetics of theory. Together, they establish a provocative and illustrative set, from which the potential permutations of theoretical literature can begin to be assessed. They sketch parameters, but do not, I repeat, exhaust the field. Quite properly, since there is hardly anything so definite and well-defined as a field to start with—only, as yet, a tendency, a disturbance, an adventure. Which of these labels is applied will depend upon one's sympathies; I hold out for the final one, and the following chapters are intended to show why I do.

II
The Creative Impasse:
The Case of Gass and Sontag

Poetry, I shall nevertheless insist, is concerned with a certain purity, fiction with purification, while prose, in essays such as this one, experiments with the interplay of genres, attempting both demonstration and display, skids of tone and decorum associated formerly with silent films, jazz bands, and the slide-trombone.

WILLIAM H. GASS, *"Carrots, Noses, Snow, Rose, Roses"*

Today's art, with its insistence on coolness, its refusal of what it considers to be sentimentality, its spirit of exactness, its sense of "research" and "problems" is closer to the spirit of science than of art in the old-fashioned sense. Often, the artist's work is only his idea, his concept.

SUSAN SONTAG, *"One Culture and the New Sensibility"*

William H. Gass and Susan Sontag are writers of (variously) stories, novels, filmscripts, cultural notes, book reviews, polemics, prefaces, and aesthetic and literary theory. Only some of these activities are credited, officially, as creative writing, yet it does not seem too farfetched to claim that for both of them, the most *creative* writing—the most daring in conception, the most arresting in its stretch of mind and language—comes, not in their conventional fictions, but in their critical apercus and the artful construction of conceptual distinctions. Their theories are, in fact, hard to localize; both are given to inserting fragments of theoretical conjecture into book reviews, interviews, lectures, and other occasional pieces and even their more sustained speculations seem to fall naturally into the confines of separate essays. They work in shards and fragments, by fits and starts—which is not to say that they lack a sustaining vision, but only that neither one is (as Barthes or Bloom are) a system builder. In the case of Sontag, it is just as hard to locate a specifically *literary* theory, to find the line of demarcation that separates it from her more general aesthetic or cultural speculations. This is in itself a significant aspect of her literary thought and certainly distinguishes her work from the ardently verbal and adamantly high cultural William Gass.

There are other interesting points of coincidence and difference. Both writers are, by academic training, philosophers, although with sharply different affiliations—Gass to the meticulously rational school of Anglo-American linguistic analysis, on the one hand, and Sontag to the cloudier and angst-ridden metaphysical dilemmas of Continental thought, on the other. Both have gained their greatest fame, not as academicians nor even as professional philosophers, but as "thinkers," philosophically inclined critics and commentators. They have, in fact, done a good deal to define the condition of lay intellectualism in this country, attempting to function as informed and literate generalists, as explicators and artists of discursive prose—a latter-day man and woman of letters, moving against the grain of increasingly narrow academic specialization. And both have met a certain amount of disparagement for their efforts: Sontag for her pretensions, for speculating beyond her professional competence, and Gass for his laxities, for refusing to play it straight—to pursue his interests rigorously or indeed to abandon his preoccupation with aesthetics and return to the more central and serious concerns of academic philosophy. Their vehicle, as generalists, has therefore been, not academic journals, but such publications as the *New York Review of Books*. There they have contributed essays that over time have helped to establish a style of reviewing as distinctive, in its way, as the fabled "*New Yorker* short story"—a style broader in scope and weightier than the usual appreciative or demeaning notices, which uses the book itself as the occasion for a more or less protracted meditation. So independent are these reviews that (as one writer has said of Gass) "one must remember to remember what he is writing about."[1] Sontag is even less dependent on books for her occasion than is Gass, given her greater curiosity about the twists and turns of politics and popular culture and her marked instinct for fashions and for fads—markedly at odds with Gass's quest for the timeless and immutable world within the word.

There are even subtle differences of ambiance and sense of place. Sontag has her energetic cosmopolitanism, her urban chic and street smarts, and Gass his plangent regionalism, his insular Ohio, Iowa, and Indiana, above the flattened planes of which towers (like Yeat's own tower) the mind-made universe of international discourse. But all of this, though interesting, is peripheral to my real subject, which is the distinctive shape each writer manages to impose on theoretical literature. What uses does each make of it, what impasses as writers does it allow them to overcome, and what can we glean from this about such larger matters as the state of contemporary letters and the nature and range of the theoretical imagination?

3
William H. Gass

Measured by his overt claims alone, by what he says in his essays if not what he does with them, William Gass is not an especially original literary theorist. One can hear the familiar strains of Valéry, of Gertrude Stein on masterpieces—influences that Gass freely acknowledges and even celebrates—and can feel the massive silent weight of American New Criticism. This last is a force that Gass leaves curiously unacknowledged save for a buried allusion ("no artist dares neglect his own world's body") to Ransom that appears but once, and then in passing, in one of his briefer essays.[1] These are hardly avant-garde critical loyalties, despite determined efforts by some readers to find in Gass a nascent structuralism, the better to embrace or repudiate him without embarassment.[2] What Gass does do is argue his formalist position more strenuously and inventively than most. He pushes his premises farther and occasionally tries to allay some of their more crippling consequences. In fact, the extreme formalism of Gass's theoretical writings curiously parallels and inverts those chilling characters—Furber in *Omensetter's Luck*, the poet-narrator of "In the Heart of the Heart of the Country," Mad Meg and narrator Kohler in "The Tunnel"—who appear in Gass's fiction, driven by a fascination with the power of words to distort and ultimately supplant reality.[3] Gass is often most interesting, however, when he turns his attention from literature narrowly construed to the conceptual "poetry" of his mathematical and philosophic systems. Here he begins, for reasons I shall treat more fully below, to exercise his imagination more freely, to complicate the strict dichotomies and qualify the hyperboles that surround his defense of poetry simpliciter. It is these apparently innocuous qualifications and ancillary concerns that ultimately push Gass into making his theoretical writings ever more literary while, at the same time, allowing theoretical concerns to cloud the ideal purity and ineffectuality of art. Despite the fact that such a mixture violates his own express contempt for: "Writers whose grasp of esthetic principles is feeble, or whose technique is poor and unpracticed, or whose minds are shallow and perceptions dim," so that they "give us stories which are never objects for contemplation, but arguments,"[4] Gass is far more prolific as a theorist than he is as a writer of fiction. His novel-in-progress, "The Tunnel," has been under way for more than ten years, during which time two collections of essays (*Fiction and the Figures of Life* and *The World within the Word*) and a separate "philosophical inquiry," *On Being Blue*, have made their appearance. Granted that volume alone is no guarantee of merit, it at least indicates facility and a significant disparity of energy and conviction. And in Gass's case, we can go beyond such superficial measures into the very quality of his prose and the richness of conception that these works display. There is an association, I would like to suggest, between the problems Gass evidently confronts when he constructs his fictions and the theory of fictions that he espouses. Yet paradoxically, it is in those theoretical writings that he overcomes his problems as a writer of fiction, transcends the confinement that he sets out to establish, and overcomes the limitations that he places on himself (and any others who would engage in *la poésie pure*).[5] The power of Gass's theory, then, is what it does for him as a writer, the release it offers him, the abundance and ebullience it brings out in him. Theory lays open to him a new breadth of technique, allowing him to move from the slightly old-fashioned solidity of character study (which as a committed postmodern, he would never dare to admit into his fiction) to a form of translucent conceptual art far more experimental than anything his narrative experiments afford.

Gass's major theoretical concern is the *ontology* of literature (a much-used term in his writing that establishes yet another link to Ransom), the peculiar mode of being that distinguishes literary language, first, from material objects, and second, from any other kind of discourse. A convenient précis of his position (ignoring for the moment any inconsistencies or changes that have cropped up during the course of his work) appears in "Carrots, Noses, Snow, Rose, Roses":

> Here is a summary of the kinds of changes which progressively take place as language is ontologically transformed in the direction of poetry....
>
> (1) Adventitious, accidental, and arbitrary properties of words, such as their sound, spelling, visual configuration, length, dentition, social status, etc., become essential; other properties, normally even more problematic and tangential (whether the word is of Anglo-Saxon origin...) make themselves available....
>
> (2) Logically necessary connections between concepts are loosened or untied altogether, and meanings which are characteristically associational become strictly implied....
>
> (3) Grammatical categories are no longer secure....
>
> (4) The language no longer denotes or names, in the ordinary sense....
>
> When a rose has been picked, popped in a vase, peered at, rearranged and watched, the flower has left its function, family, future, far behind; but language, conceived as the servant of our needs, is denied that possi-

bility.... This villain, who puts words together with no intention of stating, hoping, praying, or persuading...[Gass's ellipsis] only imagining, only creating...[Gass's ellipsis] is to many immoral, certainly frivolous.... And roses are intolerably frivolous too, and those who grow them, snowmen and those who raise them up, and drinking songs and drinking, and every activity performed for its own inherent worth.

(5) Verse forms, rhyme schemes, metrical devices, and so on, are as peculiar to poetry as the scale is to music.... These poem patterns are like hurdles. Low or high, they do define the race....

(6)... The text is surely not sacred, and, though utopian, unpolitical. Its mode is that of blandishment and seduction, but it is addressed to no one.... It certainly contains no truths, pretends to none, and will in no way ennoble its reader....

It was this quality of maintaining itself in consciousness, of requiring continued repetition, of returning attention over and over again to itself like a mirror that will not allow reflections to escape its surface, that Valéry found most significant and valued most in every art. All the transformations I've talked about have this ultimate integrity in mind; for against what do the great lines of poetry reverberate, if not the resoundings of other lines?

(7) I said that the poet struggles to keep his words from saying something, and as artists we all struggle to be poets.... The true muteness of any expression can be measured by the degree to which the justification of the symbol combinations comes to rest within the expression itself....
...only its own inner constitution (its radiance, wholeness, clarity) will guarantee its right to be read, to be repeated, praised, and pondered.... [6]

Both in substance and in style (the arched defensive back, the definitions by negation, by what literature is not, excludes, escapes) this listing bears obvious affinities with New Critical pronouncements. There is the same concern for the autonomy and integrity of the literary work, its freedom from the extratextual forces and utilitarian ends that condition other kinds of discourse, and its freedom to focus all of its resources inward, to pursue its own designs, undistracted, to their appointed end. As Richards before him, Gass lays especial emphasis (under three separate headings) on the disparity between the referring expressions of "ordinary language" and the expressions of literary language that refer to nothing and are instead justified solely by the powerful patterns they compose. An "increasing contextual interaction" between words that "respond to one another as actors, dancers, do" supplants the interaction between word and object, word and psyche—creating something that is more musical than meaningful. Literature is to be evaluated in the terms we use for architectural forms and artifacts rather than in those used for propositions. "Frozen in its formulas," literary language "invites not use, not action, not consumption, but appreciation, contemplation, conservation, repetition, praise" ("Carrots," p. 304).

There is the customary nod in the direction of Kant's "activity performed for its own inherent worth." The nature and significance of this inherent worth varies, however, from essay to essay; even in this single list one can see Gass vacillate. At one point, he speaks of it as a "hurdle," valuable as a self-imposed difficulty overcome, or as a mark that signals the ontological peculiarity of the text; then he treats it as that quality whereby literature rivets our attention and maintains itself in our consciousness, and finally as an "intolerable frivolity" that flies in the face of utilitarian narrowness, a blessed utopian inaction that blunts our cruder appetites.

Gass does attempt, in other essays, to derive humane consequences from his formalistic premises, likening the literary focus on the medium for its own sake to Kant's moral imperative that we treat human beings as ends and never as a means:

> Works of art are meant to be lived with and loved, and if we try to understand them, we should try to understand them as we try to understand anyone—in order to know *them* better, not in order to know something else. . . .
> Why are works of art so socially important? Not for the messages they may contain, . . . but because they insist more than most on their own reality; because of the absolute way in which they exist.[7]

But his efforts are ambivalent; in other places he will insist just as strongly that artistic stylization and "the amalgamation of a means with its end makes nothing moral. . . . Cruelty can be immensely refined. It can be, in this way, removed from its natural base. . . . There is, perhaps, an indirect relation, and it may be this: that such a process [of stylization] as I have here described does the best that can be done with the human nature that it's given, and in that sense, at least, may be, if not the content, at any rate the shape of civilization."[8] Amid so many *mays* and *ifs* (and even an unconscionable split between content and shape) the ethical defense of formalism falls to pieces.

Indeed, in his more delicate moments of ratiocination, when he is no longer snubbing a polemical nose at the philistines, Gass takes care to maintain a scrupulous separation between art and ethics, between what one is as a writer (or reader) of poetry and what one is when performing other acts. The distinction actually works in two ways. It protects literature from the incursion of irrelevant demands and the careless or mistaken readings these can breed, but it also protects the rest of life and language from the imperiousness or irresponsibility that would ensue were one to use the same criteria there that apply to fictions. Thus, Gass militantly opposes the confusion of "characters" with "persons" (alluding to James's creation, "Mr. Cashmore," in *The Awkward Age*):

> Now the question is: what is Mr. Cashmore? Here is the answer I shall give: Mr. Cashmore is (1) a noise, (2) a proper name, (3) a complex system of ideas, (4) a controlling conception, (5) an instrument of verbal organization, (6) a pretended mode of referring, and (7) a source of verbal energy. But

Mr. Cashmore is not a person. He is not an object of perception, and nothing whatever that is appropriate of persons can be correctly said of him.[9]

The other side of confusing literature with life is confusing life with literature. With this comes the danger that the world itself will be obliterated, "betrayed by form," and we will be tempted to live in or by these artificial shapes—"the rich eloquence of their eventual formulation may give to some 'solutions' an allure that is abnormal, one that art confers, not life."[10] Just as there are many things we can attribute to persons that we cannot logically attribute to characters, characters too have attributes that we cannot, dare not, grant to persons. We cannot and should not try to author persons or to destroy them whimsically: to pick them up, put them down, and contemplate their condition with disinterested curiosity. Gass enlarges on this theme in several of his interviews:

> Aesthetic stances and ethical stances seem to me quite different ones. . . . There are just different kinds of proficiency involved. The two things are so different that their mixture, or the importation of one into the sphere of the other, strikes me as, again, *ethically* very very very bad. . . .
> One of the things that I attribute to Furber is a general inability to contact people except through language. Now in a writer, as a *writer*, that's fine; in a writer as person it's a catastrophe. . . .
> I prefer words to anything, yet to treat people in terms of symbol systems *only* is a fundamental mistake.[11]

This category mistake (to use the philosophical name for it) is the chief concern of much of Gass's fiction; it is the distinction that his villains override and what brings his victims to their grief. In *Omensetter's Luck*, Furber supplants Omensetter, the man, with his own characterization of him, and wreaks the havoc and destruction that will follow. The poet, spending his retirement from love "in the heart of the heart of the country," fogs the window through which he tries to see his world with his own rhapsodic breathing, thus (unknowingly) sealing himself off from the renewing force of any other life. And Mad Meg, the German historian and child of Nietzsche and Vaihinger in Gass's forthcoming novel, "The Tunnel," denies the difference between history and fiction—a denial from which the Holocaust itself appears to spring:

> Historians make history. *Agricola's story has been told to posterity*, Meg declaims, *and by that he will live*. Who poisoned this paragon, Agricola? Domitan? Ha. No. His creator Tacitus, with sly suggestion. Meg stalked back and forth like a raven. Between the flags men were sitting, holding their knees. Eagles gleamed on the peaks of the standards. . . .
> . . . Events in nature, in our lives, have little power; at most, like rockets dimming, even as they flame. . . .
> Words, however, gentlemen, WORDS! words do more than fly from their tails, burning like the peacocks. . . . With words we hold back all that

going, save all that can be saved from our Niagara. And when we put our thoughts together well, men think well of us; when our speech is passionate, they feel strongly. . . .

What is this Truth we so freely prattle of. . . ? Honestly now. . . [Gass's ellipsis] my good blue-eyed gentlemen of Germany. . . [Gass's ellipsis] we do not care, give a soft stool for the august verities if what we believe is convenient, if it dashes our enemies to the ground; if it makes us rich; if it fends off our fears. . . .

. . . It's a war of lie against lie in this world where we are, fancy against fantasy, nightmare constricting nightmare like two wedded anacondas, and anyone who's taken in is nothing but a bolo and a bumpkin.[12]

The consequences Gass foresees, should fiction become indistinguishable from fact and each command precisely the same response, feed his theoretical writing with an unusual energy, a passion to contain and clarify that separates him from most of his fellow formalists, for whom the argument is asymmetrically designed to defend literature alone. If Gass does, frequently, side with Sydney in saying that "the poet nothing affirmeth," he does so to keep not only blind rejection at bay but blind acceptance as well. Censorship and philistine impatience arise when we impose the wrong demands on literature; fanaticism and madness are the fruits of carrying a literary response too far. This makes the call for purity in poetry, which Gass borrows from Valéry, the envious analogy between poetry and music, where music—with its specialized equipment and ceremonial setting—figures as the ideal of art, seems less effete than poetry.[13] "Fiction has never enjoyed the grand proscenium or gilded frame. . . . Fiction has no undermound to raise its sentences into the wind or to shadow the page with a written shout, and this has meant that the number of dunderheads reading Balzac the way they would skim Business Week is considerably larger. Language needs these signals" ("Carrots," p. 294).

The grand proscenium, the signal, is, of course, what Gass endeavors to produce by writing theory; its absence gives his own writing purpose and significance. But to avoid category mistakes requires that the categories be correctly drawn. Gass speaks as if there were one category, literature, entirely free from the considerations and interests we bring to bear on other discourse and another category, entirely utilitarian and factual, where the considerations and interests that attach to literature are likewise never brought to bear. And here it is that Gass's theory begins to turn slyly against itself, for as he begins to explore the differences between poetry and science or fiction and philosophy, the distinction (without ever vanishing) becomes far less absolute than it had seemed. Purely utilitarian acts turn out to be extremely hard to find. Just to count one's money becomes, upon inspection, an instance of imaginative "arrangement" partaking of the same mixed desire for "meaning, security, and management" that "in one lump sum, is what our science—is what our art, law, love, and magic—is principally about."[14] Philosophic systems, if one really weighs them carefully, suddenly seem to show the formal intricacy and integrity of a poem, while literary works acquire some of the conceptual value associated with philosophy. "Every sentence, in short, takes metaphysical dictation, and it is the sum of these dictations, involving the whole range of the work in which the sentences appear, which accounts for its philosophical quality" ("Philosophy," p. 14).

As Gass expands the role of the imagination and turns up beauty in unexpected places, he simultaneously allows air to seep into the carefully constructed vacuum of literary purity. Where once a term like *construct* was used solely for the patterns and musical recurrences of words in literature, it gradually shifts its use to include a second sense as well: the conceptual systems those words compose, the projections and inferences they invite. This is a marked departure from the nascent anti-intellectualism (a remnant of the Arnold-Eliot opposition to "ideas"?) one associates with New Criticism and a distinct advance over simple formalism. It turns literary "objects" into literary "models," capable of embodying logical and ethical principles, exhibiting implicational relationships, and articulating metaphysical assumptions. Though in extremis Gass would strip literary language of any meaning whatsoever, in more measured moments he acknowledges that: "The esthetic aim of any fiction is the creation of a verbal world, or a significant part of such a world, alive through every order of its Being. Its author may not purpose this—authors purpose many things—but the construction of some sort of object, whether too disorderly to be a world or too mechanical to be alive, cannot be avoided" ("Philosophy," p. 7).

Gass is careful, however, to separate such conceptual posits from empirically verifiable descriptions. "The worlds which...the writer creates are only imaginatively possible ones; they need not be at all like any real one, and the metaphysics which any fiction implies is likely to be meaningless or false if taken as nature's own" ("Philosophy," pp. 9–10). A confirmed "instrumentalist," often a "fictionalist," he insists that models—whether theoretical or fictional—are never real per se, but simply useful analogues or translations that allow us to make predictions and derive consequences.

> That light travels in straight lines; that a body set in motion will continue unchanged unless something else hinders it; that all things seek equilibrium or act to maintain themselves in any given state:...all of these are opinions so plainly desirable for the translation of data into abstract systems, as are both atoms and the void, that it seems unlikely they are more than rules of representation like the principles of perspective in painting. ["Trouts," p. 268]

To confuse a model, even when it produces satisfactory results, with whatever processes it tries to illuminate is another version of the ubiquitous category mistake: "The scientist represented motion geometrically because he wished to understand it. He did not so dangerously confuse his model with the world. But de Sade saw persons as pieces of earth in order to treat human beings like dirt" (ibid.).

Although Gass speaks loosely here and elsewhere of conceptual "worlds" and objects," what really fascinates him is the disparity between conceptual and material existence. "Concepts have no physical properties; they do not permit smell or reflect light; they do not fill space or contain it; they do not age" ("The Medium," p. 28). When it is a matter of distinguishing between literature and life, Gass speaks as if there were but one mode of being—material and locatable in time and space—but when he extends his considerations to include philosophic and mathematical systems as well, he becomes an ontological latitudinarian. (Although his explanations of what "conceptual existence" is are not quite so clear or fulsome as one could wish; characteristically, he tells us far more about what it is not.) By allowing fictional characters and events to have such an existence, Gass eliminates the absurdity of saying that what we weep or laugh over is the fate of a proper noun. Yet because fictitious characters and events seem to mimic too closely the qualities and attributes of material existence, he is never entirely comfortable with them. He wants a cleaner break, a clearer signal of the changed ontological and phenomenological status that purely verbal constructs involve. Concepts are not percepts, but another kind or level of consciousness entirely. Characterization is therefore too tempting because it invites too indiscriminate a response. We must be trained, cajoled, coerced, before we can see them for the conceptual constructions that they are.

> Only a few of the words which a writer normally uses to create a character can be "imaged" in any sense. To the extent that these images are faded sensations which we've once had, they fill in, particularize, and falsify the author's account. To the degree these images are as vivid and lively as reality is, they will often be unpleasant, and certainly can't be "feigned." Then words would act like a mind-expanding drug. . . . Constructing images of any kind takes time, slows the flow of the work; nor can imagining keep up, in complexity, with the incredibly intricate conceptual systems which may be spun like a spiderweb in a single sentence. We tend to pay attention to our pictures, and lose sight of the meaning. The novelist's words are not notes which he is begging the reader to play, as if his novel needed something more done to it in order to leap into existence. ["Character," p. 47]

In Gass's theory, the link of word to concept and thence to consciousness replaces the unreliable and frequently reductive tie of word to object. Indeed, certain states of consciousness seem to have no residence outside of language, or at least no other mode of access and expression. Language articulates our awareness, gives it a public form far more delicate than any behavior ever could, and in some cases even helps to determine its shape and shade.

The purpose of a literary work is the capture of consciousness, and the consequent creation, in you, of an imagined sensibility, so that while you read you are that patient pool or cataract of concepts which the author has constructed; and though at first it might seem as if the richness of life had been replaced by something less so—senseless noises, abstract meanings, mere shadows of worldly employment—yet the new self with which fine fiction and good poetry should provide you is as wide as the mind is, and musicked deep with feeling. ["The Medium," p. 33]

But on occasion, Gass is willing to allow matters to go further, and to move back from text, through consciousness, to the fallen material world that it had seemed designed to escape. "The artist's revolutionary activity is of a different kind. He is concerned with consciousness, and he makes changes there. His inaction is only a blind, for his books and buildings go off under everything—not once but a thousand times. How often has Homer remade men's minds?" ("The Artist," p. 288). This is the danger that Mad Meg both preaches and embodies, the power to enflame consciousness that can only be kept in control if the status of the concept—virtual and not empirical, possible but not actual—is kept firmly before us.

Naturally, there has been some shift in Gass's theoretical position over time. One subtle but important change is the increasing emphasis placed on conventions and "rules of representation" in the essays collected in *The World within the Word*, as opposed to the godlike author whose caprices seemed to rule the text in his earlier collection, *Fiction and the Figures of Life*. This seems to be the reason for using a snowman as the emblematic figure in "Carrots, Noses, Snow, Rose, Roses," a construction in which we can clearly see how great the role of rules of representation are even in the most casual acts of imitation: ". . . the human body has been divided into three pieces, but the section that is most massive in the human being is reduced in his imitation, because the stability of the snowman requires the larger roll at the bottom. Part of the art of any art consists in persuading reality to give up its mimetic demands. . . . Soon enough, indeed, genres become themselves tyrannical" ("Carrots," p. 291). And as Gass gives greater weight to the independent rules that govern literary discourse, his easy ontological analogy between philosophic and literary categories—which was so prominent in *Fiction and the Figures of Life*—has begun to come unglued. "May not grammar dictate metaphysics. . . . ? No. Subjects are subjects, not substances, and there is no quality or relation I can't turn into a noun."[15]

This new respect for mediating conventions is accompanied by a slightly altered stance in the later essays, a small but perceptible movement closer to the reader's side that surfaces in such playful asides as: "So I am pulling a poem out of this BOX. The words on the page do not contain it, but their conundrum does."[16] To give the reader so much power is, of course, a departure from Gass's official position that the form of the text determines how readers shall respond—"captures their consciousness,"—if they could but confine their wandering attention to what is actually before them on the page. But now, significantly, Gass seems far less sure of how much is actually there *on* the page and how much we as readers must supply. "One may now strike a light to the suspicion that a form without meaning is formless, and that there can be no ontology to structures without interpretation. Although some forms inhibit or deny others (it isn't easy to see the circle as a square), nevertheless I can picture my cone in a lot of different ways"("Ontology," p. 323).

But greater than all these other changes is the final plunge into theorizing as a form of literary art. There were stray glimpses of this tendency before, but confined to single passages and passing figures of speech. Oddly enough (or perhaps not oddly at all), the more oblique and playful his own essays become, the less is Gass disposed to suspend disbelief entirely, to admire the beauty or audacity of a conceptual system for its own sake—as he once did in "Philosophy and the Form of Fiction": "But the worlds of the novelist, I hear you say, do not exist. Indeed. As for that—they exist more often than the philosphers'. Then, too—how seldom does it seem to matter. Who honestly cares? They are divine games" (p. 4). It is not that the beauty has diminished or that Gass is any more willing to attribute reality (as opposed to validity) to models and conceptual systems. It is simply that now they can—still dazzling and unreal—at least be assessed and compared, their roots exposed, their consequences traced.

> Suppose I were to say, of a married couple, that in their life together the wife played left tackle. Have I made a good model? Where are the other twenty players? who are the coaches, trainers, where are the stands?...
> ...Orders vary in both their vices and their virtues, in kind as well as in degree. Some are futile, others cheap. ["Trouts," pp. 272, 269]

The latest work does not resolve all of the tensions in Gass's thought, although it does begin to tip the balance—a change of emphasis that may in fact be due to the kind of hybrid writing in which he is now engaged. What are these tensions?—principally as inconsistency with regard to the categorical distinction between literature and other kinds of discourse. In the earlier collection, Gass can, in one and the same essay, insist both that "the scientific model yields testable results,...our fictional conclusions, the inferences we draw there, remain forever in the expanding spaces of the novel" *and* that: "we see our own life in the same fashion Lowry has envisioned Firmin's; what we take away and keep is the novel's figurative form; we reconceive our own acts in his manner."[17] At a comparable moment in the later volume, he is willing to state flatly that "there are too many books in which the baby beats the nurse, in which form has been forgotten for the sake of momentary fun." Note that now it is just "books"—and not the old dichotomy of literature and sciences, literature and utilitarian prose. Moreover, the figure in contention—"the baby beats the nurse"—belongs to no less a figure than William Shakespeare: ". . . a phrase which has certainly been singled out for popular acclaim, yet the form of the flip-flop intended is not quite right, because otherwise we'd have to think that nurses beat babies as a normal and happily ordered part of their duties" ("Trouts," p. 279).

Other tensions (concerning the meaning and the modality of literary form and whether literary form imposes itself upon its readers or they must discover it) persist in even more stubborn forms in the later essays. Yet there is still something of the same diminished friction, the same tentative, if subliminal, stirrings of an altered sense of things. To these I shall return in future pages; here I wish only to show how Gass's professed theory of literature, inconsistencies and all, might inhibit him as a writer of (conventional) literature and move him towards a theoretical literature where his writing will be less constrained.

The stress on literature as a rite of purification has the consequence, at times, of reducing Gass's fiction to little more than a demonstration of the unreality of the world the words apparently project. Each text traces the same pattern; an accumulation of verisimilar details turns out, upon inspection, to be largely fantasmatic. "My blear floats out to visible against the glass, befogs its country," confesses the poet at his window "in the heart of the heart of the country," revealing as he does so that all these observations of small-town Indiana life, all these recollections of a poignant lost love, are merely verbal fabrications, "another lie of poetry."[18] This concern becomes ever more prominent in the later fiction, from "Heart of the Country" to "The Tunnel," reaching its most patent expression in the meta-fiction of *Willie Master's Lonesome Wife*, which confronts the reader with the crude but economical assertion, "You've been had from start to finish." Strangely, though, the paradoxical invitation to see something that isn't really there is more vividly and far less querulously rendered in the theoretical essays—perhaps because here there is no history of mimesis to contend with.

> Let me make a snowman and see what comes of it. . . .
> I begin by gathering snow around a tightly fisted core the way a leaper on a ledge collects a crowd, pressing it together from above, enlarging it with repeated rolls until it can't be budged. For this work I certainly don't want leaves, bare earth, or bumpy ground.
> The roll appears to stand well where it is. Good. ["Carrots," p. 287]

The present tense gives the lie to the description more subtly and pervasively than interpolated reminders that one has been had. In fact, one has not been had at all; the disillusionment is less bitter, because the illusion was never complete. It is not the rupture of illusion that is so troubling in Gass's fiction, but the reiteration of the same effect in text after text, or in different sections of the same text, as if it were a lesson we could never learn and we could never tire of repeating. If in certain theoretical passages Gass does talk of fiction (as one of his fellow philosophers complains) "as if *only* a severing were going on,...as if...the only real relation words can have to users and their world are those of reference and truth,"[19] his fiction seems even more obsessed with its own unreality. If the ordinary function of words is to name objects in the world (a narrow view, but one that Gass sometimes espouses), then literature— so the logic goes—seems fated to fill itself with antinames. Hence the long and baggy catalogs that have become the most prominent device in Gass's recent fiction, endless compilations of names that do not name, referring expressions that fail to refer. What these lists seem designed to do is defeat our hunger for mimesis with a surfeit of details so great that we cannot possibly digest them. We are to be at last forced to submit to the opacity of words, to feel them quantitatively as objects that cluster and disperse, like notes in a syntactic symphony—as in this passage from "The Tunnel":

> The books begin at the floor and continue to the ceiling as species do in Aristotle. They span the doors, in stacks crowd the closet, consume every corner, ring the radiator: four walls and a window full of *als ob*: models, fictions, phantoms, wild surmises, all the essential human gifts: dreams, preachments, poetry, and other marvels of misfeeling. There are books in the drawers, on the desk and table. Cheap. Fat. Tattered. Innocent. Grim. *Piers Plowman*. EPIHNH. *Three Weeks*. Céline. Alone. In disrepute. I could not live in such proximity with any person. With Unamuno, the beautifully named, with Marlowe—yes. Aquinas. Schopenhauer. Galileo. Bede. Call each to me with a finger that tickles the top of the spine. They play into my hands like cards. They breed....Froissart. Adams. Gobineau. Like checkers, some king the carpet's squares. Sober books. Bauds. They preoccupy my armchair like an injury. They press in. Ockham. Austen. Von Frisch. Pound.[20]

The listing continues, on and off, for some ten pages more— arresting, ornamental, almost hieratic. Yet in the mass, such passages begin to pall; one starts to expect their regular recurrence and learns to wait them out when they (inevitably) arrive, knowing in each instance what the final effect will be. It is Gass's theoretical contention that the purity of literature makes its effects eternal, ambered over and preserved against the accidents of time. Automatization and boredom are apparently among the effects of time that the theory makes no room for.

"Sterne's famous sentence: 'A cow broke in tomorrow morning to my Uncle Toby's fortifications...'[is] forever amazing; because however familiar we are with this sentence's sublime disjunctions, as we may be with Haydn's surprises, or the great sea chase in *Moby Dick*, or the eloquence of Sir Thomas Browne, these features will remain as if engraven,wholly unworn by repeated use" ("Ontology," p. 335). But plainly this is an extreme and idiosyncratic position. Gass's defense against what seem to him the contingencies and irrelevancies of social history ends by obscuring the facts of literary history as well, and even the history of our own apprehension of a literary work—the predictable dulling of curiosity and the necessary relativity of all surprises.

In reply to "Carrots, Noses, Snow, Rose, Roses," Patrick Maynard noted that for Gass the transformation of language into literature appears to mean that "it isn't really discourse anymore" but simply an assemblage, a kind of verbal sculpture.[21] The assumption that prose must sacrifice its sense to become sensuous, along with the occasional confusion of sense and reference, meaning and naming, impoverishes Gass's fiction in many cases as well. It is not the only position that he adopts, however; his interest in conceptual constructs suggests an alternative to the impasse of reference and antireference. Yet, as already indicated, Gass is suspicious of the associations and projections that begin together when words are allowed to mean as well as to sound and configure. The problem is how to control and constrain these associations, how to keep us from filling in too much detail and wandering away into our own vague images—giving Mr. Cashmore features that he plainly hasn't got.

To work with character and narrative is to risk precisely these incursions, almost to incite them, and yet character and narrative are the stuff of which novels are traditionally made. Thus, when Gass writes novels, they consist of imaginary worlds that are shattered, plots that are disrupted, characterizations that are fragmented and diffuse, often reduced to a single, sounding vocal track. As a creative writer, Gass is trying, almost frantically, to prevent our projections from outstripping his words, substituting percept for concept and faded recollections for fresh constructions. With this comes, of course, the danger that his interruptions will become too obtrusive, episodic structures too mechanical, the reshuffling of time and space too obviously that. Or worse yet, that these disruptions will themselves be read as representing something, as symptoms of the narrator's insanity, say, or of his sexual arousal, or perhaps as a generalized portrait of the workings of consciousness itself.[22] While this final interpretation might be less disturbing to Gass, any mimetic reading risks missing the productivity of the text itself by treating it as a reproduction of something else, some putative original, that we are only too ready to put in its place.

Even when Gass's tales give us no more than the play of a single voice, that voice is still too much, given his purposes. It is not that one fails to feel how much the writing deliberately denies itself, how insistently monologic it is, how lost in its own reverie, so that the other voices, the objects and events that reach us through this medium are almost wholly muffled. Nonetheless, voice remains closely tied to character. It is still an instigation to us to supply a plausible situation and a probable history to explain its shifts of mood and timbre. Gass claims that: "Character has a special excitement for a writer (apart from its organizing value) because it offers him a chance to give fresh meaning to new words. A proper name begins as a blank, like a wall or canvas, upon which one might paint a meaning" ("Character," pp. 50–51). But for him such constructions do not really start out blank enough, and thus never give him the full satisfaction of "impressing my work with inner worth the way Yeats did his symbol system" ("Carrots," p. 297). The true constructive center of "The Tunnel" is therefore not the tremulous and irrascible voice of its narrator, William Kohler, nor yet the various characters he recalls and apostrophizes—Mad Meg, his colleagues Herschel and Planmantee, his wife, his lost love, Lou, and the visionary demonic singer, Susu. It is the tunnel itself: a site, a condition, a constantly metamorphosizing image that ties the text together.

> Some years ago in a similar silence, though in another office of this building, I unscrewed with a dime a metal plate fastened low on the wall (it was like opening a tomb through the plaque of its monument), and entered a passage filled with cobweb and pipe . . . I was in one of the maintenance tunnels. . . .
>
> In one house I lived in as a child (and I lived in many), there was a long narrow arm of closet off my rooms which bent around a central chimney. Unless you pushed your way through my kiddie clothing, hanging like beaded strings to ward off flies, you couldn't know that it went out of sight like an elbow. There on the arm where the fist would be I often hid . . . totally free in the realm of the spirit. I was, as I should say now, a true self-by-itself, and so a self-inside-itself like Kant's unknowable, noumenal knower. . . . When I played Satan in the tree, or rode the New York subway later, I was not an animal in anybody's little cage of vision, but they were surely caught in mine. . . .
>
> So I built buildings full of hidden hallways with my blocks—secret stairs and unreachable rooms. Played spy. With pencil and paper drew mazes of brightly tangled hair you couldn't find your way through. And reread the designs in our rugs . . . I've lived in the landscape of that carpet ever since, beset but protected . . . my secret company, my private childhood, and my conspiracies . . . I understood at once why Alice went after the rabbit or melted in her mirror; the tunnel was more attractive than the rabbit was.[23]

Yet to construct such "symbol systems"—or as Gass calls them in an interview, "what in effect become mappings, metaphorical structures, and the development of metaphorical structures"—hardly requires the trappings of traditional fiction. It may in fact, as he acknowledges in the same interview, be impeded by them: "I want to be in any format that will let me play with language the way I want to. The traditional novel doesn't really satisfy me for that reason. Nothing does. I just want to get in the words and go. But the novel says all the time, where's the story, who are the people?"[24]

One gathers from Gass's theory that it might be possible to trust one's readers more if there were some way to signal the peculiar nature of literary language: "Language slips from mode to mode with scarely a hiss. . . .the major changes take place through the intervention of that rare reader who perceives the shift" ("Carrots," pp. 293–94). The "rare," however is telling; signals in themselves are useless unless one knows how to respond to them, and Gass seems to be convinced that nothing in either human nature or (especially) contemporary culture induces us to read literature as we ought, with patience and total attention, suppressing all extraneous associations and taking our pleasure there without a need for profit. In his fiction, the fruits of this conviction take the form of suspicion, even antagonism, towards the projected audience. The latter is particularly marked in *Willie Master's Lonesome Wife*. Although it is put into the mouth of the narrator—who is literary language personified—the hostility is so pronounced and the expectation of misunderstanding so unremitting that it seems to be more than a private quirk on the narrator's part.

> These words are all I am. Believe me. Pity me. Not even the Dane is any more than that. Oh, I'm the girl upon this couch all right, you needn't fear; the one who's waltzed you through these pages, clothed and bare, who's hated you for her humiliations, sought your love, just as the striptease dancer does, soliciting male eyes for cash and feeling the light against her like a swelling organ. Could you love me? Love me then...then love me...Yes. I know. I can't command it.[25] [Gass's ellipsis.]

None of Gass's other narrators so doubt their audience; indeed, they scarcely notice it. Yet the way those voices turn so resolutely inward, communing only and hopelessly with themselves in their private fantasies, is significant as well, and contributes to the overall impression of monotony and reduced expressive range that the fiction occasionally imparts.

Holding as he does that literature must give us objects for contemplation and not arguments or dramatized philosophy, Gass is constrained from using his novels to construct a line of thought rather than a story line. He would prefer that fictions imply a philosophy, yet has no real interest himself in the narrative devices, descriptive evocations, and character studies that normally embody these philosophical implications. The solution—and not a really happy one—is to turn his characters into orators, lecturers, and writers who, may then deliver themselves of polished pieces of doctrine. Gass does take great care to avoid making any character a simple spokesman of "the truth." Yet the stories engage us principally as a competition of views that at its best is not so very different in kind from Gass's own beloved Platonic dialogues. The issues are often the same ones that concern him in the essays—the consequences of category mistakes, the nature of consciousness, the structure of history. There is, in fact, no alternative to reading the meta-fiction of *Willie Master's* as anything other than dramatized philosophy, an ungainly allegory wherein Babs (the narrator) stands for language and Philip Gelvin (her unresponsive lover) stands for all the unimaginative and unfeeling readers and/or writers who misuse her. In spite of his ambivalence about literature's capacities as a model and his frequent claim that we can derive no consequences from a literary work, it is impossible to believe that such a determined allegory is to be entirely without issue. And yet, perhaps because of this same ambivalence, the allegory of *Willie Master's* seems forced, awkward, and dogmatic; one would prefer to take one's literary theory neat, without all this labored personification.

In *Willie Master's Lonesome Wife* especially, but elsewhere in Gass's fiction too, one senses a desperation that whatever this book is struggling to accomplish has already been accomplished. The work of purification has already been done—the depletion of that vein, the only one that the author truly cares to mine: "Joyce did data in, Mann ideas, Proust all the rest" ("Carrots," p. 305). What more remains, in the way of voiding and transforming, after Joyce's "whole world rubbed out and rearranged in music, voice, and meaning," after the modernists' "esthetic exploitation of language . . . depth of commitment to their medium . . . purity of their closed forms"? ("Carrots," pp. 305–6). For the literature of negation and antirepresentation, the line seems at an end; to repeat the same transformation transforms nothing. The experiments with typography and the revolt against linearity that fill *Willie Master's* may extend Joyce's efforts, but they do not surpass them, and while the voice of this latter-day lonely lady may be bawdier and angrier than Molly's, her own moody meditations on sexuality obviously pick up where those of Bloom's wife end.[26] The ghosts of Gass's predecessors and the efforts of his peers hang heavy on these pages, which are as much a compendium as they are an effort to exploit the devices of modern and postmodern fiction (starting perhaps where the "Oxen of the Sun" left off).

Already in "In the Heart of the Heart of the Country," Gass's fiction had begun to veer towards criticism, basing that story on a reading of Yeat's Byzantium poems.[27] (Indeed, it is in that tale that Gass establishes his own most potent rival, for the techniques he introduced there—the plot [or nonplot] broken into recurring fragments, the distribution of material under topical headings, the recirculating words and images, the dislocated catalogs—have remained with him ever since. "The Tunnel" even opens in the same mood and milieu.)[28] But Gass's movement into fiction as a form of reading—a criticism, not of life, but of ancillary texts—is not due solely to the anxiety of influence. As he says (with surprising warmth) of Colette's rich memorials: "None of us now matches her skill at rendering the actual contours of experience. How far can we see out of raised eyebrows? How straight can we speak with a curled lip? Irony, ambiguity, skepticism—these aren't attitudes any more which come and go like moods, but part of our anatomy."[29] Whatever other reasons for this increasing skepticism one might want to put forward, Gass's own explanation is based (characteristically) on the nature and (uncharacteristically) the evolutionary history of literature itself.

> . . .the novelist now better understands his medium; he is ceasing to pretend that his business is to render the world; he knows, more often now, that his business is to *make* one, and to make one from the only medium of which he is a master—language. And there are even more radical developments.
>
> There are metatheorems in mathematics and logic, ethics has its linguistic oversoul, everywhere lingos to converse about lingos are being contrived, and the case is no different in the novel. ["Philosophy," p. 24]

> Why should we be surprised to see the same development in literature? Connections in the world, the rule of thumb, the sun, the lever in the leg and arm, the yearly thaw, as we begin to understand them, are ultimately replaced by those ambitious understudies, the ideas themselves, and once where hinges were, and without oil, were squeaks, concepts oillessly swing in winds from nowhere. It's not that our studies have lost their relevance to the spit and cough and curse of daily life. It is rather that they seek their rules, and find their justifications, elsewhere. ["Carrots," p. 307]

The step to meta-fiction is one that Gass once contemplated as well, planning a massive fictional study of the history of Western literature. But eventually he abandoned that scheme as impractical and satisfied himself with *Willie Master's* alone.[30] One suspects that deeper motives operated in the abandonment as well—an unconfessed sense that the experiment was terminal, an alley all too blind. As inventive—almost hectically so—as the brief novella is, it illustrates most of the problems that can afflict auto-commentary and fiction about fiction: the tendency towards crude allegory, the awkward didacticism, the monotony and frequent poverty of self-disclosure. By personifying language, Gass allows it to speak about itself—as if to say: "I'm only a string of noises, after all—nothing more really." By making that personification a woman, Gass allows her to act out his favorite analogy between sexual and linguistic exploitation, the attentive services of a devoted lover and the parallel devotions of a committed writer or reader. Yet the personification does little to illuminate the nature of language, particularly those transcendental and inhuman qualities that Gass cares for most; often one must actually rely on one's own independent assumptions about language and literature in order to make sense of this lady's behavior. Under such conditions, it becomes too easy to be satisfied with the mere equation, to solve the puzzle of what stands for what and let it go at that.

Elsewhere, Gass himself admits obliquely to a faint uneasiness about any work that professes to "contain all its explanations"; where "logical levels rise and fall like waves" and "Only an occasional philosopher is striken with *mal du métalanguage*" ("Carrots," p. 282). In *Willie Master's*, the desire to preserve separate logical levels is expressed in the play between footnotes, marginalia, insertions, on the one hand, and the all-too-literal (nude photographs on front and back) "body" of the text itself on the other. Yet at every level, the language is still Babs's. Thus, the old problem—that some portion of the language that evaluates must forever escape its own evaluation, the irremediable blindspot of any self-scrutiny—remains unsolved. When Babs states that she is "imagination imagining itself," she is naming something but not exemplifying it. We learn nothing from the quality of this statement about the qualities of the imagination. Throughout the novella, then, there must be a constant nervous alternation of exhibition and analysis. "That I am music when most beautiful (you see? a man, a mere man, mortal, his death in his pocket like a letter he's forgotten, could not be that, could not be beautiful) is nevertheless no help against the licorice I've swallowed . . . imagine the imagination imagining . . . licorice: serpenty, twisted, sticklish, and wallowy"[31] [Gass's ellipses]. This division is exacerbated by the distrust of the reader, who might otherwise supply the higher-level analysis as s/he does in the subtler meta-fictions of Borges and Nabokov. In *Willie Master's*, Gass's covert war between language as sheer verbal music and language as a discourse that designates, argues, and instructs becomes fierce and unremitting. Plainly, for Gass metafiction cannot overcome this problematic dichotomy, but can only deepen and coarsen it.

Many of these problems and constraints disappear for Gass when he turns to theoretical writing. It is certainly much easier to pursue the conceptual questions that intrigue him most and to make art directly out of philosophical problems. Indeed, there is probably no more marked characteristic of these essays than the lush pageantry they construct out of such unpromising materials as ontology, logical levels, metaphysical categories, and the rest. The lack of initial promise actually makes them more effective (far more startling than the familiar biblical themes one encounters in his earlier fiction or the sadly worn imagery of the Holocaust that frames the study of tyranny and destruction in everyday life in "The Tunnel").

That newspaper—we might mistake it for the white wings of a passing pigeon. Do we see the line it draws? Think how Galileo would have rendered it. He'd notice neither newspaper nor pigeon. He discovered that the distance which the paper might be tossed could be expressed—how wonderful his image—as the area of a rectangle. The match-up was astonishing: Velocity could be laid out on one side, time on another, and since he knew so much more about rectangles than he did about motion, his little Euclidean model (for that's what he'd managed), to the degree it held firm, would immediately make a science of movement possible. . . in terms of dots and dashes, points and paths. . . and he went on to describe all evenly accelerating motion in the cool and classic language of the triangle. Had Dante been more daring? I think not. ["Trouts," p. 263; Gass's ellipses]

What such a passage effects is precisely a transformation—although perhaps not an ontological one, nor even one in which (to follow Gass's original recipe) the original uses of Galileo's figure must be entirely voided, or rubbed out, for its beauty and audacity to be laid bare. Actually, this is a transformation of a transformation, from the model Galileo originally proposed to the metaphorical enormity that Gass then makes of it. Perhaps by beginning with what is already a construction, Gass feels less pressed to purify. Indeed, is not his method in this instance rather to defile, to introduce again the graphic particulars that the geometric model suppresses and ignores, and to make the distance and the difference so palpable that we gasp at once at the elaborate artifice of the ideal and the precious density and fragility of the real? Moreover, as so often happens when Gass's theory turns literary, literature itself becomes as much the vehicle as the tenor. It becomes the lens that alters our regard for other kinds of discourse and, in so doing, quietly extends the domain of his theory beyond the limits of its official aestheticism.

The dichotomies that had seemed insuperable and irreconcilable in meta-fiction are more easily contained, and occasionally overcome, in theory. Because the text that comments is logically distinct from the text (here by Galileo) receiving commentary, a delicate coexistence becomes possible: What art negates, theory subsequently reasserts; if literature is a purgation, then theory is a restoration. What occurs is not a synthesis, because the levels never coincide. Affairs that never meet can never conflict—as traffic on an overpass poses no threat to traffic on the street. Gass can make his quotations from beloved literary works as mute and lapidary as he likes, can treat them exclusively as verbal objects to roll around one's mouth, and yet never cease speaking around and through them, declaiming like Demosthenes. And as Gass's own theoretical prose becomes progressively more artful, these compromise measures become less necessary, as the dividing line between the mute verbal objects and utilitarian speech is tacitly but irrevocably erased.

Writing theory helps to heal as well the debilitating split between philosophy and fiction:

> Philosophers multiply our general nouns and verbs. . .; while novelists toil at filling in the blanks in proper names and at creating other singular affairs. . . .

> ...The concepts of the philosopher speak, the words of the novelist are mute; the philosopher invites us to pass through his words to his subject...; while the novelist, if he is any good, will keep us kindly imprisoned in his language. ["Philosophy," pp. 4, 8]

Such assumptions prevent Gass from exercising many of his own highest talents—his luminous conceptual imagination, his capacity to make abstraction paradoxically tangible, his plain love of contention and argument—when he writes his fictions. The piously embraced particulars in his stories are somehow burdensome, cluttered, and inert:

> Each of these towns has acrid, yellow-tasting cloud machines, ink-streaked, redly-echoing skies, and torches one hundred feet high, burning constantly like sacred flames, discrediting the phallus as a symbol. There are piles of crates and heaps of barrels, mountains of bent, corroding metal.... I remember mostly litter, derelict cars, scarred signs, lost ground, high-tension towers which imprisoned the sky, pretending to lift vast units of electric across the valley like skiers on sagging wires...and all the residues of combustion: I remember rust, grime, glaciers of grey slag, acres of cinders, coal, smoke, acids, oiled earth.[32]

This passage from "The Tunnel" does manage to retain its grip on singular affairs, but at the expense of lapsing into nebulous enumerations. How much more palapable and particular does a general term like Galileo's "velocity" seem in contrast.

Theory supplies the frame, the signal of an altered status that unaccommodated literature lacks. This missing frame is the chief conceit of the essay "Carrots, Noses, Snow, Rose, Roses," which raises its own snowman up upon a pediment, a "primal mass [which] mainly elevates the button and the eyes, the hat, the secret smile, above the vast layer of impersonal snow which surrounds and blankets everything" (p. 292). The snowman on his pediment figures forth the elevation of indifferent language into art. And since this elevation is really effected by the theoretical text itself, pediment and prose converge. At the same time, the nature of the audience that this prose projects is transformed as well. "To be sure we understand what's going on, let's run down the figure of the snowman like a melt of ice and evaluate what's happened" (p. 289). Although that "we" is a pedagogical ploy, a generous descent to meet the pupils on their native ground, it is still a remarkable departure from the isolation and vituperation that characterized the narrator's address in *Willie Master's*. The difference is even more pronounced when one turns to *On Being Blue*, where the merger of theory and literature is almost complete. "Now this fading poet's forgotten essay furnishes us with our first example, before we are quite ready for any: the description of two figures in a painting...the prose of a shade of blue I leave to you"[33] (Gass's ellipsis).

With the signals now in place and instruction underway, there seems to be no need for mistrust and defensive maneuvers. With theory, there is something to combat the bad habits, and those dunderheads who mistook Balzac for *Business Week* can become disciples, capable of carrying out their own imaginative responsibilities. The reader of theoretical discourse is expected to be more skeptical from the start, more prone to test and query, than the reader of fiction. This, together with the clear didactic framework the theoretical text supplies, gives Gass the opportunity to explore mimesis harmlessly, even to indulge in it, without the risk of inviting category mistakes. Several of the essays collected in *The World within the Word* take the form of character studies—of Malcolm Lowry, Gertrude Stein, Colette, and Freud—an unpardonable descent into biographical irrelevancies for an avowed formalist. Yet it becomes a kind of formal exercise precisely because such characterizations are not what we expect, not the sort of argument and exegesis we had looked for in the context of a book review. As a result, the art that goes into character construction emerges as it otherwise might not. Then too, Gass's biographical essays are usually written as an oblique commentary on another biography that is the subject of a book review, thus turning that biography from fact into a version of the facts. What appears to be a simple biographical essay is actually a representative instance showing how literary biographies should be composed and a vivid reminder that they *are*, in fact, composed.

No one has written more eloquently than Gass on the resemblances between theoretical and literary constructs, and this has doubtless contributed to the growth of a more stylized theorizing. Yet another contributing factor is his sense that all the literary experiments of interest have already been performed. "It's easier, when you're writing a novel or a short story, to let the language take over. . . . In an essay or review it's a lot harder and more interesting, because it hasn't been done as much."[34] As a theorist, he seems no longer to be concerned with rivalry and belatedness; the conventions of writing are different, the demand for originality less imperious, the fact of assimilation and indebtedness no longer humiliating—as one can see from his proud endorsements of Valéry. Indeed, there seems to be an intense satisfaction in penetrating and participating in another's writing—discovering the principles of its construction, and testing that discovery by generating new examples of the same kind.

Life is rearrangement, and in a dozen different ways Gertrude Stein set out to render it. . . .

Let's begin with a sentence without any special significance, selected the same way you might curiously pick up a piece of paper in the street.

> *In the middle of the market there's a bin of pumpkins.* Dividing this sentence
> as it seems natural to do, we can commence its conquest:
>   a. There's a bin of pumpkins in the middle of the market.
>   b. There, in the middle of the market, is a bin of pumpkins.
>   c. A bin of pumpkins? There, in the middle of the market.
>   d. A bin of...pumpkins? There? In the middle of the market?
> We can make our arrangements more musical:
>   e. In the middle. In the middle of the market. In the middle there's a
> bin. There's a bin. In the middle of the market there's a bin....
> Much of this is dreadful singsong, of course, but the play has only begun.
> Besides, this is just a demonstration record. ["Gertrude Stein," pp. 112,
> 113–14]

There is great conviction and not a little fun in this demonstration
record, producing as it does something that is neither original nor
derivative, that draws its energy from Stein but at the same time makes
that energy intelligible as before it had not been. Citation frees Gass's
prose from the monologues and catalogs of his fiction, opens his theoretical writing to a richer interplay of voices, modes, and techniques. Although he claims that literary passages should reverberate only against
each other, in fact his own citational practice is far more complex:
juxtaposing Galileo and Dante, Keats and Katherine Mansfield, Hobbes
with Freud with Robert Burton. (So much for the closed text and the
sequestered universe of purely literary discourse.) Since the mode of
address of theoretical discourse is different as well—no longer confined
to meditations overheard—and since it is not so closely identified with a
single authorial voice, the range and variety of the prose is enormously
enhanced. In his theoretical writing, Gass is free to move from intimate
confession to impersonal demonstration, sliding in and out of distinct
rhetorical poses, and passing through all manner of idioms, ambiguously
stolen, cited, and absorbed. The result is something far more fluid than
poor Babs, who for all her changes of costume, stays confined throughout
the course of *Willie Master's* to her character and her couch.

The release and high spirits of the theoretical prose can be attributed to the fact that Gass need no longer work against the grain of
narrative or confine himself to the construction and subsequent destruction of situations and events. If it is true that Gass's stories work most
powerfully at the level where "semantic traits float freely in a world of
fluid identification,"[35] then this power is only enhanced when the writing
is no longer inhibited by the need to tell a story or stay in character. The
constructs of fiction are, in Gass's view, actually conceptual networks. But
the usual forms of fiction tempt us to "watch the pictures which a writer's
words have directed us to make" and thereby "miss their meaning, for the
point is *never* the picture" ("Character," p. 42). The chance to dispense
with them entirely and to work with constructs less misleading and more
patently conceptual would therefore seem a clear advantage. The rar-

efaction and abstraction of theoretical discourse would be less likely to invite our artless filling in of details that are not there. As an instrument of verbal organization and a source of verbal energy, the category, character, will serve as well or better than any given character. We will be more aware that such a conceptual distinction is a thing made of words and more attentive to the words that make it up. Gass's theoretical writing is more resourceful and trickier than this, however. Not only does he construct "pure" conceptual networks—most notably in *On Being Blue*—but he also takes the opportunity to build humbler and tauntingly particular, even visualizable objects, as in his dazzling "photos" of Colette:

> It is the hair we see in the final photographs, after arthritis has marooned her on that pillowed divan she calls her raft. She wears a futile sweater against the chill which swells from within now like a puff of cold breath, and a fur bedspread is draped over her former body. She is looking at us with Claudine's eyes and Colette's mouth. Her alertness is utterly unlike the hopelessness we earlier saw when she sat beside Willy. It is preternaturally intense. Her jaw juts as it always did; her nose has not lost its longish taper either; the brow has risen, lying beneath her frizzy hair like snow beneath a wintering bush; and her hands, thank god, can still form words. . . . One of the immortals, she will soon die, and be given a state funeral and denied consecrated ground on the same day. ["Colette," pp. 139–40]

Obviously words are not photographs—hasn't that been Gass's lesson all along?—and just as obviously these words ("a futile sweater against the chill which swells from within now") show us what no photograph ever could. With this emotionless present tense, wherein we see the reality of the pretense and not the pretense of reality, Gass at last makes his oft-repeated dictum that the lines of the novelist are not likely interpretations of anything, but are the thing itself, come to life. Here we see—not in a novel, but in theoretical prose—the chimera in the making, and we understand that what Gass means by "the thing itself" is not the opaque printers ink but the projections that we make from it. The superiority of the acquaintance-knowledge that we gain through such direct exhibition is one more reason for Gass's shift to a more *literary* theory, where exemplification and embodiment can supplement his argument.

Yet what the theoretical essays exemplify and embody need not, characteristically will not, be particulars and substances, but general categories and classes. The essays are often short on imagery—if by that we understand perceptual comparisons rather than conceptual proportions—and long on what Gass calls (referring to geometry) articulated air. In fact, they play continuously on this distinction, engaging in a persistent *discordia concors* in which ideas and objects interanimate and modify each other:

> The right triangle, for instance, will suffice for a universe. Lean a few together like subway passengers at rush hour and soon triangles of varying slopes—homologues, conjugates, and other oddities—rectangles of many sizes, stars and flowers, the uninflated sides of soccer balls, diamonds and devious parallelograms will appear—some weak in the crotch as anything aging is apt to be, some sharp, some fierce—spilling out as though we'd hit the jackpot with a nickel through the quarter slot. ["Ontology," p. 308]

While Gass elsewhere protests that the need to follow a line of thought can be as constricting as a narrative chronology, the former process is plainly nearer to his native bent. To construct cases, to subsume instances under their proper headings, is more illuminating for him, a better way of framing his philosophic interests than by trying to embody them in a sequence of situations. Nowhere is this disparity clearer than in the different treatment that the same character (originally derived from Gass's alcoholic mother) receives in "The Tunnel" and in "The Doomed in Their Sinking," an omnibus review of books on suicide. It would seem at first distinctly odd that classifying the woman as "an instance of suicide," and making her an emblem of the problem of deciding where accident and illness end and self-murder begins, should give her greater poignancy than an extended story. Granted, of course, that in the story she is filtered through the voice and apprehension of a tormented narrator, her son and sometime victim. Yet such is the constraint under which Gass's fictions operate that there is no way out of this voice, no access to the experience of the mother herself.

> I don't need to remember that they took my mother's teeth, too, before they threw her in the drunk tank. You'll not leave me here, Billy dear, will you? And the elevator covered its toothless grin to swallow down Mother with a hydraulic hiss. . . . It's only for a little while, Mother, while they get you well, and teach you how to chew without your teeth and sit nicely on a chair in the corner, Mother; soon I shall come and get you; shortly I shall fetch; certainly I shall visit: fruit, chocolates, and flowers shall spill from my lap when I part my knees. . . . Should I be sympathetic with the sick if I'm the sickness they are sick from? . . . dear old Margaret, my melted mother, mad as medicine could make her, who used me to murder her.[36]

Freed from the confinement of character and of narrative-as-voice, the essay can accomplish what the fiction cannot: a transition of consciousness, moving from son to mother within the limits of a single sentence:

> . . . (they confiscate your pins, belts, buckles, jewelry, teeth, and they'd take the air, too, if it had an edge, because the crazy can garrote themselves with a length of breath, their thoughts are open razors, their eyes go off like guns), though there was naturally no danger in these baubles to herself, for my mother was living the long death, her whole life passing before her as

she went, the way those who drown themselves are said to have theirs pass. . . a consequence, yes. . . her own ocean like a message in a bottle, so that she sank slowly somewhere as a stone sill sinks beneath the shoes of pilgrims and tourists, not like Plath with pills, or Crane or Woolf with water, Plath again by gas, or Berryman from a bridge, but, I now believe, in the best way possible, because, because the long death is much more painful and punishing than even disembowelment or bleach, and it inflicts your dying on those you are blaming for it better than burning or blowing up—during an exquisitely extended stretch—since the same substance which both poisons you, preserves, you both have and eat, enjoy and suffer your revenges together, as well as the illusion that you can always change your mind. ["The Doomed," pp. 3–4; Gass's ellipses]

"They," that mass of distant crazies and their keepers, become "her" and "my," a single couple and a singularly pained association, and ultimately "you"—that paradoxical pronoun of the generalized individual, in whose informal embrace we are all—mother, son, keepers, crazies, writers, readers too—enclosed.

Part of the power of "The Doomed in Their Sinking" is no doubt due to the daring introduction of intimate recollections in such a neutral setting, the tension between these sudden jagged edges of memory amid lists of public figures and the temperate ratiocination of a philosophical puzzle. Yet the setting does have its own value too; it transmutes and extends the significance of the confession. Suicides are particular persons—or rather, particular acts performed by particular persons—but the problem of suicide is general, one from which none of us is entirely exempt. Hence, as Gass's analysis of the problem proceeds, the seeming uniformity of suicide (and with it, the remoteness, the absolute difference between suicides and other people) begins to fray, unwinding into a multitude of separate considerations.

Definitions of suicide, like definitions of adultery, are invariably normative, and frequently do little more than reflect the shallowest social attitudes, embody the most parochial perspectives. Above all, these attitudes are for the most part deeply irrational. Failures may be executed, for example, while the corpses of successes are assaulted. Studies of suicide, including those of Alvarez and Choron, are soon elaborately confused about desire, intention, deed, and consequence, ownership and responsibility (whether we belong to ourselves, society, or God); neglect the difference between act and action, refuse to decide whether to include deaths of soul (Rimbaud?) as well as deaths of body, since holy living may indeed by holy dying, so that physical and metaphysical murders became hopelessly intertwined. . . .

If we are to call suicide every self-taken way out of the world, then even the Platonic pursuit of knowledge, involving as it does the separation of reason from passion and appetite is suicidal. . . [Gass's elipsis] as are, of course, the search for ecstatic states, and longings for mystical union. ["The Doomed," pp. 7–8]

The quest of what counts as a suicide, what the true criteria are, brings in its wake an altered attitude. We are less quickly awed or horrified as we begin to see just how unclear the outlines are and how many of the elements of which the act is presumably compounded we ourselves partake of:

> ...the same act can signify anything you like, depending on the system—even the mood or line of the eye—which gives it meaning: I cock my head one way and it appears to me that my mother was murdered; I cock it another and she seems a specially vindictive suicide; while if I face firmly forward as one in military ranks she seems to have been overcome by a rather complex illness, a chronic and progressively worsening disease. Simply examining "suicides" is like trying to establish a science of—let's say—*sallescape*, which we can imagine contains the whys and wherefores of room-leaving. The word confers a fictitious unity upon a rabble of factors, and the ironic thing about suicide itself, intrinsically considered (and what my little litanies have been designed to demonstrate), is that it is a wholly empty act. . . .
>
> ...The conditions surrounding Chatterton's suicide, for example, are certainly interesting...but which ones really count, and which ones don't, and how do they count if they do, and if they do by how much? Vivid details, picturesque circumstances...[Gass's ellipsis] my mother's cop-terlike bathroom posture, her gap-pinned robe, miscolored toes...[Gass's ellipsis] well, their relevance isn't clear. Perhaps they have mainly a vaude-ville function—to enliven without enlightening. Throughout, my mention of my mother merely mimics the problem. [Pp. 11, 13]

"Merely mimics" is too strong: suggestively configures, obscurely parallels, becomes the problem itself in an emblematic form, are better. And here the trick is turned, for what had seemed subordinate and by-the-way about the remembered mother has in the course of the essay become central and essential (one of Gass's favorite literary effects, you may recall). She stands now at the heart of the dilemma, haunting and intransigent, a figure with which we must come to terms if we are to claim that we understand anything about suicide at all. The general categories—desire, intention, consequence, and the rest—ultimately minister to the mother's particularity, refine and distinguish her from all the other suicides who she is not:

> Though Hart shed his bathrobe frugally before he jumped, my mother, also saving, would have worn hers like the medal on a hussar straight through living room and loony bin, every nursing home and needle house we put her in. . . .
>
> ...Still, she went in her own way—the way, for instance, her robe was fastened.
>
> Socrates acquiesced in his own execution, others demand theirs. The Kamikaze pilot intends his death, but does not desire it. Malcolm Lowry, who choked on his vomit, evidently desired his, but did not intend it.

Soldiers charging the guns at Verdun neither wished for death nor were bent on it, though death was what they expected. My mother accepted. [Pp. 3, 5]

How much more distinctly this figure emerges, as a microcosm and a member of a set, than as a character in Gass's novel:

Come to the head of the stairs, do. . . [Gass's ellipsis] and count all the prints on the banister where desperate hands have seized it, or see the time my mother fell on her water-laden rump going to answer the door, in a nervous hurry because she believed it might be the bread man with her booze; . . . yes, I can still sometimes discover the remains of especially bitter outbursts like the dents of kicks, dislikes which took their owners by surprise, sour and sudden as a belch may be, inspired blurts you would have to call them, since they relied for the effect upon a freshness of realization, an orgasmic intensity which is quite foreign to the more ornate, malicious, and reflective styles that have, for the most part, covered over and replaced them; . . . these thoughtless rejoinders were actually the origin and often the continuing inspiration of the cruelest and most artful gestures our civilization has so far contrived . . . the lessons that, these days, only life in the family can fully provide.[37]

Here she disappears into a general catalog of harms remembered, injuries retained long after the injured parties have themselves disappeared. "The Tunnel" begins with individuals who gradually fuse into a general image of decay and cruelty, a visionary fascism in which each instance is interchangeable with any other—"I've been in bedrooms bad as Belsen." The essay, on the other hand, uses its general parameters to frame and clarify a single instance, and in the process to illustrate how coarse are these parameters and how evanescent the meanings that we would feign assign.

The world of the suicidal is, in a certain sense (for all its familiar elements: pain, grief, confusion, failure, loss. . .), [Gass's ellipsis] a private and impenetrable one, hence the frustration of those who are trying to help, and whose offers to do so, as raps on the glass disturb fish, often simply insult the suicide immersed in his situation. . . .
Writing. Not writing. Twin terrors. Putting one's mother into words. . . [Gass's ellipsis] It may have been easier to put her in her grave. ["The Doomed," pp. 13–14, 15]

Granted, there are certain vague expectations about what belongs in a book review or a philosophical inquiry, or at least about what does *not* belong there—the latter being Gass's special province. Yet lines of thought are, on the whole, less well defined than plot lines, and the ways of constructing a concept, exploring its consequences, demonstrating its soundness and functional appeal, are far from codified. Thus, the organization of Gass's theoretical prose has a diversity and flexibility and a far happier meeting of verbal and conceptual energy than his narratives and antinarratives afford. The theoretical writing flies from mode to mode as it becomes more literary, abandoning the literal-minded call to action that characterized the earlier essays (and justified the fact that they *were* only essays). It seems deliberately to adopt antic shapes, the better to display its incredible surplus of invention. One essay poses as a series of photographs, another as a concert, another is a geography, still others are playlets, memoirs, case studies. None of these forms is quite literal, although all are serious. They give Gass the advantage of a structure he can dispense with at any moment should it prove too constricting or too unilluminating. What we might experience in fiction as digression or delay becomes the natural rhythm and inherently variable trajectory of speculation itself: the necessary pause for reassessment, the impatient exchange of one conceptual instrument for another whenever an impasse is reached or an unforeseen consequence arises. The very frivolity of these forms is charged with meaning, their vulnerability to rupture and decay a therapeutic ploy—"We confine ourselves to too few models, and sometimes live in them as if they were, themselves, the world: ("Trouts," p. 274). Amid these giddy and transparent shapes, we at least know that we cannot live for long.

Fragmentation is everywhere a part of Gass's prose, but in his theoretical essays the fragments become functional. His is really (a point to which I shall return) an art of sentences—microcosmic and motionless worlds that have their own rhythmic coherence and syntactic anatomy. "...we can regard the sentences of fiction as separate acts of creation. They are the most elementary instances of what the author has constructed" and "The sentence confers reality upon certain relations, but it also controls our estimation, apprehension, and response to them ("Philosophy," pp. 12–14). Theoretical discourse allows these sentences to become the primary units of discourse, to accumulate and converge upon a single subject from disparate angles of their own, sometimes breeding, as they do in "The Ontology of the Sentence," an entire sentence set by a playful turn of parthogenesis:

2.   He held out his hand. It was plump, pale, stubby, damp.
2.1   It was a seamed and broken, dirty hand. He held it out.
2.2   He thrust out a threatening, greedy, malicious hand. I backed away.
2.3   Nails? bitten. Palm? small. Lifeline? early broken. Skin? dry and freckled. Cuticles? unkept. Condition? loose or limp. Condition? soft. Color? pale. Condition? calm. [Pp. 328–29]

These sentences do more, of course, than exemplify a point; intricate, evocative, each is stunningly complete in its own incompletion. Moreover, when Gass thus reduplicates himself—even at one point allowing a sentence to cite itself—("In the face of this fickleness [12]— of which [13] I have provided but a sliver-sized sample—what in the name of grammar [14] does the word '*of*' do?"—"Ontology," pp. 320–21)—the pretense of a single speaker is comically undone. And in the laughter there also disappears the old fear that to write without a single controlling voice will mean the end of rhythm and modulation, a leveling of language. This fear seems to be the governing assumption of Gass's fiction, confining it to lyric monologues that are actually far more unrelieved than the stratified levels of competing sound he achieves in his essays.

Even more astounding is the triumph over the most debilitating assumption of all—that literature must consist of "words put together with no intention of stating, hoping, praying, or persuading" ("Carrots," p. 300)—and its corollary: that language used to state, hope, pray, or persuade must therefore be devoid of all aesthetic value. It may well be true that some literary texts contain no statements (which does not mean that they may not indirectly persuade us that something is or ought to be the case). And it may even be the case that it is best to read certain literary texts wholly as verbal objects, words put together into terminal patterns from which no further inferences follow. But clearly this does not apply to every text we designate as literature, and to ignore or disclaim these others is to erect the kind of normative definition that Gass specifically assails in his study of the logical grammar of *suicide*. Weaker yet is the corollary assumption that utilitarian prose must be strictly and solely that. Nuance and elegance may be irrelevant to achieving reference or logical commentary, but they are not excluded by them. Formal values contribute mightily to persuasion and to the ceremonial dignity of prayer, and theory itself, as I have tried to demonstrate elsewhere, has a large aesthetic component. Gass rarely acknowledges that a concern for truth might coexist with an appreciation of beauty, yet his own theoretical essays more and more exhibit the union of these impulses, even their mutual support—by keeping the fabricated quality of his own analogies and arguments constantly before us, lest in the absence of sufficient literariness we become entrapped in "too few models." At the very moment these essays advance the premise that literature is composed solely for the sake of contemplation and must never serve as a grounds for action, they are themselves designed to guide our action as readers—and to do so with an exuberance, an intricacy and grace, that are very much worthy of our contemplation.

These scattered reflections can be brought into focus through a reading of *On Being Blue*, Gass's most ambitious and most thoroughly ambiguated piece of theoretical literature. It is in many ways the companion piece, the inverse and more successful double, of *Willie Master's Lonesome Wife*. Both are discourses on language (although *Blue* contains much else besides): an inquiry into its nature, its relationship to human consciousness, to memory and imagination—"the imaginative use of language" being, for Gass, the definition of literature. There are even more subtle levels of comparison, since both works use sexuality and eroticism as the centerpiece for an attack on imaginative impoverishment and the crude or voyeuristic lust for copies—as opposed to constructions beloved for their own sake. In *Willie Master's* this conceit is embodied in the protagonist, Babs, her unsatisfying sexual encounter, her memories of her days as a burlesque queen, the postcoital tristesse in which she "moons" (complete with circlets dotting the page) for the love that would have fulfilled her. In *On Being Blue*, the relationship between sexuality and language is far more dispersed and multiply determined. Working within a single controlling analogy, the meta-fiction imposes an artificial uniformity on the subject of investigation that the philosophical inquiry dispels. Sex enters language (and thence literature) not only through the direct depiction of sexual material, but also through the use of sexual words, and through more or less overt association of displacements— from the steamy sexual scenes. . . to sheets and pillowcases. It may also appear via even less direct routes such as the potent mental sets that we as readers bring to bear on language, interests that may spring from our private obsessions or public occasions or traditions essential to every art. But finally:

> The true sexuality in literature—sex as a positive aesthetic quality— lies not in any scene or subject, nor in the mere appearance of a vulgar word, not in the thick smear of a blue spot, but in the consequences on the page of love well made—made to the medium which is the writer's own, for he—for she—has only these little shapes and sounds to work with, the same saliva surrounds them all, every word is equally a squiggle or a noise, an abstract designation (the class of cocks, for instance, or the sub-class of father-defilers), and a crowd of meanings as randomly connected by time and use as a child connects his tinker-toys. On this basis, not a single thing will distinguish "fuck" from "fraise du bois"; "blue" and "triangle" are equally abstract; and what counts is not what lascivious sights your loins can tie to your thoughts like Lucky is to Pozzo, but love lavished on speech of any kind, regardless of content and intention. [*Blue*, p. 43]

This passage is almost sufficient in itself to explain the shortcomings of *Willie Master's*, the awkward and distracting concretization of some-thing intrinsically abstract, the weird individuation of an inherent gen-erality, and the resulting weary seesaw of descriptions advanced and then retracted. As a character, Babs cannot but be a tease, pretending to be what she is not. But *Blue* makes no such pretense: The center of the inquiry is a term and a conception through and through. It therefore makes a more fitting model—or representative sample—of the nature and capacities of language.

On Being Blue is therefore an inquiry into the "being" of "blue"—as word, condition, color, and act. The text begins in medias res, with a sudden and unexplained immersion into a series of blues: "Blue pencils, blue noses, blue movies, laws, blue legs and stockings. . ." (p. 3)—designa-tions that are both literal and figurative, original and derived, a welter of the unconnected and the unlike that have in common only a single word. Throughout the book these "blue runs" will recur, both as a musical refrain that separates the discourse into conceptual stanzas, and as a reiteration of the theme that language is a crowd of meanings randomly connected. Yet the very randomness stimulates our intellectual need to reduce the sounds of clash and contradiction by finding or inventing some property that all these uses of the same word share.[38] It is, in fact, the burden of *On Being Blue*—the subject that the book constructs, if not the one it takes as its official point of departure—to demonstrate just how this unification may be achieved without falling for the ancient Platonic fallacy of a single word, a single thought, a single thing. Thus in the "being" of blue—a being that gradually assumes its shape throughout the course of the text, a product equally of old implications and freshly minted associations—we catch sight of the nature of linguistic constructs and of the work of literary imagination as it attempts to solve the problem of the one and the many without the excesses of idealism, reductionism, and conflation that most of the traditional solutions seem to involve.

Even aside from its conceptual protagonist, however, *On Being Blue* remains an immensely impressive compendium of language, an exercise of all its moods and registers and timbres, scaling from profanity to professional jargons, and incorporating odd bits of information of all kinds (as language does itself) along the way.

> Blue laws took their hue from the paper they were printed on. Blue noses were named for a potato. E. Haldeman-Julius' little library, where I first read Ellen Key's *Evolution of Love*, vainly hoping for a cock stand, had such covers. In the same series, which sold for a dime in those days, were the love letters of that Portuguese nun, Mariana Alcoforado, an overwrought and burdensome lady, certainly, whose existence I callously forgot until I read of her again in Rilke. [P. 4]

Decidedly this world will not be rolled into a ball, and the very erratic movements of this prose, its failure to compose itself into a coherent plot or even a predictable argument, its readiness to pursue apparently irrelevant links and private associations, is in part the point— to resist those "fair and squarely ordered thought machine[s]" that impose a false unity on language and consciousness.

> Never mind degrees, deep differences, contrasting sizes. The same blue sock fits every leg. . . . [love] is one of the passions of the mind. Furthermore, if among a perfect mélange of meanings there is one which has a more immediate appeal, as among the contents of a pocket one item is a peppermint, it will assume a center like the sum and require all others take their docile turn to go around.
> This thought is itself a center. I shall not return to it. [P. 8]

The word *blue* has many applications and the "blue words" of sex many different functions, depending on whether they are "copied, constructed, or created; they are uttered, mentioned, or used; each says, means, implies, reveals, connects; each titillates, invites, conceals, suggests; and each is eventually either consumed or conserved" (p. 56). And blue itself, the color, has many different shades. This variegation and instability makes *blue* an ideal exemplum of the promiscuity of language and a perfect analogue for the many states of mind and shades of feeling that language, used mechanically rather than imaginatively, actually suppresses and obscures.

Thus, amid apparent madness, there is method, and even the chaotic accumulative energy of the text is carefully channeled and punctuated. The inquiry is divided into four distinct chapters, and each chapter is in turn divided into smaller segments—set off from each other by a series of asterisks—each of which encloses a more or less coherent meditation. Indeed, as the text progresses, it begins to clarify and organize itself; identifiable issues emerge from its crowded and deliberately obscure opening pages like musical motifs emerging from an overture in which they were announced but not yet recognized. This introduction seems to be designed to provoke confusion, to challenge our facile clarity about what being blue is, and to wean us from our habitually narrow associations with the word, the better to construct a new associative network of its own. To throw up such an initial barrier is quite in keeping with Gass's professed anxiety that words come to literature contaminated by previous use, but in *On Being Blue* there is a more inquisitive and amused attitude toward such contamination and a greater curiosity about how language as a whole functions.

Chapter one is partly an exhibition of the arts of definition, moving rapidly through all the recognized ways we have for delimiting the meaning of a word: by synonym and antonym, by etymology, by stating its intention and extension or simply pointing to things to which the word applies, by compiling sample citations, and by magisterial stipulations. None of these definitions is final, all are demonstrably futile as the text continuously outflanks them, pouring forth new instances of blue that have escaped them. Ultimately, it is the pattern of usage embodied by the prose itself that establishes the appropriate range and value of the term. The chapter ends with an announced agenda that, omitting much that is to follow, is still accurate enough to guide us on our way. By now, from the welter of all possible blues, there has emerged a smaller set of primary associations—blue as a color or perceptual quality; blue as a condition of emptiness, absence, or transcendence (which the color is often used to represent) and the emotion associated with such absence, a "being without being" that is called in slang the blues; and finally, the most accidental association of them all and the least dependent on perception, the blue of censored material, pornography, blue movies, et al., that will (perversely) figure as the essay's central subject.

The fact that these issues initially have so little in common is an important part of the essay's demonstration. Whatever accidents originally determined the application of the same word to such diverse matters, it is now the word itself—and no shared essence common to the things it names—that unifies them. Gass is more brutal even than his master Wittgenstein, who allowed at least a "family resemblance" between different applications of the same term. The extreme disjunction between Gass's blues enacts what he argues outright elsewhere, that separate uses of the same word "involve equivocation": "Children love both hot dogs and cats, but since you eat one and pet the other, children *must* love them differently. I love to murder and create. My two loves are only metaphorically the same" ("Ontology," p. 325).

On Being Blue is built on such equivocations and metaphorical extensions: The color is not inherently sad or sexy, and the route from blue to the blues and thence to eroticism is flagrantly circuitous. The word comes first, and most of the connections are established only later: The color of a book cover (chapter one) becomes the color of its erotic subject matter; then the failure of direct depictions of sex (chapter two) is explained by the consciousness—the "subjective content"—that they leave out, just as history of metaphysics (chapter three), in subordinating color—a mere quality—beneath more reliable substances and quantities shows a similar contempt for consciousness. Such metaphysical schemes introduce an unnecessary antagonism between the abstract and the concrete, sensation and reason that turn out (in chapter three) to be analogous to the traditional false dichotomy between form and content, verbal texture and expository structure, which has for so long obscured the fact that there is no true eroticism without artful writing. For real eroticism, love must be so lavished on language that (chapter four) it can "structure the consciousness of the reader":

> . . . to use one wonder to speak of another, until in the place of the voyeur who reads we have fashioned the reader who sings; . . . the secret lies in seeing sentences as containers of consciousness, as constructions whose purpose it is to create conceptual perceptions—blue in every area and range: emotion moving through the space of the imagination, the mind at gleeful hop and scotch, qualities, through the arrangement of relations, which seem alive within the limits they pale and redden like spanked cheeks, and thus the bodies, objects, happenings, they essentially define. [Pp. 86–87]

So moves the (non)argument of the text—a slippery one, to be sure. Yet there is intellectual danger only if we somehow strive to understand this *blue* as literally the same in every case, fail to see the slippages and punning leaps of which it is composed, or take what the text puts forwards as proportional analogies as if they were substantial identities. By making the disjunctions and figurative reintegrations so overt—making the essay, in a word, so "literary"—this danger is lessened and, in addition, a more accurate record of the nature and operation of language is achieved as well.

Such antic associations also make it impossible to visualize "blue," to mistake it for an object of perception or to attribute the wrong mode of existence to it. "Blue as you enter it disappears," the text warns, "The country of the blue is clear" (p. 86). It is a conceptual construct par excellence, residing neither in the signifier itself—the physical token on the page—nor in the reader's or writer's mind, but only in their inter-action. It is something actuated by the meeting of mind (with its memories and knowledge of the language system) and word. For Gass, therefore, meaning is not a separate "thing," existing on its own, which we then arbitrarily attach to words: "From the first 'In the beginning. . .' words have been thought to have magical properties. . . . What was naive in the magician was the belief that things have names at all, but equally naive are the learned and reasonable who reject any connection beyond the simply functional between *blue* and blue. . . . Words are properties of thoughts, and thoughts cannot be thought without them" (p. 21; first ellipsis is Gass's). And neither, by the same token, are words themselves, the inky objects, sufficient on their own; they have being only when they act as "containers of consciousness," constructions capable of creating "con-ceptual perceptions." Consciousness is, then, "the privacy which a book makes public" (p. 85)—often enough a manufactured privacy, since the simple truth would be too boring. Yet though it lies so easily, language is also our only real entrance to the privacy of consciousness, all other behavioral signs being too impoverished and too vague or mute to render it.

The intertwining and interdefinition of conception, consciousness, and language is the note on which *On Being Blue* concludes. It is, however, an ambivalent and ambiguous conclusion. We have, by the final pages, entered at last into what is called "the country of the blue" (perhaps recalling, as we do so, an earlier bawdy pun to the effect that "'cunt' is concealed by a tree"—p. 26). This country is a conceptual enclosure wrought by art and wrung from words. But will we, as Henry James's protagonist Ralph Limbert (from whose tale the phrase "the country of the blue" is taken), be left to "stay there with good conscience and a great idea"? Will we ever, in a word, find our way out again? Despite occasional thrusts at the naiveté of idealism, despite the promise that "every loving act of definition reverses the retreat of attention to the word and returns it to the world" (p. 87), the return to the world seems here to go no further than the reader's consciousness.[39] ". . . will *we* enter? only if his language enters us the way God's did Adam at whose bare word, as Sir Thomas Browne reminds us, 'were the rest of the creatures made.' Then the language fills the mouth as it was meant to. We feel the need to speak it. Accepting the words as our own, speaking the words as our own, we believe at last in their denotations" (p. 88).

This points, not out, but further in, explaining how verbal constructs can achieve a *seeming* denotation, a *seeming* world. (There are even serious questions about whether one should say that such abstract constructions "denote" at all and thus whether this passage represents a return to the retrograde position that language consists only of names and pseudonames.) At the end of the book, literature stands once again as a parallel creation, an addition to the world perhaps, but even more strongly an alternative to it. This is what the final paragraphs—which suddenly alter their address from readers to potential writers—make clear, as clear as blue.

> So to the wretched writer I should like to say that there's one body only whose request for your caresses is not vulgar, is not unchaste, untoward, or impolite: the body of your work itself, for you must remember that your attentions will not merely celebrate a beauty but create one; . . . you should therefore give up the blue things of this world in favor of the words which say them: blue pencils, blue noses, blue movies, laws, blue legs and stockings . . . while there is time and you are able, because when blue has left the edges of its objects as if the world were bleached of it, when the wide blue eye has shut down for the season, when there's nothing left but language . . . shape pebbles into syllables and make stones sound; thus cautioned and encouraged, commanded, warned, persist. . . . [Pp. 89–91]

Doubtless this peroration is more than half apostrophe, and does more itself to "make stones sound" than to lay anyone under an obligation. Yet it retains just enough of the force of a directive to undermine its own position. For amid the artful return of the refrain ("blue pencils, blue noses") and the resurgence of a seemingly casual allusion to Molloy's sucking stones (first made in chapter one), there is still the phantom desire that *this* piece of literature, at least, shall "make something happen." All the blandishments of language are exercised to assure the future of language itself: "thus cautioned and encouraged, persist!"

On Being Blue advances the premise that the "being" of language is equivalent to the ghostly things that language constructs; the subjects, issues, and ideas of philosophical inquiry, the characters, scenes, acts and events of traditional fiction, are like the shapes we see on a canvas—the product of pigments artfully arranged.

> . . . shape is the distance color goes securely, . . .
> . . . every color is a completed presence in the world, a recognizable being apart from any object, while a few odd lines (since a line is only an artificial edge), a few odd lines are: nothing—thin strings of hue. [Pp. 73–74]

The analogy is unassailable insofar as it asserts that verbal texture and discursive structure are *physically* inseparable, that our acquaintance with a character or a concept can only come through our reading of individual words and sentences. This is just as true (although Gass never mentions it) of referential discourse, where the choice of words filters, organizes, and interprets the world beyond the page. In the latter case, of course, we have additional ways of getting at the world within the word; we have perceptual and tactile knowledge that is not normally available to us when we are reading fiction. Moreover, given the conventions of literary discourse, we are usually constrained from pitting one writer's formulation against another's, weighing Dickens's cityscapes against Baudelaire's as we might choose between two alternative philosophical renderings of the nature of the Good. This is why we are unusually dependent on the language of a literary text. But though plots, characters, and the rest are *made up of* sentences and paragraphs, they are not *identical to* them. The syntactic structure, phonic texture, and expository pace of any piece of discourse are logically distinct from the propositions it expresses, the narrative it tells, the arguments it makes. And, in fact, Gass wavers over this point. At times he seems to treat a text as only and wholly verbal texture; at other times he says that each text projects "its entire structure into an imaginary world." ("Ontology," p. 337). But occasionally he acknowledges that both possibilities coexist simultaneously:

> . . . to the extent a writer achieves his effects through the invention and manipulation of fictional things and people (a skill which is not a linguistic one), these effects can be suggested in another tongue or even in another medium. . . .
>
> . . . Philosophers—and others momentarily like them—are combining their concepts in amusing, instructive, or dazzling ways, and to the degree these concepts can free themselves of the language in which they were originally expressed, they can travel without too much wear and tear. Plato was an artist of ideas, as Valéry suggests all philosophers should be, and that the body is a prison for the soul is one piece of philosophical poetry with which you and I can fairly easily acquaint ourselves without knowing much Greek.[40]

One of the puzzlements—and entertainments—of reading Gass's essays is precisely this discrepancy between verbal texture and discursive structure. On one side, there is his power as an inventor and manipulator of words, and on the other, the range and durability and novelty of the ideas he constructs. In most cases, his essays seem less interested in argument and conceptual structure for the length of an entire text, while arguments fade and concepts change—and even occasionally sacrifice themselves for the sake of a more polished period. Gass's models, categories, and claims seem to function (as he says of drunkenness in Lowry's novel) largely as devices to "free the language," allowing different kinds of verbal performance—urgency for ethics, quandary for metaphysics.

Conceptual structures seem to vanish when their discursive excitement has been exhausted.

It is perhaps for this reason that Gass writes so often and so well as a reviewer of other texts, using their logic to organize his own response. This may explain as well why his counterarguments and critiques seem so much more coherent and compelling than his own abrupt and erratically defended proposals. *Blue* is therefore an unusual and happy stroke in Gass's oeuvre: a construct wherein the pursuit of shifting verbal effects manages at the same time to be the pursuit of a conceptual issue, and a text in which the exhibition of "linguistic skills" is also an illustration of a subsuming idea, the nature of language itself. And yet in all his essays, it is not a matter of empty rhetoric supplanting or subordinating logic; the writing seems, if anything, "wiser" than the propositions it conveys, acting out assumptions that are more provocative and doubts that are more searching than any it officially endorses.

Another reason for his chariness in advancing new ideas is the stringent view of truth that he adopts, the profound distinction he maintains between legitimate and illegitimate grounds for belief. "I think one can reasonably doubt the scientific status of a theory it feels too good to believe," he at one point remarks, only half in jest.[41] He has written extensively and passionately about the danger of mixing theoretical and literary values, in full sympathy with Valéry's bitter objection to "this kind of poetic play with ideas in Pascal and in other philosophers because he suspected them, lest reason fail, of using the methods of poetry, like the welcome lies of politicians, to persuade, and in this way debasing both truth and beauty" ("Valéry," p. 170). And he chastises Sartre for forgetting that: ". . . what is exactly central to philosophy is the effort to propose and argue views whose validity will transcend their occasions, and not to manufacture notions which, when squeezed, will simply squirt out causes like a sponge. If that effort cannot succeed (as we know in many cases it does not) then philosophy becomes a form of conceptual fiction, and new determinants of quality, equally harsh and public, must be employed."[42]

Again and again, Gass warns that metaphors with a certain prima facie appeal should be resisted until their root assumptions and ultimate implications have been tested. "Suppose I were to say, of a married couple, that in their life together the wife played left tackle. Have I made a good model? Where are the other twenty players? who are the coaches, trainers, where are the stands?" ("Trouts," p. 272). Untested metaphors that are "seriously meant and socially applied" can lead those who use them unknowingly to the point of talking "things into being only what [they] want to say about them" and "when we label ourselves, we try to live up or down to our titles" ("Trouts," pp. 273, 274).

The license that poetry ostensibly offers is freedom from all such questions, tests, and dismissals, but it is a freedom won by making poetic figures inapplicable to anything outside the poem itself. Thus, the terror of hybrid works is that poetic license could merge with serious application, in a sort of murderous play in which we end by committing ourselves literally to what we began by apprehending figuratively. But this dilemma is to some extent the product of the assumptions underlying it. It arises because Gass separates the being and the uses of literature too absolutely from those of any other kind of discourse; his dichotomy admits no degree of challenge or caution with respect to literature and refuses to allow utilitarian prose to be anything but wholly and immediately useful. Thus, by engaging in theory as a form of art, Gass has entered into a hitherto flatly excluded middle, a literature with serious applications, a poetry with consequences. How and why he achieves this merger will be the burden of the remainder of this section.

To begin with, there was always some ambivalence about the role of theory in Gass's work. In a very early essay, "The Case of the Obliging Stranger" (apparently under the influence of Wittgenstein's attack on artificially induced philosophical dilemmas), he states:

> For if someone asks me, now I am repentant, why I regard my act of baking the obliging stranger as wrong, what can I do but point again to the circumstances comprising the act? "Well, I put this fellow in an oven, you see. The oven was on, don't you know." And if my questioner persists, saying, "Of course, I know all about *that*; but what I want to know is, why is *that* wrong?" I should recognize there is no use in replying that it is wrong because of the kind of act it is, a wrong one, for my questioner is clearly suffering from a sort of *folie de doute morale* which forbids him to accept my final answer this early in the game, although he will have to accept precisely the same kind of answer at some time or other.
>
> Presumably there is some advantage in postponing the stop, and this advantage lies in the explanatory power of the high-level answer. It cannot be that my baking the stranger is wrong for no reason at all. It would then be inexplicable. I do not think this is so, however. It is not inexplicable; it is transparent. Furthermore, the feeling of elucidation, of greater insight or knowledge, is a feeling only. It results, I suspect, from the satisfaction one takes in having an open mind. The explanatory factor is always more inscrutable than the event it explains. The same questions can be asked of it as were asked of the original occasion.[43]

Still, as his attack on Sartre makes clear, neither is Gass entirely comfortable with "views whose validity will [not] transcend their occasions." He is quick to point out, in his review of books on suicide, that the lack of a "ruling principle" or of any effort to "rigorously differentiate sorts, define terms, regulate interpretations" reduces those accounts "to sensitively told and frequently moving *stories*" ("The Doomed," pp. 12–13). If Gass sometimes feels that theoretical explanations are artificial and irrelevant to the transparency of individual cases, he also acknowledges that choosing and weighing those cases rightly will still require some principles for distinguishing like from unlike and assigning them to the appropriate categories. "Ordinary language" can bewitch us with false classifications and misleading or irrelevant associations as easily as can the most arcane theoretical systems. And though he ends his essay on the obliging stranger with an aesthetic aside—"*King Lear*'s greatness is clear.... Nor can we get anywhere by deriving, from Shakespeare's practice, principles of judgment or rules of composition" ("Stranger," p. 241)—such confidence that artistic greatness is always clearly recognized and universally accepted (or indeed that art itself is an uncontested category) is belied by every other essay that Gass has ever written.

Thus, there is a need for theory, but theory of a most particular kind: one that, while principled, will not erase the distinctiveness of individual cases and that, while clarifying and correcting common misconceptions, will not introduce factitious explanatory terms. Gass is, moreover, hesitant to grant "reality" to even the most widely accepted theoretical models, no matter how accurately they predict or how satisfactorily they illuminate a given phenomenon. His own position is that the most that models—and indeed, all ordering frameworks, from simple enumeration on up—can provide is a compelling and memorable arrangement of information that allows one to make calculations and inferences that one could not make before. The *result* of these calculations may be true, but the model itself is neither true nor false. "The model is not to be confused with the world of ordinary experience, and the connections it establishes, made possible entirely by the rules of representation the scientist adopts, are not connections in any sense inherent in things. The model can be used to make predictions which mere observation is helpless to do, and in that manner its utility can be estimated" ("Toenail," p. 65). Similarly, he argues for an absolute distinction between "regulative principles" (which stipulate the meaning of key theoretical terms and set out a priori rules for what shall count as an instance of that term) and empirically falsifiable hypotheses. He therefore leaps to the defense of Freud, whose regulative assumption that inertia and resistance are the primary forces of psychical life has been misread by those who "fail to understand its a priori postulational status . . . and approach it as if it were an empirical conclusion of some kind. That's a little like asking about the evidence for the rules of chess" ("Anatomy," p. 221n).

In light of such positions—the fear of misrepresentation and the skepticism of representation itself, the tendency to treat large parts of theories as incorrigible, a priori and wholly unreal—one can see how Gass might be driven toward an increasingly literary theory of literature. Greater figurativeness and more overt fictions appeal to him as a remedy for the problems of theorizing. The imaginary unities that literature is capable of creating—through puns and happy coincidences and manufactured thematic linkages—are less imperious than the rigid systems that scientific and philosophic reason are wont to impose. Diversity is better tolerated; typifications are more transient in literature. And the more patent the playfulness, the less chance that readers will be tempted to confuse the framework with the subject matter, to believe that the properties of one are literally the properties of the other.

Indeed, responses to his theoretical writing indicate that Gass's playfulness may go too far for many readers. One of the commentators on "Carrots, Noses, Snow, Rose, Roses" found "the make-believe aspect of Gass's snowfigure distracting" and entirely discounted this portion of the essay.[44] Another critic, reviewing *The World within the Word*, found the new collection "teasing and brilliant," but less systematic than Gass's earlier work: "The essays on metaphor and on what he calls the ontology of the sentence do not so much deepen as exacerbate the issues pursued in earlier pieces, but they are rewarding as only the antics of a genius given to persistent verbal acrobatics can be."[45] There is, in fact, a greater archness and indirection in the later work, a desire to overturn accepted doctrines for the pleasure of the crash. Analogies are too fanciful and diction too fantastic to be taken quite seriously. Yet this is precisely the point of these essays—to make credulity more difficult and belief less literal-minded. The question remains, of course, whether Gass can still manage to retain the significance of his claims about literature, while erasing their literalness.

As the theory becomes more artful, the writing indulges more in naked juxtapositions and the ironic use of logical connectives, a tendency that reaches its extreme in *On Being Blue*:

> Loneliness, emptiness, worthlessness, grief. . .each is an absence in us. We have no pain, but we have lost all pleasure, and the lip that meets our lip is always one half of our own. Our state is exactly the name of precisely nothing, and our memories, with polite long faces, come to view us and to say to one another that we never looked better; that we seem at last at peace; that our passing was—well—sad—still—doubtless for the best (all this in a whisper lest the dead should hear). Disappointment, constant loss, despair. . .a taste, a soft quality in the air, a color, a flutter: permanent in their passage. We were not up to it. We missed it. We could not retain it. It will never be back. Joy-breaking gloom continues to hammer. So it's true: Being without Being is blue. [Pp. 11–12; Gass's ellipses]

Ellipses and digression proliferate in the later essays, as do breathless entrances and titles that seem teasingly and obliquely unhinged from their texts. Footnotes and careful documentation of sources begin to fade, and some references are even manufactured (à la Borges)—"Popeye drew his hand from his coat pocket." (*Blue*, p. 43) But even more important is the sudden density of self-reference, the newly "incestuous" (to use Gass's own word for it) nature of these texts. At the same time that the work of writing becomes more evident, it becomes more significant as well, a better demonstration (in its very excesses) of certain points about the nature of language and literary discourse that would be less convincing when put forward in the form of direct claims.

With this shift to a more playful style of writing comes a new ability to acknowledge how theory imposes its own interests on whatever other texts it incorporates. In an early essay like "In Terms of the Toenail," the central image of the toenail is pulled from Lowry's *Under the Volcano* with scant attention to how much has been left conveniently behind (particularly the tinge of Faustian self-aggrandizement that was associated with it in its original context). In later essays, however, one is almost assaulted with reminders of how much has been done to alter the citations that we actually see.

> From her window Katherine Mansfield sees a garden full of wall-flowers and blue enamel saucepans, and sets the observation down in a letter to Frieda Lawrence she'll never mail. Stephen Crane wrote and posted *The Blue Hotel*, Malcolm Cowley *Blue Juniata*, and Conrad Aiken *Blue Voyage*. Like rainwater and white chickens, KM exclaims:
>
>> Very beautiful, O God! is a blue tea-pot with two white cups attending; a red apple among oranges addeth fire to flame—in the white book-cases the books fly up and down in scales of colour, with pink and lilac notes recurring, until nothing remains but them, sounding over and over. [*Blue*, p. 6]

There is but one instance of blue in this color-drenched paragraph: the passage is presented to make Gass's point, not Mansfield's, but with no pretence of its being otherwise.

There are moments in *On Being Blue* when theories and philosophical commitments are apparently reduced to just so many different entertaining conceptual situations, positions to adopt and drop, savor and spit out for the sake of their intellectual variety alone: "Still, every one of these diligent gentlemen may be right. . .and why should we mind if every one of them is right simultaneously? Let all notes sound together and cacophony be king" (p. 70; Gass's ellipsis). Such a tendency to withhold criticism and indulge in speculation for the sake of design and novelty alone is among the predicted consequences of the merger of theory and literature. There is indeed more room for appreciating the formal beauties of different schools of thought—even obnoxious ones—when Gass writes in this hybrid mode. And there is also an implicit recognition of what he often fails to grant explicitly—the fact that literature is not the only realm where such formal values count; that scientific and philosophical systems often appeal to us for reasons above and beyond their documentation, validity, and utility; and that this appeal need not render them invalid, false, or useless. The more literary his theoretical pieces become, the more willing he is to probe the utility and truthfulness of poetic metaphors, even the most appealing ones, and to seek other grounds for choosing between models, even if they are all, ultimately, unreal.

The choice of conceptual design that prevails in these essays—and it is amazingly consistent, given their scattered and occasional nature—is perfectly congruent with the view of theory and its perils they otherwise expound. Despite (or perhaps because of) all the discussion he devotes to them, there are no real instances of theoretical models in Gass's own work. Analogies are plentiful, to be sure, but generally they are quirky, fragile, and easily dispersed. The most extended is the oft-cited snowman which (who?) figures forth the ontological transformation of language into poetry. But note that there is no actual claim that poetry *is* a snowman or even very like one. Quite the opposite; the absurdity of such a claim seems to be deliberate. It is introduced to keep the poles of the comparison from converging. The snowman merely illustrates the process of transformation and especially how the conventions of composition alter the function and value of the elements that enter into that composition. A snowman does resemble a poem to this extent, but even so, the essay does little to document the likeness, and becomes so caught up in elaborating the features of the snowman himself—his real hat and false nose, the structural significance of the dark buttons and dark eyes—that any thought of application must go rather by the board. We never learn, for instance, what element in a poem (if any) is comparable to that hat. The snowman functions less as a model than as a gloss on terms like *process, composition, function,* and *ontological value,* giving us a graphic sample of their application that is simpler and more colorful than a direct application to literature. We did not need the snowman or the bulk of his properties to arrive at these words, nor does our knowledge of him do much to extend our inferences about the nature of literature.

In contrast, the briefly sketched comparison Gass makes in earlier essays between metaphysical doctrines and sentence structures does function as a (truncated) model.

> . . .some sentences are crowded with nouns; some contain largely connectives. Some sentences are long and tightly wound; others are hard and blunt as a hammer. Some combine events of contrasting sizes, like a sneeze and the fall of Rome; others set dogs at bears, link the abstract and the concrete, quality and number, relation and property, act and thing. In some worlds the banjo and its music are two banjos, in others all the instruments dissolve into their music, that into a landscape or a climate, thus finally, through the weather, to an ear.
>
> The Humean sentence will reduce objects to their qualities, maintain an equality between them by using nonsubordinating conjunctions. . . . Henry James's sentences are continuous qualifications, nuance is the core and not the skin; and the average idealist, proceeding with a similar scrupulosity, treats his entire work as the progressive exploration and exposure of a single subject. ["Philosophy," pp. 14–15]

Here we come close to something that transforms our vision of the object of investigation, that does invite us to transfer the properties of one thing to another. Even more significant is the fact that Gass later reneges on this comparison: "May not grammar dictate metaphysics here: one of substances and their qualities? All are adjectives, and doesn't an adjective modify a noun? . . . If I understand my metaphysics, qualities don't modify substances. . . . No. Subjects are subjects, not substances" ("Ontology," p. 332). Such retractions and redefinitions are precisely what one expects from models, which must alter (as casual analogies need not) if they lead to incorrect inferences.

It is not surprising that models should be so few when the suspicion at their seductiveness runs so high. According to Gass, for our models to be anything more than arbitrary constructions that happen to facilitate correct predictions, we must be fully committed to every element in that construction: ". . . the whole net of relationships matters. But the moment the mind moves through the system establishing certain points of comparison and denying others, then the system is replaced by its interpretation" ("Toenail," p. 67). Very few scientific models, at least initially, are this systematic; in almost every case, there is some recognized area of "negative analogy" that must be discounted. "Waves" of electricity are not really wet. When Gass himself constructs a model—or, rather, a pseudomodel—the negative analogy balloons into something that is almost (as he puts it) "monstrous."

> Now imagine that Alice (the girl conceived by Carroll—minister, poet, and logician), having eaten what she's been told to and drunk according to instructions, is swelling as she tiptoes through her tunnel, and imagine in addition that there is a light like those which warn low planes of towers, chimneys, or intrusive steeples, attached to the top of her head. Can't we see her as an elongating wand whose end is then a point upon a curve? A most monstrous metaphor, yet inspired. Any curve, Descartes decided, could be considered to enclose a set of lines whose ends like trimmed logs lay against it. ["Trouts," p. 263]

Such hyperbole (so unlike Descartes's own simplicity) is meant to function therapeutically, to stand as a caveat against conflating the model and its subject matter. Yet it is curious that in all his talk about models and metaphors (which he, like his mentor, Max Black, treats as versions of each other), Gass should so consistently ignore the features that are most characteristic of his own practice as a writer. The kick of his own constructions is their incongruity, the bizarre and contradictory twists they take, the tricky irrelevancies they introduce and the gnomic paradoxes they pose.

> . . . our feelings have levels, and many are metapathetic. . . . this new mix is felt afresh as still another feeling which, when the complete self is in fine fettle, with incredible immediacy and ease, disposes qualities correctly over the embattled Europe of my experience much as we crayoned countries in sixth-grade History in order to learn who had won what in the first

World War.... We experience the world, balanced on our noses like the ball it is, turn securely through the thunder of our own applause. [*Blue*, p. 82]

Not the proximity but the distance between tenor and vehicle is prized—and the attendant shock and turmoil of disorientation this produces. Such wordplay also flies in the face of another of Gass's officially pronounced positions, that the best metaphors should be wholly reversible. "These comparisons are always unfairly one-sided.... One may decide that the nipple most nearly resembles a newly ripened raspberry,... but does one care to see his breakfast fruit as a sweetened milky bowl of snipped nips? no" (*Blue*, pp. 39–40). Note, though, that the grotesquery of this inversion is really what the commentary thrives on, the exuberance of the naughty boy in the guise of a philosopher's lament.

Interestingly, it is not metaphor but simile that is the predominant figure in Gass's theoretical writing; simile performs the work of serious instruction, while metaphors wax more and more fantastic. Since similies do not, like metaphors, assert an identity but only a similarity—my love is like a red, red rose, but is not the same thing as that rose—they are safer, saner creatures. They may be trusted to illuminate or illustrate without tempting us to make a category mistake. Even at the level of passing figures of speech, the horror of mistaken category assignments remains Gass's ruling impulse, his chief reason for theorizing. (Such moments of congruity between conceptual design and writing can be among the most compelling features of theoretical discourse, and they are especially telling when there is otherwise so much discord between what the theory claims and what it does.) In light of such a ruling impulse, it is not surprising that Gass should turn out to be a taxonomist and not a builder of models. In an interview, he even speaks of his theoretical activity as being "to build a good box" into which items may then be put.[46] What such a theory produces is not a redefinition of phenomena—which is the goal of models—but an accurate arrangement of them, honoring their own distinctive attributes and modes of being. Its excitement as a conceptual design comes from its coherence and promise of containment: "... one may contemplate the most purely abstract and most purely quantitative system for the values of the system's sake, and so far as this is done, and is the end of such pure systems, they, and the opposite pole of art, have the same appreciative aim, and are in value much akin; for creative thought and creative imagination are not so much stirred on by truth in any synthetic sense as by sublimity—a vision of absolute organization" ("Philosophy," p. 12).

Still, no ordering system is entirely pure or neutral; each arrangement is selective and brings its own criteria for what is essential or central and what is accidental or marginal to the phenomena it arranges.

...numbers are morally and metaphysically neutral. They are nothing but relations, and quite orderly relations, too, while words are deposits of meaning made almost glacially, over ages. If the systems, in mathematics, exist mainly, like glasses, to be filled, they are also clear as crystal, and are not expected to stain anyone's white radiance; while words, again, are already names for thoughts and things, acts and other energies which only passion has command of; they are not blank, Barkis-willing, jelly labels. ["Trouts," p. 275]

A classification system with four slots expects a world divided into fours; a system with four headings begins to color those divisions, to suggest what properties the members hold in common, what is crucial to them and makes them what they are, as opposed to all those merely contingent modifications, dispensible properties, and passing phases. Therefore Gass's essays usually exercise great care in establishing the array of categories under which phenomena will be subsumed, mindful that "we can put order anywhere we like. . . . Not every arrangement is equally effective. And we must keep in mind the relation of any order to the chosen good ("Trouts," p. 269). But even while acknowledging this, Gass still seems readier to treat such taxonomic orders as real—something he will not grant to models. Some orders are "right" and some are "wrong": ". . . it's like cataloguing books according to the color of their covers. . . , the color may be significant (the blue cover of *Ulysses* is), but it is scarcely a mode of classification which carves reality at the joints" ("The Doomed," p. 10).

Gass's taxonomies seem to be devised defensively, more to preserve distinctions between things in danger of being conflated than to accumulate a group of things that "belong" together. They tend, as a result, to careen wildly between brute dichotomies ("Means vs. Ends," "Literature vs. Life") and indefinitely extensible—perhaps infinite—enumerations, like the unending list of different kinds of blue. So pronounced is this passion for making distinctions that the only way to stop it, and arrive at some more manageable number, is by reaching for an analogy.

> It may be scribble, scribble, scribble, Mr. Gibbon, but scribbles differ, not only in their several aims, the nature and value of the object these activities make or their appropriate effects, but also in the character and quality of the mind and hand that makes them, and most importantly in the medium that hand shapes or mind employs. . . .
>
> The scribbles of the poet and the clerk. . . are opposed like people playing chess and checkers on the same board. ["Carrots," p. 284]

But what is most noteworthy is that these saving analogies, which reduce the threat of uncontrollable diversity, are usually invoked to protect the special status of literature.

As any reader of *On Being Blue* should be aware, members of the same taxonomic class rarely share a single essential property. Rather, they come together according to a subtler process of association: groupings based on similarities of structure, function, and behavior are preferred, but historical coincidence and even the manufactured connections of art will do, so long as they are recognized for what they are. There remains a trace of nervousness about which characteristics should be deemed "defining," since defining characteristics are simply the artifact of the classification being used.

> One might argue, of course, that a Styrofoam snowman is an imitation of a snowman the way the snowman is an imitation; but is a man with a wooden leg a man, and would we continue to say yes, if his eyes, nose, brain, and tongue were too, so long as he saw and smelled and spoke, even in wooden tone? and reasoned, and paid his bills, begot with a clothespin and died of gunshot wounds? One might as well deny that soybean steak is steak. But I shall leave such gentle questions to the metaphysicians, who in future may be formed of Styrofoam too, that splendid insulation against opposites; the wet and dry, the heat and cold, the love and strife of Reality. ["Carrots," p. 290]

This skittishness is not surprising given Gass's claim that art transforms ontology by making features "count" that never did before; these essays rely on such transformation for their own literary effects. Yet no matter how shocking or amusing, change in Gass's system can never be more than the rearrangement of old materials. The snowman is a case in point:

> Snow has been removed from snow and fastened to other snows so that the ordinary idle relation of flake to flake has been irremediably altered...
> ...changes of the kind we've been considering consist of the rearrangement of defining characteristics. [P. 290]

And as with his theory of art, so with his theoretical discourse, a discourse that adds nothing new to the world, posits no new forces or entities—no "ids" or "atoms" or "narremes." Gass invents no new theoretical terms, preferring to refine a commonplace word like *love*—or *blue* itself.

This metaphysical and terminological conservatism is consistent with the governing conceptual design, which is an effort to preserve categorical distinctions, to put everything in its proper place. But though conservative in this respect, the essays are almost perverse in others; they can effect a quiet revolution simply by putting the same old elements into a new arrangement. Thus, having demonstrated that philosophy and science concur that "qualities [like being blue], although slightly general in their character, were neither essential nor universal enough to figure importantly in knowledge" (p. 68), *On Being Blue* then inverts this judgment and insists that it is the qualities that are really primary. They are the basis of all knowledge, "without color we could not perceive, nor, I suspect, remember" (p. 68); "color is consciousness itself, color is feeling, and shape is the distance color goes securely" (p. 73). And the very sentences in which Gass's literary theory is propounded bear traces of this same concern for qualities, as opposed to entities and processes. Clauses that are ostensibly subordinate—used to modify the manner or condition of an act or event—all but overwhelm the main clauses. Similes characteristically bloom at the nether end of sentences, throwing issues open that had seemed firmly closed: "In the slag of time, numbers were forced to shed like snakes their dizzy altitudes and deeps, their splendid curvatures, their shapes which were like snowy fields dotted with stones" ("Carrots," p. 306). Indeed, another reason why similes figure so prominently in this prose is the ease with which they can be fitted onto the tail of a sentence, to render its qualities more memorable than its predications. The minute reinforcement of the writing lends plausibility to the theory's metaphysical assumptions and makes the inversion that *On Being Blue* suggests seem almost like the righting of things too long left upside down.

The mode of explanation that Gass's theory offers is one that terminates in assigning something to its appropriate category. We learn what literature is, but not how the category came to be or why this is the most desirable thing for it to be. Occasionally Gass will invoke love as the force that transforms ordinary language into literature, or will say that lovingly wrought language causes a change in the reader's consciousness that thoughtlessly constructed sentences cannot effect. But these claims about causes and consequences have little energy or substance, and are, moreover, largely tautological: Literature is said to be the result of love lavished on speech, but the only evidence of that love is the literature it makes. More serious are the efforts to introduce a form of teleological explanation, to distinguish literature from other discourse according to the ends it has (or fails to have) in view. Yet it is a most reduced teleology; there is no attempt to explain the emergence of literature itself or to say what further ends "literariness" might lead to. Apparent causal or teleological accounts turn out to be glosses on the nature of literature, further elucidations of what it is. Being is first, and all else is simply a consequence of that, following from it logically or conventionally or perhaps as a result of the ministrations of the theory itself.

In fact, the essays are torn between explanation and prescription— between the claims that literature really is this way and that it simply ought to be this way. Certainly Gass makes little effort to document his assertions about the nature of literature, nor would his fierce expostulations seem to have much point if the view of literature these essays advance were already universally accepted. Although Gass pronounces in the best of faith and the most orthodox manner that "our knowledge of a poem serves simply to explain why we were shaken. It will never, alone, do the shaking" ("Gertrude Stein," p. 107), it is a very curious sort of "cause" that shakes so selectively and requires the intervention of that rare reader who perceives. Actually, it is the insufficiency of most readings and the ease of category mistakes that makes this theory necessary; if these problems do not exist, then the theory has no force as a solution. There is something false about the bravado of: "Here is a summary of the kinds of changes which progressively take place as language is ontologically transformed in the direction of poetry. Everybody knows about them already. It is the consequences that are ignored or denied" ("Carrots," p. 297).

"Everybody knows" is a rhetorical ploy, allowing a set of premises to be introduced without defenses or documentation in the guise of a summary of accepted truths. The most tendentious claim, that literature *does* involve an ontological transformation of ordinary language, is simply presupposed, scaled off in an unassailable embedded sentence: "*as* language is ontologically transformed." In fact, the energy of the address is so extreme that several readers have complained that, far from taking his own positions to be common knowledge, Gass actually invents an enemy that does not exist, a reading public that holds impossibly naive beliefs about literature.[47]

Admittedly, it is sometimes difficult to understand where the air of daring-do and embattled discovery, which is everywhere in these essays, could be coming from. Most, if not all, of these opinions have enjoyed a long history among academic critics (despite the extraordinary ingenuity Gass employs in making the problems feel truly vexing once again, his witty reductio ad absurdums and startling creations ex nihilo—"Let's make a hand. That seems simple enough" ["Ontology," p. 317]—that renew the mystery of literary constructs and enflame our appetite for answers). But Gass does not begin from the beliefs of the academic establishment: The omitted references to New Criticism et al. are not casual or ungrateful exclusions. Rather, he establishes his own program as an antidote to the indifference to aesthetic questions that he takes to be endemic to professional philosophy, on the one hand, and to the mass of general readers, on the other.

> Philosphers distrust the subject. It has always been a stepchild, a kind of after-error, offspring of the menopause. Metaphysicians have swept it up with the rest of the dust, and nowhere can you find better examples of ignorance and arrogance cooperating against a subject than in many of their writings about art. . . .
> . . . It is not merely that the esthetician doubts the existence of clear cases; he doubts the existence of esthetics. The enjoyment of beauty simply as beauty is an intolerable frivolity. And in a world of function, purpose, and utility—this world of the drone, the queen bee, and the hive—so it is. So it is. ["Stranger," pp. 240–41]

The first group—professional philosophers—exerts the stronger force on the shape Gass's arguments take, but the second—the world of function, purpose, and utility—gives him his moments of messianic eloquence and despairing satire. (The final twist comes from the fact that he is probably read by neither camp, but by another group entirely, who must experience his ardor and invective as sheer verbal performance and his claims as comfortable reminders of doctrines they already hold dear.)

Yet Gass does model his literary theory on old and respected philosophic issues—questions about logical status, metaphysics, and ontology that have been more closely allied, historically, to scientific than to literary study. To inquire into the ontology of a literary construct or to explore the metaphysical preconceptions of a sentence by Beckett or Austen is therefore to valorize literature by operating on it with the same philosophical instruments normally reserved for more prestigious subjects. If Anglo-American philosophy has come to prize "ordinary language," Gass's response is therefore two-fold. First, he will show that one can as easily study the logical grammar of a category like literature as that of any other category. And second, he will subvert the assumption that literature is parasitic on the rules of ordinary language by asserting that it is, instead, a purification of that language and obedient to a set of independent principles of its own.

These are the interests that, officially, determine the domain within which Gass's literary theory will operate. Yet one must wonder occasionally if these particular interests were not seized upon for the sake of the domain, to constrain the issues and the information that would be relevant and keep attention riveted on form and medium alone. Very little is said, for example, about problems of epistemology, certainly a prestigious area of philosophical inquiry. Yet epistemology—unlike ontology or logic—brings in its wake all the trappings of social and psychological and historical context that Gass would clearly prefer to exclude from literary study. One commentator on "Carrots, Noses, Snow, Rose, Roses" complained that Gass treats even "the psychology of our apprehension of fictions in ontological terms."[48] (Insisting on the timeless purity of art can actually lead Gass into historical error, as when he condoles "Shakespeare, that fortunate man, who did not live to hear Hamlet say 'words, words, words,' with a Southern slur" ["Carrots," p. 290]—completely unaware that Elizabethan English has no closer modern analogue than that very Southern slur.)

Because it begins as a critique of rival notions about the nature and importance of literature, the theory's relationship to its "data"—to literature as a whole and to particular works of literature—is not always clear. For all its seeming generality, there are entire genres, whole centuries even, to which it plainly does not apply. Instead, the theory acts to select those authors who will be singled out for sympathetic attention (Gertrude Stein, Valéry, Joyce, and the early modernists at large) and determines how one can redefine the artistry of certain others who, like Malcolm Lowry, might appear at first blush too impure to rank among this pantheon. Yet the theory does not really provide criteria for evaluating individual works so much as it makes use of words (like *purify*) that carry a strong normative charge, which are then applied to any text that the theorist finds sufficiently "literary." No defense is offered for this highly evaluative language, nor can we deduce anything about the normative value of literature from the simple fact that it undergoes an "ontological transformation." As Gass himself remarks: ". . . ontological transformation is such an unassuming process it often passes unnoticed, as indeed does osmosis, and much of the time, digestion. Its action is often abrupt, simple, miraculous. A succulent center-cut porkchop, for instance, which has slid from its plate into a sack of garbage, becomes swill in a twinkling" ("Carrots," p. 285). Ontological transformation can despoil as easily as it can purify.

The elevated plane on which Gass situates his theory has no direct connection to practical criticism and offers little formal guidance for it. Most interpretations and assessments in these essays are therefore informal and ad hoc, albeit frequently dazzling. All that the theory itself provides is a certain number of proscribed responses and a general area in which one should seek the traces of ontological change. It is literature itself—as essence and defended possibility—that absorbs all the theory's energy, and that essence becomes somehow more precious, that possibility appears more fragile, for this very reason.

In theories where explanation and clarification verge ambiguously on recommendation, where what purports to account for literary activity turns out to prescribe it and sets out a program to which readers and writers must adhere, there is a tendency to be scant on justification. Since the prescriptive force is buried or ignored, there are no real arguments mounted to establish why literature *ought* to be written or read according to this program. Yet the hidden weight of prescription still prevents there being any mechanism for proving that literature is exactly what the theory claims it is. Gass relies on deduction rather than documentation to establish his claims, but his initial premises about the nature of literature either are advanced as givens, axioms that need no defense, or are defended by reducing some alternative premise to absurdity. The implicit reasoning seems to be that if another view of literature is demonstrably wrong, one's own views must then be right. The logic is unsound, of course, since to annihilate the opposition does nothing to prove one's own position unless it can also be shown that the two positions are mutually exclusive and, furthermore, that no other alternatives exist. Moreover, Gass seems to choose as his opponents only the most extreme and vitriolic antiformalists, lighting on Tolstoy in his most pugnacious and reductive moods in *What Is Art?*, or setting up a series of straw men—the "dun-

derheads" who mistake Balzac for *Business Week*, or the "oxen" who hold
worship services around their television sets. This makes refutation easy,
far too easy in fact—almost as if the goal were, not establishing a case, but
simply finding an occasion for parading the riches of one's scorn and
indulging the love of "ridicule as a weapon."[49] The finesse and fire of this
ridicule must, however, count as one of the chief ways in which the theory
becomes compelling even when it is not particularly convincing. Not only
does one hesitate to become the butt of such withering jokes, but the
elegance and the confidence of the jokester have their own cruel
fascination:

> The Frankfurt thinkers quite overpower the opponents they are
> pitted against, but the writings of this group, as well as those of many other
> Marxists, tend too often to travel from label to label and ism to ism, from
> opponent's error to enemies' mistake, with the noise and ferocity of a
> barbarian beating his shield with his sword—that is, with more clangor than
> clarity—until one feels there might be better results in future if they (and
> *their* followers) were forced to express themselves only with words like
> *banana, hausfrau, watchchain,* and *colorguard.* ["Anatomy," pp. 249–50]

Who would not, on occasion, want to exercise so fine a muscle of
disdain and move through language with such slipperiness and
versatility? And who would ever want to be left the lone barbarian amid
such high civility? There is a tacit but no less tenacious sense throughout
these essays that the ultimate reason for accepting the theory they
propound—beyond whatever applications it might have, beyond even its
delicacy of discrimination and the resplendent idea of order it
incarnates—is the kind of being one would become by failing to accept it,
the clod and vulgarian that one would prove oneself to be. And the
opportunity to shine among the elect that one would miss. Not a very good
reason for embracing any theory, perhaps, and certainly not one that Gass
himself includes among the grounds of legitimate belief, but a powerful
means for gaining our initial acquiescence. One cannot easily reject out of
hand when rejection could have so personal a weight.

The fact that the theory does rely so heavily on a rhetorical vindication explains why an authorial person is so necessary to these essays.
This "I," this word made flesh—or at least made mannerism and
memory—is an exemplary figure, less and identity than a style of being to
put on, a knowledge and a power and a promise of felicity:

> If any of us were as well taken care of as the sentences of Henry James,
> we'd never long for another, never wander away: where else would we
> receive such constant attention, our thoughts anticipated, our feelings
> understood? Who else would robe us so richly, take us to the best places, or
> guard our virtue as his own and defend our character in every situation? If

we were his sentences, we'd sing ourselves though we were dying and about to be extinguished, since the silence which would follow our passing would not be like the pause left behind by a noisy train. It would be a memorial, well-remarked, grave, just as the Master has assured us death itself is: the distinguished thing. [Blue, pp. 44-45]

The ease with which the "I" lapses into "we" is another strand in the rhetorical strategy as well, for the persona is not exemplary only, but a charmer as well—profferring and withholding companionship, approval, and above all, intimacy. This strategy of seduction has another, additional, value, partaking as it does of what the theory treats as the very essence of literary experience.

> The push toward blue in fiction has persisted from the beginning. It was immediately recognized that fiction could carry us, as the bride over the threshold, into domesticity. Suddenly there are sinks and sofas, hats and dresses, table manners. Intimacy. . . .
> The privacy which a book makes public is nevertheless made public very privately—not like the billboard which shouts at the street, or the movie whose image is so open we need darkness to cover the clad-ass and naked face that's settled in our seat. A fictional text enters consciousness so discreetly it is never seen outdoors. [Blue, pp. 83-85]

Throughout the later, more deliberately literary essays, the writing consistently serves a dual purpose; it exemplifies or "acquaints" us with what is, on another level, the subject of discussion. Ontological transformation, purification, the peculiar nature of literary constructs—these words and phrases label theoretical distinctions that the text, in turn, instantiates, providing membership for its own categories. Even such "meaningless" expository habits as Gass's predilection for breaking the text up into discrete segments acquires a certain value in relation to the taxonomic core of the theory, which similarly breaks up, sorts, and separates. And the tendency to compose each essay as a series of slightly altered demonstrations of the same point—"This is really all I have to say, but I shall not stop on that account. Indeed, I shall begin again"[50]—has its analogue in the fundamental metaphysical commitment to elements few in number but rich in combinatory possibility and to old words forming fresh patterns that utterly transform them—the paradigmatic mystery of literature as these essays celebrate it. Thus, as each essay unfolds, we experience the deceptive mobility of words, watch phrases that began as casual descriptions—"Malcolm Lowry, who choked on his vomit" ("The Doomed," p. 5)—poke through again a few pages later, elevated from a passing stage to an essential state, and no longer signifying a literal death but figuring forth the whole of life itself when it turns moribund: "The presence everywhere of decay, disease, coarseness, brutality, and death— the flow of value into a blank abyss—this death-in-life that made living like the aftertaste of drunken vomit—was the black center of the plague of melancholy which afflicted the Elizabethans" ("The Doomed," p. 7).

But perhaps the most striking feature in this prose is the supreme importance it gives to sentences, both as the basic unit of its own theoretical discourse and as the unit it most often fastens on and cites and sings in the writing of others:

> Faulkner wrote sentences—who cares?—which had never been seen before.
>
> Gertrude Stein and the Geography of the Sentence.
>
> If any of us were as well taken care of as the sentences of Henry James.[51]

In truth, the essays themselves move from one sentence to the next, in a kind of pointilism out of which there may occasionally emerge a more extended shape—a thought sequence, an argument, a block of commentary united by its subject matter—but only briefly and weakly. It is the sentences that sustain us. It is hardly a surprise, therefore, to find that the final selection in *The World within the Word* (aptly entitled "The Ontology of the Sentence, of How to Make a World of Words") is a machine for the generation and examination of sentences, projecting perfect gemlike instances bracketed off in admiring detachment from the text that gave them birth:

> Here are four more [sentences] which refine on the relation of hand-shaker to shaken, as of subject and active verb to object:
>
> 6. He doused my hand in his.
> 6.1 His huge hands, rough with toil and stained by leather, held mine as if mine were the flanks of a skittish horse.
> 6.2 With a smirk, he inserted his hand into mine.
> 6.3 What could I tell from his hand: It was the hand of a missionary. Its calm persistent skin would soon grow over and conceal mine. ["Ontology," p. 336]

But why this fixation with sentences, as opposed to paragraphs or individual words or situations or syllogisms? "They are," Gass answers, "the most elementary instances of what the author has constructed . . . . a moving unity of fact and feeling" ("Philosophy," p. 12). It is the sentence that, through its grammatical categories and syntactic arrangements, "confers reality on certain relations" and "takes metaphysical dictation" ("Philosophy," p. 14).[52] If each word is a "lens," then sentences establish "the angle at which the lens is held" ("Trouts," p. 275). Moreover, each sentence is set off from other sentences as a "different occasion" ("Ontology," p. 330), a moment of isolated apprehension, a single contour of sound and attention surrounded by silence. Thus, sentences compartmentalize, they organize ambiguously charged semantic material into more durable categories. They are taxonomies in miniature, distinguishing, articulating, ordering—performing those works of mind and language that Gass finds most necessary and least likely to distort our apprehension of the world. But the fascination with sentences is just as much an expression of indifference or an attempt to avoid certain matters. Although sentences do have a "logical form," it is a logic of categories and not yet one of premises and conclusions. And though they have tenses, the moment is frozen—time never passes there, things are never subject to fading and decay. The dream of preservation and transcendence, of the purity of the closed form, is more perfectly realized there than at any other level of discourse. By seeking sentences as isolated formal units, the theory is once again demonstrating its allegiance to a condition "ontologically of another order than that of ordinary life, its chronology, concerns, and accounts" ("Carrots," p. 304).

By the same token, the act of incorporating fragments of another text within its own discourse is itself another kind of compartmentalization and subsumption. This is clearest in *On Being Blue*, which scissors freely into the most heterogenous materials—letters, dictionaries, novels, poems, profanities, histories of art, and philosophical treatises—to gather its own compendium of blues. There is, one senses, an active pleasure in capturing and encapsulating these citations, removing them from their original contexts and turning them into discrete objects, "portable property," that can be possessed and fondled over and over again. ". . . the blues we rebreathe, always for the same reason: because the word in each case finds its place within a system so supremely organized it cannot be improved upon—what we would not replace and cannot change" (*Blue*, p. 56).

The breaking off of utterances—the separation of a portion from the whole—that is the essence of quotation is more than an unfortunate contingency in these essays. The excerpt is, as it were, saved from its surroundings, kept from being absorbed into a story, preserved with all its music under glass.

> Colette has the cat's gaze. Unhurried contemplation is her forte. Hunger cannot give us such precision.
>
> Meanwhile the shadows lengthened on the beach; the blackness deepened. The iron black boot became a pool of deep blue. The rocks lost their hardness. The water that stood round the old boat was dark as if mussels had been steeped in it. The foam had turned livid and left here and there a white gleam of pearl on the misty sand.
>
> The nouns in this passage are all nailed too firmly to their *the's*; otherwise Virginia Woolf's construction here is sensuous in the same way as Colette's: observant, thoughtful, loving, calm. [*Blue*, p. 33]

What is noteworthy about such a citation is its utter indifference to whatever value the passage had in its original (unnamed) context, what place it occupied in the progress or the structure of the text. True, there is some reference to an author's sensibility, but the references are secretly circular: The nature of the mind is derived from the nature of the sentences and not the other way around.

Not that encapsulation always has the same, rhapsodic function in these essays. Occasionally, a passage is singled out for derision too:

> The curtain rises, and Sartre, coming forward to address his audience, says:

>> The chief source of great tragedy—the tragedy of Aeschylus and Sophocles, of Corneille—is human freedom. Oedipus is free; Antigone and Prometheus are free. The fate we think we find in ancient drama is only the other side of freedom. Passions themselves are freedoms caught in their own trap.

> Observe the speech and not the speaker. There is first the round unguarded expression of essence, and the little exemplary list, notable for what it leaves out, then the ritual invocation of freedom (better than *patrie, gloire,* or god), followed by an outrageous falsehood (Oedipus is free) which is rhetorically removed with one rub of a paradox put epigrammatically. There will be a lot of this. ["Sartre," p. 177]

Of course this is not literary excerpt, and though its qualities of "speech" do not go unregarded there is no attempt to make of it a luminous object. It is still objectified, but as a piece of data, something to be counted ("There will be a lot of this") rather than "rebreathed." Here, remarks about the propositional value of the excerpt are in order, as they were not when the goal was veneration and rapturous recitation; falsehoods and fatuities are duly noted. When a real rejoinder is required, however, the offending text is more likely to be cited indirectly—as if it were necessary to strip away every trace of its verbal texture, turn it into a disembodied idea, before attacking it on argumentative grounds.

> Every biographer must measure out three qualities—space in the text, data in the dossier, and time in the life—and these should not continuously and outrageously contradict one another, as is so often the case. Blotner fills pages with the founding of New Orleans, but when, shortly after their wedding, Estelle Faulkner gets drunk and, in a gorgeous silk dress, tries to drown herself in the Gulf of Mexico, he sails peacefully past in a paragraph and won't even throw her a ring. ["Mr. Blotner," p. 53]

Yet the most seminal texts—those that give impetus to an entire essay, to which it responds or upon which it builds—are frequently never cited at all. Max Black's work on models and metaphors informs all of Gass's writing on the subject, and Wittgenstein is omnipresent, but both remain almost entirely offstage. Such silence is another kind of honor, treating these writings as so fundamental, so generally acknowledged, that citations would artificially and absurdly turn them back into private utterances, views peculiar to a certain speaker rather than generally accepted dictums. At the other extreme, but no less fully absorbed, are those Nabokovian syntactic surprises and those Shakespearean rhythms that reverberate in the form of pervasive allusions: "...imagine that somewhere nearby a snowman had been both created and destroyed, and that this was the root that was his nose, and these were the coals that were his eyes" ("Carrots," p. 288)—unidentified, and once again beyond ownership and occasion.

But perhaps most significant of all are those rare moments when the intertextual relationships into which these essays enter violate the theory's own most treasured premises. Literature "contains no truths, pretends to none.... And how much wisdom you expect to find...will depend on how foolish, unreflective, or unread you are" ("Carrots," p. 301) proclaims the theory, in an excess of aestheticism. Yet the essays return again and again to certain set passages—the closing lines of *Middlemarch* on the nature of history or (as here) Rilke on the nature of art—passages that have a force for Gass that is clearly more than just incantatory:

> No wonder the novel is long.... for such a book says...more than that two mountain chains traverse the republic; it says what Rilke wrote of another work of art, the torso of an archaic Apollo:
>
> There is no place
> that does not see you. You must change your life.
> ["Toenail," p. 76]

Rilke's lines are used and not just mentioned; coming at the very end of the essay, they do the work of theorizing and contain whatever degree of truth the theory itself pretends to.

Belying in another way the ostensible hermeticism of art is the way these essays knit together excerpts of the most diverse kinds. For a literary work to be cited in this prose is to find itself placed cheek by jowl with snippets of linguistics and mathematics, residing somewhere between Vico, Freud, and Quine (if not Marx and Durkheim) in ways that risk defiling its purity. There even seems to be some pleasure in this. The apparently clean break between language that produces its subject matter and language that merely reproduces it is muddied by the act of citation itself, which seems to do both at once—or neither one: "...let me cite without quotation the extensive pastiche of the Goncourts' *Journals* which Proust places beside the sand urn and the ficus in the foyer...in the manner later to be that of Borges, in which the Goncourts comment on characters in *A la recherche du temps perdu* as if they were in Paris and not in Proust" ("Carrots," p. 282). These words do not invent Proust or his novel, but neither are they (as the reference to Borges underscores) entirely free of invention. Language so consorts with language, and text with other texts, that the ideal of pure creation—or pure imitation—becomes implausible.

> . . . if the total presentation is what counts, and if the structures we believe we find there [in fiction] are already interpreted like laws; if we must know that only barbers use steaming towels, or that the scratched palm is a sexual invitation; then we may be inclined to suppose that the sentences of fiction reflect a world more than make one; that they rely too fully on the life we presume we lead to be other than commentary. . . . it must be this data we draw on, because the flow of the world, which often deposits itself in words like silt, is all we have; but after that . . . we can use the old to create the new, make as we imagine. ["Ontology," pp. 335–36]

That word *silt* is telling, a remnant of Gass's purification theme; yet when these essays actually draw upon old words for citations and allusions, there is no suggestion that they are being sullied in the encounter. Quite the opposite, for the otherness of the incorporated material alternatively pulls and repels the native prose, so that it must either go beyond its own initial range or redouble its effort to define and retain a character of its own. On the whole, it is the rapid twitch in the writing that takes us from one universe of discourse to another, leaving neither in control or unalloyed.

Citation circumscribes the single authorial persona—which was, in any case, partly a strategic seducer and exemplar, and partly a device for making language intimate, giving it a right to fantasy and free association. It also complicates the emphasis this theory places on individual creation. There is a defense of individualism—of the rights, the genius, and the unique reality of the isolated person—dispersed throughout the essays, at many different levels of the writing. Occasionally, however, it flairs out in a condensed and unqualified form.

> It is the principal function of popular culture—though hardly its avowed purpose—to keep men from understanding what is happening to them. . . .
> . . . People who have seen the same game, heard the same comedians, danced to the same din, read the same detectives, can form a community of enthusiasts whose exchange of feelings . . . helps persuade people that their experiences were real, reinforces judgments of their values, and confirms their addiction. . . . the products of popular culture, by and large, have no more esthetic quality than a brick in the street. Their authors are anonymous, and tend to dwell in groups and create in committees; . . . they lack finish, complexity, stasis, individuality, coherence, depth, and endurance . . .
> . . . from time to time one senses an effort to Hitlerize the culture of the Folk; . . . this, in order to put out those high and isolated fires, those lonely works of genius which still manage, somehow, amazingly, now and then, to appear. There is no Folk, of course; there are no traditions; . . . popular culture is the product of an industrial machine which makes baubles to amuse the savages while missionaries steal their souls and merchants steal their money.[53]

This lengthy quote illustrates the separate strands that enter into Gass's polemic: assumptions about what human beings are, left in a state of nature; beliefs about the inevitable effects of grouping and public life; the sense that in collectivity, human identity is lost so that all that remains is a degraded, undifferentiated mass—"all the oxen in the world," as the essay (citing Plato) goes on to call it. This is not the dispute, of course, the canniness of Gass's analysis of the manipulation and the passivity of ersatz folk culture, merely to point out that his repudiation of popular culture goes much further and his hopelessness runs far deeper than any particular form of social exploitation.[54] There is no evidence that Gass sees the situation as a historical contingency; he appears to expect no amelioration, but only an escape, a protected private space where love can govern social intercourse and art—highly wrought and individuated objects—can be treasured and preserved. Not only that condition of the individual is therefore a happy one, simply that it is the only "authentic" one. "So suicide is a disease of singularity and selfhood, because we are elevated in the social system, and authorities 'over' us are removed, as we wobble out on our own, the question of whether it is better to be or not to be arises with real relevance for the first time, since the burden of being is felt most fully by the self-determining self " ("The Doomed," p. 6). This (unacknowledged) summary of Durkheim's position significantly omits any mention of "altruistic suicide," that will to self-annihilation that comes when social bonds are too tight rather than too loose—as if such a world were utterly unimaginable, but also as if there were some secret resistance to sharing the agony and the attendant glamour of isolation.

Not a particular social arrangement, but every social arrangement—collectivity itself—is poisonous, necessarily detrimental to clear thinking and bold invention. It overwhelms by sheer bulk the fine discriminations upon which artistic value and ethical conduct alike depend. This *malaise de la masse* informs Gass's fiction as well as his theory, from the recurring vision of a visiting plague of insects to the Holocaust itself, which "The Tunnel" calls "more matter-of-fact than even brutal . . . like spraying for mosquitoes. . . ."[55] When this malaise, this horror, turns into theory, its natural machinery is taxonomy, and its most urgent goal will be discrimination and distinction. It explains as well why the array of categories should swing between brute dichotomy and sprawling infinity. Nothing intervenes between the one and the many; the only conceivable alternatives within the economy of this theory are the threatened individual and the threatening mass.

The economy makes other themes stand out as well—an acute concern for consciousness, for example, which is not only a subject matter (in *On Being Blue*) but a principle in the theory's operation. One notes that in commenting on other texts, there is never any attempt to go beneath or beyond what could be consciously intended. When Sartre is chided for omissions or excesses, it is for failing to do what he knew perfectly well how to do. Hence the impatience of the reproof. Sympathetic readings are guided by the same constraint—even when it requires some stretch of the imagination, as when a Shakespearean inversion that misfires is praised because he "didn't want us to imagine the world simply topsy-turvy" ("Trouts," p. 279). And even when it leads to outright inconsistency:

> The entire passage is held together by underlying meanings which are greatly akin and often simply repeat one another—a familiar characteristic of Stein's manifest texts....
>
> ...At the point of the first full stop, there is a definite break in the text. In order to go on, we must go back.
>
> And who are "we" at this point? Not even Gertrude would have read this far.
>
> ...So far what have I been made to do? I have been required to put roots and shoots and little stems and tendrils together...and then at some point not very pleasantly to realize that the game I'm playing is the game of creation itself, because *Tender Buttons* is above all a book of kits. ["Gertrude Stein," pp. 95–97]

Despite the Freudian talk about "manifest texts," and despite the frank admission that as a reader he has been playing a game of creation, Gass continues to insist that "I have been *made* to do it," posing as if he were still faithfully replicating the author's will—although even Gertrude wouldn't have read this far. The author's conscious will is invoked here, against the grain of strict formalism, to constrain interpretation and maintain the power that the text must exercise over its readers. Popular culture may be guilty of making spectators too passive, but making them too active endangers the "being," the determinant identity, of a work of art. Then too, it may be that the reading public at large is too numerous and too faceless to be fully trusted; if consciousness becomes diluted in the mass, then mass activity is likely to be just as pernicious (if not more so) than mass passivity.

It is consciousness—in Gass, equivalent to mind itself—that divides the human from the inhuman, merely material, modes of being: "In a fundamental way we are one with our awareness, and a certain kind of consciousness, not featherless bipedity or cleverly opposed thumbs, is the most obvious mark of man" ("Anatomy," p. 226). For all his admiration for Freud, Gass still believes it is a heroic category mistake to treat the human mind in terms of inhuman hydraulics and electronics. This is another reason for refraining from the search for traces of an unconscious force at work in writing, and for associating the creative faculty with "love" rather than with a more subliminal and driven "eros." Consciousness is, moreover, the discriminator par excellence, the great register of shades and qualities and particularities, of "feelings much more complex than sensations"—of all that rival theories would prefer to reduce to simpler quantities and more predictable, accessible behavior. This makes it both the most delicate of taxonomic machines and something too delicate for the usual theoretical discussions. The only theory that will do is one that operates like literature itself, embracing vagaries and minutiae as the coarser-grained vocabularies of scientific and philosophic discourse cannot.

Through consciousness, and through language—which is consciousness made public and permanently free of particular occasions—it is possible to transcend contingency, to escape from time and history and even society, since books will serve as well or better for our company. Transcendence is the last major theme of Gass's literary theory, sounded in the repeated cry for purity and purification and in the recurrent denigration of utility. It figures less conspicuously but no less strongly in the decision to treat literature as an "ontological" (as opposed to an epistemological or a psychological or a conventional) transformation, an entire change of being and not simply another way of seeing or responding to language. A taste for the transcendental leads to the elevation of concept over percept as well: "the clear and brilliant world of concept,...where characters, unlike ourselves, freed from existence, can shine like essence, and purely Be" ("Character," p. 54). One finds it even in the most casual imagery—the sense that language is sullied with the "silt" of previous use, making its history a kind of dirt of which literature must then be cleansed. And of course it enters into the general disregard, if not open hostility, for sociological and historical criticism. In saying that literature does not represent reality but is an addition to it, Gass is not only making a point about the logical status of literature or drawing our attention to the productive powers of writing; he is also blocking out an "other Eden"—the alternative to an unameliorable, unchangeable real world. "It is also impossible to replicate relations whenever they're wanted (I can father my firstborn but once), or refasten properties like trousers or stamps....to restore the past like dry skin, or reproduce whatever qualities might be in question...so we must bring in our names and numbers" ("Ontology," p. 314).

But when it turns to the subject of language, the theory—whose economy strives to be so solidly compacted of replicating structures and internal reinforcements—shows signs of internal strain. For—having granted language its freedom (for the sake of transcendence)—Gass must then find some way to keep it within bounds, if it is to provide a reliable refuge and a stay against all time and change. "A word," he is compelled to admit, "is a wanderer. Except in the most general syntactical sense, it has no home. 'Rose' is a name, a noun, an action: where does that put us? somewhere between Utah and the invention of the Ferris wheel" ("Carrots," p. 276). Furthermore, words do not contain their meanings, but only invite them by putting associations into play:

A hand emerged from his sleeve like a mouse from its hole.
You think you know how that is? You have observed many a mouse,
and they always bolt out as if several small cats were after them? or do they
creep out cautiously, look round and around, or saunter, whistling through
their tiny teeth? The point is that the sentence suggests that the hand came
out timidly, warily; that it was far from *thrust*. The mouse we are referring to
here is a cartoon mouse, a literary mouse, not a real mouse. Neither author
nor reader has watched mice—that's a good bet—but they have read about
them. . . . So a literary convention appears here in the guise of an observation. . . . We have had to invoke what is commonly called the pragmatic
dimension. ["Ontology," pp. 326–27]

It is a dangerous concession for one who otherwise demands eter-
nality of art to admit the need for conventional and pragmatic assistance.
It robs the literary text of the power to trigger an automatic response and
throws it open to the winds of history and the impurities of a context of
use. Not surprisingly, equivocations will reappear on the very next page—
"the text must give us the clues for its own interpretation" ("Ontology," p.
328). This remains a consistent inconsistency throughout the rest of this
essay and in several others too. After all, the very notion of transcendence
and the trick of ontological transformation requires that there be something to transcend, some ties to come undone. Thus, though the theory
calls for an art so pure that it prunes from words "any meanings they
might have been assigned," it is obvious that without these former meanings there could be no figurative departures and none of the delicious
incongruity of transformation—which these essays everywhere exploit.
Purification is not an essence but a relation; it depends upon the very
factors that it would repudiate or escape.

Gass insists that literature implies a change of status for language, a
shift that makes formerly essential features accidental and marginal
matters of form and sound criteria. This indicates a keen appreciation for
the variability and relativity of most definitions. Yet literature itself is
treated as if it were eternally fixed, its status and its features untouched by
the conceptual grid through which it is assessed. "We must keep in mind
the relation of any order to the chosen good," states the theory ("Trouts,"
p. 269), and then spends countless paragraphs on alerting us to the
dangers of reification. But all this is forgotten when it comes to literature,
where the ordering principles and chosen good of the theoretical framework are conveniently ignored, and the definitions imposed on literature
are taken for the thing itself. Even more remarkable—given the scrupulous, almost anxious, concern for making fine distinction that otherwise governs this discourse—is the way it handles literature itself as an
indivisible mass. So sensitive in other places to the haphazard way that a
single term can be extended to cover vastly different cases, so adamant
that we not allow ourselves to be bewitched into thinking that they are
therefore all the same, the theory suddenly becomes thick-fingered and

indiscriminate. This is most evident when it ranges every other conceivable use of language (as an undifferentiated mass) against literature (as another undifferentiated mass).

> Despite appearances...the words on checks and bills of lading, in guides and invoices, the words which magnify themselves on billboards, broadsides, walls and hoardings, which nuzzle together in *billets-doux* and heart-to-hearts, words which smell a lot like stools in presidential proclamations, army orders and political orations, whose heaps create each of our encyclopedias of information, our textbooks, articles of confederation, rules and regulations, charts and tables, catalogues and lists; the words whose ranks form our photo captions, chronicles, and soberest memorials, fill cartoon balloons with lies as bold as produce labels...—so many signs from every culture and accreditation—legal briefs, subtitles, shopping lists and memos, minutes, notes, reports, summations, lectures, theories, general laws, universal truths—every other mark whatever, whether sky-writ, in the sand or on a wall or water—these words are not in any central or essential sense the same as the passionately useless rigamarole that makes up literary language, because the words in poems, to cite the signal instance, have undergone a radical, though scarcely surprising, ontological transformation. ["Carrots," p. 283]

A love letter without hyperbole? A cartoon without a license for fantasy? Theories that differ not a whit from subtitles and shopping lists, but differ essentially from literature? Something is seriously amiss; there is some interest, some investment to protect, and the erstwhile principles under which the theory operated can be turned back upon itself to tell us so.

Other inconsistencies are subtler, as when—despite repeated urgings that love is the source of all fine discriminations and the one source of energy that ignites the finest prose—we cannot help but notice how often the energy of this prose comes, not from love, but from sheer aggression, and how sharply hatred can particularize its object. "Joseph Blotner's massive Egyptian work is not so much a monument to a supremely gifted writer as it is the great man's grave itself, down which the biographer's piously gathered data drops like sheltering dirt" ("Mr. Blotner," p. 47). The gaiety of Gass's review essays is a product of this passion, a far darker one than love, and the intertextual exchanges can be just as biting in other essays as well. Even when commenting on an officially beloved book, the language may betray a lust that has no place in courtship—"digging down [into Gertrude Stein]—we find a few roots," and soon "everything rattles into place like iron gates" ("Gertrude Stein," pp. 92, 97). One reason for so often citing passages without interpretation may be this strong association between interpreting and dismembering or imprisoning.

These small contradictions become important because they accompany the larger one between what the theory claims literature must be and what it then manages to do as a literary text in its own right. The result is to throw confusion over the alliances and implications that such claims would otherwise possess. The celebration of pure form is offset by an obvious effort to make the theoretical discourse itself convincing as well as formally enticing. Going by its pronouncements alone, one could easily complain (as a recent reviewer did) that "there is really no cause to pretend that novels are so special as to defy ordinary powers of comprehension."[56] At this level, the theory would indeed seem to demand specialization of the most intense sort—perhaps a staff of permanently endowed experts to keep the oxen to their proper pens, and to prevent them from trampling over necessary distinctions or getting indigestion by mistaking a page of print for the dinner it describes.

Yet the way these essays actually address their audience suggest no such fixed discrepancies of status, while the hybrid nature of the genre itself is a blow to the very notion of fixed specializations. And the further the experiment is pursued, the more the theoretical text seems to challenge the theory's own initial premises. The closed economy from which it first began—with literature absolutely opposed to ordinary language, and with use always borrowing from and eventually depleting beauty—is supplemented by the operations of the text itself. The act of writing produces values incapable of fitting back into the old system of exchange.

The literature of which this theory speaks—or chants—seems airless, static, endlessly (and tediously?) loving, confined to only a few subjects and capable of arousing a very limited range of responses. The literature that this theory *is* is sometimes hieratic and remote, but just as often bawdy, nasty, and infuriating; it delights but does not—should not—quiet our objections. Occasionally it appears to expect them— "certainly the mathematician may feel that I'm poaching" ("Trouts," p. 274). Even more often it deliberately provokes them. Hyperbole and outrageously gawdy generalizations are commonplace—"we always plate our sexual objects first. It is the original reason why we read . . . the only reason why we write" (*Blue*, p. 10; Gass's ellipses). No defense for this effrontery is offered; it is a conceit, a fond surmise for trying out. The literary excess is there to warn us against adopting too literal a response. Throughout these essays, literature acts as a check on the theoretical passion, and keeps it from waxing too intense, from making "for the sake of a certain precision, the sacrifice which Galileo had to when he took all the color from mass" ("Trouts," p. 274). More important, these overt and highly mobile figures are the best possible defense against "confining ourselves to too few models" and "living in them as if they were, themselves, the world."

Yet the play would not be so moving without the passion. The taxonomic effort (which supplants the denser and more dangerous conceptual machinery of models) is an earnest struggle to keep chaos at bay and to balance the ruthless demand for intellectual order against the fragile and infinitely divisible stuff of life. Whether one accepts it or not, Gass's *malaise de la masse* is intensely felt and ingeniously and scrupulously confronted, making the risk he has taken on by engaging in such an openly hybrid writing all the more poignant. The theory strives, moreover, for something beyond codification and discovery. It is a polemic, a defense, an effort to exercise control over writing and reading: "shape pebbles into syllables and make stones sound; thus cautioned and encouraged, commanded, warned, persist." But this command at the end of *On Being Blue* also illustrates how literature tames and curbs this appetite. When imperative lapses into apostrophe, there is a tacit acceptance that power over a reader's ultimate response is limited. The form that the will to knowledge finally assumes in these essays is closer to what Gass attributes to Freud: "His therapy, like the methods of those philosophers he most resembles, consists in the clarification of consciousness by the removal of illusions" ("Anatomy," p. 217n).

That this appears only in a footnote is all the more striking. Such diminution at once suggests and suppresses (as Freud himself well knew) a profound ambition.

4
Susan Sontag

To compare Susan Sontag's work as a filmmaker and fiction writer to her work as a writer of theoretical essays is hardly to repeat the lesson of Gass. The literature of theory is far from uniform, and its sudden rise to prominence represents the convergence of many different motives and capacities. Unlike Gass, Sontag's creative efforts have few ardent admirers and many detractors. "She is not a natural writer, certainly not a natural novelist," writes Dennis Donoghue, "She writes by insistence, the will doing the work of the imagination."[1] Even sympathetic reviews have something quizzical, embarrassed, or defensive about them, full of brusque efforts to explain away discrepancies between *Against Interpretation* and *On Photography* and novels like *Death Kit* or a story like "Dr. Jekyll" (in her recent—and more successful—collection, *I, et cetera*). Whereas readers often come to Gass's theory after reading his fiction (perhaps seeking there the principles that drive that fiction), they approach Sontag's fiction almost exclusively through her theory. The a-mount and kind of public notice the films and novels draw is almost always commensurate to her most recent theoretical achievements. Frequently, Sontag must make use of interviews and prefaces to waylay efforts to treat her creative works as simple illustrations of her critical principles—even to remind her readers that she is, in fact, a filmmaker and novelist too, and that her apparent return to the public scene in the mid-1970s (with her essays on photography) was no return at all, since she had never, properly speaking, been away.[2] There is a respectable body of academic criticism devoted to Gass, much of which alludes only in passing to his essays, but there is no comparable body of work on Sontag; though she is frequently cited, it is rarely for her fictions or her films.

One can trace problems in Gass's fiction back to the limitations and the obligations that his theory imposes on artists. One could do the same with Sontag, although the results are likely to be less illuminating—in part because it is so hard to know where to start, which of her shifting theoretical positions to pursue. Certain of her fictions do try to fabricate the pure "being," the immediate and untranslatable "luminousness of the thing itself" that she advocated in *Against Interpretation*. Yet the pure sensual awareness to which her early essays referred was less an actuality than an aspiration, valuable precisely because it stood counterposed to:

> . . . a culture based on excess, on overproduction; . . . a steady loss of sharpness in our sensory experience. All the conditions of modern life—its material plenitude, its sheer crowdedness—conjoin to dull our sensory faculties. And it is in the light of the condition of our senses, our capacities (rather than those of another age), that the task of the critic must be assessed. . . .
> . . . Our task is to cut back content so that we can see the thing at all."[3]

In the essays that follow upon this manifesto, it is the work of "cutting back" that is most evident, the careful peeling away of excrescent irritations and misapprehensions meant to bare a stirring, nearly tactile nakedness:

> In realistic terms, the motives of Bresson's characters are often hidden, sometimes downright incredible. . . .
> . . . what is central to Bresson and, I think, not to be caviled at, is his evident belief that psychological analysis is superficial. (Reason: it assigns to action a paraphrasable meaning that true art transcends.) He does not intend his characters to be implausible, I'm sure, but he does, I think, intend them to be opaque. Bresson is interested . . . in the physics, as it were, rather than the psychology of souls."[4]

Sontag's response to Bresson could hardly be called "immediate"; her negatives are central to this passage. What they retract—the psychological interpretations they withdraw—are as important to our cumulative appreciation of Bresson's art as the "physics" at which we ultimately arrive. The sheer exertion of this writing is perhaps why critics so often remark that, for someone "who is against hermeneutics," Sontag still "seems to interpret more readily than most."[5]

Against Interpretation celebrates the "incantatory, magical" qualities of a lost primeval art, but the charm of this mysterious art is distinctly comparative. When Sontag herself turns artist, the implicit comparison disappears, and we are left with only the mystery and, occasionally, with a deliberate program of mystification. One of the most patent instances of this is her film, *Brother Carl*, which she calls "a winter's tale. . . . about a present haunted by an untellable 'black' act of corruption that lies in the past, transfixed by an unmerited 'white' act of healing that waits in the future." As this description suggests, the film is almost strenuously enigmatic, full of gaps and deliberately withheld information and taking as its central figure the silent, waiflike Carl, a man damaged by nameless crimes who performs an inexplicable and gratuitous act of salvation. Both as concept and as character, Carl is troublesome without being especially troubling. He is less potently intriguing than he is meant to be, his muteness and his pain are too calculated and sentimental—as if to be speechless were in itself necessarily touching. Sontag's introduction to the screenplay has some of this same air of mingled calculation and naiveté: "...Brother Carl...[is] a tale of couples....On each side there is a 'child,' a child who is too angry or too wounded to speak. Martin has his genius protégé, who used to dance. The Sandlers have their young daughter, whom all sounds interest except words. The introduction of that refusal— that pathos and pain incarnated by the 'child'—generates the more complex interchanges of this couple story."[6]

Throughout the film there are scenes (here described in words from Sontag's own shooting script) that suggest an almost superstitious faith in the power of the dumb show of photographic images.

MARTIN...is bathing CARL in an ordinary-size metal bathtub. MARTIN's movements are gentle, without being sensual. He soaps CARL's back and neck. CARL, completely passive, seems very tense: his back and neck are particularly rigid....

...Suddenly CARL twists himself, doubles up, and plunges his head and most of his body under water. A mock drowning or a real one?

MARTIN rests one hand on the rim of the tub, pushes back a strand of hair with the other. He is waiting for CARL to surface. Thirty, forty seconds go by; it should, and will seem long. Under water, CARL (all we see is a portion of his bony back) doesn't move. MARTIN starts to get worried. He reaches out his hand to touch CARL's back, then pulls away; he doesn't dare interfere. He waits, sitting on his heels. The music stops. At least another forty seconds pass. Then, like a monster rising from the sea, CARL unfolds himself and lifts his head and upper torso out of the water; his wet hair covers his eyes. (Note: the whole action takes place within one shot, and the audience must feel that there is no trickery, that the actor who plays CARL really is staying under water for an extraordinarily long time, which will be true.) [Carl, pp. 84–85]

The scene is not unmotivated; it does suggest the strange bonds that unite Martin and Brother Carl and foreshadow a later death by drowning at the climax of the film. It also introduces a change in Carl himself, who becomes more willing to speak after this symbolic "rebirth." Yet one feels that the real fascination is with the silence, the nakedness and near caress, the risky and wholly whimsical submergence of Carl (who remains a terra incognita, an island in the bathtub, as far as the script and the camera are concerned). The fascination is in excess of anything that the narrative situation or the framing of the shot actually convey. There is, of course, the daring long take, a minor agony in itself: "Real art," according to one of Sontag's essays, should have "the capacity to make us nervous" ("A.I.," p. 7). But this is a staged trial of our nerves, and not likely to accomplish even that if we have no prior investment in Carl's survival and only a hackneyed musical cue to make his madness portentous in our eyes. The scene seems designed (in the most orthodox fashion) to repel or "undetermine" all potential interpretations and to compel us to describe instead, to stay with the sensuous surface of things. But without the mediation of Sontag's theory, little sense of urgency or dionysiac release attaches to this "pure, untranslatable, sensuous immediacy" ("A.I.," p. 19). It is appropriately carnal and totally mute, but since the silence neither defies expectation nor excites speculation, its magic and its mystery are weak at best.

In a 1978 interview, Sontag continues to speak of her fictions (as distinct from her essays) as "machines for creating strong emotions."[7] This phrase betrays a surprising sameness in her working definition of art that one does not find in her theoretical work. There, one would have to look back a decade or more to find such a commitment to art as brute agitation, a rootless and self-justifying intensity: "Whatever is wholly mysterious is at once both psychically relieving and anxiety-provoking. (A perfect machine for agitating this pair of contrary emotions: the Bosch drawing in a Dutch museum that shows trees furnished with two ears at the sides of their trunks, as if they were listening to the forest, while the forest floor is strewn with eyes.)"[8] And even here, in the lead essay to Sontag's second collection, *Styles of Radical Will*, there is more diffidence than one finds in *Against Interpretation*, a new doubleness in how the phenomenon is perceived. These later essays no longer advocate or fete the condition of contemporary art, but report upon it and probe it:

> The fact that contemporary artists are concerned with silence—and, therefore, in one extension, with the ineffable—must be understood historically, as a consequence of the prevailing contemporary myth of the "absoluteness" of art. The value placed on silence doesn't arise by virtue of the *nature* of art, but derives from the contemporary ascription of certain "absolute" qualities to the art object and to the activity of the artist.
> . . . In my opinion, the myths of silence and emptiness are about as nourishing and viable as might be devised in an "unwholesome" time—which is, of necessity, a time in which "unwholesome" psychic states furnish the energies for most superior work in the arts. Yet one can't deny the pathos of these myths. ["Silence," pp. 31, 11]

It is startling enough that her own art should remain so attached to, so trapped within an aesthetic of extremity and mystery that even ten years earlier had seemed more symptomatic than progressive. But it is even more disconcerting that the description of what she means to achieve should be so distant from what she normally does achieve. For the strongest feeling that Sontag's narratives inspire is neither awe nor horror, but a kind of moodiness, emotions in a delicately diminished minor key: nostalgia, confusion, wistfulness, irresolution. The laconic headings that appear in a recent short story like "Debriefing" are indicative—"What Is Wrong"; "What People Are Trying to Do"; "What

Relieves, Soothes, Helps"; "What Is Upsetting"—as is the resolution of the story itself:

> That late Wednesday afternoon I told Julia how stupid it would be if she committed suicide. She agreed. I thought I was convincing. Two days later she left her apartment again and killed herself, showing me that she didn't mind doing something stupid.
> Julia, plastic face in the waxy casket, how could you be as old as you were? You're still the twenty-three-year-old who started an absurdly pedantic conversation with me on the steps of Widener Library—so thin; so prettily affected; so electric; so absent; so much younger than I, who was four years younger than you; so tired already; so exasperating; so moving. I want to hit you.
> How I groaned under the burden of your friendship. But your death is heavier.
> Why you went under while others, equally absent from their lives, survive is a mystery to me.
> Say we are all asleep. Do we want to wake up?
> Is it fair if I wake up and you, most of you, don't? Fair! you sneer. What's fair got to do with it? It's every soul for itself. But I didn't want to wake up without you.
> You're the tears in things, I'm not. You weep for me, I'll weep for you. Help me, I don't want to weep for myself. I'm not giving up.[9]

There is sorrow here, but it is not insupportable, and perhaps more painful or more rueful for that. The grief is refracted through a sensibility that measures it and tests it and sets it carefully among other possibilities—that "knows" it rather than simply vibrating with it. There are no protruding edges for readers to cut themselves upon; everything is sheathed, laminated with thought. The result is something ruminative, closer to the elder Wordsworth than Sontag's own favorite eternal enfant terrible, Artaud.

It is instructive to compare this story of two women friends, one suicide and one survivor, with the more lurid version of the same situation as it appears in *Brother Carl*. The film actually shows the drowning and the discovery of the bloated body, and makes of the survivor a much more equivocal figure, "who is weak and selfish and hardly merits anything in her own right" (Introduction, p. xiv). Film (far more than writing) seems to be Sontag's preferred machine for creating strong emotions, an automaton that records without flinching and projects without judging a flood of ambiguous and nameless sensory impressions. Her prose, on the other hand, is rather spare and lean; images are few, and judgments of some sort, even when they contradict each other, are impossible to withhold. This is equally true of her writing whether one is speaking of Sontag's stories or her essays, and the fact that there is no decisive shift of verbal gears, may be one reason for the oft-heard complaint that her fiction is "thin" and gives readers too little experience. Indeed *experience* and *feeling* are the buzzwords for reviewers of her work, whether it is Denis Donoghue's guarded assessment of *Death Kit*: "Her inventions read like bright ideas driven into fictional postures; . . . an ambitious book that has never become an experience" or Louis D. Rubin's retrospective attack on *Against Interpretation* as the work of a writer who "was all ideas, and her emotions were not so much felt as thought."[10] In the midst of praise, Richard Gilman still calls her "coldness of temperature and almost complete lack of any lyric impulse," her inability "to offer the feeling of the erotic," the chief "failure and the fruitfulness of her writing"—"beneath the clean functioning, superbly armed processes of thought exists a confused, importunate, scarcely acknowledged desire that culture . . . be other than it is, in order for her to be other than she is."[11]

Both her narratives and her essays suggest the same desire for something more engulfing and less schematic—whether in the texture of her prose or in its representational detail. Ironically, those bent on defending Western culture from Sontag's alleged antiintellectualism, often betray a much greater investment in the division between reason and emotion, immediate experience and mediated intelligence, than Sontag herself. In this split, literature is allied to feeling, sensation, data, "being there"—the very alliance that Sontag then pushes to its limit by calling for an art that is entirely sensuous stimulation. The same assumption seems to draw the line between her essays and her stories, the latter being wholly concerned with formal experiment, "feeling" and "voice."[12] Yet these are precisely the areas in which she is most seriously deficient, in the pursuit of which she seems to produce her least satisfying work. There is a moment of regret, late in "Old Complaints Revisited" (another recent story), when the narrator flashes out:

> I am incapable of investigating my plight without embodying it. That leaden, bloodless tone of the true member! Anyway, other members will recognize my voice. It's my certificate of identity, like a thumbprint. . . .
> Perhaps if I rewrote what I've written here, it would be more convincing. If I could be lyrical! Unpredictable! Concise! In love with things as they are! But, alas, this thin overscrupulous voice is mine. And if I could change my voice, have written this differently, I would not be the person that I am. I would not have the problem that I have.[13]

And one almost winces, for the voice that here calls itself "thin" and "overscrupulous" is too much like other voices in this volume. If an effort has been made to be distinctive and distinguishably passionless, it has not succeeded. The one instance in which there *is* a distinctive voice (or pair of voices)—the dual soliloquy, "Baby," in which a husband and wife are heard discoursing to a silent psychiatrist about the trials of parenthood—results in a burlesque, a stilted caricature:

What we decided, doctor, was that it would be best to lay our problems before a really competent professional person. God knows, we've tried to do the best we could. But sometimes a person has to admit defeat. . . .
Of course we can afford it. We don't want to spare any expense. But to tell the truth, we picked you because your fee was more reasonable than some others. And Dr. Greenwich said you specialized in problems of this sort. . . .
How much background do you need to know. . .
Both born in this country, good native stock. Why, did you think we were foreigners? You're a foreigner, aren't you, doctor? You don't mind questions like that, do you?[14]

Far more satisfying, in this respect, are those stories like "Debriefing," "Unguided Tour," and "Project for a Trip to China," where there is only an eviscerated first person, a nearly transparent subjectivity whose history merges with that of numberless other modern urban intellectuals and whose voice is a pastiche of internalized quotations that enacts the mild lament of "Debriefing"—"Look at all this stuff I've got in my head" (p. 38). Sontag is far more compelling as an artist in those works that come closest to her theoretical essays, in the aforementioned "Project for a Trip to China" or the documentary film *Promised Lands*. Indeed, one could argue that "Project" is as much a theoretical effort as it is a piece of fiction, precisely the sort of hybrid form—part short story, part speculation—that we have been examining. The tale is laced with references that sound ambiguously autobiographical:

Invited by the Chinese Government, I am going to China.

Why does everybody like China: Everybody.

Chinese things:
    Chinese food
    Chinese laundry
    Chinese torture

China is certainly too big for a foreigner to understand. But so are most places.

For the moment I am not inquiring about "revolution" (Chinese revolution) but trying to grasp the meaning of patience. . . .

Chinese patience. Who assimilates whom? . . .

Riding around Pnom Penh in a rickshaw in April 1968, I thought of the photograph I have of my father in a rickshaw in Tientsin taken in 1931. . . .

A trip into the history of my family. I've been told that the Chinese are pleased when they learn that a visitor from Europe or America has some link with prewar China. Objection: My parents were on the wrong side. Amiable, sophisticated Chinese reply: But all foreigners who lived in China at that time were on the wrong side.[15]

The temptation to attribute these memories to Sontag herself, rather than a dramatic speaker, arises because of the allusions to Hanoi and Sontag's own well-known essay, "A Trip to Hanoi" (recounting her visit "behind enemy lines" in spring of 1968). By placing this story among her collected short fiction—in fact, putting it, tendentiously, at the *head* of the collection—Sontag gains a certain formal freedom and also dramatizes one of the major claims of "Project for a Trip to China"—for unlike most stories, this one does issue a series of claims:

> Before injustice and responsibility became too clear, and strident, mythical voyages were to places outside of history. Hell, for instance. The land of the dead.
>
> Now such voyages are entirely circumscribed by history. Mythical voyages to places consecrated by the history of real peoples, and by one's own personal history.
>
> The result is, inevitably, literature. More than it is knowledge.
>
> . . . to continue the trip, neither colonialist nor native, requires ingenuity. Travel as decipherment. Travel as disburdenment. I am taking one small suitcase, and neither typewriter nor camera nor tape recorder. Hoping to resist the temptation to bring back any Chinese objects, however shapely, or any souvenirs, however evocative. When I already have so many in my head. ["Project," pp. 27–28]

This China is a place of the mind, an awful rubble of childhood recollections and collective representations. Thus, the trip itself is not only a project (situated in the future, half desire and half potentiality) but beset by projections, "grounded in guesswork, vivified by misconception" (p. 19). There is the danger that, thus grounded, the actual visit will be lost and will leave no trace on a sensibility that is already (unwittingly) living in a fictitious China.

> Among the so-called romantics of the last century, a trip almost always resulted in the production of a book. One traveled to Rome, Athens, Jerusalem—and beyond—in order to write about it.
>
> Perhaps I will write the book about my trip to China before I go. ["Project," p. 29]

The story as a whole is an assemblage of jumbled Chinese associations, so massive and so mixed that the narrative must frequently break down into abbreviated notes and sets of "variables":

> I am going to China.
>
> I will walk across the Luhu bridge spanning the Sham Chun River between Hong Kong and China.
>
> After having been in China for a while, I will walk across the Luhu Bridge spanning the Sham Chun River between China and Hong Kong.

Five variables:
Luhu Bridge
Sham Chun River
Hong Kong
China
peaked cloth caps

Consider other possible permutations. [P. 3]

This projected China has no fixed form, only heterogeneous impressions and received ideas and news dispatches torn out of context ("There is a woman in China, twenty-nine years old, whose right foot is on her left leg"—p. 15), all susceptible to endless rearrangement and endless, contradictory readings. Thus, though China is the ostensible subject, the meditation goes beyond it to embrace such general questions as the fate of individualism, the nature of knowledge, and the relationship of both of these to literature. The narrator is caught between an ancient lie ("Entering the first grade, I told my classmates I was born in China"—p. 6) and the distortions of contemporary desire; the trip may therefore function either as a "search [for] political understanding" or as a way to "ease a private grief" (p. 19). China itself is a place of uncertainties—"The country of science fiction, where everyone speaks with the same voice. Maotsetungized" (p. 7), with its own heritage of artfulness (porcelains and veiled politeness) and a present "ruled by quotations" (p. 26). Yet it simultaneously promises idyllic simplicity, uniform and easy measures for deciding between right and wrong, truth and falsehood. The mingling of these elements—private associations and public mythologies, the single "Wary, ironic, disillusioned" (p. 20) sensibility of the narrator and the revolutionary mass—produces a speculative conflict:

> First half of second quotation from unnamed Austrian-Jewish refugee sage who died in America: "Man as such is the problem of our time; the problems of individuals are fading away and are even forbidden, morally forbidden."
>
> It is not that I'm afraid of getting simple, by going to China. The truth *is* simple.
>
> I will be taken to see factories, schools, collective farms, hospitals, museums, dams. There will be banquets and ballets. I will never be alone....
>
> "Fight individualism," says Chairman Mao. Master moralist.
> . . . .
>
> The truth is simple, very simple. Centered. But people crave other nourishment besides the truth. Its privileged distortions, in philosophy and literature. For example.
>
> I honor my cravings, and I lose patience with them.

"Literature is only impatience on the part of knowledge." (Third and last quote from unnamed Austrian-Jewish sage who died, a refugee, in America.)

Already in possession of my visa, I am impatient to leave for China. To know. Will I be stopped by a conflict with literature? . . .

Death doesn't die. And the problems of literature are not fading away . . . [Pp. 21, 26; final ellipsis is Sontag's]

Yet if literature sometimes acts as a barrier to knowledge, another and more impenetrable version of the Great Wall, it is also—for us—a necessary rite of passage, a bridge like that across the Sham Chun River with which the story opens and closes:

I shall cross the Sham Chun bridge both ways.

And after that: No one is surprised. Then comes literature. . . .

To renounce literature, I would have to be really sure that I could know. A certainty that would crassly prove my ignorance. . . .

The only solution: both to know and not to know. Literature and not literature, using the same verbal gestures. [Pp. 28–29]

"Project for a Trip to China" contains its own miniature theory of the nature of literature, thus making the story necessarily self-referring. But since the range of speculation extends beyond the text at hand, "Project" avoids the occasional coyness and the claustrophobic atmosphere of most auto-commentary. The subject matter, for example, is publicly accessible; the tale incorporates news accounts and quotations that one might actually look up and references to geographical landmarks and Chinese history that one can and does measure against other descriptions of them. But if we do so, the story will also make us more aware that we are simply pitting one set of permutations against another, making up—from differing degrees of fear and doubt and longing and guilt— different visionary Chinas. Gass's story "In the Heart of the Heart of the Country," another travelogue of sorts, resembles this story in its broken sentences, its decomposed personal anecdotes, and its overall narrative strategy of shuffling and reshuffling verisimilar details—the recognizable detritus of small-town life—into stanzaic patterns. But the final effect of "Project for a Trip to China" is not to fold back upon itself and remind us that it is, after all, only a fiction. It instead throws doubt upon the fictions that we have all been living with unwittingly, and it raises questions about what we take for facts and why.

For Gass the universe of fiction is closed, set off discretely from the opposing universe of discourse where demands for utility and truth (which he often treats as if they were almost interchangeable) hold sway. For Sontag, fact and fiction overlap—not happily, perhaps, but necessarily. Our knowledge and our discourse are compounded of diverse elements, of which truth, in the narrow sense of verifiability, is only one. Literature arises from complex motives, rooted partly in private, fantasmatic need and partly in the will to knowledge itself. And theory is the site where these motives overlap, where fact and fiction, knowledge and desire can meet. It provides an alternative to the irritations and doubts that surround traditional literature, without becoming "aggressively anti-philosophical" in the manner of those "'positive' or descriptive sciences"[16] that Sontag repudiates for their shallowness and overweaning pride. Literary discourse—as form, as play, as a machine for sheer sensation—offers too little to what she calls in *On Photography* "the possibility of understanding,"[17] to be fully engaging for her. Scientific discourse is too arrogant and too alienating in its insistence that "Being, reality, the world, the cosmos are . . . what lies 'outside' the mind" ("Thinking," p. 78). It blinds itself to the passions that condition any quest for knowledge and the larger human interests that awareness might fulfill.

"Project for a Trip to China" is therefore a piece of theoretical literature that strives to be responsible to those needs of understanding while taking their imperiousness and deviousness into account. Its mode is as much hypothetical as it is fictional; it is a set of instructions—"consider other possible permutations"—even more than a completed artifact. Sontag's writing is most effective when it thus works with, rather than against, the schematic and the generalized. She does herself a disservice by insisting that art must be always and only concrete and sensuous, either as a represented world that engulfs us or as a design that overwhelms us in an "act of comprehension accompanied by voluptuousness."[18] Her own writing provides neither the vicarious experience of realism nor the phenomenological engagement of formalism. But at its best it is capable of giving us something else—an exhilarating sense of possibility and permutation; of correlations, roots, and consequences; of the trajectory of thought as it moves across phenomena, unsettling and redistributing them.

The problem with Sontag's creative writing is not a lack of imagination but the nature of her imagination; her nonfiction, to the extent that it tries to render immediate experience, is no less awkward and no more engulfing that her fiction. There is reason to prefer the spare, categorical treatment of a potential "Oriental encounter" in a work like "Project for a Trip to China" to the extended but not quite convincing account to actual events in "A Trip to Hanoi." The latter attempts to be the record of a conversion, as several reviewers have noted. The first half of the essay is taken up with the visitor's disappointment and confusions—"the demands and limitations of the approach to Vietnam I myself was capable of"—as transcribed from the journal entries of Sontag's first week in Hanoi.[19] But suddenly, just at the point when the conversion experience should occur, the journal entries vanish, and all that we hear of this crucial change of vision is a remote, a posteriori report that it has happened.

> It wasn't that I'd expected to feel at ease in North Vietnam, or to find the Vietnamese as a people exactly like Europeans and Americans. But neither had I expected to be so baffled, so mistrustful of my experiences there—and unable to subdue the backlash of my ignorance.... By around the fifth day, as the extracts from my journal indicate, I was ready to give up—on myself, which meant on the Vietnamese as well.
>
> And then, suddenly, my experience started changing. The psychic cramp with which I was afflicted in the early part of my stay began to ease and the Vietnamese as real people, and North Vietnam as a real place, came into view. [Pp. 234–35]

This is an extreme instance of what pervades the essay as a whole, a tension between the demands of conventional autobiographical representation and ideological analysis. It is only when "Project for a Trip to China" makes autobiography itself problematic, as both a mode of and a motive for knowledge, that this tension can be reconciled.

Indeed, most of Sontag's essays treat, not artistic sensations themselves, but the *problem* of those sensations, the general "project" or "sensibility" underlying a particular aesthetic. As the introduction of *Against Interpretation* stresses:

> ...most of it could perhaps be called meta-criticism....I was writing, with passionate partiality, about *problems* raised for me by works of art, mainly contemporary, in different genres: I wanted to expose and clarify the theoretical assumptions underlying specific judgments and tastes...
>
> ...what value these essays may possess, the extent to which they are more than case studies of *my* evolving sensibility, rests not on the specific appraisals made but on the interestingness of the problems raised. [Pp. 5–6]

A careful reading of these essays will reveal that it is not, say, Godard's film that is the subject but what that film reveals about the possibilities of narrative; not the fetish objects of "camp" but the attitudes and stance that the love of camp implies. "To name a sensibility, to draw its contours and to recount its history was the problem it started from, and then I looked for an example," as Sontag remarked of her study of camp in an interview.[20] And by the time her second collection appeared, she was already arguing that art itself is "now, mainly, a form of thinking."

> For the critic, the proper question is not the relationship between the book and "the world" or "reality" (in which each novel is judged as if it were a unique item, and in which the world is regarded as a far less complex place than it is) but the complexities of consciousness itself, as the medium through which a world exists at all and is constituted.... From this point of view, the decision of the old novelists to depict the unfolding of the destinies of sharply individualized "characters" in familiar, socially dense situations

within the conventional notation of chronological sequence is only one of many possible decisions, possessing no inherently superior claim to the allegiance of serious readers. There is nothing more innately "human" about these procedures.[21]

Small wonder that when she tried to turn her speculations into conventional stories, the result is something on the order of an allegorical cartoon:

> The story begins in a crowded place, something like a Greyhound bus station, only more refined. The main character is an intrepid young woman of irreproachable white Protestant ancestry and even, regular construction. Her only visible fault was mirrored in her name, Miss Flatface.
>
> Buffeted by mechanical stares, Miss Flatface decided to enter upon a career of venery. The spirits of Ben Franklin and Tom Paine whispered hoarsely in her ears, beckoning and forbidding.
>
> Miss Flatface lifted up her skirts. A gasp was heard from one and all. "No sex, no sex," the crowd chanted. "Who could inspire desire with that face?"...
>
> ...Mr. Obscenity bounded into the room, wearing white knickers, a plaid shirt, and a monocle. "The trouble with you fellows," he said, leering at Miss Flatface, then ripping open her nylon blouse without bothering to undo the buttons, "is that you've got principles"...
>
> Something like a chariot, drawn by a team of roan horses, pulled up before the frosted-glass doors. Mr. Obscenity vaulted into his seat and, with a gesture that admitted of no refusal, summoned Miss Flatface to hers. Above the clatter of hoofs, as they sped away, moans and giggles could be heard.[22]

This forced gaiety and ungainly intellectual shorthand could hardly be more distant from Sontag's probing, utterly serious study of "The Pornographic Imagination," that appeared not long after.

> ...the extreme forms of consciousness...transcend social personality or psychological individuality.
>
> ..Art produced under the aegis of this conception certainly is not, cannot be, "realistic."...
>
> ...The ahistorical dreamlike landscape where action is situated, the peculiarly congealed time in which acts are performed—these occur almost as often in science fiction as they do in pornography. There is nothing conclusive in the well-known fact that most men and women fall short of the sexual prowess that people in pornography are represented as enjoying; that the size of the organs, number and duration of orgasms, variety and feasibility of sexual powers, and amount of sexual energy all seem grossly exaggerated. Yes, and the spaceships and the teeming planets depicted in science-fiction novels don't exist either. The fact that the site of narrative is an ideal *topos* disqualifies neither pornography nor science fiction from being literature. Such negations of real, concrete, three-dimensional social time, space, and personality—and such "fantastic" enlargements of human

energy—are rather the ingredients of another kind of literature, founded on another mode of consciousness.[25] ["Imagination," pp. 44–46]

Obviously, there is a gross discrepancy between the kind of art she here promotes and the kind of art she has produced. Not only does the essay's thoughtful, measured treatment of obscenity make the caricature of Mr. Obscenity seem adolescent and reductive, but her arguments are simply more interesting, more surprising and enlightening, than the would-be three-dimensional adventures and (literally) dimensionless figure of Miss Flatface. An even more apposite comparison can be made between her lucid analysis of Bergman's *Persona* (which also appears in *Styles of Radical Will*) and her own *Brother Carl.*

> The advantages of keeping the psychological aspects of *Persona* indeterminate (while internally credible) are that Bergman can do many other things besides tell a story... he presents something that is, in one sense, cruder and, in another, more abstract: a body of material, a subject...
>
> ...the construction of *Persona* is best described in terms of this variations-on-a-theme form. The theme is that of *doubling*; the variations are those that follow from the leading possibilities of that theme (on both a formal and a psychological level) such as duplication, inversion, reciprocal exchange, unity and fission, and repetition. The action cannot be univocally paraphrased. It's correct to speak of *Persona* in terms of the fortunes of two characters named Elizabeth and Alma who are engaged in a desperate duel of identities. But it is equally pertinent to treat *Persona* as relating the duel between two mythical parts of a single self: the corrupted person who acts (Elizabeth) and the ingenuous soul (Alma) who founders in contact with corruption.
>
> ...their enmeshment is a given, not the result of some prior situation we are allowed to understand; the mood is one of desperation, in which all attributions of voluntariness seem superficial. All we are given is a set of compulsions or gravitations, in which the two women founder, exchanging "strength" and "weakness."
>
> ...absences of utterance become more potent than words: the person who places uncritical faith in words is brought down from relative composure and self-confidence to hysterical anguish.
>
> Here, indeed, is the most powerful instance of the motif of exchange. The actress creates a void by her silence. The nurse, by speaking, falls into it—depleting herself.[23]

The ambiguous film, the misapprehensions and misreadings it has provoked, are the foundation upon which Sontag constructs something new; it rises from them in a glittering, clean-limbed clarification. The effort of refinement and simplification is moving—precisely because it must exert itself against the counterweight of Bergman's recondite, unyielding images and a confused babble of contradictory critical claims about what they mean: "Bergman's work is characterized by slowness, deliberateness of pacing—something like the heaviness of Flaubert. Hence, the excruciatingly unmodulated quality of *Persona* (and *The Silence* before it), a quality only superficially described as pessimism" (pp. 140–41).

Sontag's own interpretation (which is still that, even if her preferred categories are phenomenological and formal rather than psychological or theological) slowly emerges from this murky background during the course of the essay, shaping what had seemed shapeless and joining what had seemed impossibly disjoint. Without the original countervailing weight, however, the tension of the essay would be lost, and with it the sense of discovery. For the theme that Sontag names—"doubling"—and the narrative devices she catalogs—"duplication, inversion, reciprocal exchange"—are not terribly exciting in themselves. This is nowhere more evident than in her own film *Brother Carl*, which mechanically exploits the principles of narrative and the thematic development that she exposes here. Everything in the movie moves by twos: two couples (one degenerate, the other able to regenerate their ties), two women (one dark, one blonde), and two silent children (one autistic, the other mad and only figuratively young). The action itself is doubled—with the first attempted miracle on Carl's part a failure, and the second a success. In fact, parallel scenes are so common and so insistent that *Brother Carl* threatens to turn into a primer of elementary film technique, as here when we are prodded to see the resemblance between mute madman Carl and Karen's autistic daughter, Anna:

> KAREN, a stricken look on her face, advances slowly toward CARL (off-screen, right). MARTIN remains where he is (behind KAREN), watching.
>
> KAREN extends her hand.
>
> KAREN: Hello, CARL.
>
> Medium shot of CARL. He stares at her without making any move.
>
> Back to two-shot. KAREN turns her head to MARTIN, to look for a clue, then turns back to face CARL, more and more appalled. (Cut in flash shot: medium close-up of ANNA. Almost subliminal.) [P. 57]

What was instructive and stimulating in the essay, because it attempted to solve the problem posed by Bergman's film, becomes pedantic in *Brother Carl*, where there is no preliminary bewilderment to resolve and no excess or residual mystery to resist the clarification. The mysteries of *Brother Carl* are only too gnomic and the lessons learned from other filmmakers too programmatically applied. If Bergman and Resnais make films in which "events may form a conundrum which makes it impossible to distinguish exactly between past, present and future," *Brother Carl* must therefore have its own formulaic chronological confusions—scenes in which the same conversation is carried on in two different places at once, for example. The result (as one sardonic review put it) is a sense that "Miss Sontag is full of invention, even if some of the inventions have been tested by other film-makers." Even an enthusiastic viewer acknowledges that "*Brother Carl* is an outsider's commentary, with very personal variations, on those motifs that film-goers associate with the Scandinavian film tradition."[24]

The derivative in art and thought has been one of the key concerns of Sontag's essays throughout her career, a problem that she rightly links to modernism and the restlessness of an art with "absolute aspirations":

> . . . art is foundering in the debilitating tide of what once seemed the crowning achievement of European thought: secular historical consciousness. In little more than two centuries, the consciousness of history has transformed itself from a liberation, an opening of doors, blessed enlightenment, into an almost insupportable burden of self-consciousness. It's scarcely possible for the artist to write a word (or render an image or make a gesture) that doesn't remind him of something already achieved. ["Silence," p. 14]

Although she recognizes how consuming and finally how futile the pursuit of novelty and negation can be, Sontag offers no alternatives. Not because, like Gass, she finds the art of purification so attractive or intrinsically right, but because for her the force of artistic convention and cultural history are so overwhelming. Only in the flush of optimistic youth did she decry the weakness and intransigence of writers who give "further life to the tedious alternatives of . . . the original versus what is preconceived and ready-made."[25] In later essays, the trust that any single work can create its own context and determine its own reception gradually decays, until she is left remarking in *On Photography*: "One would like to imagine that the American public would not have been so unanimous in its acquiescence to the Korean War if it had been confronted with photographic evidence of the devastation of Korea. . . . But the supposition is trivial. The public did not see such photographs because there was, ideologically, no space for them" (p. 18).

The space in question is equally a product of aesthetic convention and social conditions. Both contribute to the situation of contemporary art: the desire for novelty, the challenging of precedents, the compromised authority, the threat of premature exhaustion. For Sontag, unlike Gass, art is always vividly contextualized; even transcendence is a historically conditioned goal. Literature is never an alternative to the world, but part of it:

> The conflict between "the two cultures" is in fact an illusion, a temporary phenomenon born of a period of profound and bewildering historical change. What we are witnessing is not so much a conflict of cultures as the creation of a new (potentially unitary) kind of sensibility. This new

sensibility is rooted, as it must be, in *our* experience, experiences which are new in the history of humanity—in extreme social and physical mobility; in the crowdedness of the human scene (both people and material commodities multiplying at a dizzying rate); in the availability of new sensations such as speed (physical speed, as in airplane travel; speed of images, as in the cinema); and in the pan-cultural perspective on the arts that is possible through the mass reproduction of art objects.

What we are getting is not the demise of art, but a transformation of the function of art.[26]

Sontag must confront the same situation whether she writes fiction or (in her own happy phrase) "reasons in public." But with this difference—her theoretical writings have the capacity to analyze and, if necessary, to dismantle the ideological space in which writing must occur. They can thus try to negate those forces that an art work, in its positivity and focus on its own constructions, must accept.

All art may be treated as a mode of proof, an assertion of accuracy in the spirit of maximum vehemence. Any work of art may be seen as an attempt to be indisputable with respect to the actions it represents.

Proof differs from analysis. Proof establishes that something happened. Analysis shows why it happened \ . . . the price of its completeness is that proof is always formal. Only what is already contained in the beginning is proven at the end. In analysis, however, there are always further angles of understanding, new realms of causality.[27]

This is from a 1964 essay in praise of Godard, and though she has changed sides in the intervening years, the opposition between artifact and analysis remains much the same in 1977:

Any photograph has multiple meanings; indeed, to see something in the form of a photograph is to encounter a potential object of fascination. . . . Photographs, which cannot themselves explain anything, are inexhaustible invitations to deduction, speculation, and fantasy.

Photography implies that we know about the world if we accept it as the camera records it. But this is the opposite of understanding, which starts from *not* accepting the world as it looks. All possibility of understanding is rooted in the ability to say no. [*Photography*, p. 23]

Contending, saying no for the sake of understanding, is what Sontag does best, and it is a source of greater power and conviction in her essays—a power to provoke and agitate, to be sure, as well as to win accord, but clearly more exciting than the bulk of her stories and films, those would-be machines for exciting strong emotions. Her theoretical writings also come close to what she once aspired to as a new sensibility:

. . . in our own time, art is becoming increasingly the terrain of specialists. The most interesting and creative art of our time is *not* open to the generally educated; it demands special effort; it speaks a specialized language. . . . The most interesting works of contemporary art are full of references to the history of the medium; so far as they comment on past art, they demand a knowledge of at least the recent past. . . . Again, a similarity with the style of science—this time, with the accumulative aspect of science—can be discerned. ["One Culture," p. 296]

The "accumulative aspect of science" (or theory) is an alternative to history experienced as a burden, the insupportable and unavoidable fear of doing derivative work. Not only for her own sake, but for the sake of those who follow her, theory is a mode that allows Sontag to continue writing and to do so without becoming one of those "writers who close off rather than inaugurate, who cannot be learned from, so much as imitated, and whom one imitates at the peril of merely repeating what they have done" ("Sarraute," p. 109). Theory also seems to allow greater coherence and control. It is a place for exercising all one's energies and uniting—if only in discourse and at the level of abstraction—the discordant particulars and competing claims (moral and aesthetic, political and psychological, high cultural and low) of contemporary life. As the narrator of "Debriefing" exclaims:

> We know more than we can use. . . . rockets and Venetian churches, David Bowie and Diderot, nuoc Mam and Big Macs, sunglasses and orgasms. How many newspapers and magazines do you read? For me, they're what candy or Quaaludes or scream therapy are for my neighbors. . . .
> And we don't know nearly enough. [P. 38]

This hectic catalog bespeaks a strained, distended field of attention—not the loving recitation of particulars, the slow, indwelling movement of the traditional novel. Such novels presuppose a solidity and continuity of detail, a coherence of experience that is immediate rather than earned, that can rely on old and trusted faculties of observation and introspection. Theoretical discourse is a way to reinstate an "earned" coherence. By simplifying and compressing, it allows one to "know less" while trying to know more.

Ultimately, Sontag's essays stand in much the same relationship to her screenplays and her stories that she herself saw between the French New Novel and *la nouvelle critique*:

> This surrender of the novel's commitment to facileness, to easy availability and the perpetuation of an outmoded aesthetic will undoubtedly give rise to a great many boring and pretentious books; and one may well come to wish the old unself-consciousness back again. But the price must be paid. Readers must be made to see, by a new generation of critics who may well have to force this ungainly period of the novel down their throats. . . .
>
> But perhaps the more valuable achievement to come out of France for the novel has been a whole body of criticism inspired by the new novelists (and, in some cases, written by them) which amounts to a most impressive attempt to think systematically about the genre. . . . The reason these essays may

prove more valuable than the novels is that they propose standards that are ampler and more ambitious than anything yet achieved by any writer. ["Sarraute," pp. 110–11]

In Sontag's writing, too, ungainly narratives stand opposed to her vivid, ample, and ambitious essays. Through theory she can more easily introduce and more consistently pursue demanding schemes that cannot yet be put to practice and exercising notions that will not fit comfortably into the generic mold of novels or screenplays.

Gass makes a good foil not only for Sontag's problems as an artist but for her powers as a theorist as well. Although both have training in philosophy, their fundamental sympathies and range of allusion are markedly dissimilar—Sontag cites Hegel, Nietzsche, and Kierkegaard; Gass is more comfortable with the Anglo-American school of conceptual analysis and the philosophy of science than with what Sontag calls "the grand continental tradition of meditation on the tribulations of subjectivity and self-consciousness."[28] While professing (in a review) to admire Sontag's "exemplary introduction" to Cioran's *The Temptation to Exist*, Gass remains impatient with Cioran himself for writing only "philosophical romance on modern themes."[29] For Sontag, however, the distinction between philosophy and philosophical romance is not easy to draw, even though she recognizes many of the same tendencies. She does not share Gass's feeling that the limits of philosophical reasoning are fixed.

> ...the objective, formalized visions of Being and of human knowledge proposed by traditional philosophy [depend] on a particular relation between permanent structures and change in human experience, in which...change is recessive. But this relation was upset— permanently?—around the time climaxed by the French Revolution, when "history" finally pulled up alongside "nature" and then took the lead.
>
> At the point that history usurped nature as the decisive framework for human experience, man began to think historically about his experience, and the traditional ahistorical categories of philosophy become hollowed out.
>
> ...philosophy's traditionally "abstract" leisurely procedures no longer appeared to address themselves to anything; they weren't substantiated any more by the sense that intelligent people had of their experience. Neither as a description of Being...nor, in the alternative conception...as a description of mind only, did philosophy inspire much trust in its capacity to fulfill its traditional aspiration: that of providing the formal models for *understanding* anything. At the least, some kind of further retrenchment or relocation of discourse was felt to be necessary....
>
> Another response was...a new kind of philosophizing: personal (even autobiographical), aphoristic, lyrical, anti-systematic. ["Thinking," pp. 76–78]

This difference in philosophic outlook becomes a difference in how each conceives the theoretical enterprise in which s/he is engaged. For Gass, the goal is verifiability and logical consistency, independent of history and desire. A theoretical model, or a philosophical system, may make other claims on us as well—by its grace and symmetry, its stirring preconceptions and powerful regulative principles—but these are utterly separate from the business of making accurate predictions and valid arguments. And though Gass everywhere promotes the glory of the aesthetic, his respect for truth (thus conceived) is so great that he must keep art from having any pretentions to it, lest he be forced to choose between them. This applies to his own artistry as a theorist as well, producing a curious imbalance between his ornate verbal surfaces and his somewhat meager and oft-repeated theoretical premises. His prose is rich, to surfeiting, but his serious claims are few and his conceptual machinery deliberately simple—in proportion to the stringency of his standards of truth. His characteristic claims are, moreover, "formal": concerned with the logic of categorization, the ontological and conceptual status of "literature."

Sontag, on the other hand, is a "substantial" theorist. Her essays bristle with generalizations about what is or ought to be the case, with detailed descriptions of the "contours" and the history of a sensibility, a school, or period. Her claims are therefore more memorable and more translatable than Gass's—witness the wide dissemination of her views on "camp" in the popular press. But they also risk inaccuracy and expose themselves to challenges and counterarguments. Mired in and admiring of his prose, few of Gass's readers dispute or even pay much attention to his claims. But whenever Sontag advances hers—even when they come close to Gass's own (as they did in *Against Interpretation*)—there is always controversy, dissension, cries of pain and outrage. In part this is because she lacks Gass's caution, but in larger part it is because one cannot make a separate peace with her prose, take an isolatable pleasure in her wordplay and leave her premises aside. Her own remarks on the difference between "style" and "stylization" apply in this connection and help us to more clearly distinguish her theoretical writing from Gass's:

> ...when the material of art is conceived of as "subject matter," it is also experienced as capable of being exhausted. And as subjects are understood to be fairly far along in this process of exhaustion, they become available to further and further stylization....
>
> "Stylization" in a work of art, as distinct from style, reflects an ambivalence (affection contradicted by contempt, obsession contradicted by irony) toward the subject-matter. This ambivalence is handled by maintaining, through the rhetorical overlay that is stylization, a special distance from the subject. ["On Style," p. 28]

Gass's ornate surfaces are in direct proportion to his attenuated and repetitive claims, but there is little chance of exhaustion in Sontag's restless pursuit of the contemporary. More to the point, hers is for better or worse an art of asseveration—which meshes rather nicely with what she values in theoretical discourse.

> Perhaps there are certain ages which do not need truth as much as they need a deepening of the sense of reality, a widening of the imagination. I, for one, do not doubt that the sane view of the world is the true one. But is that what is always wanted, truth? The need for truth is not constant; no more than is the need for repose. An idea which is a distortion may have a greater intellectual thrust than the truth; it may better serve the needs of the spirit, which vary. The truth is balance, but the opposite of truth, which is unbalance, may not be a lie.[30]

Note that Sontag is not committing one of Gass's category mistakes, not confining the truth of an idea with its "intellectual thrust"—but neither does she assume as he does that whatever "feels too good to believe" is necessarily a lie. There is simply much more room for the pragmatic "needs of the spirit" in her view of theory, which explains both her tolerance for Cioran and certain elements in her own theoretical writing.

> When Cioran describes Nietzsche's philosophy as "a sum of attitudes"—mistakenly scrutinized by scholars for the constants that the philosopher has rejected—it's clear that he accepts the Nietzschean standard, with its critique of "truth" as system and consistency, as his own. . . .
> The implication, here and elsewhere, is that what the true philosopher says isn't something "true" but rather something necessary or liberating. . . .
> . . . Nietzsche doesn't reject historical thinking because it is false. On the contrary, it must be rejected because it is true—a debilitating truth that has to be overthrown to allow a more inclusive orientation for human conciousness. ["Thinking," p. 91]

To acknowledge the force of attitude and the need for a "more inclusive orientation" is not, however, to forego all criticism. Indeed, in some instances, Sontag is more skeptical than Gass, simply because she is more attuned to hidden attitudes and their implications. Thus, Gass's response to a book like *Wisconsin Death Trip* (a collection of photographs and newspaper clippings) is to hail it as

> . . . an effort to recapture the consciousness of a neglected people . . .
> The result is an impressive example of the poetry of history. . . . As we read, we do not so much pass from death to death as we enter one life on its painful way there. . . .
> . . . There can be no question that this original work makes us deeply feel one form that misery has taken; and in causing us to feel as well as consider, *Wisconsin Death Trip* has enlarged on the uses of history.[31]

To which Sontag counters: "Of course, *Wisconsin Death Trip* doesn't actually prove anything. The force of its historical argument is the force of collage. To Van Schaick's disturbing, handsomely time-eroded photographs Lesy could have matched other texts from the period—love letters, diaries—to give another, perhaps less desperate impression. His book is rousing, fashionably pessimistic polemic, and totally whimsical as history" (*Photography*, p. 73).

Because she expects and accepts interests and attitudes to play a part in every intellectual position, Sontag has a more active, even an aggressive, conception of the theoretical enterprise. A theory of literature may pursue its own independent concerns; it need not confine itself to explaining or defending a body of completed works. *Against Interpretation*, for example, calls for a new kind of criticism—not to make particular works by Godard or Robbe-Grillet more intelligible, but to help us "recover our senses" and so bring into being the "new sensibility" that a new (perhaps as yet unborn) kind of artistry requires.

> . . . it will demand accepting new pleasures—such as the pleasure of solving a problem—to be gotten from prose fiction and learning how to get them. . . . And it will make self-conscious aestheticians, didactic explorers, of all who wish seriously to practice the form. . . . Readers must be made to see, by a new generation of critics. ["Sarraute," p. 110]

Theory constructs—and later deconstructs—ideological space; it need not await new developments in art but may operate in advance of them, or in opposition to them. This stance—so unlike the humble posture of service one associates with academic criticism—as much as any particular views she advances is what makes Sontag's work so controversial. For despite her training, she is not part of the academy, and the difficulties and pretensions of her position as a generalist, an unallied writer speaking of and to the culture at large, makes it a far gamier one than Gass's straddling of two disciplines. Without a discipline to define which problems are important, Sontag's theorizing has been obliged from the start to raise issues, invent dilemmas, project domains of thought—and to do so in a way that would make her own proposals seem not simply accurate or original but necessary. Hence, Sontag appears as a detector of tendencies, a bearer of exotic news, "a liaison critic who travels between the new art world and the intellectual community at large."[32] But this is secondary to her real genius for establishing a space of operation within which thought can work. "There can be no evidence," as she notes in *On Photography*, "of an event until the event itself has been named and characterized" (p. 19).

Not only must she bring problems into being—by importation or by discovery—but she must also invest them with glamour or distress and gather an appropriate audience for them. The latter is an especially tricky business, since an invented public is unlikely to have the unity of concern, the common stock of information and shared expectation of a group that already exists. Accidental provocations and inadvertent insults are almost inevitable. Since the general culture that is both her subject and her public is only half-perceived and half-imagined, there are bound to be many for whom Sontag's interests and sense of urgency will seem like an alien imposition. Yet all who write in Sontag's wake, even those she most annoys or who find her proposals most wrongheaded, remain beholden to her for the problems she has raised and the audience she has left behind her—an audience united largely by the fact that they have all, at least, read Susan Sontag.

Sontag herself is much indebted to European models for some portions of her subject matter, but even more for her sense of mission and the role she has tried to introduce into American intellectual life. "In France," she writes (with apparent envy): "there is more awareness of the adventure, the *risk* involved in intelligence, a man can be both a specialist and the subject of general intelligent interest and controversy."[33] Her own vocation is even more precarious than this, and her original antecedents (and one reason for claiming that her theoretical writings are artistic, even though the art is of a sharply different character than Gass's) were figures like Artaud and Breton, those artists of the manifesto. Certainly one can feel this inspiration at work in "Against Interpretation," with its terse, occasionally inflammatory dictums—"In place of a hermeneutics we need an erotics of art"—(which usually go undefended) and its discrete, highly abbreviated and separately numbered sections. The essay reads like a listing of what is to be done, or a set of these appended to some nearby wall. "Notes on 'Camp'" takes its impetus from an even more stylized oeuvre, the arch maxims and studied ironies of Oscar Wilde, while her essay on Godard's *Vivre Sa Vie*—a film in which "narrative is broken . . . by the extremely arbitrary decomposition of the story into twelve episodes . . . which are serially rather than causally related" ("Godard's *Vivre*," p. 202)—itself decomposes into seventeen episodes and an appendix that trails after it like film credits. Collage and montage, evocative fragments and incongruous juxtapositions, have continued to engage her right up to her present work, and though the engagement is more skeptical now and offset by a growing interest in continuity and history, it remains one of the identifying marks of "the artistic" in her work. Another such mark is the way in which the essays use the first person, not casually or instrumentally, but because (as she says in connection with photography) "to count as an art one must stress the individual *auteur* and 'the subjectivity of seeing' " (*Photography*, p. 136). (Comments about Sontag's "sensibility" tend to treat this first person without sufficient allowance for how mannered or strategic it is, how often the impersonation functions as a dramatized attitude and not as an incomplete autobiographical representation.)

Although there has been no vivid shift in Sontag's theoretical style—of the sort that one can see in Gass's prose—there have been certain gradual changes that suggest that her appreciation for the art of theory is undiminished—and if anything, has grown. Where once she treated her essays as strictly subordinate to "my tasks as a novelist," the balance has so altered recently that now it is more proper to speak of the influence her essays exercise on her stories and films. Even in her second collection, *Styles of Radical Will*, she ceased to treat the essays as strictly ancillary, and arranged the book itself so as to chart the progress of a dilemma from its first, quizzical appearance, through a process of exacerbation and deepening angst, to its eventual (although far from final) resolution. The collection thus has a totality and a trajectory that exceed either chance or use, and a startling continuity of theme, from the opening essay on the motives for asceticism and silence in modern art to the closing account of her visit to Hanoi, where the language barrier becomes literal and asceticism becomes a way of war-torn life. The most recent books—*On Photography* and *Illness as Metaphor*—are even more closely knit, and though sharply critical of aestheticism, they also show increasing "care for [the] means of expression as such"—which Sontag once called the defining "concern of literature" ("Imagination," p. 39). If, as Sontag claims, "the concept of art imposed by the triumph of modernism" demands that art be "subversive...of the traditional aims of art" (*Photography*, p. 127), then the line between her own literary and theoretical efforts *should* be permeable. But the fact that the artfulness of her essays has become more patent recently is due less to changes in Sontag's own writing than to changes that the artistic community at large—artists, publishers, and museum directors alike—have wrought in the definition of art itself. This general shift in public sentiment is, as Sontag notes, one of the reasons for the growing popularity of photography, which embodies: "...the characteristic direction taken in our time by both the modernist high arts and the commercial arts: the transformation of arts into meta-arts or media.... The media are democratic:...they regard the whole world as material. The traditional fine arts rely on the distinction between authentic and fake, between original and copy, between good taste and bad taste; the media blur, if they do not abolish outright, these distinctions" (*Photography*, p. 149).

On Photography and Illness as Metaphor are Sontag's finest pieces of writing to date. They are pieces that warrant our attention as art, yet they do not become art in the usual way. We are familiar enough with avantgarde extensions of "art" as a category, which arise because "modernist taste in its pop version" has a "zeal for debunking the high culture of the past (focusing on shards, junk, odd stuff; excluding nothing);...conscientious courting of vulgarity" (*Photography*, p.131). Or because of the contrary zeal to find refined but unsuspected symmetries in the most unlikely places—Paul Strand's photograph of "Abstract Patterns Made by Bowls," for example. Sontag treats both of these modes of aestheticizing in her book on photography, yet neither one of them is hers. If Gass sometimes betrays a suspicion of theory, and uses literary devices to curb and control its rapacious appetites, Sontag seems (currently) just as mistrustful of the rapacity of the aesthetic and just as eager to constrain it by applying to it the cutting edge of her analysis: ". . . every subject is depreciated into an article of consumption, promoted into an item for aesthetic appreciation. . . . reality is understood as plural, fascinating, and up for grabs"—making "the entire world available as an object of appraisal" (*Photography*, p. 110).

The crossbreeding of art and theory takes a different course in Gass and in Sontag; the former envelops theory in a deliberately disarming beauty, the latter circumscribes (without denying) beauty by standing at a willfully speculative distance from it. Reading Gass's literary theory involves a shift in where we pay attention, but the kind of attention we pay is not greatly different from that we exercise when we read his novels. Reading Sontag involves a more radical reorientation, demands a capacity to take pleasure in, and at the same time to stand ready to dispute, any given formulation—an ability to blend appreciation with skepticism, to be tantalized, engaged, but never fully submerged, always keen and questioning before the changing show.

And change it does, the breathless contemporaneity of her work earning Sontag the dubious title of "high prophetess of high fashion" in a dismissive account of her work by George P. Elliott.[34] (The association of Sontag with "fashion" is, incidentally, common enough to make one suspect that something more than a simple contempt for trendiness is involved. There is a vein of misogyny in Sontag criticism that opens even wider in essays like Rubin's "Susan Sontag and the Camp Followers," which follows up on the labored wit of its title by lamenting that Sontag prefers "to revel in concepts, treating them as if they were form-fitting silken garments."[35] Timeliness and time itself are woven into Sontag's essays in several respects. First there is the fact that, for her, art is a category that exists in time, changing its dimensions and its meaning as the world in which it is situated changes. Second, the function of theoretical activity is itself subject to change, as the consequences of a given position are revealed and as the perceived needs of the present moment alter. *Against Interpretation*, for instance, evokes the misty moment when art became "problematic, in need of defense" and establishes its own program in terms of a new moment: ". . . we have an obligation to overthrow any means of defending and justifying art which becomes particularly obtuse or onerous or insensitive to contemporary needs and practice" ("A.I.," p. 14).

Styles of Radical Will complains even more bitterly about "naively unhistorical" conceptions of art that fail to see that techniques and subject matter, indeed the scope of the aesthetic itself, are mutable. The very contemporary needs that were so honored in *Against Interpretation* have lost their power to command complete obedience, have shrunk to the position of a "prevailing contemporary myth" that would endow the art object and the artist with "certain 'absolute' qualities" ("Silence," p. 31). And by the time she writes *On Photography* and *Illness as Metaphor*, the contemporary has lost even its pathos and its fatality, its merely relative value as a source of myths "about as nourishing and viable as might be devised in an 'unwholesome' time" (p. 11). There is nothing left but to expose these contemporary myths for what they are and to keep us from becoming the witless consumers of our own mythologies.

Thus, both the subject matter and the function of the essays themselves are grounded in history. For this reason Sontag's literary theory is never a theory of literature alone. Even at the outset she argued that films "are also a subdivision of literature" and the best place to seek new developments in narrative technique ("A.I.," p. 32n). Gradually it has become, as her sense of the moment and the needs of understanding changes, a theory of collective representations of every sort, artistic or not. Both of Sontag's most recent works study ideology, in its broadly semiotic as well as its narrowly political sense. She moves to photography because, as was mentioned above, it is the "prototype of the characteristic direction taken in our time by both the modernist high arts and the commercial arts: the transformation of arts into meta-arts or media" (*Photography*, p. 149). This is obviously a transformation that affects literature as well and threatens to erode its very viability as a category—even as photography itself threatens to flood the world with images and to supplant language not only as a medium of art but as our chief means of knowing and recording our world. *Illness as Metaphor* goes on to group together documents of every sort—cinematic and verbal, fictions side by side with private letters, political theory, and bits of medical and psychiatric research. All documents are ideologically equal; each may be a vehicle for promulgating a certain vision of disease.

Time is at the core of Sontag's work in yet a third way—incorporated into the mode of writing she characteristically adopts, the essay. Gass uses essays to diminish the ambitions of theory and to prevent the emergence of a right system; he also finds them an appealing rhythmic unit. Sontag too is happiest in short bursts of rumination; her intellectual energy spends itself in a brilliant spurt of flame and trails out, into a moody and splendid ash. For her, however, the essay form is less a protest against system than a way of acknowledging the occasional and transient nature of even the most systematically developed position—a belief that is (as his remarks on Sartre illustrate) anathema for Gass. The Introduction to the 1969 paperback edition of *Against Interpretation* pays particular and unapologetic attention to this mutability:

For me, the essays have done their work. I see the world differently, with fresher eyes; my conception of my task as a novelist is radically changed. I could describe the process this way. Before I wrote the essays I did not believe many of the ideas espoused in them; when I wrote them, I believed what I wrote; subsequently, I have come to disbelieve some of these same ideas again—but from a new perspective, one that incorporates and is nourished by what is true in the argument of the essays. Writing criticism has proved to be an act of intellectual disburdenment as much as of intellectual self-expression. I have the impression not so much of having, for myself, resolved a certain number of alluring and troubling problems as having used them up. [P. 6]

And in *Illness as Metaphor*, she includes her own earlier words (from *Styles of Radical Will*) among those documents she demystifies—a stunning and justly praised moment of auto-critique:

The cancer metaphor seems hard to resist for those who wish to register indignation. . . . I once wrote, in the heat of despair over America's war on Vietnam, that "the white race is the cancer of human history."

But how to be morally severe in the late twentieth century? How, when there is so much to be severe about; how, when we have a sense of evil but no longer the religious or philosophical language to talk intelligently about evil. Trying to comprehend "radical" or "absolute" evil, we search for adequate metaphors. But the modern disease metaphors are all cheap shots. The people who have the real disease are also hardly helped by hearing their disease's name constantly being dropped as the epitome of evil. Only in the most limited sense is any historical event or problem like an illness. And the cancer metaphor is particularly crass. It is invariably an encouragement to simplify what is complex and an invitation to self-righteousness, if not to fanaticism.[36]

But minor revolutions in her doctrine just as often pass by unremarked. As a result, most critics attend only to the thematic and rhetorical continuities in her work, seeing the constancy of her preoccupations rather than the different uses she makes of them and how her assessment of the same subject matter changes. (*Illness as Metaphor* may be singled out, because of the explicit self-criticism it contains and because its antipathy to what Elliott calls the "nihilistic confusion" of the contemporary scene is so clear and unremitting.)[37] Yet, as indicated earlier, Sontag's first collection was the only place where she actually acted as an advocate of current trends. And even then, as in a remarkable essay on Simone Weil, she sharply curtailed her advocacy, taking to task "the cult of suffering" that overvalues "strength of feeling" and makes of agony "the supreme token of seriousness" rather than celebrating the classical virtues of "tranquility and equilibrium" (p. 57):

There are certain eras which are too complex, too deafened by contradictory historical and intellectual experiences, to hear the voice of sanity. Sanity becomes compromise, evasion, a lie. Ours is an age which consciously pursues health, and yet only believes in the reality of sickness. The truths we respect are those born of affliction. . . .

I do not mean to decry a fashion, but to underscore the motive behind the contemporary taste for the extreme in art and thought. All that is necessary is that we not be hypocritical, that we recognize why we read and admire writers like Simone Weil. ["Simone Weil," pp. 58–59]

The ambivalent fatalism of the collection that follows, *Styles of Radical Will*, has already been noted, and while *On Photography* is no less suspicious of traditional humanism than her two collections of earlier essays, it is just as far removed from the attitudes that marked *Against Interpretation*. Compare, for example, the battle cry of the first collection— "What is important now is to recover our senses. We must learn to *see* more, to *hear* more, to *feel* more" (*A.I.*, p. 23)—to the stern rebuke of this position in *On Photography*:

> But the aestheticizing tendency of photography is such that the medium which conveys distress ends by neutralizing it. Cameras miniaturize experience, transform history into spectacle. As much as they create sympathy, photographs cut sympathy, distance the emotions. Photography's realism creates a confusion about the real which is (in the long run) analgesic morally as well as (both in the long and in the short run) sensorially stimulating. Hence, it clears our eyes. This is the fresh vision everyone has been talking about. [Pp. 109–10]

Though *On Photography* studies a contemporary taste, it is scarcely a brief for it:

> The final reason for the need to photograph everything lies in the very logic of consumption itself. To consume means to burn, to use up— and, therefore, to need to be replenished. As we make images and consume them, we need still more images; and still more. . . . The possession of a camera can inspire something akin to lust. And like all credible forms of lust, it cannot be satisfied: first, because the possibilities of photography are infinite; and, second, because the project is finally self-devouring. The attempts by photographers to bolster up a depleted sense of reality contribute to the depletion. [P. 179]

If readers persist in seeing Sontag as the advocate or the inventor of the photographic tendencies that she simply reports, it reflects the tenacity of the *auteur* principle, the assumption that writing must express the character of the author—a character that is consistent and more or less invariant from one piece of writing to the next. Sontag is aware of how easily this principle of reading can be perverted:

> . . . some of the paltriness of the critics' reaction may be more a response to the signature that *Persona* carries than to the film itself. That signature has come to mean a prodigal, tirelessly productive career; a rather facile, often merely beautiful, by now (it seemed) almost oversize body of

work; a lavishly inventive, sensual, yet melodramatic talent, employed with what appeared to be a certain complacency, and prone to embarrassing displays of intellectual bad taste. From the Fellini of the North, exacting filmgoers could hardly be blamed for not expecting, ever, a truly great film. ["Bergman," pp. 123–24]

Of course, it is more than the "signature" alone that invites us to seek a coherent personality in Sontag's essays—there is also the persistent first person, the occasional pungent memory that makes its way into the text, and the pointed reference to "a theory of my evolving sensibility" in the headnote to *Against Interpretation* ("Note to the Paperback Edition," p. 6). Yet this persona will not bear and does not require a narrowly auto-biographical interpretation. In fact, the eagerness to make it auto-biographical is a way of robbing essays of their theoretical pretentions, making them the peculiar impulses of an idiosyncratic, (perhaps) aber-rant mind, refusing to confront either the power of the reasoning or the allure of the claims. Plainly this could not be the goal of the essays themselves, which never remain with the first person long but instead pass through it, on the way to a collective experience, a shared sensibility. *Sensibility* is the key word here—at least in the early essays, until it is displaced in *On Photography* and *Illness as Metaphor* by more impersonal terms like *photographic seeing* and *ideology*. The adoption of the first person is necessary to gain access to the subject matter or domain of her theory, which is not really a set of artifacts, but the modes of perception and the climates of belief that these artifacts imply and further reinforce.

> A sensibility (as distinct from an idea) is one of the hardest things to talk about; . . .
> . . . [to] do justice to the twin aspects of art: as object and as function, as artifice and as living form of consciousness. . . . Indeed, the entire history of the various arts could be rewritten as the history of different attitudes toward the will. . . . Emotions, longings, aspirations, by thus being named, are virtually invented and certainly promulgated by art.[38]

There are, to be sure, moments of pointed self-revelation—even in *On Photography*.

> One's first encounter with the photographic inventory of ultimate horror is a kind of revelation, the prototypically modern revelation: a negative epiphany. For me, it was photographs of Bergen-Belson and Dachau which I came across by chance in a bookstore in Santa Monica in July 1945. Nothing I have seen—in photographs or in real life—ever cut me as sharply, deeply, instantaneously. Indeed, it seems plausible to me to divide my life into two parts, before I saw those photographs (I was twelve) and after, though it was several years before I understood fully what they were about. What good was served by seeing them? They were only photographs—of an event I had scarcely heard of and could do nothing to

affect, of suffering I could hardly imagine and could do nothing to relieve. When I looked at those photographs, something broke. Some limit had been reached, and not only that of horror; I felt irrevocably grieved, wounded, but a part of my feelings started to tighten; something went dead; something is still crying. [Pp. 19–20]

Yet this "I" is ultimately a representative, and occasionally a prophetic sensibility, a convenient source of information upon which the theory may draw.[39] This explains why the memories evaporate so quickly—why the "I" is generally so faded and translucent—and what peculiar "iciness" readers complain of when they expect a more sustained presence, a furthering of confessions, a deepening of intimacy.

Purely personal or private experiences are not at issue, as the enforced personality of *Illness as Metaphor* makes clear by refusing anywhere to raise the spectre of Sontag's own cancer (lest the analysis miss its public targets and shrink into a piece of private and unrepeatable heroism). The book obeys, as it were, the dictum of the narrator of her own short story, "Old Complaints Revisited":

> I am reluctant to describe myself at all, for fear that too many particularities will make you take my problem less seriously....
> ...I don't want to go into too much detail. I'm afraid of your losing the sense of my problem as a general one. [Pp. 127–28, 126]

The scope of the sensibility (or will, or temperament) that these essays explore varies considerably, from the sensibility of a single author to what is embodied in a genre (like pornography) or a medium (like photography), to something that sets the entire tone of an age or culture. Sontag rarely writes of any state of sensibility or condition of the will as if it were utterly alien to her: To understand a phenomenon is to appreciate how it could have come about, to participate in the mood, the unconfessed motives, the inchoate desires that originate, sustain, and triumph by it. "Everyone has felt (at least in fantasy) the erotic glamour of physical cruelty and an erotic lure in things that are vile and repulsive. These phenomena form part of the genuine spectrum of sexuality, and if they are not to be written off as mere neurotic aberrations, the picture [of human sexuality] looks different from the one promoted by enlightened public opinion, and less simple" ("Imagination," p. 57). It is difficult for readers to grasp the stance of these essays because they rarely disown whatever subjects they explore, even when they are most eager to repudiate them. Take the case of her recent essay on Leni Riefenstahl, an uncompromising effort to demolish Riefenstahl's reputation, and yet an effort to comprehend her appeal as well:

> These ideals are vivid and moving to many people, and it is dishonest—and tautological—to say that one is affected by *Triumph of the Will* and *Olympiad* because they were made by a film maker of genius.

Riefenstahl's films are still effective because, among other reasons, their longings are still felt, because their content is a romantic ideal to which many continue to be attached. . . .

Riefenstahl's current de-Nazification and vindication as indomitable priestess of the beautiful—as a film maker and, now, as a photographer—do not augur well for the keenness of current abilities to detect the fascist longings in our midst.[40]

One must feel the longing to know the nature of its hold on the imagination. Such deliberately courted acquaintance-knowledge is always the first, the requisite, step in Sontag's studies of sensibility and ideology. But next must come the distancing, an emptying out and abstracting from the peculiar nature of one's own enchantment, to reveal the patterns that proximity and personality obscure. Both steps are necessary, whether the goal is to promote or to defend, to acknowledge or to subvert, the sensibility in question. Thus, most of Sontag's essays, from first to last, are rooted in the same principle of a divided intelligence that she makes explicit in her famous "Notes on 'Camp.' " "I am strongly drawn to Camp, and almost as strongly offended by it. That is why I want to talk about it, and why I can. For no one who wholeheartedly shares in a given sensibility can analyze it; he can only, whatever his intention, exhibit it. To name a sensibility, to draw its contours, and to recount its history, requires a deep sympathy modified by revulsion" (pp. 277–78).

It is characteristic of her preoccupation with motives and interests that her method should begin to take on a psychological coloring, rather than presenting itself entirely in the neutral tones of epistemology or logic. The interplay between sympathy and revulsion is always there, even though the balance tips from qualified appreciation to modified disgust—and even when the push and pull becomes so rapid and so well-matched that the "effect" (as Robert Melville puts it) is one of "ironic neutrality."[41] Yet since the essays never have the neutrality of pure technique or disinterested academicism, even if they do "refrain from bravura autobiographical performances,"[42] it is hard for many readers to know how they should respond.

It would be different if there were a clear vocational identity or official methodology to which one could attach Sontag's project—the generic figure of "the artist," or what she herself has named the "heroism" of anthropology and photography. But Sontag stands resolutely outside the boundaries of the various disciplines, outside both the academic and the artistic establishment. Her profession as an "esthetic intelligence"[43] is the product of private energy and will that strains to be public, to establish its own legitimacy and right to speak for us and to us. The nervous response these essays provoke (as her official works of art do not) is a response to all that is unplaceable, unauthorized, and willful about such a project and especially to the effort to make us all participate in it, so that she may stand before us as our (self-elected) representative. Rousseau's confessions are far less problematic for us, and Mailer's are frankly titillating, because in both cases the preoccupations belong to someone else. Not only is Sontag more theoretical than sensational, but her disclosures are—or claim to be—also our disclosures, open avowals of what we are merely keeping to ourselves. "All that is necessary is that we not be hypocritical" is one of her constant mottoes.⁴⁴ The "we" seems genuinely felt, but given the discrepancies and inconsistencies in her audience—not to mention the distended and fragmented culture of which she writes— there are bound to be as many who feel themselves (unhypocritically) uncomfortable in the embrace of the writing as there are those who find themselves relieved and purged by it.

Sontag is a public figure who has made an exemplary project of her own career, a model in which we view both what we are (made more articulate) and what we might be, if there truly were a place for generalists and if we really had a unified intellectual culture. There is reason, then, to use the principle of authorship in her case, provided that one is not using it dismissively—to ignore her theoretical pretentions or to impose an artificial uniformity on her work. A better paradigm appears in one of her own essays on Godard:

> The most profound drama of a Godard film arises from the clash between this restless, wider consciousness of the director and the determinate, limited argument of the particular film he's engaged in making. Therefore each film is, simultaneously, a creative activity and a destructive one. The director virtually uses up his models, his sources, his ideas, his latest moral and artistic enthusiasms—and the shape of the film consists of various means for letting the audience know that's what is happening.⁴⁵

Sontag's own career has some of this same quality of progressively using up enthusiasms, pursuing them until they reveal their limitations and dangers or abandoning them when they have lost their power to provoke. If, as she remarks in an interview, "the most interesting ideas, after all, are heresies," then the need for continuous revision is more or less built in. But there is more at issue than a desire to be consistently controversial, for as she states in the same interview, the chief reason for jettisoning the extreme aestheticism of *Against Interpretation* was the extremity itself, which quickly exposed the "perils of overgeneralizing the aesthetic view of life."⁴⁶ Both of these forces—heresy and generality—are evident in the kind of positions she adopts, and even more evident in the instability of her positions and the changes that take place between one collection and the next. Some of these have already been discussed: the changing definition of the nature of aesthetic experience (from a terminal voluptuousness to an interminable spiritual project), the changing role of theory (from advocacy to diagnosis to demystification and deconstruction), and the gradually expanding domain of analysis (from individual art works to entire media and ideological constructs, such as the metaphors of illness, which are confined to no particular medium or level of culture). The changes are intimately connected; a greater skepticism and tendency to read against the grain goes hand in hand with a more "indiscriminate" subject matter like photography. For example, her early defense of pornography insists that: "There is a considerable gain in truth if pornography as an item in social history is treated quite separately from pornography as a psychological phenomenon (according to the usual view, symptomatic of sexual deficiency or deformity in both the producers and the consumers), and if one further distinguishes from both of these another pornography: a minor but interesting modality or convention within the arts" ("Pornographic Imagination," p. 35). Her essays on photography, however, deliberately ignore such boundaries, as photography itself blurs the distinction between document and artwork, significance and triviality, the pursuit of information or political mastery, and the satisfaction of an addiction. To separate in this case would obscure "the confusions about truth and beauty underlying the photographic enterprise" (*Photography*, p. 112).

Although even at the height of her formalism, Sontag (unlike Gass) insisted that art does not become functionless when it is seen to be, in the last analysis, contentless, her trust in the autonomy of the aesthetic has eroded even further since her early essays. Compare her treatment of Leni Riefenstahl, in *Against Interpretation,* to her later study of the "fascinations" of fascism.

> In art, "content" is, as it were, the pretext, the goal, the lure which engages consciousness in essentially *formal* processes of transformation.

> This is how we can, in good conscience, cherish works of art which, considered in terms of "content," are morally objectionable.... Because they project the complex movements of intelligence and grace and sensuousness, these two films of Riefenstahl (unique among works of Nazi artists) transcend the categories of propaganda or even reportage. And we find ourselves—to be sure, rather uncomfortably—seeing "Hitler" and not Hitler... Through Riefenstahl's genius as a film-maker, the "content" has— let us even assume, against her intentions—come to play a purely formal role. ["On Style," pp. 34–35]

> Riefenstahl's work is free of the amateurism and naiveté one finds in other art produced in the Nazi era, but it still promotes many of the same values.... The ironies of pop sophistication make for a way of looking at Riefenstahl's work in which not only its formal beauty but its political fervor are viewed as a form of aesthetic excess. And alongside this detached appreciation of Reifenstahl is a response, whether conscious or unconscious, to the subject itself, which gives her work its power. ["Fascism," p. 27]

What is most significant in the second passage is not her changed appreciation of Riefenstahl but how this change has come about. Whereas art once seemed, by definition, to transcend political uses, now art is not uniform (there are different types of aesthetic, among which the "fascist aesthetic" is one), and faith in the transcendence of art has come to seem itself a premise with political consequences. Sontag has described this change (not wholly disingenuously) as a shift away from "the formal implications of content . . . correct insofar as it went" to a broader concern for "the content implicit in certain ideas of form" and "a less abstract understanding of the moral services a work of art performs."[47]

Clearly her more recent essays do have a greater density and diversity of concern, and a more interesting and concrete display of evidence. The generalized enthusiasms of the early manifestoes are rarely documented, and even the more refined study of the pornographic imagination appears to slant its case by considering only two works, neither of which has much in common with what generally goes by the name of pornography.[48] The generalizations in *On Photography* and *Illness as Metaphor* are no less weighty, but they are more distinctive and surrounded by a wealth of detailed textual study remarkable both for its cunning and its intricacy. To read the assembly of evidence is a pleasure itself:

> Insofar as the muckrakers got results, they too altered what they photographed; indeed, photographing something became a routine part of the procedure for altering it. The danger was of a token change—limited to the narrowest reading of the photograph's subject. The particular New York slum, Mulberry Bend, that Riis photographed in the late 1880s was subsequently torn down and its inhabitants rehoused by order of Theodore Roosevelt, then state governor, while other, equally dreadful slums were left standing.
>
> The photographer both loots and preserves, denounces and consecrates. Photography expresses the American impatience with reality. . . . Faced with the awesome spread and alienness of a newly settled continent, people wielded cameras as a way of taking possession of the places they visited. Kodak put signs at the entrances of many towns listing what to photograph. Signs marked the places in national parks where visitors should stand with their cameras. [*Photography*, pp. 64–65]

It is only appropriate that Sontag's theory should grow concrete to the extent that it functions as an analysis of present symptoms and should grow vague as it becomes a species of prophecy or vision, gesturing toward possibilities unrealized. Her shift from manifesto to *lecture symptomale* is also related to changing attitudes towards history and change itself. The early essays collected in *Against Interpretation* treat history as progress and view cultural change as an inevitable and, on the whole, exciting process. The role of the theorist is to keep abreast of those forces and, when possible, to strengthen them. *Styles of Radical Will* accepts historical necessity, but is less enamoured of it, less willing to see the present as an improvement on the past. But it is not until *On Photography* and *Illness as Metaphor* that her theory begins to move in opposition to history, not with nostalgic glances backward, but with a firm determination to circumscribe and somehow to undermine certain developmental tendencies. It is not that she ignores the forces that condition social and aesthetic change; if anything, her appreciation is fuller and far warier. The decision to devote all her theoretical energies to unraveling the present, rather than projecting a future, is a tacit admission of just how powerful those conditions are, how much one must overcome before the future will even be imaginable.

As the domain and the function of theoretical activity change, the essays become more taut and internally coherent. Aphorisms give way to sustained arguments, a discursive space is built up to protect and succour our capacity to resist the forces of the present moment. Opposition demands greater continuity and internal reinforcement than cooperation or fatalism—both of which can afford to be partial and suggestive in proportion to the forces that are already arrayed on their side. The playful and inflammatory fragments of *Against Interpretation* betoken what Sontag will later call "the overoxygenated hopes of modernism," just as the strenuousness and measured rhetoric of *Illness as Metaphor* signify a more cautious respect for the forces to be overcome and for the consequences of inflammatory rhetoric itself.

At the same time, the early emphasis on an individual sensibility—identified with the author, but not peculiar to her—fades as well. The essays become distinctly less personal as the discourse becomes more integrated and the arguments more self-sustaining. The deeper impersonality parallels the more dispersed and collective nature of the mechanisms and movements that Sontag's essays now investigate as well as the fact that such phenomena are themselves closely linked to automata and mass production.

> Less and less does the work of art depend on being a unique object, an unoriginal made by an individual artist. . . .
> . . . The media are democratic: they weaken the role of the specialized producer or *auteur* (by using procedures based on chance, or mechanical techniques which anyone can learn; and by being corporate or collaborative efforts). . . .
> . . . Indeed, the importance of photographic images as the medium through which more and more events enter our experience is, finally, only a by-product of their effectiveness in furnishing knowledge dissociated from and independent of experience. [*Photography*, pp. 147, 149, 156]

The value Sontag once unquestioningly accorded to individual authorship has been shaken. *On Photography* does not pay the same exhaustive and flattering attention to distinguished *auteurs* that characterized her earlier essays on films, where the medium was always subordinate to the individual sensibility: "The principle of intensity at the root of Bergman's sensibility determines the specific ways in which he uses new narrative forms. Anything like the vivacity of Godard, the intellectual innocence of *Jules and Jim*, the lyricism of Bertolucci's *Before the Revolution* and Skolimowski's *Le Départ* are outside his range" ("Bergman," p. 140). Now individuality of expression seems more limiting than enriching.

> Many of the published photographs by photography's greatest names seem like work that could have been done by another gifted professional of their period. It requires a formal conceit (like Todd Walker's solarized photographs or Duane Michals's narrative-sequence photographs) or a thematic obsession (like Eakins with the male nude or Laughlin with the Old South) to make work easily recognizable. For photographers who don't so limit themselves, their body of work does not have the same integrity as does comparably varied work in other art forms. [*Photography*, p. 134]

But the new impersonality of the essays seems also to reflect a new balance of attraction and repulsion towards the subject matter itself. When "camp" seemed an innocuous taste to cultivate—witty and kind-hearted and not terribly consequential—it invited a more unguarded expression of personal attachment. But now it no longer seems like a minor indulgence but more like an addiction, a habitual "pop" response— "ironic, or dead-pan, or parodistic" (*Photography*, p. 149). The attractions of the "image world" of photography, the cruel excitements of disease imagery are emotions to be purged—not "expressed" through writing, but "expunged" by it.

Some elements in Sontag's work are changeless, however, and these thematic constants make it possible to measure her variations and to appreciate the drama of her movements. Her subject was and is the condition of contemporary culture, particularly the aftermath of aesthetic and political modernism. And she continues to be drawn to abstract, difficult, and alien works, preferring demanding structures and complex (or internally divided) motives of the sort that one associates with the triumphant monuments of high modernism: "In my view, the only intelligence worth defending is critical, dialectical, skeptical, desimplifying. An intelligence that aims at the definitive resolution (that is, suppression) of conflict, which justifies manipulation . . . is not *my* normative idea of intelligence."[49]

Indeed, her commitment to "critical consciousness" has deepened as her respect for the Frankfurt School in general and for Walter Benjamin in particular, has increased. The old yearning for simplicity, immediacy, and complete fidelity that surfaced in "A Trip to Hanoi" now seems more symptomatic of our present condition than an alternative to it, an instance of the "fascist longings in our midst" ("Fascism," p. 27). Modernism appears to encourage these longings, and even to recycle them in new and more virulent forms:

To an unsophisticated public in Germany, the appeal of Nazi art may have been that it was simple, figurative, emotional; not intellectual; a relief from the demanding complexities of modernist art. To a more sophisticated public now, the appeal is partly to that avidity which is now bent on retrieving all the styles of the past, especially the most pilloried. . . . The painting and sculpture are not just sententious; they are astonishingly meager as art. But precisely these qualities invite people to look at Nazi art with knowing and sniggering detachment, as a form of Pop art. ["Fascism," p. 27]

Modernism and antimodernism are both unsatisfactory; the impression that they are real alternatives, and the only ones imaginable, simply illustrates the condition of contemporary consciousness. But rather than attempting to escape or transcend this dilemma, Sontag's solution is to turn the limits of the moment against itself, to dismantle our "knowing and sniggering detachment" with a detachment more severe and rigorous.

Like her subject matter, Sontag's favorite themes and the terms in which those themes are couched remain much the same throughout the course of her career. "The gap between the elegance and seductiveness of ideas and the brutish or lyrical opaqueness of the human condition" is a phrase that seems appropriate to *Illness as Metaphor*, but in fact, it appears in an essay on Godard in *Styles of Radical Will* (p. 183). Her preoccupations are constant and persistently paired: Skepticism alternates with fascination, moral stricture with voluptuous abandonment, silence brings on volubility, authority leads to anarchy. Excessive self-abnegation and abstinence meet and mingle with excessive desire—"pursued imaginatively enough, experienced immoderately enough" both achieve the same erosion of the "pride of individuality."[50] These preoccupations frame her discussion of art and culture in general, and provide the terms of analysis for particular works ("Spiritual Style in the Films of Robert Bresson," *A.I.*, pp. 181–98) and genres—"the religious polarities (sacred and profane)" governing pornography ("Imagination," p. 67). Occasionally, an essay will introduce a theme that is only defined in a later essay. It is not until "The Aesthetics of Silence," some years after "Spiritual Style in Bresson," that we really sense all that the evocative phrase *spiritual style* implies:

> . . . a post-psychological conception of consciousness installs within the activity of art many of the paradoxes involved in attaining an absolute state of being described by the great religious mystics. . . .
> The "spirit" seeking embodiment in art clashes with the "material" character of art itself." ["Silence," pp. 4–5]

This delay is less whimsical than it might seem, since it takes the course of several essays to work out fully the scope and meaning of her concern. *Spirituality* begins as a nonce word, a catalytic agent around which scattered features in Bresson's career as a filmmaker gradually congeal to form an intelligible pattern.

> Bresson is interested in the forms of spiritual action—. . . Why persons behave as they do is, ultimately not to be understood. . . .
> . . . In the evolution of this sensibility, Bresson's cinematic means become more and more chaste. . . .
> True, in the last, most ascetic of all his films, Bresson seems to have left out too much, to have overrefined his conception. But a conception as ambitious as this cannot help but have its extremism. [Pp. 192–95, 198]

Beginning as a description of Bresson's subject matter, the word *spiritual* evolves as the essay proceeds and leads at last to the ruling principle that controls his mise-en-scène and camera work, informing both his vision of human action and his development as an artist. By exploring the notion and seeing where it leads, the essay eventually identifies art itself with a spiritual project, an extremism that transcends any particular achievement. And this is the definition that "The Aesthetics of Silence" then advances in a summary form.

Preoccupations have their rise and fall, of course, and occasionally seem to disappear entirely—only to make a chastened return in later works. Thus, the theme of spirituality would seem to be played out by the end of *Styles of Radical Will,* when Sontag writes in "A Trip to Hanoi" of her encounter with a culture where the spiritual and the material are not so at war: "The Vietnamese are 'whole' human beings, not 'split' as we are" (p. 263). There is no mention of spirituality in *On Photography* at all. Sontag's themes seem to follow a clear trajectory across a text and from one text to the next. In each case, there is a marked tendency towards inflation, making an initially tentative position more incisive and extreme. But inflation then serves as a means of testing the power of a term and the kind of commitment it deserves. This is one way in which the value of a given theme changes, for what was tolerable in moderation may prove intolerable in extremis, and what merited defense, when it was weak and contributed to the diversity and pungency of the cultural scene, may become indefensible when it begins to swamp its rivals and to put on the colors of totalitarianism. What in prospect seemed compelling may in retrospect seem just compulsive—which is why, for example, Bergman's "almost defiling charge of personal agony," which once invested his films with strenuousness and glamour, later becomes the mark of a stunted sensibility incapable of "fruitful development. . . . He is an obsessional artist, the worst kind to imitate . . . one of those aggressively memorable geniuses of the artistic dead-end, who go very far with limited material— refining it when they are inspired, repeating it and parodying themselves when they aren't."[51]

The capacities for development and for "nourishment," however, do remain constant criteria. As a standard of value, it reminds one of

Nietzsche's vitalism, but it is more mutable in time. The very same phenomenon will be judged alternately tonic and decadent, as its consequences and correlations change. Its value depends on what it leads to, where it rose from, the energies it releases or represses, and the analogues it suggests. Because the themes themselves—silence, opacity, authority, spirituality, and the rest—are so much more palpable, it is easy to miss how much less stable they are than the principles of construction and evaluation that frame them. Any given theme may suffer a summary deflation, while the means for assigning it a meaning and a value continue to be the same. Each theme passes under the review of a small set of recurrent categories: certain basic faculties of mind (will, knowledge, and desire); the motives of a subject or the stances that a subject takes toward the world (postures of consciousness like appetite, aggression, addiction, and asceticism); situational and historical contexts; and social identities (which may be conceived in terms of individual nations or whole civilizations—indeed any group or tradition with a history and integrity of its own). Against these parameters, the fates of sensibilities and ideologies are plotted, with motive, historical contexts, and identity to give those sensibilities and ideologies separate character and color. And it is these same categories that determine a theme's fruitfulness—its ability to nourish or to interest us.

The adjectives that Sontag uses for her appraisals show little variation—a fact that is all the more remarkable when one considers that her concerns have shifted from the pristinely aesthetic to the ardently moral. Although some of these adjectives are political ("radical," "alienated") or logical ("positive," "negative") in origin, a far greater number involve degrees of difficulty ("rigorous," "strenuous," "simple," "serious," "complex") and beauty (which for Sontag is usually insipid, and is opposed to more legitimate kinds of fascination based on "intensity," "authority," and "curiosity," or "interest"). Most prominent of all are those words of praise that treat conceptual satisfaction in sensual terms, referring to the "warmth" or "coolness" of a sensibility, the thickness or "thinness" of a sense of reality, the energy of an idea, and—especially—its healthiness or unhealthiness: whether it is "nourishing," "wholesome," "tonic." No doubt this verbal habit is another reason why Sontag so often frustrates her readers by leading them to expect something more palpable and less intellectual than they will actually get. Yet so powerful and persistent is her language, that these very frustrations are often couched in her own terms; critics feel compelled to speak of the "chilliness" or "thinness" of Sontag's sensibility. But far more significant, given this commitment (perhaps addiction) to health and disease and the ambiguous fascinations of "interesting," is the way Sontag's most recent essays have managed to call the language of illness and the aesthetics of curiosity into question.

Thus, when one examines Sontag's theorizing as a continuing project, one recognizes how delicate and even how moving the connections are. Few connections are made explicit, however, and in most cases—in spite of thematic repetitions and a fairly consistent vocabulary— the intertextual dialogue is actually based on disagreement. The positions that one essay embraces are held at a distance in another. The distance itself seems to be achieved by pursuing a program of deliberate overgeneralization until the novelty of a claim has been exhausted and its hidden weaknesses exposed. Her interest in "hard cases,"[52] in uncovering or inventing problems, never flags, however. Nor does the risk she takes of falling into the errors she is engaged in condemning or of lacking the very qualities she is trying to promote. Figurative language is no easier to avoid in *Illness as Metaphor* than explication was in *Against Interpretation*. Yet to work at risk, and to dare and almost invite inconsistency, is part of the economy of Sontag's enterprise. Hers is, after all, a theory rooted in attraction modified by repulsion, one that shapes its new positions by opposing its old enthusiasms—and thus prepares itself for its own obsolescence. Each essay therefore projects another and is likely, when viewed in isolation, to be marked by what Richard Gilman calls "all the debilities and irresolution and compensatory aggression and contradiction that are inevitable in a consciousness in transition."[53] As Sontag herself put it in her reflections on Artaud, "consciousness conceived as a project condemns work to be incomplete, gives rise to anti-genres and self-cancellations."[54]

On Photography and *Illness as Metaphor* are at once Sontag's most accomplished (if not most complete) works and those texts that act most effectively as cancellations of her earlier efforts. Moreover, as the pairing is meant to suggest, they work well in tandem, if only because they seem to provoke such dissimilar responses; *Illness as Metaphor* has won universal respect, even quiet affection, while its predecessor has received equal parts of applause and denunciation.[55] Both books share much the same theoretical economy: The generalizations in *Illness as Metaphor* are not a whit less broad or biting than those in *On Photography*, and both face the same danger of indulging the very tastes (for overgeneralization and figurative distortion, or for surrealist fragmentation) against which the writing warns. Yet *On Photography* disturbs and irritates many more readers, and makes them eager to point out its inconsistencies and to report signs of ambivalence. This has more to do with its mode and rhetorical strategy—and with the positions it attacks—than it does with any logical flaws or even any opinions it actually endorses. While *Illness as Metaphor* is polemical, it is not a piece of studied heresy; it presents itself as a demystification but not as an iconoclasm. The flush of running up against an orthodoxy, defying taboos and risking punishment, is part of the gaiety and reckless energy of *On Photography*—so unlike the steady, somber flow of *Illness as Metaphor*. One could hardly imagine the latter book ending with the sort of lush and hectic anthology of quotations that is pinned on, donkey-wise, to the end of *On Photography*; the citations in *Illness as Metaphor* are not the sort that one would want to grant a second life, especially a life that is poignant and amusing.

It is not that *Illness as Metaphor* is without art. Indeed, the two books are equally handsome, the most immaculately organized and polished pieces of sustained prose in all of Sontag's oeuvre. The writing in these essays achieves a new fluidity and sheen, a shapeliness of sentence and a justice of individual wording that is only sporadically evident in her earlier works. The epigrams of *On Photography* remind one of the pithy fragments of Oscar Wilde that stud her "Notes on 'Camp' " (an essay that, in spite of this, is utterly lacking in Wilde's quickness and sureness of touch): "Photographs, which package the world, seem to invite packaging."; "Precisely by slicing out this moment and freezing it, all photographs testify to time's relentless melt." Occasionally, the prose even has the erotic qualities that seemed so often sadly absent in her earlier professions of sensual delight:

> The peppers Weston photographed in 1929 and 1930 are voluptuous in a way that his female nudes rarely are. Both the nudes and the peppers are photographed for the play of forms—but the body is characteristically shown bent over upon itself, all the extremities cropped, with the flesh rendered as opaque as normal lighting and focus allow, thus decreasing its sensuality and heightening the abstractness of the body's form; the pepper is viewed close-up but in its entirety, the skin polished or oiled, and the result is a discovery of the erotic suggestiveness of an ostensibly neutral form. [P. 98]

Although *Illness as Metaphor* is written in a diminished key and at a slower pace, it is no less sonorous. Its stately opening is a case in point (where, not by chance, the book contradicts itself by using an ornate extended metaphor): "Illness is the night-side of life, a more onerous citizenship. Everyone who is born holds dual citizenship, in the kingdom of the well and in the kingdom of the sick. Although we all prefer to use only the good passport, sooner or later each of us is obliged, at least for a spell, to identify ourselves as citizens of that other place" (p. 3). And the muted prophecy with which it closes is a model of chastened passion, of decorous sobriety and the repudiation of all self-dramatism: "The cancer metaphor will be made obsolete, I would predict, long before the problems it has reflected so persuasively will be resolved" (p. 88). The mode is different, to be sure, but no less artful for that. It extends to the very arrangement of the two texts and the layout of their pages. Both books are elegantly punctuated by small graphic emblems, and the print is centered carefully within ample borders that surround it like a mat around a photograph. The framing motif is understandably carried even further in *On Photography*, where each separate essay has its own coverleaf and ornamental heading (like a treasured family album) and the introductory note is printed in a compact block of italics, initialed and dated, in a friendly parody of the photographic image that it so pointedly is not. The effect of the graphic display in both works is to make a treasure of the printed word and to create an atmosphere of spaciousness and leisurely regard. One is visually invited to see this writing as a work of art, but the format has another function too. It is part of the effort to counter the power of the "image world" and to slow the rush of ill-considered assumptions that make up the ideology of cancer.

The new cohesiveness of Sontag's prose (already mentioned) is another aspect of this same effort. The knit is tighter in *Illness as Metaphor*, where each segment is carefully sutured to its predecessor, recapitulating the argument thus far and projecting the development to come. *On Photography* occasionally favors naked juxtaposition and thus harkens back to an earlier, more spontaneous, expository style. Yet even though the essays collected in the latter volume were written on widely separated occasions—as much as four years apart—there is still an obvious effort to integrate them and to make the book as a whole more than just a collection—as her earlier books had been. Reviewing *On Photography*, Penelope Houston points out the "way each chapter is shaped towards an essayist's elegant dying fall," while still "suggesting that the writer found her subject expanding in front of her, yielding aspects and detours, rather than that the terrain was fully mapped out before the writing began."[56] The momentum of the book is part of its appeal, like a series of waves that crest and fall, retreating and advancing and occasionally repeating themselves—fascinating because we see the integration actually coming about.

But the motion of that book also suggests what Sontag's own introduction calls her "obsession" with photography. There is nothing obsessional about the construction of *Illness as Metaphor*. The construction is solidly and rationally architectonic rather than an oscillating liquid advance. The two texts produce disparate responses because of this: *Illness as Metaphor* has been purged of its attachment to the ideas that it treats, whereas *On Photography* still retains some mixed affection for, or at least vestigial dependence on, the notions it tries to criticize. The writing is in the process of weaning itself, however, and *On Photography* is a necessary step toward positions that will be more wholeheartedly embraced in the later book. There is, for example, a new suspiciousness about what the taste for ruins and for "interesting" photographs implies:

> Photography extends the eighteenth-century literati's discovery of the beauty of ruins into a genuinely popular taste. And it extends that beauty beyond the romantics' ruins, such as those glamorous forms of decrepitude photographed by Laughlin, to the modernists' ruins—reality itself. [P. 79]

In the form of photographic images, things and events are put to new uses, assigned new meanings, which go beyond the distinctions between the beautiful and the ugly, the true and the false, the useful and the useless, good taste and bad. Photography is one of the chief means for producing that quality ascribed to things and situations which erases these distinctions: "the interesting." [Pp. 174–75]

The suspiciousness ripens in *Illness as Metaphor* into an outright attack on the glamour with which disease and the body's ruin has been invested:

... the romanticizing of TB is the first widespread example of that distinctively modern activity, promoting the self as an image. The tubercular look had to be considered attractive once it came to be considered a mark of distinction, of breeding.... What was once the fashion for aristocratic *femme fatales* and aspiring young artists became, eventually, the province of fashion as such. Twentieth-century women's fashions (with their cult of thinness) are the last stronghold of the metaphors associated with the romanticizing of TB in the late eighteenth and early nineteenth centuries

... Sickness was a way of making people "interesting"—which is how "romantic" was originally defined....

... Perhaps the main gift to sensibility made by the Romantics is not the aesthetics of cruelty and the beauty of the morbid (as Mario Praz suggested in his famous book), or even the demand for unlimited personal liberty, but the nihilistic and sentimental idea of "the interesting." [Pp. 29–31]

The difference is that although *On Photography* is skeptical of the cult of disease, it is no less skeptical of the ideal of health. Beauty, traditionally conceived, fares no better there than chic ugliness or pop indifference, and the optimism of conventional humanism seems as shallow as the mannered despair and deliberate courting of ordeal in Diane Arbus.

Arbus was not a poet delving into her entrails to relate her own pain but a photographer venturing out into the world to *collect* images that are painful....

Succeeding the more buoyant hopes for America has come a bitter, sad embrace of experience. There is a particular melancholy in the A-merican photographic project. But the melancholy was already latent in the heyday of Whitmanesque affirmation, as represented by Stieglitz and his Photo-Secession circle. Stieglitz, pledged to redeem the world with his camera, was still shocked by modern material civilization....

... a mission as rotten with doubt about America—even at its most optimistic—was bound to get deflated fairly soon....

... It is obviously too easy to say that America is just a freak show, a wasteland—the cut-rate pessimism typical of the reduction of the real to the surreal. But the American partiality to myths of redemption and damnation remains one of the most energizing, most seductive aspects of our national culture. What we have left of Whitman's discredited dream of cultural revolution are paper ghosts and a sharp-eyed witty program of despair. [Pp. 40, 47–48]

Arbus is diminished, diagnosed, by exposing her work to the larger generosity and native optimism of photographers like Stieglitz, but later the same photographers will be disparaged for sentimentality:

> The view of Stieglitz and Strand and Weston—that photographs should be, first of all, beautiful (that is, beautifully composed)—seems thin now, too obtuse to the truth of disorder. [P. 101]

> . . . displaying the perfection of the world was too sentimental, too ahistorical a notion of beauty to sustain photography.

This is not an inconsistency, since the parties to the comparison have changed and the goal of the discussion is different, but it does illustrate the persistent air of mistrust and dissatisfaction in the book. To heap doubt on humanism is not to champion nihilism. What Sontag criticizes in the name of humanism is a false-hearted optimism, a desire to scale down and narrow one's vision to comfortably domestic proportions and, in the process, to crop out the complicated interdependencies and competing interests of contemporary life, to ignore the scope and power and speed of its machinery, which photography itself must inevitably exploit:

> Steichen's choice of photographs assumed a human condition or a human nature shared by everybody. By purporting to show that individuals are born, work, laugh, and die everywhere the same way, "The Family of Man" denies the determining weight of history—of genuine and historically embedded differences, injustices, and conflicts. . . .

> . . . Photography conceived as social documentation was an instrument of that essentially middle-class attitude, both zealous and merely tolerant, both curious and indifferent, called humanism—which found slums the most enthralling of decors . . .

> . . . Social misery has inspired the comfortably-off with the urge to take pictures, the gentlest of predations, in order to document a hidden reality, that is, a reality hidden from them. [Pp. 33, 56, 55]

These are (to be sure) fighting words. *On Photography* has a penchant for turning apparent tenderness into its opposite by a simple readjustment of scale that exposes the assumptions upon which the activity rests and the kind of company it keeps. It also makes old enthusiasms noxious by making them too general. Both of these activities bear a striking resemblance to the methods of photography itself—its power to reframe and endlessly proliferate. Moreover, while disapproving of the ruthlessness and jaded sensationalism of many contemporary photographers, and especially of the tendency to mistake cynicism for truthfulness and unblinking perspicacity, the book still awards the palm to those who acknowledge their darker motives: "Cartier-Bresson and Avedon are among the very few to have talked honestly (if ruefully) about the exploitative aspect of the photographer's activities. Usually photographers feel obliged to protest photography's innocence, claiming that the predatory attitude is incompatible with a good picture, and hoping that a more affirmative vocabulary will put over their point" (p. 123).

To the extent that the high-minded side of the argument has received and will continue to receive a better press, Sontag will lean the other way. Professional photographers will still want to maintain that their work is prophetic, subversive, revelatory (and professional critics will want to preserve the justification to justify their own work in turn). And if Sontag's writing shows traces of the same stubborn thrill of heresy it castigates, so the irritation she produces comes from interfering with the potent pleasures of complacency: "In a consumer society, even the most well-intentioned and properly captioned work of photographers issues in the discovery of beauty. . . . photographs can and do distress. But the aestheticizing tendency is such that the medium which conveys distress ends by neutralizing it" (p. 109).

The greater, or at least the more uniform, popular acclaim that has attended *Illness as Metaphor* is due in part to the stable vantage point it adopts, the certain right from which it measures degrees of wrong. *On Photography* has no such certainty, no final point of rest. Perspectives shift, one value circumscribes another, then finds itself undone by yet another comparison. But unlike an exercise in deconstruction, which also makes strategic use of changing vantage points, the book is opposed both to the flabbiness of relativism and the philosophy of meaning that makes it possible:

> A photograph changes according to the context in which it is seen: thus Smith's Minamata photographs will seem different on a contact sheet, in a gallery, in a political demonstration, in a police file, in a photographic magazine, in a general news magazine, in a book, on a living room wall. Each of these situations suggests a different use for the photographs but none can secure their meaning. As Wittgenstein argued for words, that the meaning *is* the use—so for each photograph. And it is in this way that the presence and proliferation of all photographs contributes to the erosion of the very notion of meaning, to that parceling out of the truth into relative truths which is taken for granted by the modern liberal consciousness. [P. 106]

On Photography is a tendentious effort to make it possible to judge photography rather than just consume it, to find ways to see around its seeing and not submit to the claims that it makes for itself. Yet all of the available critical languages seem insufficient to the task. "The language in which photographs are generally evaluated is extremely meager. Sometimes it is parasitical on the vocabulary of painting—composition, light, and so forth. More often it consists in the vaguest sorts of judgments, as when photographs are praised for being subtle, or interesting, or powerful, or complex, or simple, or—a favorite—deceptively simple" (pp. 138–39). Formalism is too limited—"the authority of a photograph will always depend on the relationship to a subject" (p. 136)—humanism too naive, sensationalism too ruthless, aestheticism too anesthetizing. And moralism itself is too eager to gloss over the disturbing potency of the mute and polyvalent photographic image: "What the moralists are demanding from a photograph is that it do what no photograph can ever do—speak" (p. 108). Each language is, however, a useful check upon the other, and in the absence of a single, subsuming affirmation, Sontag is at least able to maintain a stance of critical repudiation. Yet these changing temporary vantage points, which alter the grounds (of time and circumstance and consequence) upon which judgment rests, recall the very "time-bound" interests and the relative, contextualized truth of photography from which these essays seek a skeptical release. Hence, the feeling on the part of many of her critics that Sontag sympathizes with what she in fact means to exorcise. The traces of entrapment, however, help to render her account of the pervasive impact of photography and the nature of our photographic age more credible. Moreover, there is a difference between accepting one's own condition and turning that condition against itself. If *On Photography* has no new alternatives to propose, it is active in its rejection of the old. This is the more impressive in light of how much there is to lose and how void is the prospect of immediate gain. Few of us will long mourn the end of the glamour of disease, or will even want to admit the attraction to decay that *Illness as Metaphor* examines. These are rooted sorrows we will be happy to believe plucked out. But our longings for a simpler beauty and domestic tranquillity are less easy to forego and far less noxious to avow. Each of the positions Sontag takes up and serially dismisses in *On Photography* has its own allure, one to which the writing is undeniably responsive. The greatest difference between these books, then, is that in one the attraction is kept entirely at bay, staged entirely as a quarrel between the discourse of the theory and the discourse it examines. But in *On Photography* the quarrel is as much internal and intratextual as it is external and intertextual. As a result, the victories can never be clear-cut.

Another problematic feature for some readers is the relationship between Sontag's reflections on photography and the work of her brilliant predecessor, Walter Benjamin, on the same subject. Indeed *On Photography* marks a decided change in this relationship: Benjamin stood out in Sontag's earlier essays on film as an admirable but fundamentally wrongheaded thinker who singularly misunderstood the value of photography. From one of the worst writers on the subject, Benjamin has now become the best: "The best writing on photography has been by moralists—Marxists or would-be Marxists—hooked on photography but troubled by the way photography inexorably beautifies. As Walter Benjamin observed. . ." (p. 107). The change in attitude is twofold, involving both a greater appreciation for Benjamin's own tormented aestheticism and an increasing respect for political and moral considerations on Sontag's own part. The ease with which she once made logical distinctions between form and function (as if this were sufficient protection against the political misuse of art) and argued the autonomy of aesthetic judgments has, in recent years, become uneasy. Thus, Benjamin's thesis that art is never simply a formal exercise, that the function and the mode of production it embodies is a necessary part of its meaning, has become far more plausible. Then too (as we shall see), the kind of conceptual design, based on formal correlations between artifacts and social processes, that Benjamin uses suggests a way of being for interpretation rather than against it. Yet for all its professed admiration, *On Photography* is neither a restatement nor a popularization of Benjamin—any more than *Illness as Metaphor* reduplicates Foucault's archeology of madness or his treatment of disease in *The Birth of the Clinic*. Both books assimilate and translate theoretical traditions that have no exact Anglo-American counterparts, but they also extend and qualify them—bringing them up to date (in the case of Benjamin) or making them a basis for action (in the case of Foucault). This is not at all what one would have expected, based on her earlier discussion of Cioran's response to the anxiety of influence:

> But he comes after Nietzsche, who set down almost the whole of Cioran's position almost a century ago. . . .
> . . .the "fact" of Nietzsche had undeniable consequences for Cioran. He must tighten the screws, make the argument denser. More excruciating. More rhetorical. ["Thinking," p. 81]

It is a mark of the maturity of Sontag's later work that she can now conceive of an honorable debt, without needing to contend for the ownership of ideas. The relationship of *On Photography* to an essay like "The Work of Art in the Age of Mechanical Reproduction" (1937) is genuinely developmental, not condemned to repetition and a tightening of the screws by outshouting what one cannot outstrip. Homage to Benjamin is the impetus for *On Photography*. It is an elaboration and elucidation of his own highly compressed and sparsely documented themes: that the development of mass production "brushes aside a number of outmoded concepts, such as creativity and genius, eternal value and mystery"; that (an insight which Benjamin himself owed to Marx) "the mode of human sense perception changes with humanity's entire mode of existence"; and therefore that our decaying sense of "aura" (the uniqueness of an object, an authentic presence that cannot be reproduced) has a social basis:

It rests on two circumstances, both of which are related to the increasing significance of the masses in contemporary life. Namely, the desire of contemporary masses to bring things "closer" spatially and humanly, which is just as ardent as their bent toward overcoming the uniqueness of every reality by accepting its reproduction. Every day the urge grows stronger to get hold of an object at very close range by way of its likeness, its reproduction. . . . To pry an object from its shell, to destroy its aura, is the mark of a perception whose "sense of the universal equality of things" has increased to such a degree that it extracts it even from a unique object by means of reproduction.[57]

On Photography takes Benjamin's suggestive but hurried and slightly remote maxims and expands upon them. It gives one time to assess the full weight of the changes they imply and to see how cunning and how manifold are the paths by which they come to pass:

The contingency of photographs confirms that everything is perishable; the arbitrariness of photographic evidence indicates that reality is fundamentally unclassifiable. Reality is summed up in an array of casual fragments. . . . the photographer's insistence that everything is real also implies that the real is not enough. . . . [as in surrealism,] a posture of alienation which has now become a general attitude. [P. 80]

Photography has powers that no other image-system has ever enjoyed because, unlike the earlier ones, it is *not* dependent on an image maker. However carefully the photographer intervenes in setting up and guiding the image-making process, the process itself remains an optical-chemical (or electronic) one. . . . the potency of the image is now experienced in a very different way. The primitive notion of the efficacy of images presumes that images possess the qualities of real things, but our inclination is to attribute to real things the qualities of images. [P. 158]

The unreal "image world" Sontag details is there in Benjamin, but she supplements his functional and epistemological analysis with an "erotic" one (of the sort *Against Interpretation* demanded but never quite achieved). This is to add what Benjamin's essay frankly and deliberately leaves out: "Needing to have reality confirmed and experience enhanced by photographs is an aesthetic consumerism to which everyone is now addicted. . . . Poignant longings for beauty, for an end to probing below the surface, for a redemption and celebration of the body of the world— all these elements of erotic feelings are affirmed in the pleasure we take in photographs" (p. 24). It is in the theoretical discourse of *On Photography*, rather than her films, that Sontag's preoccupation with the hieratic silence of photographic images receives its most satisfying expression. The numb mystifications of *Brother Carl*, the haunting but notoriously equivocal fragments that comprise her pictoral essay on Israel, *Promised Lands*, are absorbed into the writing of this book, enriching it in just those places that Benjamin's austere "theses" are impoverished. One senses how alluring, how narcotic, is the habit of photographic seeing: "both intense and cool, solicitous and detached; charmed by the insignificant detail, addicted to incongruity" (p. 99). Yet at the same time, one comes to understand that the attraction is not entirely healthy, and that describing it is an act of therapy. The most stinging invectives in the book are reflexive; the complaints about the aggression and imperiousness of documentary photography are certainly as applicable to the maker of *Promised Lands* as they are to Walker Evans or Dorothea Lang—"In these last decades, 'concerned' photography has done at least as much to deaden conscience as to arouse it." Although *Promised Lands* is easily the best of Sontag's films, it is confused about what kind of document the camera can and should produce, and at what human cost. This confusion enters *On Photography* as something to be studied. It cannot be directly solved, but it can be comprehended; the theory reveals that it is the product of technological and ideological developments that must first be understood before any practical solution is possible.

The publicity surrounding Sontag's career becomes part of *On Photography* and makes the polemic different than Benjamin's. Benjamin was always a collector and never a photographer; for him, photography represented the problem of the alien and the new, an instrument of the emerging mass society he both heralded and feared. No matter how restrained and cerebral its demeanor, "The Work of Art in the Age of Mechanical Reproduction" is a desperate effort to will the course of cultural history, to make film and photography a force for social change (rather than the pawn of Fascism). Eying the "prognostic value" of Marx's study of the economic base, Benjamin hoped to achieve the same results with his own analysis of the superstructure. His "theses about the developmental tendencies of art under present conditions of production" were designed to reveal that developments in "the processing of data" could be just as powerful as economic developments, and thus, could give potency to aesthetic speculation itself: "The concepts which are introduced into the theory of art in what follows differ from the more familiar terms in that they are completely useless for the purposes of Fascism. They are, on the other hand, useful for the formulation of revolutionary demands in the politics of art."[58]

Benjamin's analysis of aesthetic production is (or tries to be) more rigorous than Sontag's, whose strokes are broad and offer a fuller display of attitude, tending toward pensée more than a minutely scientific prognosis. Her mode, and thus the status of her claims about the relationship between economic structure and aesthetic superstructure, is far less clear, a series of scattered intimations. Still, it is evident that she does not fully agree with Benjamin and means to qualify his position. Benjamin seems to hope that the cultural revolution will precede or help to advance the economic one; Sontag (herself a filmmaker) has far less faith in the capacity of artistic production to determine its own use and to control the meanings that will be ascribed to it:

> Socially concerned photographers assume that their work can convey some kind of stable meaning, can reveal truth. But partly because the photograph is, always, an object in a context, this meaning is bound to drain away; that is, the context which shapes whatever immediate—in particular, political—uses the photograph may have is inevitably succeeded by contexts in which such uses are weakened and become progressively less relevant. One of the central characteristics of photography is that process by which original uses are modified, eventually supplanted by subsequent uses— most notably, by the discourse of art into which any photograph can be absorbed. [P. 106]

The difference between Benjamin and Sontag has more to do with the historical moment in which they write than with their respective vocations. In 1936, Benjamin could have greater (if not undivided) hopes for the untried powers of the medium and the surrealist aesthetic it promised to extend to the whole of modern life. Photography's challenge to old patterns of authority and ownership, to hierarchies based on unequal expertise and the privileges of genius, seemed the harbinger of a new egalitarian age—if, that is, it was allowed to reach its logical conclusion and was not diverted for Fascist purposes. Sontag begins by questioning Benjamin's belief that photographic reproduction will mean an end to mystery and ritual and superstitiously endowed authority. Instead, photography introduces a new kind of mystery, that of mute and deracinated surfaces rather than of hidden depths and recondite traditions: "Any photograph has multiple meanings; indeed, to see something in the form of a photograph is to encounter a potential object of fascination" (p. 23). In fact, Benjamin himself emerges as a secret follower of this latter-day cult of the numinous fragment:

> For it was Benjamin's conviction that reality itself invited—and vindicated— the once heedless, inevitably destructive ministrations of the collector....
> ... "To renew the old world," Benjamin wrote, "That is the collector's deepest desire when he is driven to acquire new things." But the old world cannot be renewed—certainly not by quotations; and this is the rueful, quixotic aspect of the photographic enterprise.
> ... what in Benjamin is an excruciating idea of fastidiousness, meant to permit the mute past to speak in its own voice, with all its unresolvable complexity, becomes—when generalized, in photography—the cumulative de-creation of the past (in the very act of preserving it), the fabrication of a new, parallel reality that makes the past immediate while underscoring its comic or tragic ineffectuality, that invests the specificity of the past with an unlimited irony, that transforms the present into the past and the past into pastness. [Pp. 76–77]

Sontag insists that authority, no matter how illegitimate, is precisely the most compelling feature of photographs—the only kind of authority that the modern world seems capable of believing in:

> Such images are indeed able to usurp reality because first of all a photograph is not only an image; . . . it is also a trace, something directly stenciled off the real, like a footprint or a death mask. . . . a material vestige of its subject in a way that no painting can be. . . .
>
> . . . Photographs—and quotations—seem, because they are taken to be pieces of reality, more authentic than extended literary narratives. The only prose that seems credible to more and more readers is not the fine writing of someone like Agee, but the raw record. [Pp. 154, 74]

Thus, the essays take issue with Benjamin's key tenet that mechanical reproduction utterly obliterates "aura"—the uniqueness of individual objects, which makes them susceptible to private ownership and authentication. Bejamin's failure to make a clear distinction between photography and film led him to miss the fact that their mass dissemination might lead to a new form of property: ". . . the force of photographic images comes from their being material realities in their own right, richly informative deposits left in the wake of whatever emitted them, potent means for turning the tables on reality—for turning *it* into a shadow. Images are more real than anyone could have supposed" (p. 180). Of course Sontag has been witness to certain later developments in the merchandising of photography that Benjamin himself could not have known of when he heralded the photograph as the antithesis of the commodity.

> Benjamin thought that a photograph, being a mechanically reproduced object, could not have a genuine presence. It could be argued, however, that the very situation which is now determinative of taste in photography, its exhibition in museums and galleries, has revealed that photographs do possess a kind of authenticity. Furthermore, although no photograph is an original in the sense that a painting always is, there is a large qualitative difference between what could be called originals—prints made from the original negative at the time (that is, at the same moment in the technological evolution of photography) that the picture was taken—and subsequent generations of the same photograph. . . . to the extent that, say, a Giotto can still be said to possess an aura in the situation of museum display, where it too has been wrenched from its original context and, like the photograph, "meets the beholder halfway" (in the strictest sense of Benjamin's notion of the aura, it does not), to that extent an Atget photograph printed on the now unobtainable paper he used can also be said to possess an aura. [Pp. 139–40]

Sontag is retrospective where Benjamin is prospective, diagnostic where Benjamin is attempting a prognosis. This is finally what makes her book necessary. Benjamin invested heavily in the surrealist challenge to

254 / The Creative Impasse

traditional high culture, hopeful that its irreverence and instinct for leveling might lead to deeper social changes. But now it seems that what photographic leveling really promotes is affectless and indiscriminate seeing, a cynical instead of a morally inflamed irreverence.

> Surrealists, who aspire to be cultural radicals, even revolutionaries, have often been under the well-intentioned illusion that they could be, indeed should be, Marxists. But Surrealist aestheticism is too suffused with irony to be compatible with the twentieth century's most seductive form of moralism. Marx reproached philosophy for only trying to understand the world rather than trying to change it. Photographers, operating within the terms of the Surrealist sensibility, suggest the vanity of even trying to understand the world and instead propose that we collect it. [Pp. 81–82]

The link that Benjamin tried to forge between political and cultural radicalism has proved too fragile. The ironies of surrealism are too facile and corrosive, its anticommodities are altogether too salable. "Photography is the most successful vehicle of modernist taste in its pop version, with its zeal for debunking the high culture of the past;...its conscientious courting of vulgarity; its affection for kitsch; its skill in reconciling avant-garde ambitions with the rewards of commercialism" (p. 131).

Standing at one edge of time, Benjamin foresaw a tendency toward totalitarianism in "the increasing formation of masses" that accompanied the rise of mechanical reproduction, and hoped only that the mass media might mean a politicized art, compatible with the dictatorship of the proletariat, and not the aestheticized politics of Fascism: "Fascism attempts to organize the newly created proletarian masses without affecting the property structure which the masses strive to eliminate. Fascism sees its salvation in giving these masses not their right, but instead a chance to express themselves."[59] In *On Photography* and in "Fascinating Fascism," Sontag continues and enlarges on this theme by suggesting that the perpetual mobility and uncertainty that photography implies creates a longing to reinstate new authoritarian controls. But her book ends, not with Benjamin's prophetic warning against approaching fascism, nor with his wistful, troubled gesture towards the possibilities of communism, but with still another possibility:

> The future may offer another kind of dictatorship, whose master is "the interesting," in which images of all sorts, stereotyped and eccentric, proliferate....
> A capitalist society requires a culture based on images. It needs to furnish vast amounts of entertainment in order to stimulate buying and anesthetize the injuries of class, race, and sex. And it needs to gather unlimited amounts of information, the better to exploit natural resources, increase productivity, keep order, make war, give jobs to bureaucrats.... Cameras define reality in the two ways essential to the workings of

an advanced industrial society: as a spectacle (for masses) and as an object of surveillance (for rulers). [P. 178]

This is the aftermath of Benjamin's apocalypse, an alliance less horrific than fascism, but more insidious and chronic. His diffuse hopes for a "food dictatorship" have congealed into the (here) unpalatable reality of China, "the dictatorship of 'the good,'" where politics have not merged with aesthetics, but have displaced them, and where it seems that "notions about the moral order of space...preclude the very idea of photographic seeing" (p. 170). Neither dictatorship seems livable. Yet Sontag's end is not desperation or numbness or even particularly ironic:

> ...there seems no way (short of undergoing a vast historical amnesia, as in China) of limiting the proliferation of photographic images. The only question is whether the function of the image-world created by cameras could be other than it is. The present function is clear enough, if one considers in what contexts photographic images are seen, what dependencies they create, what antagonisms they pacify—that is, what institutions they buttress, whose needs they really serve.

> ...And just because they are an unlimited resource, one that cannot be exhausted by consumerist waste, there is all the more reason to apply the conservationist remedy. If there can be a better way for the real world to include the one of images, it will require an ecology not only of real things but of images as well. [Pp. 178, 180]

It is appropriate that *On Photography* close on this note of uncompromising opposition—promising no utopias, but firm in its negations. It is a conclusion that fulfills the claim made in the opening: "All possibility of understanding is rooted in the ability to say no" (p. 23). Although originally a series of review essays, *On Photography* has a remarkable dynamism that connects the first moment to the last and propels each essay forward on the heels of its predecessor. It explodes ex nihilo with a brilliant burst of speed in "In Plato's Cave," which sets forth the problem all at once: What is it to be "educated by photographs?"—How does it transform our notions of what is worth seeing and what we have the right to see? What strange sort of object is a photograph and what tangled purposes does it serve? How dangerously does it inflame our instinct for aggression or flatter us that we know more, control more, than we do? Do photographs not teach us to be consumers of experience, content to accept vicarious knowledge and even to prefer it, trusting the safety and titillation of the image-world far more than the world it claims to capture for us?

Most of the book that will follow is presented in miniature here, but the announcement is much too quick to be absorbed. It has the giddy proliferation and speed of the photography itself. As one reads on, however, the movement slows, and the problem assumes a more intelligible and detailed form—each essay/chapter seeming at once a fresh beginning and a continuation, obedient to its own initial premises and the evidence at hand, yet contributing as well to the advancement of the whole. "America, Seen through Photographs, Darkly" presents a capsule history of the democratizing of the photographic object—from the visionary Whitman, who found beauty everywhere, to the heroic beautification effected by Steiglitz and his friends, to the deflation of the patronizing freak show of Diane Arbus. The next chapter, "Melancholy Objects," takes as its master term *Surrealism* rather than *democracy*, and introduces a discussion of the differences between the American and the European versions of photography. But it also pursues the paradox Sontag wishes to establish—the surrealistic nature of what purports to be the most realistic of media. This inherent surrealism subverts documentary photography, whatever its pretentions to scientific accuracy or partisan activism, making its documents unintentionally elegiac and ironic. Then, in "The Heroism of Vision," the paradox and internal inconsistencies of the photographic enterprise deepen. The competing claims of truth and beauty, subjective self-expression and objective record, "vision" in the noumenal as well as the phenomenal sense, make the heroic stance of the photographer-artist intrinsically unstable. The extended powers of awareness that photography purports to offer seem ambiguous at best—at once more than, the same as, and less than normal polysensual awareness. "Photographic Evangels" then turns to the defenses photographers themselves make of their own vocation, examining not only the terms in which these apologies are couched but the activity itself—the strange need to issue briefs for a medium that has so obviously achieved a wide acceptance. But if the prevalence of photographs is part of the problem, the automatic process that gives them their authority also challenges their artistry, leaving professionals in the awkward position of either aggrandizing their own work at the expense of the real or disguising it behind a mask of perfect neutrality. The "double standard" cited in the preceding essay now emerges as a set of distinct questions about the kind of knowledge and the kind of art photography implies. And as in the preceding essay, the expansiveness of photography corrodes the very claims it would make for itself: too indiscriminate for "vision," too automatic for knowledge, too wayward to comprise an oeuvre or an art. Whereas with paints or words, one could distinguish between the medium and the art objects made from it, photography is canonized, brought into the art museum, just when such institutions have become wary about "art"—and ready to embrace photography precisely for its indeterminacy.

With photography thus established as a generalized medium, the final chapter, "The Image-World," falls logically into place to explore the consequences of that now general condition. Neither art nor knowledge, photography becomes a "hyping of the real," thus implying that the latter is insufficient. But the final essay also goes beyond photography to consider the social matrix in which it is embedded, the uses that have made it the sort of confused instrument it is. Indeed, it is only in this larger context that it is possible to distinguish between the medium and the functions it performs; to have done so earlier would have meant treating the distinction as if it already were the case—a fact rather than a distant and difficult goal.

Thus, the essays move from problem to proposal, from the actual to the potential, and from particular and domestic history to a broad comparison of model political systems (Third World communism and Western industrial capitalism). It is hardly a linear movement, however, but one that doubles back and inches forward, a rocking motion that achieves gradual and seemingly unpremeditated advances that spring, as it were, from the intensity of the obsession itself. There is, then, an almost physical sensation of rupture when one turns to the final appended "Brief Anthology of Quotations." To be sure, the Anthology is far from casual or static, but here there is no question of advance, and the severe deracination, the abrupt alternation of inflated and deflating claims, is altogether different from the persistence of the main body of the text. It is as if the addictive incongruities of photographic seeing have reasserted themselves, as if the effort to resist them were finally too great. But with the difference that now that "seeing" is turned back upon itself (much as the illustrations on the front and back covers—the only ones in the book—are not photographic images but images of photography). Whatever apparent consistency the photographic enterprise possesses is shattered by the application of photography's own methods of framing and montage. Part of the wit of the Anthology is that, though patently discursive, it is the sole internal illustration of what photography is, thus underscoring the premise of the book that "photographic seeing" is ultimately a principle of arrangement and a structure of information, rather than a visual phenomenon per se. But since it is an album of citations instead of pictures, it still maintains the verbal resistance to images that the book as a whole embodies and enacts. The Anthology is dedicated to Benjamin and pursues an earlier reference to "Benjamin's. . .ideal project" of constructing: "a work of literary criticism that was to consist entirely of quotations, and would thereby be devoid of anything that might betray empathy" (pp. 76–77). While honoring Benjamin's "excruciating. . . fastidiousness" in wishing "to permit the mute past to speak in its own voice" (p. 77), the essay asserts what the anthology later demonstrates—that even the most fastidious quotation must result in "the fabrication of a new, parallel reality that makes the past immediate while underscoring its comic or tragic ineffectuality." Sontag's own Anthology is assembled helter-skelter and juxtaposes, out of chronological order, bits of philosophic speculation, the most earnest of professional apologetics and the gaudiest advertisements. It even excerpts the entire list of the various recognized subdivisions of photography from the thesaurus. The result is not only a demonstration of ineffectuality, but of the delight that such mobility and incongruity can produce—something that the body of the book is loath to admit. The final quotation is an abbreviated note from pioneer photographer Fox Talbot, thus a fragment of a fragment: "Make picture of Kaleidoscope." The same kaleidoscopic principle guides the recomposing patterns of the Anthology itself:

> . . . at dawn that day, a commission assigned to the task had discovered the corpse of Antonio Conselheiro. . . . They photographed it afterward and drew up an affidavit in due form, certifying its identity; for the entire nation must be thoroughly convinced that at last this terrible foe had been done away with.—From Euclides da Cunha's *Rebellion in the Backlands* (1902)

> Men still kill one another, they have not yet understood how they live . . .—tomorrow we shall be able to look into the heart of our fellow-man, be everywhere and yet be alone; illustrated books, newspapers, magazines are printed. . . . The hygiene of the optical, the health of the visible is slowly filtering through.—László Moholy-Nagy (1925)
> [P. 196]

Moholy-Nagy's dream of a new "optical ethic" is undercut in advance by da Cunha's matter of fact remarks about how useful photography is for preserving evidence of a killing. Photography has no necessary ability to reveal the heart of our fellow-man and may just as easily be used to prove how alien and deserving of death he truly is. Small wonder that the penultimate quote in the Anthology, from Kierkegaard, calls photography, sardonically, "a method of leveling down which double-crosses itself." And even Kierkegaard's irony is circumscribed by the final words from Fox Talbot, which refer to something even more sporadic and whimsical than his dialectical ironies—the kaliedoscope.

The Anthology is arch, surprising, skillful, exhilarating—in a word, seductive. We have been warned against such charm, of course; the whole of the preceding text should arm us against taking it either too seriously, as a mode of knowledge, or too lightly, as an innocent and inconsequential amusement. Yet there is a residual fascination. The rapt attention to minutiae, the enchantment with accidental effects, and the pervasive air of excited accomplishment somehow escape the book's own strictures. Evidently the willed austerity, the new "ecology of images" that *On Photography* recommends, will not be an easy thing to bring about.

In *Illness as Metaphor*, the most obvious lapse occurs at the outset, in the studied figure of the "kingdom of disease" with which the book begins. Yet this is the point from which the rest of the text departs, moving steadily forward and away, with none of *On Photography*'s wayward progress or its reliance on emergent patterns. The introduction sets forth efficiently exactly what will be at issue in the book to follow and what will not:

> I want to describe, not what it is really like to emigrate to the kingdom of the ill and live there, but the punitive or sentimental fantasies concocted about that situation: not real geography, but stereotypes of national character. My subject is not physical illness itself but the uses of illness as a figure or metaphor. My point is that illness is *not* a metaphor, and that the most truthful way of regarding illness—and the healthiest way of being ill—is one most purified of, most resistant to, metaphoric thinking. [P. 3]

To the extent that it treats something that is obviously and solely a problem, with no residual delight, the book can dispense with the strategy of exacerbation and the elaborate paradoxes that *On Photography* required. It need not hesitate to say that a solution is necessary and what that solution should be. The text proceeds with confident and implacable control, introducing us to the two diseases, tuberculosis and cancer, that have been "most encumbered with metaphor"—because they persisted after many other diseases had disappeared and because the cause and cure for them was (in the nineteenth and twentieth centuries, respectively) unknown. There then follows a brief history of the way these two, apparently fatal diseases, were at first conflated and a study of how they came to have contrasting iconographic and ideological associations—the disease that consumes and etherealizes, on one side, and the disease that invades and degrades, on the other.

Sontag traces these contradictory associations back to the responses that we have to different portions of our anatomy (the spiritual breathing apparatus vs. the vulgar lower regions) and to the changing meanings that have been assigned to death itself. Both diseases are (purportedly) symptomatic of passion, but in one case it is simply frustrated while in the other it has been strangled or was insufficient to begin with. Thus, the metaphoric network surrounding each disease is used (in opposite ways) as a means for promoting the claims of passion, "to validate subversive longings"—for leisure or bohemian impiety. By the fourth chapter, then, interest has begun to shift from the imagery of the diseases to the conditions that give rise to it, the available energies that can be funneled into disease, and how these processes work. As photography was seen as a generalized medium, a bearer of certain nascent values and an instrument for performing novel functions, so too conceptions of disease become another general vehicle, "tropes for new attitudes toward the self " (p. 28). But one could maintain a degree of troubled affection for these attitudes when the vehicle of expression was an inanimate machine; to turn human affliction into an instrument of self-expression renders the attitudes themselves far more suspect. What was voracity in the case of photography becomes vampirism here. "One must suppose," one essay comments dryly, "that the reality of this terrible disease was no match for important new ideas" (p. 30).

The indeterminate and depleting, omnipresent irony associated with photography becomes in this book the symptom of a "meta-sickness," a diseased preoccupation with disease. The comparison of cancer to tuberculosis (and later, to madness, syphilis, and finally, gangrene) lays bare an image system that invites a genealogy or conceptual archeology to explain the origin and pertinacity of that system—and to expose its artificiality at the same time. As in *On Photography*, a series of sources—or rather, social correlates—of the image system are produced, and as these change, so will the apparent value of the disease change as well. Whereas ancient epidemics were experienced collectively and were viewed as a punishment visited by the gods upon an entire community, cancer and tuberculosis individuate, and thus are more closely allied to sin and guilt than to extrinsic retribution. Faced with a mysterious disease, the ancient world took it to be the result of some determinate crime and looked only for the effect the disease might have on individual character. But the modern world treats its worst illnesses as a consequence of character, an expression of vaguely defined inherent flaws or elevated sensitivities.

> Ceasing to consider disease as a punishment which fits the objective moral character, making it an expression of the inner self, might seem less moralistic. But this view turns out to be just as, or even more, moralistic and punitive. With the modern diseases (once TB, now cancer), the romantic idea that the disease expresses the character is invariably extended to assert that the character causes the disease—because it has not expressed itself. Passion moves inward, striking and blighting the deepest cellular recesses. . . . In Karl Menninger's more recent formulation: "Illness is in part what the world has done to a victim, but in a larger part it is what the victim has done with his world, and with himself. . . ."[Sontag's ellipsis] Such preposterous and dangerous views manage to put the onus of the disease on the patient and not only weaken the patient's ability to understand the range of plausible medical treatment but also, implicitly, direct the patient away from such treatment. Cure is thought to depend principally on the patient's already sorely tested or enfeebled capacity for self-love. [Pp. 46–47]

The inner self ostensibly expressed through cancer—sterile, stoney, more a "loser" than a victim—lacks the grace of the ethereal and delicate tubercular. This betokens a historically altered understanding of the self and its resources, its inherent innocence, its just deserts. This change occurs at the same time as the rise of psychoanalysis, a new and wholly secular theology, which ultimately puts emotional disorder in the place of sin:

> Psychologizing seems to provide control over the experiences and events (like grave illnesses) over which people have in fact little or no control.

Psychological understanding undermines the "reality" of a disease. That reality has to be explained. (It really means; or is a symbol of; or must be interpreted so.) For those who live neither with religious consolations about death, nor with a sense of death (or anything else) as natural, death is the obscene mystery, the ultimate effront, the thing that cannot be controlled. It can only be denied. [P. 55]

Psychology assimilates and inflates disease—"every form of social deviation can be considered an illness" (p. 56)—and turns physical illness into one more version of the new master disease, neurosis.

Illness is interpreted as, basically, a psychological event, and people are encouraged to believe that they get sick because they (unconsciously) want to.... Psychological theories of illness are a powerful means of placing the blame on the ill. Patients who are instructed that they have, unwittingly, caused their disease are also being made to feel that they have deserved it. [P. 57]

But the change is as much in how the theoretical discourse *places* the disease metaphor in history. Earlier, the book used madness as the complement of cancer, the disease that inherited the spiritual authority and sensitivity once attrributed to TB just as cancer inherited its fatality. But later madness becomes the superordinate term that subsumes cancer, and all other disease as well. This is one instance of the way the interpretation of an illness changes; another is far more spectacular. For having said that TB is a vehicle for "validating subversive longings," the claim then shifts, and both cancer and TB become expressions of the fear of passion: "Concern about energy and feeling, fears about the havoc they wreak, have been attached to both diseases" (p. 62).

The governing correlation has changed—from manners and theology to economics—and will continue its mutations as the context of discussion becomes first military and then political. Yet because *Illness as Metaphor* is a study of discourse about disease, the correlations and the resulting changes of interpretation are not (or not entirely) a product of the theoretical framework. As Sontag remarks, "Like all really successful metaphors, the metaphor of TB was rich enough to provide for two contradictory applications" (p. 25). What the theoretical text does do is control the order in which these contradictory applications will appear. Thus, if subversive longings give way to the subjects of deepest dread, and if the uses to which the metaphor is put become increasingly primitive (and Sontag's own repudiations increasingly outspoken), one can be sure it is not accidental. The book is built upon a strategy of intensification; the implications of the metaphor grow steadily darker as its applications steadily widen: "When not being explained away as something psychological, buried in the recesses of the self, cancer is being magnified and projected into a metaphor for the biggest enemy, the furthest goal.... The equivalent of the legislation establishing the space program was the National Cancer Act of 1971, which did not envisage the near-to-hand decisions that could bring under control the industrial economy that pollutes—only the great destination: the cure" (p. 69).

The incremental violence of the book's latter chapters has two sources: the rhetorical inflation that one sees the metaphor undergo and the indiscriminate power with which one sees it exploited: "Throughout the nineteenth century, disease metaphors become more virulent, preposterous, demagogic. And there is an increasing tendency to call any situation one disapproves of a disease" (p. 74). At the same time, the analysis itself expands, going beyond its original materials—popular and literary imagery, the self-perception the ill have of themselves, and the moral or psychological explanations assigned to their condition from without—to examine the social and economic order that produces these images and explanations:

> TB and cancer have been used to express not only (like syphilis) crude fantasies about contamination but also fairly complex feelings about strength and weakness, and about energy.
> . . . In an era in which there seemed to be no inhibitions on being productive, people were anxious about not having enough energy. In our own era of destructive overproduction by the economy and of increasing bureaucractic restraints on the individual, there is both a fear of having too much energy and an anxiety about energy not being allowed to be expressed. [Pp. 61–62]

The final section of the book is also taken up with the consequences of the metaphor, the specific therapeutic procedures it encourages. However much the disease was dreaded, TB always had pathos. Like the mental patient today, the tubercular was considered to be someone quintessentially vulnerable, and full of self-destructive whims. Nineteenth- and early twentieth-century physicians addressed themselves to coaxing their tubercular patients back to health. Their prescription was the same as the enlightened one for mental patients today: cheerful surroundings, isolation from stress and family, healthy diet, exercise, rest. "The understanding of cancer supports quite different, avowedly brutal notions of treatment. (A common cancer hospital witticism, heard as often from doctors as from patients: 'The treatment is worse than the disease.') There can be no question of pampering the patient. With the patient's body considered to be under attack ('invasion'), the only treatment is counterattack" (p. 64). And the political practices that the metaphor of "invasion" can therefore be used to justify: "To describe a phenomenon as a cancer is an incitement to violence. The use of cancer in political discourse encourages fatalism and justifies 'severe' measures—as well as strongly reinforcing the widespread notion that the disease is necessarily fatal. The concept of disease is never innocent. But it could be argued that the cancer metaphors are in themselves implicitly genocidal" (p. 84).

Thus, the concluding chapter in this slim, suggestive book appropriately turns to the relationship between notions of disease and parallel conceptions of the state and of society. It is one of the most deft essays in the book, an exercise in intellectual subtlety and control that pits itself against the sprawling and inflammatory nature of the materials it studies. For though the metaphor may become distended and ferocious—descending into the stuff of science fiction and collective nightmare—and though its uses may be more freighted with invective, the theoretical discourse maintains an admirable coolness and a studied understatement. Unlike certain moments in *On Photography*, the prose of *Illness as Metaphor* is never swept up in the general excitement. The distance of which so many critics have complained in Sontag's writing here finds a purpose and a meaning—more impressive now that it clearly represents neither an incapacity nor an inexperience, but a deliberate reduction of means (which one can see by comparing it with the more sensual prose of *On Photography* and the fulsome opening passages of the text itself). The economy of expression is perfectly suited (as the prose in the earlier book was not—or not consistently) to the call for restraint with which *Illness as Metaphor* closes:

> It is, of course, likely that the language about cancer will evolve in the coming years. It must change, decisively, when the disease is finally understood and the rate of cure becomes much higher.... cancer will be partly de-mythicized; and it may then be possible to compare something to a cancer without implying either a fatalistic diagnosis or a rousing call to fight by any means whatever a lethal, insidious enemy. Then perhaps it will be morally permissible, as it is not now, to use cancer as a metaphor.
>
> ... our views about cancer, and the metaphors we have imposed in it, are so much a vehicle for the large insufficiencies of this culture, for our shallow attitude toward death, for our anxieties about feeling, for our reckless improvident responses to our real "problems of growth," for our inability to construct an advanced industrial society which properly regulates consumption. [Pp. 86–88]

On Photography proposed a similar "conservationist" remedy, although more desperately and suddenly. It is as if the earlier book had been a preparation, a struggle and a stiffening of resolve, a discovery of the means that the later book then puts effortlessly to use. The wayward progress toward a politics of art in the former work becomes here a measured march from imagery to political theory, in which all documents are ideologically equal, however greatly they may differ on other grounds. There is no special brief for fiction, poetry or film. Whether a text invents or simply exploits an available image—however elaborately it renders it, however fully it absorbs and stylizes it, however little it may seem to ask of us in the way of immediate action—it still contributes to our vision of disease.

...the virtuous only become more so as they slide toward death. This is standard achievement for TB deaths in fiction, and goes with the inveterate spiritualizing of TB and the sentimentalizing of its horrors. Tuberculosis provided a redemptive death for the fallen, like the young prostitute Fantine in *Les Misérables*, or a sacrifical death for the virtuous, like the heroine of Selma Lagerlöf's *The Phantom Chariot....* [or] *The Wings of the Dove*: after learning that her suitor is a fortune hunter, Milly Theale wills her fortune to him and dies. [Pp. 41–42]

Indeed, the figure of the suffering artist was one of the chief agencies responsible for turning TB into a glamourous affliction, and the failure even to confront cancer in most of the high arts in this century is equally (if not more) punishing—a confirmation of its unspeakable shamefulness.

As *On Photography* seeks a theoretical distance from the image, so *Illness as Metaphor* uses theory to neutralize the ideologically charged materials of literature and film, a charge that attaches to them regardless of whether they are mimetic—as in "The Death of Ivan Illych" or *Ikiru*—or symbolic—as in Bergman's *Cries and Whispers*. (For that matter, Sontag's own symbolic use of autism in *Brother Carl* is equally culpable.) There is less backsliding in this later book, however. Even the opening metaphor that likens the state of illness to a political state, a kingdom, is later rendered problematic, and becomes the subject of the book's closing meditation:

> Master illnesses like TB and cancer are more specifically polemical. They are used to propose new, critical standards of individual health, and to express a sense of dissatisfaction with society as such. Unlike the Elizabethan metaphors—which complain of some general aberration or public calamity that is, in consequence, dislocating to individuals—the modern metaphors suggest a profound disequilibrium between individual and society, with society conceived as the individual's adversary. Disease metaphors are used to judge society not as out of balance but as repressive. [Pp. 72–73]

Sontag's own initial figure, it may be recalled, joined sufferer and society—"sooner or later each of us is obliged, at least for a spell, to identify ourselves as citizens of the kingdom of the sick" (p. 3). Her final chapter expands the analogy of disease/disorder and health/order through a delicate comparative reading of Machiavelli, Hobbes, and Shaftesbury: "For Machiavelli, foresight; for Hobbes, reason; for Shaftesbury, tolerance—these are all ideas of how proper statecraft, conceived on a medical analogy, can prevent a fatal disorder." (p. 80). The disease metaphor also helps to reveal the covert ties between modern political adversaries:

> No specific political view seems to have a monopoly on this metaphor. Trotsky called Stalinism the cancer of Marxism; in China in the last year, the Gang of Four have become, among other things, "the cancer of China." John Dean explained Watergate to Nixon: "We have a cancer within—close to the Presidency—that's growing."

. . . Not gangrene—and not the plague . . . —but cancer remains the most radical of disease metaphors. And just because it is so radical, it is particularly tendentious—a good metaphor for paranoids, for those who need to turn campaigns into crusades, for the fatalistic (cancer = death), and for those under the spell of ahistorical revolutionary optimism (the idea that only the most radical changes are desirable). As long as so much militaristic hyperbole attaches to the description and treatment of cancer, it is a particularly unapt metaphor for the peace-loving. [Pp. 84–86]

The nature of her correlations and the breadth of her chosen textual domain in *Illness as Metaphor* are reminiscent of Foucault's study of "discursive formations," but with the difference that what Foucault seeks are the principles of articulation and delimitation, the techniques whereby a field of discursive operation comes into being. There are a number of passing references in this book and in *On Photography* to "rhetorics" and "codes"—to the overlapping of "discourses" of illness and urban renewal, for example, or the "deciphering" of photographs. These are, however, causal analogies rather than the leading edge of a fully developed metalinguistic model. The internal structure of a metaphor, the distinction between different tropes (which has been so much debated in recent years) are not Sontag's central concern as a theorist. The "metaphor" of her most recent book's title covers any number of distinct semiotic operations that confer figurative significance—moral, psychological, phenomenological, social—on the physical and anatomical facts of illness. These include metonymic displacements ("TB is often imagined as a disease of poverty and deprivation—of thin garments, thin bodies"—p. 15); synechdoches ("TB and cancer are thought to be much more than diseases that usually are (or were) fatal. They are identified with death itself."—p. 18); and hyperboles ("Traditional disease metaphors are principally a way of being vehement"—p. 72), as well as metaphoric resemblances and homologies: "TB is disintegration, febrilization, dematerialization; it is a disease of liquids—the body turning to phlegm and mucus and sputum and, finally, blood—and of air, of the need for better air. Cancer is degeneration, the body tissues turning to something hard" (p. 13). What matters is not how the reconstructed meaning comes about but *that* it comes about, which new qualities are annexed, and why and how this reconstruction effects our perceptions, expectations, and strength of will. Even in its opening paragraphs, *On Photography* shifts quickly from "code" and "grammar" to "ethics": "In teaching us a new visual code, photographs alter and enlarge our notions of what is worth looking at and what we have a right to observe. They are a grammar and, even more importantly, an ethics of seeing" (p. 3).

Which is not to say that Sontag's examination of photographs is entirely ad hoc. She follows regular, if tacit, procedures—is the portrait frontal or in profile? Where does the gaze of the subject fall? What degree of distance or magnification is involved? What relationship between light and shadow, central forms and background, what interplay of style and subject matter?

> Sander's eclectic style gives him away. Some photographs are casual, fluent, naturalistic; others are naive and awkward. . . . Unselfconsciously, Sander adjusted his style to the social rank of the person he was photographing. Professionals and the rich tend to be photographed indoors, without props. They speak for themselves. Laborers and derelicts are usually photographed in a setting (often outdoors) which locates them, which speaks for them—as if they could not be assumed to have the kind of separate identities normally achieved in the middle and upper classes. [Pp. 60–61]

One can learn a great deal about how to look at photographs from such a passage, but the book offers no summary procedural recommendations. Since it is the "ethics of seeing" that is most important, the categories that the theory makes explicit are functional and contextual rather than structural. Ontological questions—so central to Gass's work and of much concern to semiologists and philosophers (like Cavell) who study photographs and film—play almost no part in Sontag's own account of photography and figuration. She simply takes it as a given that metaphors have little to do with the "being" of an illness, or that photographic images have their own existence independent of their subject matter. There are moments when *Illness as Metaphor* seems almost to reach out for the unmediated experience of *Against Interpretation*—"Nothing is more punitive than to give a disease a meaning" (p. 58). As if meaning itself were illegitimate, and as if anatomical interpretations of disease were not interpretations at all: ". . . cancer was described, like TB, as a process in which the body was consumed. The modern conceptions of the two diseases could not be set until the advent of cellular pathology. Only with the microscope was it possible to grasp the distinctiveness of cancer, as a type of cellular activity, and to understand that the disease did not always take the form of an external or even palpable tumor" (pp. 10–11). Yet Sontag's concern for the ethics and politics of disease compel her to abandon her nostalgia for pure, uninterpreted being. The meanings are too consequential, whatever their metaphysical status. And because she is examining received opinions and popular beliefs, there is no need to establish an ontology of her own or to propose a new, "correct" interpretation. Thus, her more recent demystifications still avoid the kind of limiting interpretation that her earlier essays opposed.

The conceptual design of *On Photography* and *Illness as Metaphor* is expansive, favoring broad generalizations and pressing the pragmatic value of its claims. (Broad claims actually go hand in hand with pragmatic vindications, which often stress the boldness, power, and unexpectedness of a theory as grounds for accepting it.) Generality is also (as noted earlier) particularly important in Sontag's writing as a way of testing, tacitly, the viability of any given claim and of initiating a process of development in which a new claim arises in order to counter or qualify an overextended predecessor. Then too, since her theorizing is not a response to officially recognized problems—since she must somehow make her readers feel that a solution is really needed, pique their curiosity and unsettle their complacency—Sontag's tendency to adopt extreme positions and put forward very general propositions is part of her rhetorical strategy of provocation and exacerbation. By generalizing her answers—"photographic recording is always, potentially, a means of control" (p. 156)—she aggrandizes her questions (How powerful is photography? To what ends may it be put?), making the problem seem ubiquitous and universal. Even those who have never before been moved to consider it—who might, left to themselves, simply dismiss it or find the dilemma barely credible—will feel compelled to respond, if only to correct or reject what she is saying.

Sontag's unembarrassedly normative language—"it is still difficult to imagine how the reality of such a dreadful disease could be transformed so preposterously" (p. 35)—has much the same function of dramatizing the importance of the problem she has set for herself. This evaluative edge links the otherwise disparate vocabularies—of health and sensuality and difficulty—she uses; however unlike they are in other ways, they all are marked by the same extremity and vehemence. Her recent effort to make the language of disease useless for the purposes of invective is therefore more poignant, particularly the harrowing last question of *Illness as Metaphor*: "But how to be morally severe in the late twentieth century?" (p. 85).

In fact, tropes other than hyperbole are fairly rare in Sontag's prose, which becomes figurative or metaphoric only when it becomes judgmental and which otherwise ornaments itself by rearranging words—through ellipses, parenthetic pauses, parallelisms, selective repetitions, antitheses, and an occasional chiasmus—in ways that leave the literal meaning intact: "The contingency of photographs confirms that everything is perishable; the arbitrariness of photographic evidence indicates that reality is fundamentally unclassifiable" (p. 80). The result is a writing with a peculiar quality of naked insistence, because that insistence is rarely accompanied by any change of diction or lapse of literalness or exclamatory rhythm, despite its normative energy and sweeping claims. Sontag's provocations are intellectual and conceptual, pressing forward without any marked vocal gestures.

That Sontag uses metaphor, and tropes in general, so sparingly and so selectively, restricting them as much as possible to overtly polemical contexts, should scarcely surprise readers of *Illness as Metaphor*, but this aspect of her writing also corresponds to deeper levels of her theoretical design. As she avoids metaphor, so she builds no models—preferring to gather up instances and to establish correlations rather than wholly to reconstrue the phenomena she studies or to posit unseen entities and unknown forces. "Photographic seeing" is a generalization of what happens when one looks at many photographs; the disease metaphor takes shape in history but is not (as Althusser's ideology is, say) a hypothetical "motor" of history. Yet taxonomies of Gass's sort are anathema for Sontag—as they should be, given her remarks in *On Photography*:

> To take, like Sander, specimen after specimen, seeking an ideally complete inventory, presupposes that society can be envisaged as a comprehensible totality....
> ...Americans feel the reality of their country to be so stupendous, and mutable, that it would be the rankest presumption to approach it in a classifying, scientific way. [Pp. 65–66]

Inventories presuppose a closed, and especially static system, whereas the phenomena that interest Sontag most, and the nature of that interest itself, are profoundly mobile. The role time and history play in her theory may no longer be what it was in her earliest work—no longer the unequivocally progressive force it was in *Against Interpretation*, or the ineluctable decay of innocence and simplicity of *Styles of Radical Will*—but it is just as crucial. History was first a promise of release from a burdensome past. Then it became a burden in itself, a vast accumulation of the past. In "The Pornographic Imagination," she complained that historical thinking inevitably relegates works of art to the status of "documents"—symptoms and evidence. But fitfully in *Styles of Radical Will*, there also appeared snatches of historical narrative: her chronicle of the history of philosophy, for example, used to make Cioran's situation both more explicable to her audience and more excruciating. Her study of photography not only uses historical data, and shapes whole essays as narrative histories, but even stipulates: "In contrast to the amorous relation, which is based on how something looks, understanding is based on how it functions. And functioning takes place in time, and must be explained in time. Only that which narrates can make us understand" (p. 23). One of the chief reasons for disparaging photography is its failure to provide an adequate historical understanding, at the very moment when it threatens to supplant written history.

The narratives in *On Photography* no longer have the reckless sweep, the irreversible and uniform necessity of those in *Styles of Radical Will*—which proved so infectious that some of her reviewers were drawn to mirror her "story" of Cioran with another narrative that would account for Sontag's own position.[60] Originally, her histories were highly speculative proposals, genealogies written in the spirit of Nietzsche, "to conceptualize and arrange a vast realm of subtle feelings of value and differences of value which are alive, grow, beget, and perish."[61] Yet the effect in Sontag's case was often the opposite of Nietzsche's skeptical deflation, managing to make Cioran's condition seem more, rather than less, inevitable.

It is only in her later, less visionary histories that she can (in the words of *Illness as Metaphor*) use narrative for the sake of an elucidation and a liberation. As the narratives become more detailed, the treatment of chronology becomes much more complicated. Less and less is time a power in its own right; more and more it is simply the medium in which changes happen to display themselves, a site where social and economic forces become apprehensible. As *On Photography* explains the collapse of the Stieglitz circle: "Obviously, a mission as rotten with doubt about America—even at its most optimistic—was bound to get deflated fairly soon, as post–World War I America commited itself more boldly to big business and consumerism" (p. 47).

In earlier essays, Sontag was often forced to introduce arbitrary contrasts—Cocteau's name suddenly appearing in a study of Bresson, or science fiction showing up in a discussion of pornography—to illustrate the characteristic features of the sensibility or genre at hand. The historical framework of her later essays not only gives a stronger motivation to these comparisons, but also changes their value, altering the focus from the distinctive individual case to the process whereby it becomes distinct from its predecessors and successors. Thus, the deft phenomenological contrasts between cancer and tuberculosis that open *Illness as Metaphor* ("TB is a disease of time....cancer is...a disease or pathology of space" [p. 14]) not only cleverly oppose the two diseases but lead to propositions about how these different images came about: "The metaphors surrounding TB and cancer reveal much about the idea of the morbid, and how it has evolved from the nineteenth century (when TB was the most common cause of death) to our time (when cancer is the most dreaded disease). The Romantics moralized death in a new way: with the TB death, which dissolved the gross body, etherealized the personality, expanded consciousness" (pp. 19–20).

The narratives in *Illness as Metaphor* are more cautious and closely documented than those in *On Photography*: none of the neat reversals whereby "Humanism" becomes "cynicism," but changes that are more manifold and subtle—which usually require the introduction of a mediating term, a transitional category (like "the idea of the morbid," above). But the conceptual design is still only a narrative. It is capable of rendering changes more plausible or of providing a glimpse of how one set of elements might condition another, but not of establishing that one has actually *caused* the other. (The softness of its claims is one of the advantages of narrative, which depicts relationships that are too complicated or too nebulous to be reduced to a uniform and universally applicable law.) For this reason, Sontag's claims about the powers of photography show a chronic instability. "Photographic seeing" is now the antecedent, now the consequent, of a given social condition or moral attitude. The strength of the correlation will shift from a near compulsory tie ("photography is always . . .") to a vaguer mutual involvement (in which photography merely "suggests"): "Our very sense of situation is now articulated by the camera's interventions. The omnipresence of cameras persuasively suggests that time consists of interesting events, events worth photographing. This, in turn, makes it easy to feel that any event, once underway, and whatever its moral character, should be allowed to complete itself—so that something else can be brought into the world, the photograph" (p. 11).

The same pattern appears in *Illness as Metaphor*, where the images of a disease are said variously to derive from, reflect, resemble, or express the changing character of the social and ideological environment. (There is irony in this, given Sontag's explicit repudiation of the tendency to treat an individual disease as "an expression of the inner self"—an irony touching the entire basis of her book, from its symptomatic evidence to its diagnostic stance.) Thus, though Sontag's generalizations are pointed, and by far the most consistent element in her conceptual design (her "laws" outnumber even her narratives), the regularities she cites are correlations or correspondences rather than true causes. So too, her writing exploits equivalences, locatives, comparatives of all kinds rather than using sentences that stress agents and their acts or events and their effects.

Originally Sontag's laws were a priori stipulations from which certain consequences—intellectual, moral, and aesthetic—could be deduced; *Against Interpretation*, for example, sought the theoretical assumptions underlying specific judgments and tastes. The goal was not just to bare the principles from which a controversial phenomenon (like "camp") derives but, often, to replace the principles and motives generally attributed to it with others, more abstract and unexceptionable, capable of entailing the same result. Thus, pornography is subsumed under the broader principles of any "literature insistently focused on extreme situations and behavior" ("Imagination," p. 40).

It was a persuasive (if not a wholly reliable) procedure, since very different implications can be derived from the same initial premise. Generalizations are no less common and almost as unguarded in the later books, but now there is more interest in actually building generalizations (rather than simply using them to clarify individual instances). Moreover, the generalizations themselves come ever closer to the status of testable assertions, and not just useful assumptions. And although there is no real effort to discover counterevidence for these typically contentious assertions—"Nobody ever discovered ugliness through photography" (p. 85)—there is obviously greater interest (and pleasure) in documenting claims:

> In "Death in Venice," passion brings about the collapse of all that has made Gustav von Aschenbach singular—his reason, his inhibitions, his

fastidiousness. And disease further reduces him. At the end of the story, Aschenbach is just another cholera victim, his last degradation being to succumb to the disease afflicting so many in Venice at that moment. When in *The Magic Mountain* Hans Castorp is discovered to have tuberculosis, it is a promotion. His illness will make Hans become more singular, will make him more intelligent than he was before. In one fiction, disease (cholera) is the penalty for a secret love; in the other, disease (TB) is its expression. Cholera is the kind of fatality that, in retrospect, has simplified a complex self, reducing it to sick environment. The disease that individualizes, that sets a person in relief against the environment is tuberculosis. [P. 37]

Such a passage even inverts the characteristic "descending order" of Sontag's earlier prose, seeming instead to ascend from data to conclusion. But more significant is the new concern for justification and proof— where once her criteria were exlusively pragmatic, concerned solely with matters like nourishment and intellectual thrust. Yet the documentation is usually so challenging and imaginative a mix that it seems as if surprise were the primary consideration.

With the new mobility (social and geographical) made possible in the eighteenth century, worth and station are not given; they must be asserted. They were asserted through new notions about clothes ("fashion") and new attitudes toward illness. Both clothes (the outer garment of the body) and illness (a kind of interior decor of the body) became tropes for new attitudes toward the self.

. . . Consumption was understood as a manner of appearing, and that appearance became a staple of nineteenth-century manners. It became rude to eat heartily. It was glamourous to look sickly. [P. 28]

This is an art of documentation, based on an aesthetic that bears a curious resemblance to the suspect procedures of photography. There is the same fondness for samples (wistfully meant to represent the whole), for symptoms and synecdoches, for "disarticulated forms" brought "together elliptically" to achieve a "compensatory unity" (*Photography*, p. 96). Similarly, the figures and metaphoric thinking that were subjected to such intensive and skeptical scrutiny on one level, emerge again at another level to govern how she selects her evidence of metaphoric thinking. The prose itself (as mentioned earlier) is fairly free of them; the favorite operations seem to be quantification, negation, and changes of grammatical mood rather than wordplay. The measured recurrences of *all* and *only, none* and *some,* are the syntactic equivalent of a search for regularities, principles, "laws"—in the loose sense of the word. The sentences are rarely bald assertions, but (because of their carefully placed modals) studies of possibility and potentiality: "It is, of course, *likely* that the language about cancer *will* evolve in coming years. It *must* change, decisively, *when* the disease is finally understood" (p. 86; italics mine).

Yet what is strangest about Sontag's theorizing is that these wide-ranging, apparently universal claims, go hand in hand with an equally fierce commitment to time and change—not only in what she argues, or even in how these arguments change from one essay to the next, but in the way the very sentences dwell constantly on process and becoming and passing away. This is particularly so in *On Photography*: "The primitivist hankerings that inform current photographic taste are actually *being aided* by the ceaseless innovativeness of camera technology" (p. 125; italics mine). The two sides of her grammar—the emphasis on pure potentiality vs. the emphasis on temporal flux and decay—give rise to what one might call "temporary universals." But a better way to understand this incongruity is to see it as an effort to describe tendencies that are at once limitless in their scope and possible ramifications, and yet still situated in time. These necessities only *seem* like necessities when we fail to see the forces that condition them. Increasingly, it is the business of her essays to combat these necessities.

The thickly embedded sentences that have become so marked a feature of Sontag's recent prose also lend it an air of lawlike generality, by changing single instances into tendencies: "That all the different kinds of photography form one continuous and interdependent tradition is the once startling, now obvious-seeming assumption which underlies contemporary photographic taste and authorizes the indefinite expansion of that taste" (p. 132). By embedding an entire proposition as the subject of the sentence, it becomes a given, a presupposition, and thus extremely hard to challenge or to attribute to a source. Of course what the later essays study is precisely such anonymous opinion, the pervasive ideological givens of photographic seeing and disease imagery. Yet the sentence structure does not reflect this ideology, but articulates it—giving it form and accessibility. The threat and power of the anonymity is enhanced further by the vague collective nouns ("people"), the agentless activities ("the efforts," "the quarrels"), and the passive sentences that fill both books, even in the opening sentences of *Illness as Metaphor*—"Two diseases have been spectacularly, and similarly, encumbered by the trappings of metaphor: tuberculosis and cancer" (p. 5).

To take up arms against such an implacable and nameless foe is immensely inspiriting. The rhetorical strategy of Sontag's prose has always been combative; her favorite modes are all argumentative, drawn from philosophical debate and minority manifesto and even courtroom controversy. Her essay on Leni Riefenstahl and the contemporary rehabilitation of fascism is clearly the presentation of the prosecution's case—"First exhibit: Here is a book of 126 splendid color photographs by Leni Riefenstahl"; "Second exhibit: Here is a book to be purchased at airport magazine stands" ("Fascism," pp. 23, 28). This move from the defense to the prosecution in her later essays seems to come to pass right before our eyes in *On Photography* and contributes to the book's internal dissonance, the intriguing and sometimes painful impression of a struggle that it conveys.

There is always a pro and a contra in any piece by Sontag, but formerly the contest was local. The agon of the writer engaged all of our attention, even if the sensibility struggling to define and defend itself was never wholly or simply personal. Richard Gilman describes it (in *Styles of Radical Will*) as "a representative advanced consciousness" engaged in a heroic and single-handed confrontation with the new, with "all the debilities and irresolution and compensatory aggressions and contradictions that are inevitable in consciousness in transition. . . . She is the victim of their assaults . . . as much as she is their elucidator and master."[62]

Since that time, however, the heroism of the avant-garde, indeed the whole conception of an avant-garde, has been placed under a shadow. An entire chapter in *On Photography* is devoted to questioning such "Heroism of Vision": "Photography opened up a new model of freelance activity—allowing each person to display a certain unique, avid sensibility. . . . By the 1920s, the photographer had become a modern hero, like the aviator and the anthropologist—without necessarily having to leave home" (pp. 89–90). Her dismissive or skeptical treatment of photographers like Weston is inseparable from her growing skepticism of aesthetic heroism itself, with its claim to be at once aloof and purified yet capable of instigating cultural revolutions. Thus it is appropriate that in the later essays her own discourse matters more than the sensibility behind it or expressed through it. The theoretical text is the instrument for undoing the deceptions and purging the misguided affections that the sensibility still seems to labor under.

The recollections that occasionally enter into these pages may be more intensely personal than any we have encountered heretofore:

> In a hospital in Shanghai in 1973, watching a factory worker with advanced ulcers have nine-tenths of his stomach removed under acupuncture anesthesia, I managed to follow the three-hour procedure (the first operation I'd ever observed) without queasiness, never once feeling the need to look away. In a movie theater in Paris a year later, the less gory operation in Antonioni's China documentary *Chung Kuo* made me flinch at the first cut of the scalpel and avert my eyes several times during the sequence. One is vulnerable to disturbing events in the form of photographic images in a way that one is not to the real thing. That vulnerability is part of the distinctive passivity of someone who is a spectator twice over, spectator of events already shaped, first by the participants and second by the image maker. [Pp. 168–69]

But the autobiographical moment is only evidence, another document among the rest; the energy of the text is elsewhere, and it never flinches. The theory, and its conceptual machinery, is a better counter to the images and the imagery that must be undone, and is, moreover, more immune to their seductions. The immunity is signaled by the increase in indirect quotation, filtered reports, and distant summaries in the later essays, but also by the spirit in which quotations are undertaken.

With so much of her best writing devoted to film, direct citation was always problematic (and perhaps the very reason why the film essays were so memorable). Films were an incitement to her prose and a reason for it, since translating from picture to word performs a necessary service (by canceling out other, more inept, translations) and yet keeps the writing from being derivative. (Another reason why her writing often succeeds where her filming, constrained to be original, does not.) But still the study of Godard in *Styles of Radical Will* cites differently than *On Photography* does:

> In the Feuillade films, as in certain early Lang and early Hitchcock films, the director has carried the melodramatic narrative to absurd extremes, so that the action takes on a hallucinatory quality. Of course, this degree of abstraction of realistic material into the logic of fantasy requires a generous use of ellipsis. If time patterns and space patterns and the abstract rhythms of action are to predominate, the action itself must be "obscure." . . . Such film narratives attain their emotional and aesthetic weight precisely through this incomprehensibility, as the "obscurity" of certain poets (Mallarmé, Roussel, Stevens, Empson) isn't a deficiency in their work but an important technical means for accumulating and compounding relevant emotions and for establishing different levels and units of "sense." ["Godard," in *Will*, pp. 160–61]

> As the fascination that photographs exercise is a reminder of death, it is also an invitation to sentimentality. Photographs turn the past into an object of tender regard, scrambling moral distinctions and disarming historical judgments by the generalized pathos of looking at time past. . . .
> . . . A photograph is only a fragment, and with the passage of time its moorings come unstuck. It drifts away into a soft abstract pastness, open to any kind of reading (or matching to other photographs). [*Photography*, p. 71]

In the first case, the elliptical and patently obscure qualities of the films is a source of "emotional value," while in the second such "fascination" is inextricably bound up with sentimentality and scrambled moral distinctions. *On Photography* characteristically seeks in photographs what the photographer him/herself could not have been aware of—"Photography in Europe was largely guided by notions of the picturesque (i.e., the poor, the foreign, the time-worn), the important (i.e., the rich, famous), and the beautiful. . . . American photography implies a more summary, less stable connection with history; and a relation to geographic and social reality that is both more hopeful and more predatory" (p. 63). This is counterreading—which diminishes and denatures, where *Styles of Radical Will* reads into and supports. The change is even more evident in *Illness as Metaphor*, which not only sees around but seems deliberately to see through the texts it treats, to reduce them to an utterly simplified transparency. Whole novels are dismissed with an insouciant plot summary, and directly quoted materials are encapsulated within a willfully deflating prose.

275 / Susan Sontag

The thwarted passion that killed Insarov was idealism. The passion that people think will give them cancer if they don't discharge it is rage. There are no modern Insarovs. Instead, there are cancerphobes like Norman Mailer, who recently explained that had he not stabbed his wife (and acted out "a murderous nest of feeling") he would have gotten cancer and "been dead in a few years himself." It is the same fantasy that was once attached to TB, but in rather a nastier version. [Pp. 22–23]

Where once quotation seemed like a rapturous communion between one text and another, now it is the diagnosis that one text performs upon another. Even the giddy pleasure of the appendix to *On Photography* is an "Anthology," a set of labelled specimens held off at an ironic (if not, in this case, diagnostic) distance. But either way, citation is equally self-conscious—far more so than in her previous work—selecting and assembling fragments according to what are patently its own interpretive interests, "fabricating a new reality." Theoretical discourse and cited discourse operate at distinctly different levels; there is no question of contamination or direct confrontation between the two. Sontag's habit of controversy continues, but there is less scrapping. It is no longer the audience that must be chastened; the offending parties have been internalized, encapsulated and brought inside the text itself. More to the point, what is thus internalized as a quotation is not a person but an opinion, an impersonal ideological mechanism. Clearly, the use of this mechanism has moral consequences, but the condemnation, and all hope of rectification, attaches to the mechanism itself. By pitting her writing against writing, rather than against the amorphous force of time or the idiosyncrasies of temperament, the essays (as one moves from *On Photography* to *Illness as Metaphor*) seem to grow in confidence and rigor and moral control.

The rhetorical strategy changes, the suffering sensibility vanishes, precisely when the theory establishes a broader and more impersonal domain of operation. Thus, while Sontag's theorizing continues to be didactic, the emphasis falls on the teaching and not the teacher. It shifts from what she calls in an interview the virtues of teacherly "authority" to the virtues of "humility" and "skepticism" (exemplified most clearly in the self-accusation at the end of *Illness as Metaphor*). No longer are we being instructed by an adept in the mysteries of "camp" or the "new novel"; we are joining in a discipline that the text itself is in the process of inventing and the writer apparently in the process of learning. Reviewers who find her recent work more palatable are responding to this change of posture, yet the theory is really no less prescriptive. *Against Interpretation* had a program to advance, and opposed itself to other theories, not as more true or more complete, but simply as more "healthy."

Transparency is the highest, most liberating value in art—and in criticism—today. Once upon a time (say, for Dante), it must have been a revolutionary and creative move to design works of art so that they might be experienced on several levels. Now it is not. It reinforces the principle of redundancy that is the principal affliction of modern life. Once upon a time (a time when high art was scarce), it must have been a revolutionary and creative move to interpret works of art. Now it is not. ["Against Interpretation," pp. 22–23]

Illness as Metaphor offers itself as another kind of liberation, from "lurid metaphors" rather than from redundancy, but it is a program for de-creating instead of creating. Yet the credo of *Against Interpretation*—"we have an obligation to overthrow any means of defending and justifying art which becomes particularly obtuse or onerous or insensitive to contemporary needs and practices" (p. 14)—could serve the latter book just as well. The reading of those needs is doubtless different, and explanation now plays a far more central role. Yet accuracy alone is neither the sole motive nor the final grounds for Sontag's theorizing. Evidence is accumulated to assist in the larger project of demystification, and it is this project that determines where the inquiry will begin and when it will be deemed complete.

So the more fundamental change is in the economy of her theories, a concern for which emerges at the end of both of her most recent books: "our reckless improvident responses to our real 'problems of growth'. . . our inability to construct an advanced industrial society which properly regulates consumption." What are now called the problems of a "growth economy"—"expansion, speculation, the creation of new needs,. . . an economy that depends on the irrational indulgence of desire" (*Photography*, p. 65)—once were the (tacit) values upon which Sontag's own judgment rested. The superiority of the modern was, for example, its vast, even excessive, stores of sophistication; the contemporary was always an advance on, an expansion of, the past. At a subtler level, the early essays rarely envisioned a condition of scarcity or enclosure that could bring values into conflict—"As if one had to choose," cries "Against Interpretation" incredulously, "between responsible and humane conduct, on the one hand, and the pleasurable stimulation of consciousness, on the other!" (p. 32). The defense of camp or pornography is premised on an ideal openness, on there always being room for new and frequently extreme experiences. To be against interpretation was to be against constriction, single readings, and in favor of unresolvable ambiguities. But now the ambiguity of any single photographic image has become oppressive and the proliferation of all images threatening. Moreover, limits have begun to circumscribe the formerly limitless, open-ended system, giving rise to a delicate trade-off between ascendent and descendent forces: "A steadily more complex sense of the real creates its own compensatory fervors and simplifications, the most addictive of which is picture-taking" (*Photography*, p. 161).

Yet despite her overt attack on proliferation and indiscriminancy in the case of photography, on inflationary metaphors and totalitarian schemes in the case of the rhetoric of disease, Sontag's own conceptual design continues to rely on expansion, growth, and overgeneralization. From these spring the vividness of her stance and all her self-critiques and self-corrections. There are other inconsistencies between her doctrinal commitments and her theoretical design, like the recurrence of the condemned categories of "expression" and "synechdoche" in the procedures for gathering evidence in *Illness as Metaphor*. There is also the deep, if diffuse, ambivalence about the status of meaning (egregious imposition or inescapable necessity?) and the nature of the real, which is now treated as if it were uniform and transparently evident (and thus photography is condemned for distorting the reality of the "flow of time" as it "freezes moments in a life"—*Photography*, p. 81), and now as if it were mobile and eternally uncertain:

> The problem with Feuerbach's contrast of "original" with "copy" is its static definitions of reality and image. It assumes that what is real persists, unchanged and intact, while only images have changed.... But the notions of image and reality are complementary. When the notion of reality changes, so does that of the image, and vice versa. "Our era" does not prefer images to real things out of perversity but partly in response to the ways in which the notion of what is real has been progressively complicated and weakened. [P. 160]

It is possible to offset some of these internal contradictions by instead focusing (as Sontag's theory increasingly does) on other texts and whatever view of meaning and reality they seem to employ. But if these inconsistencies persist, it is not entirely detrimental to the theory. Indeed, from some points of view, it is almost a merit to thus conceive more than one can yet achieve, and in the process put the very machinery of conception in jeopardy. From the start, Sontag's speculations have always been conducted at risk. Committed to the necessity of change, each essay yet speaks in the fullness of its own (soon to be anachronistic) position. Nor is there any effort to take refuge in defensive ironies, but there is instead a resolute and fully exposed pursuit of the initial premises, wherever they might lead: "an intelligence that aims at definitive resolutions (that is suppression) of conflict" is not "worth defending."[63]

In recent essays, her skepticism has turned reflexive, subverting the sensibility, the practices, the very authority of the author and the conditions that make them possible. The mobility of Sontag's theoretical claims and her talent for posing faintly irritating, "illicit" problems that refuse to fall conveniently within the purview of any one field of expertise is another way in which these essays prevent easy assimilation and forestall certain kinds of external alliances and investments. The same concern for what "dependencies" photographic images create, "what antagonisms they pacify,...what institutions they buttress, whose needs they really serve" (p. 178), affects the theoretical discourse itself, which strives to buttress no particular institutions and to exacerbate antagonisms rather than relieving them. The discrepancies in her conceptual design and rhetorical strategy have at least the candor of their own unresolved tensions, exposing gaps between old desires and new needs that are by no means peculiar to these essays, but are rarely so intently, so strenuously, layed open. Straddling what Sontag has elsewhere called the "twin afflictions of hyperaesthesia and passivity," these essays try to embody (without yielding to) a situation in which "no position can be a comfortable one or should be completely held."[64]

Discomfort is the crucial word. It applies to the pursuit of theoretical knowledge in which these essays are engaged as much as to any particular conditions they explore. Photography and metaphorically inflated illnesses are themselves modes of knowledge and are judged in just these terms. But the questions that the essays raise about the hidden motives, the unjust profits, and the distortions that accompany photographic seeing or the rhetoric of illness do not stop there. Even when they are not openly directed at the theoretical activity itself, they linger menacingly, never out of view. From her earliest writings, Sontag has stressed that knowledge is never innocent, either in its foundations or in its effects. Inquiry is always an invasion, sometimes an aggression, disrupting by the force of its own inquisitive glance the circumstances in which a phenomenon originally existed. "The interpreter, without actually erasing or rewriting the text, *is* altering it. But he can't admit to doing this. He claims to be only making it intelligible, by disclosing its true meaning.... the contemporary zeal for the project of interpretation is often prompted not by piety toward the troublesome text (which may conceal an aggression), but by an open aggressiveness, an overt contempt for appearances" ("Against Interpretation," p. 16). The investigator, be it a mechanical apparatus (like a camera), an anonymous agency (like the collective image makers), or an individual person, always occupies its own space, uses up time and resources that might have been expended elsewhere, and must bear responsibility for this. And the interests of the investigator are always other than any the investigated could possibly (without pathology) have about itself. The complaint aimed at Diane Arbus—"Do they see themselves, the viewer wonders, like *that?*"—is something that could just as well apply to Sontag's own treatment of Arbus: does she, could she, see herself like Sontag sees her?

The crude equation between knowledge and revenge that once set her against interpretation is less certain now that her faith in the wholesomeness of appearances has declined and as different kinds and qualities of knowledge have been identified. The equivocal (often dangerous) drive to appropriate, "colonize," and "master" remains suspect, but now it is matched by the even greater threat of indiscriminate information, of images and imagery that are intelligible and satisfy the desire for knowledge without really helping to clarify our condition.

The industrialization of photography permitted its rapid absorption into rational—that is bureaucratic—ways of running society. No longer toy images, photographs became part of the general furniture of the environment—touchstones and confirmations of that reductive approach to reality which is considered realistic . . . .

The "realistic" view of the world compatible with bureaucracy redefines knowledge—as techniques and information. . . .

. . . The camera makes reality atomic, manageable, and opaque. It is a view of the world which denies interconnectedness, continuity, but which confers on each moment the character of a mystery. . . .

. . . while [photographic knowledge] can goad conscience, it can, finally, never be ethical or political knowledge. The knowledge gained through still photographs will always be some kind of sentimentalism, whether cynical or humanist. It will be a knowledge at bargain prices—a semblance of knowledge, a semblance of wisdom; as the act of taking pictures is a semblance of appropriation, a semblance of rape. [Pp. 21–24]

The superior powers of penetration and analysis that go with theory make it not simply the better of two evils but a remedial necessity. To the extent that the drive to achieve intellectual control is turned on instruments that are themselves both potent and woefully out of control, it is cleansing. And it also, surreptitiously, holds itself in check.

As a result, Sontag's theory is no longer quite so "burdened" by the accumulations of consciousness, so withered by its own skepticism. The capriciousness of *Against Interpretation* is gone, as is the dour, perhaps too eagerly embraced dilemma she described in *Styles of Radical Will*:

Cioran is not just displaying a facile ambivalence toward his own vocation, but voicing the painful, genuinely paradoxical experience that the free intellect can have of itself when it commits itself to writing and acquires an audience. . . . the use of the mind is a martyrdom, using one's mind in public—more specifically, being a writer—becomes a problematic, partly shameful act; always suspect; in the last analysis, something obscene, socially as well as individually. [P. 83]

Indeed, the tendency toward self-duplicating structures that Cary Nelson finds everywhere in her earlier work—so that comments about Cioran's problems become comments about the writer's own problems—have largely disappeared, which has made her texts less stifling. The theory can now more readily take on a variety of objects and can do so without the entropic wearing down of a self-absorbed and hence self-defeating system. What one sees in Sontag's most recent work is agon without agony, mission without martyrdom, subversion that is a steady, disciplined illumination rather than the fitful sparks of surrealistic wickedness. Writing of Cioran, Sontag stated that his "fierce, tensely argued speculations sum up brilliantly the decaying urgencies of Western thought, but offer us no relief from them beyond the considerable satisfactions of the understanding" ("Thinking," p. 94). But now the satisfactions of the understanding have become the *needs* of the understanding. The "relief " of knowledge—a mere remission, a private and rather minor indulgence—has turned into release from punitive or sentimental fantasies. For Sontag, these last produce a public sickness worse than TB or cancer—but one for which theory now seems to offer the promise of a cure.

III

The Critical Impasse:
The Case of Bloom and
Barthes

The issue is reduction and how best to avoid it. Rhetorical, Aristotelian, phenomenological, and structuralist
criticisms all reduce, whether to images, ideas, given
things, or phonemes. Moral and other blatant philosophical or psychological criticisms all reduce to rival con-
ceptualizations. We reduce—if at all—to another poem. . . .
. . . There are no interpretations but only misinterpretations, and so all criticism is prose poetry.
HAROLD BLOOM, *The Anxiety of Influence*

Fiction would proceed from a *new intellectual art* (which is
how semiology and structuralism are defined in *Système de
la Mode*). With intellectual things, we produce simultaneously theory, critical combat, and pleasure; we subject
the objects of knowledge and discussion—as in any art—
no longer to an instance of truth, but to a consideration
of *effects*.
ROLAND BARTHES, *Roland Barthes*

Gass and Sontag have, to some extent, passed from traditionally creative
work—in the form of novels, short stories and films—to theoretical
writing; Bloom and Barthes began as critics, became theorists, and
eventually passed onto the writing of hybrid texts with patently (if not
traditionally) creative pretensions. Bloom's most recent production, his
so-called gnostic fantasy, *The Flight to Lucifer*, even borders on conventional fiction—a bit too conventional, perhaps. But there are other
differences beyond the trajectory of their respective careers that make
these two couplings—Bloom and Barthes, Sontag and Gass—interesting.
Bloom and Barthes are, for example, system builders, almost notorious
for introducing their own complicated categories, inventing procedures
and borrowing postulates, that together constitute a theoretical machine
that will (ideally) outlast any immediate application. Thus, there are
"Barthesian" and "Bloomian" analyses—and anti-Barthesian and anti-
Bloomian—as there will never be sons-of-Gass or epigones of Sontag.
This is not a reflection on the sophistication of their respective theoretical
efforts, nor of its persuasiveness. Indeed, one might argue that in terms of
logical acuity and pertinacity, Gass and Sontag are the better "thinkers."
But they leave no residue, no sets of rules or teasing would-be models.

Their new hypostases are few, and those they do propose are constructed by recombining familiar words, rather than by coining new ones. *Photographic seeing* and *purification* stay close to the world of entrenched terminology; however novel they may prove to be conceptually, they fade into the light of common day as terms like *apophrades* and *narratology* do not.

Sontag and Gass are occasional theorists whose formulations are subject to the diffusion of a broad and disjointed reading public. The early essays collected in Barthes's *Mythologies* have something of this same occasional quality, graceful and deceptively insouciant, but with time, his writing became more and more closely identified with academic publications, addressing an audience of specialists on what had become (largely through his own efforts) a specialized subject. Bloom has never been other than an academic critic, although—to use his own terms—a deliberately antithetical one, a partisan of Shelley and the Romantic Sublime when both were, if not despised, at least highly suspect for their supposed self-indulgence, imprecision, and abstraction. Although Bloom has never faced the sort of organized opprobrium and academic ostracism that Barthes confronted early in his career, he has recently become the more controversial of the two, at least in Anglo-American circles. Paradoxically, the imported Barthes became an altogether less horrific figure than his Gallic original, one more easily assimilated—with his often shapely and always amusing and invigorating prose—than other of his cohorts like Foucault, Derrida, and Lacan. The domestication of Roland Barthes had gone so far, even before his recent and painfully sudden death, that his name no longer seemed intimidating or arcane enough to function as a weapon in "advanced" critical quarrels of the sort that Harold Bloom—homegrown though he be—regularly and vociferously engages in. While alternately debating and deferring to the wisdom of Lacan and Derrida, Bloom never even mentions Barthes—although one surmises that he must figure somewhere among those nameless advocates of architectonic stresses and the "anti-humanistic plain dreariness [of] all those developments in European criticism that have yet to demonstrate that they aid in reading any one poem by any poet whatsoever."[1] Yet Bloom's own theoretical efforts are clearly inspired, both negatively and positively, by the invasion of these same dreary Europeans, making Barthes the leading edge of a phenomenon of which Bloom is the wake. Moreover, Barthes (despite his identification with structuralism in the Anglo-American mind) absorbed the implications of poststructuralism far more fully than all but a few of its local partisans, Bloom included.

In their separate ways, Barthes and Bloom have come to typify the new militancy of literary theory and also a particular brand of theorizing—vaguely Continental, broadly historical, conversant with philosophy, psychology, linguistics, and ancient rhetoric, and steeped in the subterranean underside of Western rationalism (De Sade, Nietzsche, Kierkegaard, Bataille). The typification is both convenient and ambivalent, allowing some to point forebodingly at the new excesses and others to extol the new excitements of the enterprise, simply by alluding to one name or the other. There is a tendency (a fault of perspective, no doubt, induced by his early and complete deracination from his native ground) to see Barthes as an idiosyncratic and isolated figure, while Bloom is seen forever in the plural, indistinctly situated among the throng of his Yale associates. No doubt Bloom's own thickly encrusted allusions to Hartman, Hillis Miller, and de Man contribute to this vision; there is, according to David Hirsch, a form of "mutual puffery" among all these writers which manifests itself at conferences and in reviews of each others' work.[2] Yet Jerome McGann is probably right to say that the obscurity of Bloom's prose really reflects "rhetorical conventions [that] seem to be the common property of a small club whose only permanent member is Bloom himself."[3]

With Barthes and Bloom, we enter the highly charged atmosphere of competing schools and credos, of rapid accelerations and more-avant-garde-than-thou positions wherein the wrong allusion, a misplaced phrase, or a taboo word can expose one to contemptuous dismissal or charges of heresy. The overlay of citations and qualifications, the code words that fill so many recent essays (and not Bloom's alone) are a function of this need for prominently displaying one's sophistication. In such an atmosphere and amid such obvious evidence of intimidation and vested power, it is difficult for either Bloom or Barthes to assume their former postures as rebellious outsiders. Romanticism is no longer quite the neglected and maligned tradition that once it was, while structuralism and poststructuralism alike have achieved embarrassing (if not total) hegemony in the very universities that had once declined to accredit Barthes. Each of these writers, then, lived to see his own most cherished subversions become the elements of a new orthodoxy—an awkward circumstance that may have helped to push them toward greater extravagance and, ultimately, into adopting a new kind of theoretical discourse with a more ambiguously fictive status.

I therefore turn to Barthes and Bloom not for their importance as theorists of literature alone but for their distinctive efforts to write theory as a form of literature. More than refinements of style and stance are involved here. More even than strategies of vindication: The whole of the theory, from its conceptual machinery and explanatory framework to its supporting proofs and evidence, has become aesthetically charged, making it increasingly difficult to distinguish between literal claims and transient, figurative suggestions and throwing open an entire drama, a strange new sensuality of theoretical design. Yet the nature of the art that results is different in each case, as is the way that it has come about.

Originally, Barthes's theoretical writings were strictly literal—an unusually ambitious and sustained attempt to construct a "science of literature" with the aid of a model and a method of scrupulous distributional analysis borrowed from structural linguistics.

Bloom, however, became a theorist and a prose poet all at once, arriving on the scene only after the romance of scientism had begun to subside and a radical critique of the premises of structuralism—its pristine methods, its model of the sign, the systems it discovered (or imposed) on its subject matter—was already underway. As a result, Bloom's project collapsed the history of debate and self-doubt through which European structuralism gave way to various poststructuralisms; his theory became at once a system and an attack on system. This developmental difference has, in turn, had an impact on the particular balance between theory and literature that each writer achieves. Barthes's writing to the end retains vestiges of the analytic edge, the concern for lucidity and rigor, that figures in his earlier works. His conceptual machinery, however greatly it changed in value, remained chaste and almost fully operable. His aesthetic seemed, if anything, to be the product of the *askesis* (disconnectedness) in his earlier theorizing—precisely the opposite of Bloom's apparent effort to make theoretical discourse yet another version of the Romantic Sublime. Jonathan Culler captures something of the differing ideals of beauty that animate these two theoretical enterprises:

> For Barthes, one might say, the model for textual production is Bouvard and Pecuchet, whose lives are generated by an infinite network of anonymous citations. For Bloom, on the contrary, the intertextual is not a space of anonymity and banality but of heroic struggles between a sublime poet and his dominant predecessor....
>
> Turning from texts to persons, Bloom can proclaim intertextuality with a fervor less circumspect than Barthes's, for Barthes's tautologous naming of the intertextual as the *"déjà lu"* is so anticlimatic as to preclude excited anticipations, while Bloom, who will go on to name precursors and describe the titanic struggles which take place on the battlefield of poetic tradition, has grounds for enthusiasm.[4]

Not only is Bloom's writing molten, his preferred outlines somewhat vague, and his machinery itself hyperbolic, but every borrowed element must be made to conform to the principles of art (as Bloom understands them). Whereas Barthes might be described as a centrifugal literary theorist—one whose techniques and conceptual instruments take him outward (toward skepticism) from a literary center, Bloom's operations are centripedal—bent on leveling the distinctive otherness of philosophical, psychological, and semiological concerns and on returning literature to its privileged position as the source and circumference of all possible motives for critical metaphor. For Bloom, literature is special but universal; for Barthes, it is partial and particular. Like Sontag (and not accidentally so, since she wrote the preface to an early translation of his work), Barthes expanded the domain in which his theory operates, brought literature into closer contact with interests that were once deemed extraliterary, and tried to establish its position in relation to the changing forms of social life. But unlike Sontag, he expressed in later years a more marked concern for the specificity (though never the autonomy) of literature, the peculiar and irreducible nature of its pleasures. Yet, as a theorist whose theoretical operations allied him unashamedly with other disciplines and other areas of research, Barthes could still strike readers like David Hirsch as one of "those grammarians who would drain the vitality of literary texts by reducing them all to abstract representations." Hirsch in fact goes on to link Barthes with Bloom as joint proponents of the same disturbing tendencies in contemporary letters:

> What all modes of modern literary criticism seem to have in common is a desire to do away with language, to find a fiction, a deep structure, an autonomous level of plot, a psychological condition, a vision, anything just so long as it can be convincingly presented as existing outside of language itself. Under the guise of theories of literature we get theories of psychology, of sociology, of codes, of grammars, of rules, of systems. But, to paraphrase Emerson, there is no doctrine of beauty in our theories. This seems to me to be the most arresting development of modern literary criticism—that it has given up all interest in beauty and in the possible relationships between language, Beauty, and Truth.[5]

Hirsch's complaint is not incomprehensible, if indiscriminate. For though Bloom's theory begins as a fight to preserve poetry, the autonomy he eventually wins for it is more a necessary fiction than a fact. And though his subject is still the same literary monuments with which he began his career as a practical critic, the effort to enrich that criticism, to enlarge its gestures and enhance its powers without expanding its domain, has had equivocal consequences. For in trying to wrest back from rival disciplines the excitement and the sense of purpose that literary studies seem to have lost, Bloom has tacitly acknowledged that excitement. He is acutely attuned to the grandeur of rhetorical estrangement, the éclat of intellectual combat, the "scenic value" of the conceptual machinery he would borrow—indeed, this is the chief motive for his borrowings. But whether one can thus steal the thunder and hold the lightning at bay is another question. In the process of enriching his interpretations, Bloom may have unleashed forces beyond his power to control.

5
Harold Bloom

Both in his status and in his style as a theorist, Bloom mirrors the condition of contemporary literary studies. Uneasy and ambitious, suspicious of, or simply bored with, the confinements of New Criticism—its methodological and intellectual isolationism, its appeal to gentlemanly understatement and the ostensible dictates of common sense, and its controlling critical fiction of the self-contained literary artifact—he (and it) are therefore tempted by the fresh theoretical impetus of Continental thought. There is something grasping, desperate, and overfull about Bloom's theoretical prose; almost overwhelmed by its own newly discovered powers and the fresh ranges of permissible references that have been thrown open to it, it remains far from comfortable with the assumptions upon which this new power seems to rest and the consequences it might yet have. Hence, the quick changes of temperature, the inconsistent sympathies, the wary, sidelong glance seeking signs of approval or the encroachments of competitors—all symptoms of a gnawing uncertainty that keeps perfect pace with each advance.

Bloom's emergence as a theorist was accompanied by "a staggering burst of energy,"[1] a sudden eruption in the 1970s of productivity that in many ways parallels the flood of activity—the new journals, the massive accumulation of books—in the academy at large during the same period. The energy is made up of equal parts of stimulation and sting: as much a frantic effort to right a vertiginous sense of imbalance as an excited application of new ideas. Thus, responding to what has since become Bloom's prolegomena, *The Anxiety of Influence*, Paul de Man notes how problematic a book it really is and, indeed, must be: "In this essay, literature is not the well-defined subject matter of a traditional discipline. It is a volatile term, in the midst of undergoing dramatic changes of content and value."[2] And in an omnibus review of the books that follow *The Anxiety of Influence*, Joseph Riddel develops the full irony and discomfort of Bloom's position:

> . . . his assertiveness has fated Bloom, a "man without a handle" as the elder Henry James called Emerson, to be the academy scapegoat for the very kind of unregenerate thinking he so passionately resists.
> . . . Whatever else one says of recent continental thought, it has. . . . broken the immediateness of the text. . . . erased the margins of "literature"

as a distinct thinking of primary and secondary texts, imaginative and interpretive discourse. Bloom is not at all certain that this interruption of the old
paradigm is desirable, but like original sin, once it has been thought it continues to produce extraordinary images. It can only be resisted or tran-
sumed, not denied. So that Bloom's disturbing performances of late can
only be understood as restagings of an inevitable and necessary play—the
revenge of self-consciousness.[3]

Riddel argues that what Bloom has created in his twistings and
turnings is "the 'unreviewable' essay," an unwitting or unwilling instance
of the principle of textual indeterminacy that he had hoped instead to
master: "That a text is 'undecidable' (rather than plurisignificant or
inexhaustible) is one of those disturbing notions of the *nouvelle critique* that
divides the vanguard from the old guard."[4] Riddel's reading of Bloom is
subtle and convincing in this respect, yet it also illustrates why writing
about Bloom at such a cultural moment is so difficult and so revealing.
The "undecidable" nature of these texts compels one to assume some
strategy of confrontation and appropriation, to choose among the available ways of overcoming or coming to terms with that very indeterminacy.
A neutral reading of Bloom is impossible. Thus, his criticism functions as
a litmus test for the preconceptions and preoccupations of the commentators themselves. Reading Bloom exposes not only which particular
theories one accepts or tolerates, but what one holds a theory of literature
to be and how one defines *literature* itself. One is forced to make
decisions—to establish contexts (or suspend them), to determine values
(or determine that value is irrelevant)—all of which will ultimately reveal a
good deal about one's own preferred conventions of reading, assumptions about authorship and intention, along with more fugitive feelings
about the character of Bloom himself, his capacities and his limitations.
Even Riddel's witty and urbane acceptance of the inconsistencies in
Bloom's writing as necessary and irreducible does not escape this rule. As
one of the most knowing and noteworthy American proponents of
deconstruction, his delighted discovery that Bloom has written a self-
defeating text is hardly surprising.

> Bloom's effort to overcome what de Man calls the *aporia* between two views
> of language, two senses of rhetoric [as persuasion and trope] has stunned
> critics who are accustomed to making a more modest choice between the
> two. . . . Characteristically, Bloom nearly always situates himself in the ab-
> surd "between" of any systematic formulation, only to construct there his
> own Tinguely-like device, a vast mechanism that would overthrow critical
> entropy by building into it a reversal of its own reversals. . . .
>
> The crucial point is irresistible: that like all theories of language it
> harbors an internal contradiction.[5]

The same features that delight Riddel, however, prove intolerable
to Culler, for whom theories of language are not, a priori, impossible, and

internal contradiction therefore bespeaks a contingent inadequacy in the theoretician himself:

> Bloom...has now effectively slain his past and fully acceded to a new oracular role. One hopes to learn from his book how to recognize a relation of influence, how to identify in a poem the slaying of a precursor, what it looks like for one poem to be a misreading of another, or for a late poet to become in his poem the ancestor of his predecessor. Juxtapositions and assertions we have in plenty, but demonstrations and explanations I think only twice, neither of which even begins to illustrate the scope claimed for the theory.[6]

Culler further laments Bloom's need to go on generating readings rather than explaining (for Culler, the only valid goal of literary theory) "how interpretation is and has been possible: on what grounds, through what codes and conventions."

> To read an author's poem as a misinterpretation of a poem which he never read is simply an act of interpretation, a decision by the critic that valuable meaning and energy will be produced if one poem is applied to the other.
>
> ...ultimately his theory bears not on tradition, intertextuality, and presupposition, but on what I shall call "application": the rubbing together of two texts in order to release energy....a decision made for the purposes of interpretation and not as a motivated axiom of the theory.[7]

For other readers, Bloom's interest in producing rather than explaining interpretation is no problem: Instead the complaint is variously (and inconsistently) that the theory Bloom proposes *restricts* his freedom and flexibility as a reader, or *contradicts* the readings he actually produces ("For all the talk about wandering meaning, the meanings Bloom finds...are too often fixed and unambivalent"),[8] or is simply *irrelevant* to them ("To this ability [for noticing specific things about specific poems,] his theories, like his categories and terminologies, seem unnecessary.")[9]. Similarly, Bloom has been praised by some for returning us all, once again, to the question of literary value and blamed by others for obscuring real values—"If you accept Bloom's systematic theorizing,...whether or not it's true you will begin to see the last poems of Hardy to which it's applied become portentous, exemplary, and therefore great."[10] Most discordant of all are the responses to Bloom's historical pretensions, with some writers lauding him for seeing that "literature is produced in time and in society by human beings, who are themselves agents of, as well as somewhat independent actors within, their actual history"[11]—and others for situating "the concept of influence well beyond any naively empirical event." Paul de Man, whose phrase this is, goes on to claim that what seems to be a history is actually the mask of a "still unformulated theory of the imagination": "Frustrated by the difficulty of stating his insight into the nonreferential quality of the imagination, Bloom has become the subject of his own desire for clarification. His theoretical concerns are now displaced into a symbolic narrative."[12]

Because Bloom's writings are susceptible to such inconsistent readings, several reviewers have suggested that one would do better treating them as if they were frankly fictions or poems, rhetorical displays that "rewrite Borges' legendary Library of Babel in Stevensian metaphors."[13]

> Like most good books, Harold Bloom's latest essay is by no means what it pretends to be. It calls itself, in subtitle, "a theory of poetry.". . .
> Despite the subtitle, it is not really a *theory* of poetry, or only to the extent that it conforms literally to the quotation from Wallace Stevens which serves as a motto: "that the theory/Of poetry is the theory of life,/As it is. . . ."... It is not every day, after all, that one has a chance to watch literature fight itself over its own claims.[14]

Yet to call what Bloom is writing literature in no way solves the problem, for as literature it is equally unstable and difficult to define. If responses to his theoretical pretensions are divided between enthusiasm, disappointment, and regret, responses to his pretensions as a poet are even more extreme—from parody to embarrassment to solemn litany. Sometimes the distaste is an expression of discomfort over any effort to blur the responsibilities of writer and reader, or to inflate criticism while diminishing the presence of the poem as an absolute and original thing-in-itself. "Bloom, like Hartman, strives mightily to establish literary criticism as a form of 'primary' writing. The argument for criticism as a primary activity is doomed to fail, however, because it is repugnant to common sense. The critic must start by recognizing that whereas the great poet (novelist, playwright, etc.) converts energy into matter by translating undifferentiated experience into language, the critic starts with that which is already shaped into language."[15]

But just as often the response cuts across any vocational gap between "primary" and "secondary" writers, reflecting the (tutored) expectations and tastes we apply to writing as a whole. Thus, Howard Nemerov (himself a poet) discourses at length on Bloom's failure of logic, his rhapsodic excesses, the hackneyed fatality of his master plot, and ends by remarking "that the effort to render English unintelligible is proceeding vigorously at the highest levels of learning."[16] While fiction-writer Ronald Sukenick, far from disowning Bloom as an aberrant academic, embraces him as a fellow practitioner of his own postmodernist experiments, calling him "the intriguing example of a critical intelligence in the process of thinking like a poetic intelligence":

> Bloom is a provocateur.... moving literary commentary...out of the realm of systematic "concept thinking" into that of contingency and the progressive qualification of relativism. There is no such thing as truth. But if there is no such thing as truth, perhaps there is no such thing as theory. In

fact, Bloom's purpose is to return criticism from systematic theory to practical criticism. And yet, his own theoretical system is pervasive and heavy-handed and constantly gets in the way of his practical criticism. And yet, if his theory is consistent, it should evolve in the direction of self-destruction, thereby providing an escape from theory. And yet, Bloom does not mean to be consistent. And yet, and yet, and yet. Which is the point.[17]

One is tempted (I am tempted) to say that the problem is an effort to reduce Bloom to the position of either a (flawed) theorist or a (misguided) rhetor, assuming that the two must completely exclude each other and leave no room between. (Even if Bloom himself often seems to accept this dichotomy, too, switching uneasily from one side to the other in one and the same essay: "A theory *of* poetry must belong *to* poetry, must *be* poetry" vs. "the difference between a reading that is criticism and a reading that is a new poem. . . is that criticism frequently has a stronger apparent presence than the poem upon which it comments.")[18] Yet this is no more neutral than any other reading; one is still deciding how to read Bloom and which features of his indeterminate text should count and why.

No reading is ever fully determined by the evidence of the text, but Bloom's work, with its haste and capacity for indiscriminate engulfment, *radically* underdetermines whatever we have to say about it—or even what the "it" in question should be. Should it be all of Bloom or only the most recent works? Bloom alone or in the context of ongoing critical debates? Such is the force of Bloom's own stirring account of the relationship between a text and its precursors, however, that most of those who write about him—admiringly, angrily, or ironically—feel compelled to note how his own formulas have been influenced by precursor and/or rival theories. A characteristic response is Riddel's, who—while dismissing Bloom's proposals as examples of "the superficiality of American criticism"—still ends up applying Bloom to Bloom: "Bloom's combativeness with rival theories reduplicates his theory of the battle of the books, . . . [and] only barely conceals the exclusively contemporary or sibling competitiveness of his argument."[19]

Riddel is not the only writer to suggest that Bloom's appeals to Freud, Vico, Nietzsche, and Emerson are actually a smokescreen for other and more immediate rivalries.[20] But again, the rivals who are discerned vary with the reader's training and alliances. This is yet another way in which Bloom is exemplary, for the range and the ambiguity of his critical affiliations place him squarely at the crossroads of contemporary Anglo-American letters. Some see Leavis as the unnamed competitor—a writer against whom Bloom holds an ancient grudge for his treatment of Shelley, who also comes too close to Bloom's emphasis on great traditions and even shares his style of strong, sometimes cantankerous, opinion.[21] For others, Bloom's "revealing habit of acknowledging with extravagant praise distant and therefore safe precursors" is a cover for his embarrassing affinities with the measured humanism of Arnold and Eliot. Bloom may try to make his literary theory a negative theology but he is no less priestly than Arnold in his claims for the study of poetry: "Our profession is not genuinely akin any longer to that of the historians or the philosophers. Without willing the change, our theoretical critics have become negative theologians, our practical critics are close to being Agaddic commentators, and all of our teachers, of whatever generation, teach how to live, what to do, in order to avoid the damnation of death-in-life."[22]

Even more embarrasing (or anxious) than the tie to Arnold is the link to Northrop Frye, Bloom's acknowledged master in *The Visionary Company*, whose view of Romanticism as a form of "secular humanism" and imaginative quest—rather than as nature poetry—set the terms for a reevaluation of that poetry (of which reevaluation Bloom himself became one of the chief proponents). Then too, Frye's own *Anatomy* remains one of the most formidable pieces of American literary theory, its taxonomic design bearing more than a chance resemblance to Bloom's own map of misreading. James Kinkaid notes that in "Bloom's wrestling with Frye" one still "hears the echo of Frye's insistence that poetry can only be made out of poetry, his dialectic between desire and anxiety, his analysis of the role of parody and revision."[23] The fact that for Frye influence is something that expands the individual and is thus a means of freeing him by a sense of the accumulated resources of the past, from the narrowness of the present, gives Bloom both the impetus for and the site of his own ironic or tragic version of the same process. As *A Map of Misreading* misreads Frye: "The student is a cultural assimilator who *thinks* because he has *joined* a larger body of thought. Freedom, for Frye as for Eliot, is the change, however slight, that any genuine single consciousness brings about in the order of literature simply by joining the simultaneity of such order" (p. 30).

Misreadings become even more blatant when one turns to Bloom's dreary European rivals, Lacan and Derrida, whom Riddel and Culler naturally (given their own critical perspectives) see as the true instigators of Bloom's precipitous emergence as a revisionary theorist.[24] According to Culler:

> One begins to understand that Bloom boldly creates a theory of influence because it is the best way of disarming his critical opponents and of sustaining the myth of poetic genius and human tragedy which can rescue and inform his own style of apocalyptic interpretation. . . .
> Bloom sees himself locked in battle with "the school of Deconstruction, the heirs of Nietzsche, among whom Derrida, de Man, Hillis Miller are the most distinguished." Nietzsche's ephebes threaten to "despiritualize" literature by suggesting that "language itself writes the poems and thinks."[25]

Yet de Man himself insists (modestly or sophistically) that "the precursor who worries [Bloom] perhaps most of all is not Frye, or Bate, or contemporary rivals, but Bloom himself."[26]

Not only do the names of Bloom's putative precursors change but so does the conception of influence itself. Influence, as Riddel and Culler imagine it, is much more complicated, in its displacements and inversions than even Bloom deems it to be, with revisions coming, not (as Bloom suggests) to avoid repeating an admired precursor, but in an effort to put on the power of alien rivals. Other readers of Bloom see him fleeing influences that are almost shameful, revising in order to remove all traces of his own anachronistic roots. Neither of which is quite what *Bloom* means by the anxiety of influence—an anxiety born of the effort to be unlike a father figure whom one must be like in order to be the sort of poet one desires to be. "Weaker talents idealize; figures of capable imagination appropriate for themselves. But nothing is got for nothing, and self-appropriation involves the immense anxieties of indebtedness, for what strong maker desires the realization that he has failed to create himself?"[27]

Clearly there are still other ways to conceive of influence, based on different permutations and redefinitions of debt, identification, anxiety, and desire—which merely shows how fertile and how teasing Bloom's key notions are. This explains why it seems to be impossible either to ignore him or to reach consensus about his achievement, and why he should inspire so much commentary, a near industry of detractors and defenders. If, as he has sometimes stated, "a critic is strong if his readings . . . provoke other readings" (*Kabbalah*, p. 125), then in this respect, at least, his own strength as a theorist is certain.

Since talk about Bloom seems inevitably to show as much about the speaker as about Bloom himself, it is probably best to probe one's own interests from the start. My own approach to Bloom is governed by a concern for how well his work confronts current impasses in literary theory and in writing itself, what possibilities he opens up or forecloses. I begin by searching Bloom's own history for whatever may have moved him to abandon practical criticism for theory, and for some clearer understanding of why his theorizing has taken the eccentric shape it has. Moreover, I accept de Man's proviso that "the books may be somewhat hard to follow unless one is familiar with Bloom's earlier work"—not only in an evolutionary sense, but also in the sense that Bloom frequently uses in one text phrases of which the significance is only revealed in another. Thus, in *The Anxiety of Influence*, he alludes to "the deep tautology—of the solipsist who knows that what he means is right, and yet that what he says is wrong" (p. 96)—a mysterious statement that recurs in his later books (*Map of Misreading, Kabbalah and Criticism, Poetry and Repression*) with some changes of emphasis and rhythm, but no further elucidation. It is only by tracing the reference back to an essay on Mark Strand and A. R. Ammons (later collected in *Figures of Capable Imagination*) that one unearths the tutor text from which this recurring echo is excerpted:

> "What the solipsist *means* is right," a gnomic Wittgensteinian truth, is in traditional American terms the Emersonian admonition "Build therefore your own world," which in turn is founded on the central Emersonian motto: "What we are, that only can we see.". . . Pears, expounding early Wittgenstein, reads to me like an exegete of Emerson:
> . . . So the only thing that he can legitimately say is that what is reflected in the mirror is reflected in the mirror. But this is neither a factual thesis nor a substantial necessary truth about what is reflected in the mirror, but a tautology. It means only that whatever objects exist exist. So when solipsism is worked out, it becomes clear that there is no difference between it and realism.[28]

Leaving aside the misreading of Wittgenstein (who is scarcely defending solipsism, but instead undercutting it by showing how easily it reverses into its presumed opposite), one can still see how complex an intertextual event Bloom's later allusions are, merging Emerson with Wittgenstein by means of Pears's mediating exegesis. The allusions compress and embed one text within another to form a single intertextual knot—a citation of his own earlier quotation of a commentary on a quotation. This knot becomes progressively more difficult to untie with each subsequent appearance, each additional act of self-citation. (Even the original is actually incomplete; only part of Wittgenstein's sentence is quoted, with the rest simply presupposed, to be restored in later allusions.)

This kind of complex interchange between one text and another—half recapitulation, half anticipation—is characteristic of Bloom's work, which endlessly redeploys its own verbal resources in a process of development that is neither progressive nor regressive, but an endless oscillation or recirculation. Whether one sees this as a fault of composition or as a mark of heated thought that must overflow the traditional closure of the text, it is surely grounds for reading Bloom's work as a set of interdependent writings.

When one does examine the whole of Bloom's career, one is struck first by how fragile the theoretical impulse is. The notion that *The Anxiety of Influence* is the natural outgrowth of his practical criticism, making explicit the principles that had tacitly guided him all along, is (as Cary Nelson notes) a fiction of Bloom's own devising. While the book seems to provide theoretical grounds for his earlier judgments, it is actually an effort to "repossess and renew his past" by reformulating it in the light of his later theory.[29] It is true that at the outset of his career, in *Shelley's Mythmaking*, he adopted a theoretical framework of sorts, deploying Martin Buber's distinction between two different kinds of relational events—the intimate confrontation of an "I" and a "Thou," the estranged contemplation of an "it" by an "I"—to combat the critical censure of Shelley. While later he would claim that what is most characteristic about Romantic poetry are precisely its estranged landscapes, in this first book he is concerned instead to show that Shelley's apostrophes, his notorious lack of concreteness, and his seeming self-absorption are actually the traces of a different kind of "mythmaking" intelligence. To describe concretely would be to confront an "it," to reify the fleeting intimacy of a meeting that is not that of a subject and an object—or even that of two subjects—but something prior to the division of I and not-I, human and inhuman. For Bloom, Shelley is unique in his capacity to bear the burden of knowing both how transient such visionary meetings must be and that the "Thou" one seems to meet is ultimately an invention of the poetry itself. Bloom uses Buber to exculpate Shelley and to open up the possibility of another line of poetry, different from the reigning line of wit. His choice is extraordinarily apt, but one is always aware that Shelley's poetry, and not Buber's framework, is what truly interests him. First came the poetry, and a canny assessment of the assumptions governing Tate and Leavis in the disparaging of that poetry. Only afterward did Bloom light upon his chosen (antithetical) theoretical apparatus.

Bloom even takes pain in this first book to emphasize his indifference to the ultimate truth of his borrowed premises—"I am concerned with looting the work...for my own purposes"[30]—and sounds more careless still in his Preface to the paperback edition—"The use of Buber in this study is of course heuristic" (p. vii). *Heuristic* is a much misused word in literary studies, but here it seems to mean something like "convenient" or "suggestive," something that happened to fit one's needs on a given occasion but requires no further inquiry or allegiance. The preface goes on to point out (with apparent pride) that his later studies of Shelley manage to "avoid for the most part both the polemics and the various technical vocabularies" (p. vii) of this early book. And indeed, the books that followed—*Visionary Company, Blake's Apocalypse,* a number of essays and prefaces—have no isolatable theoretical machinery, and the writing is as untechnical as possible, adopting the ostensibly ordinary language and understated good manners of New Critical prose. These may not be the books of a man speaking to other men, but they are plainly those of a critic writing to other critics within familiar and widely shared conventions, using terms that have become so entrenched that they seem transparent.

Yet the retreat from theory—even one so halfhearted and abbreviated as the one that frames *Shelley's Mythmaking*—is not just a repudiation of a labored style. Indeed, Bloom's initial choice of frameworks suggests a deep suspicion that categorization of any kind must always be reductive, too static for the inherently transient stuff of which poetry and myth are made. The appeal of Buber's theory is its paradoxical opposition to theory: "I hardly know what a reductive use of the *I-Thou, I-It* dialectic would be, since what Buber calls 'relationship' has to vanish when analyzed, or discussed" (p. vii). This sounds as if Bloom were opposed to analysis per se, not out of any special reverence for the ineffable but out of a commitment to the special, the privileged status of poetry itself: ". . . Fogle draws sanction and critical vocabulary for this matter from outside Shelley's poetry; I do not. I urge mythopoeia and its principles . . . as the proper technique for reading here precisely because sanction and vocabulary for it can be drawn from the poetry. Platonism, or anything akin to it, is another kind of discipline entirely" (p. 185).

The attack on extrinsic categories becomes more pronounced in his next book, *The Visionary Company*, although it remains covert except for occasional slaps at Freud (which anticipate, in mirror-reversal, his singular attachment to Freud in later work): "This poem can help explain Keats's life; his life cannot explain the poem. Alternatively, the poem can help explain certain contemporary psychological reductions of human desire, but *they* cannot explain *it*."[31] *Blake's Apocalypse* acknowledges the example of Northrop Frye (as did *Visionary Company*), but keeps its distance from Frye's synoptic tabulation of Blake's system, instead moving slowly and diachronically through a poem-by-poem close reading. Still, like *Visionary Company*, this book contains a number of passages that presage some of the tenets of Bloom's own theoretical system:

> I have never found a knowledge of Blake's supposed esoteric sources to be of much use in reading *The Four Zoas* or other poems by Blake. Usually the hunt for those sources is all too successful in the results, and the reading of the sources takes the place of reading Blake's poems as poems. One can imagine Blake's unhappiness at having a "tradition" of hidden wisdom or a "perennial philosophy" substituted for the meanings of his very original poems. . . .
>
> . . . Blake does not need anybody to elucidate his ideas for the alert reader. What a critic can do for that reader is to increase his alertness, to help him recognize much that is left implicit.[32]

In the ironic light of retrospect, one can see how Bloom will both ignore his own warnings ("the reading of the sources takes the place of reading Blake's poems as poems") and yet, in the choice of his sources, try to obey them. For the only way of protecting poetry against deadening scholarship and the hunt for irrelevant esoteric sources will turn out to be a systematic insistence on *poetic* sources and a personally devised theoretical framework in which the esoteric becomes pure rhetoric. That this system will make Blake's (or any other poet's) originality highly problematic is part of the paradox of Bloom's development—the changes he must introduce just to stay the same.

Side by side with Bloom's mistrust of all that is reductive and alien in theories of literature (and indeed any theory must be somewhat reductive—or selective—and must translate its subject matter into another language, or there will be no gain in knowledge) is a marked distaste for the rigidity of any system—especially if one has not invented it for oneself. Shelley and Blake stand out as writers who refuse to "adhere to formulated myth" (*Shelley*, p. 8), who thrill us by their apocalyptic disdain for the world as it is given and the antinomian pride of the visionary poetry they create. Thus, in Bloom's reading of these two poets one can see the first stirrings of what will later be identified as the anxiety of influence, the inability of any strong poet to accept a prior authority, the need to believe (even if the belief is only an illusion) that one's imaginings are self-begotten. The fullest expression of this theme, in its incipient form, is in an essay entitled "To Reason with a Later Reason: Romanticism and the Rational," collected in *The Ringers in the Tower* (a volume of Bloom's prose from the sixties and early seventies, just prior to his emergence as a theorist). The essay is one of several in *Ringers* that attempt to distinguish between Romanticism and irrationality, defending Romantic antinomianism against (what were to Bloom) the cruder frenzies of the sixties counterculture:

> The great enemy of poetry in the Romantic tradition has never been reason, but rather those premature modes of conceptualization that masquerade as final accounts of reason in every age. It is not reason that menaces the shaping spirit, but the high priests of rationalization, the great men with the compasses who have marked out circumferences from Descartes, Bacon, Newton, and Locke down to subtler limiters of the imaginative horizon in Hegel, Marx, Freud, and their various revisionist disciples. Romanticism, in what seems its central tradition, at least in our language, is a revolt not against orderly creation, but against compulsion, against conditioning, against all unnecessary limitation that presents itself as being necessary.[33]

How one determines when a conceptualization is "premature" is never explained, but clearly Bloom has come to doubt the efficacy of anarchy and to appreciate for himself Blake's claim that "I must Create a system, or be enslav'd by another Man's." *The Ringers in the Tower* continues the contrast that informed *Visionary Company* between those who, like Blake, construct a "personal myth" and those who, like Wordsworth, follow "the tradition of nakedness or decreation, of a poetry of confrontation that hesitates at the threshhold of myth, but declines altogether to cross over into it." This is a reformulation of the distinction in *Shelley's Mythmaking* between "primitive" mythopoeic poetry and a more "complex" stage of mythmaking in which "the poet can dare to make his own abstractions," but here Bloom is wary of the costs of nakedness: "The price of failure is madness, or death-in-life; the reward of success is only to have written the poem, and to be free for the struggle with the next poem. *Resolution and Independence* is a poem about not being able to do what Blake's Milton does, to cast off the coverings of anxiety and of self-torturing analysis" ("To Reason," p. 326). The language is reminiscent of the theory-to-come, but here "anxiety" is the result of living without a myth, rather than with a borrowed one. All that is needed, however, to put the full Bloomian system into play is the recognition that Blake's Milton does not, in fact, cast off the coverings of anxiety, but is actually a product of anxiety.

The essays in *Ringers* are (at least in the fictitious teleology of hindsight) transitional—preparing us for a new, less celebratory view of Romanticism and, equally important, for a more aggressive and highly formalized view of it. Even in his first book, Bloom had been too acute to believe that theory was the only form that "premature conceptualization" might take—recognizing that the silent norms of practical criticism could be just as dogmatic and just as rigid as the most carefully articulated theory.

> "Abstract and intangible" is the implied comment of Cleanth Brooks and Robert Penn Warren in their popular poetry textbook, where they invite neophytes to the demonstration that the images of "Hymn [to Intellectual Beauty]" do not make its "abstract and intangible quality" concrete. I deny the relative abstractness of the poem's subject to begin with, for it is no more abstract than personal religious experience seems when verbally presented. Next, I deny that it is the proper business of this poem to make concrete, by its images, its supposedly abstract and certainly intangible subject phenomenon. Rather, the success of its images is in their consistent reinforcement of the impression upon us of the subtle nature of the Power behind this subtle influencing, the intangible grace, the spiritual beauty that constitutes the poem's subject. . . . Only our recent dogma which dictates the universal necessity of concrete imagery could provide a basis for condemning the imagistic pattern of the "Hymn." [*Shelley*, pp. 38–39]

The Ringers in the Tower is bluntly critical of our tendency to confuse any "myth in which we believe without conscious effort" ("To Reason," p. 324) with truly spontaneous and unconditioned thought, and equally warm in its praise for Stevens's "supreme fictions," those consciously constructed myths that we recognize as such because we have constructed them:

> The mind is the terriblest force in the world, father,
> Because, in chief, it, only, can defend
> Against itself.
> [P. 326.]

Cautiously, Bloom has begun to edge toward the construction of his own explicit conceptual framework; Blake's maxim for strong poetry is becoming a maxim for strong criticism as well: "The quest for interpretive models is a necessary obsession for the reader who would be strong, since to refuse models explicitly is only to accept other models, however unknowingly."[34]

But why was it only at this point that the conversion from practical to theoretical criticism took place? Bloom had obviously been aware for some time of the power of silent orthodoxies, and of Blake's recommended strategy for circumventing them, but he never felt the need to build a system of his own. Something more was necessary to push him over that threshold. One contributing factor must have been his prolonged study of Yeats's *Vision* and *Per Amica Silentae Lunae* (from whence the title *The Ringers in the Tower* comes) and of Stevens's *Notes toward a Supreme Fiction*, which occupied him during the decade separating *Blake's Apocalypse* and *The Anxiety of Influence*. These are works that belong to "the tradition of the marmoreal reverie" (as Bloom describes it in his later study of *Yeats*)[35]—the opaque splendors of which *The Anxiety of Influence* obviously hopes to emulate.[36] Then too, it is in these works that Yeats and Stevens establish (respectively) the notions of "mask" and "necessary fiction," a knowing artifice that is at once a philosophy of invention and an invented philosophy:

> Yeats distinguishes between the Mask or Image that is fated, because it comes from life, and the Mask that is chosen. Though in *Anima Hominis* he says that all happy art is but Solomon's hollow image, he means by this that tragic art is happy, yet expresses also the "poverty" of its creator, this use of "poverty" being strikingly similar to Stevens's use of it to mean "imaginative need," or a need that compels the imagination to come into full activity. . . . When the poet has seen *and foreseen* the image of all he dreads, while still seeking the image of desire to redress his essential poverty, then he will have his reward. [*Yeats*, pp. 180–81]

This is close to Blake's paradoxical escape from an imposed order through an order of one's own imposition, but with an additional turn of the screw: The self-imposed order must be consciously unreal, strictly an effect of art, as Blake's mythological system was not. Yeat's "mask" and Stevens's "fiction" are plainly seminal for Bloom's conception of poetic "strength" and seem to shape his own stance as an antithetical theorist who devises deliberately "fantastic" and "desperate" frameworks. There are traces of this notion as far back as *Shelley's Mythmaking*. Indeed, throughout Bloom's work one can discern the recurrence of the same cyclic pattern: An endangered or deluded success is succeeded by a quick decline or disillusionment, to be followed in its turn by an "antithetical" return of energy (or certainty, or a sense of purpose). This renewal, however, is forever colored by the memory and the prophetic certainty of failure; it is "an image of desire to redress an essential poverty." Although the "story" stays the same, its setting and its stages seem to change. Frequently, the narrative is truncated, and one enters it only in medias res, when the former glories are already past. Still the pattern itself is remarkably stable. In the case of Shelley, it serves as a frame for the poet's entire career: "From idealistic dream-making of the fulfillment of desire, he had passed to fully conscious mythopoeia with its knowledge that desire is unfulfillable. From an attempt to mix vision and history, he had moved to vision alone" (*Shelley*, p. 167).

It also shapes the passage from "the Promethean phase of the Romantic quest" to that quest's "mature phase" in *The Visionary Company*, a pattern that can be observed at several different levels, in the careers of particular poets and in the history of the Romantic movement as a whole.

> The outward form of the inward grace of Romantic imagination was the French Revolution, and the Revolution failed. . . . Milton, after the failure of his Revolution, turned inward like Oedipus, making of his blindness a judgment upon the light. Wordsworth's movement to the interior was more gradual, and ended in defeat, with the light of imagination dying into the light of another day, in which existing conceptions of the world seemed acceptable. Coleridge found the blinding light of theology, and forgot that "a whole Essay might be written on the Danger of *thinking* without Images," and so left the essay unwritten.
>
> Blake's response, like that of Shelley after him, was to strengthen the myth or self-made account of reality given by his own poetry. [*Visionary Company*, p. xiv]

The stages of the cycle thus form a typology of poets, distinguishing them, as here with Blake, according to the degree of "displacement of antinomian desire from an outer actuality that had ceased to be very extraordinary, to the intense warfare of consciousness against itself" (ibid., p. xiv). Ultimately—although it is no more than a vague suggestion at this point—the cycle becomes a pattern of literary history itself, tracing the decline from the supreme achievements of the first two generations of Romantic poets to Beddoes and Clare "expiring in a graceful but tenuous indefinable," and ending with the renewal of a chastened Romanticism in "our own day" in such figures as Hart Crane and Wallace Stevens: "the Romantic imagination ends, if at all, in an open question, and in the humanist conviction that mortality itself stirs the sense of possible sublimity . . ." (ibid., pp. 449–50).

By *The Ringers in the Tower*, the cycle has achieved far greater definition and prominence; each phase is isolated, specified, and subdivided (forming a pattern very close to the six "revisionary ratios" of Bloom's theory). Thus, according to the preface, the prevailing themes of the (now uninterrupted) Romantic tradition are: "Promethean quest and its failure; the estrangement of landscape from the imaginative quester; the sensibility of skepticism when intimately allied with the 'privileged moment' or secularized epiphany. One purpose of this book is to suggest that our poets, if they are to survive the anxieties of influence, must learn to master and unify these themes, which remain inescapable" (p. xi). One is tempted to read the final directive reflexively, as an edict the critic directs to himself as much as to "our poets," a command to learn to "master and unify" these glistening but still inchoate pieces of a promised order. (The reading gains plausibility if one recalls that these are the words of a preface, prospective in its position but retrospective in fact, with the belated writer [now turned reader] catching sight of possibilities as yet unrealized.) Bloom's effort to regain control over himself after the fact will become more and more apparent as his theoretical project unfolds. The effort at control seems to be one of that project's chief motivations, a source of his ceaseless and restless productivity.

The essays themselves bear out the premise that Bloom's prefatory announcement is more potential than actual, for in the body of the book the "three prevailing themes" take the shape of separate and overlapping claims about the nature of Romanticism. Thus, one essay explains the movement as an internalization of the old quest romance, both incorporating and circumventing a Freudian explanation by rooting the pattern of the quest in literary conventions and making Freud himself just one more Romantic writer who instantiates it:

> Freud thought that even romance, with its element of play, probably commenced in some actual experience whose "strong impression on the writer had stirred up a memory of an earlier experience, generally belonging to childhood, which then arouses a wish that finds fulfillment in the work in question, and in which elements of the recent event and the old memory should be discernible." Though this is a brilliant and comprehensive thought, it seems inadequate to the complexity of romance, particularly in the period during which romance as a genre, however displaced, became again the dominant form. . . .

> The movement of the quest-romance, before its internalization by the High Romantics, was from nature to redeemed nature, the sanction of redemption being the gift of some external spiritual authority, sometimes magical. The Romantic movement is from nature to the imagination's freedom (sometimes a reluctant freedom), and the imagination's freedom is frequently purgatorial, redemptive in direction but destructive of the social self. . . .

> Wordsworth is a crisis-poet, Freud a crisis-analyst; the saving movement in each is backward into lost time.[37]

The argument with Freud turns on the fact that the poetic movement inward was not to a subjectivity already constituted but to one in the process of being invented, a process that, pursued fearlessly and thoroughly enough, might manage to overcome the solitary self-love to which Freud apparently condemned human nature:

> All romance, literary and human, is founded upon enchantment; Freud and the Romantics differ principally in their judgment as to what it is in us that resists enchantment, and what the value of that resistance is. For Freud it is the reality-principle, working through the great disen-

chanter, reason, the scientific attitude, and without it, no civilized values are possible. . . .

. . . [The love that transcends selfhood] is, to use Shelley's phrasing, a total going-out from our own natures, total because the force moving out is not only the Promethean libido but rather a fusion between the libido and the active or imaginative element in the ego; or simply, desire wholly taken up into the imagination. . . .

. . . "outward" and "inward" become cloven fictions or false conceptual distinctions in this triumph. ["Quest Romance," pp. 23, 24, 28]

This salvation of the Romantic imagination at the expense of Freudian pessimism will, of course, be reversed in subsequent books. Indeed, there are hints, scattered throughout *Ringers*, that the inward movement may in fact be final, that the redemption of imagination may be only a solipsistic mirage. The effort to see the distinction between subject and object as a false dichotomy, or "cloven fiction," proves a difficult one to maintain—especially when Bloom's private cyclic myth demands a stage of genuine loss, to be recuperated by a purely visionary gain. The glamour and the pathos of the final stage of affirmation are strictly commensurate with the fictive nature of what is being affirmed, a pattern of heroic desperation.

It is hardly surprising, then, to find Bloom sliding back, in other essays, to dualism and worrying about the estrangement of the landscape and the sadly temporary reunion of subject and object that Romantic poetry effects. Most worrisome of all is the figure of Emerson, whose oscillations between asserting the imagination's autonomy and then urging a "merging with Necessity" (literally identifying the imagination with Fate, so that it is at once inescapable and unreal) form yet another, nihilistic version of the cycle of loss and gain:

Like Wordsworth, Stevens yields to a version of the Reality Principle. Blake and Emerson do not, but Emerson departs from Blakean affinities, when, in his extraordinary impatience, most fatedly American of qualities, he seeks terms with his Reality Principle only by subsuming it. . . .

. . . "why should we fear to be crushed by savage elements, we who are made up of the same elements?" We are ourselves strokes of fate, on this view. . . . The dangers, social and solipsistic, of so amazingly unconditioned a bardic vision crowd upon us.[38]

The status of Emerson rises and falls in the later writing, in proportion to Bloom's own fatalism. In the passage above—as in his nearly contemporaneous book on Yeats—there is a dim but persistent association between fatalism and "shamanism," a link between the too eager "abdication" of imaginative autonomy and "the idea of man to a conception of destiny" (*Yeats*, p. 471) with the superstitious hope of somehow gaining magical, rather than figurative, control over those forces. Yeats and Emerson are therefore castigated for a terrifying failure of imagination (rather like what Gass would call, exploiting a different critical vocabulary, a category mistake): They ask at once too much and too little of human vision.

Emerson continues to haunt *Figures of Capable Imagination*—the putative companion volume to the "four tractates of influence" that form the theory proper (p. ix)—but though Bloom still points out the dangerous machinations of those "failed Orphics who refuse to accept defeat," the phrasing itself is telling. Such an admission of defeat bespeaks a new level of fatalism on the part of "A critic who has learned, ruefully, to accept the reductive view that imagination is only decaying sense." No more visionary triumphs; at best, there are only different ways of embracing an inevitable failure. Thus, the way of solipsistic excess now seems far less repugnant than it did in *Ringers*, and far more inescapable: "Stevens fulfilled the unique enterprise of a specifically American poetry by exposing the essential solipsism of our Native Strain."[39]

As Bloom's own defeatism deepens, then, his sense of the purely defensive role of the imagination quickens, and the example of Emerson is gradually ennobled, until he becomes the supreme liar against fate, the writer who has given up the delusions of "Freedom" for the riches of rhetorical "Power." This is a power that comes only to those who have confronted the full force of "Fate," yet have managed ingeniously and deviously to deny their own subjection to it. The triad—Freedom, Fate, and Power (or, alternatively, Logos, Ethos, and Pathos)—provides the framework for Bloom's most recent book as well, a study of Wallace Stevens. By thus collapsing Stevens into Emerson and turning Stevens's own pattern—"One must have a mind of winter, or reduce to the First Idea; one must discover that to live with the First Idea alone is not to be human; one must reimagine the First Idea"[40]—into a version of Emerson's movement toward the illusory power of solipsism, Bloom abolishes the last distinction between (self-)deception and vision. If all imagination is an elaborate lie, a more or less provocative display of willfulness, then one can no longer discriminate between self-inflation and supreme fictions—each becomes a critique of the pretensions of the other. The solipsist may be deluded about the efficacy of his visions—which turn out to be nothing more (if nothing less) than a rhetorical flourish—but the supremely knowing fabulist is equally deluded about the extent to which he is in control of his own fictions, and even the extent to which his fictions are his own. Whereas Emerson once threatened to upset the unfolding of the Romantic cycle from experiential loss to imaginative gain, now he has been brought back into the fold, but at the cost of making imaginative gain wholly equivocal and turning the visionary gleam into a paradoxical blindness.

Readers familiar with Bloom's narrative habits will be quick to recognize the foundation upon which his gnostic fantasy *The Flight to*

Lucifer is built. The book traces the well-worn path from the memory of a mythic lost "Fullness," through the emptiness and meaninglessness of a fallen cosmos, to the diminished good of the climax in which Valentinus (the eternally recurring voice of gnosticism) "went on, but speaking [*n.b.*] now more to himself. 'Or, is this the measure of our strength? That we admit to ourselves, and without perishing, that the world of original being had ceased to be true?' "[41] Valentinus's remark wins an unwilling response from his companion, Olam (the normally secretive fallen angel or aeon, who together with twenty-nine other aeons once constituted the cosmos in its unfallen, uncreated form): "The aim is not to return to the Pleroma as it was, at the origin! For that All was less than All, that Fullness proved only an emptiness. The aim must be to gain a past from which we might spring, rather than that from which we seemed to derive" (*Flight*, p. 193).

These two (not unexpectedly) are the remnants of an original triad of questors who set out together to find the lost ground of the Pleroma (located on the alien planet, Lucifer, where the destructive Demiurge still survives among a population divided into competing spiritual dogmas). The third, the fiery Promethean Perscors, dies in combat—thus allowing the more contemplative Valentinus to achieve his ultimate epiphany. "The will to follow the maimed Demiurge ebbed in Perscors. He felt neither pain nor desire but only the peace of exhaustion. After a few moments, a fire broke forth from his loins. When he realized that it was indeed his own fire, he smiled in contentment. Triumph was his final thought as his head became the fire" (p. 231).

This reenacts the timeworn movement from experiential loss to imaginative gain—save that the vision that Valentinus is granted is ambiguously associated with "the hill of the Therapeutae" (where it takes place) and is linked as well to some final loss of memory on the seer's part:

> In the calm twilight, memory of his own speculation became complete for him. The ancient cause of his failure of nerve remained hidden, but he had accepted that lapse. . . .
> He knew freedom. . . .
> He passed into reverie, and from reverie into his own Pleroma, his own place of rest. [Pp. 239–40]

Although far gentler than Emerson's flagrant willfulness, this remains a visionary lie—a separate and invented peace the soul builds for itself. A therapy rather than a victory.

One assumes, of course, that the pattern of *The Flight to Lucifer* is intensely, even parodically, self-conscious. The name Perscors—the man who "follows the quest through," and burns himself out in doing so—is too close to Bloom's doctrine of the precursor to be accidental, and Perscors's final battle reads like a pastiche of Childe Roland's arrival at the dark tower (the most frequently cited text in Bloom's theoretical tetralogy):

Perscors detected a light neither from above nor from himself. All about the open, circular, darkened space in which he stood, a horizon of fire burst forth like an imprisoning dawn. Between that distant fire and himself, uncertainly in the midst, Perscors felt rather than saw a wilderness of spectators. Whoever they were, he knew that they came to view the last of him. [P. 229]

There they stood, ranged along the hill-sides, met
    To view the last of me, a living frame
    For one more picture! in a sheet of flame
I saw them and I knew them all. And yet
Dauntless the slug-horn to my lips I set,
    And blew. "Childe Roland to the Dark Tower came."

Yet if *Flight to Lucifer* is the aftermath of the theoretical writings— and it is noteworthy that the aftermath should be an externalized, third-person narrative, rather than a lyric rhapsody—the pattern of the tale existed long before the "novel," long before the theory itself was constructed. This in itself should do something to blunt the common complaint that Bloom lost his spontaneity and freedom from preconception when he confined himself to a theoretical framework. The confinement, such as it is, had been there all along. Yet it also casts a strange light on the flourish with which Bloom announces that he needs a more formalized framework, a new "poetics that will foster a more adequate practical criticism" (*Anxiety*, p. 5). What, in effect, has happened in the passage from a private mythic cycle to an explicit poetics?

First, the stages of the cycle have been isolated and provided with portentous titles—*apophrades, clinamen, kenosis,* and the rest—although even this is not entirely new, since several essays in *Ringers in the Tower* attempt to fix and designate poetic tendencies, using such labels as "Promethean" or "Merlin." The chief difference is that the labels in *The Anxiety of Influence* no longer come from the poetry itself, but are borrowed from theology, antique rhetoric, and psychology—thus departing from Bloom's former strenuous commitment to intrinsic criticism, as well as making the proposed categories stand out boldly from the poetry to which they are applied. Indeed, the gap that is thus opened up between the discourse that Bloom analyzes and the discourse of his analysis will never again be closed, giving a new theatricality to Bloom's writing. It also helps to generate one text out of another, as each new book struggles to span the gap by introducing new categories—which open up a new gap, and the need for yet another mediating book. Thus, the six different revisionary relationships that a poet establishes with his precursors (introduced in *The Anxiety of Influence*) are later glossed by six separate rhetorical tropes and six distinct types of defense mechanisms, all inscribed within a larger six-phase movement called "the Scene of Instruction":

The Scene—really a complete play, or process—has six stages, through which the ephebe emerges: election (seizure by the precursor's power); covenant (a basic agreement of poetic vision between precursor and e-phebe); the choice of a rival inspiration (e.g., Wordsworth's Nature vs. Milton's Muse); the self-presentation of the ephebe as a new incarnation of the "Poetical Character"; the ephebe's interpretation of the precursor; and the ephebe's revision of the precursor. Each of these stages then becomes a level of interpretation in the reading of the ephebe's poem.[42]

Such hectic growth gives rise to a search for some way to contain it, some new ordering principle, sought now in a "dialectic of revisionism" derived from the Kabbalah (in *Kabbalah and Criticism* and *Poetry and Repression*). Yet this dialectic, meant to explain the movement from one revisionary strategy (or trope or defensive posture) to another, ultimately fails to subsume the other categories, becoming just one more element among the rest. Thus, in his most recent study, *Wallace Stevens*, Bloom adds yet another layer to the system, a set of poetic crossings to supplement the dialectic of revisionism with a further explanation of how and why the gap between one kind of figurative thinking and another is overstepped. Although apparently discarding nothing, Bloom's charts and tables can be misleading, however. In practice, he tends to scant one or another category, offering the full array more as a promissory note or as part of a strategy to undermine his theoretical antagonists. Thus, the "Scene of Instruction" (which is designed to circumscribe Derrida's "scene of writing") is scantily developed and disappears entirely from the study of Stevens. Moreover, as one moves from book to book, old categories are quietly redefined—the revisionary ratios, for example, are subsequently reduced to a simple set of names for a given combination of trope, image, and defense, with no independent value of their own. A process of beneficent forgetting helps to keep the system in homeostatic balance.

In constructing his theory, Bloom introduced new values for the different stages of his cyclic myth—installing (at least at first) a precursor poet in the place of the "lost fullness" and measuring the decline and modest reappropriation of poetic power in the descending generations. This was, of course, a tendentious move; it is one thing for Wordsworth to have lost his own visionary gleam and quite another for him to have lost the glory that was Milton. The internalization of the quest romance that the Romantic poets accomplished was formerly explained as the result of failed revolutionary hopes or as a response to an even more pervasive crisis of epistemological estrangement and social isolation—vaguely cultural explanations that Bloom offered without much apparent conviction. Indeed, the passage in *The Ringers in the Tower* that treats this change reads like a classic instance of repression—not of intellectual debts or even of sexuality, but of any hint that social forces might somehow condition consciousness:

308 / The Critical Impasse

Changes in consciousness are of course very rare, and no major synthesizer has come forth as yet, from any discipline, to demonstrate to us whether Romanticism marks a genuine change in consciousness or not. From the Freudian viewpoint, Romanticism is an "illusory therapy" (I take the phrase from Philip Rieff) or what Freud himself specifically termed an "erotic illusion." The dialectics of Romanticism, to the Freudians, are mistaken or inadequate, because the dialectics are sought in Schiller or Heine or in German Romantic philosophy down to Nietzsche, rather than in Blake or the English Romantics after him. Blake and Coleridge do not set intellect and passion against one another, any more than they arrive at the Freudian simplicity of the endless conflict between Eros and Thanatos. ["Quest Romance," pp. 14–15]

Interestingly, Freud's name enters this discussion precisely at the point where one might expect some further reference to social history. Although Freud seems to pose the threat of an extrinsic analysis, his notion of the "Family Romance" is conveniently confining—all the more so when, in later works, Bloom revises it into a strictly literary family, an Oedipal struggle between poetic fathers and sons.[43] This suggests that Freud's role in Bloom's theoretical studies is as a crucial distraction or displacement of the energy of inquiry. Freud is offered here as a false lead; his reductive account of Romantic internalization—really more descriptive than explanatory—allows Bloom to counter with an alternative description of his own. Rather than trying to answer the more disturbing question of why or how all this came about, Bloom substitutes the question of whether the internalization was truly an advance or only an illusory respite.

It is significant that Bloom's interest in explaining the change in consciousness that Romanticism comprised increased remarkably when he found a way to prevent the explanations from becoming extraliterary. And equally significant that the effort to devise a strictly intrapoetic account—and the construction of a theoretical apparatus to accomplish just that—began during a period of intense political unrest, precisely when the question of "relevance" and the social implications of literary studies were being publicly debated. This is not, of course, to deny the specificity of literary history or to reduce to a mere reflection of social forces Bloom's own change from practical criticism to theoretical criticism. But it is worth noting that Bloom's emergence as a theorist took place under much the same conditions that saw Sontag's passage from aesthetic to ideological analysis. Moreover, Bloom himself acknowledges the existence of such pressures in his Map of Misreading—however much he might object to seeing his own work as a reaction to them:

I do not believe that I am talking about an ideology, nor am I acknowledging any shade whatsoever of the recent Marxist critiques of our profession. Whatever the academic profession of letters now is on the Continent, . . . it is currently in America a wholly Emersonian phenomenon. Emerson abandoned his church to become a secular orator, rightly trusting that the lecture, rather than the sermon, was the proper and luminous melody for Americans. . . .

. . . Instruction, in our late phase, becomes an antithetical process almost inspite of itself, and for antithetical teaching you require antithetical texts, that is to say, texts antithetical to your students as well as to yourself and to other texts. . . . Any teacher of the dispossessed, of those who assert *they* are insulted and injured, will serve the deepest purposes of literary tradition and meet also the deepest needs of his students when he gives them possession of Satan's grand opening of the Debate in Hell. [Pp. 29–30, 40]

Explaining the Romantic internalization of romance as the product of a hypothetical struggle with a prior talent is thus a sly revisionary tactic. It allows Bloom to treat the rise of Romanticism in solely literary terms— as a renaissance of the Renaissance, unable either to ignore or equal its epic predecessors, if only because the second can never be precisely the same thing as the first. Wordsworth's transformation of the Miltonic epic into an egotistical sublime becomes a desperate maneuver to confront the impossible task of trying to become another Milton while yet remaining a different poet than Milton, a separate poetic self. Wordsworth's solution, however, merely increased the burden for his own poetic progeny, for how could one be more a self than he, and how experience that selfhood as one's own when the stance, the very project of realizing a self, had come from Wordsworth?

The revisionary ratios that *The Anxiety of Influence* proposes are six different strategies for departing from such a compound precursor and overcoming not only the appearance but the very consciousness of indebtedness. The new poet begins in a "flooded" apprenticeship, a moment of "oceanic bliss" when s/he has no separate identity—"before his strength began to assert itself in the revisionary ratios" (p. 16). The first stage of self-assertion is to continue valuing the precursor, but to discover an "error" that one may then correct (through a *clinamen,* or revisionary "swerve") or to find something not yet complete that one may then bring to completion (*tessera*). The second stage involves an effort to break with the precursor, first by seeming to abandon (through *kenosis*) all of one's own pretentions as a poet—and thus denying the power of the predecessor to inspire emulation—and then an attempt to seek a renewal of inspiration based on an even greater power, one to which the precursor was also, ostensibly, indebted, hence, "to generalize away the uniqueness of the earlier work" (*Daemonization*). The final stage is a return to the precursor, but a return that now is willed and undertaken only after one has managed to clear an imaginary space for one's own poetry. The return begins with an *askesis,* a deliberate curtailment of one's own powers (as opposed to the denial or surrender of those powers in *kenosis*) that also involves a purgatorial period of isolation and retreat into the self, and ends when "burdened by an imaginary solitude that is almost a solipsism," the poet enters a stage of *apophrades* and, of his or her own accord, "holds his own poem so open again to the precursor's work that at first we might believe the wheel has come full circle, and that we are back in the later poet's flooded apprenticeships. . . . But the poem is now *held* open to the precursor, where once it *was* open, and the uncanny effect is that the new poem's achievement makes it seem to us, not as though the precursor were writing it, but as though the later poet himself had written the precursor's characteristic work" (*Anxiety*, pp.14–16).

One can see how these ratios continue the familiar pattern of glory, fall, and qualified recovery, in the form of affiliation, denial, and renewed affiliation. Bloom proposes them both as stages in the life cycle of any strong poet and as distinct revisionary operations that a given poem applies to the precursor poem that inspired it. Since neither claim receives sustained illustration in *The Anxiety of Influence*, Bloom goes on to write his *Map of Misreading*, purportedly to do just that. Yet the *Map* actually effects a series of small changes in the theory itself. The cycle is now identified with the internal movement of an individual poem, from one revisionary ratio to another. (The "life cycle" of the poet now has its own separate schema, the aforementioned "Scene of Instruction" that leads from the poet's first exposure to the predecessor to his adoption of his own revisionary stance.) To chart the movement of the poem from ratio to ratio, one must attend to clusterings of characteristic images (of presence and absence, fullness and emptiness, and so forth), and watch for changes in rhetorical trope (from irony to metalepsis) and the way one psychic defense supplants another (from reaction-formation to introjection, projection). Eventually, the effort to prove that individual poems "map" as they should (which can become quite elaborate, given the number and the vagueness of the categories) threatens to become an end in itself, entirely supplanting the original intertextual focus of the theory. This kind of play within the system—this easy substitution of one object of analysis for another, along with rapid changes in the site or level at which the categories are said to apply—is not far from the kind of variability one noted in Bloom's pretheoretical days. Again it would appear that the construction of a more or less formalized framework has done less to curb Bloom's habits of mind than his critics might suppose.

What Bloom's more formal framework does do is to isolate insights that had formerly seemed casual and to endow them with an air of logical or historical necessity. From repeated discoveries that the same triadic pattern "happened" to occur in instance after instance, Bloom has moved to an overt claim that it *had* to occur. This change has probably provoked more consternation among his opponents than any other element in his theory. Decadence is sad as fact but horrifying as inevitability. To say that certain "original" effects are actually the product of a tormented effort to overcome influence is a plausible, even a pleasing, paradox—until it becomes the only force propelling literary history and solely responsible for whatever form each new poem takes. It is, then, the totality and the (fitful) determinism of the claim that is disturbing, something that Bloom himself obviously appreciates and even makes one of the defining characteristics of "strong reading": *strong* reading can be defined as one that itself produces other readings—as Paul de Man says, to be productive it must insist upon its own exclusiveness and completeness, and it must deny its partialness and its necessary falsification."[44]

As with Sontag, generality becomes the source of subsequent challenges and corrections, although Bloom seems to admire the totalitarian stance itself more than its subsequent corrections and modifications. The more expansive Bloom's claims are, the greater the opportunity for attacking them, for finding instances that contradict them. Something of this sort was what Popper (whose *Conjectures and Refutations* Bloom cites in passing in *Poetry and Repression*—p. 8) meant when he commended powerful hypotheses—those that are broadest in scope and hence most exposed to falsification on all sides—over weaker claims whose falsehood might escape detection longer. Thus, Bloom's theoretical stance may tempt him to inflate his findings, but it also makes them more corrigible—or at least (to use Bloom's own word for it) more "combattable." What once posed as a mere response to the subject matter—whether Shelley's whole career or a single ode of Keats—now patently rests on a set of initial premises. True, Bloom continues to waver about the status of those premises. The patterns he observes may be a product of the theoretical framework itself, or something that the theory and poetry have in common (because both are "poetic" in their inspiration and design), or an independent hypothesis that the evidence of the poetry happens to bear out. Yet for the first time, his cycle has been acknowledged and named, elevated to a new logical and discursive level where it can be subjected to question and complaint—as it formerly could not be.

The social upheaval of the 1960's was not alone enough to inspire Bloom, and it is appropriate that the other influences should have come from inside the academic literary establishment. Bloom presents his own explanation and "apologia for the use of so esoteric and extravagant a model" in *Kaballah and Criticism*, drawing upon the work of Thomas Kuhn:

> Kuhn says that even when confronted by severe and prolonged anomalies, scientists tend not to renounce the paradigm that has led them into crisis, because no paradigm can be rejected without accepting another paradigm substituted for it. . . .

> . . . critics, meaning all readers, must have paradigms, and not just precursors. Western literary criticism has followed the paradigms provided by Aristotle and Plato, with the later modifications of Christian Aristotelianism and Christian Platonism, down to the recent models provided by theories as diverse as those of W. K. Wimsatt and Northrop Frye. Out of an amalgam of Nietzsche, Marx, Heidegger, Freud, and the linguists, another paradigm is now coming from France, moving upon us like that apocalyptic crimson man of Edom that Blake both celebrated and feared. [Pp. 86–87]

By substituting *paradigm* for *precursor*, Bloom hopes to avoid inconsistencies; his claim is that precursors are known only a posteriori, by their power to make their helpless progeny nervous. One could not, then, write theory as a precursor, both because one could not guarantee recognition and because a theorist does not limit, but rather facilitates, the efforts of his or her followers. The substitution then is not simply self-serving, for it shows that Bloom is capable of constructing an alternative to the struggle for dominion on which his conception of influence is based. Or at least of envisioning such an alternative—for in practice, it may be his (singular) achievement to try to "own" his own paradigm, to individuate and absorb into his own (writerly) personality the multiple and anonymous sources that usually make up such paradigms, becoming, as it were, the Norman Mailer of our speculative prose.

By this substitution, Bloom is also trying to suggest, not that his own work is unprecedented, but that it is possible for him to reject his theoretical predecessors wholly and without residual anxiety—as his own Romantic poets cannot. Bloom poses as the "savior" of the Anglo-American tradition of humane letters, holding off the incursions of alien systems that threaten to level all distinctions of quality and to destroy the centrality and autonomy of the human will. For James Kinkaid, this is "one hidden and great source of power in these books: Harold Bloom's creative and losing struggle to misread and thereby escape the influence of structuralism."[45] For Riddel, this defensive struggle is instead an index of Bloom's theoretical limitations:

> . . . he is the last Romantic, the last proponent of the "self," the last archivist of the wearying struggle for "identity." . . .
> The whole of *Anxiety* is an appropriation by expropriation . . . a model of exclusions. . . . It almost wholly ignores the linguistic problematics [of] Lacan . . . [and] represses or ignores the challenge of Derrida's "scene of writing," a rigorous anti-mimetic theory of language uncovered in Freud.[46]

Yet one must beware of taking Bloom at his own word too literally. His heroic blindness and native humanism are as much a deliberately cultivated difference as symptoms of an inherently limited or martyred vision. Bloom's refusals and repudiations set him apart from other of his contemporaries, while the lost causes he defends add a shade of pathos, and provide a raison d'être, for his work. All of these—pathos, blindness, desperate and losing battles—come much too close to the kind of art that his theory seems to favor for the similarity to be wholly accidental: "To equate emotional maturation with the discovery of acceptable substitutes may be pragmatic wisdom, particularly in the realm of Eros, but this is not the wisdom of the strong poets.... The argument of this book is that strong poets are condemned to just this unwisdom: Wordsworth's Great Ode fights nature on nature's own ground, and suffers a great defeat, even as it retains its greater dream" (*Anxiety*, pp. 9–10).

In such passages, the taste for a certain kind of twilight tableau is so powerful that it is difficult to tell whether the theory is narrowing Bloom's sense of aesthetic possibility or if taste is deriving the theory towards ever more mordant claims and anguished postures. One suspects that the apocalypse brought on by the arrival of structuralist and poststructuralist criticism was *more* celebrated than feared. The European invasion cast a sudden poignancy over familiar critical attitudes (which were now imperiled), while at the same time fanning new ambitions with its display of breadth, its sense of risk and rebellion, and its intricacy and difficulty. These atmospheric values may not be the only or the best ways to assess a body of theoretical doctrine, but they are always powerful and do seem to be what Bloom was most keenly attuned to, and what he made the greatest effort to incorporate in his own work. While resisting the alien premises (especially the displacement of human subjectivity from the center to the periphery of language, and making it the effect rather than the cause of certain social, intellectual, and discursive operations), Bloom seems to have found the consequences—the sheer pyrotechnics of reading— irresistible. He was drawn to emulate the ornateness and portentousness of the criticism, even as he rejected the principles behind it: "'Deconstruction' *is* reading, but this is Over-Reading, or the reading of an Over-Man, who knows simultaneously how to fulfill and to transcend the text" (*Stevens*, p. 386).

Similarly, while heaping ordure on the European tendency to reduce literature to language, and vowing to keep himself from "yielding to any purely rhetorical criticism, however imported, however newfangled" (*Map*, p. 79), all of Bloom's theoretical work presupposes this reduction. Without this initial equation between literature and language, language and "the discourse of the Unconscious," there would be no common denominator, none of the translations between psychological mechanisms and poetic patterns upon which Bloom's own system depends. Once the basis for exchange and substitution has been established, however, it also becomes possible for Bloom to reverse it, asking (as he does at the start of *Poetry and Repression*): "Jacques Derrida asks a central question in his essay on Freud and the Scene of Writing: 'What is a text, and what must the psyche be if it can be represented by a text?' My narrower concern with poetry prompts the contrary question: 'What is a psyche, and what must a text be if it can be represented by a psyche?' " (p. 1). If the French try to render humanity transparent, to see through to the language that comprises it, Bloom can work to impassion the impersonal structures of poetic (and theoretical) discourse, by a selective use of those psychological terms (like *defense* and *romance*) that already carry the overtones of human figures locked in battle or embrace: "A poetic 'text,' as I interpret it, is not a gathering of signs on a page, but is a psychic battlefield upon which authentic forces struggle for the only victory worth winning, the divinating triumph over oblivion" (*Poetry*, p. 2).

Although Bloom gradually learned to overleap his immediate precursors and to claim that his analogies had come from Freud himself—"I seek to take back from Freud precisely what he himself took from the poets" (*Map*, p. 89)—it is clear from a reading of his earlier essays that his sense of Freud as a fount of rhetoric or a student of poetry arose only after he was exposed to Lacan's gnomic formula, "the unconscious is structured like a language." Bloom is, of course, a revisor of Lacan, who is himself a revisor—or rereader—of Freud. Indeed, though Bloom's own interest in revisionism is confined to poetry, this process of revisionary reading, which he not only studies but practices, is symptomatic of the entire movement to which he has ambivalently allied himself. Most of the recent French "innovators"—Lévi-Strauss, Lacan, Althusser, Derrida, and Barthes himself—are actually revisionists. However much Saussure may have owed to the neo-grammarians, or Freud to Charcot, or Marx to Hegel and Ricardo; however great Nietzsche's debt to Schopenhauer and Heidegger's to Husserl and Nietzsche, they did not so thoroughly station themselves in the shadow of a monumental master. But Lévi-Strauss is (scandalously) content to reread and reconstruct the findings of Mauss according to a framework of a differential analysis that is itself borrowed (from Saussure). Lacan and Althusser have returned to the most disturbing implications of Freud and Marx, from which milder, intervening generations ostensibly fled. Derrida has made it his sole business to work in and through the language of precursor texts to disclose the workings of internal contradictions, the mechanisms whereby the writing seeks to evade its own fluid and unstable condition. Of course the motives and the meanings of revision differ, as does the status ascribed to the precursor texts, which are alternately offered to us as new universal languages or as a shield for writers who wish to avoid erecting any such language of their own. Such rereaders arrive in this country, in turn, with their own apologists and revisionists, and it is against these (in yet another turn of the screw) that Bloom directs the bulk of his own revisionary energies.

There are many who would accuse Bloom of being by now too far removed from the source, failing to catch Derrida's drift or missing the full force of Lacan (however strangely this reverence for the source accords with what they otherwise have to say about both reverence and sources). To such critics Bloom would no doubt respond that there are already pious and "Talmudic" interpreters in sufficient number; his is the kabbalistic misinterpretation:

> Revisionism is a reaction to the double priority and authority of both text and interpretation, Bible and the normative Judaism of rabbinic tradition.... [As revision, the Kabbalah was] a collective, psychic defense of the most imaginative medieval Jews against exile and persecution pressing on them *inwardly*. So some Kabbalists spoke of a missing twenty-third letter of the Hebrew alphabet, hidden in the white spaces between the letters. From those openings the larger Torah was still to emerge, yet it was there already. This revisionist notion hoped to bring forth the invention of the Kabbalists themselves. [*Kaballah*, pp. 53–54]

That Bloom is a latecomer to European criticism is no accident; that he was moved very little by phenomenology and not at all by the earliest and most aggressively scientific phase of structuralism only illustrates how selective of his own influences he has been. It was not until structuralism had become openly self-critical and ready to acknowledge the limitations inherent in its own preconceptions that Bloom allowed himself to be "flooded." The strategic and slippery quality of the new theoretical stance was more to the taste of someone whose primary allegiances were to poetry and myth. He has been (consciously or not) equally careful about which particular elements he will assimilate and which he will choose to combat—antagonism and engulfment being the twin poles of Bloom's intertextual operations. The traces of these operations are apparent even to one who knows nothing about Bloom's sources and sees only the swell and fall of references, the sudden fits of fury or the beatitude of a brief rest. Yet in some ways Bloom's intertextual relations belie his theory. Even the most summary reading of Bloom's various combats with and debts to his reviewers makes one aware of how much each new book owes to his commentators, and in how many different ways. His development is not the gradual, self-engendered evolution of Sontag's (ideal) project but is produced in the heat of rapid interchange. Thus, if Jerome McGann claims (in a review of Bloom in *Critical Inquiry*)[47] that Whitman is an obvious exception to the rule of the anxiety of influence, then in *Poetry and Repression* Bloom will make a point of demonstrating that Whitman is the most uncanny of them all, the poet whose anxiety borders on psychosis:

> Whitman's ego, in his most Sublime transformations, wholly absorbs and thus pragmatically forgets the fathering force, and presents instead the force of the son, of his own self or, in Whitman's case, perhaps we should say of his own selves. Where Emerson *urges* forgetfulness of anteriority, Whitman more strenuously *does* forget it, though at a considerable cost. Emerson says "*I and the Abyss*"; Whitman says: "*The Abyss of My Self*." The second statement is necessarily more Sublime and, alas, even more American. [Pp. 265–66]

316 / The Critical Impasse

If Geoffrey Hartman states that there is a tacit, as yet undeveloped "counter-theology" at work in *The Anxiety of Influence*, then *A Map of Misreading* will lay claim to that theology and *Kabbalah and Criticism* will expand it into a full-fledged antithetical "orthodoxy," capable of outnegating the most negative of European thought. Characteristically, Bloom absorbs from Hartman his descriptions and his summaries, using them to clarify his own goals for himself:

> Bloom engages the sky-gods of Modern Criticism and Romantic Scholarship....
>   Though Bloom stands close to Bate's general view he expunges from it the residual idealism of believing, like Keats, in a "freemasonry" of great spirits....
>   ...the intensest struggle (because of the greatest debt) is with Northrup Frye [who] proposes a clear and simple theory of cultural assimilation. It holds that both as artists and critics we join ourselves necessarily to a larger body of thought without which we could not think. The de facto continuum is stressed rather than the anxiety for continuity; the communicable categories rather than the psychomachia of ephebe and ghostly father.[48]

> Northrop Frye, who increasingly looks like the Proclus or Iamblichus of our day, has Platonized the dialectics of tradition....The student is a cultural assimilator who *thinks* because he has *joined* a larger body of thought....This [belief] is a noble idealization. [*Map*, p. 30]

Hartman's latent tendencies become part of the manifest design, until eventually Bloom will speak as if the effort to "de-idealize" Frye and his ilk were the origin and aim of his theory from the start.

But if Hartman is brought in seamlessly, Paul de Man's opinions are handled more gingerly. After de Man's not unadmiring remark that Bloom's "interest in the methodological debates that agitate American and European criticism is peripheral," Bloom responds by saturating his writing with methodological debate. Just as influential (by inversion) is de Man's wry attempt to extract a hidden "linguistic" framework from Bloom's first book:

> It would be a somewhat trivial exercise to transpose Bloom's six ratios back to the paradigmatic rhetorical structures in which they are rooted. *Clinamen,...*symbolizes the universality of the substitutive pattern. The five other ratios describe more specific types of rhetorical substitution: *tessera* defines the potentially misleading totalization from part to whole of synecdoche; *apophrades* rightly figures in the climactic last place as the sixth ratio, because it destroys the principle on which the system itself is patterned: it substitutes early for late in a metaleptic reversal. *Askesis*...the substitutive play of an inside-outside polarity that is characteristic of...[a] type of metaphor that figures prominently in romantic diction. *Daemonization*...uses another set of spatial antinomies:...high and low, as in hyper-

bole; . . . precisely the rhetorical mode, the type of misreading, favored by Bloom in his own works. *Kenosis* is a more complex case because it is the only class in which a figure is used to undo systematically the substantial claim implied in the use of another figure; it is the figure of a figure, in which the one de-constructs the universe proposed by the other. . . . it substitutes a contiguity for an analogy or resemblance and thus rediscovers in its turn, the familiar metaphor-metonymy opposition. . . .

What is achieved by thus translating back from a subject-centered vocabulary of intent and desire to a more linguistic terminology? If we admit that the term "influence" is itself a metaphor that dramatizes a linguistic structure into a diachronic narrative, then it follows that Bloom's categories of misreading operate not only between authors, but also between the various texts of a single author, or within a given text, between the different parts.[49]

De Man "discovers" a pair of binary oppositions (early/late, strong/ weak) and a pattern of substitution and inversion that mediates between them—precisely the structure Lévi-Strauss finds at the root of the myth; he then turns Bloom's diachronic pattern into a "dramatization" of a set of timeless paradigmatic oppositions that can be characterized with rhetorical labels. Bloom counters this—in *A Map of Misreading* first, but ultimately in all his texts to date—by absorbing de Man's categories, in an effort to circumscribe them. The effort takes several different forms—simply by increasing the intricacy of his framework, Bloom may be hoping to prevent his system from falling into predictable binary oppositions (or at least to make such oppositions harder to discern beneath the hysterical excess). Second, while he accepts de Man's rhetorical labels, he redistributes them and slyly alters the defining properties of several tropes in such a way as to undermine de Man's priorities. As the six tropes are added to Bloom's *Map of Misreading*, they become notoriously difficult to apply. In fact, they are (perversely, but one suspects deliberately) both ill-defined and over-defined; they seem to partake of too many different traditions:

> Vico says that all tropes reduce to four: irony, metonymy, metaphor, and synecdoche, which agrees with Kenneth Burke's analysis of what he calls "The Four Master Tropes." . . . I will follow both Vico and Burke in my own analysis, except that I will add two more tropes—hyperbole and metalepsis—. . . following Nietzsche and de Man. . . .
>
> Burke associates irony with dialectic, metonymy with reduction, metaphor with perspective, and synecdoche with representation. Hyperbole and metalepsis I add as progressively more blinded or broken representation, where "blinding" or "breaking" is meant to suggest the Lurianic breaking-of-the-vessels or scattering-of-the-light which I have carried over into the poetic realm as substitution. As tropes of contraction or limitation, irony withdraws meaning through a dialectical interplay of presence and absence; metonymy reduces meaning through an emptying-

out that is a kind of reification; metaphor curtails meaning through the endless perspectivizing of dualism, of inside-out dichotomies. As tropes of restitution or representation, synecdoche enlarges from part to whole; hyperbole heightens; metalepsis overcomes temporality by a substitution of earliness for lateness. [*Map*, p. 94–95]

As one reads on, the definitions slide and begin to shift: *Metonymy* is particularly subject to such changes, now associated with the interplay between container and contained (and thus overlapping with *synecdoche*), now with any instance where a name takes the place of the object itself and its properties, and finally with fragmentation and collage, with any description in which properties seem to be excerpted and recombined in an arbitrary manner. This allows Bloom, of course, enormous latitude for locating examples of metonymy and makes it extremely difficult to test the accuracy of his map against the patterns of actual poems. Metonymy can be made to appear in any passage where the map predicts it should appear, and the chief interest (for the reader) becomes just how Bloom will manage to manipulate the poem or to redefine his own categories to achieve the necessary fit. The result can be quite striking—as most of Bloom's creative misreadings of Browning are:

> Now blotches rankling, coloured gay and grim,
>   Now patches where some leanness of the soil's
>   Broke into moss or substances like boils;
> Then came some palsied oak, a cleft in him
> Like a distorted mouth that splits its rim
>   Gaping at death, and dies while it recoils.

> This landscape is a landscape of repetition, but in the deadliest sense, one in which all questions of genesis have yielded to mere process, to one-thing-after-another. Here, in the long middle part of Browning's poem, one is in a world of contiguities, in which resemblances, if they manifest themselves at all, must be grotesque. Roland describes his landscape like Zola describing an urban scene, yet Roland's world is wholly visionary, its "realism" a pure self-imposition. Roland's landscape is a kind of continuous metonymy, in which a single, negative aspect of every thing substitutes for the thing itself. [*Map*, p. 110]

Critics have accused Bloom of reading just those poems that best fit the system he has devised, but this passage should make clear that the "obsession" with Browning (to which Bloom confesses in *Poetry and Repression*) has little to do with fit. Rather it is simply the fact that Browning-cum-Bloom makes an especially arresting composite text, full of tensions and surprising convergences. That other combinations are less suspicious may be an indication of the aesthetic limits of Bloom's theory (or of Browning's poetry.) Indeed, it is perhaps better to treat the long swatches of poetry that dot *A Map of Misreading* and *Poetry and Repression* as extensions of the theoretical discourse, rather than as a body of evidence or even as a set of convenient illustrations. Even the sequence of Bloom's books, with its apparent alternation of pure speculation and practical demonstration (the orphic prose of *Against Interpretation* or *Kabbalah and Criticism* as opposed to the utilitarian *Map of Misreading* and *Poetry and Repression*) is misleading in this respect.

But if Bloom's notion of metyonymy seems vague and his definitions apt to wander, it is not just a matter of interpretive convenience. For metonymy is also one of de Man's favorite tropes, a figure based on arbitrary ties that opposes the traditional privileges of metaphor, with its nostalgia for meanings based on natural resemblances. Bloom retains (on different grounds) de Man's demotion of metaphor, but his unstable treatment of metonymy reflects a desire to absorb de Man while also circumventing him. Bloom therefore places both metonymy and metaphor among the "figures of limitation"—where he also classes irony, a figure that plays a crucial role in de Man's own rhetoric of temporality. Bloom treats irony as part of *Clinamen*, the *first* of his own revisionary ratios. In doing so, he is reasserting the power of time and sequence over timeless structural principles like irony and metonymy, which become henceforth only passing phases. Bloom's ever expanding program is designed to subvert synchronic structures and to reemphasize diachrony—not (as some would have it) by constructing an actual history, but simply by establishing a plot sequence, a passage from before to after. Culler accurately depicts Bloom's limits as a historian, his tendency to choose precursor texts "on grounds of interpretive convenience" and his decision to keep his history entirely "in the family. . . . wholly within the traditional cannon of major poets."[50] Bloom himself has come increasingly to insist that this poetic family history is largely figurative:

> What I mean by "influence" is the whole range of relationships between one poem and another, which means that my use of "influence" is itself a highly conscious trope, indeed a complex six-fold trope that intends to subsume six major tropes: irony, synecdoche, metonymy, hyperbole, metaphor, and metalepsis, and in just that ordering.
> . . . ["influence" is] a figuration for poetry itself; not as the relation of product to source, or effect to cause, but as the greater relation of latecomer poet to precursor, or of reader to text, or of poem to the imagination, or of the imagination to the totality of our lives. [*Map*, pp. 70–71]

The passage echoes de Man, yet the one thing Bloom refuses to call a trope is "ordering." He goes far enough to call influence a trope, a designation of any number of structural relationships one might wish to establish between one poem and another. But still he preserves the idea of sequence. "Before" and "after" may be only a trope, a trick of rhetoric, but the illusion is precious. Without sequence there is not drama, none of the suspense or sense of loss upon which anguished expectation and heroic resignation depend. The threat of structuralism and poststructuralism, then, seems to have less to do with the traditions of literary humanism than with the traditional sources of intensity and excitement. Bloom objects to linguistic models not just because they are reductive (his own are no less so, in the sense of ignoring and overriding textual particulars), but because they are deflationary.

A sense of drama also governs what Bloom assimilates and rejects from his European antagonists—Derrida and Lacan, in particular. There seems to be no consistency if one considers only logical coherence, but the only consistency Bloom truly cares for is atmospheric and passional. A concept may prove titillating and be adopted for the sake of a temporary frisson, to be dropped again for the sake of some new excitement. Sustained ordeal is a difficult condition to maintain and may require what in other ways seem hectic and incoherent changes of opinion. It is common to attribute these changes to backsliding, to an inability to confront the full consequences of the positions he adopts. Bloom himself contributes mightily to this impression by continuously stressing what he finds unbearable: "Some of the consequences of what I am saying dismay even me. . . . Still, I cast my vote for Oscar Wilde's insight: a strong poem lies against time, and against strong poems before it, and strong criticism must do the same. Nothing is gained by continuing to idealize reading, as though reading were not an art of defensive warfare. Poetic language makes of the strong reader what it will, and it chooses to make him into a liar" (Kabbalah, pp. 125–26).

Culler and Riddel are both eloquent on the theme of Bloom's evasions, his attempt to "repress the enervating theory of belatedness," his struggle to "arrest the dissolution of the subject."[51] Yet Bloom is less consistent in his "repressions" than his more consistent readers would imply. It is not simply a matter of avoiding, for instance, Derrida's unnerving notion of the indeterminacy of writing—suspended between the object it replaces and interpretations yet to come, forever "differing" and never anything in itself. Bloom is perfectly capable, on occasion, of accepting and exploiting this argument, if not following it in all its finer details. The reasons for believing that texts are indeterminate are simply less compelling for him than the mood that indeterminacy induces: "Poetic meaning, despite the awesome interpretative self-confidence of both Vico and Emerson, is therefore radically indeterminate. Reading, despite all humanist traditions of education, is very nearly impossible, for every reader's relation to every poem is governed by a figuration of belatedness. . . . A poet interpreting his precursor, and any strong subsequent interpreter reading either poet, must falsify by his reading" (Map, p. 69).

While concluding (as de Man does), that reading is impossible, Bloom's reasoning for why this should be so has little to do with epistemology or metaphysics and everything to do with the rapacity and cussedness of the reader. Bloom consistently substitutes the solipsist shudder "it's all in the mind" for Derrida's contention that the meaning of the text can never be localized anywhere at all. *Kabbalah and Criticism* begins with Derrida, but soon moves to other grounds:

> An empirical thinker, confronted by a text, seeks a meaning. Something in him says: "If this is a complete and independent text, then it *has* a meaning." It saddens me to say that this apparently commonsensical assumption is not true. Texts don't *have* meanings, except in their relations to other texts.
>
> . . . Meaning wanders, like human tribulation, or like error, from text to text, and within a text, from figure to figure. What governs this wandering, this errancy, is defense, the beautiful necessity of defense. For no just interpretation is defense, but meaning itself is defense, and so meaning wanders to protect itself. [*Kabbalah*, pp. 106, 82]

It is not finally the indeterminacy of meaning that intrigues Bloom, but meaninglessness, the experience of emptiness and the soul in isolation. "For Emerson, meaning is concerned with survival, and signification is only an instrumentality of meaning. What holds together rhetoric as a system of tropes, and rhetoric as survival, is the necessity of defense, defense against everything that threatens survival, and a defense whose aptest name is 'meaning' " (*Repression*, p. 240). An empty text, where meanings must be imposed rather than discovered, offers a larger field for the exercise of will and makes that exercise appear more desperate and strenuous, investing it with a (slightly shopworn) existential angst. Thus, *Poetry and Repression* retracts Bloom's earlier harsh assessment of Yeats's gnosticism (prefiguring Bloom's own "gnostic fantasy" to come): "his Gnostic tendencies aided Yeats by giving him a wider context in a traditional ontology, however heterodox, for his own *antithetical* longing. . . . Yeats, like Nietzsche, implicitly decided that he too would rather have the Void as purpose, than be void of purpose" (p. 234).

Bloom invokes gnosticism and the Kabbalah in the hope of containing the infinite regress of meaning; Luria's story of Creation through Divine withdrawal or "contraction" is said to share the same paradoxical union of presence and absence of Derrida's "writing." Yet the Lurianic paradox is fixed; it has the quality of a primordial event rather than a pure potentiality. Bloom stops the trace, drops the notion of indeterminacy, when it is no longer an inducement to dramatic struggle but a dizzying and indefinite impasse: "Kabbalah too thinks in ways not permitted by Western metaphysics, since its God is at once *Ein-Sof* and *ayin*, total presence and total absence, and all its interiors contain exteriors, while all of its effects determine its causes. But Kabbalah stops the movement of Derrida's "trace," since it has a *point* of the primordial, where presence and absence co-exist by continuous interplay" (*Kabbalah*, p. 53). He fears not the relativism of the deconstructive school, but what he calls its nihilism—meaning, apparently, the mood of wry acquiescence to logical necessity. *Nihilism* is a loaded word, of course, and may be used here more because of something that Bloom feels he is being denied (definite outlines and the thrill of conquest) than because of anything inherently defeatest in deconstruction itself. (Indeed much poststructuralism is anything but acquiescent, prescribing deconstruction as part of a program of militant skepticism.)

Bloom's distrust for what he now names nihilism is actually a recurrent element in his work, part of his original attachment to Romanticism, which he defines as the last poetry to exist without resorting to continuous irony. This makes him almost unique among literary theorists in his active distaste for ironic distance, the acute state of critical consciousness that one normally associates with the theoretical impulse itself. Nor does this ancient grudge recede into the background when he begins to construct a theory of his own. In 1969, he complains of Borges (whose thinking on the subject of influence he will later cite admiringly): "What Borges lacks, despite the illusive cunning of his labyrinths, is precisely the extravagance of the romancer; he does not trust his own vagrant impulses. He sees himself as a modestly apt self-marshaller, but he is another Oedipal self-destroyer. His addiction to the self-protective economy and overt knowingness of his art is his own variety of the Oedipal anxiety, and the pattern of his tales betrays throughout an implicit dread of family romance."[52] But even in the heat of *The Anxiety of Influence* itself, in the midst of setting forth his own antithetical program, Bloom pauses to remark: "The strong imagination comes to its painful birth through savagery and misrepresentation. The only humane virtue we can hope to teach through a more advanced study of literature than we have now is the social virtue of detachment from one's own imagination, recognizing always that such detachment made absolute destroys any individual imagination" (*Anxiety*, pp. 86).

Bloom is therefore more and more caught up in the effort to save the imagination from the deflationary effects of rival theories by making his own theory a bulwark against them: "The function of criticism at the present time, as I conceive it, is to find a middle way between the paths of demystification of meaning, and of recollection or restoration of meaning, or between limitation and representation. But the only aesthetic path between limitation and representation is substitution, and so all that criticism can hope to teach, whether to the common reader or to the poet, is a series of stronger modes of substitution" (*Repression*, p. 270). *Strength* is the keystone of Bloom's defense against demystification and the most frequently used word in his entire lexicon. It is not as prepossessing as some of his other terms, trailing their clouds of Latin or Hebraic glory, but it is no less theoretical for all that and must be ranked as his chief conceptual instrument. The word acquires different values at different moments in the course of Bloom's unfolding argument, but it never loses its normative force as a word of praise for those who achieve personal success and individual authority. What changes are the conditions under which strength is tried and proved. Whereas strength was formerly the gift of those poets capable of revising (or of believing that they have revised) their precursors, gradually it has become the power (of readers as well as writers) to confront and overcome the emptiness of writing itself. (Or again, since this is not really possible, of believing that one has overcome it and persuading others to believe it too.) It is much the same position de Man labeled "blindness," but with the values reversed and with the understanding, as well, that it is a deliberately courted blindness, a *conscious* unconsciousness. According to *Poetry and Repression*, "tropes or defenses are primarily figures of willed falsification rather than figures of unwilled knowledge" (p. 25). The strong poet continues to hold onto an enforced belief in his or her capacity to impose a final meaning, and the strong reader does the same, knowing all the while that the belief is self-induced, the effort bound to fail in the end. The *structure* is still that of a contest, however, exactly as it was in the battle between poet and precursor. It is not by chance that Bloom finds himself obsessed with *Childe Roland*, a hero whose greatest discovery is the absence of an adversary.

To examine Bloom's doctrines and the kind of theoretical instruments he has constructed, borrowed, and repudiated is to find the persistent application of the same psychopoetic standard. Thus, of all the instruments he has either absorbed or refused from the deconstructionist camp, there is one notable omission. De Man's review of *Anxiety of Influence* credits Bloom with a longstanding appreciation "that, all appearances to the contrary, the romantic imagination is *not* to be understood in dialectical interplay with the presumably antithetical category of 'nature.'. . . Increased misgiving about the validity of this model led to a shift in valorization: whereas romanticism often used to be described as a cult of nature. . .the positive emphasis on nature. . .was reversed and replaced by its opposite. Terms such as "interiorization," "mind," "consciousness" and "self" gained currency. . . . [which] clearly shows that, as long as the polar structure is not itself questioned, a reversal of valorization is in fact immaterial."[53] Although Bloom takes over whole phrases from this essay, he does not seem to heed the warning about the futility of "reversed valorization" and the structures that facilitate it. For it *is* the structure that is at issue—not a particular pair of terms, but the impasse that results whenever two sides of a dichotomy are hopelessly interlocked. Since one term is defined by the other, a simple change of status will do nothing to undo the deadlock or to fundamentally alter the underlying assumptions. Indeed, dichotomies in which one party is elevated over the other form the very core of Bloom's theory of poetic influence. Similarly, when the theorist himself does battle with his rivals, he employs the same dichotomous distinctions and the same (futile) strategy of celebrating one side in order to disparage the other. This is so even when Bloom is at his best, attacking the narrowness of deconstruction as a theory of literature based solely on epistemology:

> Why do we believe one liar rather than another? Why do we read one poet rather than another? . . .
> Deconstruction touches its limit because it cannot admit such a question. For the deconstructive critic, a trope is a figure of knowing and not a figure of willing, and so such a critic seeks to achieve, in relation to any poem—or to find in that poem—a cognitive moment, a moment in which the Negative is realized. . . . But what can a cognitive or epistemological moment in a poem be? Where the will predominates, even in its own despite, how much is there left to know? How can we speak of degrees of knowing in the blind world of the wish. . . .
> . . . The issue of the limits of deconstruction will be resolved only if we attain a vision of rhetoric more comprehensive than the deconstructors allow, that is, if we can learn to see rhetoric as transcending the epistemology of tropes and as re-entering the space of the will-to-persuasion. [*Stevens*, pp. 387–88]

In the midst of apparent clarification, the writing recoils and re-instates the old disjunction. Poems are not susceptible to a psychopoetic *as well as* an epistemological approach; one or the other must be triumphant. We are instructed to transcend conceptual rhetoric by seeing that poetry is actually governed only by the rhetoric of persuasion, that whatever seems to be a figure of knowing is in reality a figure of willing—blinded, lustful, and gloriously lying. In fact, Bloom's argument here conforms precisely to the pattern of inverted dualisms that he elsewhere associates with the (defective) trope of metaphor. Note too that the bold lie, the blind world of the wish, is defined only in terms of what it excludes—truth, cognitive value, renunciation. Bloom does not present a more com-prehensive rhetoric, but in fact inscribes his proposed new rhetoric in terms of the old dichotomies—heart and mind, reason and emotion—even if the heart in question is now less tender and the emotion far more violent and ungenerous than any that Wordsworth or Coleridge would have acknowledged.

What could be responsible for this (one is tempted to say) willful reinstatement of a dichotomy that Bloom has in several places called simplistic? Of an inversion that his own *Map* treats as a passing phase to be undone by a later and more sophisticated trope in which the strong poet recognizes an entrapping structure and so turns to "troping on a trope" to make the fact of a conditioning structure obvious through "word-consciousness" (*Map*, p. 138)? The clue is in the very wording of

Bloom's charge to contemporary criticism—to study the problematics of loss. Bloom uses such structures because his study requires it. As de Man notes, the stories constructed out of dichotomies and inversions are intricate, complicated, suspenseful, and it is this intricacy, suspense, and (one should add) pathos that Bloom is loath to surrender. For the poignancy of loss, there must be something to lose; a foregone disenchantment like de Man's affords little drama. A similar need for drama seems to govern the alternatives to deconstruction Bloom advances. There is, for instance, his studied rejection of sublimation and the reality principle:

> My theory rejects also the qualified Freudian optimism that happy substitution is possible, that a second chance can save us from the repetitive quest for our earlier attachments....
> ...To equate emotional maturation with the discovery of acceptable substitutes may be pragmatic wisdom, particularly in the realm of Eros, but this is not the wisdom of strong poets. [*Anxiety*, pp. 8, 9]

It is possible, of course, to read this as one of Bloom's own revisionary ratios, a *clinamen* whereby his theory becomes a corrective of Freud: "Both Nietzsche and Freud underestimated poets and poetry, yet each yielded more power to phantasmagoria than it truly possessed. They too, despite their moral realism, over-idealized the imagination" (*Anxiety*, pp. 8, 9). In later books (as *Beyond the Pleasure Principle* becomes his tutor text), Bloom will move to *tessera* and will claim only to "complete" Freud's work by including poetry among the defenses against the death instinct. Yet the pessimism of Bloom's own stance fails to encompass the full despair of the late Freud, for Bloom's theory treats repression as the warding off of an inevitable decay, while Freud would rank this warding off itself as an effort to avoid undue stimulation, pursuing an ideal equilibrium or homeostasis of which death is the most perfect example. Hence, for Freud, exertion is paradoxically directed toward the end of exertion, a life force bent on bringing itself back to death. This is not the doomed drama of a struggle for survival, nor even the sad depletion of limited resources that (in Bloom's theory) makes each new instance of poetic success a step towards the exhaustion of poetry as a whole. These exertions at least retain a dim if baffled grandeur, which the Freudian version of the death drive—less martial in every way—would make impossible, even risible.

Still more striking is the way that Bloom reformulates Freud's family romance (or rather revises Lacan's revision of it) by collapsing the primordial triangle into a dyadic structure in which the father seems exclusively responsible for the incarnation of the son. As a result, the real problem is no longer jealousy but a tortured and ambivalent identificaton.

> But who, what is the poetic father? The voice of the other...—*the dead poet lives in one....*

A poet, I argue in consequence, is not so much a man speaking to men as a man rebelling against being spoken to by a dead man (the precursor) outrageously more alive than himself. A poet dare not regard himself as being *late*, yet cannot accept a substitute for the first vision he reflectively judges to have been his precursor's also. Perhaps this is why the poet-in-a-poet *cannot marry* whatever the person-in-a-poet chooses to have done. [*Map*, p. 19]

Any reader of Lacan must be struck by how closely the situation Bloom posits resembles what Lacan (assisted by Melanie Klein, Sartre, and Hegel) has identified as the *pre*-Oedipal stage of development, the so-called "mirror stage."[54] Briefly, this stage lasts from the first emergence of consciousness—which erupts in the form of a sudden awareness of deprivation and, subsequently, as a desire for the fantasized "lost object" that once (putatively) supplied the lack—to the Oedipal struggle itself. In passing through the Oedipal stage, the subject leaves behind crude efforts to repossess the lost object (identified with the mother) and enters into the reign of "the Symbolic," where the object itself no longer appears as a fixed (chimerical) image but as a freely interchangeable sign. This rite of passage is, of course, precisely what Bloom repudiates; poets cannot as poets accept "substitutions." Yet for Lacan, the lost object was *already* a substitution, an image set up to explain the sudden perception of dissatisfaction—a dissatisfaction that can never, in the nature of things, be satisfied by the object of desire, since subjectivity and desire alike are products of that initial sense of loss.

If one follows Lacan's analysis of the mirror stage proper, one discovers that the coherence of the desiring subject is also a delusion. The phrase *mirror stage* refers to the formation of an image of the self, an image that is internalized by observing the integrated outline of another being—so different from the disorganized experience of one's own body—or by viewing one's "own" estranged image in a mirror. As in Hegel's "master/slave dialectic," the "self " thus constituted and internalized both depends upon and fears the other to whose gaze the new self-image is offered—at once eager to preserve the gaze and fearful of its power to withdraw, disconfirm, undo, the image that was unstable and extrinsic from the start. Without the other, there is no sense of self, yet with the other there is the constant threat that the self will be snuffed out, when the other goes its own way or enforces its own demands for confirmation. For Hegel and Lacan alike there is no escape from this dilemma until the basic structure of the relationship is changed and the subject is freed from its delusory "specular identification."

Thus, the desire to repossess the lost object is paralleled by the desire to own one's own being in the form of an object, a reified self-image. Lacan terms this stage "the Imaginary" because the full structure of the exchange between subject and object is hidden and the image is treated as if it were a natural rather than a differential value. The story of poetic incarnation that Bloom's theory endlessly retells is just such a tale of specular identification.

> To evade the precursor's imagined glance, the ephebe seeks to confine it in scope, which perversely enlarges the glance, so that it rarely can be evaded. As the small child believes his parents can see him around corners, so the ephebe feels a magical glance attending his every movement. The desired glance is friendly or loving, but the feared glance disapproves, or renders the ephebe unworthy of the highest love, alienates him from the realm of poetry. [*Anxiety*, p. 105]

Clearly Bloom is aware of the cost of such an identification and in a passage in *Poetry and Repression* even makes explicit the analogy with Lacan's punishing Imaginary:

> I am tempted to adopt here the notion of what Jacques Lacan calls the Imaginary Order, which has to do with a world of what Blake called the Crystal Cabinet, a Beulah-world of doubles, illusive images, mirrors and specular identifications. . . . I do find useful in poetic, rather than general human terms, Lacan's remark that the ego, the *moi*, is essentially paranoid. The poetic ego is a kind of paranoid construct founded upon the ambivalency of opposition and identity between the ephebe and the precursor. [*Repression*, p. 145]

There is something decidedly amiss in this affirmation of paranoia, even if—as is usually the case—Bloom distinguishes between "real" paranoia and the paranoia that is deliberately entered for the sake of stronger poetry. *The Anxiety of Influence* even lashes out at Lacan for leaping to the conclusion that because the self thus defined is so punishing, it should therefore be exchanged for: ". . . the humanizing acts of the child's verbal imagination, in which subjectivity combines its own abdication and the birth of the symbol, . . . [for Lacan] 'the moment in which desire becomes human is also that in which the child is born into Language'"(*Anxiety*, p. 81). What Bloom calls the "abdication" of subjectivity, Lacan sees as the surrender of a narcissistic fixation on delusory images (of the lost object, of the self) for a more supple symbolic system based on arbitrary, relational values and shifting, subjective positions. Granted that Lacan thus threatens to turn self-consciousness and autonomous identity into an illusion, a trick of presymbolic perspective, it is not this that Bloom seems to oppose. For on several occasions, both by the peculiarity of his syntax and by a series of asides, Bloom hints that he too feels that the self-consciousness of the ephebe is a mirage and that the whole encounter with the precursor—indeed, the precursor himself—is artificially staged, phantasmatic.

> He errs in seeking imagoes—the Muse was never his mother nor the precursor his father. His mother was his imagined spirit or idea of his own

sublimity, and his father will not be born until he himself finds his own central ephebe, who retrospectively will beget him upon the Muse, who at last and only then will become his mother. Illusion upon illusion. . . .

We need to stop thinking of any poet as an autonomous ego, however solipsistic the strongest of poets may be. [*Anxiety*, pp. 61, 91]

Why then such hostility when Lacan (whose work, in later books, Bloom denigrates as "gorgeous nonsense") suggests that the subject is an "error"? The answer is that for Bloom certain errors are indispensable, worth any effort to preserve, even if preserving them involves a confession of their unreality. Thus, in the process of saving the self, Bloom is willing to incur enormous losses. Self-knowledge and self-reliance are shored up, but at the cost of making them necessary fictions, repressions that conceal the real limits of the self to beget or even to know itself. And this despite his constant invocation of the Gnostic doctrine that "what makes us free is the Gnosis of who we were, of what we have become, of where we were, of wherein we have been thrown." Bloom's own Gnostic fantasy ends with a failure of self-knowledge, a forgetting; criticism may be born of gnosis, but "poetry is born of our ignorance of causes, . . . if any poet knows too well what causes his poem, then he cannot write it, or at least will write it badly" (*Repression*, p. 5). If, in Bloom, defenses and repressions are consciously willed rather than being unconscious "mechanisms" (the mechanical analogies in Freud and his French followers come in for a great deal of ridicule, while *Poetry and Repression* finally discards the unconscious altogether), the gain for human dignity is equivocal at best. For the result is of a consciousness that is wholly self-serving, cunning in its devotion to a certain saving ignorance, strong to the extent that it can cover all traces of its weakness and aware only to the extent of what it cares to know. Such a self is condemned to a constant, paranoiac whirligig of mastery and slavery. It is symptomatic that the most powerful and convincing reading that *Poetry and Repression* produces should be of Tennyson's *Mariana*:

> . . . what Mariana is longing for is not her belated swain but . . . her really deadly obsession . . . nevertheless is giving her an intense quasi-sexual pleasure, a kind of sublime perversion that no sexual satisfaction could begin to hope to match. Mariana is much more than half in love with easeful death, and in the poem's closing lines she all but identifies death with her own primal narcissism.
>
> . . . The poem is more deliciously unhealthy than all its Pre-Raphaelite and Decadent progeny were to be, and remains the finest example in the language of an embowered consciousness representing itself as being too happy in its unhappiness to want anything more. [Pp. 151–52]

This is no demystifying reading, as Bloom had promised, but it resists demystification in a most peculiar way; Bloom is perfectly ready to read against the grain of the manifest text, not to *reveal* but to revel in its latent emotion. "Too happy in its unhappiness" is a phrase that one might easily apply to the anguished announcements of decline, the steadfast devotion to baring the problematics of loss, which fill the theoretical text as well. If the theorist insists upon remaining in the Imaginary, or refuses to see the fruitlessness of inverted polarities, it is not because he has failed to understand their demystification. Rather, it is because to abandon them would be to lose their satisfactions. Thus, Bloom responds to Lacan's translator and interpreter, Anthony Wilden: "Wilden speaks of 'transcending the individualistic identities and oppositions of the Imaginary by entering the *collective differences* of the Symbolic.' I would say against this Marxist idealizing that the study of poetic misprision demonstrates the necessity of fresher and greater repressions if strong poetry is to survive.... There are no dialectics of liberation that will work in the world of the antithetical" (*Repression*, p. 146).

But is what survives the onslaught of Bloom's revisionary defense still strong poetry? One could answer this by noting that Browning, Emerson, and Tennyson have waxed progressively stronger in Bloom's canon, while Blake, Wordsworth, and even Shelley have grown weaker and Whitman and Stevens have turned decidedly demonic. A better response, however, would be to examine the quality of the theoretical discourse itself, for it is here that Bloom's version of strength has been embodied in its most direct and uninhibited form. It is clear enough in the case of *The Anxiety of Influence* that we are faced with a text with pretensions to "severe poetry," even without the carefully worded introductory notice:

> A theory of poetry that presents itself as a severe poem, reliant upon aphorism, apothegm, and a quite personal (though thoroughly traditional) mythic pattern, still may be judged, and may ask to be judged, as argument. Everything that makes up this book—parables, definitions, the working-through of the revisionary ratios as mechanisms of defense—intends to be part of a unified meditation on the melancholy of the creative mind's desperate insistence upon priority. [*Anxiety*, p. 13]

Such moments of self-observation are frequent in Bloom's writing and, though rarely prolonged, they have an air of nervously estimating the impression that is being made. The effect is alternately disarming and an unwitting analogue of the mirror stage itself. Here, the writing seems to be "reviewing" itself, suggesting the appropriate degree of seriousness and the most appropriate categories for appreciating what is to follow. However accurate the assessment, it clearly indicates the mode to which the writing aspires and gives us further purchase on the qualities of stance and construction that are deemed provocative and strong. The adjectives, from *severe* to *desperate*, establish the "deep" but narrow channel that will continue throughout Bloom's theoretical writings—the unremitting extremity and agony of the dying Gaul. The substantives are more diverse and more interesting, however; the mixed set includes poems, aphorism, apothegm, mythic pattern, argument, parable, definition, meditation—all only loosely conjoined. Together they suggest both the slipperiness of the enterprise as a whole and the heterogeneity of its parts. Yet the mixture is not wholly arbitrary; the stirring and obscure fragment, the compressed pronouncements and gnomic hints, the suggestive but recondite patterns of myth share a common element of mystery and indirect revelation. The example of Nietzsche is no doubt relevant, both as a stimulus and as a sanction for assuming certain *Ubermensh*-ly postures. (Bloom's Nietzsche is all *Sturm und Drang* and has little in common with the skeptical hermeneut the French have championed.) The description, then, evokes the fascination of what's difficult, what just exceeds our grasp, vision which cannot be reduced to visualization.

This last is an old preoccupation with Bloom, who warmed to the apocalyptic and antimimetic qualities of Romantic imagery when other critics seemed confused and irritated by the lack of visual coherence and concrete detail. Argument has always interested him, perhaps not in the sense of logical entailment but in the sense of intuitions that need not be either palpable or perceptible to be effectual—that need not obey the spatiotemporal continuities of domestic realism. Not unexpectedly, Bloom has had little to say about the novel, despite his predilection for narrative. An interest in prose fiction seems only to emerge when the tale is suitably remote and ultramundane, when desire predominates over imitation, and when, in addition, the outlines are stark, the movement highly selective and compact. The adventures he favors are peopled by giant forms that are also curiously abstract. At best, this produces his sensitivity to Blake and Borges; at worst, his tendency to overestimate the value of ersatz ballads and to call anything that is fantastic or Titanic enough sublime.

Somewhere in the middle range of this severe, demanding, strong taste fall the parables that form the Prologue and the Epilogue of *The Anxiety of Influence*. The first is an (unidentified) citation from a Gnostic text; the second is presumably a pastiche of the author's own invention. The Prologue differs in its graphic design from the rest of the book, set off (as are the Epilogue and the central "interchapter"—"A Manifesto for Antithetical Criticism") by means of an italicized title, a larger and more wiry typeface, and by a spacing that is strongly reminiscent of verse or liturgy. It is a solemn, even a ceremonial, setting and, together with the epilogue, immediately distances this text from the usual utilitarian books of academic criticism and ultimately from the fallen condition of ordinary language itself. The otherworldliness of the prologue is enhanced by plunging the reader (shades of Milton), into the midst of the story, amid the aftermath of a mysterious fall—"After he knew that he had fallen, outwards and downwards, away from the Fullness, he tried to remember what the Fullness had been"—that is rendered even more mysterious by being excerpted from a mythology few if any readers will be able to recognize. (One feels that Milton was somehow derelict, fell short of full sublimity, by stooping to familiar biblical materials rather than prolonging his reader's disorientation and ignorant wonder.) The Prologue traces the cause of the fall back to a mythic excess of passion that destroyed the perfectly balanced embrace of the original primordial lovers; from excess came cosmic division and thereafter reckless passion become a force without limit. The excerpt ends by condemning the "strengthless and female fruit" responsible for allowing the passion to escape.

We are never told explicitly how this fragment, with its closing reference to strength, relates to the theory that follows, but the omission is obviously studied. If there is no further elucidation, it is not because the passage is held to be self-explanatory but because the inexplicable is a source of awe and holy dread. The Epilogue is less mystifying, coming as it does after the full exposition of the theory (a rather chaotic exposition, to be sure, since the revisionary ratio that is the nominal subject of each chapter is usually only a point of departure for further meditations on the general problem of anxiety and influence). One is, in fact, tempted to read the Epilogue as an allegory of the process of misreading, with each obstacle representing one of the six revisionary ratios:

> Riding three days and nights he came upon the place, but decided it could not be come upon.
> He paused therefore to consider.
> This must be the place. If I have come upon it, then I am of no consequence.
> Or this cannot be the place. There is then no consequence, but I am myself not diminished.
> Or this may be the place. But I may not have come upon it. I may have been here always.
> Or no one is here, and I am merely of and in the place. And no one can come upon it.
> This may not be the place. Then I am purposeful, of consequence, but have not come upon it.
> But this must be the place. And since I cannot come upon it, I am not I, I am not here, here is not here.
> After riding three days and nights he failed to come to the place, and rode out again. [*Anxiety*, p. 157]

But the fit is skewed, suggesting that what we confront here are Laing-like knots of fresh anxiety and not duplications or refinements of the original six revisionary ratios. This is another instance of the fundamental instability of Bloom's conceptual design; his unlocalized conception of the anxiety of influence gives rise to a continual displacement and redefinition of his basic categories. Such wandering is perhaps the most intriguing feature of his writing and far outstrips in its complex machinations his deliberate efforts to mystify or the self-conscious sublimities of his posture and vocabulary. Occasionally, Bloom does employ a consistent imagery, as here when he constructs a play on inundation, flood, and dessication that even crosses the divide between quotation and commentary:

> The precursors flood us, and our imaginations can die by drowning in them, but no imaginative life is possible if such inundation is wholly evaded. In Wordsworth's dream of the Arab, the vision of a drowning world brings no initial terror, but a prior vision of dessication immediately does. Ferenczi in his apocalypse, *Thalassa: A Theory of Genitality*, explains all myths of deluge as a reversal:
>
>> The first and foremost danger encountered by organisms which were all originally water-inhabiting was not that of inundation but of dessication. The raising of Mount Ararat out of the waters of the flood would thus be not only a deliverance, as told in the Bible, but at the same time the original catastrophe which may have only later on been recast from the standpoint of land-dwellers. [*Anxiety*, pp. 154–55]

Yet the pleasures of a persistent image pattern belong to Wilson Knight, to other and earlier schools of criticism. They are distinctly out of place in a theory like Bloom's that lays such stress on discontinuity and poetic crossings, and disputes the integrity of the text.

If one probes the organization of *The Anxiety of Influence* in more detail, one finds a fairly standard literary chronology lurking beneath its apparently chaotic processes of association. The examples upon which each chapter draws follow the chronology of Romantic tradition, with Milton at one end and Artaud and Ashberry at the other. The organization becomes overt in later books: The last third of *A Map of Misreading* traces the "line of Milton," and then the "line of Emerson," a linear history that *Poetry and Repression* recapitulates at even greater length. The chronological arrangement of Bloom's texts turns his literary history into a steadily descending spiral, downward and inward, as each new poet tries to establish his own position within the circle that his precursor has drawn defensively around himself. Thus, each writer sinks ever further from the glory that was Milton and comes ever closer to the nadir of an internalization so complete that there is nothing, literally no thing, left:

> The problem of surpassing Wordsworth is the fairly absurd one of going beyond Wordsworth in the process of internalization. . . .
>
> . . . Nothing is got for nothing, and it need not surprise us that Stevens's last poem sublimely celebrates a "Mere Being" that is beyond not only reason but also beyond all "human meaning" and even "human

feeling." The American Sublime ends as the abyss, as the void beckoning just beyond the palm at the end of the mind. [*Repression*, pp. 60, 292–93]

Looking only at the structure of the narrative, without even raising questions of accuracy, one is struck by its extreme simplicity—the unbroken continuity, the utter singularity of the decline, without gap or throwback or syncopation. This simplicity actually seems to grow from book to book, gradually eliminating the twist, or *apophrades*, that reverses the decline at the end of *The Anxiety of Influence*. The old mythic cycle becomes ever less cyclic as the final stage becomes, not imaginative triumph over experiential loss, but the delusion of triumph, a more and more transparent lie. Thus, in *Poetry and Repression*, Shelley does not triumph over his precursor: "Yet in what I have called the *apophrades* or final part of Shelley's poem, . . . the meaning that returns is wholly a Wordsworthian kind of meaning, and the colors of the return flicker a little uncertainly, so that we cannot tell at times if they are Shelley's transformations, or if they are survivals still very much Wordsworth's own" (p. 107). Bloom's second treatise, *A Map of Misreading*, still holds out the possibility of an evanescent resurgence of the prophet's power to make meaning over the skeptic's power to destroy it.

Poems and dreams alike may *remind* us of what consciously we never have known, or think we never have known, or they make us *recall* kinds-of-knowing we thought no longer possible for us. Such tokens are not merely illusions to be dissolved. . . . Blake, Balzac, Browning are among the nineteenth-century giants who in their work exemplified such a deconstruction of the ego more strikingly than Nietzsche did, yet all of them finally *interpreted* more in the mode of recollecting than of demystifying meanings. . . .
At issue is the evaluation of consciousness, since to Nietzsche and to Freud consciousness is, at best, a mask, yet to Blake and Browning (and Emerson) it need not be false but can prophesy the truth. [*Map*, pp. 85–86]

And (again) the later *Poetry and Repression* despairs of this; all that remains is the *will* to power without the promise that it will ever prove effectual. "So in effect, the strong poet wants pleasure and not truth; he wants what Nietzsche named as 'the belief in truth and the pleasurable effects of this belief.' No strong poet can admit that Nietzsche was accurate in this insight, and no critic need fear that any strong poet will accept and so be hurt by demystification" (p. 2).

As Bloom moves from text to text, to preserve the fine edge of anguish, the purest sensation of loss, seems to be an ever greater problem—which is just what one might expect of a closed system, where there can be no new influx of energy and no diminution of desire. Hence, the strength needed for survival becomes progressively more cruel, violent, and deceitful, and survival itself becomes almost indistinguishable from death. Whether Bloom's story of decay is an accurate history of poetry or not, it replicates his own development as a theorist, for the cycle of his earlier work (up to and including *Anxiety of Influence*) has itself spiraled steadily inward and down, until at last the mythmaking that had promised a marginal "divinating triumph" has become the last lie that the poet tells to himself; "We know that we must be misinterpreted in order to bear living, just as we know we must misinterpret others if they are to stay alive" (*Repression*, p. 140).

It is appropriate, then, to compare *The Anxiety of Influence* to the final volume in this tetralogy of theoretical writing, *Poetry and Repression*. Here the focus falls inexorably on thanatos rather than on the baffled and anxious eros of the earlier book. Nominally, it is a far more complicated system that Bloom brings to bear in *Poetry and Repression*, incorporating elements of the two intervening books—*A Map of Misreading* and *Kabbalah and Criticism*—and offering a more reasoned defense of his sixfold framework (which *The Anxiety of Influence* was content to say "could as well be more, and could take quite different names than those I have employed"—pp. 10–11). The expanded framework (as noted earlier) reflects a continuing effort to bridge the gap between the theory and its object, and to engulf the apparatus of rival theorists by subordinating them to a larger, more sophisticated scheme. Yet all of this growth, all of these efforts at improvement, are inconsistent with Bloom's basic premises—as if theory might improve with each fresh formulation while poetry necessarily declines.[55] Indeed, by thus expanding and retaining all that has gone before, the true function of Bloom's framework seems to be to act as a bulwark against the displacement of meaning that his system is constantly undergoing. Unlike his rival Derrida, whose instruments are quickly appropriated and disposed of, Bloom's categories accumulate, refuse to submit to the indignity of translation and replacement. The map in chapter 5, the center of *A Map of Misreading*, stands as a graphic display, an icon of Bloom's desire for "presence"—for meanings that are immanent, final, and fixed—even as his successive reformulations foil this.

Poetry and Repression reproduces this map, just as the intervening *Kabbalah and Criticism* repeats the device of the framing parables from *The Anxiety of Influence*. Yet though *Kabbalah and Criticism* harks back to the first book, it is not a perfect analogue: The prose is not so rhapsodic, the "manifesto" for future criticism comes at the end instead of the middle of the argument, and the theory itself is no longer styled as a theory of poetry, but as a "theory of *reading* poetry" (*Kabbalah*, p. 12; my italics). This verges on a confession of what *A Map of Misreading* would not admit, that the theory has wandered from its original mark. (Elaborating new schemes, appending new categories begins to seem like projecting a series of transitional objects, allowing the theorist to attach himself to a new enterprise while seeming to stay with the old.) *Kabbalah and Criticism* still insists, however, that there has been no real change, and that all Bloom is doing is searching for a "primordial scheme after which the revisionary impulse seems to model itself " (p. 12). Yet this search, which *Poetry and Repression* continues, is always, secretly, an abandonment. For though *Poetry and Repression* displays the old map prominently, it is now at the head of the text, and operates more as a point of departure than as a guide for the book that follows. The opening chapter pays only cursory attention to the categories that the map so ardently compiles and quickly hurries on to establish its own, narrower concerns: "I too offer a 'machine for criticism,' though I sometimes fear that poetry itself increasingly has become the last formula. . . . the strongest artists, but only the strongest, can prevail even in this entrapment of dialectics. They prevail by re-attaining the Sublime, though a greatly altered Sublime, and so I will conclude this chapter by a brief speculation upon that fresh Sublime, and its dependence upon poetic equivalents of repression" (*Repression*, p. 21). The six separate revisionary ratios have been swallowed up by the Sublime (an expanded version of the daemonization and hyperbole of old), and the six distinctive categories of defense have become part of one global operation that Bloom labels repression, or, as he would say of poems, defensive processes in constant change:

> I conclude by returning to the poetic equivalent of repression, to the Sublime or the Counter-Sublime of a belated *daemonization*, because the enigma of poetic authority can be resolved only in the context of repression. [*Repression*, p. 26]

For Bloom the primal poetic repression is what allows poetry to go on producing Sublime works (by forgetting the sublimity of former poets and the dilemmas of wandering meaning); it also fuels the extremity we associate with the Sublime. Thus, only repression, and the refusal to forego the tepid comforts of sublimation, allows strong poetry to survive. Yet "the hyperbole or intensified exaggeration that such boundlessness demands exacts a psychic price" (p. 24), making of each poem not only a battle with its precursor but "a fierce, proleptic debate with itself." To survive under such circumstances is wearying and melancholy, a paradoxical situation in which restitution, the resurgence of creative power, is a form of loss: "It is only by repressing creative 'freedom,' through the initial fixation of influence, that a person can be reborn as a poet. And only by revising that repression can a poet become and remain strong. Poetry, revisionism, and repression verge upon a melancholy identity, an identity that is broken afresh by every new strong poem, and mended afresh by the same poem" (*Repression*, p. 27).

As mentioned earlier, Bloom's apparent alternation between books of theory and books of application, with books of speculative poetry followed by pieces of sober, prosaic illustration, is not quite what it seems. *Kabbalah and Criticism* may include no sample readings, but the exposition is far from flamboyant, and is even conservative in the first chapter, with its lucid summary survey of Jewish mysticism. *Poetry and Repression* is filled with readings, yet the theory that they seem to illustrate is really in the process of being written. Moreover, the interplay between quoted passage and commentary is curiously internalized and ambiguous. Citations well up from a mysterious private repository, without the usual marks of identification—"Repression is, as Derrida surely remarks somewhere, a difference in contending forces" (*Repression*, p. 154). They are swept up in an ongoing meditation that they do not so much document as extend and energize:

> ...and I
> Was left alone once more, and cried in grief,
> "Lo, if I find the Holy Grail itself
> And touch it, it will crumble into dust."

I have quoted all of this sequence, so as not to lose any of its cumulative force. But what is this force? I think we recognize in it, all of us, one of our own nightmares, the nightmare that is centered upon our own self-destructiveness, and so upon our own murderousness also, our aggressive instinct whose aim is the destruction of the object. [*Repression*, p. 171]

In spite of that suave, inviting "we," the atmosphere of these pages is too close; the overall impression is that of a sustained monologue. Here the questioner is being fed all the appropriate lines and only those—calling for an answer that is already known. There is never an intrusion, never a hesitation, never an unanswered question that might provide an opening for alien lines of speculation. Every inch of verbal space seems covered.

The writing in *Poetry and Repression* is much subdued in comparison to the incantatory *Anxiety of Influence*, with its "deep comprehension," "strong imagination," "dreadful greatness" (to cite but a single page). Apparently the pieces of poetry that have been absorbed into the text make it less necessary to try to simulate sublimity, to call it magically into being by reciting certain formulaic phrases. *Poetry and Repression* relies for its sublimity on the nature of the argument itself and the grim pertinacity with which the book pursues each new intimation of mortality. The first thing that a reader of Bloom's former books is likely to notice is how greatly the powers of the Imagination have been curtailed. Always before it was possible to distinguish the more valuable from the less valuable ratios and defenses, to discriminate (following the Kabbalah) between the tropes of limitation (irony, metonymy, metaphor) that contract or shatter meanings and the "tropes of representation" (synecdoche, hyperbole, metalepsis) that expand, restore, regain in imagination what is lost in experience. In *Poetry and Repression*, however, the distance between limitation and restoration has been collapsed and the tropes of representation (or restoration) are merged into a single continuum that measures only the relative intensity of exaggeration. Thus, troping becomes quantitative rather than qualitative, a simple matter of the energy expended, the cost or risk incurred. Indeed, the whole notion of restoration is now identified as a trope; what we take to be a return or re-presentation is always and only a persuasive lie or error that we accept because it is more pleasant than the truth. The very desire for a restoration of meaning has become almost vulgar: "Any poetaster or academic imposter can write a poem for us that oozes a plentidue of 'meaning' " (*Repression*, p. 140). If the strong poem is now identified by its "dearth of meaning" (which therefore compels us as readers "to invent if we are to read well"), then restoration is not only illusory but puny.

The strongest tropes in *Poetry and Repression*—or the strongest reading of what troping is and how it functions—is the least idealizing. The book restates Bloom's earlier objections to the demystifiers, but in the absence of any possible restoration of meaning, the sole alternative to deflation is a demonic deidealization:

> . . . I wish to acknowledge two very different readings or misreadings of the poem, the powerfully revisionist or deconstructive one implied by Paul de Man, in which the whole poem is an *aporia*, . . . or the powerfully canonical one, in which Keats pioneered and which culminates in Hartman's *The Unmediated Vision*. . . . Or is it, as an antithetical reading or misreading would seem to tell us, a very great visionary lie, not as much a myth of memory as it is a utilization of memory as a lie against time? . . . Which of the three readings/misreadings would cost us too much of the poem's strength? Or to say it in more Nietzschean terms, of these three errors, these three composite tropes, which is the most necessary error?
>
> Why, mine of course, though of the three it is the one I like the least, because it increases the problematics-of-loss in the poem. [*Repression*, pp. 79–80]

By increasing the problematics-of-loss (now an indivisible quality) of poetry, one preserves its power—to shock or shame or wound, if not to restore meaning to the world. Thus, *Poetry and Repression* presents a series of anticanonical readings that invert the received opinion (at times one that Bloom must first invent in order to attack) of Blake, Wordsworth, Shelley, Keats, Browning, and Stevens. When a poem enters the canon, we are told, it is assumed to be a repository of humane values and is consistently misread because of that assumption. But Blake's "London" is not really such "a prophetic outcry, not a vision of judgment. . . . We misread Blake's poem when we regard it as a prophecy, and see it as primarily sympathy with the wretched of London, because we have canonized the poem, and because we cannot bear to read a canonical poem as being truly so altogether negative and self-destructive a text" (*Repression*, p. 44).

The route by which Bloom reaches this assessment is circuitous; the entire chapter that leads up to it is a dramatization of the kind of strong "over-reading" announced in the book's introduction, "strong only by virtue of a kind of textual usurpation." "A strong poem does not *formulate* poetic facts any more than strong reading or criticism formulates them, for a strong reading *is* the only poetic fact, the only revenge against time that endures, that is successful in canonizing one text as opposed to a rival text" (*Repression*, p. 6). Thus one watches a performance of a reading as an instance of the Sublime—embattled and perverse, capable of desperate or cunning acts of inflation:

> Blake begins: "I wander thro' each charter'd street," and so we begin also, with that wandering and that chartering, in order to define that "I." Is it an Ezekiel-like prophet, or someone whose role and function are altogether different? To "wander" is to have no destination and no purpose. A biblical prophet may wander when he is cast out into the desert, . . . but he does not wander when he goes through the midst of the city. . . . There his inspired voice always has purpose. . . . Blake knew all this, and knew it with a knowing beyond our knowing. When he begins by saying that he *wanders*, . . . then he begins also by saying "I am not Ezekiel, I am not a prophet, I am too fearful to be the prophet I ought to be, *I am hid*." [*Repression*, p. 37]

The essay makes great use of wordplay, ringing variations on *to know*, as above, and laying a new stress on etymology: "to weave is to wind is to wander is to turn is to blight and blast" (*Repression*, p. 39). Such associations leave a dizzying aftertaste of Gertrude Stein, although they are doubtless designed to make the methods of Heidegger and Derrida serviceable for severe poetry. But where Derrida is exposing the instability of writing, Bloom is imposing upon it, displaying his own arbitrariness as a strong reader and not the arbitrariness of the sign. Over-reading words by drawing on arcane roots is a way of refiguring the poem, inscribing within the old terms a new allegorical value. In this case, an allegory of the powers of "voice" as opposed to the powers of writing. ". . . the poem is precisely anti-Nietzschean, anti-Derridaean, and offers us a terrifying nostalgia for a lost prophetic *voice*, the voice of Ezekiel and religious logocentrism, which has been replaced by a demonic *visible trace*, by a mark, by the writing of the apocalyptic *taw*" (*Repression*, p. 40).

The same allegory makes its way into Wordsworth's "Tintern Abbey," where Bloom traces the tension between seeing (the sense associated with writing) and hearing (the sense of voice) back to Wordsworth's fixation on the blinded Milton:

> For Wordsworth, unlike Milton, "the day is come," and the season is seasonally bestowing its fruits to the seeing eyes. The mist that Milton prays be purged from his mind is sent up, to Wordsworth's sight, from the fire of the Hermit's cave. And if all this transposition seems far-fetched, then examine the very strangely phrased opening of the poem's very next verse-paragraph:

The beauteous forms,
Through a long absence, have not been to me
As is a landscape to a blind man's eye:

Need we question who this blind man is? [*Repression*, p. 73]

This is deliberately strained and could hardly be more at odds with the distaste for allegorical readings Bloom expressed in his study of Shelley's mythmaking—but Coleridge's organicism and New Critical immanence have given way, first, to Saussurian arbitrariness and post-structuralist dissemination and then to Bloom's own doctrine of the empty sign. Moreover, strain is not inappropriate to sublimity (especially Bloom's version of the Sublime as an extended hyperbole). Now that the text is no longer presumed to have a meaning in itself, faithful reading is no longer fidelity to a poem but enslavement to a canon. True fidelity to the spirit of poetry, so *Poetry and Repression* implies, is to use the same means that poets themselves use—the great and persuasive lie—with the goal of enhancing the fading potency of major poems that now seem threatened by Continental skepticism, on the one hand, and canonical tedium, on the other. Thus, far from allegorical substitutions, now all reading is translation: "the only aesthetic path between limitation and representation is substitution, and so all that criticism can hope to teach, whether to the common reader or to the poet, is a series of stronger modes of substitution" (*Repression*, p. 270).

Yet, characteristically, the writing retreats from this exposed position only two sentences later—"there are patterns...that resist the power, however strong, of any reader and of every writer." And with this, the book gradually leaves off from its audacious allegorizing to focus on the subject of repression and the Sublime. The "patterns...that resist any reader and every writer" take over the argument, and the readings become less reliant on the extraordinary, ad hoc ministrations of the Over-reader. One scarcely knows how to treat this disappearance of the reader into his own system—is it the discovery of a more convincing lie? Is it an act of repression through which the reader masterfully forgets his own responsibility and convinces himself that the patterns are not imposed, but are truly there (because without such a conviction he could not go on)? Indeed how to go on—in the face of mounting doubts about one's own abilities and the reality of one's goals—is the chief problem of the book. In earlier books, *Kabbalah and Criticism* in particular, one watched the writing hurl itself against imaginary interlocutors, parrying questions about the worth of the enterprise:

But again, I hear the question: "Why do you insist upon *misreading*?" My answer is that a reading, to be strong, must be a misreading, for no strong reading can fail to insist upon itself. . . .
The sad truth is that poems *don't have* presence, unity, form or meaning. Presence is a faith, unity is a mistake or even a lie, form is a

metaphor, and meaning is an arbitrary and now repetitious metaphysics. . . . [A poem's] presence is a promise, part of the substance of things hoped for, the evidence of things not seen. Its unity is in the good will of its reader. [*Kabbalah*, pp. 125, 122]

A difficult credo to maintain: It requires great strength—even arrogance and oblivion—to continue reading into things what one no longer believes to be there. The strong reader can neither wholly admit to his own skepticism nor wholly do without it, since it is only the struggle with skepticism that makes credulity heroic, soaks it with the sunset colors of a desperate lie. Thus, as *Kabbalah and Criticism* also warns, the strongest criticism will end by confusing its own operations of the text under study—"according to the strong reading, it and the text are *one*" (*Kabbalah*, p. 125). Bloom's theory requires a certain stationing of the reader in relation to text (or of the text in relation to other texts—the two are interchangeable); their relative positions must be such that the result is always the same pained delight. This in turn condemns his own writing to vacillate between absolute suspicion and absolute conviction, between total solipsism and what he calls (almost punning) a relatively empiricist stance. Yet stance is precisely what it is not, for the polarity between faithless relativism and realism is so drawn that composure is impossible; the two positions must forever chase and torment one another if the situation is to have the requisite dynamism and intensity.

Thus, *Poetry and Repression* slips from reading-as-performance to reading-as-discovery, finding in the poetry it examines the very dilemmas of flagging desire and failing certainty that assail the reader himself. The book becomes a quest after the fading genre of the quest, a search for how other searchers have managed to sustain their drive and sense of direction when no longer sure of what, if anything, they are seeking. This becomes evident in the fifth chapter, after the debacle of Shelley, who had the sadness of knowing overtly what other poets have simply evaded knowing, that is, his inability to either equal Wordsworth or avoid repeating him. In the face of this, Shelley wrote his last poems in which mundane life triumphs over poetic vision and in the process won for himself a temporary, parodic ascendancy over Wordsworth—even at the price of killing himself as a poet. When we turn to Keats in the following chapter, then, we are in the aftermath of this poetic extinction and watch for how Keats will confront the problem of going on with what is now explicitly an impossible task.

> . . . in Keats's poem, Moneta, as what Freud calls the symbol of negation, mediates for Keats not so as to free his thought from the consequences of repression but so as to show him that his thought cannot be so liberated, if it is to remain *poetic* thought. . . . Romance, as Keats teaches us to understand it, cannot break out of the domain of the pleasure-principle even though that means, as Keats knows, that romance must accept the vision of an endless entropy as its fate. [*Repression*, pp. 141–42]

The solution, such as it is, is to absorb futility into the project, make the fear of it a spur to further effort and the opportunity to allay that fear the real goal of the quest. Desire is thus whetted by the horror of the absence of desire, the wish revived by the will never to lose the excitement of wishing. Indeed, the reference to the pleasure principle in such a context seems out of place, and soon gives way to the death instinct that Freud posited to account for the compulsion to repeat unpleasurable experiences. Freud's belief that we are driven by the need to reduce excessive stimuli and ultimately to return to a state of inorganic rest is not one that Bloom could ever finally endorse, however. *Poetry and Repression* flirts with thanatos: "I have invoked all of this Freudian speculation in order to get us to the Nirvana Principle, for that is the actuality of Percivale's Quest....where desire shall vanish, the individual self fade away, and quietude replace the strong poet's search for a stance and word of his own" (*Repression*, p. 173). But it does so for the sake of increasing stimulation, to terrify and awe us, and to replenish what we may have lost due to the boredom of repeated exposures to the same canonical poems. Thus, Keats is said to reinvent the vocation of the poet and to reinvigorate the self as a defense against "the severities of repetition" that threaten to make one's efforts "meaningless" unless one sees them as "the perpetual and difficult possibility of becoming a strong poet" (*Repression*, p. 142). So too the "embowered consciousnesses" in Tennyson, the loveless lovers and landlocked travellers, are transformed and their narcissism is praised as a defense against the death instincts [p. 152]—these instincts being equated with whatever thwarts desire and threatens to call an end to the perpetual chase. "What Vico saw is that truly poetic metaphysics was founded upon a sacred solipsism, which Vico called 'ignorance,' or rather that imagination takes its flight when the mind *represses* its own knowing and its own understanding. What Tennyson's Ulysses represses is his own knowledge, of himself and of his relation to others, so that by this repression he can be driven out, away from home, to seek knowledge again" (*Repression*, p. 159).

At whatever cost, the quest and its satisfactions must be preserved. Eventually cost, pain itself, becomes another source of satisfaction, as the egotistical Sublime of Wordsworth turns into the paranoiac and self-destructive counter-Sublime of later poets. It is therefore the self-destructive peculiarities of Browning's men and women that preoccupy the theory next. Browning is described as:

> ...[the] uncanny creator, whose poetry never suffers from a lack of ambition, who is always Sublime where he is most Grotesque, and always Grotesque when he storms the Sublime....
>   ...what Browning could never bear was a sense of *purposelessness*. It is purposelessness that haunts Childe Roland, and we remember again what may be Nietzsche's most powerful insight....[that] The...ideal,...by which he meant also the aesthetic ideal, was the only *meaning* yet found for

human suffering, and mankind would rather have the void *for* purpose than be void *of* purpose. [*Repression*, pp. 192–93]

The link between Browning's (supposed) fears and Nietzsche's proposed solution is interesting both because it mirrors the anxiety of the strong reader and because of the way it introduces the problem of suffering into the discussion. Bloom is not saying that the question of why we suffer plays any role in Browning's poetry; rather his problem is aimlessness, which suffering might even ease by providing us with a motive and a cause for action. Bloom then goes on to drop a few dark hints that project the movement of the remainder of the book: "In the final phases of Browning, Hardy, Yeats, and Stevens, the poet's Will raises itself against Nature, and this antithetical spirit breaks through a final anxiety and dares to represent itself as what Coleridge called self-determining spirit. Whether Freud would have compounded this self-realizing instinct with his 'detour towards death' I do not know, but I think it is probable" (*Repression*, p. 194).

All trace of doubt is removed in the next chapter, when it is announced that "we cannot distinguish the daemonic, or uncanny, or Sublime, from a particular variant of repetition-compulsion, whose affect is morbid anxiety" (*Repression*, p. 210). The Sublime is brought to life again by making it deadly, discovering in it symptoms of morbid anxiety and making the repetition of the same devices compulsive rather than banal. To call this history of poetry a repetition-compulsion also neatly presupposes that the canon is forever closed, not by the theorist, but by drives inherent in poetry itself. Bloom here uses the death instinct as a compositional resource to arouse and to excite—in ways that seem the precise reverse of Freud's intentions. The fact that it is chiefly a rhetorical stimulant explains the otherwise inconsistent treatment it receives—now invoked as that against which poetic repression provides a healthy defense, now as the abyss towards which poetry and repression alike secretly tend. "For though defense takes instinct as its object, defense becomes contaminated by instinct, and so becomes compulsive and at least partly repressed, which rhetorically means hyperbolical or Sublime" (*Repression*, p. 10).

In *Poetry and Repression* the defensiveness, the wholly nugatory quality of revision is clearer than in any of Bloom's previous books; the wish to engender oneself or to be the sole possessor of poetic power reduces to a more or less tormented denial. The object of that denial varies—it may be a repudiation of one's own narcissism, or of one's aggressive impulses, or of the fear of one's own impotence—but the process of denial itself is what matters most. Hence, the single name for all of them, *repression*—which is more Bloom's own category than Freud's. Bloom's *repression* is an active force that produces exaggerated representations and is not the silent process (inferred, never observed) that prevents representations from reaching consciousness. Indeed, in Freud *repression* both defines and constitutes the unconscious mind, which primary repression Bloom claims to find unintelligible. Since the aesthetic of Bloom's theory requires a vivid sense of loss and failure, a process that by definition is unknowable would be anathema. Thus, *repression* here becomes a paradoxically knowing ignorance, a willed gap in consciousnss. It is negative in two different senses—a heroic or cunning denial, on the one hand, and a depletion of the ever-more-limited resources of poetry, on the other: "Any poet (meaning even Homer, if we could know enough about his precursors) is in the position of being "after the Event," in terms of literary language. His art is necessarily an *aftering*, and so at best he strives for a selection, through repression, out of the traces of the language of poetry; that is, he represses some of the traces, and remembers others" (*Repression*, p. 4).

Whatever small or passing increments were possible in preceding versions of revisionism are eliminated here. To revise is to subtract from former glory, and troping can neither alter, undo, nor add to the true condition of the world, which is one of continual erosion and decay. Even as a practical critic, Bloom had associated poetic power with mundane disappointment, defining the imagination as that faculty exlusively concerned with myth and the formulation of desires that could never come to be. The theory makes this working assumption an official (if impoverishing) postulate, and *Poetry and Repression* pushes it to its most tragic limits—imagination, poetry, figurative language do not transcend loss, but depend upon it and incarnate it:

> Wordsworth and Coleridge had viewed the Imagination as compensatory, as trading off experiential loss for poetic gain, a formula that we can begin to believe was an unmitigated calamity. Is it the peculiar fascination of *Childe Roland* as a poem, that it undoes every High Romantic formula, that it exposes the Romantic imagination as being merely an accumulative principle of repression? But such negation is itself simplistic, and evades what is deepest and most abiding in this poem, which is the representation of *power*....
>
> ...Roland learns, and we learn with him, that the representation of power *is* itself a power, and that this latter power or strength is the only purposiveness that we shall know.... For Roland, as persuasively as any fictive being, warns us against the poisonous ravishments of truth itself. [*Repression*, pp. 199–201]

Thus, perversely, Browning seems to become a stronger poet than his High Romantic forebearers, and the admittedly grotesque and timeworn patterns of *Childe Roland*, its narrowness and almost brutal simplicity of design, are hailed as a new and feverishly immediate power. A passage near the close of the book expands upon this strangely impotent potency, this tragedy of compensation that is presented to us as the history of poetry, but seems more like a gothic story the theory is telling, raptly, to itself:

> . . . sublimation is a *re-seeing* but repression is a *re-aiming*, or, rhetorically, a metaphor re-sees, that is, it changes a perspective, but an hyperbole *re-aims*, that is, redirects a response. . . .
>
> . . . In re-seeing, you have translated desire into an act, but in re-aiming, you have failed to translate, and so what you re-aim is a desire. . . .
>
> . . . I would add, as a surmise, that all of us tend to value poetry more for its desires than for its acts, more for its re-aimings or purposiveness, than for its re-seeings. The Sublime, and particularly the American Sublime, is not a re-seeing but rather is a re-aiming. To achieve the Sublime is to experience a greater desire than you have known before, and such an achievement results from a failure to translate anterior or previous desires into acts. [*Repression*, pp. 253–54]

Ingeniously, then, the poverty of poetry has become a guarantee of strength, an inflammation of the will and a replenishing of desire. This is the solution to the problem of doubt and flagging interest that has dogged the theory from the start—or perhaps was the motive for starting out, in quest of "an enrichment of rhetorical criticism." For after all, the canon has not been changed in twenty years. How to continue reading with fresh appetite and to preserve the same degree and kind of enchantment is a question of some delicacy. And the answer is cast in the very terms of the aesthetic it is designed to save. Hence, the above formulation outstrips Blake (and even perhaps Lacan) in its determination to nurse unacted desires, achieving a crude sublimity all its own—which is doubtless more the point than its probity or accuracy. Auden's poems make nothing happen, but Bloom has made of the instances when nothing happens a higher form of poetry. *Poetry and Repression* is not simply an un-canonical reading of particular poems but of the Sublime itself: "*Within a poem the Sublime can only result when translation fails, and so when misprision is heightened, through hyperbole, to a daemonic climax*" (p. 135). For the idealizing view of the Sublime is that it is a mode that overwhelms its reader with the breadth of its vision, with the massiveness of its events and personages, and above all, with the elevation and power of its language. *Poetry and Repression* inverts this formula and turns heightened language into hysteria, a power that is always and only a desperate imitation of power, sound and fury that swells only when it is assured of signifying nothing—"that self-negation in loss, bewilderment, error, even in an approach to death, that always haunts the *unheimlich* or daemonic aspect of poetic sublimity" (*Repression*, p. 225).

A Sublime poem does not overwhelm us, but summons from the Over-reader in us a response to its disavowals, dessications, and consequent dearth of meaning. Bloom's antithetical reformulation of the Sublime is a studied reversal of received opinion: "By defining poetic strength as usurpation or imposition, I am offending against civility, against the social conventions of literary scholarship and criticism" (pp. 6–7). In effect, Bloom's own discourse strives to reinstate the fading pleasures of a Sublime that finds its roots in the rebellion of Milton's Satan. Yet his particular revisionary swerve may be too predictable, too obviously antithetical, and too sentimental in its effort to make unremitting pathos the source of further pathos—all in all too facile to produce the effect of strength to which the book aspires. For those with no prior commitment to the Sublime, it may all seem only a bewildering, phantasmagorical display; for those who are committed, the impulses out of which the book constructs its case may make that commitment embarrassing. In *Poetry and Repression* negative theology has become a kind of fundamentalism that may, in its literal-mindedness, do more to cloy than to increase our appetite for the Sublime.

Critics of Bloom, even the most virulent, often show a curious forebearance when it comes to the mode of his writing. The prose is, of course, open to caricature. Yet even while pointing out its "large-mannered notions," its pugnacity and pratfalls from stupendous heights, there is a mildness (bred perhaps of not taking it all too seriously) in William Pritchard's satiric rebuke: "The 'strong' way of writing about poems is often a barbarous and sometimes a bathetic way. 'I am myself an uneasy quester after lost meaning,' says the on-stage troubled critic, sinking as he speaks."[56] A more sympathetic reader like Kincaid arrives at much the same conclusion—"we simply cannot base a reasonable objection on anything so simple as manner."[57] Thus, it is Bloom's conceptual machinery that draws the most sustained and intricate commmentary, even from those who view it as hopelessly garbled or self-consuming. But the knot is not so easily undone; Bloom's theoretical framework is as mannered as his vocabulary. Aesthetic concerns are paramount in determining the whole of his conceptual design, down to its very discrepancies and absurdities. The categories and initial premises, the way the arguments are pressed, documented, or left without documentation have the same obscurity and largesse as the sentence construction. It is a theory of literature that is literary to the core; the opinions that he parries or absorbs and the operations that he borrows or invents have a theatrical power first and a function to perform only after that. This is not to preclude the need to examine the logic and the application of the theory more closely, but only to suggest that its literary pretentions must receive the same scrutiny. It is, moreover, on the strength of these pretentions that Bloom must ultimately be judged, since other vindications, like feasibility and plausibility (which normally complement whatever aesthetic appeal a theory may possess) are notoriously weak in Bloom's case. Indeed, Bloom's positions become stronger, to use his own term, precisely to the extent that they are implausible. Moreover, his repeated efforts to demonstrate how useful and productive his framework is, in book after book, have had the effect of convincing many readers that it works only for the theorist himself. There is something odd, and no doubt willfully piquant, about any attempt to advance for general adoption a theory that makes the claim that ". . . we can only understand what we ourselves have made. A reader understanding a poem is indeed understanding his own reading of that poem. If the reading is wholly a received one, then it will not produce other readings" (*Kabbalah*, p. 107).

Bloom's own defense for such "systematic mappings" is far from consistent. At times, he argues that his apparatus reflects "what is truly *there* in the poem, yet might never have been observed if we had not first seen it flatted out upon a necessarily somewhat distorting surface" (*Repression*, p. 225); other times, that "whether the theory is correct or not may be irrelevant to its usefulness for practical criticism" (*Map*, p. 10). Often it is only the preternatural strength of the readings it produces that matters, not the clarity or the fruitfulness of the orientation it provides. In this last case, the strength of the theory is beyond logical demonstration, and it must instead convince us through the majesty of its impositions. The grounds for accepting the theory shift as the theory itself changes from a theory of poetic influence to a theory of misreading, altering both its scope and its goal. The already ambiguously worded promise of *A Map of Misreading*—to chart "*how meaning is produced* in Post-Enlightenment strong poetry" (p. 87)—shows that questions about who is really producing that meaning could not be far behind. Such ambiguities and shifts make it extremely hard to disapprove of Bloom's contentions, let alone to disprove them—although invitations to contest or disapprove are scattered everywhere. It is the *air* of combat and extremity that counts; the theory, like the poetry it (mis)construes, "when it aspires to strength, is necessarily a competitive mode, . . . because poetic strength involves self-representation that is reached through trespass" (*Repression*, p. 7). There is strength enough in making claims, issuing instructions, constructing schemes—or in the increasingly militant wording of *Poetry and Repression*: "The strong word and stance issue only from a strict will, a will that dares the error of reading all of reality as a text, and all prior texts as openings for its own totalizing and unique interpretations" (p. 2).

Thus, gradually and secretly the vindication of the theory narrows to a preoccupation with design values alone and with the stance of the implied subject who operates the theory. Yet a theory that is nothing more than a particularly powerful stance must ultimately collapse, for the power of theory depends on the values we have come to associate with it—rigor, control, illumination, a stay against uncertainty and a standard for future conduct. If these expectations are consistently disappointed, the glamour and apparent strenuousness must disappear as well. And despite Bloom's confidence that we are more moved by displays of purposiveness than by purpose, that permanently dysfunctional desires have a grandeur that fulfillment plainly lacks, the theoretical enterprise (and perhaps imagination too) must eventually wither under such confining conditions. Unless, that is, the writing manages to conceal the evidence of failures past and prospective, or to persuade its readers to forget them in exchange for the compensation of calamitous sublimity and the inexhaustible pleasures of the problematics-of-loss.

Concealment, persuasion, and compensation all play some part in the rhetorical strategy of Bloom's theory. One finds evidence of repression less in particular passages than in the contradictions between them, the continual reformulation of the framework and the claims themselves. It is not an especially devious or manipulative strategy, not bent on blinding other readers any more than it blinds itself. There is enough baring of its own devices, and the inconsistencies are sufficiently transparent to disabuse anyone who has no wish to be taken in, for the sake of the pleasurable effects of belief. To take just one example from *Poetry and Repression*: "An image is necessarily an imitation, and its coverings or maskings in poetic language necessarily center in certain fixed areas: presence and absence, partness and wholeness, fullness and emptiness, height and depth, insideness and outsideness, earliness and lateness. Why these? Because they are the inevitable categories of our makings and our becomings, or as inevitable as such categories can be, within the fixities and limits of space and time" (pp. 8–9).

The argument is perfectly and hyperbolically circular: The imagery of great poetry is "necessarily" of a certain character because such a character is "inevitable." Here is explanation as a form of incantation, with the theater of finitude and the atmosphere of fatality as the goal. In fact, Bloom's bold departures from logical consistency are ill-matched with his grieving posture of determinism, an incongruity that is pervasive in these writings. The effort to keep the rhetoric forever at the same pitch of extremity leads to a number of such odd couplings—yoking Emerson and Ecclesiastes, the anxiety of interpretive freedom gone mad with the angst of absolute confinement. It is impossible to control a rhetorical strategy so driven by the demand for strength and so dependent on pastiche. With each new resource the theory appropriates, with each new exercise of the will to power, the speaking subject is pulled further off center, until all that remains is a swarm of incompatible citations: "Lunatic as the juxtaposition may seem, I want to contrast Peirce's vision of triads with the Neoplatonic triads of Proclus, in his *Elements of Theology*" (*Kabbalah*, p. 57). The lunatic juxtapositions dazzle us with their subjective whimsy, and yet what does that subject turn out to be except a vanishing point in the infinite regress of borrowed references?

Kabbalah and Criticism squarely faces the charge of logical (if not rhetorical) contradiction and resolves it by appealing to the example of poetry:

...look at the language of the poets, and not at any theory of language, including the poet's own, and...observe in the language of the poems a perpetual self-contradiction between empirical and dialectical assumptions. I knowingly urge critical theory to stop treating itself as a branch of philosophical discourse, and to adopt instead the pragmatic dualism of the poets themselves....A theory *of* poetry must belong *to* poetry, before it can be of any use in interpreting poems. [P. 109]

It is difficult to imagine a more extravagant fictionalism (although it is hardly the sort of fictionalism the philosophers of science had in mind). Here to endow theory with the logical and ontological peculiarities of literature, is to make it *more* accurate, more adequate to its object, rather than just more attractive or convenient. "A theory of poetry must be poetry" is even a plausible slogan (although it neglects to mention that what poetry "is" is still defined by the theory itself). Generally, fictionalism attributes the success of theory to its economy, elegance, and symmetry, but these are not the operative aesthetic values of Bloom's theory, which instead treasures abundance, imbalance, and the capacity to provoke awe. This is apparently why (above and beyond his defense of humane values) Bloom heaps sarcasm on the French Freudians who, "at their most hilarious, [reduce] Freud to a kind of Chaplin or Buster Keaton of the memory-machine" (*Repression*, pp. 54–55). In fact, there is no need to "reduce" Freud to mechanical conceptions. He draws mechanical analogies readily enough on his own, along with a number of others based on hydraulic systems, grammatical categories, and electrical impulses—all of which Bloom shuns in his own prose. From Freud he takes only the theatrical "scenes," the rhetorical "tricks," the martial "defenses" and "aggressions," along with the geometric figures of "introjection" and "projection." In Bloom's work, the ego becomes a protagonist, while the language of legal and moral judgment (*guilt* and *narcissism*) that Freud carefully plucked from its normative ground, Bloom just as carefully replants again. Avoiding a reductive use of Freud in this case seems to mean absorbing only those categories that have the appropriate poetic ambiance, just those metaphors that can be reanimated to perform grand and horrible deeds. Note how this intertextual operation works in the following passage from *The Anxiety of Influence*:

> We live increasingly in a time where soft-headed descriptions of anxiety are marketable, and cheerfully consumed. Only one analysis of anxiety in this century adds anything of value, in my judgment, to the legacy of the classical moralists and Romantic speculators and necessarily that contribution is Freud's. First, he reminds us, anxiety is something felt, but it is a state of unpleasure different from sorrow, grief, and mere mental tension. Anxiety, he says, is unpleasure accompanied by efferent or discharge phenomena among definite pathways. These discharge phenomena relieve the "increase of excitation" that underlies anxiety. The primal increase of excitation may be the birth trauma, itself a response to our first

situation of *danger*. Freud's use of "danger" reminds us of our universal fear of domination, of our being trapped by nature in our body as a dungeon, in certain situations of stress. [P. 57]

Bloom clearly does prefer what he thinks of as the active powers of mind to the mechanical drives and "discharge phenomena" that Freud had recourse to, but this is not repudiation of determinism. *The Anxiety of Influence*, after all, thrills to the possibility that "Influence is *Influenza*—an astral disease" (p. 95). It is just that to be determined by the stars is a more gorgeous and exotic fatality than to be ground up by the gears of one's own psychical machinery. Bloom's active mind is not free, but it is in motion and at war, a more dramatic and stimulating prospect than automatic processing. "If influence were health, who could write a poem? Health is stasis" (p. 95). As Freud's writing mingles with Bloom's, it loses its finer articulations; sharp distinctions and minute structural discriminations give way to larger and more deliciously vague forces: "Freud's very problematic final theory of the instincts posits a group of drives that work towards reducing all tensions to a zero-point, so as to carry everything living back to an inorganic state. Freud's formulation is difficult, because it suggests that a self-destructive drive back towards origins is a universal phenomenon. As a theory, Freud's notion here is frankly daemonic" (*Repression*, p. 172).

Bloom finds in Freud the language he had always sought, one no longer based on visual representation yet still capable of generating intrigue and sustaining dramatic engagement. The same applies to his imported theological terms and kabbalistic categories, which (as he himself notes) have nothing to do with any theosophical leanings and everything to do with atmospheric effect. The vocabulary thus accumulated provides an alternative to the equally abstract but deflationary grammars and inscriptions of the Europeans. Bloom's revision of Freud (like his revision of Nietzsche) is no more accurate than his rivals'; it simply saves the hermetic Freud as Lacan and Derrida save the "hermeneutic" Freud. And beyond any particular use he makes of Freud (or Gnosticism or kabbalism or even deconstructionism), there is his predilection for importation itself, and the deliberate policy of eclecticism he seems to be pursuing. At several junctures, Bloom alludes to the mixture of "beauty and strangeness" that (for him) characterizes the Romantic tradition. The way in which his own writing incorporates borrowed terms, savoring their strangeness and frequently withholding complete definitions, is consonant with this taste for exoticism. It also ambiguously recalls his own much-cited passage from Van den Berg on the "historical psychology" of Romanticism:

> The estrangement of things . . . brought Romanticism to ecstasy.
>
> . . . I think it correct . . . to say of Wordsworth what Van den Berg says of Rousseau, that the love of that answering subject, nature, is a love that

distances and estranges nature. Internalization and estrangement are humanly one and the same process. [*Repression*, pp. 64, 65]

Thus, the theory can be expected to move on to new and stranger categories whenever the enchantment of the old has worn away. Traditionally, theory is either an effort to come to terms with what is already estranged or an attempt to estrange what is too familiar for the sake of arriving at a fresh understanding. But here it seems that estrangement is an end in itself, an intoxication that never gets beyond what *Poetry and Repression* calls "the dialectical character of lyrical subjectivism," a curiously truncated and inverted version of Vico's "poetic logic":

> For Vico, then, the trope comes from ignorance. . . .
>
> . . . man in his ignorance makes himself the rule of the universe. . . . for when man understands he extends his mind and takes in the things, but when he does not understand he makes the things out of himself and becomes them by transforming himself into them. [P. 8]

This is an ignorance from which there can be no exit, nor is this an accident, for the excitements of estrangement are too great to renounce. What seems to be an "extension of the mind" to take into the theory the alien materials of Freudian psychology, theology, and philosophy is really an effort to preserve the hegemony of the subject, the self in search of (what it takes to be) exotic sensations (even if the result is only a subtler version of entrapment or narcotic dependency).

The pursuit of estrangement for its own sake becomes even more apparent when one examines the conceptual design as a whole. The design is far too unstable to be really workable. Narrative in structure (even speaking of the story of intra-poetic relationships), it tries for the appearance of a taxonomy (the map, with its various headings and subheadings for dividing and classifying revisionary devices) and at the same time calls itself a model of how influence-anxiety shapes individual poems, the life cycle of different poets, and ultimately the history of poetry as a whole:

> These patterns—evident as sequences of images, or of tropes, or of psychic defenses—are as definite as those of any dance, and as varied as there are various dances. But poets do not invent the dances they dance, and we *can tell* the dancer from the dance. The stronger poet not only performs the dance more skillfully than the weaker poet, but he modifies it as well, and yet it does remain the same dance. I am afraid that there does tend to be one fairly definite dance pattern in post-Enlightenment poetry, which can be altered by strong substitution, but still it does remain the same dance. [*Repression*, p. 270]

It is notoriously difficult to construct a genuine model of historical processes, or even a set of laws that are applicable in every case. Bloom's model is famously vague even about such basic questions as its intended scope. Does it cover all of poetry or only English poetry since the Enlightenment? All Sublime poetry or only those particular poems that are judged to have sufficient strength? It is equally famous for its resistance to falsification, since any work that fails to perform as the model predicts it should can be summarily dismissed as weak or outside the model's range, or can be made to agree with it by equivocal definitions and surreptitious changes in the model itself. When Jerome McGann complains that "one cannot know the 'truth' or 'meaning' of statements and demonstrations generally, unless one can show as well under what circumstances the demonstration would *not* be true,"[58] Bloom can then take refuge in the fact that Freud too

> . . . had to create a myth of an archaic fixation, as though he were saying: "in the beginning was repression, even before there was any drive to be repressed or any consciousness to be defended by repression." If this is science, then so is the Valentinian Speculation, and so is Lurianic Kabbalah, and so is Ferenczi's *Thalassa*, and perhaps all of them are. But clearly they are also something else, poems that commence by defensive processes, and that keep going through an elaboration of those processes. [*Repression*, p. 26]

The balance between literature and theory is just enough to give the theory, as poetry, a certain pleasant (painful) mien of strictness and "severe" ratiocination, while also allowing it, as poetic speculation, the freedom to forego documentation and demonstration. The books suspend disbelief at will and then pluck it back again. Thus, *Kabbalah and Criticism* will at one point assert "I take it that I am stating obvious truths. Why do we resist such truths?" (p. 102); then, a scant twenty pages later, it will claim "it would be a hopeless quest for criticism to follow philosophy in its benighted meanderings after truth" (p. 124).

As many of Bloom's readers have noted, however, his favorite notions—"lies" and "misreading"—presuppose that truth exists.[59] He requires it not just logically but dramatically, for in his system there must always be something to lose. Bloom's use of *lie* and *misreading* is not mistaken, but tactically stubborn; he is simply unwilling to accept the affective consequences of having no standard of truth (or beauty or the good) to lose. These standards must command at least a passing emotional commitment for his antithetical or deidealizing postures to inspire the desired response. An aesthetic based on skepticism and self-irony is too tepid, and so is any theory of reading that (like deconstruction) is too skeptical of its own premises—"a reading to be strong must be a misreading, cannot fail to insist upon itself." If the usual goal of treating theory as a literary mode is to make its claims less absolute, more transient and indisposable, the effect of Bloom's aesthetic is to make the text more bellicose, more unyielding and totalitarian. Its superficial mobility and constant displacement are ways of assuring that more fundamental changes will never have to be made.

In the case of Gass and Sontag, it was clear how discrepancies in the economy of the theory can push the theory further than it had meant to go or can demonstrate why it is so difficult to go as far as was intended. In Bloom's writing, the inconsistencies between different levels of the text tend rather to increase the entropic closure of the whole. For example, Bloom dismisses causal explanations—following Nietzsche's reasoning that the seeming separation between cause (as a superadded force) and effect (as the passive receptor of that force) is really a matter of interpretation and might have looked entirely different if we began by drawing the boundaries in another way:

> Influence, as I employ it, is not a doctrine of causation. It does *not* mean that an earlier poem causes a later one.... [It] does away not only with the idea that there are poems-in-themselves, but also with the more stubborn idea that there are poets-in-themselves. If there are no texts, then there are no authors—to be a poet is to be an inter-poet, as it were. But we must go farther yet—there are no poems, and no poets, but there is also no reader, except insofar as she or he is an interpreter. "Reading" is impossible because the received text is already a received interpretation, is already a value interpreted into a poem. [*Kabbalah*, pp. 114–15]

Yet the syntax of each passing sentence betrays Bloom's professed antipathy to cause. His preferred form is the passive—"The moral psychologist, philosopher or psychoanalyst *is discovered* to be talking about poems"—a construction in which the agent of discovery vanishes and the discovery seems to impose itself of its own accord. There are a number of sentences that invest the text with a preternatural power that goes well beyond being an "object-in-itself." Texts and poems become mysteriously conscious, strategically aware of what they are about and bent on bringing readers to their knees: "A strong poem starts out strong by knowing and showing that it *must be mis-read*, that it must force the reader to take up a stance that *he* knows to be untrue" (*Kabbalah*, pp. 111–12).

To do away with cause in principle is to strike a strong pose, yet it leaves Bloom free to exploit cause whenever he needs it for local effects—as here where the theorist describes how his own obsession forced him to embrace an extravagant model: ". . . I did not set out upon this enterprise with a Kabbalistic model consciously in view. But it was there nevertheless, as I groped to explain to myself why I had become obsessed with revisionary ratios, and then with tropes and defenses of limitation and of substitution" (*Kabbalah*, p. 87). When pressed to say what kind of posit "influence" is, if it is *not* a cause, and thus what explanatory value it actually has, Bloom calls it a trope, empowered to explain poetry because poetry too is made of tropes. But this leads to another impasse—for poetic tropes have been defined as willed falsifications. Hence, for a theoretical posit to behave like a figure in a poem is for it to lose all possibility of rendering an accurate account of poetry.

In Bloom's system, *trope* is the category that helps to hold together the contradictory energies of explanation and prescription; it hovers between illumination and invitation, claiming to do both but responsible for doing neither. Promises of accuracy and "adequacy to the text" alternate with what are openly proposals "to enrich criticism by finding a more comprehensive and suggestive trope for the act of interpretation" (*Map*, p. 74). There is no a priori reason why a theory may not prescribe a course of action rather than explain why something is the case, especially when knotty questions of value are involved. Bloom clearly appreciates how difficult it is to explain what literature is without straying accidentally into stipulations about what ought to count as literature, what and how we ought to read, and why. "For the ultimate question a strong reading asks of a poem is: Why? Why should it have been written? Why must we read it, out of all the too many other poems available? Who does the poet think he is, anyway? Why is his poem?" (*Repression*, p. 6). His (somewhat garbled) suggestion that the word *tradition* is necessarily "numinous" shows his alertness to the fact that most definitions of tradition are normative, as are most claims about which texts belong to it: ". . . rhetorically considered tradition is always an hyperbole, and the images used to describe tradition will tend to be those of height and depth. There is then something uncanny about tradition. . . . Tradition is itself then without a referential aspect, like the Romantic Imagination or God" (*Kabbalah*, pp. 97–98).

Culler complains that Bloom abandons the legitimate goals of literary theory (that is, trying to account for how prior texts condition later texts) and produces only "an act of interpretation." Bloom's claims reflect "a decision by the critic that valuable meaning and energy will be produced if one poem is applied to the other. . . . a decision made for purposes of interpretation and not as a motivated axiom of the theory of intertextuality."[60] It is, of course, a serious failing to confuse explanation and prescription (as Bloom occasionally does), but it is equally serious to treat prescription as wholly unmotivated, which is what happens when Bloom calls his framework a trope. If tropes are simply *willful*, then there is no need to justify them and no way to choose between them, except in terms of their forcefulness or stubbornness. All that we hear is that the worthiest tropes are "strong," more memorable and imposing—or whatever the theory happens to find memorable and imposing. To demonstrate its own strength, the theory must become capricious, insistent, unexpected in its tastes. Browning must be better than Yeats, Stevens must have no irony—simply because "I [the willful theorist] do not recognize this Stevens in the poetry" (*Repression*, p. 273). Decisions about what is strong must be total and "daring," and the defense must be in the confidence with which they are expressed rather than in tedious definitions or timid rationalizations. One understands more about the nature and the narrowness of strength as a criterion of value by observing Bloom's tactics as a writer than by any formulation he actually presents—and especially by seeing how his need for outrage grows from book to book. *The Anxiety of Influence* is rapt and perhaps too mired in its own afflatus, but *Poetry and Repression* is martial and inexorable in its pronouncements. The taste for extreme states now demands not just tragedy but decadence and destruction, as strength becomes quantifiable, equal to a certain *amount* of repression: " . . the degree of represson in one poem, as opposed to another, can be judged by a comparison of estrangement, distortion, and malforming, in tropes and images. The formula may well be that catachresis, or abuse of all figurations, attends really intense poetic repression, so that images, in consequence, become not only more grotesque where repression is augmented, but also more outlandishly hyperbolical" (*Repression*, p. 223).

Although all of this is designed to advance the thesis that poetry is in decline, there is certainly no suggestion that we give up the tastes that have brought us to such a pass. The decision to tell a story of inescapable decline is itself governed by the same taste it examines. If Bloom's desire to display his will and thus to awaken the latent powers of every Overreader, that desire still seems to follow to its own implacable course, thus making the strong subjectivity, the "I" whose tactics the discourse seems to reflect, more possessed by the will to power than possessing it. Ultimately, the problem of literary value is dismissed, or evaded, as the theoretical discourse itself struggles to become a thing of value. The strong stance cannot afford to question the roots or meaning of its own strength.

Many of Bloom's critics (even those who otherwise regard his entire program with dismay) acknowledge that his books do raise the vexing problem of the value of pursuing literary studies at the present time.[61] This is no negligible contribution, although the problem may be something to which he is responding rather than something he has bravely chosen to open up. The nature of his response also vitiates his contribution. The theory is deliberately obscure. Its apparatus is formidable, tantalizing, mutable; its operations are vivid but erratic—rich with promised applications, it yet remains difficult to take hold of and operate for oneself. Familiar poems that pass through Bloom's machinery become suddenly unfamiliar, full of new impediments, impossible to read.

> What then would an antithetical as opposed to a canonical reading of *The Fall of Hyperion* be? All canonical readings (my own earlier one included) have *naturalized* the poem; an antithetical reading would abstract the poem from the irrelevant context of nature, in every sense of "nature." Poems are not "things" and have little to do with a world of "things," but I am not endorsing either the Stevensian notion that "poetry is the subject of the poem." There is no subject *of* the poem or *in* the poem, nor can we make the

poem into its own subject. There is a dearth of meaning in a strong poem. . . . *The Fall of Hyperion* is a very strong poem because it impels every reader to return upon his or her enterprise as a reader. [*Repression*, pp. 139–40]

All of this is dazzling and challenging, sweeping us as readers into an interminable problematic that can never be completely resolved. Yet to embroil us in this insoluble problem is actually to solve (or to allay) another and deeper problem: how to keep desire active, how to continue reading the same canon with the same degree and kind of satisfaction— how to maintain the critical enterprise itself without succumbing to internal ennui or external challenge. By asking only *why* we read what we read, Bloom quietly assumes that the limits of our reading have been fixed. Most of the questions that the theory poses to itself—and the writing in the later books is almost entirely taken up with self-interrogation—are built upon such preoccupations. "Is the peculiar fascination of *Childe Roland*. . ." is a question that takes that fascination as a given, just as the tortured "Why is poetry in decline? Why must we misread canonically?" makes the comfortable assumption that poetry is declining and that the canon now is closed. This precludes the search for other poems or the effort to imagine an alternative kind of literature, while also making it unnecessary to justify the claim that any given poem is or deserves to be canonized.

The domain of Bloom's theory (much the same poetry his practical criticism treated) remains unchanged while the angle of approach changes and the framework itself expands. Evidently it is preferable to absorb alien influences at this level rather than to try to reexamine the canon or the nature of literature itself. Of course the alien is only absorbed as something that promises to be exotic, and all too quickly it too is reduced to familiar patterns, so that Freud and Nietzsche become "two of the strongest poets in the European Romantic tradition" (*Repression*, p. 2). This makes any influx of new information impossible. Every new element that is added to Bloom's repertory only increases the entropy of the system as a whole and moves us ever further from any possibility of imaginative renewal. The fruitful tension of exchange that ordinarily characterizes the relationship between the theoretical text and the texts that it examines or responds to is eliminated; all becomes a numb redundancy. The theoretical prose swells until it is awash with allusions and indirect quotations, many of which refer to its own previous formulations ("Let me return to and now adumbrate a distinction I ventured in *A Map of Misreading*. . . .") The result is a continuous recirculation of swatches of Wittgenstein and Freud, Vico and Kenneth Burke, Nietzsche, de Man, and Derrida, that float, unmoored and anonymous, among Bloom's own recurrent pet phrases (antithetical, central man, severe, ephebe, covering cherub), which themselves turn out to be derived from Yeats, Blake,

Emerson, and Stevens. So powerful is the effect of this transumptive operation, that when one comes across these fragments in their original setting, one does indeed have the uncanny impression that "the mighty dead return" in Bloom's own voice (*Anxiety*, p. 141)—an acute sense of *déjà lu* that need not aggrandize the ephebe but certainly helps to deaden our capacity to attend closely to his precursors.

Bloom's texts blur the distinction between commentary and quotation in several ways. Long, undifferentiated blocks of words ("here is a canto of Nuttall on Wordsworth") are introduced without further remark and left there to impose upon and often weary the eye. Or just the opposite: poems are reduced to summary of how they "map," until all that remains is "a very rough revisionary pattern" (*Repression*, p. 66). Allegorical readings may sheer off all but a few selected lines, or translate everything into Bloom's own governing tropes and images:

> Blake dares to see himself, in succession to Milton, ascending the chariot in the introductory quatrains of his own poem, *Milton*:
>
>> Bring me my Bow of burning gold:
>> Bring me my Arrows of desire:
>> Bring me my Spear: O clouds unfold!
>> Bring me my chariot of fire!
>
> The emphasis is on "my," as Blake moves to be the Enthroned Poet riding the chariot that is at once drawn by, and constituted of, the Four Zoas, the "living creatures" of Ezekiel and Revelation. [*Repression*, p. 92]

Gone are the bow, the gold, the clouds; the theory is concerned only with the devolution of the image of the chariot (from Ezekiel to Milton to Blake to Shelley), and so the chariot is all that will appear.

Both sides of the theory's intertextual operations—its dialogue with rival theories, its encounter with poetic texts—show the same tendency to ignore, undo, and undermine the otherness of the other text, no matter how distended the theoretical prose must become in the process. The narrator is lost and pulled apart by the power of his own constant quotations, even as these quotations lose their own distinctiveness. Such composition-by-quotation is one of several ways in which the theory becomes its own best illustration, but what does the economy of the theory as a whole portend? As mentioned earlier, most of the apparent internal inconsistencies become quite consistent if one asks what taste they express and what effect they hope to achieve. The lateral displacement of the theory, from one book to the next, conceals a fundamental sameness in the aesthetic principles that govern its design. Not surprisingly, the overall assumption that literature is a closed and decaying system is borne out at every level of the writing. The paradigmatic revisionary ratio, *clinamen*, comes from Lucretius, "where it means a 'swerve' of the atoms so as to make change possible in the universe" (*Anxiety*, p. 14); the dialectic of revisionism is based on Luria's "regressive" theory of creation whereby "God clears a space for creation" by "contraction" to leave room for what is "not-God" (*Kabbalah*, p. 40). "Repression"—the source of the Sublime—is a process of omission and selection. In each case a common metaphysic: The elements are constant, and change itself is only a redistribution (or an outright loss) of the same elements. Since one's chosen metaphysics will define what counts as a change, the theory seems to have ruled out from the start any possibility of growth or significant transformation.

The same powerful preconception governs Bloom's account of tropes. Figures are fruitless because (for Bloom) they involve a simple reshuffling of labels; the conditions that they name and the language system that they violate cannot be changed. Thus, troping can only display a tragic intensity of will. One need not explore Bloom's philosophy of meaning at length. Simply note that the language system is treated as immutable and kept entirely distinct from actual language use (over which it seems to exert a dictatorial control); that one can putatively know what things are in themselves before any of the distorting labels have been applied to them; and that sense is consistently subordinated to reference, so that differences of sense seem trivial and "subjective." It is enough to see how easily such assumptions would lead to the disparagement of metaphor and the apotheosis of hyperbole, which becomes the figure that most accurately reflects the true condition of all figurative language— able to change the mood and the sheer quantity of affect, but nothing more. There is nothing new under the sun and all that can be sought is the temporary solace of Kabbalah's "power of the mind over the universe of death" (*Kabbalah*, p. 47).

As we have seen, the various cycles of loss and partial or deluded renewal that figure so prominently in all of Bloom's work are also closed systems. Although it begins as a sequence of three stages, the triad has a tendency to collapse into two stages, just enough to establish a transition and to supply the excitement of departure or arrival. So too the various "dialectics" and triadic structure that the theory borrows from other sources—Freud's family romance, the kabbalistic creation cycle—tend to collapse into polarities and binary oppositions from which there is no escape. These dyads and polarities favor simple reversals: Everything is measured on the same scale and so verges on its opposite; every positive is only a version of a negative. In a decorous aside, Geoffrey Hartman probes the roots of Bloom's choice of the term *ratio* and arrives at a conclusion that associates it with this same leveling tendency:

> Blake associates "ratio" with Newtonian science, and uses it to denote a proportionate (ratio-nal) and yet—in his view—reductive or uncreative relation between two or more terms of similar magnitude. . . . For Bloom since the two terms are always precursor-source and later poet, or literary

"father" and "son," the revisionist relation is basically a tricky attempt to establish commensurability between incommensurables. The "ratio" turns out to be a false and, ultimately, "fearful" attempt at "symmetry."[62]

Thus, the internal economy of the theory imposes, by fiat and presumption if not by argument, a condition within which all things—literature and literary theory alike—must compete for the same limited resources: "Poems fight for survival in a state of poems, which by definition has been, is now, and is always going to be badly overpopulated. Any poem's initial problem is to make room for itself—it must force the previous poems to move over and so clear some space for it. A new poem is not unlike a small child placed with a lot of other small children in a small playroom with a limited number of toys, and no adult supervision whatever" (*Kabbalah*, p. 121). The justification for such statements is the excitement they can generate, ostensibly because we find them persuasive or aesthetically compelling, but equally if we simply find them disconcerting or repellent. For the function of the theory, in terms of its external economy, is to offset doubts about the institutions (critical and educational) of literary study and to distract us from questions about the value of reading what we do and how we do. In *A Map of Misreading* and in each of the subsequent volumes, Bloom takes up the issue of the canon and of the role of the academy in forming and sustaining literary tastes:

> What we call "literature" is inescapably connected to education by a continuity of twenty-five hundred years, a continuity that began in the sixth century B.C. when Homer first became a schoolbook for the Greeks. ... Curtius makes the central formulation: "Education becomes the medium of literary tradition: a fact which is characteristic of Europe, but which is not necessarily so in the nature of things."
>
> This formulation is worth considerable dialectical investigation, particularly in a time as educationally confused as ours recently has been. Nothing in the literary world even sounds quite so silly to me as the passionate declarations that poetry must be liberated from the academy, declarations that would be absurd at any time, but peculiarly so some twenty-five hundred years after Homer and the academy first became indistinguishable. [*Map*, pp. 33–34]

The start is promising, although it glosses over any distinction between the different uses that the academy has made of literature (for moral instruction, philological and historical information, and only lately for distinctively "aesthetic" ends), and ignores the fact that separate departments of literature and the study of modern literature, in particular, are recent inventions. By reifying both literature and the academy, the writing moves away from Curtius's historical understanding of the situation and his specific assertion that it "is not necessarily so in the nature of things." Bloom begins with an open question, "Do we choose a tradition or does it choose us, and why is it necessary that a choosing take place, or a being chosen?" (*Map*, p. 32). But the book gradually closes it, and instead of clarifying the processes by which a literary tradition is formed, it makes them more opaque:

> When the first literary scholars wholly distinct from poets created their philology in Alexandria, they began by classifying and then selecting authors, canonizing according to secular principles clearly ancestral in relation to our own. The question we go on asking—"What is a classic?"—they first answered for us by reducing the tragedians initially to five, and later to three. Curtius informs us that the name *classicus* first appears very late, under the Antonine emperors, meaning literary citizens of the first class, but the concept of classification was itself Alexandrian. We are Alexandrians still, and we may as well be proud of it, for it is central to our profession. [*Map*, p. 34]

"What is a classic?" has already been answered for us, and curiously, in this ostensibly antithetical theory, the ground for our current practices is our ancestors' practice. And within the course of a few pages more, traditions of both literature and academic authority will have become self-justifying and self-perpetuating:

> . . . we need Milton, and not the Romantic return of the repressed Milton but the Milton who made his poem identical with the process of repression that is vital to literary tradition. But a resistance even in myself is set up by my counsel of necessity, because even I want to know: what do I mean by "we?" Teachers? Students? Writers? Readers?
>
> I do not believe that these are separate categories, nor do I believe that sex, race, social class can narrow this "we" down. If we are human, then we depend upon a Scene of Instruction, which is necessarily also a scene of authority and of priority. If you will not have one instructor or another, then precisely by rejecting all instructors you will condemn yourself to the earliest Scene of Instruction that imposed itself upon you. . . .
>
> All literary tradition has been necessarily élitist, in every period, if only because the Scene of Instruction always depends upon a primal choosing and a being chosen, which is what "élite" means. . . .
>
> . . . Do the dialectics of literary tradition yield us no wisdom that can help with the final burden of the latecomer, which is the extension of the literary franchise? What is the particular inescapability of literary tradition for the teacher who must go out to find himself as a voice in the wilderness? Is he to teach *Paradise Lost* in preference to the Imamu Amiri Baraka?
>
> I think these questions are self-answering, or rather will be, with the passage of only a few more years. [*Map*, pp. 37–40]

In a series of circular definitions and substitutions, with new and more amenable questions supplanting the old, time has insinuated itself as the true motor of literary and academic history, removing any burden of institutional or personal responsibility for making choices and in the same move upholding the necessity of whatever choices have been made and the authority of those who have (covertly) made and continue to make them.

One can see here too how the question of literary influence has foreclosed other questions about the relationship between literature and professional literary studies on the one hand and about other aspects of our cultural and personal life on the other. As noted earlier, the borrowed Freudianisms have much the same effect as well, especially when Freud has been redefined to suit the purpose of the theory:

> ... the proper use of Freud, for the literary critic, is not so to apply Freud (or even revise Freud) as to arrive at an Oedipal interpretation of poetic history.... In studying poetry we are not studying the mind, nor the Unconscious, even if there is an unconscious. We are studying a kind of labor that has its own latent principles, principles that can be uncovered and then taught systematically. Freud's lifework is a severe poem, and its own latent principles are more useful to us, as critics, than its manifest principles. [*Repression*, p. 25]

The whole of Bloom's elaborate framework seems to be designed more to determine what cannot be said about poetry—the various debarred deconstructions and the disallowed semiotic parallels—than what can be. The lateral slide from term to term (from "Oedipal interpretation" to "labor" with "its own latent principles" in this instance) is another aspect of this same defensive effort, since each freshly borrowed piece of conceptual equipment threatens to open up the study of literature to alien interests that must be summarily dismissed by borrowing or inventing yet another set of terms.

Joseph Riddel calls the operation of Bloom's theory "nostalgic": "... a particularly modern nostalgia, which reconceives the Romantic poem (or quest-romance) as a universal model which overmasters aporia and contains every tendency of deconstruction. This is not nostalgia for a lost meaning that can be recuperated, even in a fiction one knows not to be true. It is a nostalgia for power, a resistance to the modern sense of entropy or impotence."[63] A most suggestive reading, although the "resistance to entropy or impotence" in Bloom's case takes the peculiar form of embracing them in order to make the theoretical framework more arresting and the story that it projects more terrifying. Similarly, by assuring the impotence of human actions and institutions before the sway of time, by insisting on the "poverty of the imagination" and limiting it to the role of providing figurative compensations for literal and inevitable losses, the theory strives to preserve its own preferred traditions and the power of those who minister to it. If the will to know that expresses itself in theory often borders dangerously on the will to dominate and possess, this antithetical theory suggests that intricately sustained "ignorance" may be driven by an even more powerful will to impose and master. Perhaps even fearful that too much knowledge might drain that will and make possession and mastery feel impossible or valueless.

In plain terms, I am asking: What is the difference between two closely related interpretative stances, one that asks, with Nietzsche: Who is the Interpreter, and what kind of power does he seek to gain over the text? While the other says, with Emerson, that only the truth as old as oneself reaches one.... How, for interpreters, do the Will to Power and Self-Reliance differ?... for Nietzsche, the trope is an error, albeit necessary and valuable; for Emerson, the trope is a defense, a life-enhancing defense. [*Kabbalah*, p. 118]

...we seek only what can aid the continuity of our own discourse, the survival of those ongoing qualities that will give what is vital in us even more life. This seeking is the Vichian and Emersonian making of signification into meaning, by the single test of aiding our survival. [*Repression*, p. 244]

It is not uncommon for theories to proliferate during periods of challenge and intellectual transition, when old principles have been discredited and the burden of doubt, skepticism, and estrangement is greatest. Yet the function of Bloom's theory is not to embody this exacerbated critical consciousness, whether as a passing stage through which one moves toward fresh and more sophisticated foundations or as a permanent condition in which systematic doubt becomes the one reliable instrument, the sole article of (negative) intellectual faith. It is, rather, to deflect it. Against the "negative thinking" of the Frankfurt School, with its "effort to contradict a reality in which all logic and all speech are false" and arrive at the conditions that give rise to such distortions, *Kabbalah and Criticism* urges instead the wisdom of the Kabbalah that one cannot recover tabooed meanings and that each effort to do so is only a defense against the unbearable permanence of our ignorance. If all systems of thought and all methods of investigation are ultimately defensive, why not adopt the most pleasing defense? Bloom's invocations of Kabbalah, Vico, Emerson, et al., to support his claims is a mode of reasoning by authority and precedent, rather than by laboriously constructed arguments. And despite his protests, they betray a powerful attraction to the idea of solipsism and utter meaninglessness, for the sake of the sensations such doctrines are capable of producing. It is not the authority or the cogency of the Kabbalah that is at work, but a decision to draw upon its most titillating premises—that we cannot ever really know (rather than, say, that our knowledge is not quite what we had thought), and that since all knowledge is contaminated by will, every willful act must therefore be a kind of knowledge. From this position it becomes possible for the theory to adopt only those opinions that are most thrilling, which is to say, "distressing":

My commentaries have been canonical ... in that they organized themselves around the assumption that Shelley was in the canon of major poetry in English, and so a vital element of meaning in him had to come out of his counterpointing his vision of mythmaking against his own reception of tradition. This now seems to me too idealizing and optimistic a view of

Shelley's, or any poet's, relation to a strong tradition. Poets no more fulfill one another than the New Testament fulfills the Old.... Modern theories of mutually benign relations between tradition and individual talent, including those of T. S. Eliot and of Northrop Frye, have added their idealizations, so that it becomes an enormous labor to clear away all of this noble obfuscation. [*Repression*, p. 95]

Thus, Bloom's enormous (by implication, Heraclean) labor takes the form of deidealizing rather than demystifying, of performing a set of simple Satanic reversals on a theme rather than exploring why that theme should have taken hold, what its roots and final consequences are. Indeed, to achieve the look (without the trouble) of critical thinking, the theory must often invent impossibly banal and sentimental orthodoxies against which it can then turn its own rather narrow and moody infidelities. The posture of iconoclasm may even require the sacrifice of "the received misreadings of the earlier Bloom" (*Repression*, p. 46)—thus undoing the integrity and continuity of the ego that the theory is ostensibly designed to defend and making its claims for self-preservation ring hollow. In fact, the strong trope has become a rule unto itself, a law far more imperious than the will it was to serve.

In the hybrid text that Bloom composes, the literary impulse does little to loosen the absolutism of theory, and the theoretical impulse nothing at all to alter or enliven literature. The attraction to theory is almost wholly aesthetic to begin with, and that aesthetic is inflexible and all-engulfing, tolerating difference only on its own terms—when it provides the frisson of the foreign or the fascination of what's difficult. For this reason, Bloom's experiment in theoretical literature cannot possibly invent a way out of old aesthetic impasses. Indeed, it seems to strengthen them, to mire us further in the polarities—of literature vs. life, heart vs. head, imagination vs. reason, beauty vs. truth—which such hybrid texts would seem most fit to overcome:

> Wilde, as a good disciple of Walter Pater, was a superb antithetical critic. As his spokesman, Vivian, says ... what is fatal to the imagination is to fall into "careless habits of accuracy." Art, fortunately, is not accurate, for it "has never once told us the truth." In a remarkable vision, Wilde's Vivian shows us Romance returning to us, by all the tropes of poetry coming to life, by all "the beautiful untrue things" crowding upon us.... Against Arnold, Wilde insisted that "the primary aim of the critic is to see the object as in itself it really is not." Wilde's superb denial that interpretation is a mimesis, is a good starting-point for ridding our judgments of the notion that good criticism establishes itself through sound descriptiveness. We do not speak of poems as being more or less useful or as being right or wrong. A poem is either weak and forgettable, or else strong and so memorable. [*Kabbalah*, pp. 124–25]

Once again, we are asked to choose—without much appetite for such a choice—between strong but useless art and sound but unappealing arguments.

6
Roland Barthes

It is possible, indeed common, to read Bloom's entire theoretical opus as an unfortunate aberration brought on by too extended an exposure to foreign influences. Left to himself, the story goes, Bloom (who here stands for the whole upheaval in Anglo-American letters) might have gone on as a productive and useful practical critic, happily innocent of the distorting ambitions and distorted syntax of theoretical writing. In this melodrama of innocence seduced, Barthes (in type, if not in fact) would no doubt figure as the villain, the alien intoxicating guileless minds with dazzling but deceptive promises. Such, at any rate, is the tableau upon which Bernard Bergonzi's review of *S/Z* opens (although, to be sure, with a good deal of delicate irony):

> A former pupil, now doing research in another university, writes to me in praise of Foucault and Barthes and speaks dismissively of the "Leavisite school.". . . Only the very young and the very intelligent can muster quite such purity of scorn, and it would be easy to discount it as the result of a passing enthusiasm. Not all the most able students respond so warmly to French ideas. In the end, the implications of that drab old maxim, "Be neither the first to accept change nor the last to resist it," have to be accepted. Teachers of Eng. Lit. may want to pick up some of these new notions, if only for the same practical reason that dedicated teachers in comprehensive schools watch mindless television programmes and listen to pop songs—so as to know what their pupils are talking about.[1]

One must, in fact, acknowledge from the start how great a role exoticism has played in the superficial popularity of imported literary theories, Barthes's included. And it is as an imported, a translated, figure that I shall be treating him—a being constructed from a name and a body of writings that made their appearance on the Anglo-American scene at a particular moment and have established there a function and a meaning independent of whatever they might have meant or been in their original context. If Bloom may be used, loosely, to exemplify the native strain, Barthes may serve us as the representative foreigner. As Bloom's career incorporates or rebuts most of the assumptions and methods that have governed the local scene for the past twenty years, so too in Barthes one can discern (according to Fredric Jameson) "a veritable fever-chart of all the significant intellectual and critical tendencies since World War Two:

Bachelardian phenomenology and Sartrean existentialism, Marxism, Freudianism, Structuralism and post-structuralism."[2] This catalog may be less feverish, however, than it at first appears. For if Bloom's writing collapses the separate stages of theory and theory-as-literature, in Barthes it is the pattern of an entire career that has been telescoped, even rearranged, under the pressure of translation. The order and the tightly compressed form of the translated oeuvre means that Barthes's work is, like Bloom's, capable of provoking wildly discrepant enthusiasms and complaints. The tangle of his references, artificially superimposed on one another, and the seemingly abrupt, almost whimsical shifts of critical position arrived here all at once, to be met by our own more diffuse and slowly formed allegiances. And as with Bloom, the interplay that results reveals as much about the current state of our own literary establishment—its contradictions and contending factions, its strange mixture of fascination and uncertainty—as anything the texts themselves actually embody.

Yet the representative issues are there, too. One finds in Barthes as well as in Bloom the same concern for the machinery of reading, and hence for creative (rather than purely receptive or responsive) critical writing:

> It is language which speaks, not the author; to write is, through a pre-requisite impersonality (not at all to be confused with the castrating objectivity of the realist novelist), to reach that point where only language acts, "performs," and not "me.". . .
>
> . . . there is no other time than that of the enunciation and every text is eternally written *here and now*. The fact is (or, it follows) that *writing* can no longer designate an operation of recording, notation, representation. . .
>
> . . . a text is made up of multiple writings, drawn from many cultures and entering into mutual relations of dialogue, parody, contestation, but there is one place where this multiplicity is focused and that place is the reader, not, as hitherto said, the author. The reader is the space on which all the quotations that make up a writing are inscribed without any of them being lost; a text's unity lies not in its origin but in its destination. Yet this destination cannot any longer be personal: the reader is without history, biography, psychology; he is simply that *someone* who holds together in a single field all the traces by which the written text is constituted.[3]

At the root of this concern, however differently they may express it, is a set of nagging epistemological questions that have touched them both—doubts about the stability of meaning and the grounds and nature of our knowledge. One even finds them invoking Nietzsche in similar ways—"What does nihilism signify? *That the higher values are losing their value*. The ends are lacking, there is no answer to this question 'What's the use?' "[4] What Bloom and Barthes seem to share is a common situation, bred by the problematic condition of the literary establishment itself—the impasses of reading, writing, and teaching at the present time. For Hirsch, this means that they are simply stray symptoms of this larger problem:

> The "crisis" (if there is one) is not in literary criticism but in literature itself, and perhaps not only in literature but in Western culture as it has developed over two millennia. The problem is not to free criticism from "an exclusively interpretive role" but to demonstrate that "literature" bears "truths" or "values" or something worth interpreting. If literature itself could no longer inspire a pleasure once associated with the apprehension of "truth," then what point would there be in defending literary criticism as "a mode of knowledge"? Knowledge about what?[5]

A critic less antipathetic than Hirsch might argue, though, that it is more than the symptom of a crisis we are seeing; it is also (at least potentially) an effort to overcome it, by defining and so reinventing the situation in which the reading, writing, and teaching of literature must take place. Thus, the interest of juxtaposing Bloom and Barthes is not just in their shared preconceptions or common predicaments but in the distinctive ways in which each writer defines his dilemmas and begins to chart a response to them. It is in these terms that one must finally distinguish between them and weigh their individual achievements— indeed, weigh the potential value of theoretical literature as a whole. One may use theoretical writing to write oneself into a corner—as Bloom appears to—or to begin, with Barthes, to try to write one's way out.

Translations of Barthes's work tend to fall into clusters, beginning with the first brief essay, "Criticism as Language" (actually commissioned for publication in English), which appeared in the *Times Literary Supplement* in 1963, within a year of the cresting of "structuralism" as a public phenomenon in France. As Jacques Ehrmann describes the scene: "Around 1962, structuralism, from a working method known to and practiced by specialists, became a fashionable philosophy discussed in as many circles as Sartre's existentialism had been after World War II; that year saw the publication of Claude Lévi-Strauss' *La Pensée Sauvage* which contained a chapter-length refutation of the importance given to history by Jean-Paul Sartre in his *Critique de la raison dialectique* (1960)."[6] This first essay was quickly followed by the American translation of *On Racine* (New York: Hill and Wang, 1964), again within a year of the French publication date. There was then a slight break until the next wave of translations began, stretching roughly between 1967 (which saw the British appearance of the combined edition of *Writing Degree Zero* and *Elements of Semiology*) and 1972 (when the American translation of *Critical Essays* appeared, along with the joint Anglo-American publication of Annette Lavers's selections from *Mythologies*.) Finally, around 1975, another series of translations was issued in both the United States and Great Britain, at the rate of one or two a year: *S/Z* (1976), *Image/Music/Text* (1977), *Roland Barthes by Roland Barthes* (1977), and *A Lover's Discourse* (1978).

But these clusterings have more to do with the rise and fall of Anglo-American appetites than they do with Barthes's own productive rhythms—something that is clearly visible if one compares the dating of the translations with the date of original publication.

Le degré zéro de l'écriture (1953)	
[*Michelet par lui-même* (1954)]	
Mythologies (1957)	
Sur Racine (1963)	"Criticism as Language" (1963)
Essais Critiques (1964)	*On Racine* (1964)
Eléments de Sémiologie (1964–65)	
[*Critique et Vérité* (1966)]	
[*Système de la Mode* (1967)]	*Writing Degree Zero and Elements of Semiology* (1967)
S / Z (1970)	[Various anthologized essays, 1968–1972]
[*L'Empire des Signes* (1970)]	
Sade, Fourier, Loyola (1971)	*Mythologies* (1972); *Critical Essays* (1972)
Le Plaisir du Texte (1973)	
Roland Barthes par Roland Barthes (1975)	*S / Z; The Pleasure of the Text* (1975);
	Sade / Fourier / Loyola (1976)
Fragments d'un discours amoureux (1977)	*Image / Music / Text; Roland Barthes by Roland Barthes* (1977)
	A Lover's Discourse (1978)

The Anglo-American Barthes began as his own contemporary and passed through a period of retrospective appreciation, to finally become, once again, nearly the contemporary of his French counterpart. The effect of this redistribution was to define Barthes's structuralist writings as the core of all that came before and after them, the goal and crowning a-chievement of the earlier work, the point of departure for his last (and ostensibly uniform) poststructuralist phase. This is even more patent if one considers the intertextual network into which these transported writings were inserted: the 1963–64 translations of Lévi-Strauss's *Structural Anthropology* and *The Savage Mind* (not yet fully differentiated from the general flood of Continental thinking that at this time included fresh translations of Bachelard and Poulet as well); the flurry of conferences and special issues in the later sixties (most notably, the Johns Hopkins conference on "The Languages of Criticism and the Sciences of Man"—later published as *The Structuralist Controversy*—which Barthes himself attended, and the *Yale French Studies* issue on structuralism of the same year (1966), mingling with anthologies of recovered Russian formalist pronouncements, on the one hand, and the appearance of a number of new journals devoted to linguistic stylistics, on the other; all of which activity reached its peak of self-conscious and sometimes militant expression by the early 1970s. The publication of Jonathan Culler's *Structuralist Poetics*, Fredric Jameson's *The Prison-House of Language*, and Robert Scholes's *Structuralism in Literature* between 1972 and 1974 marked at once a retrospective synthesis and an effort to critique the assumptions of structuralist methods, and was accompanied by a second wave of translations (some dating from as far back as the middle fifties) of Althusser, Foucault, Derrida, Lacan, and Deleuze/Guattari that gradually crystallized into a poststructuralist assault on scientism. At the same time, there emerged a group of even newer journals—*Diacritics, Glyph, Semiotexte*—with a more loosely philosophical or speculative, rather than a militantly scientific, basis.

That the imported Barthes should fall so neatly into this same three-stage chronology and be read in terms of these same categories of intellectual and ideological controversy can hardly be accidental. But by locating these patterns, I do not mean to dismiss them as false to the original. Rather I wish to note what they invite us to make of Barthes's career, the story that they tempt us to tell about him—from his first appearance as an upstart intruder to his decline into an aging and outmoded writer, struggling to keep up with newer trends. Or (in another version) a writer who grew embarrassed and unsure and began to betray his own best work, or (in another version still) *matured* to the point where he could disdain the changing whims of fashion and write solely for himself. One can easily find strains of one or another of these narratives, these different Barthesian myths, in almost any book review one happens to pick up:

> The science of literature is a timid response to the risks of an indeterminate, infinitely prospective interpretation.... An art of multiple interpretations invites a criticism of multiple interpretations—an exuberant excess of language which would be one of the effects of that subtle subversion of bureaucratic structuralism which I find already begun in Derrida and in Deleuze. Barthes seems to be moving in a similar direction.[7]

> There is a far more generous outflow of the personality into the text than Barthes has allowed himself before. The analytical power is as great as ever; but the rattle of formulas has been replaced by contemplative thoughtfulness that lifts the writing to a new level.[8]

> [The claim] that Barthes went beyond semiology because he found it wanting implies that he mastered it and then discovered its limits.
> ... [but] the passage from poetics to *semanalyse* cannot involve a rejection of poetics, since one can only describe literature's violation of codes if

these codes have been studied and formulated. This formulation is precisely what Barthes, in the name of self-transcendence, refuses to countenance, and no assessment of his contribution to literary theory can ignore this refusal.[9]

The distance, the lag of time, and the loss of context that translation introduces was just enough to turn Barthes into a malleable figure that one could twist into any number of different and aesthetically arresting poses—tragic, heroic, or laconic—at will. Indeed, the now fixed habit of marketing his books beneath an imposing cover picture of the author makes Barthes even more the star—a frozen and fantasmatic face, curiously (now cruelly) removed from time and change. And beyond whatever peculiar features distinguished him, Barthes was also an outsider, fascinating in his remoteness and made even more so by virtue of his status as an import—as one who did not seek us out, but came at our behest, bearing unfamiliar knowledge and not in the least curious about whatever we might, in turn, know. Actually, the exchange was not entirely one-sided, but Barthes's references to Anglo-American sources are few, and the structure of importation itself is such that translations are never directed at the audience they ultimately reach. As a result, they retain a certain alien aura, thrilling or irritating according to one's tastes. The alien quality can become a source of fear and/or power as well, inducing a terror of falling out of step and out of fashion, which anyone with the requisite missing information may then exploit. There is no little irony in this, given Barthes's own efforts to dismantle "fashion" (both the tyranny of haute couture in *Système de la Mode* and of intellectual trends—what can be said, what it is expected one would say—in *Pleasure of the Text* and *Roland Barthes*). In Barthes's later excursions into the discourse of desire, the relation of the obsessed lover to his (imagined) love-object bears a curious resemblance to the relation between the Anglo-American audience and the wandering, translated text:

> The other is in a condition of perpetual departure, of journeying; the other is, by vocation, migrant, fugitive; I—I who love, by converse vocation, am sedentary, motionless, at hand, in expectation, nailed to the spot, *in suspense*. . . .
>
> . . . To make the other into an insoluble riddle on which my life depends is to consecrate the other as a god. . . . the other is not to be known; his opacity is not the screen around a secret. . . . I am then seized with that exaltation of loving *someone unknown*, someone who will remain so forever. [*Discourse*, pp. 13, 135]

For all the hackles it may raise, importation is not invasion. The fact that Barthes occasionally indulged in reflex anti-Americanisms—"an American (or positivist, or disputatious: I cannot disentangle) student"[10]—is proof only that the native sense of dearth and self-doubt was deep enough to make such insults seem bracing and confirming. Besides, the disdain is perfectly in keeping with certain homegrown stereotypes about the Frenchman and his snobbery, what one reviewer of Barthes called "a lot of Gallic P. R. about the supposed lack of 'rigor' and the 'provincialism' of 'Anglo-American' criticism."[11] The phrase "Gallic P. R." is interestingly ambiguous—both advertisements *by* and *of* the French— and reminds one of Barthes's analysis of how French advertising in turn uses the image of "the Italian":

> Here we have a Panzani advertisement: some packets of pasta, a tin, a sachet, some tomatoes, onions, peppers, a mushroom, all emerging from a half-open string bag, in yellows and greens on a red background....
>
> ... the sign *Panzani* gives not simply the name of the firm but also, by it assonance, an additional signified, that of "Italianicity.". . .
>
> ... not Italy, it is the condensed essence of everything that could be Italian, from spaghetti to painting . . . *Italianicity* belongs to a certain axis of nationalities, alongside Frenchicity, Germanicity or Spanishicity.[12]

As a translated writer, then, Barthes was identified with all that is "typically French"—including fashion, hauteur, sensuality, and hedonism—i.e., all that opposes Puritan constraint. This includes a certain worldly cynicism (dating back to La Rochefoucault, but now associated more closely with attacks on humanism, with demystification, a preference for political and economic, rather than moral, explanations and a general suspicion of professed motives, while relishing wicked or subversive or deterministic accounts of human behavior). It embraces Cartesian rationalism as well (a skeptical tendency to doubt appearances, ultimately to forego evidence—as in Lévi-Strauss's notorious arm-chair anthropology—matched with a stylistic taste for absolutes, for a priori rules and inflated generalizations that take the form of pithy maxims all the more annoying for being witty and dexterous). Doubtless Barthes owed much of his sheer celebrity (though not his well-earned intellectual fame) to how well he fulfilled our nascent expectations of what a typically French writer should be—"he belongs to the antique tradition that includes Montaigne and Cocteau, a quite traditional man of letters—an animator of taste, stylist, vagrant commentator, phrase maker, master of revels, mediator, gadfly."[13] While fulminating at his "arcane" conceptual machinery, critics were nonetheless more willing to accept such excesses in a Frenchman than in an American like Bloom:

> *S/Z* is more brilliant but comparatively useless: it stays in the mind like a piece of beautiful advanced technology or an object in a science fiction film....
>
> Like *S/Z*, Mr. Bloom's book may, in the end, tell us more about its author's mind than about literature. And mind for mind, Barthes' seems to me more powerful, more ingenious, less ostentatious and more elegant in its operations.[14]

And they have positively warmed to those elements in his later work—the fragmentary pensées and dark confessions, the eroticism and hedonism, the self-consciously staged "perversions"—which seem to conform even more precisely to the stereotype.

The power of this stereotype is evident in Bloom's own persistent tendency to confuse deconstruction and demystification with de-idealization, and thus (try to) render himself more Continental by the simple expedient of uttering heresies at every turn. Reviews, even by those who operate as official liaisons between French and Anglo-American intellectual life, continue to reinforce the stereotype too. "France, as everyone knows, is the country of fashion. Intellectual jargons and artistic personalities are picked up as passionately and dropped as ruthlessly as the perpetually daring inventions of Givenchy and Saint Laurent. . . [which] makes some of us understandably suspicious of the intellectual revolutions which the French perpetually announce."[15] (Perhaps it is precisely such writing that is most prone to perpetuate the stereotype because the need for a liaison arises only when knowledge is otherwise inaccessible, quixotic, difficult to attain and hold.) Sontag's idealizations of French intellectual life are no less distorted than the detractions, to judge from the frequent complaints about French anti-intellectualism that pepper Barthes's own prose—"ideas are noxious if they are not controlled by 'common sense' and 'feeling.'. . . one gets rid of intellectuals by telling them to run along and get on with the emotions and the ineffable."[16] The public airing of intellectual debate (which Sontag found so enviable) instead made Barthes more vulnerable, in his native country, to attacks as a dilletante, rejected both by traditional literary scholars and by professional linguists who ranked him only as "an essayist or critic."[17] Apparently it is only a trick of perspective that makes it seem to us that "the French" (whether they embody our collective fears or our collective longings) have achieved a condition in which the boundaries between action and contemplation have been erased and intellectual life rendered universally accessible, public, and effectual.

When Geoffrey Hartman says: "these are still the Banquet Years in France. . . . New fantastic words appear on the scene to express the mixture of disciplines: 'economimesis,' 'ana-semantics,' 'mimology,' "[18] he, and we, are perhaps too ready to believe (a strangely antistructuralist delusion) that if the words exist, so must the institutional arrangements that they apparently name. The delusion is fostered by the nature of the texts we choose to import and by the very fact that we have the texts and nothing more—words ripped from their contexts make it hard to test or measure the degree of hyperbole or fantasy involved. Such texts float enigmatically—promisingly, threateningly—in the middle distance between what we are and what we take to be possible. Our translations therefore are a better index of our own intellectual life—its founding assumptions, its felt lacunae—than they are of intellectual preoccupations in France. One need not wonder, then, at the sudden popularity of French theoreticians, nor blame it on alien conspirators in our midst; the influx of foreign thought came to remedy our own native sense of tedium or uncertainty. And the selective fascination that the French writers, in particular, have exercised, suggests an already extant disenchantment with English humanism and empiricism looking for relief in its antipode. However faithful to its origins this outburst of French thought in English letters may eventually prove to be, it has at least fulfilled the function which Barthes himself ascribed to his own "taste for the very exotic languages, . . . whose structure *represents* for him—image and remonstrance—the organization of an altogether different subject" (*Roland Barthes*, p. 116).

With a writer as supple as Barthes and one as intoxicated by enantiosemes (words with the same form, but contradictory meanings) and amphibology (phrases where the grammar allows two or more distinct readings) as he gradually became, translation will always present problems. French is close enough to English in its fundamental grammatical categories to allow broad semantic distinctions and even some of the syntactic rhythm of Barthes's prose to filter through—a proximity of language that is doubly important given Barthes's predilection for constructing critical distinctions out of grammatical ones: the pronoun system, tense markers, the separation between substantives and adjectives, subjects and predicates. "The adjective is inevitable: this music is *this*, this execution is *that*. No doubt the moment we turn an art into a subject (for an article, for a conversation) there is nothing left but to give it predicates. . . . the predicate is always the bulwark with which the subject's imaginary protects itself from the loss which threatens it. The man who provides himself or is provided wth an adjective is now hurt, now pleased, but always *constituted*."[19]

Even so, there is some loss, since though English does have a tense system, for example, it does not perfectly parallel the French, nor do we have the same conventionalized specialization of tenses into those that are appropriate for writing and those that are not. Thus, part of the argument of *Writing Degree Zero*—indeed something of the special status that Barthes gives to *écriture* (writing) itself—is destined to be dampened by the translation:

> Obsolete in spoken French, the preterite, which is the cornerstone of Narration, always signifies the presence of Art; it is a part of the ritual of Letters. . . . Through the preterite, the verb implicitly belongs with a causal chain, it partakes of a set of related and oriented actions, it functions as the algebraic sign of an intention. . . . it calls for a sequence of events, that is, for an intelligible Narrative. This is why it is the ideal instrument for every construction of a world; it is the unreal time of cosmogonies, myths, History

and Novels. It presupposes a world which is constructed, elaborated, self-sufficient, reduced to significant lines, and not one which has been sent sprawling before us, for us to take or leave.[20]

In Barthes's later writing, with what Culler calls its "preference for loose and evasive appositional syntax,"[21] the emphasis falls more heavily on the individual word and especially on its shimmering capacity to mean many different and inconsistent things at once, once syntax no longer constrains it to a single value. Moreover, Barthes always played with and against the standards of linguistic purity as determined by the French Academy (an institutional commitment to the national tongue that neither England nor America can match), and if the aura of each separate word becomes greater, so too must the delicate interplay between the common and the arcane, the polite word and the vulgarism. Thus, according to Richard Howard: "The French has a vocabulary of eroticism, an amorous discourse which smells neither of the laboratory nor of the sewer.... In English, we have either the coarse or the clinical.... we lack the terms acknowledged and allowed in polite French utterance; we lack *jouissance* and *jouir*, as Barthes uses them."[22] At the same time, the sonorous and rhythmic qualities of the prose also becomes more insistent, in an effort to suggest the polymorphous play of language inside the body, the "grain" of the voice. On every side, then, translation grew increasingly difficult, and the translator was forced to choose between trying to render the sonorous texture of a phrase—"Le paradox comme jouissance/Paradox as pleasure" (in Richard Howard's translation of *The Pleasure of the Text*) or instead suggesting its full range of implications and associations, as Stephen Heath does in his Translator's Note to Image/ Music/Text:

> *Jouissance*...includes enjoyment in the sense of a legal or social possession (enjoy certain rights, enjoy a privilege), pleasure, and, crucially, the pleasure of sexual climax.... I have no real answer to the problem and have resorted to a series of words which in different contexts can contain at least some of that force: "thrill" (easily verbalized with "to thrill," more physical and potentially sexual than "bliss"), "climactic pleasure," "come" and "coming" (the exact sexual translation of *jouir, jouissance*), "dissipation" (somewhat too moral in its judgement but able to render the *loss*, the fragmentation, emphasized by Barthes in *jouissance*). [P. 9]

Indeed, such choices allow one to assess the sympathies and alliances of different translators, what each takes to be essential to Barthes's prose—the conceptual machinery, the social subversions, or the cadences—and to judge, as well, when a new period of reception had begun placing Barthes in an entirely new category. The fluidity and grace of Richard Howard's Barthes—"Foreseeability is a structural category, since it is possible to give the modes of expectation or of encounter (in short: of *suspense*) of which language is the theater" (*Roland Barthes*, p.

149)—is clearly distinct from Heath's deliberately "difficult" writer—
"The absence of code disintellectualizes the message"—whose language is
kept from merging too easily with entrenched, and idiomatic, English. (As
a result, the recent return of Howard as Barthes's principal translator—
after the "poststructuralist" interim of *S/Z*, *Sade/Fourier/Loyola*, and *The
Pleasure of the Text* [all translated by Richard Miller]—unwittingly suggested the emergence of a more accessible, more "readable" Barthes,
hailed by reviewers uncomfortable with his earlier works as a convert to
common language and common sense.)

Translators of Barthes also face the problem of *faux amis*—in this
case, of hidden discrepancies of academic disciplines and methodological
traditions, rather than the usual purely verbal associations. Stephen
Heath suggests: "There is (as yet?) no real overlap in theoretical context
between the two languages in question,"[23] but this is often hidden when
the disciplinary labels are the same. For example, since the Cartesian
cogito has never held the same central position in Anglo-American philosophy that it has in France, the studied assault on the primacy of
consciousness and the subject are difficult for us to place. The same
applies to the effort to invert Sartrean existentialism, to call unmediated
experience and being-in-itself into question—whether by insisting (with
Lévi-Strauss) that knowledge has its own, autonomous structures or, later,
emphasizing the will that conditions our experience, or the infinite
regress of semiosis, where each sign presupposes yet another sign, in an
endless chain of transformation that eradicates things-in-themselves.
Because the philosophical and academic status of Marxism is more uncertain in England and especially in America, the early structuralist debates
over the relative power of synchronic as opposed to diachronic accounts
of social order, and the implicit critique of historical progress and economic determinism that structuralism implied, are likely to have less
resonance. As is the reemergence in "poststructuralist" writing of a new
and displaced materialism. The key words that mark Barthes's own
change of attitude in this respect—*enunciation, praxis, semioclasm*—therefore evoke less to his Anglo-American readers.

Heath's fine Translator's Note to his edition of *Image/Music/Text*
struggles with this difficulty and tries to indicate where the crucial theoretical and ideological distinctions fall and how they might be translated
into analogous Anglo-American distinctions. But the Saussurian categories of *langue* and *parole* ("the system or code . . . which allows the
realization of the individual messages" vs. "the individual moments of
language use"—p. 7) are not a perfect match for the familiar Chomskian
distinctions between *competence* (the speaker's intuitive knowledge of the
rules of his language) and *performance* (what that speaker happens, on
occasion, to produce, including accidents and gaffs). Saussure's *langue* is
an instrumentally useful posit, one that allows linguistics (as Heath put it)

to delimit "its specific object and [fix] as its task the description of that object.[24] Chomsky's *competence* is an explanatory category rather than a methodological aid, a posit that (putatively) exists and thus affords verifiable predictions instead of mere descriptions. *Competence* is linked to the properties of the (idealized) individual mind; *langue* is linked to social norms that are shared by an entire speech community. Moreover, Saussure's understanding of the language system was rooted in phonology. The set of phonetic distinctions that any language employs is small and relatively fixed; one can discover them by locating points where substitutions occur until all the available paradigmatic alternatives and the permissible syntagmatic sequences have been inventoried. Chomsky starts out, however, with the sentence—where the set of potential combinations is infinite and cannot be inventoried, and structural relationships are often difficult to identify by observing surface patterns alone. Chomsky's quarrel with American structural linguistics was that while methodological categories like syntagm and paradigm might be useful enough for isolating bits of language structure, this in no way proved that they were actually part of the language system itself. Sentences are not just syntagmatic sequences of contiguous words, but consist of more abstract relationships that are ultimately hierarchical and logical rather than sequential. In addition, Saussure held that syntagmatic patterns above the level of the word were more or less fluid, a matter of *parole*, while Chomsky sees sentences as the embodiment of "rule-governed creativity"—it being a part of every native speaker's competence to know how to transform syntactic structures into a number of alternative surface patterns.

Thus, Chomsky's transformational grammar not only altered Saussure's conception of language as a fixed and delimited code but also made the chief source of evidence about the language system the speaker's judgments of what patterns are "acceptable." In place of an external, socially codified reservoir of linguistic items and the rules for properly combining them—from which speakers are obliged to draw—there were now the intuitions of the speaking subject. Instead of focusing on categories that are learned, and that vary from language to language, transformational grammar stresses the formal properties that are shared by all languages and that (by implication) reflect the innate capacities of the human mind. Hence, the founding assumptions, the sort of evidence employed, and the ideological implications—the position of the individual relative to the social order, for example—are enormously different, as is the status of linguistic theory (descriptive or explanatory, taxonomic or hypothetico-deductive) in each case.

In fact, the importation of American linguistics played no small part in the breakup of French structuralism, although only certain elements of Chomsky's program were actually assimilated. Thus, Julia Kristeva (Barthes's former student, and later colleague at *Tel Quel*) introduced a distinction between the *geno-texte* (a productive core, a symbolizing capacity) and the *pheno-texte* (in which that infinite capacity is channeled into a narrow, finished product)—a cleavage inspired by Chomsky's competence/performance, save that Chomsky identifies the former with *orderly* syntactic rules and the latter with relatively uninteresting variations and mistakes. The Chomskyan affirmation of the primacy of the speaking subject has also been useful for subverting the power of rigid Saussurian codes and introducing an element of play and change into what had seemed to be an oppressive system of a priori constraints. Strangely, as in *Language and Mind*, Chomsky's ideal automata—with its "rule-governed creativity"—has become a dionysiac force, what Culler calls a "presymbolic state [that] offers a 'natural' basis from which to contest the conventional orders of literature and society,"[25] closely associated with the undifferentiated "pulsions" of pregenital sexual energy. There is a paradox, however, in the poststructuralist account of the speaking subject. To the extent that this subjectivity is organized and self-conscious, it is a delusion, an imposition of the culture, an effect and not (as Chomsky would have it) the source of the symbolic order. Yet as a pure site, a mobile energy and place of praxis, subjectivity itself is held to be capable of undoing (however fleetingly) the constraints of that symbolic order and exploding its falsely imposed and confining cohesiveness.

Similarly, the notion of the "speech act" (derived from J. L. Austin's work in the philosophy of language, *How to Do Things with Words*) has been used in France, as it has here, to offset the limitations of the *langue/parole*, competence/performance dichotomy by suggesting that *parole* (or "performance") is not so arbitrary after all. But where the Anglo-American study of speech acts stresses the link between speech and its functional context, insisting on the highly structured and predictable nature of those links (and hence on their legitimate place in the scientific study of language), the French study of *langue* and social and psychological context stresses (following Lacan) the absolute "disjunction of the *sujet de l'énoncé* and the *sujet de l'énonciation*"; "the ways in which it [the *langue*] structures the possibilities of *énonciation*" (Heath, Translator's Note in *Images*, p. 8), and not the way the act reflects a preexistent context or an already constituted subject. Thus, the emphasis falls on the process of *énonciation*, as distinct from the product it produces, whereas, in Anglo-American studies the act of speaking is not distinguished from the speech act that results. *Enonciation* signals the primacy of the work of production, a signifying practice that surpasses the end product and may even subvert the whole fixation with products and results. The Anglo-American speech act would be (in French terms) both socially conformist and prey to the twin delusions of representation and expression, to the assumption that signs are simply vehicles for communicating what already exists without them, rather than for shaping the distinctions they convey. Indeed, the effect of assimilating Austin's notion of "illocutionary" activity to the Marxist notion of "praxis" is to stiffen the already stern structuralist antipathy to reference and mimesis. In an exemplary passage from Barthes himself, which Heath uses in his Translator's Note:

> It becomes necessary to distinguish signification, which belongs to the plane of the product, of the enounced, of communication, and the work of the signifier, which belongs to the plane of the production, of the enunciation, of symbolization. . . . what immediately distinguishes it from signification is thus precisely a work: not the work by which the (intact and exterior) subject might try to master the language (as, for example, by a work of style), but that radical work (leaving nothing intact) through which the subject explores—entering, not observing—how the language works and undoes him or her. [*Image*, p. 10]

The notion of linguistic acceptability, which Barthes adopted from American linguistics, is similarly skewed with respect to its original meaning. In transformational grammar, judgments of acceptability are used to determine whether potential sentences that the theory generates are, in fact, permissible sentences in the eyes of a native speaker. For Barthes, however, such judgments of what is acceptable suggested, not scientific evidence, but the antithesis of science, a way to wrench theory away from strict determinations of truth and falsehood. Acceptability became (perhaps willfully) a license for replacing the patient accumulation of data—at first making validity the chief criterion, and then simply "preference":

> The science of literature (should it ever exist) will not have to prove any particular meaning, but to say 'why a meaning is acceptable.' . . .
> This virtually scientific notion (in that it is of linguistic origin) has its emotional side; it substitutes the validity of a form for its truth. . . . the *acceptable*, on the structural alibi, is a figure of desire. [*Roland Barthes*, p. 118]

This kind of intertextual exchange, by the way, approximates Barthes's own notions of literary influence far more closely than Bloom's; for Barthes, writing "is transmittable only on condition it is *deformed*."[26] Thus, the career of Roland Barthes (according to Roland Barthes), "evolves according to the authors he treats. . . . The inducing object, however, is not the author I am talking about but rather *what he leads me to say about him*: I influence myself *with his permission* (*Roland Barthes*, p. 106).

Translation has even more bizarre side-effects than these—as in Barthes's unlikely advocacy of Bruno Bettelheim, in *A Lover's Discourse*, or his use of (the—for us—passé) Norman O. Brown to counter (the—for us—formidable) Lacan. And on the other side, there is the problem of determining just how seriously *we* ought to take Barthes's own pretensions as a thinker and a theorist. Stephen Koch, for instance, has complained that:

Here in America, instead of becoming the arbiter of taste he is in France, Barthes has seen his books fly—as Edmund Wilson once remarked that *Finnegan's Wake* went flying—direct from his desk (via Richard Howard's) into the classrooms of the academe, without even a brief rest in what teachers might wistfully call the "real world." Nonetheless in those classrooms, he has become *extremely* influential as a "theoretician" of literature. There is something very depressing about this development.[27]

The problem is compounded by the fact that so much of Barthes's later writing was directed at the proposals of other writers, whose status is similarly difficult for us to assess. Some of these—like Kristeva and Sollers—are scarcely available in translation at all; others—like Blanchot and Deleuze—have been translated only spottily (and often not in those particular texts that Barthes seemed to take for granted his readers would know well—"This entire fragment, of course, takes its departure from Deleuze's *Nietzsche et le philosophie*"). Others still (Foucault and Derrida) are now easily accessible in English, but have been translated in a way that situates them chronologically as Barthes's disputatious progeny rather than his theoretical coevals. Moreover, while Barthes's own writing passed through the hands of several different translators, other translators still have rendered his colleagues into English, making it difficult to trace a common vocabulary. One has trouble recognizing (for instance) that what is glossed as "the wrong object" in Barthes is called "the bad object" in translations of film theorist Christian Metz, and that both of these refer to Melanie Klein's study of the way children split the mother into two, opposed "objects" of desire and aggression. Similarly, what is rendered as "the Imaginary" in translations of Lacan occasionally becomes in Barthes the "image-repertoire," while the term *méconnaissance*—which has accumulated the combined force of Lacan's psychoanalytic skepticism and Althusser's Marxist critique of ideological blindness—is hardly palpable beneath the limp, respectable English of "proud organ of misapprehension" in *A Lover's Discourse* (p. 126). But, of course, the decisions of different translators make it almost as difficult to follow the (often checkered and rarely "progressive") development of a crucial term in Barthes's own writing, where (as he himself described it): "Each word *turns*, either like milk, spoiled in the disintegrated space of phraseology, or else like a tendril, down to the neurotic root of the subject. And other words, finally, are crusiers: they follow what they meet up with: *imaginary*, in 1963, is no more than a vaguely Bachelardian term; but by 1970—in *S/Z*—it has been rebaptized, transformed (even deformed) into the Lacanian version" (*Roland Barthes*, p. 126).

Although most of Barthes's writing is now available in English, there remain certain key omissions: *Critique et Vérité*, Barthes's response to Raymond Picard's attack on *Sur Racine* (and the whole gamut of Marxist, phenomenological, psychoanalytic, and protostructuralist studies roughly grouped together by Picard under the rubric of *la nouvelle critique*), which is his fullest effort to distinguish between literary science and literary criticism; *Système de la Mode*, the only attempt Barthes ever made to analyze completely the structure of a semiotic system—the code of high fashion, in this case; *L'Empire des Signes*, the sumptuously illustrated and delicately written meditation on things Japanese that *Roland Barthes* names as Barthes's finest achievement in prose. And with respect to *Roland Barthes* itself, the fact that Barthes's earlier *Michelet par lui-même*, published in the same series, has never been translated makes the later book seem far more "expressive" and "personal" (to use two common adjectives from the reviews), far more an autobiography of the "first degree" than it actually is.

> As everyone with an interest in French will know, these books have provided in the past chiefly useful short cuts (cribs even) to both the work and the life of great writers. The usual practice has been for the editor to select extracts from the writer in question in order to illustrate not merely what he wrote but "what kind of person he was" and (since the arrangement of extracts is usually chronological) the shape and development of his life and career. . . . The radical originality of Barthes' contribution is that he is his own editor of extracts nearly all specially composed for the occasion. His book is autobiographical but only by dint of calling in question the idea of autobiography as it has been practised in the past, questioning by adoption the future possibilities of a literary form.[28]

The net effect of the deracination, the ruptures, and the redistributions that translation effects is curiously close to Barthes's own ideal of textuality: a floating signifier without origin or owner, permeable to uncertain echoes and open to a hundred inconsistent readings as it wanders from place to place:

> The author is reputed the father and the owner of his work: literary science therefore teaches *respect* for the manuscript and the author's declared intentions, while society asserts the legality of the relation of author to work. . . . [But] the Text reads without the inscription of the Father. . . . the metaphor of the Text is that of the *network*; if the Text extends itself, it is as a result of a combinatory systematic (an image, moreover, close to current biological conceptions of the living being). Hence no vital "respect" is due to the Text: it can be *broken*; . . . it can be read without the guarantee of its father, the restitution of the inter-text paradoxically abolishing any legacy. . . .
>
> The Text is plural. Which is not simply to say that it has several meanings, but that it accompishes the very plural of meaning: an *irreducible* (and not merely an acceptable) plural. . . . The plural of the Text depends, that is, not on the ambiguity of its contents but on what might be called the *stereographic plurality* of its weave of signifiers (etymologically, the text is a tissue, a woven fabric). . . . what [the reader of the Text] perceives is mul-

tiple, irreducible, coming from a disconnected, heterogeneous variety of substances and perspectives: lights, colours, vegetation, heat, air, slender explosions of noises, scant cries of birds, children's voices from over on the other side, passages, gestures, clothes of inhabitants near or far away. All these *incidents* are half-identifiable: they come from codes which are known but their combination is unique.[29]

Yet even in this (plainly) utopian account of textuality, Barthes continues to invoke a fairly stable network of intertextual associations made up of "codes which are known," without which it might be impossible to recognize the plurality and irreducibility of the text. Something closer to the experience of *pure* textuality occurs when an English reader, unversed in French, confronts the handwritten script scattered throughout the English version of *Roland Barthes*. Preserved in their original form—as the mysterious traces of the absent hand that wrote them—these fragments are for English readers) not quite words—infinitely suggestive and utterly unplaceable, their graphic slash and curve is nearly indistinguishable from the doodles placed on the book's back cover to represent "signifiers which have no signified."

Still, the rootless translated text seems peculiarly vulnerable to reductive forms of recuperation. The most common kind of recuperation is the "star system," through which each text finds a secure resting place in the shadow of a glowing name. The market value of the name of Roland Barthes has preserved the myth of authorship ten years after Barthes himself proclaimed it defunct. Oddly enough, it is a native author like Bloom who comes to seem more mystifying; the more remote the author, the less discontinuity and unpredictability he is allowed. According to Steven Ungar:

> On the basis of a solid commercial market (almost all his books have been translated into English), he is the most visible of current French critics. But as a result of the voluble polemic with Raymond Picard which sprang up in the wake of *On Racine* (1962), Barthes is still linked with the *nouvelle critique* of the 50's and early 60's. Among more conservative American and British critics, he continues to incarnate a false image of Structuralism which refers less to a particular kind of inquiry or focus than to its reception in an academic environment prone to resist critical concepts that are not home-grown.....
>
> If Barthes is no longer the Structuralist he may never have been, where does that leave him and where does that leave his readers? Who, in other words, is Barthes for *us*?[30]

It is in answer to these final questions—and especially in terms of the project at hand, a study of the interplay between literary theory and theoretical literature—that I mean to write of Barthes. The account will have its own interests and artificial limits; but without them, other processes of recuperation are only too ready to set in. Thus, Barthes's later writing will inevitably be read as a fall (from more rigorous theory) or a return (to common sense and a more personal form—although the subjectivity that returns in *The Pleasure of the Text, Roland Barthes,* and *A Lover's Discourse* could hardly be the same after all that went before). Because of Barthes's position as the original, the essential, literary structuralist, he will be supplied with appropriate rivals—made by his readers utterly unlike or utterly (and therefore uninterestingly) the same as the Anglo-American New Criticism he and his fellows threatened to supplant.

> Already a century ago, Matthew Arnold denounced the 'French mania' for translating ideas into a revolutionary program. The Anglo-Saxon reserve in matters of theory has something to do with the assertiveness of theory. (Compare Barthes' propaganda for a radical change in our perception of past works of art with T. S. Eliot's laconic statement of 1919 that a new work of art changes the 'order' of all existing works.[31]

> ...There is nothing *as* theory in *A Lover's Discourse,* or any other book by Barthes, that comes within hailing distance of...the theoretical rigor and sophistication of—to choose two long-standing but underestimated Anglo-American theoreticians—Kenneth Burke or William Empson.[32]

And he will be championed or disparaged with reference to post-structuralists like Foucault and Derrida, his position changing according to the needs through which we perceive him. Thus, Said faults Barthes for treating the text as:

> ...a wholly integrated and equilibrated system....
> Reading and writing become, at such moments, instances of regulated, systematized production, as if the human agencies involved were irrelevant....

> ...[whereas] Foucault [has] gone very far in determining the social (and external) constraints upon production, as well as the discursive and cultural (that is, internal) systems that provoke and assimilate literary production.[33]

While, in the same volume, Hayden White groups Barthes *with* Foucault (and Derrida as well) as writers who have pushed the inherent inflation of structuralism to its logical conclusion—"A sickness unto death with language seizes upon the notion of arbitrariness...making of the arbitrariness of the sign a rule and of the 'freeplay' of signification an ideal."[34]

The combativeness and controversy of the French intellectual scene is not solely an Anglo-American invention, but surely it does have a strong appeal for the Anglo-American Imaginary. Something more than accident ties the sudden and excited outpouring of theoretical activity in this country—visible at fever pitch in Bloom—and our first taste of the imported blood of causerie. Despite a generally dismissive tone toward the French cultural scene, Stephen Koch admits that though "*Tel Quel* is nothing but an instrument of fashion, we should not perhaps altogether despise fashion. Whatever else, fashion provides focus and focus in turn provides energy."[35] Yet, interestingly, whatever Barthes was in France, he did not become for us the standard of intellectual fashion. Though read widely, even avidly, he had no real flock of epigones, no coterie, no secondary industry here to dispense him and explain him and offer final verdicts in his name. Jonathan Culler, who (with Stephen Heath) would seem best equipped to fulfill this role, patently refused to indulge in what he calls "intellectual hagiography"[36] and instead remained a commentator and highly skeptical critic for an entire corpus of theoretical operations of which Barthes was simply one practitioner. No one seems (at least, not now) to be able to stop the arguments by ritually invoking Barthes's name—as, say (without his willing it), Derrida's name has come to be used. To be thus open to cool and irreverent appraisal, to be utterly useless as a weapon in critical disputes, is a unique achievement in these much embattled and polemically divided times.

Indeed, the translated figure of Roland Barthes stands precisely in that utopian position that his final books struggled to construct:

> When I used to play prisoner's base in the Luxembourg, what I liked best was not provoking the other team and boldly exposing myself to their right to take me prisoner; what I liked best was to free the prisoners—the effect of which was to put both teams back into circulation: the game started over again at zero.
>
> In the great game of the powers of speech, we also play prisoner's base: one language has only temporary rights over another; all it takes is for a third language to appear from the ranks for the assailant to be forced to retreat: in the conflict of rhetorics, the victory never goes to any but the *third language*. The task of this language is to release the prisoners. [*Roland Barthes*, p. 50]

In this passage (as in so many others), Barthes stands decidedly apart from Harold Bloom, deducing from the current intellectual and institutional turmoil, not the need for heroism and the strength to impose meanings where none are guaranteed, but the need for fluidity and the grace to let go of what one cannot hold. The difference is not simply epistemological or even political, but simultaneously (and inseparably) aesthetic as well. The dialectic of warring opposites that is the source of drama in Bloom's theoretical narrative is specifically assailed by Barthes, in *The Pleasure of the Text,* as a trivial pattern of thought that simply substitutes one reification for another: "dialectics only links successive positivities; whence the suffocation at the very heart of anarchism. How *install* the deficiency of any superior value?" (p. 44). So too does Barthes's vision of intertextuality, with its infinite and slippery impersonality, eschew the definite outlines and the martial intensity of Bloom's embattled giants:

To try to find the "sources," the "influences" of a work, is to fall in with the myth of filiation; the citations which go to make up a text are anonymous, untraceable, and yet *already read*: they are quotations without inverted commas.

. . . each piece is self-sufficient, and yet it is never anything but the interstice of its neighbors.[37]

In such a system of continuous interchange and dispersed identity, of continual and unrepeatable permutation, the theatrical confrontations and disputes over possession that Bloom's theory stages become impossible, literally unthinkable. Not only is there nothing to possess, but there is no one—in the sense of an isolate and self-contained being—to possess it. There is, in fact, probably no more unequivocal expression of real loathing anywhere in Barthes's writing than when he describes the sort of "scenic" construction upon which Bloom's art seems to depend.

This theater, of the stoic genre, magnifies me, grants me stature. By *imagining* an extreme solution (i.e., a definitive one; i.e., a definite one), I produce a fiction, I become an artist, I set a scene, I paint my exit; the Idea is *seen*, like the pregnant moment (pregnant endowed with a strong, chosen meaning) of bourgeois drama. [*Discourse,* pp. 142–43]

If scenes have such a repercussion, it is because they lay bare the cancer of language. Language is impotent to close language—that is what the scene says: the retorts engender one another, without any possible conclusion, save that of murder; and it is because the scene is entirely bent on, aims toward this ultimate violence, which nonetheless it never assumes (at least among "civilized" people), that it is an essential violence, a violence which delights in sustaining itself: terrible and ridiculous, like some sort of science-fiction homeostat. [*Roland Barthes,* p. 159]

In Bloom, of course, the violent and melodramatic tableaux in which the ephebe confronts his precursor are staged to arrest the flight of meaning. Without such scenes, in which the ephebe—or the critic—takes his stand, there would be only the eternal advance of an omnivorous and inhuman void, a pervasive meaninglessness excluding not just sense and definition, but desire as well, threatening to destroy the excitement of the contest and the rewards of mastery. For Barthes, however, (at least in his later work) replete and static meanings were far more threatening: "We do not form oppositions of *named*, fractionized values; we skirt, we avoid, we dodge such values: *we take tangents*; strictly speaking, this is not a change of course; the fear is that we fall into opposition, into aggression, i.e., into meaning" (*Roland Barthes,* p. 140). At his most subtle moments, Barthes tried to avoid or to rewrite the very opposition upon which Bloom's entire aesthetic depends. Whereas Bloom feels that one must either treat meaning as a stable thing-in-itself (even if one believes this to be a heroic lie) or succumb to nihilism, cynicism, and despair, for Barthes there is another alternative, or perhaps a series of alternatives. In the words of Steven Ungar, Barthes tried "to dislodge clear and precise meaning in favor of the kind of continuous instability":

> Those who see the model of the two pleasures [in *Pleasure of the Text*] as leading to a critical paradigm of unbridled subjectivism should not fail to observe that this nihilistic moment in Nietzsche's meditations on interpretation yields to a subsequent yes-saying to the subjective nature of truth as a human (all too human) valuation. Nietzsche thus upholds a vision of the truth which contains error—"not the error which has been overcome in a new truth, not the error which those who like to themselves accept, but the inescapable error which is present even in the new truth." [Wilcox, *Truth and Value in Nietzsche*, p. 170][38]

Both Bloom and Barthes drew from Nietzsche's "fictionalism" the conclusion that portions of every theoretical framework are permanently beyond verification, and therefore subject to one's own peculiar tastes. In both cases, this led to an increased emphasis on the nascent beauties of theoretical discourse itself, encouraging the leap into theory as a form of literature. But for Bloom, fictionalism has meant that theory is wholly subjective, even solipsistic, with the victory going to the strongest will—to he who provides the most stirring or terrifying schema. For Barthes, the choice of a theoretical framework involves will and taste as well, but it remains possible to explore the grounds for choosing one theory over another; strength alone will not prevail. If values play a part in all our knowledge, this does not imply that we can never really know, only that our knowledge is not the neutral thing we once conceived it to be. Moreover, *Value* is, in Barthes, a theoretical category and not a given. *Bliss* is a value that his theory must construct, a new mode of pleasure we must learn to recognize and distinguish from those other meaner joys we have been taught to pursue. Indeed, pleasure itself is something that we must learn to separate from the culturally imposed assumptions that surround it, making it seem antithetical to all serious intellectual and political pursuits. Even in the (wryly seditious) embrace of hedonism, Barthes is never solipsistic—since the subjectivity of which he writes is too mobile to be possessed and too patently a product of the act of writing itself to be mistaken for a preexisting being. Barthes's is a nominal hedonism, meaning, not that it is unreal, but that its reality begins with and is sustained by language.

The critical response to Barthes is proof enough of how correct he was about our embarrassment and uncertainty in the face of pleasure.

> An entire minor mythology would have us believe that pleasure (and singularly the pleasure of the text) is a rightest notion. On the right, with the same movement, everything abstract, boring, political, is shoved over to the left and pleasure is kept for oneself: welcome to our side, you who are finally coming to the pleasure of literature! And on the left, because of morality

(forgetting Marx's and Brecht's cigars), one suspects and disdains any "residue of hedonism." On the right, pleasure is championed *against* intellectuality. . . . On the left, knowledge, method, commitment, combat, are drawn up against "mere delectation" (and yet: what if knowledge itself were *delicious?*). [*Pleasure*, pp. 22–23]

The very fact that Barthes's prose is often and frankly charming, even voluptuous, makes it suspect—as if duress in reading were somehow equivalent to rigor of thought. In fact, Barthes's popularity among Anglo-American readers, though broad, is hardly uniform. It tends to be divided between those who read him primarily as a theorist (even while expressing disappointment at the "fragmentary and random"[39] quality of his recent efforts) and those who, like Stephen Koch, feel that:

> there is an atrocious—and even 'theoretical' misjudgment involved in the elevation of Barthes to the role of theoretician, however much he himself may have sought it. . . .
> On the contrary, Barthes strikes me as a quite different kind of writer: a highly intuitive, intensely private (even personal) quite unsystematic aphorist and essayist in a very old-fashioned sense. It is true, there is a sort of aging child prodigy's fascination with grandly theoretical sounding abstractions.[40]

Even Geoffrey Hartmann, sympathetic as he is to the effort to "make criticism creative" and "reconcile learning with the love of language," applies epithets to Barthes that seem (unwittingly) condescending or trivializing—"Barthes as critic, semiotician, master of metalanguage, constructs an elegant confection out of his struggle with both fictional and systematic forms of learning."[41] The severity of Bloom's more orphic writing, its tendency towards the massive and the ponderous, seems to make his claims to serious attention more secure than Barthes's (increasingly) delicate and evanescent effects. This suggests an interesting, subliminal association in the popular mind: The more deeply embedded the sentence structures, the deeper (read: more Teutonic) the thought; the more the syntax works by "simple" conjunctions and appositions, the more superficial (read: Gallic, or "confectionary") it is likely to be. (This is not all superstition; apposition often suggests only the vaguest relationship between one phrase and the next, and conjunctions tend to mark rhetorical or topographical connections. Embedded phrases, on the other hand, become part of the subject or the predicate, and thus participate directly in the internal logic [causal, locative, attributive] of the sentence.)

Yet Barthes's characteristic manner has a "theoretical" rationale; it is part of his effort to make the "work" of the writing visible: hence, the need for effects that can be seen on the surface of the text. It was also his hope (perhaps more wish than hope) to avoid the dichotomizing and reifying logic of the subject/predicate construction. As he put it in *Pleasure of the Text*:

> ...tiny syntagms, bits of formulae, and *no sentence formed*, as though that were the law of such a language. This speech, at once very cultural and very savage, was above all lexical, sporadic; it set up in me, through its apparent flow, a definitive discontinuity: this *non-sentence* was in no way something that could not have acceded to the sentence, that might have been *before* the sentence; it was: what is eternally, splendidly, *outside the sentence*. Then potentially, all linguistics fell, linguistics which believes only in the sentence and has always attributed an exorbitant dignity to predicative syntax (as the form of a logic, of a rationality). [*Pleasure*, pp. 49–50]

The impetus for Bloom's "serious" sentences, on the other hand, is almost solely stylistic—its Germanisms are operatic, with closer affinities to Wagner than to Heidegger.

Barthes has argued, eloquently, against our tendency to confuse poverty of form with "spiritual seriousness":

> Discrediting the form serves to exalt the importance of the content: to say: *I write badly* means: *I think well*. Classical ideology practices in the cultural order the same economy as bourgeois democracy does in the political order: a separation and a balance of powers, a broad but closely watched territory is conceded to literature, on condition that the territory be isolated, hierarchically, from other domains.... Thus once again the place our society assigns to language is confirmed: decoration or instrument, it is seen as a sort of parasite of the human subject, who uses it or dons it at a distance, like an ornament or tool picked up and laid down according to the needs of subjectivity or the conformities of sociality. [*Sade*, p. 39]

Like Bloom, Barthes is a hybrid writer, but the balance is different. Bloom attempts to assimilate theory to extant rhetorical and poetic models (compounded of the Emersonian essay, the Shelleyan defense, the "marmorial reveries" of Yeats and Stevens, and the parabolic utterances of Kaballah and Gnosticism); Barthes tried to use theory to write his way beyond familiar models—which in his case, went beyond a single tradition of poetry, to include plays by Brecht and Racine, novels by Robbe-Grillet, Proust, and Balzac, and films by Eisenstein and Mankiewicz. Both men borrowed a good deal of their theoretical apparatus, and effected a change in the meaning of that apparatus in the process, but Bloom appears to borrow terms for their decorative qualities, treasuring their hieratic remoteness more than the operations they allow. Barthes borrowed words, entire frameworks, for the labors they could perform and, since they *were* put to use, they quickly lost their exotic otherness: "Right from the start, the notion of myth seemed to me to explain these examples of the falsely obvious. At that time, I still used the word "myth" in its traditional sense. But I was already certain of a fact from which I later tried to draw all the consequences: myth is language" (*Mythologies*, p. 11).

Bloom imports and adapts to his own prior purposes, but Barthes's interaction with other texts was more an effort to export himself—to "displace" himself from his own former positions (in the deft formulation of Stephen Heath).[42] It is therefore no surprise that the domain of Bloom's theory should remain largely unchanged, fixed upon the same body of poetry, however much his chosen framework alters, while Barthes's work continually extended, contracted, and redefined the object of investigation. More to the point, Bloom's theory is designed to preserve a certain notion of what literature is by engulfing anything that might oppose it; Barthes's theory—first in its subject matter, and then in the theoretical writing itself—was bent on changing the place that literature occupies in relation to other aspects of contemporary life and letters—from mass communication to political practices to scientific research. For Bloom, literature is threatened by the extrinsic claims that are made upon it—in the name of politics, philosophy, and science—and the problem is somehow to finesse these claims, to allow literature to stay as it has always been and to maintain the position and the traditional authority of literary studies, while reanimating them with the zeal and sense of purpose of rival disciplines. For Barthes—more closely associated with the problems of contemporary literature and more interested in furthering its experiments than in conserving its traditions—the chief threat to literature is isolation and impotence, a threat that arises neither wholly from the outside nor entirely from the inside, since literature is *constituted* as an autonomous institution by the culture in which it operates. The relationship between literature (or writing in general) and the larger culture was redefined again and again in Barthes's career, from his early Marxist analysis in *Writing Degree Zero* to his more recent, utopian proposals, but the necessity of the relationship itself was never in doubt. His concern remained to establish what it is possible to write, and why it should be possible, which gives his decision to embark on his own writerly experiments—rather than to await changes in poetry, novel, or film—far more weight.

> Literature is a *mathesis* an order, a system, a structured field of knowledge. But this field is not infinite: on the one hand, literature cannot transcend knowledge of its period; and on the other, it cannot say eveything: as language, as *finite* generality, it cannot account for objects, spectacles, events which would surprise it to the point of stupefying it; this is what Brecht sees when he says: "The events of Auschwitz, of the Warsaw ghetto, of Buchenwald certainly would not tolerate a description of literary character. Literature was not prepared for such events, and has not given itself the means to account for them."
>
> Perhaps this explains our impotence to produce a realistic literature today: it is no longer possible to rewrite either Balzac, or Zola, or Proust, or

even the bad socialist-realist novels, though their descriptions are based on a social division which still applies. Realism is always timid, and there is too much *surprise* in a world which mass media and the generalization of politics have made so profuse that it is no longer possible to figure it projectively: the world, as a literary object, escapes; knowledge deserts literature, which can no longer be either *Mimesis* or *Mathesis* but merely *Semiosis*, the adventure of what is impossible to language. [*Roland Barthes,* pp. 118–19]

In Bloom the effort to produce a hybrid text at once presupposes and reinforces the distinction between literary and theoretical discourse, but in Barthes the dichotomy itself is at issue.[43] As he put it in his study of Loyola: "Indifferent to suitabilities of genres, subjects, and ends, the seriousness of the form. . . has nothing to do with the arrangement of "fine" works; it can even be wholly parodistic and make fun of the divisions and hierarchies our society, for conservationist ends, imposes on language acts" (*Sade,* p. 40). *Writing* and *the text*—two key terms in Barthesian theory—are words designed to designate this interstice, this currently excluded middle between concrete description and abstract speculation, lyrical pseudostatement and flat assertion. It is this same interstice that his own writing strove ever more, if not to occupy (since it is as yet only a virtual space, and perhaps must always stay so), at least to mark out and project as a possibility.[44] The merger of theoretical and literary writing in Barthes parallels those other blurrings and neutralizations of which he was (and always had been, even before the advent of Derrida) so fond: "The Neutral is not an average of active and of passive; rather it is a back-and-forth, an amoral oscillation, in short, one might say, the converse of an antinomy" (*Roland Barthes,* pp. 132–33).

Which may, perhaps, help to explain an enigmatic wish expressed in *Roland Barthes* to write "not comedy of the Intellect but its *romanesque,* its novelistic theory" (p. 90). The comedy of the intellect would be its simple opposite, its parodic rejection; to write a *romanesque* of the intellect would be to complicate—to neutralize, transgress, and retranscribe—the usual distinctions and definitions, and to do so ceaselessly. One gets a better sense of what Barthes meant by *romanesque*—not merely novellike but closer to the wavering shadow between pure fiction and pure fact—by examining the writing that precedes *Roland Barthes.*

We are accustomed to considering the "real" and the residue as identical: the "unreal," the fantasmatic, the ideological, the verbal, the proliferating, in short, the "marvelous," may conceal from us the "real," rational, infrastructural, schematic; from real to unreal there may be the (self-seeking) production of a screen of arabesques, whereas from unreal to real there may be critical reduction, an alethic, scientific movement, as though the real were at once more meager and more essential than the superstructures with which we have covered it. Obviously, Fourier is working on a conceptual material whose constitution denies this contrast and which is that of the *marvelous real*...what we might call, contrasting it directly with the novel, the novelesque. [*Sade*, p. 96]

The specific filmic (the filmic of the future) lies not in movement, but in an inarticulable third meaning...the possiblity of configuration...

...[that] calls for a *vertical* reading....at once parodic and disseminatory....[seeking] the trace of a superior *distribution* of traits of which the film as experienced in its animated flow would give no more than one text among others....a second text *whose existence never exceeds the fragment.*[45]

The suffix (rendered by different translators as "-ic" or "-istic" or "-esque") seems to suggest a departure from a given genre, be it novel or film, and especially from the key assumptions upon which that genre is based. In addition, Barthes seems to use it to isolate "*possibilities* of configuration" from any particular configuration—something for which theoretical writing, with its abstraction and generality, may be better suited than most primary texts. Above all, the added suffix prods us to rethink any opposition that claims to separate the interests of fantasy from those of ideology, or the accidents of writing from the simple truth, stripped bare of the extrinsic shapes that interest and language impose on it.

Barthes's self-consciousness does not mean, however, that his effort to alter the position of literature by merging it with theory was uniformly successful. No critic has given a more exacting description of the temptations to which such a project exposes the writer, or been more savage in his assessment of the places where Roland Barthes succumbs to these temptations:

> In what he writes there are two kinds of important words. Some are simply ill used: vague, insistent, they serve to take the place of several signifieds ("Determinism," "History," "Nature"). I feel the limpness of these important words, limp as Dali's watches. The others ("writing," "style") are remodeled according to a personal project, and these are words whose meaning is idiolectal....
>
> The "reasoning" consists, in short, of a series of metaphors: he takes a phenomenon (connotation, the letter Z) and he submits it to an avalanche of points of view: what replaces argumentation is the unfolding of an image:...the metaphoric application will play the part of an explanation....
>
> ...What carries all before it is the flavor of paradox....
>
> ...What he says about the large objects of knowledge (cinema, language, society) is never memorable: the treatise (the article *on* something) is a kind of enormous falling off. Whatever pertinence there happens to be comes only in the margins, the interpolations, the parentheses, *aslant*: it is the subject's voice *off*, as we say, off-camera, off-microphone, offstage.
>
> On the other hand, he never makes explicit (never defines) the notions which seem most necessary to him and which he constantly makes use

of (constantly subsumed under a word). The *Doxa* is invariably allegated, but is not defined: no piece on the *Doxa*. The *Text* is never approached except metaphorically: it is the field of the haruspex, it is a banquette, a faceted cube, an excipient, a Japanese stew, a din of decors, a braid, some Valenciennes lace, a Moroccan wadi, a broken television screen, a layered pastry, an onion, etc. And when he comes up with a treatise "on" the Text (for an encyclopedia), without denying it (never deny anything: in the name of what present?), it is a labor of knowledge, not of writing. [*Roland Barthes*, pp. 125–26, 152, 98, 73–74]

One could go on and on with the obsessive musings of *Roland Barthes* by Roland Barthes, but it is important to break off, both because the book is a piece of the Imaginary, forever distorted by the longings and the loathings of all self-analysis, and also because one must avoid making it the master text for every other text by Roland Barthes.

> What I write about myself is never *the last word*. . . . Open (and how could they be otherwise?) to these different futures, my texts are disjointed, no one of them caps any other; the latter is nothing but a *further* text, the last of the series, not the ultimate in meaning: *text upon text*, which never illuminates anything.
> What right does my present have to speak of my past? Has my present some advantage over my past? [Pp. 120–21]

If *Roland Barthes* by Roland Barthes is the summary of neither a life nor a career, writing such a book—so dangerously close to the now forbidden territory of autobiographical self-indulgence—is still a significant gesture. It is part of the embarrassment of Barthes, relative to the rest of the "Continental invasion," that his prose retains a stubborn animation, a capacity to inspirit a given subject matter, to color it with euphoria or nausea. This evaluative and affective edge was never entirely absent from his texts, even when they were busy proclaiming the triumph of the abstract linguistic machine and the "death of the author." It is somehow easier to believe, reading the neutral tones of Foucault, that the "author" is truly dead; Derrida's critique of value and valorization is convincing precisely to the extent that he himself succeeds in settling nowhere, remaining perpetually suspended between different systems of value. Yet it is the peculiar task of Barthes to establish a space for value that will survive the general critique of evaluation and to disentangle the mobile energies and pleasures of affect from the traditional belief in a self who contains or possesses those pleasures.

For all his protests against the idea of development, Barthes's later writing still appears to build upon—rather than to retreat from—what went before, both in his own writing and in the intellectual (or intertextual) scene that surrounded him during his last ten to fifteen years. (As with Bloom, the emergence of an overt art of theory is closely tied to an

390 / The Critical Impasse

atmosphere of intense polemical exchange in which theoretical discourse begins to be measured more by the relationship between contending theories than by how well those theories fit the data.) Hence, a cautious developmental sketch is in order, tracing some of the factors that conditioned the change from literal theorizing to a self-consciously figurative theory—recognizing that the change may only be a matter of "returning," as *Roland Barthes* puts it, "in a new place." For in Barthes's case, the aesthetic and pragmatic features that play a part in the design of any theoretical framework were openly acknowledged, even at the height of (what he himself called) the "scientific delirium" of structuralism. Indeed, one might almost say that his change from one theoretical position to another *was* a change of aesthetics (and politics), that even such an unprepossessing book as *Elements of Semiology*—"a very dreary little book quite unlike the rest of his writing," according to Koch[46]—is not without its beauty. Indeed, the distaste that Koch and others have expressed for this phase of Barthes's work is exactly that—the expression of a taste that does not recognize itself as such.

> Public opinion does not like the language of intellectuals. Hence he has often been dismissed by an accusation of intellectualist jargon. And hence he felt himself to be the object of a kind of racism: they excluded his language, i.e., his body: "you don't talk the way I do, so I exclude you." . . .
> And yet (a frequent trick of any social accusation), what is an idea for him, if not *a flush of pleasure?* "Abstraction is in no way contrary to sensuality" (*Mythologies*). Even in his structuralist phase, when the essential task was to describe the humanly *intelligible*, he always associated intellectual activity with delight. [*Roland Barthes*, p. 103]

Thus, it is not too farfetched to claim that moving from *Writing Degree Zero* to *A Lover's Discourse* is like passing from *Daisy Miller* to *The Golden Bowl* or (since there is no reason to stay within the artificial bounds of a single oeuvre) from cubism via abstract expressionism to minimalism and the color field. In fact, Barthes gained a certain amount of notoriety for proposing just such an analogy between analysis and art in "The Structuralist Activity," comparing structuralism, not to the "hard sciences" nor even to the other "sciences of man," but to the principled procedures of certain contemporary artists:

> The goal of all structuralist activity, whether reflexive or poetic, is to reconstruct an "object" in such a way as to manifest thereby the rules of functioning (the "functions") of this object. Structure is therefore actually a *simulacrum* of the object, but a directed, *interested* simulacrum, since the imitated object makes something appear which remained invisible or, if one prefers, unintelligible in the natural object. . . .
> We see, then, why we must speak of a structuralist *activity*: creation or reflection are not, here, an original "impression" of the world, but a veritable fabrication of a world which resembles the primary one, not in

order to copy it but to render it intelligible. Hence one might say that structuralism is essentially *an activity of imitation*, which is also why there is, strictly speaking, no *technical* difference between structuralism as an intellecutal activity, on the one hand, and literature in particular, art in general, on the other: both derive from a *mimesis*, based not on the analogy of substances (as in so-called realist art), but on the analogy of functions (what Lévi-Strauss calls *homology*).[47]

Although Barthes's later books seem to retract this comparison, and to deny that art can follow the same principles as theory, they are actually championing a new kind of art (and calling for a more fluid kind of theorizing, as well).

> Many (still unpublished) avant-garde texts are *uncertain*: how to judge, to classify them, how to predict their immediate or eventual future? Do they please? Do they bore? Their obvious quality is of an intentional order: they are concerned to serve theory. Yet this quality is a blackmail *as well* (theory blackmailed): love me, keep me, defend me, since I conform to the theory you call for; do I not do what Artaud, Cage, etc., have done?—but Artaud is not just "avant-garde"; he is a kind of writing *as well*; Cage has a certain charm *as well*. . .—But those are *precisely* the attributes which are not recognized by theory. [*Roland Barthes*, p. 54; Barthes's ellipsis]

Theory is always identified with an activity or an operation in Barthes; this is perhaps the single most stable element in all his writing, the one principle that holds firm through all the changes of conceptual design and domain. Documentation and evidence alone were never enough; one must still somehow decide what to document and why. This emphasis on "choice" (even after it no longer goes by that name) is doubtless the residue of Sartre's early influence. In *Writing Degree Zero* (which both builds upon and takes issue with Sartre's call for a "committed" literature), Barthes invokes the notion of choice as a "meaningful gesture of the writer" that, though it can never be free of literary and linguistic history (both of which Sartre underestimates), yet establishes an authentic moment of freedom: "Thus the choice of, and afterwards the responsibility for, a mode of writing point to the presence of Freedom, but this Freedom has not the same limits at different moments of History" (p. 16). Barthes's goal is to defend, as a historically and politically responsible choice, the efforts of writers like Queneau and Robbe-Grillet to purge writing of all signs of literary status (a bourgeois heritage) rather than using their books to urge social revolution. But this same freedom to choose and take responsibility for one's writing is obviously available to critics and theorists as well. Thus, in *Mythologies*, Barthes insists yet more strongly on the pragmatic (here political) value of his own methods, above and beyond their simple accuracy. Indeed, since the mythic constraints of the modern imagination can only be appreciated by positing what one might be able to imagine, were those constraints removed, there is no way for demystification to be strictly factual or value-free. "The unveiling which it carries out is therefore a political act: founded on a responsible idea of language, mythology thereby postulates the freedom of the latter" (p. 156).

In the *Critical Essays* and *On Racine*, the argument has changed a bit, but the place of choice, or value, in formulating one's critical positions is no less prominent. Now, however, it takes the shape of an irreducible ethnographic relativism rather than political interests or the freedom of the Sartrean "project."

> Our knowledge never divides itself from our culture....
>
> ... How could we believe, in fact, that the work is an object exterior to the psyche and history of the man who interrogates it, an object over which the critic would exercise a kind of extraterritorial right? By what miracle would the profound communication which most critics postulate between the work and its author cease in relation to their own enterprise and their own epoch? Are there laws of creation valid for the writer but not for the critic? All criticism must include in its discourse (even if it is in the most indirect and modest manner imaginable) an implicit reflection on itself; every criticism is a criticism of the work *and* a criticism of itself. In other words, criticism is not at all a table of results or a body of judgments, it is essentially an activity, i.e., a series of intellectual acts profoundly committed to the historical and subjective existence (they are the same thing) of the man who performs them. Can an activity be "true"? It answers quite different requirements.[48]

Hence, structuralism itself becomes subject to the same principled skepticism that it directs towards its objects:

> Nothing in principle prevents a metalanguage from becoming in its turn the language-object of a new metalanguage; this would, for example, be the case with semiology if it were to be "spoken" by another science.... each science, including of course semiology, would contain the seeds of its own death, in the shape of the language destined to speak it. This relativity, which is an inherent part of the general system of metalanguages, allows us to qualify the image which we might at first form, of a semiologist over-confident.... his objectivity is made provisional by the very history which renews metalanguages.[49]

At about the same time, Barthes mounted another attack on absolute truth based on the fact that the object of criticism is not physical but verbal (as the critic's own framework is verbal):

> The object of criticism is not "the world" but a discourse, the discourse of someone else: criticism is discourse upon a discourse; it is a second language, or a *metalanguage* (as the logicians would say) which operates on a first language (or *language object*)....
>
> For if criticism is only a metalanguage, this means that its task is not at

all to discover "truths," but only "validities." In itself, a language is not true or false, it is or is not valid: valid, i.e., constitutes a coherent system of signs.... One can say that the critical task (and this is the sole guarantee of its universality) is purely formal: not to "discover" in the work or the author something "hidden," "profound," "secret" which hitherto passed unnoticed,... but only to adjust the language his period affords him (existentialism, Marxism, psychoanalysis) to the language, i.e., the formal system of logical constraints elaborated by the author according to his own period.... critical "proof," if it exists, depends on an aptitude not to *discover* the work in question but on the contrary to *cover* it as completely as possible by its own language. ["What Is Criticism?" in *Essays*, pp. 258–59]

As different arguments can have equal validity, so too can different criticisms. There is some sophistry in this passage, however—why should the critic be constrained to choose among "the languages his period affords him," if in fact any language will do? And how, if one is condemned to the language of one's own period, can one be certain of recognizing the formal system that an author has elaborated according to the constraints of his own period—how to know when one has truly "covered" it? Questions of this sort helped to precipitate the next (and final) phase of Barthes's theoretical progress, in which no language is privileged and validity itself is circumscribed, reduced to just one more value among the rest. It is, indeed, a suspect value, given the consistency and the immobility it demands, its mutually exclusive choices and insistence on noncontradiction: "Simply, a day comes when we feel a certain need to *loosen* the theory a bit, to shift the discourse, the ideolect which repeats itself, becomes consistent, and to give it the shock of a question. Pleasure is this question. As a trivial, unworthy name (who today would call himself a hedonist with a straight face?), it can embarrass the text's return to morality, to truth: to the morality of truth" (*Pleasure*, pp. 64–65).

Thus, though the particular standard of value, the "word-as-mana" may change, the site of Value itself remains constant. As *Roland Barthes* describes it (discounting the characteristically reductive asperity of autocritique): "In an author's lexicon, will there not always be a word-as-mana, a word whose ardent, complex, ineffable, and somehow sacred signification gives the illusion that by this word one might answer for everything?... This word has gradually appeared in his work; at first it was masked by the instance of Truth (that of history), then by that of Validity (that of systems and structures); now it blossoms, it flourishes; the word-as-mana is the word 'body' " (pp. 129–30).

It is only in these later books that Barthes calls aesthetic those values that impel and help to vindicate the choice of one theory over another aesthetic. In the past, aesthetic grounds were always tempered by other interests, subordinate to other (existential or political or ethnographic or systematic) ends. Even here, the aesthetic is assimilated to the psychoanalytic—"it is the extreme of perversion which defines [bliss]"

(*Pleasure*, p. 52)—and to the dream of a utopian social order where pleasure would no longer be suppressed:

> It is still a political alienation which is in question: the foreclosure of pleasure (and even more of bliss) in a society ridden by two moralities: the prevailing one, of platitude; the minority one, of rigor (political and/or scientific). As if the notion of pleasure no longer pleases anyone. Our society appears to be both staid and violent; in any event: frigid. . . .
>
> . . . The important thing is to equalize the field of pleasure, to abolish the false opposition of practical life and contemplative life. The pleasure of the text is just that: . . . for what the text says, through the particularity of its name, is the ubiquity of pleasure, the atopia of bliss. [*Pleasure*, pp. 46–47, 59]

But perhaps it is the psychoanalytic and the social that have been assimilated to pleasure: Different "states" (in the sense of either psychological conditions or political arrangements) come to be measured by their capacity to produce pleasure; different theories are assessed according to their tolerance for or interest in it: "These are books of Desire, not of Pleasure. Or, more mischievously, they represent Pleasure *as seen by psychoanalysis*. A like meaning says, in both instances, that *the whole thing is very disappointing*" (*Pleasure*, p. 58).

Thus, the "perversions" that figure so prominently in Barthes's work from *S/Z* and *Sade/Fourier/Loyola* on, are in reality subversions "as seen by psychoanalysis"; seen from the opposite shore, they are visions of heavenly delight. Fetishism, hysteria, obsessional neurosis become a convenient nomenclature for cataloging distinctive styles and structures of intoxication:

> We can imagine a typology of the pleasures of reading: . . . it could only be psychoanalytic, linking the reading neurosis to the hallucinated form of the text. The fetishist would be matched with the divided-up text, the singling out of quotations, formulae, turns of phrase, with the pleasure of the word. The obsessive would experience the voluptuous release of the letter, of secondary, disconnected languages, of metalanguages (this class would include all the logophiles, linguists, semioticians, philologists: all those for whom language *returns*). A paranoiac would consume or produce complicated texts, stories developed like arguments, constructions posited like games, like secret constraints. As for the hysteric (so contrary to the obsessive), he would be the one who takes the text *for ready money*, who joins in the bottomless, truthless comedy of language, who is no longer the subject of any critical scrutiny and *throws himself* across the text (which is quite different from projecting himself into it). [*Pleasure*, p. 63]

These categories lose their strictly symptomatic quality when they become identified with the aesthetic—which for Barthes includes all "meaning insofar as it is sensually produced" (*Pleasure*, p. 61). Without ceasing to operate, they now operate according to new premises and with a sly air of fiction. It is characteristic of Barthes that categories that once applied to the "object language" under study should later become applicable to the theorist's own "metalanguage" as well. In his later writing, categories of every kind and every level undergo sudden elevations and depressions; the language of analysis shows traces of the very perversions it had once presumed to analyze, and political values that formerly passed judgment are themselves judged by the new standard of pleasure.

> His (admissible?) dream would be to transport into a socialist society certain *charms* (not *values*) of the bourgeois art of living:. . . this is what he calls the *contretemps*. . . .
>
> (Might it not be possible to take one's pleasure in bourgeois [deformed] culture *as a kind of exoticism?*)[50]

While paradox became more frequent and more taunting in the later books, hyperboles and shifts of level were never entirely lacking in Barthes's prose. Take, for instance his coy decision to use Sartre's favorite terminology ("History," "Freedom," and "choice") to rebut Sartre's own position in *Writing Degree Zero*:

> Nobody will deny that there is such a thing, for instance, as a writing typical of *Ésprit* or of *Les Temps Modernes*. What these intellectual modes of writing have in common, is that in them language, instead of being a privileged area, tends to become the sufficient sign of commitment. . . . Writing here resembles the signature one affixes at the foot of a collective proclamation one has not written oneself. So that to adopt a mode of writing—or, even better, to make it one's own—means to save oneself all the preliminaries of choice. . . . Whereas an ideally free language never could function as a sign of my own person and would give no information whatsoever about my history and my freedom, the writing to which I entrust myself already exists entirely as an institution; it reveals my past and my choice, it gives me a history, it blazons forth my situation, it commits me without my having to declare the fact. Form thus becomes more than ever an autonomous object. [Pp. 26–27]

And certainly, in *Michelet par lui-même*, Barthes's "existential thematics" are more than a bit overdrawn; to summarize Michelet's relationship to substance as "munching on history" and to focus so much attention on his response to menstruation is to exaggerate the Sartrean/Bachelardean framework and to make a scandalous and hyperbolic game of applying it to texts. Going on to *Mythologies*, one finds that the "psychoanalysis of substances" has become a compositional resource, covertly creeping into the language of analysis itself and no longer located solely in whatever subject matter Barthes happens to be treating. Density of substance becomes one aspect of the ideal against which the mystified can be measured; it becomes as well an instrument of invective, a means for rendering our mystified condition hideous to us:

Plastic, sublimated as movement, hardly exists as substance. Its reality is a negative one: neither hard nor deep, it must be content with a "substantial" attribute which is neutral in spite of its utilitarian yielding. In the hierarchy of the major poetic substances, it figures as a disgraced material, lost between the effusiveness of rubber and the flat hardness of metal; it embodies none of the genuine produce of the mineral world: foam, fibres, strata. It is a "shaped" substance: whatever its final state, plastic keeps a flocculent appearance, something opaque, creamy and curdled, something powerless ever to achieve the triumphant smoothness of Nature. But what best reveals it for what it is is the sound it gives, at once hollow and flat; its noise is its undoing, as are its colours, for it seems capable of retaining only the most chemical-looking ones. Of yellow, red, and green, it keeps only the aggressive quality, and uses them as mere names, being able to display only concepts of colours. [*Mythologies*, p. 98]

Indeed, density becomes a more or less permanent resource of Barthes's writing. Philip Thody, in the midst of his intentionally deflationary "conservative estimate" of Barthes's career, still pauses to remark on "this almost physical delight in the handling of language which is one of Barthes's most attractive characteristics."[51] And other readers have been struck by it as well, to the extent of calling it an "obsession" or being tempted to perform their own thematic analysis of Barthes.[52] Yet such an undertaking is faced with the problem that Barthes's thematics is derived—his relationship to substances springs from and is mediated through his earlier theoretical commitments. Which does not mean that it is false or insincere, but rather that the exact degree of sincerity or hypocrisy is undecidable, perhaps irrelevant. What those who relish Barthes solely for his succulent phrases—and wish that he had left all his tedious theoretical machinery behind—ignore is that the pleasures of his prose are tied directly to his chosen theoretical design. Koch speaks of Barthes's "aging child prodigy's fascination with grandly theoretical sounding abstractions,"[53] as if it were somehow ancillary and irrelevant to the reality of his writing. Yet the fascination is inseparable and irreducible. It inspires the writing, often serving as a preliminary "logic of invention" (of which I will have some more to say later on). And it shines through the writing, a source for its ebullience and energy, its movements of attraction and repulsion. Ultimately, Barthes's peculiar gift, and no small part of the structuralism he helped to popularize, is to *make* "theoretical abstractions" sound grand, to turn a conceptual machine into something one longs to watch at work and to try out for oneself—for the sheer exhilaration of it. Hence, one must resist taking *Roland Barthes* too literally:

> In relation to the systems which surround him, what is he? Say an echo chamber: he reproduces the thoughts badly, he follows the words; he pays his visits, i.e., his respects, to vocabularies, he *invokes* notions, he rehearses

them under a name; he makes use of this name as an emblem (thereby practicing a kind of philosophical ideography).... In this way, no doubt, words are shifted, systems communicate, modernity is tried (the way one tries all the push buttons on a radio one doesn't know how to work), but the intertext thereby created is literally *superficial*.... No doubt the reason for this is that one cannot at one and the same time desire a word and take it to its conclusion: in him, the desire for the word prevails, but this pleasure is partly constituted by a kind of doctrinal vibration. [P. 74]

What Barthes, at his best, accomplishes is a transformation, not just an echo; his writing is a "development" in Merleau-Ponty's sense of a discovery of previously unrecognized possibilities that were both always there and never there before. Barthes's theoretical prose discloses latent capacities for bliss and ethical/political force in what had seemed prosaic beyond recall. It disturbs the value of a concept by prying it free from its original sphere of use, denaturing it, and making it signify anew. What had formerly seemed a necessary or at most a convenient way of organizing information (whether into thematic categories or linguistic paradigms) becomes a poetic device—sensual, mobile, unpredictable. It may be true that Barthes never completely "takes to their conclusion" the various categories he borrows. And when at last he openly declared himself a theoretical esthete, the threat of empty figures that require no intellectual commitment at all and excite no effort to test their adequacy—a kind of literary nihilism—became especially great. If everything is only "as it were," it is easy to treat all metaphors as equals, allowing them to fade and blur into one another in an indistinct subjunctive mumble. Yet Barthes remained alert to this temptation, far more attuned to the distinctive consequences of each new metaphoric transformation than *Roland Barthes* admits. Indeed, it is only in their follow-through that his borrowed figures come to life, only in moving from a dim "what if?" to an excited "why then": if clothing is a sign, why then there must be a grammar and semantics of fashion. If pleasure is the banished place, the blind spot of every system, then there can be no direct approach to it, but only continuously renewed subterfuges and asides. If love is discourse, then it has its own peculiar reservoir of figures and its own poetics. And whatever the transformation thus effected, the underlying question remains, why is this metaphor worth pursuing and under what conditions should we cease pursuing it?

Long before he officially proclaimed himself a follower of Nietzsche, Barthes's practice as a literary theorist and semiologist, his evident satisfaction in transferring models from one domain to another, was of a piece with Nietzsche's dictum that " 'truth' is only the solidification of old [or entrenched] metaphors" (*Pleasure*, p. 42). The course of his writing is actually a gradual accumulation of metaphorically extended models—the thematics of substance is temporarily supplanted by abstract structural analysis but emerges once again to make something distinctly corporal of the "body" of the Text and of the "material signifier" stripped of its ghostly signified. "Thematic criticism has come under a certain suspicion in recent years. Yet we must not abandon this critical notion too readily. The theme is a useful notion to designate that site of discourse where the body advances *under its own responsibility*, and thereby thwarts the sign" (*Roland Barthes*, p. 178). So too, the grammatical model is first stretched beyond its literal application to words and sentences (to account for the structure of narratives and certain other nonverbal signifying systems, along with secondary significations, connotations, and ideologies). Next, with a further and willfully exaggerated straining of the model, it is applied to the "language" of spiritual practices in Loyola and of pornographic combinations in de Sade: "For Sade, there is no eroticism unless the crime is reasoned; . . . in short, to subject crime (a generic term designating all the Sadian passions) to a system of articulated language; but it also means to combine according to precise rules the specific actions of vice, so as to make from these series and groups of actions a new 'language,' no longer spoken but acted; a 'language' of crime, or new code of love, as elaborate as the code of courtly love" (*Sade*, p. 27).

But by thus establishing a "grammar" of perversion, *Sade/Fourier/Loyola* also allows one to invert the figure and speak of the "perversion" of the grammarian:

> The pornogram is not merely the written trace of an erotic practice, nor even the product of a cutting up of that practice, treated as a grammar of sites and operations; through a new chemistry of the text, it is the fusion (as under high temperature) of discourse and body. . . . so that, that point having been reached, the writing will be what regulates the exchange of Logos and Eros, and that it will be possible to speak of the erotic as a grammarian and of language as a pornographer. [Pp. 158–59]

"To speak of language as a pornographer" is precisely what Barthes's next book, *The Pleasure of the Text*, sets out to do, while laying the foundation for a further figurative displacement—in *Roland Barthes* by Roland Barthes—in which the notion of perversity itself will be found insufficiently perverse:

> Political liberation of sexuality: this is a double transgression, of politics by the sexual, and conversely. But this is nothing at all: let us now imagine reintroducing into the politico-sexual field thus discovered, recognized, traversed, and liberated . . . *a touch of sentimentality*: would that not be the *ultimate* transgression? the transgression itself? For after all, that would be *love*: which would return: *but in another place*. [*Roland Barthes*, pp. 65–66; Barthes's ellipsis]

And so, logically enough, the next step is *A Lover's Discourse:*

> The necessity for this book is to be found in the following consideration: that the lover's discourse is today *of an extreme solitude*. . . . ignored, dis-

tude....ignored, disparaged, or derided..., severed not only from authority but also from the mechanism of authority (sciences, techniques, arts). Once a discourse is thus driven by its own momentum into the backwater of the "unreal," exiled from all gregarity, it has no recourse but to become the site, however exiguous, of an *affirmation*. [P. 1]

This kind of accumulative method, with its growing emphasis on transgression, is risky; it presupposes a shared body of acquired assumptions, a reservoir accessible to all. How else will readers recognize that a metaphor has "returned" or appreciate what *Roland Barthes* calls "that disturbing (comical and banal) strabismus of an operation that comes full circle: something like...a breakdown of levels" (p. 49)? Many of Barthes's Anglo-American readers, deprived of such a reservoir, have leapt upon passages in *Roland Barthes* and *A Lover's Discourse* as evidence that Barthes had simply abandoned theory, rather than doubled back, cunningly, upon it.

He had always, up to now, worked successively under the aegis of a great system (Marx, Sartre, Brecht, semiology, the Text). Today, it seems to him that he writes more openly, more unprotectedly; nothing sustains him, unless there are still patches of bypassed languages (for in order to speak one must seek support from other texts). [*Roland Barthes*, p. 102]

Everything follows from this principle: that the lover is not to be reduced to a simple symptomal subject, but rather that we hear in his voice what is "unreal," i.e., intractable. Whence the choice of a "dramatic" method which renounces examples and rests on the single action of a primary language (no metalanguage). [*Discourse*, p. 3]

But if this new writing evades metalanguage, it does so only by defining itself against various other available metalanguages—some of them of Barthes's own devising. It is an "innocence" achieved a posteriori and never (an impossible condition, in Barthes's view) a priori. Hence, the peculiar features of this ostensibly "primary language": hot and cool by turns, intimate then suddenly remote, full of shattered pieces of the very theoretical systems it repudiates, which stud the surface of the text like mock jewels.

The person with whom I can in fact talk about the loved being is the person who loves that being as much as I do, the way I do: my symmetric partner, my rival, my competitor (rivalry is a question of place). I can then, for one, discuss the other *with someone who knows*; there occurs an equality of knowledge, a delight of inclusion; in such discussion, the object is neither distanced nor lacerated; it remains interior to and protected by the dual discourse. I coincide simultaneously with the Image and with this second mirror which reflects what I am (on the rival countenance, it is my fear, my jealousy which I read). Bustling gossip, all jealousy suspended, around this absent party whose objective nature is reinforced by two converging visions: we give ourselves over to a rigorous, successful experiment, since there are two observers, and since the two observations are made under the same conditions: the object is *proved*: I discover that *I am right* (to be happy, to be injured, to be anxious). . . .

Jealousy is an equation involving three permutable (indeterminable) terms: one is always jealous of two persons at once: I am jealous of the one I love and of the one who loves the one I love. The *odiosamato* (as the Italians call the "rival") is *also* loved by me: he interests me, intrigues me, appeals to me (see Dostoevsky's *Eternal Husband*). [*Discourse*, pp. 65–66]

Algebra, mock-science, Lacan, and Sartre—all are here, albeit carefully dismembered so that none can form a full and consistent language or begin to exercise a mastery over any of the others. This primary language, so-called, is not really a single action (as the book's introduction suggests) but a jostling of separate analytic languages that pull each other down whenever any one of them threatens to establish itself on a higher, privileged level, to set itself up as the "last word" on jealousy. In fact, the last word here goes to Dostoevsky, whose novella is situated at the same level as other putative authorities on the subject (even temporarily promoted over them: "see Dostoevsky" we are told, not "see Lacan"). Such play is carried out consistently throughout *A Lover's Discourse*, which not only reanimates and reinterprets the all but dead metaphor of the Family Romance—"we shut ourselves up in a mutual kindness, we mother each other reciprocally; we return to the root of all relations, where need and desire join" (p. 224)—but also uses bits of Freud's intimate biography and his personal love letters rather than his psychoanalytic papers, preferring the analyst's own symptomatic behavior to his magisterial symptomatic readings.

Thus, *Roland Barthes* and *A Lover's Discourse* do not really dispense with metalanguages so much as treat them as if they were primary language—which indeed any of them may rapidly become if one lives with them over time and uses them as the mundane stuff of daily intellectual life. The result is two not quite consistent effects. The bold, reductively suspicious gaze of certain powerful analytic systems is abashed by denying them the power to coalesce and by preventing any one of them from having the final say. At the same time, the writing accepts the fact that we must all live with the consequences of these suspicions by treating these terms as part of our common parlance, an inescapable element of modern subjectivity. This raises new questions about where "the unconscious" can be now, when so much has been dredged up and forced into our consciousness—into, that is, our language. Barthes's writing is therefore almost the opposite of Bloom's frantic efforts to use language to wall out consciousness and to preserve a comfortable unconscious, full of oddly cozy and perfectly predictable mysteries. For Barthes, unlike Bloom, the power of a metaphor does not cease when its figurative nature has been recognized; one must still live with the concretions of intellectual and discursive history, even if one refuses to accede to them.

Ideological systems are fictions.. . . Every fiction is supported by a social jargon, a sociolect, with which it identifies: fiction is that degree of consistency a language attains when it has *jelled* exceptionally and finds a sacerdotal class (priests, intellectuals, artists) to speak it generally and to circulate it. . . .

He used to think of the world of language (the logosphere) as a vast and perpetual conflict of paranoias. The only survivors are the systems (fictions, jargons) inventive enough to produce a final figure, the one which brands the adversary with a half-scientific, half-ethical name, a kind of turnstile that permits us simultaneously to describe, to explain, to condemn, to reject, to recuperate the enemy, in a word: *to make him pay.* [*Pleasure,* pp. 27–28]

If there was always more than a touch of the figurative and the fictive in the models Barthes deployed, if his metalanguage was always a shade too opulent, too savory, to be the ideal disembodied and disinterested instrument of intellect, still, the balance shifted dramatically in the works he produced during the seventies. One need only compare the controlled, deliberately restrained treatment that the concept of "phonological opposition" receives in *Elements of Semiology* to the broad strokes and escalating metaphoric chain it inspires in *S/Z*:

The opposition between *biére* and *pierre*, although very small (*b/p*), cannot be split into indefinite intermediate states; an approximate sound between *b* and *p* cannot in any way refer to an intermediate substance between *beer* and *stone*; there are two parallel leaps: the opposition is still in the *all-or-nothing* category. We again find the principle of difference which is the foundation of opposition: it is this principle which must inspire the analysis of the associative sphere; for to deal with the opposition can only mean to observe the relations of similarity or difference which may exist between the terms of the oppositions. [*Elements,* p. 74]

SarraSine: customary French onomastics would lead us to expect SarraZine: on its way to the subject's patronymic, the *Z* has encountered some pitfall. *Z* is the letter of mutilation: phonetically, *Z* stings like a chastising lash, an avenging insect. . . . *S* and *Z* are in a relation of graphological inversion: the same letter seen from the other side of the mirror: SarraSine contemplates in La Zambinella his own castration. Hence the slash (*/*) confronting the *S* of SarraSine and the *Z* of Zaambinella has a panic function: it is the slash of censure, the surface of the mirror, the wall of hallucination, the verge of antithesis, the abstraction of limit, the obliquity of the signifier, the index of the paradigm, hence of meaning.[54]

Obviously, a great deal must have occurred in a very short space of time (a mere six years) to have made the nature of theoretical discourse so different. To some extent, the more richly figured, "aesthetic" writing serves as a defense against polemics, both those directed at the theory from without and those that the theorist himself might be tempted to mount. According to *Roland Barthes*:

This is perhaps the role of the aesthetic in our society: to provide the rules of an *indirect and transitive* discourse (it can transform language, but does not display its domination, its good conscience).

He attempts to compose a discourse which is not uttered in the name of Law and/or Violence: whose instance might be neither political nor religious nor scientific; which might be in a sense the remainder and the supplement of all such utterances. What shall we call such discourse? *erotic*, no doubt, for it has to do with pleasure; or even perhaps: *aesthetic*, if we foresee subjecting this old category to a gradual torsion which will alienate it from its regressive, idealist background and bring it closer to the body, to the *drift*. [Pp. 104, 84]

Yet such an aesthetic cannot wholly escape polemics (even if it does evade mystery), since to champion it—as this paragraph demonstrates—is obviously to be controversial. Barthes's formulation dares the contempt of militant demystifiers while at the same time patently aiming to outrage traditional aesthetes and literary Humanists, by coolly labeling them "regressive idealists." Thus, the aesthetic to which Barthes here returns cannot be the familiar one, but one that has been (and is still being—the groping of the prose continues) redefined in light of Barthes's own previous work and the proposals of his contemporaries.

We need, then, to examine Barthes's conception of the aesthetic, and how and why it has changed. But this depends, in turn, on the fate of several (interlocking) concepts, some of which have received their own official designations—like *writing* and *Nature*—and others that are more diffuse: a set of persistent, overlapping preoccupations with, for example, meaning and the binary. It was in his very first book, *Writing Degree Zero*, that Barthes posited the existence of "writing"—a posit that may be his most enduring contribution to literary theory, however often it has been redefined both in his own writing and in the writing of his *Tel Quel* colleagues. *Writing Degree Zero* situated "writing" between "style" and "language." Of these two, the former was understood as an ineluctable fatality, the rhythms and thematic obsessions that a writer cannot choose, but simply has. (Related to the Sartrean notion of "immanence," style seemed slightly repugnant at this point, but was capable of being recuperated through Bachelard's more "wholesome" phenomenological poetics and, much later, through the notion of the subversive "perversity" and "intractibility" of the body.) Barthes treats "Style" as asocial, while "language"—understood as a field made up of both codified meanings and grammatical habits that are "the undivided property of men"—"is a social object by definition, not by option" (p. 9). Language establishes the limits within which a writer must work if s/he is to make any sense at all—and therefore cannot be the arena wherein one may define one's peculiar moral choices and political commitments. That arena is writing, both a site of potential choices and the historical residue of choices that have already been made—for, as Barthes points out, writing easily becomes institutionalized and associated with different professions, times, and places. The past is always with us and thus constrains the range of choice: One cannot will away the fact that the language patterns one would prefer to use have been used before, so that to use them will be necessarily to sound like a butcher or a politician or a professor—or simply, sadly hackneyed, a situation to which the preface to *Critical Essays* refers:

> A friend has just lost someone he loves, and I want to express my sympathy. I proceed to write him a letter. Yet the words I find do not satisfy me: they are "phrases": I make up "phrases" out of the most affectionate part of myself; I then realize that the message I want to send this friend, the message which is my sympathy itself, could after all be reduced to a simple word: *condolences*. Yet the very purpose of the communication is opposed to this, for it would be a cold and consequently inverted message, since what I want to communicate is the very warmth of my sympathy. I conclude that in order to correct my message (that is, in order for it to be exact), I must not only vary it, but also that this variation must be original and apparently invented.
>
> This fatal succession of constraints will be recognized as literature itself (that my final message struggles to escape "literature" is merely an ultimate variation, a ruse of literature). [P. xiv]

Writing Degree Zero is concerned primarily with the moment when writing became recognizably "literary" and a "fatal succession of constraints" forced novelists and poets to formulate a stance toward this institutionalized literary language, to feel the weight of the accumulated values interfere between themselves and anything that they might, individually, choose to express or do with their language.

> The ideological unity of the bourgeoisie periods (classical and romantic), literary forms could not be divided because consciousness was not; whereas, as soon as the writer ceased to be a witness to the universal, to become the incarnation of a tragic awareness (around 1850), his first gesture was to choose the commitment of his form, either by adopting or rejecting the writing of his past. Classical writing therefore disintegrated, and the whole of Literature, from Flaubert to the present day, became the problematics of language.
>
> . . . Classical art could have no sense of being a language, for it *was* language, in other words it was transparent. . . .
>
> From an initial non-existence in which thought, by a happy miracle, seemed to stand out against the backcloth of words, writing thus passed through all the stages of a progressive solidification; it was first the object of a gaze, then of creative action, finally of murder, and has reached in our time a last metamorphosis, absence: In those neutral modes of writing, called here "the zero degree of writing," we can easily discern a negative momentum, and an inability to maintain it within time's flow, as if Literature, having tended for a hundred years now to transmute its surface into a

> form with no antecedents, could no longer find purity anywhere but in the absence of all signs, finally proposing the realization of this Orphean dream: a writer without Literature. Colourless writing like Camus's, Blanchot's, . . . represents the last episode of a Passion of writing, which recounts stage by stage the disintegration of bourgeois consciousness. [*Zero*, pp. 2–3, 5]

Writing in general, and literary writing in particular, is therefore an autonomous institution, one that is conditioned by other social forces, to be sure, yet also capable of conditioning itself, as it acquires its own independent history. A "committed" writing of the type that Sartre calls for is impossible because it ignores the specialized functions that literature has been assigned to play within the social order as a whole, and the fact that there is no writing common to all members of complex societies, some members even lacking any writing at all. No writer can speak for all the members of a divided society, nor can s/he hope to address them all in their own, native writing. At this point in his career, Barthes is ambivalent about the autonomy of writing. Ideally, it suggests a freedom of choice offered by neither "style" nor "language"; in reality, it has become burdened by its own past choices and corrupted by its position among other social institutions. The power of writing to subsist beyond the moment of its origin is liberating—it is not a thing confined to natural decay and determinism; it is projected towards a future; it is subject to one's will. But this same subsistence ultimately makes it confining—one is faced with all the writing one has not created; one cannot control the value of the options from among which one has to choose. The result is both an existential (the writer feels "inauthentic") and a political quandary (the writer is alienated).

> However hard he tries to create a free language, it comes back to him fabricated, for luxury is never innocent: and it is this stale language, closed by the immense pressure of all the men who do not speak it, which he must continue to use. Writing therefore is a blind alley. The writers of today feel this; for them, the search for a non-style or an oral style, for a zero level or a spoken level of writing is, all things considered, the anticipation of a homogeneous social state; most of them understand that there can be no universal language outside a concrete, and no longer a mystical or merely nominal universality of society. [*Zero*, p. 87]

One can see how writing embodies all the paradoxes of history itself, which both liberates us from natural necessity and becomes its own artificial necessity—a guilty heritage, a structure that complicates our moral choices, confines our practices, and may blind us to the possibility of introducing further changes and seeking a fuller human development. Human nature discovers itself in artifice and fabrication—one form of which is the fabrication of meaning—"it reveals my past and my choice, it gives me a history, it blazons forth my situation, it commits me without my having to declare the fact" (*Zero* p. 12). When a writer manages to fabricate his or her own meaning, this artificiality is a good; when s/he inherits a prefabricated meaning, it is instead experienced as an imposition. All the struggles to circumvent this situation through literary inventiveness cannot prevent such writing, in its turn, from bearing the secondary signs of self-conscious literariness. "Modern writing is a truly independent organism which grows around the literary act, decorates it with a value which is foreign to its intention, ceaselessly commits it to a double mode of existence, and superimposes upon the content of the words opaque signs which carry with them a history, a second-order meaning" (*Zero*, p. 84).

The most that writers can do, short of a political revolution (for which writing itself can never be a substitute) or a sudden end to history (in which writing is so hopelessly intertwined), is to operate on the writing they inherit and to strive to purge it of the signs of specialization and literariness in anticipation of a more homogeneous social order to come:

> In this same attempt towards disengaging literary language, here is another solution: to create a colourless writing, freed from all bondage to a pre-ordained state of language. A simile borrowed from linguistics will perhaps give a fairly accurate idea of this new phenomenon; we know that some linguists establish between the two terms of a polar opposition (such as singular-plural, preterite-present) the existence of a third term, called a neutral term or zero element: thus between the subjunctive and the imperative moods, the indicative is according to them an amodal form. [*Zero*, p. 76]

One act of neutralization is not enough, however; writers must keep on neutralizing each time a form threatens to become ossified. "Literature becomes the Utopia of language": "It hastens towards a dreamed-of language whose freshness, by a kind of ideal anticipation, might portray the perfection of some new Adamic world where language would no longer be alienated....[It] invents its language only in order to be a project" (*Zero*, p. 88).

It is striking to realize how much of *Writing Degree Zero* anticipates Barthes's later emphasis on "self-consuming" metaphors and how clearly it establishes, as well, the basic premises from which Foucault (with his discursive archives), Kristeva (with her poetics of the presymbolic), and Derrida (with his critique of presence and intentionality) will draw such sharply different conclusions. As one moves on to *Mythologies*, the problems of writing, of the natural and the artificial, of meaning and meaninglessness, become more tangled still. The autonomy, or "intransitivity," of writing is now more openly and crudely disparaged:

> If I am a woodcutter and I am led to name the tree which I am felling, whatever the form of my sentence, I "speak the tree," I do not speak about it. This means that my language is operational, transitively linked to its

object.... But if I am not a woodcutter, I can no longer "speak the tree," I can only speak *about* it, *on* it.... I no longer have anything more than an intransitive relationship with the tree.... Compared to the real language of the woodcutter, the language I create is a second-order language, a metalanguage in which I shall henceforth not "act the things" but "act their names." [*Mythologies*, pp. 145–46]

To operate on primary language in any other way than to neutralize or demystify it is to risk mythology:

Myth is a peculiar system, in that it is constructed from a semiological chain which existed before it: it is a *second-order semiological system*. That which is a sign (namely the associative total of a concept and an image) in the first system, becomes a mere signifier in the second. We must here recall that the materials of mythical speech (language itself, photography, painting, posters, rituals, objects, etc.) are reduced to a pure signifying function as soon as they are caught by myth. [*Mythologies*, p. 114]

"Writing" now becomes identified with such second-order value; it is reconceived as a higher-level sign composed of what are already, on a lower level, simple verbal signs: "I began to discuss this problem in *Writing Degree Zero*, which was, all told, nothing but a mythology of literary language. There I defined writing as the signifier of the literary myth, that is, as a form which is already filled with meaning and which receives from the concept of Literature a new signification" (*Mythologies*, p. 134).

Barthes wavers, in *Mythologies*, between several different and inconsistent accounts of *meaning*. One is (loosely) based on labor and use-value (hence the "object language" is praised for bearing the traces of the original labor and the interests of the user), another treats *meaning* as (variously) the signified object to which a signifying form refers or the conceptual value that it has been made to bear. As several of his critics have noted, there is little real appreciation yet of Saussure's emphasis on the purely differential nature of both signifier and signified. The signifier is construed as an independent material form and the signified as a freestanding "idea" or even as a physical object, rather than seeing each as relationally defined values. This is why transitive language is preferred; denotation and reference seem to provide unproblematic, immediate ties to objects, events, and concepts, which myth then pollutes with a disgusting overlay of illicit associations. There are also moments when *Mythologies* gestures nostalgically toward a mute Nature, a state of ideal purity and uncongealed process that even transitive language distorts with its fixed and artificial categories. Yet at other moments, the aesthete breaks through, and the artificial is valued more than the natural, because it promises a lucidity and purity greater than Nature itself could ever afford. Both attitudes converge in the famous essay on wrestling:

Such a precise finality demands that wrestling should be exactly what the public expects of it. Wrestlers, who are very experienced, know perfectly how to direct the spontaneous episodes of the fight so as to make them conform to the image which the public has of the great legendary themes of its mythology. A wrestler can irritate or disgust, he never disappoints, for he always accomplishes completely, by a progressive solidification of signs, what the public expects of him. In wrestling, nothing exists except in the absolute, there is no symbol, no allusion, everything is presented exhaustively. Leaving nothing in the shade, each action discards all parasitic meanings and ceremonially offers to the public a pure and full signification, rounded like Nature. This grandiloquence is nothing but the popular and age-old image of the perfect intelligibility of reality. What is portrayed by wrestling is therefore an ideal understanding of things; it is the euphoria of men raised for a while above the constitutive ambiguity of everyday situations and placed before the panoramic view of univocal Nature, in which signs at last correspond to causes, without obstacle, without evasion, without contradiction. [*Mythologies*, pp. 24–25]

The book later explains this wavering between nature and artifice, meaning-as-pollution and meaning-as-purification, as a response to the artificial naturalness that myth imposes on what is actually arbitrary and historical. Yet the divided attraction to the truth of uninterpreted nature, *and* to classical intelligibility (where, as in Molière's theater, all that matters is the refinement of the gesture and "there is no more a problem of truth"—*Mythologies*, p. 18) is not so easily reconciled. It will linger as a resource and a threat throughout the whole of Barthes's career. Indeed, though *Mythologies* claims to take on the analysis of myth as a thankless political task, when it actually unveils the intricate machinery of mythological imposition, there is a queer tremor of excitement, an unmistakeable trace of what *Roland Barthes* will later dub the *frisson du sens*: "that first state according to which the 'natural' begins to stir, to signify (to become once again relative, historical, idiomatic); the abhorred illusion of the *self-evident* chips, cracks, the machine of languages starts up, 'Nature' shudders with all the sociality compressed, sleeping, within it: I am astounded by the 'natural' aspect of sentences, as Hegel's ancient Greek was astounded by Nature and in it heard the thrill of meaning" (*Roland Barthes*, p. 97).

In *Elements of Semiology*, the sign itself—and not just second-order systems like mythology and writing—at last becomes autonomous, and language and its fellow signifying systems are granted their own "systematized set of conventions necessary to communication" (*Elements*, p. 13). This means that *all* uses of language, even reference, are mediated. Though plainly interested in establishing the nature of the *langue* or system itself, Barthes notes in passing that "it is speech which makes language evolve" and that the abstract language system "is at the same time the product and the instrument of speech" (*Elements*, p. 16)—a source of change that will gain added importance when the *Tel Quel* attack on closed systems begins to take shape. *Elements* also shows a far more sophisticated grasp of the differential nature of the sign, and exercises far more care to make its peculiar mode of existence clear: "Being neither an act of consciousness, nor a real thing, it can be defined only within the signifying process, in a quasi-tautological way.... a purely functional definition: the signified is one of the two *relata* of the sign; the only difference which opposes it to the signifier is that the latter is a mediator" (*Elements*, p. 43). The value of the sign is now clearly perceived to be the product of its relationship to other signs:

> For a sign (or an economic "value") to exist, it must therefore be possible, on the one hand, to *exchange* dissimilar things (work and wage, signifier and signified), and on the other, to *compare* similar things with each other. One can exchange a five-franc note for bread, soap or a cinema ticket, but one can also compare this banknote with ten- or fifty-franc notes, etc.; in the same way, a "word" can be "exchanged" for an idea (that is, for something dissimilar), but it can also be compared with other words.
> ...Saussure used the analogy of a sheet of paper: if we cut out shapes in it, on the one hand we get various pieces (A,B,C), each of which has a *value* in relation to its neighbours, and on the other, each of these pieces has a recto and a verso *which have been cut out at the same time* (A-A', B-B', C-C'): this is the signification. This comparison is useful because it leads us to an original conception of the production of meaning: no longer as the mere correlation of signifier and signified, but perhaps more essentially *as an act of simultaneously cutting out* two amorphous masses, two "floating kingdoms" as Saussure says. [*Elements*, pp. 55–56]

The economic analogy is here only a convenience, an illustration, but it will have portentous consequences in later volumes, when "the ideology of the sign" and the parallel between the assumptions that govern linguistics and those that govern economics comes under scrutiny: "Sign, language, narrative, society function by contract... the controlled exchange on which the semantic process and collective life are based.... [is, on one level] a bourgeois value which merely legalizes a kind of economic talion: *nothing for nothing*" (*Roland Barthes*, p. 59). Equally important, in later critiques, will be the apparently casual slip that turns Saussure's purely "functional" signified back into an entity, a "thing" for which the signifier is exchanged. Lacan will be the first to argue that the signified is just a hallucinatory resting place, that signification is in reality an endless chain of substitutions. Kristeva, Sollers, et al., will add to this their own insistence on the "materialism" of the process, each signifier giving way only to another signifier (rather than a disembodied conceptual signified). And Derrida will argue for the undecidable nature of the signifier, neither material nor conceptual, neither here nor there, but always in transition between the signifier it necessarily anticipates and the signifiers against which it distinguishes itself. Indeed, Derrida will take as his text the very passage in Saussure that Barthes (rectifying his earlier explanation of the "zero degree") cites in *Elements of Semiology*:

The element which is common to all the terms of a paradigm (-*ation* in *education* and *saturation*) appears as a positive (non-differential) element, and this phenomenon seems to contradict the reiterated declarations by Saussure on the purely differential, oppositional nature of the language: "In the language, there are only differences without any positive terms." . . . In fact, what seems the common element in a paradigm, is itself *else-where*, in another paradigm, that is, *according to another relevant factor*, a purely differential term: broadly speaking, in the opposition of *le* and *la*, *l* is indeed a common (positive) element, but in *le/ce*, it becomes a differential element. . . .

. . . The zero degree is therefore not a total absence (this is a common mistake), *it is a significant absence*. We have here a pure differential state; the zero degree testifies to the power held by a system of signs, of creating meaning "out of nothing." [*Elements*, pp. 72–73, 77]

Thus, even in this most serious and circumspect of all Barthes's structuralist texts, there are passages that anticipate the excess and the deliberate courting of uncertainty one identifies with poststructuralism. Even the binary opposition (that most sacred of all high structuralist instruments) comes in for some (polite) disparagement:

The importance and the simplicity of the privative opposition (*marked/ unmarked* . . . have led to the question whether all known oppositions should not be reduced to the binary pattern. . . .

. . . If we leave the plane of the "logo-techniques," to come back to that of the systems which are not artificial, which concerns us here, the univer- sality of the binary principle appears far less certain. Paradoxically, Saus- sure himself never did conceive the associative field as binary: for him, the terms of a field are neither finite in number, nor determined in their order: "A term is like the centre of a constellation, the point where other co- ordinate terms, the sum of which is indefinite, converge." [*Elements*, pp. 80–81]

In time, this gentle reservation grows into the wild "disturbance in classification" that *S/Z* finds at the (absent) center of Balzac's *Sarrasine*:

It is fatal, the text says, to remove the dividing line, the paradigmatic slash mark which permits meaning to function (the wall of Antithesis), life to reproduce (the opposition of the sexes), property to be protected (rule of contract). In short, the story *represents* (we are in a readerly art) a generalized collapse of economies: the economy of language, usually protected by the separation of opposites, the economy of genders (the neuter must not lay claim to the human), the economy of the body (its parts cannot be inter- changed, the sexes cannot be equivalent), the economy of money (Parisian Gold produced by the new social class, speculative and no longer land- based—such gold is without origin). . . . By abolishing the paradigmatic barriers, this metonymy abolishes the power of *legal substitution* on which meaning is based: it is then no longer possible regularly to contrast op- posites, sexes, possessions; it is no longer possible to safeguard an order of just equivalence; in a word, it is no longer possible to *represent*, to make things *representative*,individuated, separate, assigned; *Sarrasine* represents the very confusion of representation, the unbridled (pandemic) circulation of signs, of sexes, of fortunes. [*S/Z*, pp. 215–16]

Although *Elements of Semiology* continues to harbor a certain amount of confusion about the logical and/or metaphysical status of meaning, there is none of the apparent yearning for unmediated nature one finds in *Mythologies*, and none of the alternating horror and fascination in the face of artificially imposed sense. The very split between nature and artifice disappears, replaced by a benign acquiescence to the arbitrariness of the sign and a growing belief that all our knowledge and all our behavior—even when it seems most natural—is mediated through different semiological codes. At times, the mood is more than acquiescent, as in this passage from "Introduction to the Structural Analysis of Narratives" (an essay from the same period as *Elements of Semiology*):

> The "reality" of a sequence lies not in the "natural" succession of the actions composing it but in the logic there exposed, risked and satisfied. Putting it another way, one could say that the origin of a sequence is not the observation of reality, but the need to vary and transcend the first *form* given man, namely repetition: a sequence is essentially a whole within which nothing is repeated. Logic has here an emancipatory value. . . . [The excitement of reading narrative is] that of meaning, that of a higher order of relation which also has its emotions, its hopes, its dangers, its triumphs. "What takes place" in a narrative is from the referential (reality) point of view literally *nothing*; "what happens" is language alone, the adventure of language, the unceasing celebration of its coming.[55]

This celebration of meaning never loses sight of the possibility of distortion; it simply rejects the possibility of naked truth. "There is no reality except when it is intelligible," according to *Elements*, although there are different levels of intelligibility:

> Once the sign is constituted, society can very well refunctionalize it, and speak about it as if it were an object made for use: a fur-coat will be described as if it served only to protect from the cold. This recurrent functionalization, which needs, in order to exist, a second-order language, is by no means the same as the first (and indeed purely ideal) functionalization: for the function which is re-presented does in fact correspond to a second (disguised) semantic institutionalization, which is of the order of connotation. [*Elements*, p. 42]

"Second-order meanings" remain a principal concern in *Elements*, as they were in *Mythologies*, and the relationship between primary and secondary values is visualized in precisely the same way: as a spatial hierarchy in which one system is literally fastened on top of the other. *Elements*, however, introduces a distinction between two different kinds of second–order values—"connotation," in which an existing sign becomes the signifier of a supplementary signified, and "metalanguage," in which a new signifier is applied to an extant sign to isolate and label the elements that compose it.

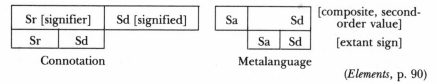

| Sr [signifier] | Sd [signified] | | Sa | | Sd | [composite, second-order value] |

| Sr | Sd | | | Sa | Sd | [extant sign] |

Connotation   Metalanguage

(*Elements*, p. 90)

The diagram is visually elegant but difficult to use; one cannot really separate secondary and primary meanings without first establishing when meanings are equivalent in all other respects and differ only in certain "secondary" features. Usually this means appealing to referential or to functional equivalence: "House" and "home," e.g., are equally domiciles, but differ in their secondary associations. Yet this is to prejudge which features of language are really primary, truly essential. It grants reference a secret privilege and reifies a certain pattern of "normal" usage, while ignoring the fact that different features of meaning will appear inessential or secondary as the situation of use changes. Paradoxically, it was precisely Barthes's appreciation for the relativity of "essential" and "accidental" features that led him to propose a "linguistics of connotation" in the first place:

> This linguistics, hardly foreseen by Saussure, can assume a great importance wherever fixed syntagms (or stereotypes) are found in abundance, which is probably the case in mass-languages, and every time non-signifying variations form a second-order corpus of signifiers, which is the case in strongly connotated languages: the rolled *r* is a mere combinative variant at the denotative level, but in the speech of the theatre, for instance, it signals a country accent and therefore is a part of a code, without which the message of "ruralness" could not be either emitted or perceived. [*Elements*, p. 20]

Such (inadvertant) reification of norms is a by-product of Barthes's linguistic methodology, which naturally grants precedence to those distinctions that establish different phonological and syntactic categories over those that seem functionless in this regard. This is one reason for his subsequent disaffection with linguistics:

> Denotation would here be a scientific myth: that of a "true" state of language, as if every sentence had inside it an *etymon* (origin and truth). *Denotation/connotation*: this double concept therefore applies only within the field of truth. Each time I need to test a message (to demystify it), I subject it to some external instance, I reduce it to a kind of uncouth rind, which forms its true substratum. The opposition therefore functions only in the context of a critical operation analogous to an experiment in chemical analysis: each time I believe in the truth, I have need of denotation. [*Roland Barthes*, p. 67]

Indeed, one of the chief complaints against science as a whole, in the later books, will be the fact that it demands replication, reproducible results, and hence cannot avoid reifying the phenomena it studies. Science must treat every difference as an accidental and unimportant departure from what is (underneath it all) the "same thing."

> We are today incapable of conceiving a true science of becoming (which alone might assemble our pleasure...): "A tree is a new thing at every instant; we affirm the *form* because we do not seize the subtlety of an absolute moment" (Nietzsche).
> The Text too is this tree whose (provisional) nomination we owe to the coarseness of our organs. We are scientific because we lack subtlety. [*Pleasure*, pp. 60–61]

Significantly, Barthes's analysis of Balzac in *S/Z* breaks with the notion that denotation and connotation are separate levels. He refuses to place any of the five codes of reading he isolates there on a plane above or below any of the others. "The five codes create a kind of network, a *topos* through which the entire text passes (or rather, in passing, becomes text). Thus, if we make no effort to structure each code, or the five codes among themselves, we do so deliberately, in order to assume the multivalence of the text, its partial reversibility" (*S/Z*, p. 20). The static and literal-minded box diagram gives way to a deliberately mobile tree diagram in which nodes unfold and branch out in several different directions at once.

> As the utterance proceeds, the rhetorical code is superimposed on the proairetic [action] code,...but the discourse expands by branching out....we thus arrive at a proairetic (often trellised) tree whose forks and new joints represent the incessant transformation of the sentence line into textual volume:

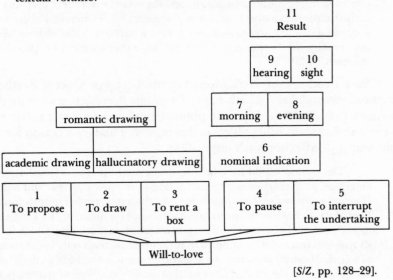

[*S/Z*, pp. 128–29].

Another break between Barthes's later work and *Elements of Semiology* is the status accorded to metalanguage. Whereas *Mythologies* treats any second-order languages as a "fall" from primary, "transitive" speech, *Elements* seems to honor the transparency of scientific metalanguages, which (purportedly) do nothing more than analyze the object language, without assigning parasitic values to it. True, the book ends by arguing that this objectivity is only "provisional," that, with time, each metalanguage must submit to newer metalanguages that will reveal its biases and the arbitrariness of its distinctions. Yet the prose retains the aloof tone of the dispassionate expert—so unlike the political vehemence of the mythologist. It is this expert who will be the butt of endless jokes to come, which will stress instead his lustfulness, his compulsiveness, and the concealed self-interest that lies buried beneath his airs of neutral specialization.

> The obsessive would experience the voluptuous release of the letter, of secondary, disconnected languages, of metalanguages (this class would include all logophiles, linguists, semioticians...).
>
> What relation can there be between the pleasure of the text and the institutions of the text? Very slight. The theory of the text postulates bliss, but it has little institutional future....this theory can produce only theoreticians or practitioners, not specialists (critics, researchers, professors, students). [*Pleasures*, pp. 63, 60]

Of course, Lévi-Strauss himself had acknowledged (in 1964, the same year that saw the publication of *Elements of Semiology*) that the metalanguage in which he isolated the basic units of a myth was itself no more than one more transformation, one more version of that myth.[56] But even this renunciation of the privileges of the analyst was too little. The belief that one was simply transforming, providing a structural equivalent of the original, soon seemed too sanguine. Why should one even try to preserve the structure of the original, rather than disrupting it or exposing its exclusions and its blind spots?—transformations only reinforce the impression that the structure has the inevitability and the oiled efficiency of a machine. Why should one even assume that the closed and perfectly symmetrical systems that structuralism was so fond of positing were truly "there"—and not, at least in part, the product of the analyst's own fondness? Lévi-Strauss's much vaunted claim to be studying "being in relation to itself " began to seem epistemologically naive in light of his own confessed "mythology of the mythologist" and in light of the difficulty of "proving" the truth of any given taxonomic framework.[57]

But rather than following the Anglo-American example and tightening the scientific claims of the linguistic model (making it predictive, demanding independent evidence), the French dissatisfaction turned toward critique instead—at least in Barthes's own circle.[58] Interest shifted to identifying the presuppositions and the passions invested in structuralism—why it favored balanced oppositions and discrete categories, preferring finality and closure to less rigid and immutable designs. As attention turned to the epistemological preconceptions and political consequences of a given conceptual instrument (rather than its adequacy and reliability), Barthes's earlier, almost lyrical enthusiasm for the semiological machine began to fade. Compare the exhilarated sense of imaginative possibility in his *Critical Essays* to his bemused (though not entirely unsympathetic) tone in *Sade/Fourier/Loyola*:

> The sign is chosen from a finite organized reservoir, and this summons is the sovereign act of signification: imagination of the surveyor, the geometrician, the owner of the world who finds himself at his ease on his property, since man, in order to signify, has merely to choose from what is presented to him already prestructured either by his brain (in the binarist hypothesis), or by the material finitude of forms. The syntagmatic imagination no longer sees the sign in its perspective, it *foresees* it in its extension: its antecedent or consequent links, the bridges it extends to other signs; this is a "stemmatous" imagination of the chain or the network; hence the dynamics of the image here is that of an arrangement of mobile, substitutive parts,... a strictly fabricative or even *functional* imagination.[59]
>
> It is in this negative, repellent sense that—at least at the outset—the Ignation imagination must be interpreted....
>
> ...The *Exercises* is somehow machine-like, in the cybernetic sense of the term....
>
> ...The obsessional character of the *Exercises* blazes forth in the accounting passion transmitted to the exercitant: as soon as an object, intellectual or imaginary, appears, it is broken up, divided, numbered. The accountancy is obsessional not only because it is infinite, but above all because it engenders its own errors; being a matter of accounting for his sins,...the fact of accounting for them in a faulty way will in turn become an error that must be added on to the original list....In fact, it is the neurotic nature of obsession to set up a self-maintaining machine, a kind of homeostat of error, constructed in such a way that its function alone provides it with operating energy. [*Sade*, pp. 49, 57, 70]

Yet if the semiotic machine now seems, occasionally, "repellent," the detour through structuralism and the postulated autonomy of the sign had profound consequences for Barthes, particularly for his aesthetic. From it, he gained the sense of meaning as a differential play of forms, rather than a grotesque and unnatural imposition. From it, he also gained a "propensity for division" (as *Roland Barthes* calls it), for "partitions, glittering details,...a bird's-eye view of fields, windows, haiku, line drawing, script,...all the articulation of the semanticism or all the raw material of the fetishist" (p. 70). This taste never entirely deserted him, even when it became a subject for parody and transgression. Structuralism also taught Barthes to be critical of mechanical causation and to reject brute determinism in either social or literary history. Though his later books no longer agree with "Literature Today," in *Critical Essays*, that "to write" is "an intransitive verb," they preserve the same blissful sense of the vacancy of sheer signification. His ability to savor the pure and uninterpreted play of the signifier is the result of his initial interest in the operations of the signifying system itself, rather than in supplying interpretive readings. *Critical Essays* goes far beyond his earlier, ambivalent remarks in *Mythologies* and *Writing Degree Zero* in this regard:

> Once a language ceases to be incorporated into a *praxis*, once it begins to recount, to recite reality, thereby becoming a language for itself, second meanings appear, reversed and evasive, and consequently the institution of something which we call, precisely, *literature*.
>
> . . . literature is only language deprived of all transitivity, forever doomed to signify itself just when it wants to signify only the world, literature is a motionless object, separated from a world in the making. But also, each time we do not *close* the description, each time we write ambiguously enough to suspend meaning, each time we proceed as if the world signified though without saying *what*, then writing releases a question, it troubles what exists, though without ever preforming what does not yet exist, it gives the world an energy: in short, literature does not permit us to walk, but it permits us to breathe.[60]

If one turns from this to a more recent book like *Roland Barthes*, it is obvious how much has been retained, even if it does occupy a new place:

> Meaning, before collapsing into insignificance, shudders still: *there is meaning*, but this meaning does not permit itself to be "caught"; it remains fluid, shuddering with a faint ebullition. The ideal state of sociality is thereby declared: an enormous and perpetual rustling animates with countless meanings which explode, crepitate, burst out without ever assuming the definitive form of a sign grimly weighted by its signified: a happy and impossible theme, for this ideally thrilling meaning is pitilessly recuperated by a solid meaning (that of the *Doxa*) or by a null meaning (that of the mystiques of liberation). [*Roland Barthes*, pp. 97–98]

As was the case with Bloom (and even Sontag), the social turmoil of the late sixties established a climate of challenge that led Barthes to reevaluate his own work and to seek fresh justifications for literary studies and for theory in general. Indeed, the abrupt and dramatic rupture of May 1968 (with its subsequent public rites of intellectual self-criticism) has no perfect Anglo-American equivalent. But if such events posed the questions, writers themselves were responsible for their own answers, which could be strikingly different. Sontag became more social theorist and less esthete and novelist; Bloom redoubled his defense of Romanticism and, as it were, backed into his own version of theory-as-severe-poem. At the same moment, Barthes was seeking ways to *reduce* the severity of his theory and to defend textual pleasure as far more radical than conventional politics. Part of that defense was the reshaping of his own writing into a utopian text merging theoretical and aesthetic interests indistinguishably. As *The Pleasure of the Text* describes it:

> What it establishes, its precise accomplishment, its assumption, is a practice (that of the writer), not a science, a method, a research, a pedagogy....
>
> ...There is only one way left to escape the alienation of present-day society: *to retreat ahead of it*: every old language is immediately compromised, and every language becomes old once it is repeated. Now, encratic language (the language produced and spread under the protection of power) is statutorily a language of repetition; all official institutions of language are repeating machines: school, sports, advertising, popular songs, news, all continually repeat the same structure, the same meaning, often the same words; the stereotype is a political figure, the major figure of ideology. Confronting it, the New is bliss....a (marginal, eccentric) impulse toward the New—a desperate impulse that can reach the point of destroying discourse: an attempt to reproduce in historical terms the bliss repressed beneath the stereotype. [Pp. 60, 40–41]

The basis for a critique of structuralism's "encreatic" tendencies was already present in structuralism itself: especially in the notion of differentiation, which eventually threatens the self-containment and stability of any system. If meaning is only difference, then there is (in Derrida's words) no "center which arrests and founds," making possible a "joyous affirmation of the freeplay of the world without truth, without origin, offered to an active interpretation."[61] But it also makes possible an interminable suspicion, a profound uncertainty about how any chosen site of observation distorts what can be observed. Such is the thrust of Lacan's teasing question, "Is the subject I speak of when I speak the same as the subject who speaks?"[62]—a question ultimately touching analytic patient and analyst alike. The theoretical subject is no safer from the delusions of his or her discourse than the ordinary speaking subject—had not Lacan himself his nostalgias (for "presence," as revealed in his treatment in *Écrits* of the "lost object" at the root of semiosis), his a priori limits (e.g., his stress on the "normal" subject's acceptance of the authority of the *"Nom du Père"*) his hidden "phallocentrism" (the phallus functioning for him as the "gold standard" functions to pin down the value of the signifier in monetary matters)?[63] Thus, the pursuit of structuralist premises stimulated both guilt-ridden autocriticism and its opposite—bold affirmations of biases and interpretive activism that now seemed inevitable.

To write theory in such a context is necessarily to write at risk—exposed on all sides to warring claims and a widening array of methods and countermethods. Barthes had himself contributed his share to the available store of theoretical weapons by extending the notion of language and semiosis to include economic, political, and psychological structures. As a result, there was no way to safely posit a model of "the

Text" without at the same time raising questions about its economic, political, and psychological predilections—its implicit bourgeois or totalitarian or neurotic leanings. If Barthes's later writing is flooded with teasing proposals for theories that will never be developed—"active Philology" (to evaluate the "force which directs (or attracts)" an utterance), a "linguistics of value" (to study the worth signs have for the Imaginary), and so forth[64]—the incompletion is neither casual nor careless. Rather, it is the exercise of a care so extreme that no proposal can escape unscathed. Ultimately, it is no longer a matter of allowing one's theory to be contaminated by a particular ideology but of allowing it to solidify around any fixed position at all. As *The Pleasure of the Text* puts it:

> For each jargon (each fiction) fights for hegemony; if power is on its side, it spreads everywhere in the general and daily occurrences of social life, it becomes *doxa*, nature: . . . but even out of power, even when power is against it, the rivalry is reborn, the jargons split and struggle among themselves. . . .
>
> . . . "Every ideological activity is presented in the form of compositionally completed utterances." Let us also take Julia Kristeva's proposition in reverse: any completed utterance runs the risk of being ideological. In fact, it is the power of completion which defines sentence mastery and marks, as with a supreme, dearly won, conquered *savoir-faire*, the agents of the Sentence. [Pp. 28, 50]

The problem of ideological recuperation is an old one for Barthes; *Mythologies* devotes several pages to the question of whether any language can resist it:

> Are all primary languages a prey for myth? Is there no meaning which can resist this capture with which form threatens it? In fact, nothing can be safe from myth, myth can develop its second-order schema from any meaning and, as we saw, start from the very lack of meaning. . . .
>
> When the meaning is too full for myth to be able to invade it, myth goes around it, carries it away bodily. This is what happens to mathematical language. In itself, it cannot be distorted, it has taken all possible precautions against *interpretation*: no parasitical signification can worm itself into it. And this is why, precisely, myth takes it away en bloc; it takes a certain mathematical formula ($E = mc^2$), and makes of this unalterable meaning the pure signifier of mathematicity. [Pp. 131–32]

But over time, ideology changes from a parasite that violates the purity of formalized languages "after the fact" to something that is invested in them from the start. Even an "uninterpreted calculus" has its ideal of order, its preferred logic, its tendency to harden and congeal. Thus, in "Change the Object Itself: Myth Today," Barthes turns his attention to the analytic pretensions of *Mythologies* itself:

> A mythological doxa has been created: denunciation, demystification (or demythification), has itself become discourse, stock of phrases, catechistic

declaration; in the face of which, the science of the signifier can only shift its place and stop (provisionally) further on: . . . it is no longer the myths which need to be unmasked (the doxa now takes care of that), it is the sign itself which must be shaken; the problem is not to reveal the (latent) meaning of an utterance, of a trait, of a narrative, but to fissure the very representation of meaning. . . . "mythoclasm" is succeeded by a "semioclasm" which is much more far-reaching and at a different level.[65]

The deepest ideological menace of formalized systems is their implied promise of mastery and control. The intimate connection between the desire to know—to categorize and comprehend—and the "will to possess" (as Richard Howard renders *"vouloir-saisir"* in *A Lover's Discourse*) is particularly problematic for theory. It is because Barthes strove to continue writing theory that he began to write it less literally, as an antidote to its domineering tendencies:

> His (sometimes acute) discomfort—mounting some evenings, after writing the whole day, to a kind of fear—was generated by his sense of producing a double discourse, whose mode overreached its aim, somehow: for the aim of his discourse is not truth, and yet this discourse is assertive.
>
> (This kind of embarrassment started, for him, very early; he strives to master it—for otherwise he would have to stop writing.) [*Roland Barthes*, p. 48]

When the operations of theory have lost their innocence, when its objects have become its victims, when the very bases of research and the logic of proof itself are under attack, the entire enterprise is obviously in jeopardy. There is the threat of an infinite regress of auto-critique, already mentioned. Or the threat of silence and paralysis, which weighs heavily in the paragraph from *Roland Barthes*. Yet a third threat is vicious relativism, where efforts to sort out competing claims seem useless, and (in the absence of accepted standards) all positions are deemed equally worthwhile—or worthless.

Even the claim that everything is relative must somehow be justified. Yet if one really takes to heart the work of a Kristeva or a Deleuze and Guattari (where the principles of logic—noncontradiction, strict implication, disjunction and identity—are ploys erected for the sake of a more predictable and controllable social order), there is no way to distinguish between justification and vindication. Judging a theory good or bad on the grounds of its validity, coherence, and ability to withstand repeated empirical tests becomes equivalent to judging it on the grounds of its usefulness or ideological soundness or the compelling beauty of its design. The result is a flowering of deliberately unrealistic claims, reflecting not what literature is, but what it could or should become. (Roughly, this was one cause of the *Tel Quel* group's break with Derrida in 1971, an impatience with the endless analyzing of logical quandaries rather than setting forth revolutionary proposals.)[66]

Yet vindication can never be certain or final—especially when there is no common sense of purpose, no shared criterion of the good or the beautiful to serve as the court of last appeal. One could, like Bloom, make this a new source of purpose and stress the value of taking a stand, any stand at all, rather than losing the only possiblity of excited endeavor that is left. The danger is that this position will either prove impotent—and leave one standing Lear-like, commanding the heedless winds to blow—or potent to the point of tyranny. At either extreme—sheer willfulness or will-less relativism—theory becomes not only unverifiable but unconvincing and uninteresting, and usually inoperable to boot.

At one time or another, Barthes was drawn in each of these directions and towards the pitfalls associated with them. It is an easy matter to find passages, from *S/Z* on, that seem to celebrate the end of certainty, indeed, of meaning itself—not as the yawning of Bloom's fearful void but as the transformation of signs into voluptuously tactile signifiers:

> ...that exemption from meaning which does indeed illumine so many works of the East and which we are scarcely able to comprehend, since for us to attack meaning is to conceal or oppose it, never to absent it....
>
> ...In Bunraku,...the codes of expression are detached from one another, pulled free from the sticky organicism in which they are held by Western theatre...
>
> ...The narrator's voice gathers together extravagant declamation, tremulous quiver, shrill feminine tones, broken intonations, tears, paroxysms of anger and lamentation, supplication and astonishment, indecent pathos, the whole concoction of emotion openly prepared at the level of this visceral, inner body of which the larynx is the mediating muscle.... Thus what the voice exteriorizes finally is not what it carries in it ("feelings") but itself.[67]

Yet Barthes may just as easily stress the translucency of the signifier, beckoning us into an ever-opening labyrinth where each signifier gestures toward another signifier and another:

> Signs, endlessly deferring their foundations, transforming their signifieds into new signifiers, infinitely citing one another, nowhere come to a halt...["Change the Object," pp. 167–68]
>
> ...the signifier must not be conceived of as "the first stage of meaning," its material vestibule, but, in complete opposition to this, as its *deferred action*. Similarly, the *infinity* of the signifier refers not to some idea of the ineffable (the unnameable signified) but to that of a *playing*; the generation of the perpetual signifier...is realized...according to a serial movement of disconnections, overlappings, variations. ["Work to Text," p. 158]

Barthes had his experiments in deconstruction, particularly in *S/Z*, where he manipulates the language of the text until it exposes its own hollowness and contradicts its own desire for solid and stable signs.

Hence, Balzac's realistic representation turns out to be based (like the society he writes about) on a logic of signification that will eventually undo it:

> The difference between feudal society and bourgeois society, index and sign, is this: the index has an origin, the sign does not: to shift from index to sign is to abolish the last (or first) limit, the origin, the basis, the prop, to enter into the limitless process of equivalences, representations that nothing will ever stop, orient, fix, sanction.... the two elements *interchange*, signified and signifier revolving in an endless process: what is bought can be sold, the signified can become signifier, and so on. [*S/Z*, p. 40]

But, characteristically, the task of locating such aporias will not detain him long, and he will turn from demonstrating the impossibility of the text's pretentions to enumerating those devices—the various "codes" of reading and writing—that help to conceal this impossibility. For Barthes, these habits of interpretation continue to have "real" effects, no matter how unreal or unsound their premises are. Thus, *S/Z* does not so much deconstruct as decompose and "pluralize" the texts of Balzac's story. This is to follow the example of the Bunraku theater that Barthes so much admired, which achieves Brechtian disillusionment by introducing a "discontinuity of codes, . . . so that the *copy* elaborated on the stage is not destroyed but shattered" ("Lesson in Writing," p. 177). The shattered text is *both* demystified and delectable.

In later books—*Roland Barthes, A Lover's Discourse*—"shattering" and distancing alone are enough, supplanting the effort to isolate and analyze different semiotic codes. Even in *S/Z* the codes were hardly more than suggested avenues of association that, by their multiplicity and contention, might help to keep the signifier in play. The point was not to comprehend the codes—and perhaps make them seem inevitable—but to lay bare the semiotic work behind seemingly natural appearances. By the very insouciance of its analysis, *S/Z* illustrates that irreverence remains possible, accomplishing what *The Pleasure of the Text* calls a "*subtle subversion . . .* what is not directly concerned with destruction, [and] evades the paradigm" (p. 55). Deconstruction is no less subversive, but Barthes is too much a writer, too seduced by discourse, to remain forever poised in skepticism. "There are those who want a text (an art, a painting) without a shadow, without the 'dominant ideology'; but this is to want a text without fecundity, without productivity, a sterile text.... The text needs its shadow: this shadow is *a bit* of ideology, *a bit* of representation, *a bit* of subject: ghosts, pockets, traces, necessary clouds: subversion must produce its own chiaroscuro" (*Pleasure*, p. 32).

Moreover, Barthes seems convinced that one can never really transcend the position of the theoretical subject; even without commitment to a formal system, awareness itself is subject to preferences and distastes, the accumulated history of what *The Pleasure of the Text* calls "the body";

Whenever I attempt to "analyze" a text which has given me pleasure, it is not my "subjectivity" I encounter but my "individuality," the given which makes my body separate from other bodies and appropriates its suffering or its pleasure....for it is at the conclusion of a very complex process of biographical, historical, sociological, neurotic elements (education, social class, childhood configuration, etc.) that I control the contradictory interplay of (cultural) pleasure and (noncultural) bliss, and that I write myself as a subject at present out of place:...anachronic subject, adrift. [Pp. 62–63]

Barthes's writing fluctuates between affirming this subject and undercutting it. Or rather, it does both at once—pointing out its inevitability, exploring its positive pleasures and subversive potential, yet disrupting and reshaping it at every opportunity. The inconsistencies are especially apparent in *Roland Barthes*, which is less an autobiography than a debate between the (brutal) claims of autocriticism and the temptation of a complete regression into the Imaginary. This tension, in fact, is what keeps the subject from congealing into a stable self-image: "[A]...student identifies, as if it were self-evident, *subjectivity* and *narcissism;* no doubt he thinks that subjectivity consists in talking about oneself, and in speaking well of oneself....Yet today the subject apprehends himself *elsewhere,* and 'subjectivity' can return at another place on the spiral:...why should I not speak of 'myself' since this 'my' is no longer 'the self'?" *(Roland Barthes,* p. 168).

What do these nods towards a new subjectivity amount to—intimations of a coming polymorphous identity?[68] Or an effort to belie Lacan by catching oneself in the act of composing one's own fantasies and correcting for this?[69] Or perhaps a prologomena to a new subjective praxis, where the subject reinvents itself as it goes along? Or is all this mobility and discontinuity simply a defense against falling into predictable patterns? "*Pigeonholed*: I am pigeonholed, assigned to an (intellectual) site, to residence in a caste (if not in a class). Against which there is only one internal doctrine: that of *atopia* (of a drifting habitation)" *(Roland Barthes,* p. 39).

Such inconsistencies about the role and nature of the subject are partly tactical, partly indications of a process of deliberation that remains (bravely) unresolved. Indeed, *Roland Barthes* indulges in stylized trial and error. For example, it will carefully chart the stage of the rise and fall of structuralism in Barthes's own career, with interest shifting from structures to "the Text" and thence to "Value" (under the influence of Kristeva-Derrida-Lacan and Nietzsche, respectively). Then within the next few lines it will promptly renounce such neat divisions and propose entirely new stages: "Between the periods, obviously, there are overlappings, returns, affinities, leftovers;...political and moral obsession is followed by a minor delirium, which in its turn sets off a perverse pleasure (with its undercurrent of fetishism);...the articulation of a period, of a work, into phases of development—though this be a matter of an imaginary operation—permits entering the interaction of intellectual communication: one makes oneself *intelligible"* (*Roland Barthes*, p. 145). The effect is to redivide, indeed to put in doubt the whole chronology—in the same way that the table of contents to *The Pleasure of the Text* slyly rearranges the body of the text, redescribing its divisions rather than recapitulating them.[70] In fact, *Roland Barthes* doesn't stop with just two versions of Roland Barthes's intellectual history, but allows them to proliferate as new vantage points and new languages arise in the act of writing:

> Let us follow this trajectory once again. . . . the first impulse, the first shock, then, is to demystify (*Mythologies*); then when the demystification is immobilized in repetition, it must be displaced: semiological *science* (then postulated) tries to stir, to vivify, to arm the mythological gesture, the pose, by endowing it with a method; this science is encumbered in its turn with a whole repertoire of images: the goal of a semiological science is replaced by the (often very grim) science of the semiologists; hence, one must sever oneself from that, must introduce into this rational image-repertoire the texture of desire, the claims of the body: this, then, is the Text, the theory of the Text. But again the Text risks paralysis: it repeats itself, counterfeits itself in lusterless texts, testimonies to a demand for readers, not for a desire to please: the Text tends to degenerate into prattle (*Babil*). Where to go next? That is where I am now. [*Roland Barthes*, p. 71]

"Where I am now" is an antic tautology—where "I" (the marker and the emergent identity) am in the text is literally "now," the moment when the reader's eye meets this particular line and this stage in the argument. But it also illustrates the instability of Barthes's overall position (and far from his alone). At such a pass, the aesthetic comes into its own, as a means for avoiding commitments, to be sure, and resisting reappropriation for ideological ends—but equally as a motive for theorizing when all the old ones seem tainted. Art is more tolerant of inconsistent, incomplete, and tentative positions; it more easily accepts mixed and heterogenous languages. It provides a place for conducting "thought experiments" in which the weaknesses and the unforeseen consequences of a theoretical framework can be gauged at less expense. And the traditional association between the aesthetic, fiction, and the figurative is the best possible expression of the status of theory during a period of suspicion and intense self-scrutiny, when each new posit is guarded and each new claim bracketed with a whispered "as it were."

In the happy formulation of *Roland Barthes*, art supplies what "we lack in French (and perhaps in every language) a grammatical mode which would speak *lightly* (our conditional is much too heavy), not intellectual doubt, but the value which strives to convert itself into theory" (p. 55). Unlike Bloom, Barthes is able to imagine a position for theory that lies somewhere between assertion and command, neither absolute truth

nor a desperate lie. The mix of theory and literature produces an intimation or an invitation, rather than an imposition; the design must
engage us, not dominate us. The residue of his scientific delirium was
strong enough in Barthes to make it necessary to test the value of a figure,
even one clearly recognized as figurative—to examine it critically, beyond
the immediate flush of novelty. One can and should evaluate fictions by
the practices they make possible, and test those practices in turn by criteria
beyond scholarly productivity and the power to alleviate disciplinary
ennui.

Undoubtedly, the increasing artfulness of Barthes's prose changed
the kind of theory that he wrote, emphasizing theorizing itself as a kind of
practice, beyond whatever other reading and writing practices it explains
or recommends:

> From the moment a piece of research concerns the text (and the text
> extends very much further than the literary work) the research itself
> becomes text, production: to it, any "result" is literally *im-pertinent*. . . . recall
> the research to its epistemological condition: whatever it searches for, it
> must not forget its nature as language—and it is this which renders finally
> inevitable an encounter with writing. In writing, the enunciation deludes
> the enounced by the effect of the language which produces it, a good
> enough definition of the productive, dissatisfied, progressive, critical ele-
> ment which is indeed ordinarily granted to "research.". . . teach the scientist
> or scholar *that he speaks* (but if he knew it, he would *write*—and the whole idea
> of science, the whole of scientificity would be changed thereby).[71]

From what was (roughly) an explanatory theory, Barthes's texts ultimately became almost entirely programmatic and critical: "The work
must increase lucidity, manage to reveal the implications of a procedure,
the alibis of a language, in short must constitute a *critique* (remember once
again that to *criticize* means to *call into crisis*)" ("Writers," p. 201). Yet since
the major modes of critique have a tendency to accept their own premises
uncritically, one must call them into crisis as well—first by stressing the
fact that they are discourse too, and then by posing questions that lie
outside the range of that discourse. This is the function of "pleasure"
(both aesthetic and erotic) or simply "Value"—that area that even the
most skeptical and/or engaged critiques usually ignore. It is noteworthy
that even Bloom defends his theory as something necessary for our
survival, rather than as something that delights us. And yet—as Barthes
might argue—where Bloom's apparent pragmatism ends, there his real
will-to-theory begins, for his proposals are nothing if not exciting.

But how to construct a theory of Value, of what is (by Barthes's own
definition) inherently fugitive, unpredictable, and intensely idiosyncratic? "No 'thesis' on the pleasure of the text is possible," according to *The
Pleasure of the Text:*

I can only *circle* such a subject....

> The bliss of the text is not precarious, it is worse: *precocious*; it does not come in its own good time, it does not depend on any ripening. Everything is wrought to a transport at one and the same moment. This transport is evident in painting, today's painting: as soon as it is understood, the principle of loss becomes ineffective, one must go on to something else....
>
> ...whence the impossibility of speaking about this text from the point of view of positive science (its jurisdiction is that of critical science: pleasure is a critical principle). [Pp. 34, 52–53, 52]

Under these conditions, the provocative and performative qualities of the theorist's own prose will become more crucial than ever before—and even these must inevitably prove insufficient to the task. "As soon as it is understood, the principle of loss"—the shock of dissolution that is bliss— "becomes ineffective."

Why, then, attempt to write a theory of it at all? If Barthes often accused metalanguage of rigidity and a constitutive lack of subtlety, he had not faith that "ordinary language" is any more supple or capable of nuance. If anything, the unmarked language of common intercourse is more deadening, its stereotypes more ubiquitous, its structures more entrenched. Because its assumptions are far more uncritically accepted, its tyranny is far more absolute. "It takes itself seriously, believes itself to be closer to the truth because indifferent to its nature as language. It is at once corny and solemn" ("Writers," p. 197). Thus, while recognizing the dangers of "a fixation with Method," Barthes was unwilling to forego it, "because it realizes the highest degree of consciousness of a language *which is not forgetful of itself* ("Writers," p. 201). All things considered: "A system calling for corrections, translations, openings, and negations is more useful than an unformulated absence of system—one may then avoid the immobility of prattle and connect to the historical chain of discourses, the progress (*progressus*) of discursivity" ("Writers," p. 200).

Then too, promoting a particular value like "bliss"—or trying to improve the status of "Value" in general—demands innovation and not a return to what we already know. If anything, such proposals must subvert familiar standards of value:

> Pleasure is continually disappointed, reduced, deflated, in favor of strong, noble values: Truth, Death, Progress, Struggle, Joy, etc. Its victorious rival is Desire: we are always being told about Desire, never about Pleasure; Desire has epistemic dignity, Pleasure does not. It seems that (our) society refuses (and ends up by ignoring) bliss to such a point that it can produce only epistemologies of the law (and of its contestation), never of its absence, or better still: of its nullity. [*Pleasure*, pp. 57–58]

Perhaps the greatest paradox in *The Pleasure of the Text* is precisely its insistence that pleasure is not innate, that even boredom is acquired (and may therefore be shed, with the help of theory): "Just as the pleasure of the text supposes a whole indirect production, so boredom cannot presume it is entitled to any spontaneity: there is no *sincere* boredom: if the prattle-text bores me personally, it is because in reality I do not like the demand. But what if I did like it (if I had some maternal appetite)? Boredom is not far from bliss: it is bliss seen from the shores of pleasure" (pp. 25–26).

Without the intervention of theory, operating both to critique present assumptions and to prescribe alternatives, one could not understand where and how Barthes means to resituate pleasure. In fact, most of the key terms in his later work are similarly displaced; "fetishism,"[72] "the body," the "Imaginary," even "love" no longer have the same status that they have in other texts—even some written by Roland Barthes himself. "Then perhaps the subject returns, not as illusion, but as *fiction*. A certain pleasure is derived from a way of imagining oneself as *individual*, of inventing a final, rarest fiction: the fictive identity. This fiction is no longer the illusion of a unity; on the contrary, it is the theater of society in which we stage our plural: our pleasure is *individual*—but not personal" (*Pleasure*, p. 62). Yet the fact that these terms have returned as hypothetical or prescriptive "inventions" may be hard to recognize. As the reviews reveal, it is only too easy to take new fictions as old descriptions, and hail the glee of Barthes's postscience as a repudiation of science, a return to more spontaneous writing. But for Barthes, spontaneity is usually veiled habit; nuance can only be rediscovered on the far side of reduction. "Always remember Nietzsche: we are scientific out of a lack of subtlety.—I can conceive, on the contrary, as a kind of utopia, a dramatic and subtle science, seeking the festive reversal of the Aristotelean proposition and which would dare to think, at least in a flash: *There is no science except of differences*" (*Roland Barthes*, p. 161).

One needs categories to sense differences, modulations, the refined subversions Barthes so excelled in. Even the much-maligned signified is needed to foreground the fluidity of a process of signification without fixed and final meanings, only endless signifiers. As *Roland Barthes* insists, repeatedly: "It is not a question of recovering a pre-meaning, an origin of the world, of life, of facts, anterior to meaning, but rather to imagine a post-meaning: one must traverse, as though the length of an initiatic way, the whole meaning, in order to be able to extenuate it, to exempt it" (p. 87). Thus, just when it seems to risk obscurantism, Barthes's writing reasserts its dependence on theory. It is "only at a certain moment" that one dare abandon—or better, bend—one's theoretical framework: "*At a certain moment*, therefore, it is necessary to turn against Method, or at least to treat it without any founding privilege as one of the voices of plurality— as a *view*, a spectacle mounted in the text" ("Writers," p. 201).

But is the result still really theory? True, seeing the elements of theory—its conceptual design, the procedures it sanctions and the field of operation it opens up, the various kinds of documentation and/or argumentation it accepts—as a "spectacle mounted in the text" requires a high degree of theoretical sophistication. One must be capable of relishing the machinery, know how it works and what it will produce. And one must also have some principle or rule for recognizing the right moment to make the break, when and especially how to put an entire theoretical apparatus at crisis. This higher, or rather later, procedure need never achieve the consistency and formality of theory proper; it may—in Barthes's opinion, it should—be heterogeneous and plural, eclectic and unpredictable, "a tactics without a strategy." One tactic for inducing crisis is to permit the clash of different metalanguages, each defining the limits (and the enticements) of what the other has to say—as in *S/Z*, *The Pleasure of the Text*, and *Roland Barthes*. But *Roland Barthes* introduces yet another tactic, which will continue to operate in *A Lover's Discourse* as well. Here crisis or critical distance is achieved by a simple staging of the metalanguage as a spectacle, asking us to hear it as if it were the speech of a "character in a novel" or a drama of theoretical ideas—on the model of Plato's dialogues or Dostoevsky's passionate debates or (more directly) the disembodied recitation of Bunraku. It is in these last two books that Barthes appears to be least theoretical—most disposed to treating metalanguage as a primary language and least willing to seek a position superior to that language or a new set of terms for analyzing it. Thus, while *The Pleasure of the Text* wickedly labels each theory according to its perversion, *Roland Barthes* simply pits Bachelard against Lacan, Brecht against Barthes, and even Barthes against Barthes. *A Lover's Discourse* gives only the scantest headnotes and relies on the awful blank of the surrounding margins to bracket and suspend the fragment of "love-speech," to make the labor of the discourse stand out without presuming to structure it or deconstruct it or set a value on it. Of course, there always remains some slight interference and mediation. The fragments are presented in a sequence, and in spite of Barthes's attempt to arrange them alphabetically so that the "figures occur to the lover without any order. . . . they stir collide, subside, return vanish. . . . like a perpetual calendar, an encyclopedia of affective culture" (pp. 6–7), the book still has a compelling melodic line, if not a plot. The fragments move from the first frantic crisis of "engulfment" to the final, sober intoxication when the will-to-possess at last declines.

The vaulted and echoing space of the page in *A Lover's Discourse* recalls the ideal set forth in *S/Z*:

> Here it is impossible to attribute an origin, a point of view, to the statement. Now, this impossibility is one of the ways in which the plural nature of a text can be appreciated. The more indeterminate the origin of the statement, the more plural the text. . . . in the classic text the voice gets lost, as though it had leaked out through a hole in the discourse. . . . listen to the text as an iridescent exchange carried on by multiple voices, on different wavelengths

and subject from time to time to a sudden *dissolve,* leaving a gap which enables the utterance to shift from one point of view to another, without warning: the writing is set up across this tonal instability (which in the modern text becomes atonality), which makes it a glistening texture of ephemeral origins. [*S/Z,* pp. 41–42]

Barthes took care to distinguish this atonality from the classical mode of distancing we call irony. Irony always operates from a secure position of its own, rooted in another language that it takes to be the true or final one and from which it presumes to ridicule or parody the language it examines: "irony acts as a signpost, and thereby it destroys the multivalence we might expect from quoted discourse. . . . For multivalence (contradicted by irony) is a transgression of ownership. The wall of voices must be passed through to reach the writing: this latter eschews any designation of ownership and thus can never be *ironic*; or, at least, its irony is never certain (an uncertainty which makes several great texts: Sade, Fourier, Flaubert)" (*S/Z,* pp. 44–45).

Thus, the Barthesian plural differs from the New Critical ideal of controlled ambiguity, the integrated tone of civilized and genteel detachment. For Barthes, ironic distance was not distant enough; it secretly reinstates a new absolute, one step removed, and reinstitutes a proprietary attitude toward language. Instead, Barthes's later writing establishes unnerving mergers and, occasionally, an utter absence of tone—related to the impersonality and tonelessness of his structuralist tracts, but without the guarantee of scientific neutrality. In place of the utopia of science, there is now the "atopia" of shattered, infinitely suspended points of view, each with its own idiosyncracy but together having no integrity or identity. The tonelessness of the later writing is sometimes harder to hear; one tends to take up one of the opposing voices in *Roland Barthes* and subordinate the others to it—here is Barthes "himself," and there are his moments of doubt, the instances when he is temporarily not himself. But such a reading not only eliminates the multivalence of the text, it also insists on seeking out a person outside of and above the writing—in spite of *Roland Barthes*'s hints that this personality is the effect and not the cause of the writing—or, rather, that the two coincide: "*In the field of the subject, there is no referent*[.] The fact (whether biographical or textual) is abolished in the signifier, because it immediately *coincides* with it: *writing myself,* . . . I myself am my own symbol, I am the story which happens to me: freewheeling in language" (*Roland Barthes,* p. 56).

Yet, as *Roland Barthes* goes on to admit, this sense of the subject is hard to preserve. The very conventions of writing (character and story), the categories of language itself (person, tense, and number) conspire to build up the image of a self and the illusion of a preexistent referent.

Very frequently, the image-system creeps in stealthily, gently skating over a verb tense, a pronoun, a memory, in short, everything that can be gathered together under the very device of the Mirror and of its Image: *Me, myself, I*.

Hence the ideal would be: neither a text of vanity, nor a text of lucidity, but a text with uncertain quotation marks, with floating parentheses (never to close the parentheses is very specifically: *to drift*). This also depends on the reader, who produces the *spacing* of the reading. [Pp. 105–6]

The odd and touching way this text gradually shifts the responsibility for critical distance onto its reader is the point of departure for the *Lover's Discourse* which follows it:

A figure is established if at least someone can say: *"That's so true! I recognize that scene of language."* For certain operations of their art, linguists make use of a vague entity which they call linguistic feeling; in order to constitute figures, we require neither more nor less than this guide: amorous feeling. . . .

Each of us can fill in this code according to his own history: rich or poor, the figure must be there, the site (the compartment) must be reserved for it. . . . What we have been able to say below about waiting, anxiety, memory is no more than a modest supplement offered to the reader to be made free with, to be added to, subtracted from, and passed on to others. [Pp.4–5]

Here the detachment is more sympathetic than in *Roland Barthes*; the goal is an appreciation for the "citational" nature of love that still manages to avoid the usual reductive and domineering skepticism of critique. (Hence, the fun when bits of psychoanalytic, philosophical, and political jargon can be smuggled into the lover's declamation's.) Yet the risks of this sort of operation are enormous; readers can too easily fail to view the figures as figures and can take the discourse as a piece of unmediated confession. They may become caught up in the dilemmas, identify with the lover, or watch him voyeuristically, without recognizing that the book means to offer them only "a discursive site."

It is bizarre, in fact, to find Barthes, of all writers, invoking "intuition" (here translated as "feeling") as a guide, when the weight of all his preceding writings was on the other side, arguing that even our capacity for pleasure must be acquired. Perhaps the systematic ambiguity of transformational grammar, where the theoretical model is deliberately conflated with the "model" of language that governs a native speaker's intuitions about acceptable sentences, has influenced him. Yet if there are reliable and partially innate linguistic intuitions, it is extremely doubtful that larger discursive patterns—like the discourse of love—are innate in just this way, that they are not greatly mediated by differences of experience and education. In practice, *A Lover's Discourse* takes acculturation for granted, and also presupposes a healthy exposure to psychoanalytic, economic, and political theory, along with a fair degree of familiarity with Barthes's own previous speculations. For the uninitiated or unwilling reader, however, the alienation effect that Barthes means to achieve by staging these languages may never take place; his pleas for sympathy will be heard directly and sentimentally, their antithetical echoes lost.

Thus even Barthes's final, most "atopic" texts presuppose at the very least a theory of atopia. The tactics that control the interruptions and the displacments in the writing are stochastic—unpredictable in any given case, but intelligible in general. Indeed, *Roland Barthes* almost formulates a set of rules—then reneges, for such a formulation would violate its own rules. But to presuppose a theory is not the same thing as constructing one. There is reason, then, to call all of Barthes's writing up to and including *The Pleasure of the Text* theoretical—or at least theoretical literature—and to label his more recent books posttheoretical. No doubt the usual criteria that apply to theoretical discourse—formality, generality, operational adequacy, and justification—must be stretched to cover everything from *Writing Degree Zero* to *The Pleasure of the Text*, but not entirely abandoned. Justification may be edged out by vindication, but no proposal ever goes undefined or undefended. The formalism may become less consistent; metalanguages may contend with, or play upon, one another, rather than forming a single, coherent model. But they never entirely lose the crucial capacity to illuminate and remodel the object of analysis, however transiently, and thus (in the antique formula of "The Structuralist Activity") they "make something appear which otherwise remained invisible, or unintelligible."

There is, of course, increasing skepticism as Barthes goes on about how much is actually in the object of analysis and how much in the language that one applies to it. And, as the theory shifts from efforts to explain the structure of a text or a semiological system to a criticism of the proposed explanations themselves, there is a marked change in the grounds on which the theory rests. *Elements of Semiology* recommended testing one's hypotheses against recurrent features in the corpus under study; "Introduction to the Structural Analysis of Narrative" shifts to a hypothetico-deductive logic, in which one "[works] down from [the] model towards the different narrative species which at once conform to and depart from the model" (p. 81) (though with few provisions for testing when the data do indeed conform and with far more emphasis on the abstract merits of various competing models of narrative structure). By the time of "The Struggle with the Angel" (a study of the narrative structure of Genesis), competing models are beginning to be weighed by their capacity to *produce* new readings, rather than by their fidelity to preexisting structures: "The contemporary theory of the text . . . [should be] understood as production of *signifiance* [without any possible reference to fixed signifieds] and not as philological object."[73]

Both in this essay and in *S/Z*, Barthes continues to allude to "codes," but these codes are placed ambiguously between reading practices that are already commonplace and practices that the theory itself constructs in order "not to reduce the Text to a signified. . . . but to hold its *signifiance* fully open" ("Struggle," p. 141). In fact, "The Struggle with the Angel" actually advances three quite different models of reading, less for the sake of comparing and ranking them, than to "savor the friction between them." "What is given here is not a 'result' nor even a 'method' (which would be too ambitious and would imply a 'scientific' view of the text that I do not hold), but merely a 'way of proceeding' " (p. 127).

By *The Pleasure of the Text*, the domain of the theory has become openly inter-theoretical, almost wholly concerned with the claims of various competing models and what they make it possible (or impossible) to see in any given text. Still refusing to offer itself as a science, the book does not prescribe a particular program of reading but instead clears a space in any and every program for pleasure to operate. The goal is to give pleasure theoretical dignity. This naturally means paying as much attention to the assessment of other frameworks as to developing one's own. The measure of Barthes's argument thus becomes either its power to undo the pretensions of the alternatives, or its capacity to open up a new practice. (Capacity, in this case, includes not just the feasibility of the proposal, but also whether it is worthy of being realized.) *Pleasure* and *bliss* are nevertheless theoretical categories: posits or "sites" of potential fulfillment that remain general in themselves, however idiosyncratic and changeable the means of achieving them may be. "What we are seeking to establish in various ways is a theory of the materialist subject. . . . It can generalize the subject . . . —which does not mean collectivize it" (*Pleasure*, pp. 61–62).

As with *value, pleasure* and *bliss* are extraordinarily difficult to define; the usual theoretical definitions, with their absolute distinctions and closures, threaten to level the very nuances and surprises upon which they depend. "(*Pleasure/Bliss*: terminologically, there is always a vacillation—I stumble, I err. In any case, there will always be a margin of indecision; the distinction will not be the source of absolute classifications, the paradigm will falter, the meaning will be precarious, revocable, reversible, the discourse incomplete.)" (*Pleasure*, p. 4). Hence, *The Pleasure of the Text* can only construct temporary approximations, work by indirection and circumlocution, rather than offer the complete and self-contained equations (Let x = any y, such that y . . .) of a fully formalized language. Yet such traditional definitions remain important, for in the process of exposing their limitations, one begins to indicate what they leave out—the interstices, the blind spots (the "intractable," as *A Lover's Discourse* will eventually call it), which the available languages cannot name.

Illumination can only come about through the ongoing labor of the writing, proposing names and claims and then disposing of them. The definition of pleasure cannot be isolated in any single passage—even in the deceptive lushness of the book's finale, which seems to reach the pitch of verbal tumescence, yet remains only a prologue:

> ...the articulation of the body, of the tongue, not that of meaning, of language....the sound of speech *close up* (this is, in fact, the generalized definition of the "grain" of writing)...[makes] us hear in their materiality, their sensuality, the breath, the gutterals, the fleshiness of the lips, a whole presence of the human muzzle (that the voice, that writing, be as fresh, supple, lubricated, delicately granular and vibrant as an animal's muzzle), to succeed in shifting the signified a great distance and in throwing, so to speak, the anonymous body of the actor in my ear: it granulates, it crackles, it caresses, it grates, it cuts, it comes: that is bliss. [*Pleasure*, pp. 66–67]

The final "that" is simply a pointer; it circumscribes, but does not and cannot describe. Note too how this passage uses its *nots*—a linguistic operator that turns aside the insufficient definition, but puts no positive term in its place. It is not that bliss, or Value, are ineffable, but that they are part of the process of this writing, revealed in the motion of the unfolding discourse. *The Pleasure of the Text* provides no rules for locating instances of pleasure, no descriptions of it, no synonyms or antonyms, not even a recipe for attaining it. Yet it ceaselessly and persistently inscribes the missing place of pleasure, and leads one to the threshold that one must then cross for oneself.

If Barthes's art is the antidote for the tendency of theory to become dogmatic and literal-minded, forgetting its own discursive nature, his theoretical passions are equally unsettling to conventional standards of art. His writing mixes the graceful and the technical indiscriminately, asking us to take precisely the same degree and kind of interest in the finer points of methodology and the unlooked-for simile. Saussure's struggle with the anagram is not a whit less interesting than Jacob's struggle with the angel: "Not situated structurally, a semantologist would not agree to its objective existence (but then what is an objective reading?); and if to me it is clear..., that is *still* perhaps (for the moment) by the same 'aberration' which compelled the lone and unhappy Saussure to hear in ancient poetry the enigmatic voice of the anagram, unoriginated and obsessive" ("Third Meaning," pp. 60–61). Not that Barthes is pitting intellectual "adventure" against narrative suspense. Rather than redefining the *objects* that we should find absorbing, he is making the process of being absorbed in a text something new. Representation was offensive to him because it conceals its own discursive practices and limits itself to the plausible, the acceptable, the recognizable—to just those discursive forms and turns of language that are already familiar—as if this were the height of imaginative accomplishment. "The stereotype is the word repeated without any magic, any enthusiasm, as though it were natural, as though by some miracle this recurring word were adequate on each occasion for different reasons, as though to imitate could no longer be sensed as imitation: an unconstrained word that claims consistency and is unaware of its own insistence" (*Pleasure*, pp. 42–43).

Representation is built upon prefabrication; the readerly values of classical realism are associated with the familiarity and security of the reader. This, rather than the metaphysical or epistemological "errors" of mimesis, is Barthes's chief concern. Error or no, representation succeeds and provides a form of stability and satisfaction that will not be shaken simply by exposing its fallacies. Perhaps because of his early Marxism, and certainly after his structuralism, the real in Barthes is less an ontological category than a cultural and semiological one. The fears of the solipsist— that it is all only in the mind—are remote for one who recognizes what power the collective mind can exercise. Bloom's "reality" is both un-knowable and inexorable; Barthes's is equivalent to what is currently accepted, and thus more mutable, since the acceptable does not exhaust the possible.

Barthes's resistance to representation became increasingly evident in his prose, in the growing delicacy of the assertions, in the questions and the constant qualifications, in the way it breaks off whenever there is the threat of becoming too insistent. The instability, the constant re-formulation, disappearance, and return of Barthes's vocabulary are as far from Bloom's hammering repetitions as his general air of modulation and qualification is from Bloom's hortatory mode. Barthes's search for some degree between "is" and "is not" was not merely polite; it reinforced his repudiation of limits, of the prefabricated real. In fact, there was even room for realism in Barthes's canon, provided that the labor of achieving the reality effect is fully exposed. By revealing the codes at work in Balzac's *Sarrasine*, *S/Z* purges it, as *Mythologies* (less knowingly, perhaps) sucked out the poison and released the pleasure in the tawdry myths of modern life. Even so discredited and underbred an activity as "identifying with" a character can be repatriated, if one appreciates that it *is* an activity and *has* a structure:

> The subject painfully identifies himself with some person (or character) who occupies the same position as himself in the amorous structure.
>
> ...In the theory of literature, "projection" (of the reader into the character) no longer has any currency: yet it is the appropriate tonality of imaginative readings: reading a love story, it is scarcely adequate to say I project myself; I cling to the image of the lover, shut up with this image in the very enclosure of the book (everyone knows that such stories are read in a state of secession, of retirement, of voluptuous absence...). [*Discourse*, pp. 129, 131]

Of course, *projection* and *identification*, so rendered, have quite a different force than they had before. As does *character* when it has been processed, rearticulated, and redistributed, by Barthes's theoretical machinery in *S/Z*:

> When identical semes traverse the same proper name several times and appear to settle upon it, a character is created.... The proper name acts as a magnetic field for the semes; referring in fact to a body, it draws the semic configuration into an evolving (biographical) tense.... to say *I* is inevitably to attribute signifieds to oneself; further, it gives one a biographical duration, it enables one to undergo, in one's imagination, an intelligible "evolution," to signify oneself as an object with a destiny. [Pp. 67–68]

The analysis is reminiscent of William Gass, but it illustrates as well how, for Barthes, structural analysis might be *at once* an explanation of literary conventions and a way of reconstructing or rewriting the text at hand. The transformation of character is delicious in its own right and, unlike Gass, does not collapse discourse back into mere words. Indeed, the result is a new site of reading and writing, one that is capable of undergoing even further modifications. Thus, the paragraph goes on from this analysis of character to posit a new locus of semantic energy it calls "figure," moving from actual representational fiction to a (hypothetical) postrepresentational text: "The figure is altogether different: it is not a combination of semes concentrated in a legal Name, nor can biography, psychology, or time encompass it: it is an illegal, impersonal, anachronistic configuration of symbolic relationships.... As a symbolic ideality, the character has no chronological or biographical standing; he has no Name; he is nothing but a site for the passage (and return) of the figure" (*S/Z*, p. 68).

By thus "discovering" the figures hidden in the text of *Sarrasine*, Barthes manages to preserve both intelligibility and its dissolution. Although the "text of bliss" was, putatively, his ideal, and he was an enthusiastic (and instructive) reader of the radical experiments of Sollers, et al., Barthes's own writing remained permanently transitional. He himself did not write texts of bliss, although he gestured towards them.[74] His own work came closer to what he admired in Flaubert:

> Flaubert: a way of cutting, of perforating discourse *without rendering it meaningless*....
> This is a very subtle and nearly untenable status for discourse: narrativity is dismantled yet the story is still readable: never have the two edges of the seam been clearer or more tenuous, never has pleasure been better offered to the reader—if at least he appreciates controlled discontinuities, faked conformities, and indirect destructions. [*Pleasure*, pp. 8–9]

Indeed, *The Pleasure of the Text* suggests that it may be impossible for experimental art, unaided by theory, to do what it sets out to do:

> Art seems compromised, historically, socially. Whence the effort on the part of the artist himself to destroy it. . . .
> Unfortunately, this destruction is always inadequate; either it occurs outside the art, but thereby becomes impertinent, or else it consents to remain within the practice of the art, but quickly exposes itself to recuperation (the avant-garde is that restive language which is going to be recuperated). [P. 54]

Paradoxically, Barthes's hybrid, impure text may be the only defense against compromise.

The attack on representation took Barthes beyond epistemology and even politics to a (highly tentative) psychoanalytic critique as well.

> Representation is not defined directly by imitation: even if one gets rid of the notions of the "real," of the "vraisemblable," of the "copy," there will still be representation for so long as a subject (author, reader, spectator, or voyeur) casts his *gaze* towards a horizon on which he cuts out the base of a triangle, his eye (or mind) forming the apex. . . .
> . . . a pure cut-out segment with clearly defined edges, irreversible and incorruptible; everything that surrounds it is banished into nothingness, remains unnamed, while everything that it admits within its field is promoted into essence, into light, into view. . . .

> In the theatre, in the cinema, in traditional literature, things are seen *from somewhere.* Here we have the geometrical foundation of representation: a fetishist subject is required to cut out the tableau. This point of meaning is always the Law: law of society, law of struggle, law of meaning. Thus all militant art cannot but be representational.[75]

Such a criticism runs cruelly (doubtless deliberately) counter to the marked taste for segmentation in structuralist methodology; in other writings, the "fetishist" will be less rudely handled, even (equivocally) redeemed.[76] The fragmentary sentences and broken bits of discourse in the writing from *S/Z* on seem designed to undo the unity of the writing/reading subject by not allowing any fixed tableaux to form. But this remedy for fetishism is itself another form of fetishism, a dependence upon partial objects. Despite brief flirtations with undifferentiated, pulsional writing, Barthes was always drawn back to discontinuity and distinction: "Resistance to the cinema: the signifier is always, by nature, continuous here; . . . the film (a skin without puncture or perforation) *follows,* like a garrulous ribbon: statutory impossibility of the fragment, of the haiku" (*Roland Barthes,* pp. 54–55).

Fragmentation in Barthes is at once—and undecidably—symptomatic and aesthetic. It is also tactical, so that writing is kept an open-ended praxis rather than a finished product. To this end, his texts repeatedly undo what has just been done—only to undo this in turn. Sometimes, though, Barthes tries to catch writing in the act of manufacturing sense, as in *Roland Barthes,* where "I" am only what "my" writing makes of me at any given point. Or as in *A Lover's Discourse*, where a summary headnote fails to mesh with its meditation, undermining any belief that two different labors of writing can ever really "say the same thing."

> *disreality*
>
> Sentiment of absence and withdrawal of reality experienced by the amourous subject, confronting the world.
>
> 1.   I.   "I am waiting for a telephone call, and this waiting makes me more anxious than usual. I try to do something, but without much success. I walk back and forth in my room: the various objects—whose familiarity usually comforts me—the gray roofs, the noises of the city, everything seems inert to me, cut off, thunder struck—like a waste planet, a Nature uninhabited by man." [P. 87]

Although *labor* is Barthes's own word, it seems unfortunate to call his writing that or to limit it to endless unmaskings and demystifications. Barthes's writing characteristically defies such an atmosphere of pain and duty. As *The Pleasure of the Text* complains, "All socio-ideological analyses agree on the *deceptive* nature of literature. . . . [forgetting] the formidable underside of writing: bliss: bliss which can erupt, across the centuries, out of certain texts" (p. 39). Reading Barthes it becomes briefly possible to feel that the labor of writing is simultaneously a pleasure and to experience disillusionment as voluptuous release.

But to appreciate such a claim, one needs to take a more sustained look at one of his texts. I choose for this purpose *Sade/Fourier/Loyola*, a crucial text because it is situated precisely at the divide between structuralism and poststructuralism, and embodies this change of theoretical design directly in its prose. The book consists of four essays, rather than the three the title might lead one to expect: one each on Loyola and Fourier (published in 1969 and 1970, respectively) and two separate pieces on the Marquis de Sade, the first dating from 1967 (just one year after "Introduction to the Structural Analysis of Narratives" and a year prior to the 1968 rebellion) and the second written expressly for this volume. Indeed, the arrangement of the book—Sade I, Loyola, Fourier, Sade II—underscores both the order of composition and the return to Sade, as if to stress the passage through Loyola and Fourier and make the question of change more prominent. The separate studies of Sade are kept from coalescing into one, or even from serving as a corrective to one another. Sade recurs but does not repeat; the second reading displaces but does not cancel out the first. One can see in this arrangement, then, traces of Barthes's emerging appreciation for the sign as a ceaseless chain of substitution. The ordering of these essays is, in fact, one of the few instances of imitative form anywhere in Barthes's work; usually the organization of a book is strictly chronological or typological. *Elements of*

Semiology, for example, follows a careful sequence of basic structuralist distinctions and procedures, while *S/Z* willfully braids alternating bits of close textual analysis and broad digressive meditations (on subjects like the readable, the economy of classical realism, and so forth). Later books more often employ the deliberately arbitrary order of the alphabet to organize the fragments into some kind of whole. Not only in its gross outline, but also in its Preface, *Sade/Fourier/Loyola* continues to play upon the problems of order and development by permuting the three names:

> From Sade to Fourier, sadism is lost; from Loyola to Sade, divine interlocution. . . . Here they are all three brought together, the evil writer, the great utopian, and the Jesuit saint. There is no intentional provocation in this assembling (were there provocation, it would rather consist in treating Sade, Fourier, and Loyola as though they had not had faith: in God, the Future, Nature), no transcendence (the sadist, the contestator, and the mystic are not redeemed by sadism, revolution, religion), and, I add (which is the meaning of this preface), no arbitrariness: each of these studies, although first published (in part) separately, was from the first conceived to join the others in one book: the book of Logothetes, founders of languages. [P. 3]

When the three writers are compared, their differences fall away; a new category arises that no one of them, taken individually, would suggest— the category of the "logothete," or a founder of a language. This grouping may or may not have been designed for provocation, but clearly the disparity between the three writers still matters. Without it, there would be no sense of wonder at the abstract structural identity that underlies the very different uses to which these invented languages are put—saintly, utopian, and sadistic, respectively

Yet this is still and stubbornly a strange corpus, one that belies the straight-faced procedural pronouncements of the Preface. According to *Elements of Semiology*, the corpus that structural analysis requires is "a finite collection of materials" that "must be as homogeneous as possible" (pp. 96–97), according to some adopted "principle of relevance" (p. 95). But, as the wild heterogeneity of *Sade/Fourier/Loyola* reveals, the principle of relevance may be at war with the scrupulous collection of a corpus, since it determines long before the evidence is in what will count as evidence: what materials to collect and what "as homogeneous as possible" really means. *Sade/Fourier/Loyola* takes further liberties with semiological science as it goes on. The self-isolation that these three logothetes demanded (each in his own way and for his own purposes) coyly echoes Saussure's attempt to "isolate the systematic *langue* from the chaos of the *parole*," as *Elements of Semiology* describes it (pp. 15–17). "Disorder disappears if, from [the] heterogeneous whole, is extracted a purely social object"—and "this social product is autonomous, like a game with its own rules" (*Elements*, pp. 13–14). It is but a short step from this to the literal closeting prescribed by a Sade or a Loyola: "The new language must arise from a material vacuum; an anterior space must separate it from the other common, idle, outmoded language, whose 'noise' might hinder it: no interference of signs; in elaborating the language in which the exercitant can interrogate the Divinity, Loyola requires retreat: no sound, little light, solitude; Sade shuts his libertines up in inviolable places" (*Sade*, p. 4). The echo is not parodic, any more than it is earnest. A peculiar air of delectation (or mild astonishment? or commiseration?—it is difficult to define but clings, luminous as a fog, to the surface of the writing) hangs over the entire book, leaving shapes slightly distorted and sounds slightly removed from their source. The life studies of Sade and Fourier that are appended to the end are, for example, said to be made up of "biographemes." Is this category simply a passing piece of wit, or is it something more enduring?

> The author who leaves his text and comes into our life has no unity; he is a mere plural of "charms," the site of a few tenuous details. . . . In the total disengagement from value produced by the pleasure of the Text, what I get from Sade's life is not the spectacle, albeit grandiose, of a man oppressed by an entire society because of his passion, it is not the solemn contemplation of a fate, it is, *inter alia*, that Provençal way in which Sade says "milli" (mademoiselle); . . . what I get from Fourier's life is his liking for *mirlitons* (little Parisian spice cakes); . . . what I get from Loyola's life are not the saint's pilgrimages, visions, mortifications, and constitutions, but only his "beautiful eyes, always a little filled with tears." . . . how I would love it if my life, through the pains of some friendly and detached biographer, were to reduce itself to a few details, a few preferences, a few inflections, let us say: to "biographemes" whose distinction and mobility might go beyond any fate and come to touch, like Epicurean atoms, some future body, destined to the same dispersion. [*Sade*, pp. 8–9]

Clearly this is fairly shady structuralism—no commutation tests, no distributional analysis establishes the existence of these biographical units. They are based only on "preferences" and a "total disengagement" from conventional values that "the pleasure of the Text" effects, units defined by the winnowing intertextual friction between "the author who leaves his text and comes into our life" (pp. 7–8).

But Barthes's prefatory note, along with his appended life studies, are actually the aftermath of his study of Sade, Loyola, and Fourier—the untrammeled and irreverent treatment the linguistic model receives in the opening and closing pages of the book is not consistently the case throughout. What is consistent (and no doubt contributes to the gradual erosion of the book's scientific pretentions) is the analogy between what Loyola, Fourier, and Sade do in their writings and what happens in the construction of any artificial metalanguage, linguistics and semiology included. Barthes's earlier *Elements of Semiology* had called for the study of "any system of signs, whatever their substance and limits" (p. 9). Thus, the fact that "the language they [Sade, Fourier, and Loyola] found is obviously not linguistic" (*Sade*, p. 3), but instead composed of devotional exercises, erotic postures, and utopian projects, would not debar them from serious semiological analysis. At this level of structure, there is no way to distinguish between saint and sadist—or, for that matter, semiologist. Indeed, it seems that Barthes's first study of Sade may have begun as a more or less conventional piece of narrative analysis, trying to locate the grammar of eroticism to which Sade's texts conform, rather than as a study of Sade's own ventures as a logothete. The opening of "Sade I" sounds remarkably like the opening of *On Racine*, Barthes's first structuralist success:

> Whether Astrakhan, Angers, Naples, or Paris, cities are merely purveyors, countrysides are retreats, gardens are scenery, and climates are operators of lust; it is always the same geography, the same population, the same functions; what must be gone through are not the more or less exotic contingencies, but the repetition of an essence, that of crime (and let us include in this word once and for all torture and debauchery). If, therefore, the voyage is varied, the Sadian site is unique. [*Sade*, p. 15]

> Although there is only one setting [in Racine], according to the rules, one might say that there are three tragic sites. . . .
> The Chamber is contiguous to the second tragic site, which is the Antechamber, the eternal space of all subjections, since it is here that one *waits*. The Antechamber (the stage proper) is a medium of transmission; it partakes of both interior and exterior, of Power and Event, of the concealed and the exposed.[77]

It is only later in the essay that Sade is seen to be an analyst himself, "eager to define beings by their functions and to regulate the entry into play of those functioning classes" (p. 17). This shift in the level of analysis puts the Sadian imagination on the same plane as the theoretical imagination: manipulating data, abstracting and compiling classes, identifying rules and functions. (The shift seems to take place under the auspices of transformational grammar, where the theoretical model conforms to the competence of a native speaker. Barthes nowhere makes his "conversion" to a new linguistic theory explicit, but it is in the Sade essay that he begins to use tree diagrams, rather than compiling syntagms and paradigms.)

The semiologist differs from the sadist (at least initially) in proposing a metalanguage for an existing language, trying to make its functioning more intelligible. It cannot be the need for intelligibility that drives Sade. Or can it? "The function of the discourse is not in fact to create 'fear, shame, envy, an impression,' etc., but to conceive the inconceivable, i.e., to leave nothing outside the words and to concede nothing ineffable to the world: such it seems is the keynote repeated throughout

the Sadian city" (*Sade*, p. 37). Having raised the possibility that a (perverse) rage for order is precisely what obsesses Sade, Barthes goes on to
enumerate the elements of this obsession: a desire to divide into significant units (since transgression demands clear distinctions to overcome, barriers looming larger than whatever they happen to forbid); a
drive to combine these units according to the rule of transgression
(putting together what does not belong together is the chief libertine
delight, constituting him as a libertine); and finally a need to order these
combinations into larger tableaux or episodes, ultimately composing
entire "scenes" according to a set of principles similar to the traditional
rhetorical prescriptions that govern all extended discourse (the requisite
refinements of pacing, order, symmetry).

Thus, it seems that Sadian eroticism and violence are shaped by the
same operations of isolation, articulation, composition, and ordering that
semiology itself exploits. If Sade's pleasures depend on order, then
perhaps the reverse is also true: "any form of text is always and only the
ritual that orders pleasure" (p. 5). The elaborate methodological constraints of semiology then become just another ritual for the sake of
pleasure. The logic of this reversal is imperfect—if Sade is a logothete, it
does not follow that that is *all* he is nor that *all* logothetes are therefore
Sadian. Yet here, as so often in Barthes, what we are seeing is a logic of
invention rather than of proof, a means for generating plausible hypotheses: If Sade took such pleasure in sorting, classifying, and devising rules,
might not the semiologist—or any other theorist—as well? To pose the
question thus is not to answer it, but the way it is posed endows it with a
certain prima facie credibility and solubility. It constitutes the problem as
a problem, sending us in search of the relationship of subjectivity to
theory—the interests, the drives, the unspoken ecstasies it breeds.

Not by accident does Sade come first in this book; his reputation for
salaciousness and uncivil desire colors the normally austere activities of
the logothete, even as the abstraction and the orderliness of logothesis
purge him of any simple evil. In fact, the wickedness of Sade's conceptual
design turns out to be inversely proportional to any actual wickedness:
"On every page of his work, Sade provides us with evidence of concerted
'irrealism': what happens in a novel by Sade is strictly fabulous, i.e.,
impossible; or more exactly, the impossibilities of the referent are turned
into possibilities of the discourse" (p. 36). According to "Sade I," there is a
perfect isomorphism between the syntax and rhetoric of the Sadian
sentence and the character alignments and crimes that comprise his story.
"The erotic code benefits totally from the logic of the language, mani-
fested through the artifices of syntax and rhetoric. The sentence (its
ellipses, its internal correlations, its figures, its sovereign progress) is what
looses the surprises of the erotic combinative and converts the network of
crime into a marvelous tree" (p. 32).

One can see how this putative correlation of erotic and grammatical code derives from Barthes's "working hypothesis" in the "Introduction to the Structural Analysis of Narratives": "the most reasonable thing is to posit a homological relation between sentence and discourse insofar as it is likely that a similar formal organization orders all semiotic systems" (p. 83). Yet the application in Sade's case somehow sours the air of a perfectly "reasonable" posit. If indeed all semiotic systems possess the same organization, and if for Sade that organization is conducive to perverse delight, then reason verges suddenly on madness. One might agree with Michael Riffaterre that Barthes never really establishes his initial premise but simply "imposes on the text. . . an associative system." Yet Riffaterre's principal objection is that Barthes is "superimposing the *wrong* code [italics mine]" and not the reasonable assumption that Sade's work *is* coded.[78] Riffaterre's review in fact proposes its own analysis of Sade's code, an analysis that follows to the letter Barthes's earlier demand (in *Critique et Vérité*) that all proposals must be tested by their "fit," their power to exhaust the given corpus and still remain within its limits. It is doubtful, however, that Riffaterre's analysis is truly more "immanent" than Barthes's; he invokes Plato on "bestiality" just as Barthes invokes Lacan on 'fetishism' (an appeal that Riffaterre finds artificial and extrinsic). It is not that Riffaterre's polarity of "human vs. beast" is inconsistent, simply that one could find so many others in Sade's texts (e.g., "masters vs. dependents" or "torturers vs. victims" work just as well). Nor is there any guarantee that Sade's logic was really and exclusively binary (women, for example, seem to occupy an ambiguous position *between* beasts and men).

Barthes does, as Riffaterre complains, "make cuts, retrace his steps, 'forget' some of the meanings," particularly in "Sade II," the essay that is the real locus of Riffaterre's impatience. But no matter how serious-minded and thorough Riffaterre's analysis is, it cannot escape making its own initial leap of invention—that moment when an initial (leading) question is posed—"How is Sade's text like a language?" cannot prove that his is the only possible solution to the question and, still less, that the question he has posed is superior to any other. For this, one must seek other (never conclusive) arguments. And the arguments that *Sade/Fourier/Loyola* advances are no longer based on methodological rigor alone, but on the pleasure of manipulating certain analytic instruments (something Sade himself could have appreciated).

> In Sadian grammar there are two principal rules of action: they are, we might say, the regular procedures by which the narrator mobilizes the units of his "lexicon" (postures, figures, episodes). The first is a rule of exhaustiveness: in an "operation," the greatest number of postures must be simultaneously achieved; . . . and . . . in each subject every part of the body be erotically saturated; the group is a kind of chemical nucleus, each "valence" of which must remain free: all of Sadian syntax is thus in search of

the total figure. . . . In the scene, all functions can be interchanged, everyone can and must be in turn agent and patient, whipper and whipped,
coprophagist and coprophagee, etc. This is the cardinal rule, first because it
assimilates Sadian eroticism into a truly formal language, where there are
only classes of action, not groups of individuals . . . ; second, because it keeps
us from basing the grouping of Sadian society on the particularity of sexual
practices (just the opposite of what occurs in our own society; we always
wonder whether a homosexual is "active" or "passive". . .). [Pp. 29–30]

Already there is something askew in this technical passage: the
analytic operations grate against each other—the cool grammar (or geometry) of lust explodes with strange eruptions like "coprophagist" and
"coprophagee." The very mixture of technical languages (the jargon of
linguistics and of chemistry) is telling—as are the quotation marks pluck-
ing terms like *lexicon* and *operation* out of the body of the text, squirming
with their own autonomous life. Add to this the pert parenthetical
aside—where the good conscience of "normal" sexual prejudice seems
even more bizarre and tyrannical than Sade—and one arrives at a writing
that is too buoyant, too amused, too interested, for science. It is only later
that Barthes will actually stipulate that "excess" is the sign of pleasure, but
clearly that definition is being worked out here. Clearly too, the writing
has begun to function as its own vindication, directly exhibiting (instead of
arguing) the value of its operations. It is the extremist rigor of Sade,
Loyola, and Fourier that attracts Barthes to them; in them, principles and
procedures become utterly, blissfully gratuitous: "this economy is not
appropriative, it remains "excessive": . . . the ultimate vacation, the denial
of any reciprocal economy, is itself obtained only by means of an economy" (p. 5). (In much the same spirit, *Roland Barthes* will complain that "it
was because it could not be *carried away* that semiological science had not
turned out well"—p. 160).

Thus, in *Sade/Fourier/Loyola,* Barthes begins to pursue an "excessive" (as opposed to a scientific) semiology. This aestheticized conceptual
design unites interest and disinterest, a paradoxical bliss-in-loss that
comes from producing more than one needs for merely instrumental
ends. Unrealistic? No doubt, and deliberately so. Yet the new concern for
the "economy" of theoretical discourse is nonetheless an effort to bring
writing back into the world. Literary pleasure should neither be irrelevant
to the social order nor reduced to it; Barthes is positing a human capacity
for pleasure as fundamental as the capacity for language.

One fears (not without warrant) that thus grounding theory on
critique and pleasure might lead to flippancy. Of course, choosing a set of
operations for the intoxication they afford, or the preconceptions and
consequences they avoid, does not preclude making them well-defined
and adequate to the textual evidence. In this respect, one notes how few
direct quotations *Sade/Fourier/Loyola* contains; excerpts from the texts

appear only at the bottom of the page—even as the next book, *S/Z*, will be excessive in its citations, omitting not a single sentence of the story and placing the entire, uninterrupted text in the appendix of the book. *S/Z* is a witty demonstration of how easily one may reproduce each jot and tiddle, yet wholly alter their functions, since the citations occupy a new place, in a new, "disseminative" text.

Still, the exchange between object-text and theoretical-text is no less intense in *Sade/Fourier/Loyola* simply because it is less explicit. One can read the entire book with only the slightest knowledge of the writers it considers—but this is a sign and warning that the theoretical discourse is rewriting its materials (a warning Bloom's bulky quotations fail to provide). It is significant that though Riffaterre fears the demons Barthes has loosed, he can still quarrel with his claims. The principles and procedures that produce the readings are still lucid and operable enough to allow them to be tested. This is one stay against unbounded relativism; another is Barthes's respect for writing itself. Structuralism left two not quite consistent attitudes toward writing in its wake: one, that since writing is only a play of differences, there is nothing to prevent the freest possible reading; the second, that every reading is itself another "writing," a text with its own specific qualities. Writing as pure difference, and writing as material practice stand counter to each other; Barthes struggled to assimilate them both. The second reading and altered writing of "Sade II" exalt the play of differentiation, precluding any final rest, but Barthes's final preference was for praxis—as more conducive to pleasure and value, perhaps. This show, not in his actual claims (which are fairly evenly divided, but in the way his own text encounters other texts—be they other theories or bits of advertising or works of literature. One always feels in Barthes's prose the gravitational pull of that other writing, not in borrowed phrases (in the manner of Bloom) but in fundamental changes of procedures affecting everything from sentence rhythms to levels of abstraction and styles of argumentation and documentation. Indeed, the very paucity of quotation in *Sade/Fourier/Loyola* recalls the isolation, the filtering out of extrinsic noise that characterizes the writers he is studying. But, of course, it is Barthes himself who calls this isolation "characteristic," and this characteristic only emerges as such when he has classed the writers together as comparable "logothetes."

The paradox of intertextuality, as Barthes both conceived and practiced it, is that the character of any piece of writing is revealed only in its power to transform other writing. More than revealed, it is here that it actually comes into "being" (and subsequently vanishes, when new intertextual connections are made). When texts act upon each other, they produce something new that belongs to neither text in isolation. The very notion of a text in isolation becomes an abstraction in Barthes's scheme; each text is "woven entirely with citations" ("From Word to Text," p. 160), and its individuality can be gauged only by its variations and departures from the "already read" which each reader brings to it. *Sade/Fourier/ Loyola* is an unusual opportunity to see this intertextual exchange at work, as Barthes "meets" Sade, and the product of that meeting then goes on to meet Loyola and Fourier in turn. When the writing has been reconstructed by these further encounters, it returns to Sade once more and finds him strangely altered. In fact, it is the assumptions governing the reading and the language of analysis that have changed, as a result of all that has come between. It would be hard to read Sade in the same way even after "Sade I"—that is, after the link between pornographer and semiologist has been suggested: "All of Sade is supported on the writing of Sade. Its task, at which it is brilliantly successful, is to contaminate reciprocally the erotic and the rhetoric, speech and crime, to introduce suddenly into the conventions of social language the subversions of the erotic scene" (p. 33).

These sentences introduce a different vision of the value and function of artificial language. For Sade, the work of constructing classes and rules of combination is prospective and prescriptive, rather than retrospective and explanatory. What he establishes is a program *for* and not an account *of* fantasies. Treating Sade as the inventor of an artificial language allows Barthes to propose that some writing is "programmatic" rather than mimetic. In this way, he can challenge the misconceptions that have led to Sade's condemnation as a boring or immoral writer.

> Sade is boring only if we fix our gaze on the crimes being reported and not on the performances of the discourse. . . .
>   . . . The Society that bans him . . . sees in Sade's work only the summoning forth of the referent; for it, the word is nothing but a window looking out onto the real; the creative process it envisions and upon which it bases its laws has only two terms: the "real" and its expression. The legal condemnation brought against Sade is therefore based on a certain system of literature, and this system is that of realism: it postulates that literature "represents," "figures," "imitates"; that the conformity of this imitation is what is being offered for judgment. [P. 36–37]

The Sadian text is neither referential nor pseudoreferential, nor is it "pure" verbal music (as William Gass would have it). Its status is presented far more incisively in "Sade II":

> Indeed, if some group conceived the desire to realize literally one of the orgies Sade describes (like the positivistic doctor who crucified an actual cadaver in order to show that the crucifixion described in the Gospels was anatomically impossible, or in any case would not have produced the painter's Christ on the Cross), the Sadian scene would quickly be seen to be utterly unreal: the complexity of the combinations, the partners' contortions, the potency of ejaculations, and the victims' endurance all surpass human nature. . . . (why not test the "realism" of a work by examining not

the more or less exact way in which it reproduces reality, but on the contrary the way in which reality could or could not effectuate the novel's utterance? Why shouldn't a book be programmatic, rather than painting?). [P. 136]

This sense of text-as-program would have been hard to achieve based on Sade's texts alone, since it was the impossibility of putting his words into practice that make them so exciting, such fit meat for fantasy: "Sade radically contrasts language with reality, or more precisely, he places himself at the sole instance of the 'reality of language' " (p. 137). Barthes needed the example of Loyola to crystallize his notion of the programmatic value of artificial languages. The *Exercises* is a multiple text, composed of directives on four separate levels of instruction—from the author to those wishing to direct a spiritual retreat; from these directors to prospective excercitants; from the excercitant to his own mind and body, translating advice into actions that become a language directed to God; and from God back to the excercitant (a reply that can only be achieved by offering a scrupulously narrowed "paradigm" of alternatives through which one can recognize when one has indeed received a sign). As Barthes notes, Loyola's art is "mantic" rather than "mystical"; what he presents is not an account of becoming one with God or even advice on how to achieve that state. Instead, he offers ways for correctly "signaling" to God and assuring a divine response in return:

> The model of the task of prayer here is much less mystical than rhetorical, for rhetoric was also the search for a second code, an artificial language, elaborated on the basis of a given idiom; the ancient orator disposed of rules (of selection and succession) for finding, assembling, and constructing arguments designed to reach the interlocutor and obtain from him a response; in the same way, Ignatius constitutes an "art" designed to determine divine interlocution. [Pp. 44–45]

The analogy to a secondary language seems more apposite here than in Sade. It is also clearer in Loyola's case that the metalanguage is a prescription for a future action and not an explanation of an "object" language or semiotic practice that is already in use. Actually what Loyola prescribes is a logic of intervention, "general rules . . . set down which can enable the subject to find what to say" (p. 45). *Saying* here includes not only verbal signs, but gestures, tears, the appropriate organization of time and space, and even what mental images one may safely, with assured sanctity, allow oneself to entertain. Thus, Loyola is (heretically) bound up with Sade as another architect of fantasy, and like Sade too, he is a writer persistently misread, although not as an imitator but as if he were simply (if gloriously) an instructor: "Purified of any contact with the seductions and illusions of form, Ignatius's text, it is suggested, is barely language: it is the simple, neuter path which assures the transmission of a mental experience" (p. 40).

To say that there is something peculiar or arresting about Loyola's writing is irreverent enough, but to treat it as the "rhetoric manual" of the contemplative life is gross impiety—although the only real piety being flouted is the belief that writing is ever strictly instrumental. But in ridiculing such assessments of Loyola, Barthes is ridiculing himself as well, for semiology had heretofore involved the same blind faith in the neutrality of its own language. Thus, if Sade supplies the initial suggestion that literature (and theory) may be prescriptive rather than descriptive, Loyola provides the second step: A text may be prescriptive without serving as a "simple, neuter path" of instruction. By this point, Barthes has begun to disparage openly "the image of literary creation we set up" (p. 39), and to insist on a more general category that will embrace Barthes's own prose as well; the essay on Loyola remains fairly constrained, save for a few abrupt topical headings ("Articulation," "The Tree," "Assemblages," "Fantasm") that appear almost like placards in a performance of Brecht—or like Loyola's own prized system of *topoi*: "A form pre-existent to any invention, the topic is a grill, a tablature of cases through which the subject to be treated (the *questio*) is guided.... Thus the topic contains all the wonders of an arsenal of latent powers" (p. 58).

The joke of these headings is small, close to the bone, but it is part of the growing disenchantment with articulation and classification that pervades the essay:

> Ignatius has linked the image to an order of discontinuity, he has articulated imitation, and he has thus made the image a linguistic unit, the element of a code....
>
> ...We have seen how this punctuation, which we know to be the condition necessary and proper to all language, reigns in the *Exercises*, cutting up, subdividing, bifurcating and trifurcating, combining every strictly semantic operation designed to combat relentlessly the vague and the empty. [Pp. 56, 67]

The discussion gathers force like the progress of an irritation, secretly and patiently enflamed until it finally erupts in phrases like "exasperated punctuation" (p. 68) and outright complaints about Loyola's mechanistic accountancy, his obsessional neurosis. Sade's instruments of torture were redeemed by being made the elements of a metalinguistic system, but Loyola's metalinguistic apparatus is itself an instrument of torture and brutal censorship: "As voluntary action, speech energy, production of a formal system of signs, the Ignatian imagination thus can and must have an apotropaic function; it is first and foremost the power of repulsing foreign images; like the structural rules of a language—which are not normative rules—it forms an *ars obligatoria* that determines less what has to be imagined than what it is not possible to imagine—or what it is impossible not to imagine" (p. 51).

If the structuralist phase of Barthes's own writing relied heavily on linguistics for its logic of invention, that reliance is nearly at an end. Already in this essay, he refuses to compile lists of basic units and rules of combination as he does, almost lasciviously, in "Sade I," where he celebrates the Sadian erotic as "assertive, combinatory," a "marvelous" tree diagram (p. 32). Now such euphoria gives way to a sense that the *Exercises* is somehow machine-like, repellent (p. 37). And though he still uses the same analytic categories, still attempting to construe Loyola in terms of a code and a set of rhetorical operations, the analysis is fractured, scattered, as if brakes were being applied to the semiological machine. If the "punctuation" of Loyola's system "permits a gradual development, the same rhythm as that of logical progressions," Barthes's own treatment of Loyola is closer to what he (in a sudden and unexplained aside) calls *torin*. "Buddhism has doctrines called (in Chinese) *torin*, wherein the opening up of the spirit is a separate, sudden, abrupt, discontinuous. . . event" (p. 68).

Though only at the edges of the argument, a desire to "decentralize the plenitude which is part of every closed language" (p. 75) has begun to show. It is difficult not to read the critique of Loyola and his Church as a veiled attack on structuralism, (perhaps not fully recognized as such):

> We see the ambiguity of the *Exercises;* it establishes a psychotherapy designed to awaken, to make resonate, through the production of a fantasmatic language, the dullness of this body which has nothing to say; but at the same time it provokes a neurosis. . . . A situation with which must be contrasted—if we want truly to understand the Christian particularity toward which we can be blinded through force of habit—another type of ascesis, Zen for example, whose entire effort is on the contrary to "de-obsessionalize" meditation by subverting, in order better to supersede them, classes, lists, enumerations—in short, articulation, or even: language itself. [P.71]

Still, it is not until the essay on Fourier that the programmatic elements in Barthes's own theory come fully to the fore, and the book becomes a commendation and a demonstration of a reading practice rather than a simulacrum of a system. In fact, what guides the essay (although this is kept secret until well past the middle) is a principle of disruption that is the antithesis of system:

> The *system* being a closed (or monosemic) one, it is always theological, dogmatic; it is nourished by illusions: an illusion of transparency (the language employed to express it is purportedly purely instrumental, it is not a writing) and an illusion of reality (the goal of the system is to be *applied*, i.e., that it leave the language in order to found a reality that is incorrectly defined as the exteriority of language); it is a strictly paranoid insanity whose path of transmission is insistence, repetition, cathechism, orthodoxy. . . . *systematics* is the play of the system; it is language that is open,

infinite, free from any referential illusion (pretension); its mode of appearance, its constituency, is not "development" but pulverization, dissemination (the gold dust of the signifier); it is a discourse without "object" (it only speaks of a thing obliquely, by approaching it indirectly: thus Civilization in Fourier) and without "subject" (in writing, the author does not allow himself to be involved in the imaginary subject, for he "performs" his enunciatory role in such a manner that we cannot decide whether it is serious or parody). . . . systematics is not concerned with application (save as purist imagining, a theater of the discourse), but with transmission, (significant) circulation; further, it is transmittable only on condition it is *deformed* (by the reader). . . . Here, we are not explaining Fourier's system (that portion of his systematics that plays with the system in an image-making way), we are talking solely about the several sites in his discourse that belong to systematics. [Pp. 109–10]

The excerpt is long (in spite of ellipses); the paragraph from which it comes contains but three sentences in all. It is not just the unbroken thread of language that one notices here—as if all must be said simultaneously, and each word moved in several directions at once—although this is surely a departure from the cleanly punctuated prose of the earlier passage. Where once the only problem was defining one's theoretical terms, now one must also weigh the assumptions they embody, the faculties they flatter, the illusions they sustain. By merging all of these considerations in a single sentence, the writing refuses to make any of them secondary. Indeed, the closure of syntactic structure itself is shaken by the perverse way these sentences suddenly stop and start, not at all where one would expect them to. With no real violation of grammar, the writing still manages to make it hard to find and hold one's place. The multiplication of predicates ("insistence," "repetition," "catechism," "orthodoxy," "open," "infinite," and "free") has the same disorienting effect. There is no place to rest; each epithet slides out from under us, calls into play another and equally tentative epithet.

Changes of theoretical position are directly embodied in the prose then. If not wholly "pulverized" (characteristically, this writing can only gesture toward a condition it cannot itself achieve without making that condition unintelligible), it has still taken quite a pounding. Obviously, other influences than Fourier alone are at work. Derrida's "dissemination" makes its way into the discussion, along with the general attack on the signified; these doom any effort to apply Fourier's principles, since application is a foreclosure of dissemination, a fatal last word. Fourier is, like Sade and Loyola before him, a writer easily misread, but now misreading means not just an appetite for mimesis or for transparent instruction but any desire to turn writing into a finished product:

Fourierist invention is a fact of writing, a deploying of the signifier. These words should be understood in the modern sense: Fourier repudiates *the writer,* i.e., the certified manager of good writing, of literature, he who guarantees decorative union and thus the fundamental separation of substance and form; in calling himself an inventor ("I am not a writer, but an inventor"), he places himself at the limit of meaning, what we today call Text. Perhaps, following Fourier, we should henceforth call *inventor* (and not *writer* or *philosopher*) he who proposes new formulae and thereby invests, by fragments, *immensely and in detail,* the space of the signifier. [P. 88]

This is to make literal Fourier's utopian schemes by insisting that they are just that—nowhere realizable. Fourier's plans become an ideal type that we localize at our peril. Indeed, the only safe site for putting them into practice seems to be in writing. One may enact Fourier's programs only by constructing one's own "theater of discourse."

The essay on Fourier is designed to keep the "systematics" of Fourier's writing in play and to prevent the text from collapsing into a system: "Not explaining Fourier's system" (pp. 109–11) is one part of this effort. Barthes at last emerges fully as a designer of programs for reading rather than a scientist of structure. Thus, there is no orderly summary of Fourier's opinions, not even a step-by-step examination of the units and the rules that make up this metalanguage. "We can distinguish bits of *perspective* and bits of *theory*. . . . It follows that the book (a somewhat Mallarméan view) is not only pieced out, articulated (a banal structure), but, further, mobile, subject to a rule of *intermittent* actualization: the chapters will be inverted, the reading will be speeded up (expedited movement) or slowed down" (p. 89). The essay is itself "intermittent," even scrappy; we stumble without a key from talk about discourse to discussions of rancid butter, from a diatribe against system to a top-ographical map of "Harmony" (Fourier's ideal city). Along the way, we catch glimpses of the machinery that generates Fourier's schemes, but only when it is about to deviate—or, rather, when Fourier's writerly instincts have left room for deviation.

> As a classifier (a taxonomist), what Fourier needs most are passages, special terms that permit making transitions (meshing) from one class to another, the kind of lubricator the combinatory apparatus must use so as not to creak; the reserved portion is thus that of Transitions or Neuters (the neuter is what comes *between* the mark and the non-mark. . . . it is the class in which everything that attempts to escape classification is swallowed up: . . . the *supplement of classification,* it joins realms, passions, characters; the art of employing Transitions is the major art of Harmonian calculation. [Pp. 107–8]

The evaluative edge is obvious in this essay, supplanting the clinical neutrality that was just beginning to become ridiculous in "Sade I." But neither is evaluation quite so painfully judgmental as it was in "Loyola." As value becomes thematic, the writing turns antic and jubilant, like Fourier's own ideal of the good.

By forcing me to lie about my likes (or dislikes), society is manifesting its *falseness* i.e., not only its hypocrisy (which is banal) but also the vice of the social mechanism whose gearing is faulty: . . . society cannot rest until it has guaranteed (how? Fourier has clearly explained it, but it must be admitted that it hasn't worked) the exercise of my manias, whether "bizarre" or "minor," like those of people who like old chickens, the eater of horrid things. [P. 77]

Though patently normative, the essay invokes no one, superior norm, "for Fourier, and this is his victory, there is no normality" (p. 78). The bulk of the essay is devoted to exploring (intermittently of course) how Fourier has managed to conceive, defend, and indulge a value that is not a Master Value. One can see how, for a theorist in Barthes's position, this would be a consuming question. For having abandoned the old justifications of scientific accuracy, how is one to defend one's own proposals? Where can one find support for using this reading practice, rather than some other—outside the sanction of an Absolute?

But value has a double sense for Barthes. It is not only the motive or foundation for a practice; it is also an economic or linguistic concept, the "value" conferred on any item by its relation to and distinction from the other items in the same system. The loss of all distinctions would produce valuelessness and indifference. Yet the usual means for evaluating and distinguishing are contaminated; the systems harden, and values become absolute. To this dilemma Fourier brings the promise that if the process of differentiation is carried far enough, it will ultimately cure itself:

> For [Fourier], the basis of meaning is not substitution, equivalence, but the proportional series. . . . by virtue of the number of its terms, not only *livable* (whereas the semantic paradigm is subject to the law of rival, inexpiable opposites, which cannot cohabit), but even *felicitous*. . . .
>
> . . . Fourier attacks the civilized (repressive) "system," he calls for an integral freedom (of tastes, passions, manias, whims); thus, we would expect a spontaneistic philosophy, but we get quite the opposite: a wild system, whose very excess, whose fantastic tension, goes beyond system and attains systematics. [Pp. 97–98, 110–11]

Fourier's passionate calculations overturn binary oppositions by subjecting them to ever further subdivision. Thus, one makes room for composite cases, even invents a special class for those things that have no other class. Nietzsche's complaint that system is necessarily without subtlety is met by Fourier's even gayer science of nuance.

> One need only subdivide a class in order triumphantly to achieve this paradox: detail (literally *minutia*) magnifies, like joy. . . .
> . . . Nuance, the game being stalked in this taxonomic hunting expedition, is a guarantee of pleasure. [Pp. 104, 105]

The tyranny of value, in which one thing is worth more than another, is brought to an end not by erasing differences but by allowing them to proliferate, until it is no longer possible to hold one up as the norm from which all the rest depart.

Although *Roland Barthes* names Nietzsche as the writer most responsible for the change in Barthes's later theoretical program, it is evident that Fourier was no less influential. It is Fourier (or at least Barthes's reading of him) who suggests how one might exceed the blind drive of the pleasure principle by using pleasure as the measure of principle. And, since Fourier situates pleasure in the process and not the product, logothesis can finally be rehabilitated by viewing it, too, as a process:

> Fourier is like a child (or an adult: the author of these lines, never having studied mathematics, has been very late in experiencing this feeling) discovering with enchantment the exorbitant power of combinatory analysis or geometrical progression . . .
>
> . . . Fourier's speech itself is sensual, it progresses in effusiveness, enthusiasm, throngs of words, verbal gourmandise (neologism is an erotic act, which is why he never fails to arouse the censure of pedants). [Pp. 104, 81]

Such pleasurable systematizing is impractical no doubt, but this only illustrates what is lost by being practical:

> What Fourier lacks (for that matter voluntarily) points in return to what we ourselves lack when we reject Fourier: to be ironic about Fourier is always—even from the scientific point of view—to censure the signifier. Political and Domestic (the name of Fourier's system), science and utopia, Marxism and Fourierism, are like two nets whose meshes are of different sizes. On the one hand, Fourier allows to pass through all the science that Marx collects and develops; from the political point of view (and above all since Marxism has given an indelible name to its shortcomings), Fourier is completely *off to one side*, unrealistic and immoral. However, the other, facing, net allows pleasure, which Fourier collects, to pass through. [P. 87]

The phrasing echoes passages to come in *The Pleasure of the Text* and *Roland Barthes* especially. What will eventually result is an unending play of alternation, a critique of one system by another in which each reveals what the other allows to "pass through" and none can dominate. In this essay, however, there is still a master word—*systematics*—even as it calls for the demise of all dominant metalanguages: "Naturally, Fourier was aware of the 'ridiculousness' of his demonstrative objects (of his rhetoric). . . . 'The melon has among its properties that of *ironic harmony.*'. . . What reader can hope to *dominate* such an utterance—adopt it as a laughable or a critical object, *dictate to it,* in a word?—in the name of *what other language?*" (pp. 94–95).

As the title *Sade/Fourier/Loyola* suggests, Fourier is the center of the book, even if his doctrines and his placement in the text itself make him a deliberately eccentric one. Sade and Loyola both have their circles, but Fourier is forever outré, off somewhere to the side of both orthodoxy and fashionable heresy. The book's title forms a delicate syllabic progression—one beat, two beats, three—and thus introduces into the arbitrariness of a group of proper names the poetic intelligibility of a proportional series, Fourier's favorite figure. As the study of Loyola dispenses with the notion of merely instrumental writing, so the encounter with Fourier affirms the potential sensuality of all writing: "Somewhere, Fourier speaks of 'nocturnal furnishings.' What do I care that this expression is the trace of an earthshaking transport? I am carried away, dazzled, convinced by a kind of *charm* in the expression, which is its delight. Fourier is crammed full of these delights: no discourse was ever *happier*. . . . I do not resist these pleasures, they seem 'true' to me: I have been 'taken in' by the form" (pp. 90–91). There is a dialogue going on in this passage—a tacit quarrel with those who measure writing by its truth alone and believe that being "charmed" is the same thing as being "fooled." Against the dogma that writing should empty itself for the sake of higher things, Barthes's prose reasserts its own shape and weight and specificity.

The disorderly progress of the Fourier essay is almost too well-planned. The discourse breaks strategically just where and when the principle of "systematics" declares it should. But in the last essay in the volume, "Sade II," the fragmented text no longer seems to follow a preordained design but proceeds according to mysterious rhythms of its own. The length of the segments varies; topics are pursued as they emerge rather than distributed in a spirit of willed transgression. The result resembles Sade's own cherished dinner menus, which "have the (non-functional) function of introducing pleasure (and not only merely transgression) into the libertine world" (p. 125). Disruption is no longer the only way to show writing at its work; now we feel it in the voluptuous density of the prose:

> The (polychromatic) languages of the libertine and the (monotonal) language of the victim coexist with a thousand other Sadian languages: the cruel, the obscene, the ironic, the polite, the pointed, the didactic, the comic, the lyric, the novelistic, etc. A text is thus created which gives (as do few texts) the sensation of its etymology: it is a damask fabric, a tapestry of phrases, a changing luster, a fluctuating and glittering surface of styles, a watered silk of languages: a discursive plural uncommon in French literature is achieved. [P. 135]

Epithets continue to displace and translate one another, but the passage is more than a demonstration of dissemination at work. One lingers over phrases; there is something savory in this chromaticism that is not exhausted when the point about the plurality of Sade's languages has been made. Indeed, it *is* part of the point to allow us to sample, to feel the sensation of texture. Not that the writing in "Sade II" is simply and conventionally pretty—any more than it refuses to be charming when urgent philosophical and political questions are at issue. This sensual text, with its rhapsodic fragments that can be recombined at will, approaches the ideal reversibility Barthes attributes to Sade's novels:

> To recount, here, does not consist in developing a story, . . . i.e., to subject the series of episodes to a natural (or logical) order, which becomes the meaning imposed by "Fate" on every life, every journey, but in purely and simply juxtaposing iterative and mobile fragments: then the continuum is merely a series of bits and pieces, a baroque fabric of odds and ends. . . . This construction frustrates the paradigmatic structure of the narrative . . . and . . . constitutes and outrage of meaning: the rhapsodic (Sadian) novel has no *meaning* or *direction*, nothing compels it to progress, develop, end. [P. 140]

The use of deictic pronouns in this passage ("to recount *here*," "*this* construction") is systematically ambiguous; it applies to either the object language of the Sadian novel or to the language Barthes himself employs to analyze that novel. This is one of those passages in *Sade/Fourier/Loyola*, by the way, that incite Riffaterre's most serious objections: Sade's novels clearly are progressive, *if* one analyzes them thoroughly (and seriously) enough. "Each episode is indeed a paroxysm, but not a paroxysm reached at once: it is attained via an ascending scale of variants. In other words, it has an order, a direction, and even an end, when the troupe of actors is exhausted or eliminated. . . . The direction of progress here is governed by the combined restrictions of polarization and nomenclature."[79]

But such "ifs" hang heavy for any programmatic theory, and (by this point in the book) Barthes's has become just that:

> If I say there is a Sadian erotic grammar (a porno-grammar)—with its erotemes and combining rules—that does not mean I have a hold over the Sadian text in the manner of a grammarian (in fact, who will denounce our linguists' image reservoir?). I merely mean that to Sade's ritual (structured by Sade himself under the name of *scene*) must respond (but not cor-respond) another pleasure ritual, which is the labor of reading, reading at work: there is labor as soon as the relationship between the two texts is not a mere *compte-rendue*; my hand is not guided by truth, but by the game, the truth of the game. [Pp. 165–66]

Without repudiating his own stricter analysis of "Sade I," Barthes puts it on another footing, placing it—strictness and all—among the "rituals" of pleasure. Theoretical discourse is now measured by its angle of de-parture, the supplementary labor it adds to the text by "responding" to it rather than "corresponding" to it. Barthes thus introduces a third alterna-tive *between* fidelity and infidelity—something to allay the threat of utter solipsism commonly associated with programmatic theories (and the very cornerstone of Bloom's program for strong reading). Yet, in point of fact even a *compte-rendue* departs from the original. As Barthes himself noted, in "The Structuralist Activity," a successful simulacrum necessarily transforms our experience, making it more intelligible. Otherwise, there would be no need for it.

If, then, there is no such thing as simple correspondence, one is faced with evaluating theoretical constructions in some other way. Predictive accuracy is a common value, but Barthes now finds it too "stifling." "The ultimate censorship does not consist in banning, . . . but in unduly fostering, in maintaining, retaining, getting bogged down in (intellectual, novelistic, erotic) stereotypes" (p. 126). This objection is at once ideological, epistemological, and aesthetic, for relying on the "repetitious matter of common opinion" (p. 126) to verify one's predictions raises it to the status of a given—unconditioned and immutable. Thus, from "Sade II" on, the book foregoes analysis based on insistence and repetition and concentrates instead on "(significant) circulation" (p. 110). In the appended "Lives" of Sade and Fourier, this means stringing anonymous reports together so that each hangs englobed like a small, separate pearl:

> FOURIER . . .
> 9. His knowledge: mathematical and experimental sciences, music, geography, astronomy.
> 10. His old age: he surrounded himself with cats and flowers.
> 11. His concierge found him dead in his dressing gown, kneeling among the flowerpots.
> 12. Fourier had read Sade. [Pp. 183–84]

But it may also involve more drastic interventions, as when "Sade II" takes Sade's favorite tableaux and postures (which "Sade I" had simply cataloged) and breaks them down into pieces. The redistribution and renaming of the elements of the Sadian text is not, as in "Sade I," for the sake of greater intelligibility but for increased delectability:

> The Sadian body is in fact a body seen from a distance in the full light of the stage; it is merely a *very well lit* body . . . rendered in dull expressions (*perfect body, ravishing body, fit for a painting,* etc.). . . . perhaps it is the function of this touch of hysteria which underlies all theater (all lighting) to combat this touch of fetishism contained in the very "cutting" of the written sentence. However that may be, I had only to experience a vivid emotion in the presence of the lit bodies in the Parisian nightclub for the (apparently very tame) allusions Sade makes to the beauty of his subjects to cease to bore me and to glitter in their turn with all the illumination and intelligence of desire. [P. 128]

This passage gives the already stretched theoretical vocabulary of "Sade I" a further strain. Not only does Barthes drop bits of the psychology of object-relations into a once predominantly grammatical model, but his references to stagecraft emphasize the metaphoric incongruity of all his terms. In this respect, the programmatic theory is truer than its explanatory predecessor, ready to display how its own discursive labors can make a "boring" text glitter with desire.

Thus, in *Sade/Fourier/Loyola*, the theorist comes out as a writer, with all the risks for theory that such a change entails:

> Nothing is more depressing than to imagine the Text as an intellectual object (for reflection, analysis, comparison, mirroring, etc.). The text is an object of pleasure. The bliss of the text is often only stylistic: there are expressive felicities, and neither Sade nor Fourier lacks them. However, at times the pleasure of the Text is achieved more deeply (and then is when we can truly say there is a Text): whenever the "literary" Text (the Book) transmigrates into our life, whenever another writing (the Other's writing) succeeds in writing fragments of our own daily lives. [P. 7]

Plainly, Barthes hopes to get beyond mere "expressive felicities" and to reach a pleasure that is "achieved more deeply" in his own art as well. His words betray his impatience with those reverential treatments of "fine writing" that condemn it to permanent ineffectuality. Yet as this passage goes on, it too threatens to confine the circulation of writing:

> It is a matter of speaking this text, not making it act, by allowing it the distance of a citation, the eruptive force of a coined word, of a language truth; our daily life then itself becomes a theater whose scenery is our own social habitat; . . . (it is not a matter of taking into ourselves the contents, convictions, a faith, a cause, nor even images; it is a matter of receiving from the text a kind of fantasmatic order: of savoring with Loyola the sensual pleasure of organizing a retreat, of covering our interior time with it, of distributing in it moments of language: the bliss of the writing is barely mitigated by the seriousness of the Ignatian representations). [Pp. 7–8]

Barthes's choice of Sade, Fourier, and Loyola as his exemplary writers begins to tell, for their convictions are particularly difficult to accept—at least, no one could consistently advocate the opinions of *all three*. When these extreme positions meet, it is indeed their fantastic and fantasmatic qualities that one sees. Does this mean, then, that the value of writing must stop forever short of "content" (*contents* evidently meaning whatever residue one cannot live with or refuses to enact)? Are we to be condemned again to the tired dilemma of form and content, and thereby to reinstate the banished signified as well? It is even more surprising for a student of general semiology, like Barthes, to constrain the economy of writing in this way. After all, he begins *Sade/Fourier/Loyola* by arguing that praxis *is* a language (p. 26). But somewhere in the course of this book's discovery that language is, in turn, a praxis, the other languages of life seem to fall away. Perhaps this is because Barthes's chosen writers have so often been misread as flawed imitators and staid instructors. Or perhaps because action seems doomed to irrevocable finality and literality as language is not. Whatever the reason, the result is to restrict the exchanges into which the ideal text may enter, with a palpable shrinking of Barthes's normal range of extra literary reference. In later years, he became increasingly concerned with the relationship between one piece of writing and another, although in other ways his theory had expanded—no longer limiting itself to immanent analysis, and emphasizing the inexhaustible plurality of the text.

Still, one is moved to ask whether the invitation to speak this text, not to make it act, applies equally to Barthes's writing too. Does the theoretical text practice what it preaches—can it, and still remain a theory? Of course, *Sade/Fourier/Loyola* still leaves room for experimental fantasy in which we try out a conceptual design by using it to order and articulate our own experience. For this, one must at least be able to operate the theory, to occupy the place of its subject and discover what it is like to *know* by means of these devices. What Barthes commends is really a sensual pleasure of knowing—a possibility much trampled under-foot by the recent emphasis on the politics and the psychopathology of knowing. For Barthes, such versions of knowledge are unduly impoverished; they narrow the powers of subjectivity and make language falsely disincarnate, merely symptomatic.

But must the greater richness that Barthes promises come at the expense of all conviction? Can we partake of the pleasure of Loyola's writing (or Barthes's own) only if we hold off any questions about the credibility and the consequences of his framework? Yet, to read in this way and seek pleasure in these terms means following Barthes's instructions—and, hence, accepting some of his arguments. Barthes must, then, allow some room between accepting a theory servilely and treating it as only an amusing design. And here, in this "between," Barthes tried to situate his own theoretical texts.

The status of Barthes's theory clearly altered over time. Even if his earlier metalinguistic models had a tendency to degenerate into taxonomic systems (with no provision for prediction and independent verification of the sort that a true theoretical model requires), still they were internally consistent and seriously proposed. They came with instruction for applying them and were readjusted when they proved inadequate. Barthes never seemed to doubt the major premise of his model: that literature (or drama, or fashion, or furniture) was truly a signifying system—and not just that one could conveniently look at things that way. In later years, however, this faith in the simulacrum faded. "When I resist analogy, it is actually the imaginary I am resisting: which is to say: the coalescence of the sign, the similitude of signifier and signified, the homeomorphism of images, the Mirror, the captivating bait. All scientific explanations which resort to analogy—and they are legion—participate in the lure, they form the image-repertory of Science" (*Roland Barthes*, p. 44).

The grammar of Sadian eroticism is largely "as it were"; there are needs to rival models, and any given metalanguage is tentative and revocable. All of Barthes's later books follow the imperative of *Roland Barthes*: "let the essay avow itself *almost* a novel: a novel without proper names" (p. 120). A fictive or metaphoric operator now binds the entire text—an operator with many functions: It warns against the deluded literalism of the Imaginary; it stands between the theory and the phenomena that it would master. These bound or 'staged' words are displaced from their origin and resist recuperation. Bracketed, their status never certain, they will less easily enter the cycle of repetition that sustains stereotypes: "It is a kind of intellectual 'sport': he systematically goes where there is solidification of language. . . . Like a watchful cook, he makes sure that language does not thicken. . . . it is a pure language tactic, which is deployed *in the air*, without any strategic horizon" (*Roland Barthes*, p. 162).

For the reader, this bracketing or near-novelizing is both a caveat and a diminution of the force of any utterance; the martial tones of instruction give way to the discreet elegance of an ambiguous solicitation. In fact, one of Barthes's chief theoretical preoccupations became how to indicate and explain the peculiar status of his own discourse: "In him, another dialectic appears, trying to find expression: the contradiction of the terms yields in his eyes by the discovery of a third term, which is not a synthesis but a *translation*: everything comes back, but it comes back as Fiction, i.e., at another turn of the spiral" (*Roland Barthes*, p. 69). The writing fumbles between various analogies—novel, theater, scenography—a fumbling that is a necessary part of the definition.

> Were logothesis to stop at setting up a ritual, i.e., a rhetoric, the founder of language would be no more than the author of a system (what is called a philosopher, a savant, or a thinker). . . . In fact, to found a new language *through and through*, a fourth operation is required: *theatricalization*. What is theatricalization? It is not designing a setting for representation, but unlimiting the language. . . . [to] never stop the weighing and elaborating operation; as the style is absorbed in the writing, the system disintegrates into systematics. [*Sade*, pp. 5–6]

The posits of Barthes's theory—"writing," the "signifier," "the readerly" and "the writerly"—were always abstract, relational, hypothetical, but at the end they were often pure idealizations. Thus, "the Text" is really a limit case, a pole towards which any piece of writing may tend but none will ever reach. So too "bliss," and, of course, "utopia." Still, there was some range to Barthes's notion of theoretical "fictions"—from the hypothetical to the ideal to the purely fantasmatic. At the furthest pole was that fiction that can inhabit no possible world outside writing itself, whose sole function is to stimulate further discursive invention. "One borrows from science certain conceptual procedures, an energy of classification: one steals a language, though without wishing to apply it to the end.... Then what good is it? Quite simply, it serves *to say something*: it is necessary to posit a paradigm in order to produce a meaning and then to be able to divert, to alter it" (*Roland Barthes*, p. 92).

But this is the most reductive voice in the chorus that makes up *Roland Barthes*. Not false, but not exhaustive either, it does suggest why Barthes's later writing would invite increasingly ambivalent and divided responses. For Steven Ungar, Barthes's novelistic theory recapitulates Nietzsche's gay science, embracing the necessity of error without succumbing to nihilism.[80] For Gregory Ulmer, Barthes was instead pursuing "an alternative mode of reading and writing—a whole new set of conventions to replace the dead metaphors of realistic or representational reading and writing."[81] Stephen Heath finds the true value of Barthes's writing in its technique of displacement—an achievement at once epistemic ("faire éclater l'intelligibilité de l'habitual"), ethical (setting a higher standard of delicacy and tact, suspending conflict), and writerly (embodying what Heath calls the "lesson of astonishment"—"non pas au sens philosophique [il n'est pas question de quelque naiveté retrouvée] mais un sense où un diament peut être dit 'étonné'; leçon de dispersement...dans la langue").[82] Gay science, or the equally gay disbanding of all science? A plan of production, or a strategy of deconstruction? And these are the supporters of Barthes's later work, against whom Jonathan Culler advances his own more guarded assessment:

> One's complaint is not that he has failed to fill in details—there is, after all, a limit to what one man can accomplish—but that having sketched a perspective, he turns against it and speaks as though the programme were complete and must now be transcended. What from Dr. Heath's vantagepoint is an exciting intellectual displacement may equally be seen as a refusal to accept responsibility, a nimble and stylish evasion.... One finds the tendency of a radical structuralism to denigrate and undermine those realms in which it might accomplish most, to speak enthusiastically about the destruction of meaning without specifying what is destroyed.... In Barthes' work this matters less, for in his latest writing he undertakes no large analytical project, but offers in its place a "euphorie de l'écriture," an experience of language.[83]

Culler lays out with great finesse the damage that Barthes's hybrid ambitions might do to his theory, while the subtle disagreements among more enthusiastic readers show the difficulty of trying to 'fictionalize' in advance of any shared definition of 'fiction.' Barthes never fought his own way clear of these dilemmas; on many occasions, he disagreed with himself. But if the fight became his most consuming interest, the result was not only a contribution to "fine writing" but a legitimate problem for a theory of writing to take on. The struggle to establish an "effectual fiction" was inseparable from Barthes's own practice as a writer, knit into what the writing *does* as well as what it *says*.

One returns therefore to the sense that theory is a practice, an activity carried out in writing, one of the constant themes of Barthes's career. It remained constant despite immense upheavals of taste and rhetorical strategy, in spite of gross changes in conceptual design and in the purported status of theorizing itself. Perhaps it even facilitated those changes. Culler may be too quick to dismiss the mutability of the late work as evasion, for Barthes's changes were an effort to remain responsible— not to the completion of an explanation or a program, but to the constant probing of one's initial premises and their most grievous consequences. Barthes was, in fact, always more suggestive than exhaustive; his characteristic mode was the prolegomena:

> He has a certain foible of providing "introductions," "sketches," "elements," postponing the "real" book till later.. . .
> Now let us reverse all this: these dilatory maneuvers, these endlessly receding projects may be writing itself.. . . the work is never monumental; it is a *proposition* which each will come to saturate as he likes, as he can.. . . the work is a tangle; its being is the *degree*, the step: a staircase that never stops. [*Roland Barthes*, pp. 173, 174–75]

Prolegomena have, of course, a proud history of their own, and Culler is among the many writers who have benefited from Barthes's prospectuses, in all of their vulnerability and incompletion. Indeed, this is central to the economy of Barthes's writing, which strives to make itself vulnerable (to dispute, qualification, remonstrance) rather than 'recuperable' (useful as a weapon in the war of words). Vulnerability is a function of being open to inspection, so that inconsistencies will inevitably be discovered. And among these inconsistencies is the fact that though Barthes uses Aristotle to define *praxis* for him—as an activity "which produces no work as distinct from the agent" (*Sade*, p. 26 n. 11)—his own writing practice in no way centers on its agent (who is simply the site of praxis).[84] Nor is his writing practice entirely bereft of external goals. It is just that Barthes's goals can be achieved only by abandoning all goals, all that we normally think of as instrumental or practical activity. Even in its most inward-looking moments, this prose projects its own ideal against which one can measure the actual, doubt the "natural," and resist the inevitable. As *A Lover's Discourse* puts it:

> I hallucinate what is *empirically* impossible: that our two profferings be made *at the same time*: that one does not follow the other, as if it depended on it.. . . Simultaneous proffering establishes a movement whose model is socially unknown, unthinkable: neither exchange, nor gift, nor theft, our proffering, welling up in crossed fires, designates an expenditure which relapses nowhere and whose very community abolishes any thought of

reservation: we enter each by means of the other into absolute materialism. [Pp. 150–51]

Oddly enough, it is the fiercely apolitical Bloom whose system allows one to most easily infer a social order; one can predict what a state built on his premises would be like and can even say what kind of institutions, what distribution of power and authority, this theory allies itself with. Barthes never claims his theory is apolitical, but its politics are more and more antithetical—designed to ward off, in advance, a fixed institutional future. "This theory," according to *The Pleasure of the Text*, "can produce only theoreticians or practitioners, not specialists" (p. 60)—only users and speculators, never governors or owners. Its politics is critical: to call to mind the ramifications of various powerful metalanguages and to remind us of the values that escape their nets. *Roland Barthes* even names the actual circumstances of theorizing itself:

> I live in a society of *transmitters* (being one myself): each person I meet or who writes to me, sends me a book, a text, an outline, a prospectus, a protest, an invitation to a performance, an exhibition, etc. The pleasure of writing, of producing, makes itself felt on all sides; but the circuit being commercial, free production remains clogged, hysterical, and somehow bewildered; most of the time, the texts and the performances proceed where there is no demand for them [P. 81]

This is the opposite of Bloom's effort to stimulate an artificial demand and to substitute the excitement of manufactured problems for the deeper problem of knowing what is *worth* demanding and how the academy and literature itself might meet those needs. Bloom's economy is also a closed system, and Barthes had a horror of such closure. At first this horror expressed itself only in the restlessness of his changing theoretical affiliations—Sartre, Bachelard, Saussure, and Hjelmslev. But at last it became a principle. In describing the machinery of "making scenes" in *A Lover's Discourse*, Barthes is also describing the (abhorred) economy of any system that closes in upon itself and breeds only endless rivalry:

> The partners know that the confrontation in which they are engaged, and which will not separate them, is as inconsequential as a perverse form of pleasure. . . .
>
> . . . Each argument (each verse of the distich) is chosen so that it will be symmetrical and, so to speak, equal to its brother, and yet augmented with an additional protest; in short, with a *higher bid*. This bid is never anything but Narcissus's cry: *Me! And me! What about me!* . . .
>
> No scene has a meaning, no scene moves toward an enlightenment or a transformation. . . .
>
> Each partner of a scene dreams of having the *last word*. To speak last, "to conclude," is to assign a destiny to everything that has been said, is to

master, to possess, to absolve, to bludgeon meaning; in the space of speech, the one who comes last occupies a sovereign position, held, according to an established privilege, by professors, presidents, judges, confessors:...by the last word, I will disorganize, "liquidate" the adversary, inflicting upon him a (narcissistically) mortal wound, cornering him in silence, castrating him of all speech. [Pp. 204–8]

Bloom conceives the situation of writing scenically—hence the anxiety of influence—and his own theoretical writing is a scenic art of combat and heroic imposition. But Barthes was ever less—or other—than heroic: "What is a hero? The one who has the last word.... To renounce the last word (to refuse to have a scene) derives, then, from an anti-heroic morality....a more subversive because less theoretical riposte" (p. 209).

Barthes's texts often stop short of giving answers, preferring instead to pose and re-pose the problem. He risked (as he well knew) deluding himself about the power of such subversions: "I have the illusion to suppose that by breaking up my discourse I cease to discourse in terms of the imaginary,...attenuating the risk of transcendence; but since the fragment (haiku, maxim, *penseé*, journal entry) is *finally* a rhetorical genre and since rhetoric is that layer of language which best presents itself to interpretation, by supposing I disperse myself I merely return, quite docilely, to the bed of the imaginary" (*Roland Barthes*, p. 95). Yet in the absence of ready and really satisfactory solutions, perhaps the best one can do is to hold the problem open. Perhaps Barthes's writing goes as far as writing, by itself, can go in solving problems that are in the deepest grain of our culture.

"Modestly, by a simple *intelligence* of language—by the knowledge of its own effects—an author produces a political text at once strict and free...this is what Brecht does in his writings on politics and society" (*Roland Barthes*, p. 50). What *Roland Barthes* praises (p. 52) as the via media of Brecht seems to be the way of Roland Barthes as well—or at least of all those essays, books, and sketches marketed in his name. There are few texts where the intelligence of language is greater and that are more sensitive to the fate of common discourse or more scrupulous about the exploitation, curiosity, and pleasure they may produce.[85] This is one measure of Barthes's acute 'critical self-consciousness,' a consciousness that we share with him in the face of that vast accumulation of metalanguages that have so complicated for us all the known and the knowable. Our very sophistication makes ignorance more tempting than ever before—and more impossible to achieve. In the face of this, *Roland Barthes* pursues two complementary policies. First, it engages in what it calls "dramatized science," restoring the "textuality" of awareness, so that what had seemed merely laborious reveals itself as tense with passion:

He suspected Science, reproaching it for what Nietzsche calls its *adiaphoria*, its in-difference, erected into a Law by the scientists who constituted themselves its procurators. Yet his condemnation dissolved each time it was possible to *dramatize* Science . . . ; he liked the scientists in whom he could discern a disturbance, a vacillation, a mania, a delirium, an inflection; he had learned a great deal from Saussure's *Cours*, but Saussure had come to mean infinitely more to him since he discovered the man's desperate pursuit of the Anagrams; in many scientists, he suspected a similar kind of happy flaw. [P. 160]

The second tactic is to regress—to take up the newly extended consciousness, yet know that this cannot eliminate the unconscious, only shift it to a new position:

> This book consists of what I do not know: the unconscious and ideology, things which utter themselves only by the voices of others. I cannot put on stage (in the text), *as such*, the symbolic and the ideological which pass through me, since I am their blind spot (what actually belongs to me is *my* image-repertoire, my phantasmatics: whence this book). I can make us of psychoanalysis and of political criticism, then, only in the fashion of Orpheus: without ever turning around, without ever looking at them. . . .
> . . . Beyond that zone of diffraction—the only one upon which I can cast a glance, though without ever being able to exclude from it the very one who will speak about it—there is reality, and there is also the symbolic. For the latter, I have no responsibility (I have quite enough to do, dealing with my own image-repertoire!): to the Other, to the transference, and hence *to the reader*. [Pp. 152–53]

The unconscious belongs to others, to readers who will transpose the writing in terms of their own interests and trace in it the patterns that are forever hidden from the writer's view. In fact, it is up to readers to discover who and what the writer is, for as his writing unfolds, the writer changes his position and can be recovered only by whoever then rewrites him: "The pleasure of the Text also includes the amicable return of the author. Of course, the author who returns is not the one identified by our institutions (history and courses in literature, philosophy, church discourse); he is not even the biographical hero. . . . he is a mere plural of 'charms,'. . . a discontinuous chant of amiabilities" (*Sade*, p. 8).

Ultimately, the (mobile) subjective space that Barthes's writing circumscribes is neither personal nor antiseptic. Alight with curiosity, tense with ardor and dexterity, it is also benignly untenanted and un-owned. It realizes that "figure" *S/Z* posited some years ago—not a character but a site to be traversed. As such, it remains perennially open to others. We too can occupy it and learn there what it might be like to savor—instead of to suffer—the burdens of contemporary critical awareness.

Afterword, Notes, Index

Afterword

Literature is no longer organized as a system of values along the same principles it once was. . . . There are no great leaders: A new type of *"scripteur"* is born, often more of an intellectual than a writer. There is a loss of interest in "style," a crisis of the novel (many minor novels, but no "great novel"), a relegation of poetic activity to very limited groups. This disintegration of old values should not necessarily be read as an apocalypse, but rather as a mutation within society. We don't know yet where it is leading.

      ROLAND BARTHES, *"Twenty Writers Select the New Classics"*

As it happens, all four of the writers we have been considering—Gass, Sontag, and Bloom as well as Barthes—were among those the *New York Times* chose to question when it was trying to determine "which post–World War II books have already established themselves in a group of a hundred or so of the most important books of Western literature?"[1] Although the question was framed in terms of Western literature, and most of the respondents (aside from Barthes) dutifully replied by citing poets, playwrights, and novelists, few of the writers the *Times* approached were themselves poets or playwrights or novelists. The majority (sixteen out of the twenty respondents) came much closer to being the kind of *scripteur* Barthes describes. Although he carefully hedged his remarks by saying that they apply "in France at least," judging from the nature of the choices that the *Times* itself made, he need not have been so circumspect. Something has happened to the Anglo-American literary scene as well, even if we acknowledge it more often in our practice than in our pronouncements. Bloom (whose own writing has been so profoundly enflamed by the Continental invasion) named only American poets when he was asked; Gass's "candidates for literary immortality" were the same as Sontag's: Beckett, Borges, and Nabokov (the same postmodern triumvirate whose work so overawes their own, beyond whom they cannot seem to get when they try to construct fictions). It is doubtful, in fact, that Gass and Sontag were really asked to speak in their character as novelists. Instead, like their fellow *scripteurs* (Bloom and Barthes included), they

were called upon because of their conceptual and analytic writings—
because such writing interests us, engages us as little of the more conventionally literary writing has been able to in the decade after Borges,
Beckett, and Nabokov achieved their greatest fame.

Gass and Sontag, Barthes and Bloom, are four quite different
writers. Four seems a necessary, if scarcely sufficient, number if we are
trying to understand an "event" in the history of discourse, a moment—of
what significance or duration, it remains to be seen—in the evolution of
writing. Looking at four different writers can at least establish that
something really has occurred, something collective that exceeds
peculiarities of temperament and training and even talent. Our writers
come from different places, both metaphorically and physically, but they
have all converged, at roughly the same time, on much the same experiment. This much they all share—however different their reasons for
engaging in it, however differently they conduct it, however openly they
acknowledge it.

These four writers do not, then, represent a phenomenon; they
instance or exemplify it. They do not stand for other writers whose work I
might also have considered—although they do stand prominently *among*
them—they read and misread, are read and misread, by any number of
others. A certain density of such intertextual relations was one reason for
selecting these four in particular. Bloom and Barthes are patently figures
at the center of a nexus, as interesting for the intellectual history in which
they have participated and for the various attacks and defenses that they
have inspired, as for their own individual achievements. Bloom would, of
course, resist this decomposition of his authorial integrity; his entire opus,
in postulate and practice, is a defense of the boundaries of the solitary
soul. Barthes would probably have welcomed any opportunity to make
these boundaries more diffuse. Sontag too has her camp followers and
especially her detractors, the latter being (one senses) necessary and
invigorating to her, and therefore as important to any study of the
changes in her writing as the unsettling lack of any serious opposition is to
the study of William Gass.

One must read all of these writers intimately, with full particularity.
It is one of the peculiar features of the new theoretical impulse that it will
not suffer us to forego the delicacy and intensity of the old close reading,
whether in the treatment it asks for other texts or in what it demands of us
when we scan its own pages. The net has grown, if anything, even
finer—in Barthes's case, almost deliriously reticulate. Avoiding snap
generalizations is especially important when it is a question of a new mode
in the making, generalizations that could hamper or limit it. We must
exert every effort to keep from treating these texts as if they were all
versions of the same thing and must be on guard against our own natural
urge to tame these unfamiliar (and therefore disquieting) texts by assimi-

lating them into familiar patterns. Reading theory requires that we recognize and respond to its conceptual design: how it constructs its explanations and prescriptions (by model or metalanguage, by laws or narratives, by taxonomies or simple procedural recommendations), as well as what these operations do to resituate or reconstrue the object of analysis (and how drastically), and for what purposes—to master that object, to estrange it, to glamorize it, or to denude and demystify it. These purposes depend, in turn, on the nature of the theoretical problematic, the goals a theory establishes for itself and the field of operation it opens up (or forecloses) as a result, the rules of argument and evidence that supply a sense of sufficiency and completeness. But no matter how "radical" a theory's goals appear to be—whether it answers its own questions cleanly or instead deliberately exacerbates them, whether the questions themselves are shocking or comfortable, profound or trivial—the reader of theory cannot rest there. For, frequently, the manifest problematic conceals a latent one—and here one begins to probe the economic motives that posing a certain problem in a certain way might serve. For example, the evident desire in Bloom's theory to disturb and deidealize is actually designed to quell anxieties of another kind. Gass's ready answer to the problem of literature's peculiar mode of being displaces other (social and political) questions he is unwilling even to raise. Sontag must keep inventing problems to sustain her own unsanctioned role as a cultural diagnostician; Barthes must keep reopening them or fall from (quicksilver) systematics into (symptomatic) system.

To read theory, then, is to be at once engaged and questioning—better, to be engaged *through* questioning, as other forms rarely demand. One is required to "see through" where normally one is only asked to "see." Theory offers no events, no voices, no images to cling to—although uneasy readers frequently struggle to project them, to make the theoretical text into an expression of an idiosyncratic psyche or, failing that, an allegorical drama of personified ideas. (Which may explain the appeal of Bloom's unusually scenic texts.) What theory does offer are operations and practices to perform, figures of thought to detect and test, which may lack phenomenological presence but need not therefore lack integrity and even beauty.

Indeed, theory as a form of art challenges the seemingly unbreakable tie between presence and aesthetics. One *can* have the experience of one without the illusion of the other. There is a penetrating pleasure in the scope, the starkness or the intricacy, the sheer ingenuity of a conceptual design, and in the thoroughness or eccentricity of its application, the surprise (even the incongruity) of its operations compared to operations that we already know. One learns, in fact, to appreciate just how a theory arouses interest and commitment—through provocative contrasts or through assimilation to more familiar matters; through placement in a broader (genetic or environmental or functional) context or through stunning ruptures and deracinations; by means of sly inversions, invaginations, and paradoxes, or with calming reassertions of fundamental harmony. All this is possible without returning theoretical discourse to the status of a description—and without surrendering the requisite posture of (amused, ravished, fierce) interrogation. Yet to read for such figures of thought is not quite the same as reading theory literally—for where one might have sought only neutral modes of explanation, one now faces the unleashed power of desire, ambivalence, and repugnance. A simple true or false will no longer suffice.

But it may be too much to call theoretical literature a mode in the making—instead of a termination or a point of stalemate. After all, what happens within a piece of prose need not spread any further; the institutions responsible for dispensing and sustaining discourse may withdraw their support. Institutions may allow marginal experiments as long as they remain marginal—or they may just as easily disallow and censor them. There is nothing inevitable about theoretical literature, no guarantee of how it might develop or even if it will develop at all. Then too, no matter how cautiously or ingeniously a text is constructed, structure alone cannot determine the uses to which it will be put—at best, it can only make certain ways of using it more awkward.

It is fitting that a mode that so often concerns itself with the problematic nature of writing, that emerged during a crisis over the powers and/or impotence of writing, should find itself in this position. A writing crisis begins when discourse confronts us with its opacity—whether this means its beauty as a formal object or its ability to impose its own structure on our world. Yet this need not be immediately experienced as a crisis—not until the first flush of discovery has faded and left us to confront its consequences. The exhilaration of pure formalism is soon exhausted; the novelty of baring the device cannot go on forever. If at first cracking the codes is intoxicating, living with them soberly is quite another matter. The autonomy of discourse that was once (and truly) a promise of liberation becomes, by degrees, imprisoning: Savoring it no longer seems like a sufficient end in itself, nor quite so innocuous.

It is tempting, of course, to regard the atmosphere of crisis as if it were entirely a theoretical invention, a French conspiracy, a sophist's self-induced and self-interested hysteria. Thus, Irvin Ehrenpreis complains:

> The crises of interpretation . . . are derived from the most general kind of theoretical speculation. When critics strive to produce a science of hermeneutics or interpretation, they want broad, abstract principles that will apply to many works of different genres. Once we turn from such ambitions to the actual experience of interpretation, the crises shrink into

manageability. Away from the blackboard of the theoretician, they are barely visible.

Yet Ehrenpreis is himself constrained to add that:

> In colleges and universities today, the study of literature is a troubled discipline. Undergraduates drawn to it press into courses dealing with the twentieth century. The competition of other kinds of entertainment has narrowed their experience, and the diversified curricula of their high schools have not supplemented the meager diet of recent novels that constitute imaginative literature for them. . . .
>
> Serious attention to literature tends to direct itself to an audience of specialist students and teachers. . . .
>
> Before an audience of students whose first analogies are with television plays and movies, any problem of literary meaning can swell into the size of a metaphysical dilemma.[2]

These are not really separate issues. As I argued at the outset, theory arises in response to problems in literature itself and in the literary establishment. If there is an audience of specialists, if literature has grown dependent on academic intermediaries, if the academy itself has experienced a crisis of confidence as it struggles to meet the expanding and inconsistent demands being placed upon it, this could not all be the doing of a band of literary theorists (no matter how determined). The problems of literature and literary study are clearly overdetermined and doubtless took the work of centuries to reach such a pass. Theory is part of an effort to regain legitimacy for the study and appreciation of literature after it has *already* been challenged. The artificial rules and broad ambitions of which Ehrenpreis complains have rushed in to fill the vacuum left behind when the old consensus collapsed—a consensus with ambitions just as broad and patterns of interpretation just as consistent as anything the theorists have tried to foist upon us. So broad, so consistent, in fact that there was no need to make them more explicit.

If our condition is problematic, disclaiming it or trying to behave as if the problems did not really exist will do nothing to alter it. One cannot will collective norms back into being; standards become no surer by rebuking those who demonstrate how easily we can be made uncertain. Moreover, the ease and comfort of our old, pretheoretical understandings had a price—flattering here, suppressing and ignoring there— as anything that seems too obvious to bear examination is bound to do. It may be impossible, even repellent, to recover this condition. But if the complaint is, rather, that some theorists revel in their (and our) dilemma, engage in mystifications where they claim to be exposing an essential mystery, then this is clearly reason for concern. We are unjust to theoretical writing if we ignore the situation that engendered it, but such writing should also be something more than a symptom or an exploitation of that situation. It should do as much as writing, by itself, can do—illuminate wherever it can, complicate wherever it must. It is only in relation to the crisis that gave it rise that one can hope to judge the literature of theory, its individual writers, and the movement as a whole. What does it do for literary studies, for literature itself? What possibilities of writing and knowledge does it create or foreclose?

Theory as a literary form stands opposed to mimesis and formalism alike. Mimetic writing faces an unprecedented problem of growing discrepancies between what we know (or at least suspect) about the actual organization of our lives and how we nonetheless must continue to experience them. The machinations of the unconscious, the distortions of ideology, are constitutively out of sight; even those political and economic ties that our media can show to us seem out of moral reach, beyond our ability to feel and to act upon them. Our awareness has been extended, our suspicion and self-consciousness have been increased in ways that make our former realistic representations seem inadequate. Nor can we simply revise those representations, for any revision capable of encompassing this newly distended world, with its complicated interdependencies and invisible forces, would destroy that sense of familiarity—that ease of recognition and reassuring confirmation of a stable center of observation—that is the chief delight of realistic representation. In addition, with this general extension of our awareness, there comes a much more sophisticated appreciation of the structures of language and the effect of discursive conventions. Could we effect a return to representationalism on other grounds, we would still find ourselves encumbered by the knowledge that our medium of representation is neither transparent nor innocuous—is not really a medium at all, but a complex organization in its own right.

Obviously, the rise of theory as a literary form is connected to the opening up of such new theoretical domains, and so, in this sense, the crisis can be called self-induced. But is crisis necessarily a bad thing to be in? The compromise between formalism and mimesis, which left discourse divided between sacred objects of art and profane instruments of commerce and communication, was neither durable nor healthy. It forced art to apologize for itself as an escape or a decoration. It rendered literature intransitive and ineffectual, while so distorting the nature of transitivity and effectuality in other cases that it almost encouraged nonliterary discourse to remain crudely instrumental. For, to appear to be nothing more than an instrument or a reflection, discourse must be firmly based on the already-known and (especially) the already-said: The formulations must be so entrenched that they come to seem inevitable and invisible. It is unlikely that such entrenched forms of writing are really what we need at this moment in our intellectual and discursive history. How could they help us to comprehend what they themselves will not explore, or to control complexities that they, by definition, must ignore? But it is equally unlikely that we need writing that prides itself on its uselessness and purely formal values. What we do need is a kind of discourse that will help us come to terms with our distended responsibilities, to overcome our sense of helpless spectatorship, and to clarify our restless, unconfirmed suspicions. Theoretical literature turns decorative figures back into conceptual instruments, offers us posits and programs in the place of fictions—hence the rush of interest that it has inspired, even when it fails to achieve everything it promises. Even when it irritates or offends—for at least the offended parties can contest it, as one cannot contest a pseudostatement. Many find the recent spate of theoretical writing distasteful—abstract, pretentious, toneless—but no one seems to find it inconsequential. And nowhere is the hunger for consequential discourse—for debatable positions and applicable ideas—plainer than in these very cries of outrage and repudiation.

Yet we cannot recover consequence by going back to mimesis.[3] If discourse is to be transitive and effectual, it must achieve this in new ways that will respect what we now know about the status of signs and the workings of discourse. Theory can, of course, become so preoccupied with problems of discourse that there seems to be no hope of exit. The Anglo-American understanding of structuralism and poststructuralism has been particularly prone to emphasize the rhetoricity and self-decomposition of the text. But one cannot make such theoretical claims about discourse without violating one's own principles—without, that is, referring to other texts, or without sufficient internal consistency to make the claims themselves seem plausible. If one cleaves to such principles, one must eventually abandon theorizing and be satisfied (in Barbara Johnson's apt description) with "readings [that] can only *enact* the impossibility of any ultimate analytical metalanguage."[4] (And even then, that telltale judgment of "impossibility" sounds suspiciously categorical.)

If theoretical writing stays theoretical, however, then it necessarily forges an exit for itself back into the world—albeit the route is indirect and the world does not exist with the same independence and imperviousness it had before. Rather than mirroring the world, such writing becomes something *of* that world, operating *in* it and *upon* it. It articulates the world, it isolates and differentiates, thus making it possible for us to locate what we could not otherwise locate, to make distinctions and to compare. It constitutes the world for us as something we can know. It positions us in a certain relationship to the world, allowing us to manipulate it in different ways—to describe it, to explain it, to deny and reimagine it. The categories it establishes can be compared, in turn, to the other ways of classifying and arranging that a given culture affords; the labors one performs in and through writing can be measured against other forms of labor. The relationship of word to world can be even more direct than this—since discursive labor needs the support of other institutions (of education and publication, and so forth). Different kinds of writing, according to their structure and the conventions governing their use, are more or less accessible to would-be readers or writers, and more susceptible to control and private ownership. Thus, though theory may not be responsible for specialization, it can help to protect it—or to undermine it.

It is in these terms that one must consider the defensiveness of Bloom's theory, its effort to absorb any extraneous threat and all external distractions into itself, to make literary study (and those institutions currently responsible for it) a world sufficient unto itself. Sontag's effort to make problems appear where none seemed to be before is the reverse of this, for though it surely helps to provide a sanction for her own writings, it also chips away at the authority of established disciplines that cannot even pose her questions, far less answer them. Barthes was faced with the emergence of an official field of study that he himself helped to create, with all the dangers of rigidity, the potential vested interests and discrepancies of power that such an official structure can entail. His eclecticism and fragmentation were designed to resist this emergent system of authority from the inside—just as Sontag made her discourse more coherent to resist the power of well-established institutions from the outside. Gass is in the peculiar position of writing against himself, denying by his own example the very division of imaginative labor that he is arguing for. And, judging from the way his essays have affected other writers, his example seems more influential than his arguments.

But the same forces that have made mimesis difficult also make it hard for theory to trust its own devices fully. Thus, if theoretical literature gains its transitivity from theory, it owes to literature its ability to survive its own self-doubts. This is especially clear in the writing of Roland Barthes, who could only contain an otherwise endless cycle of self-criticism by making his framework ever more fragile and amused. Literature licenses his wry fragments and playful inconsistencies, as it does the stark hyperboles in Sontag, the extravagant disgressions and punning sleight-of-hand in Gass or the operatic postures of Bloom. Were we forced to take any of them entirely at their word, we would have to dismiss a good deal of what they say. Literature allows us to take them seriously without having to take them literally. This is why we cannot read them well unless we appreciate their literary pretensions. Indeed, nowhere does the problem of literary taste, the predilection for certain stances and narrative structures, become more acute than in the writings of Harold Bloom. And no one illuminates the meaning of our tastes more trenchantly than Susan Sontag, or with more intricacy than Roland Barthes.

Each of these four writers has studied the dilemmas of contemporary writing (which may be why they have all been led to experiment with their own writing). Yet each frames the dilemma differently. Gass longs for purity, yet sees that most of the work of "purification" has already been performed. Sontag sees us driven to a self-martyring "silence." Barthes fastens on the independence and persistence of writing and the way this interferes with the desire for authenticity. Bloom bears witness to an overwhelming anxiety in the face of "prior" writers. Within these differences, one can pick out a common theme, a shared awareness that writing accumulates and achieves a durable history of its own that no writer can ignore. All four know themselves to be revisionists, writing at a "revolutionary moment." And they know as well that this reflects, not a lack of will or individual talent, but the fact that so much has been done without yet being assimilated or has been assimilated and so no longer has to be done. For Bloom, the problem is how to be original at such a moment; Sontag worries less that forms have been used up than that they have been compromised. Gass finds himself trying to perform alchemy on materials that have already been made into gold—and yet unable to find anything else *worth* doing. Barthes faced the eerie afterlife of his own writing, the indelible record of his own blind spots and false positions, and recognized that there were some errors he could never help committing.

For all four, then, theory offered the attractions of a kind of writing that is from the start revisable and collective. And certainly they all had much to gain from a less strict division between literary and nonliterary discourse. Gass and Bloom receive a chance to be (or feel) original once more by employing familiar devices in a new setting. Sontag gains a place to exercise her talent for generalization and negation, which is constricted in traditional narrative and lyric forms, with their demands for a specificity of description that she finds inimical to "the needs of the understanding." Barthes found a space for exploring questions of value and trying to effect a renovation of pleasure and a redefinition of fiction. Since neither Gass nor Bloom really tries to create new possibilities of writing, the results of their experiments are more likely to be short-lived. Bloom's aesthetic is actually more confining than the one he is ostensibly trying to preserve; the Sublime seems less awesome than exaggerated in his hands. Gass does not diminish the power of his favorite literary effects but simply finds something new he can submit to an "ontological transformation." Only in the cases of Sontag and Barthes do we see a sustained effort to alter the nature of aesthetic experience itself, to change the values that animate it and the attitudes and activities that are deemed appropriate to it, for readers and writers alike. Yet a belief in the potential similarity of readers and writers is something that all four share. Bloom's most significant contribution may be his intransigent demand that readers recognize that they are condemned to "writing" their own interpretations, as writers are condemned to the influence of all that they have read. Bloom's own efforts as an over-reader are an encouragement to his readers to dispute with and to extend his claims in ways that he can never fully control. This is the saving excess of his (or any other) conceptual machine: To the extent that it achieves the requisite generality and definition, it must always produce more (and for other hands) than it was intended to.

Still there is scarcely any uniformity about the way these writers exploit the possibilities of theoretical writing. For Gass, theory is all edge; its business is to differentiate cleanly—indeed, it becomes dangerous when it attempts to do anything more. His taxonomies function to prevent massing, to separate and preserve individual distinctiveness. His writing laminates and encapsulates his chosen literary objects, protecting them from the ravages of time and use. Gass's is a theory designed to preserve; its economy is closed, its categories conservative, despite the fact that transcendence and transformation are his favorite themes. And because of this, his theory can neither place nor account for his own theoretical writings.

There is tension between text and claim in Sontag's case as well, but here the theory is more, rather than less, powerful than the writing. The habits of mind of which Sontag complains—symptom hunting, generalizing, and leveling—are not yet purged from her own discourse. Perhaps they are ineradicable, for hers is above all a diagnostic theory, which reaches its diagnoses by establishing very general correlations between different aspects of the same culture. Sontag's progress from one theoretical position to another is based on a refined extremism: to appreciate the signficance of any position, she must push it to its limit. She is a bolder theorist than Gass, since the correlations she draws can actually change the value of the texts and artifacts she studies, even though she rarely tries to restructure them. Her themes change constantly—as they must, for her true theme is the cultural present tense and how best to move with or against it. Her proposed "laws" therefore take the paradoxical shape of a series of temporary universals. Not surprisingly, the economy of her theory is unstable as well. Formerly expansive, intolerant only of intolerance, it has been steadily contracting in recent years. Resources seem more limited now; one is forced to choose between alternatives and to limit one's demands.

Resources are even more limited in Bloom's system, but changing the scope or nature of one's demands is, by definition, impossible. The economy of the theory is at once absolute and annihilating (although the threat of annihilation is really meant to bring flagging interests back to life). Bloom is a melodramatic theorist, even lurid, but the strength of his "strong" claims is hard to determine, since their status and application shifts so rapidly. (This makes Bloom's boldness as a theorist unlike Sontag's, who more often and more openly risks being caught in an error.) It is difficult, too, to tell what kind of conceptual design Bloom is actually using. We are presented with what seems to be a set of taxonomic categories, but the desire to classify runs fairly thin; there is little of Gass's passion to preserve distinctions. More often than not, examples seem to be revised to fit the categories, with opportunities for eccentric revision exploited to the full. Bloom also claims that his theory is a model that explains the necessary shape of poetry, but covertly he is using it to reshape familiar poems (and thus to preserve the old poetic canon even as he "deidealizes" it). And underlying both taxonomy and model is the same narrative design, a myth of loss and regeneration that recently has lost even its promise of cyclic return, and has become a simple and linear story of decay. The problems that Bloom makes thematic—solipsism, rivalry, insuperable priority, and inevitable decline—are not the problems that he uses his theory to resolve, however. The study of the anxiety of influence displaces a deeper and less engaging fear of aimlessness and disaffection.

Like Bloom, Barthes's theoretical writing frequently reworks the texts and artifact he studies. At first, the revisions seemed almost accidental, a by-product of his search for principles of structure that, in the process, stripped away the most immediately recognizable features. Thus, even at their most extreme, Barthes's revisions rarely produced the kind of allegorical translations one finds in Bloom. Normally, Barthes stopped short of substituting new thematic values, preferring to rearticulate and regroup features in the text to achieve his characteristic effects. Passing through Barthes's theoretical machinery, a text becomes instantly etherealized, transformed into a play of permutations, a translucent circulatory system. To keep the circulation moving, while complicating his notions of the system, became at last one of his chief reasons for writing, so that programmatic demonstrations gradually supplanted explanations and catalogs. The writing also became more demonstrative in another sense as well—although even when it strove for scientific accuracy, it was never truly neutral. To unveil an underlying structure was to find release from delusion and perhaps a kind of ecstasy—for the demystifier's hell soon became the artifical paradise of the semiologist. In time, these same pains and pleasures became the central issue, as Barthes began to probe the values that impel metalanguages and to question the status of the structures they reveal (or impose). His prose had always managed to invest whatever objects he studied with amazement or disdain, until such values, and Value itself, became his chief object of study—albeit a most peculiar object, which we distort and reify by trying to know it too objectively. Thus, he was compelled to make his writing more demonstrative, an exhibition of what could not be described directly. Revelation had to occur in the labor of the writing, with superfluities and absences to circumscribe unspoken desires. And when there was no longer the prospect of a stable signified, existing prior to and outside of this discursive labor, structures could no longer be unveiled. The veil of the signifier became impenetrable and the process of analysis interminable—a new kind of wholly skeptical transport was born.

All these changes came about because of Barthes's explicit (perhaps exaggerated) concern for the economy implicit in any theory of signs. His own earlier model of signification was condemned as too miserly, too given to constraining the value of the signifier by restricting it to the most predictable and stereotypic circuits of exchange. The problem now was to "unlimit" the range of potential values without making it so great as to leave the signifier valueless. (The same infinitely expanding abyss of deconstruction drove Bloom to impose a set of final values of his own.) Value exists only when we can make distinctions, but distinctions too easily harden as the process that gave birth to them is forgotten. Barthes's hope was that by moving between different systems of value, he could keep that process of differentiation constantly in view, thus preserving value but avoiding categorical commitments. He hoped as well to incorporate the skepticism of deconstruction without entirely abandoning the pursuit of theoretical understanding. Playing off one metalanguage against another, the inadequacies of each could be exposed, but also the peculiar powers of illumination—even if the light was no longer absolute.

Like Sontag's, Barthes's writing falls short of the ideals he proposed, although there was no surprise or bitter irony in this. The completely plural text, the value that can never be reified or systematized, and the metalanguage that clarifies but never dominates its object are known to be beyond attainment from the start. All one can do is gesture toward them, but to make that gesture intelligible, one must accept some of the very limits one is striving to overcome. Some of these limitations can be recognized as such (and thus used or abandoned strategically), but others are beyond recognition, since they are the assumptions on which the theory rests. Yet Barthes was unconvinced that one could evade assumptions simply by abandoning all theoretical frameworks. As a result, his writing never quite lost its anchoring in theory—its affection for formalizations and definitions, general structures and rules—even when he felt the need to loosen them a bit.

Still, the effort to preserve something of theory by stressing its value as intellectual spectacle is costly if what one wants from theory is verifiable predictions or a program to which one can be fully committed. Barthes's later work was designed to subvert confident predictions and leave us in a new and paradoxical theoretical mood of mutable curiosity, indulgent skepticism, wistful speculation. It is just as difficult (although for different reasons) to be confident about what counts as an instance of revision or as evidence against Bloom's claim that reading and writing are necessarily defensive. Sontag's correlations are a bit less slippery, but they still stand like brilliant flashes in the dark; the mechanisms responsible for them are never named, and evidence that runs counter to her proposals is never really sought. What moves us is the sweep of her assertions and denials, what it would mean to us if they were true; we are drawn by our own need for something more than the constant and chaotic flood of atomistic impressions. Yet art reveals Gass's claims to be just as conservative, while swelling his illustrations and allowing his style of argumentation to become lush and extravagant. Because he is so fearful of mixing the appealing with the true, his experiment in writing theory as a literary form produces a deliberately top-heavy and ornamental text. The effect is to make his claims appear more marginal, especially when the very text that he is writing violates them by introducing a utilitarian desire to make a case into what should be pure aesthetic play.

Thus, strangely, the same aesthetic impulse that drives Bloom to make the most aggrandized and disturbing claims has just the opposite effect on Gass. So too art makes Sontag more strenuous while it renders Barthes more and more tentative and evanescent. To say that theory is a literary form is to say surprisingly little about what kind of literature it is or even what kind of theory. To the extent that Bloom and Barthes, Gass and Sontag, are all writing hybrid texts, they are participating in the same movement, and their separate efforts can offer encouragement to each other. Together they help to establish a general realm of possibility for writing, but not the particular uses that will be made of it. There is no way of knowing in advance how any given piece of theoretical literature will effect our ideas about literature or how it will advance or hinder efforts to arrive at a more adequate theory of cultural phenomena than the frameworks borrowed from the natural sciences have proved to be. There is a very real danger that, in the end, the entire literary experiment will have done little more than made our theories wilder—too vague to draw the necessary consequences from them, too arch to tell if they are even feasible or plausible. If the result is a form of theorizing that seeks no further justification than its design value alone, content to vaunt its symmetries or novel turns of thought as ends in themselves, then the loss for theory will be greater than the gain. Has the sound and fury surrounding Bloom actually improved the quality (as opposed to the notoriety) of literary theory—expanded its resources, introduced new questions or new ways of arguing? More to the point, does the severity of his theoretical design—and his alternately tortured and impudent reasoning on its behalf—really make it a better theory? Surely it does gain attention for it, and in so doing, attracts other writers capable of extracting useful frameworks of their own from Bloom's surcharged and perpetually wandering system.[5] Bloom has indisputably helped to excite a new interest in literary history by showing that tracing the lineage of a poem need not be dull, pedantic work—and why it might even be compelling and important. Whether the relationships he prefers to trace are the most fruitful ones is another matter. Since he himself equivocates, and will not finally say whether his theory explains literary history or only animates it, it is hard to push it beyond the first burst of excited speculation. Bloom's penchant for grandeur and obscurity means that there is no way to test whether another theory might better accomplish his professed goals or even whether there are better goals to seek.

With Barthes, one knows at least that one is faced with a program (or perhaps a series of programs), and there is some effort to suggest reasons for preferring one framework to another (at least for certain purposes). The advantages of a looser and more highly colored presentation are also clearer: The relationship of means to end that underlies a program is not as strict as the relationship between premise and conclusion. If an explanatory theory is always underdetermined (since many different accounts are compatible with the same evidence), programs commonly, and often violently, disagree with one another. The recommended means for reaching the same end can actually contradict one another and be equally valid. And contention becomes even harder to resolve when it comes to choosing which ends are actually *worth* reaching. Pluralism is to be expected in programmatic theories—although Barthes obviously stretches this beyond "reasonable limits"; his fragmented competing languages will allow no single victor, no dominant value. Any theory must, at some level, appeal to our fastidiousness or impatience, our need for security or our desire for surprise, but these pragmatic and aesthetic attractions become even more important when (as in programmatic theories) we are invited to do something we might not otherwise do. In such circumstances, persuasion is not only legitimate but necessary. By writing theory as a literary form, Barthes could make freer use of an entire array of rhetorical inducements and assume the antic role of a missionary tease.

Still, we can and must examine such inducements, and ask of any theory—programmatic or explanatory—what hidden tastes it appeals to and perhaps inflames. The way that Sontag's recent writing wars upon itself—generalizing about the dangers of generalization, seeking out the symptoms of our tendencies to accept symptomatic reasoning—keeps us from fully indulging these tastes, even as it provides a compelling demonstration of just how potent and how prevalent they are. Though her writing has taken a more explanatory tack, the shift is for the sake of making her advocacies more convincing and her warnings more effective. It is because the dangers she means us to see are not self-evident, because we so easily ignore them (lest they disrupt our comfort and good conscience), that she must construct her explanations more carefully and provide enough evidence to make them plausible to resisting readers. In fact, what she now most wants to inspire in us is a desire to reason more curiously and coherently; the "needs of the understanding" must be awakened from their artificial sleep just as the senses once needed to be saved from atrophying. This imparts to her unstylized prose a peculiar intensity: The act of explaining itself takes on a new aesthetic urgency. Gass, however, seeks a release from the demands of literal and sequential argument that is equally functional. Through his flights of phrase and sudden, oblique connections, he can incarnate what are for him the most intoxicating and unnerving qualities of the art that is his subject. In addition, the more blatantly his terms indulge in rhetorical excess, the closer that the quixotic behavior of a word like *blue* approaches the pure contingency of a pun, then the weaker will be our temptation to make category mistakes and the better our understanding of the seductions of language. But, at the same time, such writing cannot but make Gass's own favorite categories seem mistaken. Whether the absolute distinction between literature and other discourse is "real" or just convenient, whether it explains the special status of literature or instead only persuades us to treat it differently, Gass's own purposive playfulness completely straddles (and so escapes) the classes he has constructed.

It is easy enough to see (and perhaps decry) what the effort to be artful does *to* theory. Seeing what it can do *for* theory is harder, since we must first agree on what we want from theory—explanations or prescriptions, novelty or clarity, comprehension or control—and what domain and range of application our ideal theory would have. Only then can we assess whether a given conceptual design is actually enriching rather than just unwieldy or erratic. However artful, a theory should continue to meet at least the minimal standards of generality and replicability; we should be able to operate and challenge it, and to recognize (however loosely they are sketched) the kinds of evidence and arguments that count for it and against it. The abiding sins of theory as a literary form are too much drama, on the one hand, and too much delicacy, on the other—the unleashed will to power that rejects all need of justification and the will-lessness of the *belle-âme* that shrinks before committing itself to any framework. One can see how close Sontag and Bloom (on one side), Barthes and Gass (on the other) come to these two poles, beyond which all theoretical pretensions must collapse. Yet through their writing one can also see why it might be worth the risk—what drama does to make the habitual suddenly problematic and to prod the phlegmatic will to inquiry and action, how a deliberately light touch shows us how much inevitably escapes any theoretical net, where generalizations fail and masterful predictions go awry. Theory as a literary form can help us to preserve the ingenious balance necessary to literary theory, which must at once acknowledge the way that art resists our formulas, yet push the threshold at which we lapse into speechless wonder ever higher. Theory too is a raid on the inarticulate, and in its more literary forms, it illustrates the desperate absurdity and heroism of that raid, and initiates us in the ways of graceful retreat.

But whatever the experiment may do for the theory of literature, there remains the question of its impact on literature itself. Such writing may do more to influence our taste and expectations than even the boldest claims, may challenge our imagination more radically—or more forcefully constrain it. It is tempting to think that the writerly qualities of these texts are compensations for their theoretical failings, making up in spectacle or wit whatever has been lost in the way of precision or feasibility. But to accept this as a necessary trade-off is to reinstate the same tired opposition between creation and reflection, beauty and use, that theoretical literature was meant to overcome. Indeed, what contribution would there be to literature if such writing were to exploit the same effects and to function in precisely the same way as novels and poetry do? For theoretical literature to be aesthetically valuable—whether as a subversion or a stimulant—it must retain something of its identity as theory. Only to the extent that it is arguable, practicable, deniable, can theoretical literature alter our sense of the potential transitivity of literature. Only because a theory allows each reader to operate it, and so play a part in its development, can it challenge the more oppressive features of the notion of artistic originality—the scramble for the private ownership of an idea and the perpetual exhaustion of forms that goes with it, the mystifying and inaccessible genius of the artist and the concommitant irresponsibility and passivity of the "consumer." If Bloom's theory is evasive and difficult for others to operate, this would seem to be another expression of his unyielding (if endlessly disappointed) yearning for total originality. If Barthes's design became ever more fragmented and unstable, so too was he ever more disenchanted with the scientific ideal of perfectly replicable results and bent on inscribing within his own text some place for subjective novelty. Yet this subjectivity remained a general one, a potentiality belonging to no one in particular. As such, its operations had to be defined (or circumscribed) with enough precision to allow others to perform them. Thus, however great his retrospective irony for the delirium of science, Barthes could never quite put aside his predilection (which was moral and political, as well as aesthetic) for formality and generality. The most actively antistructuralist of his texts still lack the intense hermeticism one associates with a good deal of poststructuralist writing.

But then, there is something antithetical and deeply disquieting about a hermetic theory. It violates the economy of theory in its largest sense when abstract and difficult formulations are used to intimidate and to mystify. Not that theory is required to make things simpler and more accessible. Scientific theories must often complicate and estrange the phenomena they study before they can become truly comprehensible. And since aesthetic appreciation demands excited attention, it may well be a legitimate goal of aesthetic theory to renew our sense of the stubborn strangeness of artifacts and texts we have normalized. But it is not legitimate when theory makes itself inaccessible, and through vagueness, secrecy, and whimsy works against a more general participation in critical activity, allowing an exclusive group of experts unimpeachable authority. When and if literary experiments give rise to obscurantism and permit cults to collect around a potent proper name or fetish phrase, theory has not been extended but perverted.

As with any experimental literature, the value of theoretical writing must be in its ability to innovate and renovate, to suggest new ways of organizing our imagination and apprehension. Much of the experimental literature in this century has been negative—that is, lampooning traditional literary constructs (like character and narrative) and playing havoc with the silent expectations that attend familiar genres. In some ways, theoretical literature is a logical outgrowth of this, continuing and making systematic the spirit of antithetical critique. But, ironically, theory is also capable of giving rise to new and positive constructions. Barthes's *écriture*, for instance, has made possible an extended series of elaborations and reworkings in the hands of other writers, as purely antithetical devices (among them, the "degree zero" that led Barthes to first propose the term) do not. Sontag's "photographic seeing" builds on Benjamin's "mechanical reproduction" as James's refinements of "point of view" built on the novelists preceding him—and not as, say, one of Borges's deflationary detective tales plays off Chesterton and Poe. Both Sontag and Gass seem able to achieve more striking results in their essays than in their fictions, where the effort to exploit deflation and purification seems all too derivative, barren, and played out. Indeed, in posits like purification, Gass comes closer to realizing his definition of a literary construct—"a complex system of ideas, a controlling conception, an instrument of verbal organization"—than in his less focused and self-exploding literary creatures. In Sontag's writing it is even more apparent that conventional literary constructions lack the scope and shape she needs to characterize what interests her most and seems most vital to an imaginative grasp of the workings of the modern world. Her failure to create graphic adventures or distinctive voices is the corollary of her success in shaping a set of categories that isolate, not individual persons and events, but social and historical relationships and pervasive ways of being—"styles of will." Bloom's "Gnostic novel" is the inverse of this—an effort to individualize and concretize historical (or transcendental) processes, which actually diminishes them by shrinking them to fit the incongruous dimensions of a science-fiction allegory. Although his theoretical writing is clearly "scenic" in its structure, manipulating categories to create familiar patterns of dramatic conflict, it still has the novelty of finding conflict in such unexpected places and of lifting literary history out of the doldrums of the catalog.

Yet novelty of this sort does not go very deep and in the long run can do little to renew literature itself, since all of its devices have come from well-established (sometimes anachronistic) literary traditions. The same applies to Gass's effort to find a new place to practice his favorite transformations; the setting may be different, but the aesthetic standards remains the same. Again, one must ask how long the sense of novelty can last and what opportunities for fresh develpment have been opened up. It is only in Sontag and Barthes that new demands are placed upon aesthetic contemplation, demands that now include what had seemed wholly antipathetic to it: skepticism, disputatiousness, an eagerness to put to the test. Perhaps what matters most, then, is not the kind of posits that these writers produce but the act of positing itself, which alters the status of literary constructions—which henceforth act as prescriptions that might yet be put into practice or hypotheses that could yet turn out to be "true." Even when Bloom submits that his entire framework is a "noble lie," a rhetorical trick, the rhetoric is not quite that of fiction; to posit an "anxiety of influence" is to challenge us to reconceive our literary histories and to send us back to reexamine the evidence for traces of revision or forward to reread familiar poems in terms of epic struggle. (Obviously, we cannot in the same way search for traces of Emma Bovary or vow to treat her differently the next time that we meet her.) Bloom's theoretical constructs are situated somewhere tensely in between the fictional and the actual, slipperier than lies and less transient than the emphatic coloring of a hyperbole. And surely without this tension he would lose the very ability to excite controversy on which his "strong" stance depends.

After Sainte-Beuve, Arnold, and (later) Randall Jarrell, it has been common to assume that an age preoccupied with criticism must therefore be devoid of any active and initiating imagination. But such warnings sound odd in a situation like our own, where creative writing has for so long been engaged in critique and parody, and critical writing (at least in its theoretical forms) is so patently boisterous and venturesome, full of innovations that may not always be profound but are seldom less than lively. Surely there is nothing one could fairly call timid in the sort of theorizing that has gained such prominence in the past decade. The presupposition that the rise of theory must signal a general cultural decline, a pervasive passivity and derivativeness, fails in the face of what we have experienced. Barthes's rereading of Balzac, for example, is hardly a work of patient and pedantic homage. Instead, it strives irreverently to wring new possibilities of writing out of an old text. Perhaps there is something faintly conserving (if not conservative) about exploiting an already extant text to do this, recycling the writing as it were. One may find in this an echo of Sontag's recently voiced concern for a more careful husbanding of scarce resources, or even traces of Bloom's more apocalyptic sense of diminishing returns. Yet though such parallels are tempting, one must recall that the fundamental theme of *S/Z* is not saving but anarchic expenditure. By taking pieces of Balzac's text one by one, and removing them from their subordination to the progress of the story, Barthes hoped to place the writing once again in circulation. And by focusing on general types of circulation—whether the orderly channels of the five readerly codes or the disorderly digressions of wilder writerly associates—*S/Z* also manages to hold off the closure of a single reading. Since this focus is one of the distinguishing features of all theoretical (as opposed to practical) criticism, Sontag, Gass, and Bloom share this trait as well. Although none of them is as committed to irreducible plurality as Barthes, the fact that they focus on general problems of readability means that they do not take all of the play out of the texts they study by giving them the finality and closure of a single interpretation. There is still the shimmer of unexplored possibility.

They are all, moreover, "rereaders" in some sense, if not precisely to the same extent or in the same ways as *S/Z*. Sontag's earliest form of rereading, for example, was proscriptive (as Gass's continues to be); she stripped away impeding interpretations just as he removes distracting visualizations and misguided instrumentalism. In her later essays, Sontag revises our sense of the commonplace by treating it in terms of its contextual and intertextual relations, as Bloom (more emphatically) revises familiar pieces of Romantic poetry in terms of their "ratios" to their epic ancestors. Such revisions clearly distinguish themselves from received or "normal" readings, and in so doing cannot but trouble our impressions of transparency and immediate accessibility. This would seem to put all our theorists squarely on the side of literature, where wordplay has always clouded the ideal transparency of language and has frustrated desires for immediacy. And such an alliance would seem particularly valuable now when increasingly sophisticated commercial and political uses of language and imagery strive to conceal their own rhetoric and to impress upon us, from every side, the ease and inevitability of every formulation. Yet literary theory continues to be received by some as if it were an alien or antagonistic presence from whose leaden and reductive grasp it is imperative to keep literature protected. It is rare, however, that it is the literary, as such, that is being protected, rather than a certain comfortable accommodation with it—not irreducible strangeness and surprise, but the security of knowing that one's expectations will be fulfilled and one's competence as a reader rewarded. The pleasures of accommodation and immediate assimilation are the first that theory asks us to forego—which may do as much to make it seem forbidding and "inhumane" as anything it actually proposes.

But these feelings of estrangement may also be a clue to the real value that theoretical writing has for us, why it should have gained such prominence now and exercised enough fascination to draw the attention of serious readers away from more conventionally literary forms. For, if it were simply a question of finding fresh means of expression and new aesthetic satisfactions, why take such an indirect route to reach them— why bother with revisionary readings, or, indeed, with studying other texts at all? It cannot really be a dearth of novel ideas that compels this kind of study. Even those theories that deliberately present themselves as commentaries on another writer—a return to Marx or Freud or to the forgotten writings of Saussure—have an emphasis so profoundly altered and a range of applications and connections so unlike the original that it is hard to accept this modesty at face value. The insistence on mounting one text on another is too determined; the effort to preserve enough distance from the other text to observe it critically and then to operate upon it is too strenuous to reflect nothing more than a desire for borrowed glory. Instead, it is as if the need for doubleness were irreducible, as if there must always be a secondary scrutiny capable of watching over every primary act—assaying, placing it, tracing its complications and likely consequences.

Of course, a piece of writing can try to study its own devices, but self-absorption like this all too easily leads to sterility—to facile bits of self-exposure or paralyzing self-doubt. Self-reference lacks the richness of an interchange between different texts because the opportunities for profound transformations are fewer. Moreover, it is compromised from the start, for it can only examine what it had been doing and not what it is in the midst of doing—that is, examining itself. The studied irony of classical modernism, which became ever more self-ironic as the sense of heroism and discovery declined, is clear evidence that such double-mindedness has been with us for some time. Indeed, when it becomes a formal textual division in theoretical literature, the scrutiny seems somehow kinder, and certainly it takes more varied forms. Being less subject to the insoluable ambivalence of self-regard, it is less likely to fall into defensive postures of apology, aggrandizement, and mockery. Of course, this is not to say that theoretical writing is therefore immune to self-consciousness. The change that turned theories of literature into literature themselves came precisely because of a declining trust in the neutrality of theoretical instruments, and a rising interest in the spectacle of their operation. But at its best, contemporary theory seems to be warier of indulging the pleasant pains of self-scrutiny, skeptical above all of its own capacity for skepticism. Then too, a theory that becomes too absorbed in its own design soon ceases to be theoretical; it must be put into operation, for its nature as a theory depends on how it works and not on how it looks. The workings of a theoretical text can only be assessed by bringing to bear a further set of operations. No theory can hope to justify or to critique its own workings, for it can only appeal to the same values and use the same logic that are in question. Theory escapes the closed and sticky world of self-consciousness, then, by giving way to new theories—through Barthes's game of topping hands or Sontag's restless reformulations.

There is probably no way out of our watchfulness, which is the fruit of our accumulated history, our innured acceptance of projections and predictions, the speed and scale of our communications. It is what we are because of all we know and how we know it—and of all that now seems permanently unknowable. The internal division and the provisional and revisible nature of theoretical writing are well suited to our condition. But more important, they are suited to making it intelligible and liveable. The only way out that theory offers us is to go further in, to construct texts that will embody and explore our dilemmas rather than trying to escape them. If we are haunted by suspicions, then theory will illuminate the structure of suspicion and will even help us to savor the workings of an unavoidably critical consciousness. If we both distrust and cannot do without our will to know, theory can display that will in action and, by making literature of it, can keep it from assuming too absolute a form. If we cannot wholly trust our representations, yet find formalism ineffectual, theoretical literature can show us what discourse as discourse can do—its capacity to transform, even to construct as such, domains of study—and can train us both to applaud and to contend with these constructions. If we can no longer experience directly all that we know to be the case about our world and our actual position in it, theory can help us to make the necessary inferential leap that alone can narrow this gap. Our sense of estrangment will not vanish, it may even be intensified, but estrangement we can comprehend is less likely to produce numbing anomie.

If we need instruction to locate the contours of unfamiliar literary shapes or fresh incentives for reading when the pleasure of recognition has been denied to us, theoretical literature seems ideally formed to do this work. It alone can shame or seduce us into new efforts, while at the same time demonstrating of what they should consist and the grounds on which they are based. Above all, theoretical writing can teach us the uses of artifice, how to live with standards that we know we have constructed for ourselves and will always have to test and argue for, because we have gone beyond the point of taking them on faith. Theory is the faith of the faithless, and what more appropriate form could our literature take?

Notes

Part I
1. Statistics gathered from the *MLA International Bibliography of Books and Articles on the Modern Languages and Literatures*, comp. Harrison T. Meserole et al. (New York: New York Univ. Press, 1967–77).
2. This list reflects only the new Anglo-American journals or international journals with a large English audience. The same developments could be traced as well in European journals, and one might also cite the many new journals in other disciplines (art, music, linguistics, etc.) in which literary theory also makes an occasional appearance.
3. Bernard Bergonzi, "Critical Situations: From the Fifties to the Seventies," *Critical Quarterly* 15, no. 1 (1973): 64.
4. Stephen Heath quoted ibid., p. 66, from *Signs of the Times: Introductory Readings in Textual Semiotics*, ed. Heath, Colin McCabe, and Christopher Prendergast (Cambridge: At the University Press, 1971).
5. Dorrit Cohn, "Kafka's Eternal Present: Narrative Tense in 'Ein Landarzt' and Other First-Person Stories," *PMLA* 83, no. 1 (1968): 144–50.
6. Henry Sussman, "The Court as Text: Inversion, Supplanting, and Derangement in Kafka's *Der Proseß*," *PMLA* 92, no. 1 (1977): 41–55.
7. Significantly, further comparisons would be difficult to pursue, since there has also been a marked change in the choice of writers to be most frequently studied.
8. See Geoffrey Hartman, "Crossing Over: Literary Commentary as Literature," *Comparative Literature* 28, no. 3 (1976): 257–76.
9. Jonathan Culler, "In Pursuit of Signs," *Daedalus* 106, no. 4 (fall 1977): 106.
10. Hartman, "Crossing Over," p. 262.
11. See, for instance, William Pritchard's "The Hermeneutical Mafia," *Hudson Review* 28, no. 4 (winter 1975–76): 601–10; or Wallace Martin, "Literary Critics and Their Discontents," *Critical Inquiry* 4, no. 2 (1977): 397–406; or the response of a less satiric reader like Richard Klein, "That He Said That Said Said," *Enclitic* 2, no. 1 (1978): 81–96.
12. Geoffrey Hartman, "The Recognition Scene of Criticism," *Critical Inquiry* 4, no. 2 (1977): 408n.
13. Edward Said, "Michel Foucault as an Intellectual Imagination," *Boundary–2*, 1, no. 1 (1972): 4.
14. Randall Jarrell quoted in Stephen C. Moore, "Contemporary Criticism and the End of a Literary Revolution," *Centennial Review* 15, no. 2 (1971): 147.
15. Murray Krieger, *Theory of Criticism: A Tradition and Its System* (Baltimore: The Johns Hopkins Univ. Press, 1976), p. x.
16. See Jonathan Culler's frequent and explicit attacks on "theory for interpretation's sake," for example, in *Structuralist Poetics* (London: Routledge and Kegan-Paul, 1975) and "Beyond Interpretation: The Prospects of Contemporary Criticism," *Comparative Literature* 28, no. 3 (1976): 244–56.
17. M. H. Abrams revives Coleridge's phrase in "What's the Use of Theorizing about the Arts?" in *In Search of Literary Theory*, ed. Morton W. Bloomfield (Ithaca, N.Y.: Cornell Univ. Press, 1972), pp. 36–37 especially.

18. See several articles to this effect in *Directions for Criticism*, ed. Murray Krieger and L. S. Dembo (Madison: Univ. of Wisconsin Press, 1977), and Robert Weimann's *Structure and Society in Literary History: Studies in the History and Theory of Historical Criticism* (Charlottesville: Univ. Press of Virginia, 1976), among many others.

19. Bergonzi, "Critical Situations," Moore, "Contemporary Criticism"; and Hayden White, "The Absurdist Moment in Contemporary Theory," in *Directions for Criticism*, ed. Krieger and Dembo, offer convenient summary histories of New Criticism.

20. John Wain quoted by Bergonzi in "Critical Situations," p. 64.

21. This is a common theme of English Romanticism and survives in Arnold's prefaces as well as in I. A. Richards's discussion of the "problem of belief," in "Doctrine in Poetry," chap. 7 of *Practical Criticism* (New York: Harcourt Brace, 1929).

22. Culler, "Beyond Interpretation," p. 257.

23. Krieger cites Eliseo Vivas to this effect, in *Theory of Criticism*, p. 11.

24. See Benjamin R. Tilghman's critique of the literary "object" in "The Literary Work of Art," in *Language and Aesthetics: Contributions to the Philosophy of Art*, ed. Tilghman (Lawrence: Univ. Press of Kansas, 1973), pp. 131–53.

25. William Righter, *Logic and Criticism* (New York: Chilmark Press, 1963), p. 113.

26. Culler, "Beyond Interpretation," p. 245.

27. Ralph Cohen, "On a Shift in the Concept of Interpretation," in *The New Criticism and After*, ed. Thomas Daniel Young (Charlottesville: Univ. Press of Virginia, 1976), p. 62.

28. Edward Wasiolek, "Wanted: A New Contextualism," *Critical Inquiry* 1, no. 3 (1975): 627.

29. White, "The Absurdist Moment," pp. 99, 101–2.

30. Wasiolek, "Wanted," p. 624.

31. Cohen, "On a Shift," p. 63.

32. Righter, *Logic and Criticism*, p. 115.

33. For a fuller discussion of the similarities and differences see Denis Donoghue's *The Sovereign Ghost* (Berkeley: Univ. of California Press, 1976), pp. 59–68 especially.

34. Monroe C. Beardsley, *The Possibility of Criticism* (Detroit: Wayne State Univ. Press, 1970).

35. René Wellek, *Theory of Literature*, 2d ed. (New York: Harcourt, Brace, 1956), p. 261, quoted in Cohen, "On a Shift," p. 66.

36. See Cary Nelson's "Reading Criticism," *PMLA* 91, no. 5 (1976): 801–15, and "The Paradox of Critical Language," *MLN* 89, no. 6 (1974): 1003–16.

37. Culler's "Beyond Interpretation" discusses the problem posed by this need to interpret texts that are, in the same breath, said to "contain" their own meaning, pp. 250–51.

38. Cohen, "On A Shift," p. 69.

39. Lionel Abel, "It Isn't True and It Doesn't Rhyme: Our New Criticism," *Encounter* 51, no. 1 (July 1978): 49.

40. Or at least a version of perception; see Louis O. Mink's "History and Fiction as Modes of Comprehension," in *New Directions in Literary History*, ed. Ralph Cohen (Baltimore: Johns Hopkins Univ. Press, 1974), pp. 107–10, for a brief but lucid account of perceptual as opposed to inferential knowledge.

41. The literature on this subject is vast, but it is usefully summarized in Robert Brown, *Explanation in Social Science* (Chicago: Aldine, 1963).

42. R. Harré, *The Philosophies of Science* (London: Oxford Univ. Press, 1972), p. 23.

43. Werner Heisenberg, *Physics and Philosophy*, quoted in Claudio Guillén, *Literature as System: Essays toward the Theory of Literary History* (Princeton: Princeton Univ. Press, 1971), p. 371.

44. Harré, *Philosophies of Science*, p. 25.

45. Mary Hesse, *Models and Analogies in Science*, chap. 1, cited in Ian G. Barbour, *Myths, Models, and Paradigms* (New York: Harper and Row, 1974), p. 33; Barbour's intro-

duction is also a useful summary of the changes in the philosophy of science during the past two decades.

46. See Stephen Toulmin, "From Form to Function: Philosophy and History of Science in the 1950s and Now," *Daedalus* 106, no. 3 (summer 1977): 143–67.

47. The situation is not unique to English and American education, but extends throughout almost the whole of Western European culture.

48. Jean-François Halté, Raymond Michel, and André Petitjean, editors of *Pratiques*, discuss this in broad terms in "Littérature/Théorie/Enseignement," *Poétique* 30 (April 1977): 156–66, as does John Fekete in *The Critical Twilight* (London: Routledge and Kegan-Paul, 1977).

49. Gerald Graff, "Fear and Trembling at Yale," *American Scholar* 46 (fall 1977): 477.

50. Both Krieger (*Theory of Criticism*) and Donoghue (*Sovereign Ghost*) discuss the fate of humanism in their respective studies of recent literary theory.

51. Jean Starobinski, "Criticism and Authority," *Daedalus* 106, no. 4 (fall 1977): 7.

52. Peter Hohendahl, "Introduction to Habermas," *New German Critique* 1, no. 3 (1974): 47.

53. Fekete, *Critical Twilight*, pp. 196–97.

54. Cohen, "On A Shift," pp. 70–71.

55. Cf. Raymond Williams's Introduction to Fekete, *Critical Twilight*, and Klaus Garber, "Thirteen Theses on Literary Criticism," *New German Critique* 1, no. 1 (1973), p. 132.

56. Graff, "Fear and Trembling," p. 476.

57. The position most notably expressed by Paul de Man in his *Blindness and Insight* (New York: Oxford Univ. Press, 1971) and later essays.

58. This is Terrence des Pres's version of Paul Ricoeur's "restorative criticism," in "Prophecies of Grace and Doom: The Function of Criticism at the Present Time," *Partisan Review* 42, no. 2 (1975): 277.

59. Fekete, *Critical Twilight*, p. 202.

60. Robert J. Matthews, "How Is Criticism Possible?" *Diacritics* 2, no. 2 (spring 1972): 24.

61. Cf. Weimann, *Structure and Society*, pp. 30–31.

62. Geoffrey Hartman, "Literary Criticism and Its Discontents," *Critical Inquiry* 3, no. 2 (1976): 211.

63. An attempt apparent even in the diagrams and the paragraphing protocols, as well as in the actual wording and style of argumentation adopted. The point itself is taken from Starobinski, "Criticism and Authority," p. 14.

64. Nicholas Rescher, *Scientific Explanation* (New York: The Free Press, 1970), p. 6.

65. See Krieger, *Theory of Criticism*, chap. 1 passim.

66. Halté et al., "Littérature," p. 159.

67. Edward Said, "Eclecticism and Orthodoxy in Criticism," *Diacritics* 2, no. 2 (spring 1972): 3.

68. Leon S. Roudiez, "With Structuralism and Beyond," *Books Abroad* 49, no. 2 (1975): 208.

69. Hayden White, *Meta-History* (Baltimore: Johns Hopkins Univ. Press, 1973), p. 21.

70. Stephen Melville, "The Situation of Writing," *Chicago Review* 29, no. 2 (1978): 103–16.

71. Barbour, *Myth, Models, and Paradigms*, p. 96.

72. Richard H. Brown, *A Poetic for Sociology* (Cambridge: At the University Press, 1977), p. 3.

73. Abel, "It Isn't True," p. 36; Hartman, "Crossing Over," p. 262.

74. Hartman, "The Recognition Scene," p. 410.

75. des Pres, "Prophecies of Grace," p. 278.

76. Hayden White, "The Problem of Change in Literary History," *New Literary History* 7, no. 1 (1975): 106.

77. Said, "Michel Foucault as an Intellectual Imagination," p. 4.

78. Arnold, "The Function of Criticism at the Present Time," in *Poetry and Criticism of Matthew Arnold*, ed. A. Dwight Culler (Boston: Houghton-Mifflin Co., 1961), p. 239.

79. Ibid.

80. Warner Berthoff's remarks appear in the closing statement to *New Literary History*'s issue on "thinking in the arts and sciences"—"The Way We Think Now: Protocols for Deprivation," vol. 7, no. 3 (1976), p. 600.

81. Krieger, *Theory of Criticism*, p. 53.

82. Starobinski, "Criticism and Authority," p. 14; see also his fuller account "On the Fundamental Gestures of Criticism," *New Literary History* 5, no. 3 (1974): 491–514.

83. George Watson, *The Literary Critics* (Harmondsworth, England: Penguin Books, 1962); Hans Jauss, *Literaturgeschichte als Provokation*, is cited by Richard T. Segers, "Readers, Text, and Author: Some Implications of Rezeptionsasthetik," in *Yearbook of Comparative and General Literature* 24 (1975): 16.

84. Weimann, *Structure and Society*, p. 31.

85. See Michel Charles, "La lecture critique," *Poétique* 34 (April 1978): 129–51.

86. Edward Said, "Notes on the Characterization of a Literary Text," *MLN* 87, no. 7 (1972): 769–70.

87. Cohen, "On a Shift," 73.

88. Gerard Genot, "Rules of the Game: Regulation of the Text," *Sub-stance* 17 (1977): 77–79.

89. Walter L. Reed, "The Problems with a Poetics of the Novel," *Novel* 9, no. 2 (1976): 102.

90. This is what Starobinski cites as the moment when criticism emerges from the communal world of ritual in "The Fundamental Gestures," pp. 495–96.

91. Stephen J. Spector, "The Dummy in Critical Discourse," *Boundary-2*, 4, no. 1 (1975): 141–47.

92. Paul Ricoeur, from "The Critique of Religion," in *The Philosophy of Paul Ricoeur*, ed. Charles E. Reagan and David Stewart (Boston: Beacon Press, 1978), pp. 214–15.

93. R. Meager, "Art and Beauty," *British Journal of Aesthetics* 14, no. 2 (1974): 103.

94. Hartman, "Crossing Over."

95. Michel Foucault, *The Archeology of Knowledge*, trans. A. M. Sheridan-Smith (New York: Irvington, 1972), pp. 182–83.

96. Lionel Abel, "It Isn't True," p. 36.

97. Starobinski, "The Fundamental Gestures," p. 494.

98. Oscar Wilde quoted in Ihab Hassan, "The Critic as Innovator: A Paracritical Strip in X Frames," *Chicago Review* 28, no. 3 (1977): 12.

99. Matthew Arnold, "The Function of Criticism at the Present Time," in Arnold, *Lectures and Essays in Criticism*, vol. 3 in *The Complete Prose Works of Matthew Arnold*, ed. R. H. Super (Ann Arbor: University of Michigan, 1962), p. 283.

Chapter One

1. *Oxford English Dictionary*, s.v. "Theory," 1st ed. (1919).

2. See Jacques Derrida, *La Dissémination* (Paris: Seuil, 1972). In an interview with J-L. Houdebine and Guy Scarpetta ("Positions," *Diacritics* 2, no. 4 [winter 1972]: [35–43], Derrida speaks of his general project as exploring "certain marks...which escape from inclusion in the philosophical (binary) opposition and which nonetheless inhabit it, resist and disorganize it....The *pharmakon* is neither the cure nor the poison, neither good nor evil." Following Derrida, we might say that "theory" is neither fact nor fiction, neither the

real nor the imaginary, but establishes a point where such dichotomies break down and an apparently exhaustive taxonomy shows itself inadequate.

3. R. Harré mentions these as among the logical, epistemological, and metaphysical questions that any theory raises (*The Philosophies of Science* [London: Oxford Univ. Press, 1972], pp. 2–6).

4. Richard H. Brown, *A Poetic for Sociology* (Cambridge: At the University Press, 1977), p. 25.

5. See, for example, Wladyslaw Tatarkiewicz, "Abstract Art and Philosophy," in *Selected Essays*, ed. Jean G. Harrell and Alina Wierzbiańska *Aesthetics in Twentieth Century Poland*: (Lewisburg, Pa.: Bucknell Univ. Press, 1973), pp. 127–42, for a fuller discussion of these matters, especially the distinction between "aspecticism"—a concern for outward form—and "prospectism"—a concern for essence, which rules most so-called abstract art.

6. Brown, *A Poetic for Sociology*, p. 26.

7. W. V. O. Quine, "Posits and Reality," in *Theories and Observation in Science*, ed. Richard E. Grandy (Englewood Cliffs, N.J.: Prentice-Hall, 1973), p. 158.

8. Hayden White, "The Fictions of Factual Representation," in *The Literature of Fact*, ed. Angus Fletcher, Selected Papers from the English Institute (New York: Columbia Univ. Press, 1976), p. 30.

9. The words are Harré's (*The Philosophies of Science*, p. 180), but they build upon Karl Popper's famous claim that theories originate in a "cloud of conjecture." Harré does not dispute the primacy of conjecture, but does dispute the cloudiness and lack of system Popper attributes to it.

10. Harré, *Philosophies of Science*, p. 25.

11. Ian G. Barbour, *Myths, Models, and Paradigms* (New York: Harper and Row, 1974), p. 95.

12. Harré, *Philosophies of Science*, p. 17.

13. Ibid., p. 170.

14. Barbour, *Myths, Models, and Paradigms*, p. 7.

15. This is Nicholas Rescher's position—adapted from Carnap, Hemple, and the later work of Nagel—in *Scientific Explanation* (New York: The Free Press, 1970), p. 129.

16. See Wesley C. Salmon, "Theoretical Explanation," in *Explanation: Papers and Discussions by Peter Achinstein et al.*, ed. Stephan Körner (New Haven: Yale Univ. Press, 1975), p. 165.

17. Ibid., p. 145.

18. Barbour discusses this at length in his introduction to *Myths, Models, and Paradigms* and on pp. 71–78.

19. Nicholas Rescher, *Scientific Explanation* (New York: The Free Press, 1970), p. 12.

20. The distinction is Herbert Feigl's in "De Principiis Non Disputandum . . . ?" in *Philosophical Analysis*, ed. Max Black (Ithaca, N.Y.: Cornell Univ. Press, 1950), pp. 119–56.

21. Harré (*Philosophies of Science*) and Rescher (*Scientific Explanation*) each treat this division between the "metaphysical" or "conceptual" framework and the falsifiable portions of the theory—a distinction that is rooted in Karl Popper's work.

22. Grover Maxwell, "Theories, Frameworks, and Ontology," in *Theories and Observation*, ed. Grandy, p. 107.

23. Imre Lakotos, *Criticism and the Growth of Knowledge* (Cambridge: At the University Press, 1970), p. 133. W. V. O. Quine makes much the same point in *From a Logical Point of View* (New York: Harper and Row, 1953)—see especially "On What There Is," pp. 1–19, and "Two Dogmas of Empiricism," pp. 20–46.

24. Harré notes (*Philosophies of Science*, pp. 92–95), how the status of theoretical posits may vary over time and from theory to theory in just this respect.

25. In an earlier work, *Theories and Things* (London: Sheed and Ward, 1961), R. Harré develops the heavy reliance on aesthetic considerations (what he dubs "Platonic Induction") in most theories, pp. 72–76.

26. See Stephen Toulmin's historical account, "From Form to Function: Philosophy and History of Science in the 1950s and Now," *Daedalus* 106, no. 3 (summer 1977): pp. 143–67.

27. Some writers would, in fact, go even further and insist not only on theory as explanation but that such explanations be limited to mechanical causality, as opposed to teleological or configurational explanations. Then too, some insist in addition that, for theory, explanation must be symmetrical with prediction. Suffice it to say that these restrictions are neither universally accepted nor borne out by the history of science itself.

28. Cf. Peter Geach, "Teleological Explanation," in *Explanation*, ed. Körner, pp. 88–90.

29. Harré offers a brief history of different explanatory frameworks in *The Philosophies of Science*, pp. 130–50; and cf. Geach's remarks in "Teleological Explanation," as well.

30. Harré, *The Philosophies of Science*, p. 171.

31. M. H. Abrams, "What's the Use of Theorizing about the Arts?" in *In Search of Literary Theory*, ed. Morton W. Bloomfield, Studies in the Humanities (Ithaca, N.Y.: Cornell Univ. Press, 1972), pp. 36–37.

32. Arthur Moore, *Contestable Concepts of Literary Theory* (Baton Rouge: Louisiana State Univ. Press, 1973), p. 218.

33. Leonard B. Meyer, "Concerning the Sciences, the Arts—AND the Humanities," *Critical Inquiry* 1, no. 1 (1974): 195.

34. Rescher, *Scientific Explanation*, p. 154.

35. Abrams, "What's the Use," p. 40.

36. William Righter, *Logic and Criticism* (New York: Chilmark Press, 1963), p. 87.

37. Abrams, "What's the Use," p. 10.

38. An amalgamation of several writers in Benjamin R. Tilghman's collection *Language and Aesthetics: Contributions to the History of Art* (Lawrence: Univ. of Kansas Press, 1973) have refined and extended William Kennick's well-known essay "Does Traditional Aesthetics Rest on a Mistake?" (*Mind* 67 [1958]: 317–24), asking whether the concept is not only "open," but also "perenially debatable" and unresolvably "vague." The phrase —"candidate for appreciation" comes from William Dickey's "The Institutional Conception of Art," a proposal for an "institutional definition" of art—both flexible and historically variable, yet determinate for any given community. Allowing for differences in what will be deemed worthy of appreciation, Dickey still argues that the property of "being a candidate" is common to all art objects (see, pp. 21–30).

39. See Jay Schleussener, "Literary Criticism and the Philosophy of Science," *Critical Inquiry* 1, no. 4 (1975): 892–900.

40. See the editors' introduction to *Aesthetics in Twentieth Century Poland*, ed. Harrell and Wierzbiańska, pp. 3–5.

41. Thomas A. Mayberry, "Aesthetic Pleasure and Enjoyment," in *Language and Aesthetics*, ed. Tilghman, p. 123.

42. Editors' introduction to *Aesthetics*, ed. Harrell and Wierzbiańska, pp. 5–6.

43. Righter, *Logic and Criticism*, p. 23.

44. Mary Hesse, "The Explanatory Function of Metaphor," in *Models and Analogies in Science* (New York: Sheed and Ward, 1963), p. 249.

45. Rescher, *Scientific Explanation*, p. 137.

46. Abrams, "What's the Use," p. 21.

47. M. H. Abrams, "Theories of Poetry," in *Princeton Encyclopedia of Poetry and Poetics*, ed. Alex Preminger, enl. ed. (Princeton, N.J.: Princeton Univ. Press, 1974), p. 648.

48. Jonathan Culler, *Structuralist Poetics* (London: Routledge and Kegan Paul, 1975), p. 26–31.

49. Meyer, "Concerning the Sciences," p. 196.

50. Louis O. Mink, "History and Fiction as Modes of Comprehension," in *New*

Directions in Literary History, ed. Ralph Cohen (London: Routledge and Kegan-Paul, 1974), p. 114.

51. Grover Maxwell, "Theories, Fragments, and Ontology," in *The Nature of Scientific Theories*, ed. Robert G. Colodny (Pittsburgh: Univ. of Pittsburgh Press, 1970), p. 10.

52. Harré, *Theories and Things*, pp. 72, 76.

53. W. V. O. Quine, "Grades of Theoricity," in *Experience and Theory*, ed. Lawrence Foster and J. W. Swanson (Amherst: Univ. of Massachusetts Press, 1970), pp. 16–17.

54. The opposition appears in Meyer, "Concerning the Sciences," owing something in turn to Suzanne Langer.

55. David Basch, "A Proposed Definition of Aesthetics through the Extension of the Logical Syllogism," *Connecticut Review* 5, no. 1 (1971): 13–25.

56. Peter Achinstein, *Law and Explanation* (Oxford: Clarendon Press, 1971), p. 82.

57. Norbert Hanson, "A Picture Theory of Theory Meaning," in *Nature of Scientific Theories*, ed. Colodny, p. 237.

58. This is Meyer's summary in "Concerning the Sciences," pp. 181–84, although his dichotomy between science and the humanities is too simple.

59. Roy Pascal, "Narrative Fictions and Reality," *Novel* 11, no. 1 (1977): 40–44, citing Frank Kermode's *The Sense of an Ending*, with further qualifications of his own. Yet Barbour similarly disputes in *Myth, Models, and Paradigms*, the notion that scientific theories rise and fall on "crucial tests" alone.

60. Hilary Putnam's words are directed to the difference between moral systems and scientific theories, but seem applicable to aesthetics matters too—see "Literature, Science, and Reflection," *New Literary History* 7, no. 3 (1976): 491.

61. R. D. Braithwaite, *Scientific Explanation* (Cambridge: At the University Press, 1968), pp. 80, 82.

62. R. D. Braithwaite, "Symposium: Imaginary Objects," in *Proceedings of the Aristotelean Society*, suppl. vol. 12 (London: Harrison and Sons, 1933), pp. 44, 49, 50–51.

63. W. V. O. Quine, "Posits and Reality," in *Theories and Observation in Science*, ed. Richard E. Grandy (Englewood Cliffs, N.J.: Prentice-Hall, 1973), pp. 157–58.

64. John R. Searle, "The Logical Status of Fictional Discourse," *New Literary History* 6, no. 2 (1975): 330.

65. R. D. Braithwaite, quoted in Jerzy Pelc, "Nominal Expressions and Literary Fiction," in *Aesthetics*, ed. Harrell and Wierzbiańska, p. 215.

66. Harré, *Theories and Things*, pp. 61–62—who ends by distinguishing between "objects" (both meeting stable expectations and locatable in space-time) and "entities" (which meet only the first criterion).

67. See Francis X. Coleman, "A Few Observations on Fictional Discourse," in *Language and Aesthetics*, ed. Tilghman, pp. 31–42, and Eva Scheiper, "Fiction and the Suspension of Disbelief," *British Journal of Aesthetics* 18, no. 1 (1978): 29–44.

68. Pascal, "Narrative Fictions and Reality," treats this question at length.

69. Harré, *The Philosophies of Science*, pp. 10–18.

70. Ibid., pp. 80–94.

71. Barbour, *Myths, Models, and Paradigms*, pp. 34–42.

72. Quine, "Posits and Reality," pp. 157–58.

73. Harré, *Theories and Things*, pp. 26–27, and further refined in *The Philosophies of Science*, pp. 25–28, to show which constructs could be eliminated and which could not.

74. This is not to deny that other literary motives are equally compelling—fantasm, "criticism of life," and so forth—nor to conflate literary fictions and theoretical posits. Harré (*Philosophies of Science*, pp. 80–89) and Robert Brown (*Explanation in Social Science* [Chicago: Aldine, 1963], pp. 179–83) propose various distinctions between theoretical posits that have empirical claims and "ideal types" or "formal concepts" that lack them. The latter would seem closer to literary fictions, since they are not revisable on empirical grounds, but instead

serve to classify or hold together in "one intelligible system" facts for which no necessary logical or empirical connection is claimed. Thus, one who finds a pattern of behavior and calls it "Pickwickian" is not claiming that the pattern is evidence that the person must be Pickwick, but simply that the same structure of behavior is also ascribed to a fictional character called Pickwick. It is simpler to use one word than to list the various actions and their relationship. Moreover, in citing Pickwick, the speaker is probably also alluding to what first led him to focus on that pattern—or to what he expects will lead his listeners to focus on the pattern. Of course, the example of Pickwick could also serve as the basis for discoveries about the way behavior is likely to cluster, about "character formations" and the circumstances associated with them that could be candidates for reality, even if Pickwick himself is not. In the latter case, however, one eventually ceases to speak of the fictional character at all; Pickwick would be one of Wittgenstein's ladders to be kicked away. (See also Mary Hesse, "Is There an Independent Observation Language?," in *Nature of Scientific Theories*, ed. Colodny, pp. 159–60; David Papineau, "Ideal Types and Empirical Theories," *British Journal for the Philosophy of Science* 27, no. 2 (1976): 145–46; Pascal, "Narrative Fictions and Reality"; Harrell and Wierzbiańska's introduction to *Aesthetics*; and Jerzy Pelc's article "Nominal Expressions and Literary Fiction," pp. 205–228 in the same volume.)

75. Oscar Wilde, "The Decay of Lying," in *Critical Theory since Plato*, ed. Hazard Adams (New York: Harcourt, Brace, Jovanovich, 1971), pp. 680–81, 683.

76. Quine, "Posits and Reality," pp. 158–59.

77. Harré, *The Philosophies of Science*, p. 80. See also Robert Scholes, "The Fictional Criticism of the Future," *Tri-Quarterly*, no. 34 (fall 1975), 233–47.

78. See Maria Eaton, "Liars, Ranters, and Dramatic Speakers," in *Language and Aesthetics*, ed. Tilghman, pp. 43–63, and Roman Ingarden, "On So-Called Truth in Literature," in *Aesthetics*, ed. Harrell and Wierzbiańska, pp. 164–204.

79. William Ray, "Recognizing Recognition: The Intra-textual and Extra-textual Critical Persona," *Diacritics* 7, no. 4 (winter, 1977): 20–33.

80. Searle makes this point in "Logical Status," pp. 326–28, as does (more forcefully, and without the usual claim that fiction is therefore "parasitic") Eaton in "Liars, Ranters, and Dramatic Speakers."

81. Paul Feyerabend, "On the 'Meaning' of Scientific Terms," in *Theories and Observation in Science*, ed. Grandy, p. 181, argues that in fact, even scientific theories are untranslatable and unparaphraseable, that each theoretical text gives a new meaning to its key terms (like *energy*). Feyerabend has, however, been countered by Stephen Toulmin and others as discussed by Barbour in *Myths, Models, and Paradigms*, pp. 106–8.

82. Hesse, "Is There an Independent Observation Language?" p. 57.

83. Donald Davidson, "What Metaphors Mean," *Critical Inquiry* 5, no. 1 (1978): 33. There continue to be lively arguments about whether metaphor produces a new meaning. Monroe Beardsley's "Metaphorical Sense," *Nous* 12 (1978): 3–16, opposes Davidson's view that meaning should be kept entirely distinct from the effect a metaphor produces ad hoc. Both writers concur with Max Black's view that metaphor results in a new organization of our usual associations, either altering a word's implications or its applications.

84. Grandy's Introduction to *Theories and Observation in Science*, p. 10.

85. Ibid., p. 9.

86. Hesse, "Is There an Independent Observation Language?" p. 50.

87. Hesse, *Models and Analogues in Science*, pp. 164–65.

88. Ibid., pp. 164–65.

89. See Paul Ricoeur's synthesis of several analyses of metaphor (notably Max Black's classic treatment in *Models and Metaphors*, 1962) in *The Rule of Metaphor* (Toronto: Toronto Univ. Press, 1977), pp. 237–43. In contrast, Rescher stresses that scientific models need not be more familiar, just more intelligible, in *Scientific Explanation*, p. 2.

90. Cf. Barbour, *Myths, Models, and Paradigms*, on Black and Hesse. pp. 43–9.

91. Ibid., passim, and Harré, *The Philosophies of Science*, pp. 172–80.
92. Cf. Barbour's introduction to *Myths, Models, and Paradigms*, pp. 29–48.
93. Brown, *A Poetics for Sociology*, pp. 74–128.
94. Beardsley, "Metaphysical Senses," pp. 14–15, and Ina Loewenberg, "Creativity and Correspondence in Fiction and Metaphors," *Journal of Aesthetics and Art Criticism* 36, no. 3 (1978): 341–50.
95. Meyer, "Concerning the Sciences," p. 180.
96. Hayden White, "The Absurdist Moment in Contemporary Literary Theory," in *Directions for Criticism*, ed. Murray Krieger and L. S. Dembo (Madison: Univ. of Wisconsin Press, 1977), p. 103.
97. Jonathan Culler, *Ferdinand de Saussure*, Penguin Modern Masters (Middlesex, England: Penguin Books, 1976), p. 77.
98. Jacques Derrida, *Of Grammatology*, trans. Gayatri Chakravortky Spivak (Baltimore: Johns Hopkins Univ. Press, 1976), p. 20.
99. Ibid., p. 19.
100. Jonathan Culler, "In Pursuit of Signs," *Daedalus* 106, no. 4 (fall 1977): 108.
101. Culler, *Structuralist Poetics*, p. 40.
102. Hazard Adams, "Contemporary Ideas of Literature: Terrible Beauty or Rough Beast?" in *Directions for Criticism*, ed. Krieger and Dembo, p. 69.
103. Culler, *Saussure*, pp. 79–82.
104. Edward Said, "Contemporary Fiction and Criticism," *Tri-Quarterly*, no. 33 (spring 1975), pp. 254–55, both citing and commenting on Foucault, *The Archeology of Knowledge*.
105. Richard Klein discusses Said's ambiguous attraction to "performance" as a category in somewhat different terms, in "That He Said That Said Said" (*Enclitic* 2, no. 1 [1978]: 88).
106. Maurice Nadeau, "Le brancher sur la machine Deleuze," *Le Livre de la Quinzaine*, 15 February 1978, pp. 4–5.
107. Culler, *Structuralist Poetics*, pp. 138–39, quotes from Julia Kristeva, *Semiotike*.
108. Edward Said, "Roads Taken and Not Taken in Contemporary Criticism," in *Directions for Criticism*, ed. Krieger and Dembo, p. 50.
109. Layla Perrone-Moisés, "Intertexte and autotexte," *Poétique* 27 (1976): 373.
110. Culler, "In Pursuit of Signs," p. 108.
111. Jean Franco, "The Crisis of the Liberal Imagination," *Ideologies and Literature* 1, no. 1 (1976–77): 18.
112. Ibid., passim.
113. Ibid., p. 6.
114. Fredric Jameson, "Of Islands and Trenches: Neutralization and the Production of Utopian Discourse," *Diacritics* 7, no. 2 (spring 1977): 7.
115. Nadeau, "Le brancher," pp. 4–5.
116. Tzvetan Todorov, "The Notion of Literature," *New Literary History* 5, no. 1 (1973): 5–16, mentions the forms that literary and non literary discourse share; Searle, "The Logical Status of Fictional Discourse," notes that even fiction is not exclusively literary; and Wilbur Samuel Howell treats the changing boundaries between literature and "rhetoric" in *Poetics, Rhetoric, and Logic: Studies in the Basic Disciplines of Criticism* (Ithaca, N.Y.: Cornell Univ. Press, 1975).
117. Sylvère Lotringer, "The Game of the Name," *Diacritics* 3, no. 2 (summer 1973): 9.
118. Paul de Man, "The Crisis of Contemporary Criticism," *Arion* 6, no. 1 (1967): 55.
119. Alan Bass, " 'Literature'/Literature," *MLN* 87, no. 7 (1972): 860.
120. Stephen Melville, "The Situation of Writing," *Chicago Review* 29, no. 2 (1978): 104.
121. Harré, *The Philosophies of Science*, p. 81.

122. See Hugh Kenner, "The Poetics of Error," *MLN* 90, no. 6 (1975): 738–46.

123. Frank Kermode, "The Way We Live Now," *New York Times Book Review*, 14 January 1979, p. 27.

124. Robert Alter, "The Self-Conscious Moment: Reflections on the Aftermath of Modernism," *Tri-Quarterly* 33 (spring 1975): 218–19. See also Ihab Hassan's reflections on the "new Gnosticism,"—"Abstractions," *Diacritics* 5, no. 2 (spring 1975): 15.

125. Jean-François Lyotard, "For a Pseudo-Theory," *Yale French Studies*, no. 49 (1973), 116–17.

126. David Hayman, "An Interview with Maurice Roche," *Tri-Quarterly* 38 (winter 1977): 74.

127. Ray (discussing Wolfgang Iser) in "Recognizing Recognition," pp. 26–30.

128. Terrence des Pres, "Prophesies of Grace and Doom: The Function of Criticism at the Present Time," *Partisan Review* 42, no. 2 (1975): 280.

129. Alter, "The Self-Conscious Moment," pp. 214–15.

130. Robert Scholes, "The Fictional Criticism of the Future," quoted in Gerald Graff, "Fear and Trembling at Yale," *American Scholar* 46 (fall 1977): 470.

131. Linda Hutcheon, "The Outer Limits of the Novel: Italy and France," *Contemporary Literature* 18, no. 2 (1975): 198–200.

132. Robert Scholes, "The Fictional Criticism of the Future," p. 239.

133. Des Pres (following Ricoeur), "Prophesies of Grace," p. 274.

134. Fredric Jameson, "T. W. Adorno, or Historical Tropes," *Salmagundi* 2, no. 1 (1967): 20.

135. Leo Bersani, "The Subject of Power," *Diacritics* 7, no. 3 (fall 1977): 7.

136. Hutcheon, "The Outer Limits," pp. 214–16.

137. Stanley Cavell, "A Matter of Meaning It," in his *Must We Mean What We Say?* (Cambridge: At the University Press, 1969), pp. 219–20.

138. See Hans R. Jauss, "Interview," *Diacritics* 5, no. 1 (spring 1975): 55, and "Levels of Identification of Hero and Audience," *New Literary History* 5, no. 4 (1974): 283–317.

139. Jean François Halté et al., "Littérature/Théorie/Enseignement," *Poétique* 30 (April 1977): 156–66.

Chapter Two

1. Geoffrey Hartman, "Crossing Over: Literary Commentary as Literature," *Comparative Literature* 28, no. 3 (1976): 259.

2. See Paul Ricoeur, *The Rule of Metaphor* (Toronto: Toronto Univ. Press, 1977), on the logic of prediction in metaphor, and particularly the tension between asserting and disavowing metaphoric identities, pp. 178–79.

3. Leonard B. Meyer, "Concerning the Sciences, the Arts—AND the Humanities," *Critical Inquiry* 1, no. 1 (1974): 167.

4. C. P. Snow, *Public Affairs*, quoted by Meyer, ibid., p. 186. Against this view there stands the work of Paul Feyerabend and (to a lesser extent) Kuhn; for an account of the quarrel see Ian G. Barbour, *Myths, Models, and Paradigms* (New York: Harper and Row, 1974).

5. Meyer, "Concerning the Sciences," pp. 183–84.

6. See Jonathan Culler's *Structuralist Poetics* (London: Routledge and Kegan Paul, 1975) for a general discussion.

7. Roman Ingarden, "On So-Called Truth in Literature," in *Aesthetics in Twentieth Century Poland: Selected Essays*, ed. Jean G. Harrell and Alina Wierzbiańska (Lewisburg, Pa.: Bucknell Univ. Press, 1973), pp. 164–204.

8. Gerald Graff, "Fear and Trembling at Yale," *American Scholar* 46 (fall 1977): 477.

9. Hayden White, "The Absurdist Moment in Contemporary Literary Theory," in *Directions for Criticism*, ed. Murray Krieger and L. S. Dembo (Madison: Univ. of Wisconsin Press, 1977), pp. 85–110, also treats the related problems of specialization and mystification.

10. William Rueckert, "Literary Criticism and History," *New Literary History* 6, no. 3 (1975): 501.

11. Richard Brown, *A Poetics for Sociology* (Cambridge: At the University Press, 1978), p. 99.

12. Ibid., pp. 183, 102.

13. Cf. William Ray, "Recognizing Recognition," *Diacritics* 7, no. 4 (winter 1977): 20–33, and Robert Scholes, "Toward a Semiotics of Literature," *Critical Inquiry* 4, no. 1 (1977): 105–20.

14. Hillary Putnam, "Literature, Science, and Reflection," *New Literary History* 7, no. 3 (1976): 490.

15. Jean Starobinski, "On the Fundamental Gestures of Criticism," *New Literary History* 5, no. 3 (1974): 497.

16. Jan Mukarovsky, "Standard Language and Poetic Language," in *Critical Theory since Plato*, ed. Hazard Adams (New York: Harcourt, Brace & Janovich, 1971), pp. 1053–54.

17. Brown, *A Poetics for Sociology*, p. 3.

18. Barbour, *Myths, Models, and Paradigms*, pp. 142–46.

19. Nelson Goodman, *The Languages of Art* (Indianapolis: Bobbs-Merrill, 1968), p. 264.

20. See Jean-François Lyotard, "Jewish Oedipus," *Genre* 10, no. 3 (1977): 395.

21. George Dickie, "The Institutional Conception of Art," in *Language and Aesthetics: Contributions to the Philosophy of Art*, ed. Benjamin R. Tilghman (Lawrence: Univ. Press of Kansas, 1973), pp. 21–30.

22. See Brown's summary in *A Poetics for Sociology*, pp. 50–51.

23. Jens Allwood, et al., *Logic in Linguistics* (Cambridge: At the University Press, 1977), treats the logic of "opaque" and "oblique" sentences, pp. 117–18. A different orientation may be found in Gilles Deleuze, who builds upon Nietzsche's "repetition" (as opposed to representation or reflection) to arrive at a vision of recurrence that is not a "copy"—in *Nietzsche et la philosophie* (Paris: Presses Universitaires de France, 1962).

24. Cary Nelson, "Reading Criticism," *PMLA* 91, no. 5 (1976): 802.

25. Lionel Abel, "It Isn't True and It Doesn't Rhyme: Our New Criticism," *Encounter* 51, no. 1 (July 1978): 38.

26. Emir Rodriguez Monegal, "Borges and *La Nouvelle Critique*," *Diacritics* 2, no. 2 (summer 1972): 118.

27. Hans Robert Jauss, "Levels of Identification of Hero and Audience," *New Literary History* 5, no. 2 (1974): 285–86.

28. Helene Cixous, "The 'Character' of Character," *New Literary History* 5, no. 2 (1974): 401–2.

29. Cary Nelson, "The Paradox of Critical Language," *MLN* 89, no. 6 (1974): 1005; Richard Klein, "That He Said That Said Said," *Enclitic* 2, no. 1 (1978): 86; Leo Bersani, "The Subject of Power," *Diacritics* 7, no. 3 (fall 1977): 6.

30. Cf. Hayden White's *Meta-History* (Baltimore: Johns Hopkins Univ. Press, 1973) and Paul de Man's essay "Political Allegory in Rousseau," in *Critical Inquiry* 3, no. 3 (1976): 649–75, for exemplary studies in which the subject of prose and the revived interest in rhetorical categories merge; another case in point is the "rediscovery" of Kenneth Burke.

31. See Julian Moynahan et al., "Character as a Lost Cause," *Novel* 11, no. 3 (1978): 207 (the phrase is credited to Arnold Weinstein).

32. R. Harré, *The Philosophies of Science* (London: Oxford Univ. Press, 1972), p. 80.

33. Edward Said, "Contemporary Fiction and Criticism," *Tri-Quarterly*, no. 33 (spring 1975), pp. 241–42.

34. Stephen Melville, "The Situation of Writing," *Chicago Review* 29, no. 2 (1978): 103–16.

35. Culler, *Structuralist Poetics*, p. 148.

36. Cf. Peter Achinstein's "The Object of Explanation" (along with its responses) in *Explanation: Papers and Discussions by Peter Achinstein et al.*, ed. Stephan Körner (New Haven, Conn.: Yale Univ. Press, 1975).

37. William Charlton, "Is Philosophy a Form of Literature?" *British Journal of Aesthetics* 14, no. 1 (1974): 9.

38. Charles Alteieri, "Wittgenstein on Consciousness," *MLN* 91, no. 6 (1976): 1406.

39. I here substitute three sites for Brown's original two in *A Poetics for Sociology*, p. 172.

40. Gilles Deleuze and Felix Guattari, *Anti-Oedipus* (New York: Viking, 1977).

41. See Stephen J. Spector, "The Dummy in Critical Discourse," *Boundary–2*, 4, no. 1 (1975): 141–47.

42. See Fredric Jameson, "The Vanishing Mediator," *New German Critique* 1, no. 1 (1973): 52–89.

43. Hayden White, "The Problem of Change in Literary History," *New Literary History* 7, no. 1 (1975): 104.

44. Fredric Jameson, "The Symbolic Inference," *Critical Inquiry* 5, no. 2 (1978): 517–18.

45. Nicholas Rescher, *Scientific Explanation* (New York: The Free Press, 1970), p. 33.

46. Louis Marin, "Interview," *Diacritics* 7, no. 2 (summer 1977), p. 49; Jameson, "The Vanishing Mediator," p. 75; Brown, *A Poetics for Sociology*, p. 182.

47. See Barbour's introduction to *Myths, Models, and Paradigms*.

48. Harré, *Philosophies of Science*, pp. 175–76.

49. Max Black, *Models and Metaphors*, cited in Barbour, *Myths, Models, and Paradigms*, p. 43.

50. See Harré, *Philosophies of Science*, p. 176 and throughout, for a discussion of when the status of a model changes.

51. Barbour, *Myths, Models, and Paradigms*, pp. 71–78.

52. See the "Métalanguage" issue of *Littérature* (no. 27; October 1977), especially Claude Abastrado's Introduction, pp. 3–5.

53. Bernard Bergonzi, "Critical Situations," *Critical Quarterly* 15, no. 1 (1973): 67.

54. See Culler's debate with "structuralist poetics" on this question.

55. See Claude Abastrado's introduction to the "métalanguage" issue of *Littérature*, pp. 3–5.

56. Rescher, *Scientific Explanation*, p. 153.

57. Ibid., pp. 131–38, 150–56.

58. Jauss, "Levels of Identification," pp. 293–94.

59. Louis Marin, "Disneyland: A Degenerate Utopia," *Glyph* 1 (1977): 53.

60. Cf. Culler, *Structuralist Poetics*, p. 224.

61. Lewis O. Mink, "History and Fiction as Modes of Comprehension," in *New Directions in Literary History*, ed. Ralph Cohen (Baltimore: Johns Hopkins Univ. Press, 1974), p. 111.

62. Jauss, "Levels of Identification," p. 294.

63. Wilhelm Dilthey, "The Rise of Hermeneutics," *New Literary History* 5, no. 2 (1974): 229–44.

64. See Frank Kermode, *The Sense of an Ending* (New York: Oxford Univ. Press, 1967).

65. Sande Cohen, "Structuralism and the Writing of Intellectual History," *History and Theory* 17, no. 2 (1978): 176–80.

66. Cf. Frank Kermode, "An Approach through History," in *Towards a Poetics of Fiction*, ed. Mark Spilka (Bloomington: Indiana Univ. Press, 1977), pp. 23–30; Mink, "His-

tory and Fiction"; Roy Pascal, "Narrative Fictions and Reality," *Novel* 2, no. 1 (1977): 40–50.
67. Culler, *Structuralist Poetics*, pp. 209–10.
68. Roland Barthes, "Introduction to the Structural Analysis of Narratives," in his *Image/Music/Text*, selected and trans. Stephen Heath (New York: Hill and Wang, 1977) provides a useful summary, as do Culler's chapters on Greimas and on the study of narrative in *Structuralist Poetics*.
69. Pascal, "Narrative Fictions," pp. 45–46, and Mink, "History and Fiction," pp. 120–22.
70. J. L. Gormer, "Review of Leon J. Goldstein's *Historical Knowing*" (*History and Theory* 16, no. 1 [1977]: 66–80) discusses the question of counterfactuals in narrative history.
71. Cf. Barthes, "Structural Analysis," p. 94.
72. Harré, *Philosophies of Science*, p. 119.
73. See Lyotard, "Jewish Oedipus," pp. 395–98.
74. Culler, *Structuralist Poetics*, pp. 222–23.
75. White, *Meta-History*, p. 7.
76. For a more detailed treatment of taxonomy and theory, see Rescher, *Scientific Explanation*, pp. 1–35, 129–37; Culler, *Structuralist Poetics*, pp. 45–90; William Righter, *Logic and Criticism* (New York: Chilmark Press, 1963), pp. 87–88, 110–20.
77. Mink, "History and Fiction," p. 116.
78. Fredric Jameson, "Figural Relativism," *Diacritics* 6, no. 1 (spring 1976)): 6, 8.
79. Kenneth Burke, *A Rhetoric of Motives* (Berkeley, Calif.: Univ. of California Press, 1969); Roman Jacobson and Lawrence G. Jones, *Shakespeare's Verbal Act in "Th'expense of Spirit"* (The Hague: Mouton, 1970).
80. White, *Meta-History*, pp. 35–38; although White's central interest is not taxonomy and he tends to conflate different relationships, mixing part/whole with cause/effect and agent/instrument.
81. Daniel Delas, "Confondre et ne pas confondre: de quelques précautions métalinguistiques concernant le changement définitionnel," in the "Métalanguage" issue of *Littérature*, pp. 97–99.
82. M. H. Abrams, "Theories of Poetry," in *Princeton Encyclopedia of Poetry and Poetics*, ed. Alex Preminger, expanded ed. (Princeton: Princeton Univ. Press, 1965), p. 648, quoted in Arthur K. Moore, *Contestable Concepts in Literary Theory* (Baton Rouge: Louisiana State Univ. Press, 1973), p. 216.
83. Nelson's words about Barthes, in "Reading Criticism," p. 802.
84. Culler, *Structuralist Poetics*, p. 257, calls this "rigorous irrelevance."
85. Ricoeur, *Rule of Metaphors*, pp. 241–43.
86. Jonathan Culler, "Beyond Interpretation: The Prospects of Contemporary Criticism," *Comparative Literature* 28, no. 3 (1976): 245–46.
87. John Reichert, "Model-Making and the Usefulness of Criticism," *College English* 34 (1973): 922.
88. Said, "Contemporary Fiction and Criticism," pp. 232–33, names Mallarmé, Nietzsche, and Proust in this respect.
89. Johnathan Culler, "In Pursuit of Signs," *Daedalus* 106, no. 4 (fall 1977): 110.
90. Harré calls this the level of "micro-explanation," in *Philosophies of Science*, p. 132; cf. also White, *Meta-History*, p. 14.
91. Harré, *Philosophies of Science*, pp. 120–32.
92. Reichert, "Model-Making," p. 918.
93. M. H. Abrams, "Rationality and Imagination in Cultural History," *Critical Inquiry* 2, no. 3 (1976): 454.
94. Donald S. Taylor, "Literary Criticism and Historical Inferences," *Clio* 5, no. 3 (1976): 348–49.
95. Abrams, "Rationality and Imagination," p. 459.
96. De Man, "Political Allegory in Rousseau," p. 674.

97. Marin, "Interview," p. 45.

98. Ibid., p. 50.

99. Leo Bersani, "The Subject of Power," *Diacritics* 7, no. 3 (fall 1977), 5.

100. Cf. Charlton, "Is Philosophy a Form of Literature?"

101. See Richard Gullon, "On Space in the Novel," *Critical Inquiry* 2, no. 1 (1975), 12–13.

102. Hayden White, "The Fictions of Factual Representation," in *Selected Papers of the English Institute*, ed. Angus Fletcher (New York: Columbia Univ. Press, 1976), p. 35.

103. White, *Meta-History*, p. 22.

104. Marin, "Interview," p. 51.

105. Culler, *Structuralist Poetics*, p. 146.

106. Ihab Hassan, "The Critic as Innovator," *Chicago Review* 28, no. 3 (1977): 18.

107. Laurent Jenny, "La strategie de la forme," *Poétique* 27 (1976): 280–81.

108. Monegal, "Borges and *La Nouvelle Critique*," p. 32.

109. Claude Abastrado, "La glace sans tain," in the "Métalanguage" issue of *Littérature*, pp. 61–64.

110. Michel Charles, "La lecture critique," *Poétique* 34 (1978): 132–33.

111. Jenny, "La strategie," p. 266, and Layla Perrone-Moises, "Intertexte," *Poétique* 27 (1976): 372–84.

112. Francis C. Ferguson, "Reading Heidegger," *Boundary–2* 4, no. 2 (1976), p. 195.

113. Charles, "La lecture critique," pp. 150–51.

114. Jenny, "La strategie," p. 267.

115. Perrone-Moises, "Intertexte," p. 373.

116. M. Bakhtin, *Voprosy esteki literatury i* (Moscow: 1975), p. 433. Translated as *The Dialogic Imagination* by Carl Emerson and Michael Holquist, University of Texas Slavic Series no. 1 (Austin: University of Texas Press, 1981), p. 433.

117. See Culler, *Structuralist Poetics*, p. 144, on presupposition vs. construction.

118. Robert R. Magiola, *Phenomenology and Literature* (West Lafayette, Ind.: Purdue Univ. Press, 1977), p. 63.

119. Lucien Dallenbach, "Intertexte et autotexte," *Poétique* 27 (1976): 290–95.

120. Charles, "La lecture critique," p. 142.

121. Ibid., pp. 147–49.

122. Ibid., pp. 131–32.

123. Michel Foucault, "Monstrosities in Criticism," *Diacritics* 1, no. 3 (fall 1971): 58.

124. Jenny, "La strategie," pp. 275–79.

125. Virgil Nemorianu, "Recent Romanian Criticism," *World Literature Today* 51, no. 4 (1977): 560—citing George Calinescu.

126. Nelson, "The Paradox of Critical Language," discusses the alternation of ascent and descent.

127. Klein, "That He Said That Said Said," 95–96.

128. Gayatri Chakravorty Spivak, "*Glas*-piece," *Diacritics* 7, no. 3 (fall 1977): 22–43.

129. Culler, "Beyond Interpretation," p. 254.

130. Charles, "La lecture critique," pp. 149–50.

131. Nelson, "Reading Criticism," p. 803.

132. Charles, "La lecture critique," Perrone-Moises, "Intertexte," Jenny, "La strategie" and Dalenbach "Intertexte et autotexte" usually show one text mastering the other—or losing its mastery.

133. Melville, "The Situation of Writing," passim.

134. Sande Cohen, "Structuralism," p. 204.

135. Hartman, "Crossing Over," p. 260; see also Friedrich Waismann, "Language Strata," in *Logic and Language*, ed. Anthony G. Flew (New York: Philosophical Library, 1952), pp. 226–47.

136. Kenneth Burke, "Introduction," *A Grammar of Motives* (Berkeley: Univ. of California Press, 1945), pp. xv–xxiii.

137. John Searle, *Speech Acts* (Cambridge: Cambridge Univ. Press, 1969); see chapter three in particular.

138. V. V. Ivanov, "The Significance of M. M. Bakhtin's Ideas on Sign, Utterance, and Dialogue for Modern Semiotics," *Soviet Studies in Literature* 11, no. 2–3 (1975): 199.

139. Wilbur Samuel Howell, *Poetics, Rhetoric, and Logic: Studies in the Basic Disciplines of Criticism* (Ithaca, N.Y.: Cornell Univ. Press, 1975), pp. 62–63, 81. See also Edwin Black, *Rhetorical Criticism* (Madison: Univ. of Wisconsin Press, 1978), pp. 106–7.

140. William G. Lycan and Peter K. Machmer, "A Theory of Critical Reasons," in *Language and Aesthetics*, ed. Tilghman, pp. 87–112.

141. Black, *Rhetorical Criticism*, p. 146.

142. Murray Krieger suggests a further distinction: between the critical "persona"—"the public personality" adopted in conformity with the principles of a system that may well exceed any single text and that seeks to achieve agreement with the audience—and the critical "person," who strives for authenticity even at the expense of system and palatability (*Theory of Criticism: A Tradition and Its System* [Baltimore: Johns Hopkins Univ. Press, 1978] pp. 46–47).

143. Cf. Scholes, "Toward a Semiotics of Literature," and Ray, "Recognizing Recognition," for further treatment of the distinction between the "ideal," the "real," and the "implied" audience of the text.

144. See Bakhtin on varieties of dialogism, quoted in Ivanov, "Significance of Bakhtin's Ideas," p. 203.

145. Brown, *A Poetics for Sociology*, p. 45.

146. Jean-François Lyotard, "For a Pseudo-Theory," *Yale French Studies*, no. 49 (1973), 115.

147. Nelson, "The Paradox of Critical Language," p. 1004.

148. Sande Cohen, "Structuralism," p. 202.

149. Meir Sternberg, *Expositional Modes and Temporal Ordering in Fiction* (Baltimore: Johns Hopkins Univ. Press, 1978), pp. 35–55.

150. Richard A. Lanham, *A Handlist of Rhetorical Terms* (Berkeley: Univ. of California Press, 1968), p. 125.

151. Jean-Marc Blanchard, "The Pleasures of Description," *Diacritics* 7, no. 2 (summer 1977): 29.

152. Berel Lang's system is threefold, with philosophical empiricism, idealism, and reflexivism each having its associated temporal and spatial perspectives: *Art and Inquiry* (Detroit: Wayne State University Press, 1975), pp. 162–63.

153. Harré, *The Philosophies of Science*, p. 18; see also Lang, *Art and Inquiry*, p. 163.

154. Culler, "Presupposition and Intertextuality," *MLN* 91, no 6 (1976): 1389–90, also illustrates the difference between "logical" and "pragmatic" presupposition, the latter being the necessary contextual and conventional conditions.

155. See David Hayman, "Some Writers in the Wake of the *Wake*," *Tri-Quarterly* 38 (winter 1977): 30–31.

156. See Nelson, "Reading Criticism," p. 804n.

157. See Marc Shell, *The Economy of Literature* (Baltimore: Johns Hopkins Univ. Press, 1978); S. Todd Lowry, "The Archeology of the Circulation Concept in Economic Theory," *Journal of the History of Ideas* 35 (July–September 1974): 424–44; and a very early adaptation of Lévi-Strauss by Jacques Ehrmann, "Structures of Exchange in the *Cinna*," *Yale French Studies*, nos. 36/37 (1966): 169–200.

158. Anthony Wilden, *System and Structure* (London: Tavistock, 1972), p. 134.

159. Jameson, "Figural Relativism," pp. 7–8, provides a convenient summary of Karl Marx's stages of exchange.

160. Terry Eagleton, *Criticism and Ideology* (London: New Left Books, 1976), p. 167.
161. See Jacques Derrida, *L'écriture et la différence* (Paris: Ed. du Seuil, 1967).
162. Lyotard, "Jewish Oedipus," speaks of such "figures" in Freud's text, p. 398.
163. Derrida, *L'écriture*, p. 44.
164. Lyotard, "Jewish Oedipus," p. 392.
165. Edward Said, "Roads Taken and Not Taken in Contemporary Criticism," in *Directions for Criticism*, ed. Kreiger and Dembo, p. 39.
166. Edward Said, "An Ethics of Language," *Diacritics* 4, no. 2 (summer 1974): 30.
167. Peter Caws, "Projections and Restrictions," *Diacritics* 3, no. 2 (summer 1973): 20.
168. Michel Foucault, *Language, Counter-Memory, Practice*, ed. Donald F. Bouchard, trans. Donald F. Bouchard and Sherry Simon (Ithaca, N.Y.: Cornell Univ. Press, 1977), p. 200.
169. Michel Foucault, *Discipline and Punish*, trans. Alan Sheridan (New York: Pantheon Books, 1977), p. 15.
170. Foucault, *Language, Counter-Memory, Practice*, p. 201.
171. Fredric Jameson, "T. W. Adorno, Or, Historical Tropes," *Salmagundi* 2, no. 1 (1967): 6.
172. Max Weber, quoted in Robert Brown, *Explanation in Social Science* (Chicago: Aldine, 1963), p. 180.
173. Dennis Donoghue, *The Sovereign Ghost* (Berkeley: Univ. of California Press, 1976), pp. 40–41.
174. Maurice Blanchot quoted in John Blegen, "Writing the Question," *Diacritics* 2, no. 2 (summer 1972), 14.
175. Monegal, "Borges and *La Nouvelle Critique*," p. 33.
176. Fredric Jameson, "Of Islands and Trenches," *Diacritics* 7, no. 2 (summer 1977), p. 2.
177. Geoffrey Hartman, "Remarks on the Psychology of the Critic," *Salmagundi*, no. 43 (winter 1979), p. 133.
178. Perrone-Moises, "Intertexte," p. 383.
179. Sylvere Lotringer, "The Game of the Name," *Diacritics* 3, no. 2 (summer 1973): 8–9.
180. Ray, "Recognizing Recognition," pp. 32–33.
181. Jean Franco, "The Crisis of the Liberal Imagination," *Ideology and Literature* 1, no. 1 (1976–77): 12.
182. Starobinski, "On the Fundamental Gestures of Criticism," p. 513.
183. Eagleton, *Criticism and Idealism*, p. 89.
184. Hans Robert Jauss, "Interview," *Diacritics* 5, no. 1 (spring 1975): 55.

Part II

1. William Rueckert, "Love Lavished on Speech," *Chicago Review* 29, no. 4 (1978): 53.

Chapter 3

1. See Gass, "The Medium of Fiction," in *Fiction and the Figures of Life* (New York: Alfred A. Knopf, 1970), p. 29. (Hereafter cited as *Fiction*; article cited in text as "The Medium.")
2. See, for instance, Robert Boyers, "The Realism of Reading" (review of Gass's *World within the Word*), *Times Literary Supplement*, 3 November 1978, pp. 1274–75, and R. E.

Johnson, "Structuralism and the Reading of Contemporary Fiction," *Soundings* 58, no. 2 (1975): 281–306.

3. Richard J. Schneider, "The Fortunate Fall in William Gass's *Omensetter's Luck*," *Critique* 18, no. 1 (1976): 5–20.

4. "Philosophy and the Form of Fiction," in *Fiction*, p. 10. (Cited in text as "Philosophy.")

5. Ned French proposes a somewhat different line of development in "Against the Grain: Theory and Practice in the Work of William H. Gass," *Iowa Review* 7, no. 1 (1976): 96–107.

6. Gass, "Carrots, Noses, Snow, Rose, Roses," in *The World within the Word* (New York: Alfred A. Knopf, 1978), pp. 297–302. (Hereafter cited as *World*; article cited in text as "Carrots.")

7. "The Artist and Society," in *Fiction*, pp. 284, 282. (Cited in text as "The Artist.")

8. "The Stylization of Desire," in *Fiction*, pp. 204–5. (Cited in text as "Stylization.")

9. "The Concept of Character in Fiction," in *Fiction*, p. 44. (Cited in text as "Character.")

10. "The Doomed in Their Sinking," in *World*, p. 14. (Cited in text as "The Doomed.")

11. Jeffrey L. Duncan, "A Conversation with Stanley Elkin and William Gass," *Iowa Review* 7, no. 1 (1976): 66, 68.

12. Gass, "Mad Meg" [from "The Tunnel"], *Iowa Review* 7, no. 1 (1976): 90–93.

13. Larry McCaffery discusses the debt to Valéry in "The Art of Metafiction," *Critique* 18, no. 1 (1976): 29–30.

14. "Groping for Trouts," in *World*, p. 263. (Cited in text as "Trouts.")

15. "The Ontology of the Sentence, or How to Make a World of Words," in *World*, p. 332. (Cited in text as "Ontology.")

16. "Gertrude Stein and the Geography of the Sentence," in *World*, p. 97. (Cited in text as "Gertrude Stein.")

17. "In Terms of the Toenail: Fiction and the Figures of Life," in *Fiction*, pp. 75, 70. (Cited in text as "Toenail.")

18. Gass, "In the Heart of the Heart of the Country," in *"In the Heart of the Heart of the Country" and Other Stories* (New York: Harper and Row, 1968), pp. 172–206. A very suggestive reading of this story is Frederick Busch, "But This Is What It Is to Live in Hell," *Modern Fiction Studies* 19, no. 1 (1973): 97–108.

19. David Hills, "Reply to Gass," *Journal of Philosophy* 73, no. 19 (1976): 740.

20. Gass, "Koh Whistles Up a Wind" [from "The Tunnel"], *Tri-Quarterly*, no. 38 (winter 1977), p. 197.

21. Patrick Maynard, "Professor Gass's Transformations," *Journal of Philosophy* 73, no. 19 (1976): 743.

22. All of these suggestions have been made, at one time or another, by readers of *Omensetter's Luck* and *Willie Master's Lonesome Wife*. Tony Tanner's "Games American Writers Play" is one of the few essays that manages to avoid a mimetic reading of the latter (despite its extravagant and forbidding formal pyrotechniques)—see *Salmagundi* 35, no. 4 (fall 1976): 110–40.

23. Gass, "Why Windows Are Important to Me" [from "The Tunnel"], *Tri-Quarterly*, no. 20 (winter 1971), pp. 292–98.

24. Duncan, "Conversation," pp. 74, 64–65.

25. Gass, *Willie Master's Lonesome Wife*, published as *Tri-Quarterly* supplement no. 2 (Evanston, Ill.: Northwestern Univ. Press, 1968). While the text itself is unpaginated, I follow McCaffery ("The Art of Metafiction") in numbering each colored section separately—here, white section, p. 4.

26. McCaffery takes the opposite view, that Gass enormously expands on Joyce's simpler framework, in "The Art of Metafiction."

27. See Busch, "But This Is What It Is to Live in Hell," and Gass's own comments in "Pole-Vaulting in Top Hats: A Public Conversation with John Barth, William Gass, and Ishmael Reed," *Modern Fiction Studies* 22, no. 2 (1976): 147.
28. Bruce Bassoff, "The Sacrificial World of William Gass," *Critique* 18, no. 1 (1976): 41.
29. "Three Photos of Colette," in *World*, pp. 144–45. (Cited in text as "Colette.")
30. See McCaffery, "The Art of Metafiction."
31. *Willie Master's*, olive section, pp. 22–24.
32. Gass, "Susu, I Approach You in My Dreams," *Tri-Quarterly*, no. 42 (spring 1978), p. 124.
33. Gass, *On Being Blue* (Boston: David R. Godine, 1976), p. 5. (Hereafter cited as *Blue*.)
34. Duncan, "Conversation," p. 64.
35. Bassoff, "Sacrificial World," p. 37.
36. "Susu, I Approach You," pp. 126–29.
37. Ibid., pp. 133–34.
38. For an alternative reading, see William Rueckert, "Love Lavished on Speech," *Chicago Review* 29, no. 4 (1978): 54.
39. Rueckert has a more hopeful reading, ibid., p. 59.
40. "Paul Valéry," in *World*, p. 169. (Cited in text as "Valéry.")
41. "The Anatomy of Mind," in *World*, p. 217. (Cited in text as "Anatomy.")
42. "Sartre on Theater," in *World*, pp. 182–83.
43. "The Case of the Obliging Stranger," in *Fiction*, pp. 230–31. (Cited in text as "Stranger.")
44. Maynard, "Professor Gass's Transformations," p. 742.
45. Boyers, "The Realism of Reading," p. 1274.
46. Duncan, "Conversation," p. 56.
47. Hills, "Reply to Gass," p. 739.
48. Ibid., p. 741.
49. Ibid., p. 740.
50. That this quote appears in "The Case of the Obliging Stranger" (p. 262) shows that this tendency actually antedates Gass's more literary indulgences.
51. "Mr. Blotner, Mr. Feaster, and Mr. Faulkner," in *World*, p. 57 (cited in text as "Mr. Blotner"); "Gertrude Stein," p. 63; *Blue*, p. 44.
52. This position is later refined to make the relations that a sentence establishes wholly verbal rather than "metaphysical."
53. "Even if, by All the Oxen in the World," in *Fiction*, pp. 272–74.
54. Ned French is both right and wrong in saying that Gass's aestheticism has social roots. Gass does repudiate commodity culture, but does not seem to see it as a passing historical stage, nor does the condition Gass associates with arts seem to be capable of serving as a model for social renovation. See French, "Against the Grain," pp. 100–101.
55. "Why Windows Are Important to Me," p. 306.
56. Boyers, "The Realism of Reading," p. 1274.

Chapter Four

1. Dennis Donoghue, "Sweepstakes," *New York Review of Books*, 28 September 1967, p. 6.
2. See Robert Boyers and Maxine Bernstein, "Women, the Arts, and the Politics of Culture: An Interview with Susan Sontag," *Salmagundi*, nos. 31–32 (fall 1975/winter 1976), pp. 29–30, for example.
3. Sontag, "Against Interpretation," in *Against Interpretation and Other Essays* (1966;

rpt. ed. New York: Dell Publishing Co., 1969), p. 23. The volume is hereafter cited as *A.I.*, the article is cited in text as *A.I.*).

4. "Spiritual Style in the Films of Robert Bresson," in *A.I.*, pp. 191–92.

5. Paul Velde, "Polymorphous on Sunday: The Sontag Sensibility," *Commonweal*, 24 June 1966, p. 391.

6. *Brother Carl: A Filmscript by Susan Sontag* (New York: Farrar, Straus, and Giroux, 1974), pp. viii–ix, xiv. (Hereafter cited as *Carl*.)

7. In an interview on "The Dick Cavett Show," 1 December 1978.

8. Sontag, "The Aesthetics of Silence," in *Styles of Radical Will* (New York: Farrar, Straus and Giroux, 1969), p. 29. (The volume is hereafter cited as *Will*; the article is cited in text as "Silence.")

9. Sontag, "Debriefing," in *I, etcetera* (New York: Farrar, Straus and Giroux, 1979), pp. 51–52. (Hereafter cited as *I, etc.*)

10. Donoghue, "Sweepstakes," pp. 6, 8; Louis D. Rubin, Jr., "Susan Sontag and the Camp Followers," *Sewanee Review* 82, no. 3 (summer 1974): 503.

11. Richard Gilman, "Susan Sontag and the Question of the New," *The New Republic*, 3 May 1969, p. 25.

12. In the 1978 Cavett interview.

13. "Old Complaints Revisited," in *I, etc.*, p. 142.

14. "Baby," in *I, etc.*, pp. 147–48.

15. "Project for a Trip to China," in *I, etc.*, pp. 10–12. (Cited in text as "Project.")

16. " 'Thinking Against Oneself ': Reflections on Cioran," in *Will*, p. 78. (Cited in text as "Thinking.")

17. Sontag, *On Photography* (New York: Farrar, Straus and Giroux, 1977), pp. 23–24. (Hereafter cited as *Photography*.)

18. "On Style," in *A.I.* , p. 38.

19. "Trip to Hanoi," in *Will*, p. 207. (Cited in text as "Hanoi.")

20. Boyers and Bernstein, "Women, the Arts," pp. 39–40.

21. "The Pornographic Imagination," in *Will*, pp. 34, 41–42. (Cited in text as "Imagination.")

22. "American Spirits," in *I, etc.*, pp. 55–56.

23. "Bergman's *Persona*," in *Will*, pp. 132, 135–36, 142, 144–45. (Cited in text as "Bergman.")

24. Martin Tucker, "Please Don't Eat the Cannibals," *Commonweal*, 5 December 1969, p. 306; Edgardo Cozarinsky, quoted on back cover of *Carl*.

25. "Nathalie Sarraute and the Novel," in *A.I.*, p. 117. (Cited in text as "Sarraute.")

26. "One Culture and the New Sensibility," in *A.I.*, pp. 296–97. (Cited in text as "One Culture.")

27. "Godard's *Vivre Sa Vie*," in *A.I.*, pp. 200–201. (Cited in text as "Godard's *Vivre*.")

28. "The Death of Tragedy," in *A.I.*, p. 140.

29. William Gass, "The Evil Demiurge," in *Fiction and the Figures of Life* (New York: Alfred A. Knopf, 1970), p. 257.

30. "Simone Weil," in *A.I.*, p. 59.

31. William Gass, "Wisconsin Death Trip," in *The World within the Word* (New York: Alfred A. Knopf, 1978), pp. 40, 44.

32. Velde, "Polymorphous on Sunday," p. 390.

33. "The Anthropologist as Hero," in *A.I.*, p. 78.

34. George P. Elliott, "High Prophetess of High Fashion" (review of *On Photography*), *Times Literary Supplement*, no. 3964 (17 March 1978), p. 304.

35. Rubin, "Susan Sontag and the Camp Followers," p. 504.

36. *Illness as Metaphor* (New York: Farrar, Straus, and Giroux, 1978), pp. 84–85. (Hereafter cited as *Illness*.)

37. Elliott, "High Prophetess," p. 304; see also Benjamin DeMott, "Susan Sontag: To Outrage and Back," *Atlantic*, October 1978, pp. 96–99.

38. "Notes on 'Camp,'" in *A.I.*, p. 277 (cited in text as "Camp"); "On Style," p. 40.

39. Richard Gilman, "Susan Sontag and the Question of the New," *New Republic*, 3 May 1969, p. 24.

40. Sontag, "Fascinating Fascism," *New York Review of Books*, 6 February 1975, pp. 23–30.

41. Robert Melville, "Images of the Instant Past," *Encounter*, November 1978, p. 69.

42. DeMott, "Susan Sontag," p. 96.

43. Gilman, "Susan Sontag," p. 23.

44. See Emile Caporiya, "The Age of Allegiance," *Saturday Review*, 3 May 1969, p. 29, on this point.

45. "Godard," in *Will*, pp. 170–71.

46. Boyers and Bernstein, "Women, the Arts," pp. 45, 32.

47. Ibid., p. 32.

48. Gilman, "Susan Sontag," p. 25.

49. Boyers and Bernstein, "Women, the Arts," p. 47.

50. Ibid., p. 42.

51. Ibid., p. 35.

52. Ibid., p. 30.

53. Gilman, "Susan Sontag," p. 24.

54. Sontag, "Reflections: Approaching Artaud," *New Yorker*, 19 May 1973, p. 40.

55. See Elliott, "High Prophetess," and DeMott, "Susan Sontag," for split reviews; Melville, "Images of the Instant Past," and Penelope Houston, review of *On Photography*, in *Sight and Sound* 47, no. 4 (1978): 265, are among the more enthusiastic reviewers of *On Photography*.

56. Houston, review of *On Photography*.

57. Walter Benjamin, "The Work of Art in the Age of Mechanical Reproduction," in *Illuminations*, ed. Hannah Arendt and trans. Harry Zohn (New York: Schocken Books, 1969), pp. 218, 222, 223.

58. Ibid., p. 218.

59. Ibid., p. 241.

60. Cf. Caporiya, "Age of Allegiance."

61. Nietzsche, "Natural History of Morals," in *Basic Writings of Nietzsche*, ed. Walter Kaufmann (New York: Modern Library, 1966), p. 287.

62. Gilman, "Susan Sontag," p. 24.

63. Boyers and Bernstein, "Women, the Arts," p. 47.

64. Ibid., p. 47.

Part III

1. Bloom, *The Anxiety of Influence: A Theory of Poetry* (New York: Oxford Univ. Press, 1973), pp. 12–13.

2. David Hirsch, "Deep Metaphors and Shallow Structures," *Sewanee Review* 85, no. 1 (1977): 162.

3. Jerome McGann, "Formalism, Savagery, and Care: The Function of Criticism Once Again," *Critical Inquiry* 2, no. 3 (1976): 629.

4. Jonathan Culler, "Presupposition and Intertextuality," *MLN* 91, no. 6 (1976): 1386.

5. Hirsch, "Deep Metaphors," p. 160, 166.

Chapter 5

1. Donald Marshall, "Beyond Formalism," *Partisan Review* 44, no. 1 (1977): 191.

2. Paul de Man, review of Bloom, *The Anxiety of Influence*, in *Comparative Literature* 26, no. 3 (1974): p. 270.

3. Joseph Riddel, review of Bloom, *Kabbalah and Criticism* and *Poetry and Repression*, in *Georgia Review* 30 (summer 1976): 989, 990–91.

4. Ibid., p. 989.

5. Ibid., pp. 992, 995, 998.

6. Jonathan Culler, "Reading and Misreading," *Yale Review* 65 (autumn 1975): 92.

7. Jonathan Culler, "Presupposition and Intertextuality," *MLN* 91, no. 6 (1976): 1382, 1387–88.

8. Joseph R. Kincaid, "Antithetical Criticism, Harold Bloom, and Victorian Poetry," *Victorian Poetry* 14, no. 4 (1976): 377.

9. Vincent Miller, "The American Sublime," *Yale Review* 47 (autumn 1977): 123.

10. William H. Pritchard, "The Hermeneutical Mafia," *Hudson Review* 28, no. 4 (winter 1975–76): 610.

11. Edward Said, "Roads Taken and Not Taken," in *Directions for Criticism*, ed. Murray Krieger and L. S. Dembo (Madison: Univ. of Wisconsin Press, 1977), p. 47.

12. De Man, rev. of *Anxiety*, p. 272.

13. Riddel, rev. of *Kaballah* and *Repression*, p. 1005.

14. De Man, rev. of *Anxiety*, p. 269–70.

15. David Hirsch, "Deep Metaphors and Shallow Structures," *Sewanee Review* 85, no. 1 (1977): 163.

16. Howard Nemerov, "Figures of Thought," *Sewanee Review* 83, no. 1 (1975): 169.

17. Ronald Sukenick, "Misreading Bloom," *Partisan Review* 45, no. 4 (1978): 635–36.

18. Bloom, *Kabbalah and Criticism* (New York: Seabury Press, 1975), pp. 109, 121. (Hereafter cited as *Kabbalah*.)

19. Riddel, rev. of *Kabbalah* and *Repression*, pp. 991, 996.

20. See Kincaid, "Antithetical Criticism," p. 271.

21. William H. Pritchard, "Mr. Bloom in Yeatsville," *Partisan Review* 38, no. 1 (1971): 107.

22. Bloom, *A Map of Misreading* (New York: Oxford Univ. Press, 1975), p. 29. (Hereafter cited as *Map*.)

23. Kincaid, "Antithetical Criticism," p. 373.

24. Riddel, rev. of *Kabbalah* and *Repression*, p. 1005.

25. Culler, "Reading and Misreading," p. 93.

26. De Man, rev. of *Anxiety*, p. 270.

27. Bloom, *The Anxiety of Influence: A Theory of Poetry* (New York: Oxford Univ. Press, 1973), p. 5. (Hereafter cited as *Anxiety*.)

28. Bloom, "Dark and Radiant Peripheries: Mark Strand and A. R. Ammons," in *Figures of Capable Imagination* (New York: Seabury Press, 1976), pp. 154–55. (Hereafter cited as *Figures*.)

29. Cary Nelson, "Reading Criticism," *PLMA* 91, no. 5 (1975): 803.

30. Bloom, *Shelley's Mythmaking* (1959; rpt. ed. Ithaca, N.Y.: Cornell Univ. Press, 1969), p. 3. (Hereafter cited as *Shelley*.)

31. Bloom, *The Visionary Company* (Garden City, N.Y.: Doubleday, 1961), p. 427.

32. Bloom, *Blake's Apocalypse* (Garden City, N.Y.: Doubleday, 1963), pp. 190–91.

33. Bloom, "To Reason with a Later Reason: Romanticism and the Rational," in *The Ringers in the Tower: Studies in Romantic Tradition* (Chicago: Univ. of Chicago Press, 1971), pp. 323–24. (Hereafter cited as *Ringers*; article cited in text as "To Reason.")

34. Bloom, *Poetry and Repression* (New Haven: Yale Univ. Press, 1976), p. 14. (Hereafter cited as *Repression*.)

35. Bloom, *Yeats* (New York: Oxford Univ. Press, 1970), p. 179.

36. Stuart Ende, review of *A Map of Misreading*, *Georgia Review* 29, no. 2 (1975): 509–10.

37. "The Internalization of Quest Romance," in *Ringers*, pp. 13–54, 16, 17. (Cited in text as "Quest Romance.")

38. "Bacchus and Merlin: The Dialectic of Romantic Poetry in America," in *Ringers*, pp. 301, 303.

39. "Wallace Stevens: The Poems of Our Climate," in *Figures*, pp. 118, 119.

40. Bloom, *Wallace Stevens* (Ithaca, N.Y.: Cornell Univ. Press, 1977), p. 1. (Hereafter cited as *Stevens*.)

41. Bloom, *The Flight to Lucifer: A Gnostic Fantasy* (New York: Farrar, Straus and Giroux. 1979), p. 193. (Hereafter cited as *Flight*.)

42. *Repression*, p. 27.

43. Jonathan Culler, "Presupposition and Intertextuality," *MLN* 91, no. 6 (1976): 1386.

44. *Kabbalah*, p. 97; see also p. 125.

45. Kincaid, "Antithetical Criticism," p. 372.

46. Riddel, review of *Kabbalah* and *Repression*, pp. 991–93.

47. Jerome McGann, "Formalism, Savagery, and Care: The Function of Criticism Once Again," *Critical Inquiry* 2, no. 3 (1976): 617.

48. Geoffrey Hartman, "War in Heaven," *Diacritics* 3, no. 1 (spring 1973): 27, 28.

49. De Man, review of *Anxiety*, pp. 271, 274–75.

50. Culler, "Presupposition and Intertextuality," pp. 1386, 1388.

51. See Riddel, review of *Kabbalah* and *Repression*, p. 994, and Culler, "Misreading," p. 94.

52. "On Ginsberg's *Kaddish*," in *Ringers*, p. 213.

53. De Man, review of *Anxiety*, p. 271.

54. Jacques Lacan, in *Ecrits* (Paris: Seuil, 1966), and in the translated selections as well (*Ecrits: A Selection*, trans. Alan Sheridan [New York: W. W. Norton, 1977]).

55. Riddel, review of *Kabbalah* and *Repression*, p. 995.

56. Pritchard, "Hermeneutical Mafia," p. 85.

57. Kincaid, "Antithetical Criticism," p. 70.

58. McGann, "Formalism," p. 610.

59. Cf. Robert Scholes's review of *The Anxiety of Influence*, in *Journal of English and German Philology* 73 (April 1974): 266–68.

60. Culler, "Presupposition and Intertextuality," pp. 1387–88.

61. See McGann, "Formalism," and Gerald Graff, "Fear and Trembling at Yale," *American Scholar* 46 (fall 1977): 467–82.

62. Hartman, "War in Heaven," p. 31.

63. Riddel, review of *Kabbalah* and *Repression*, p. 1004.

Chapter Six

1. Bernard Bergonzi, "A Grid of Codes," *Encounter* 45, no. 1 (July 1975): 52.

2. Fredric Jameson, "The Ideology of the Text," *Salmagundi*, nos. 31–32 (fall 1975/winter 1976), p. 208.

3. Barthes, "The Death of the Author," in *Image/Music/Text*, selected and trans. Stephen Heath (New York: Hill and Wang, 1977), pp. 143, 145, 148. (Hereafter cited as *Image*.)

4. Barthes, *A Lover's Discourse: Fragments*, trans. Richard Howard (New York: Hill and Wang, 1978), p. 186n. (Hereafter cited as *Discourse*.)

5. David Hirsch, "Deep Metaphors and Shallow Structures," *Sewanee Review* 85, no. 1 (1977): 161.

6. Jacques Ehrmann, *Structuralism* (New York: Anchor Books, 1970), p. viii.

7. Leo Bersani, "Is There A Science of Literature?" *Partisan Review* 39, no. 4 (1972): 553.

8. Graham Hough, "The Importation of Roland Barthes," *Times Literary Supplement*, no. 3951 (9 December 1977), p. 1443.

9. Jonathan Culler, "The Ever-Moving Finger," *Times Literary Supplement* no. 3782 (30 August 1974), p. 934.

10. *Roland Barthes by Roland Barthes*, trans. Richard Howard (New York: Hill and Wang, p. 168. (Hereafter cited as *Roland Barthes*.)

11. Stephen Koch, "Melancholy King of Cats," *Saturday Review of Books*, 2 September 1978, p. 34.

12. "Rhetoric of the Image," in *Image*, pp. 33, 48–49.

13. Koch, "Melancholy King of Cats," p. 34.

14. Bergonzi, "Grid of Codes," pp. 57–58.

15. Leo Bersani, "From Bachelard to Barthes," *Partisan Review* 34, no. 2 (1967): 215.

16. Barthes, *Mythologies*, trans. Annette Lavers (New York: Hill and Wang, 1972), pp. 34–35.

17. For the critical reception of Barthes in France, see Louis-Jean Calvet, *Roland Barthes: Un regard politique sur le signe* (Paris: Payot, 1973), p. 129 and passim.

18. Geoffrey Hartman, "Signs and Symbols," *New York Times Book Review*, 4 February 1979, p. 12.

19. "The Grain of the Voice," in *Image*, p. 179.

20. Barthes, *Writing Degree Zero*, trans. Annette Lavers and Colin Smith (Boston: Beacon Press, 1970), p. 30. (Hereafter cited as *Zero*.)

21. Culler, "The Ever-Moving Finger," p. 934.

22. "A Note on the Text," in Barthes, *The Pleasure of the Text*, trans. Richard Miller (New York: Hill and Wang, 1975), p. v. (Hereafter cited as *Pleasure*.)

23. Stephen Heath, Translator's Note, in *Image*, p. 7.

24. Ibid.

25. Culler, "The Ever-Moving Finger," p. 934.

26. Barthes, *Sade/Fourier/Loyola*, trans. Richard Miller (New York: Hill and Wang, 1976), p. 110.

27. Koch, "Melancholy King of Cats," p. 33.

28. David Ellis, "Barthes and Autobiography," *Cambridge Quarterly* 7, no. 3 (1977): 253.

29. "From Work to Text," in *Image*, pp. 160–61, 159.

30. Steven Ungar, "RB: The Third Degree," *Diacritics*, 7 no. 1 (spring 1977): 72–73.

31. Hartman, "Signs and Symbols," p. 34.

32. Koch, "Melancholy King of Cats," p. 34.

33. Edward Said, "Roads Taken and Not Taken in Contemporary Criticism," in *Directions for Criticism*, ed. Murray Krieger and L. S. Dembo (Madison: Univ. of Wisconsin Press, 1977), pp. 38, 39, 48.

34. Hayden White, "The Absurdist Moment in Contemporary Literary Theory," ibid., p. 106.

35. Koch, "Melancholy King of Cats," p. 33.

36. Culler, "The Ever-Moving Finger," p. 934.

37. "From Work to Text," p. 160, and *Roland Barthes*, p. 34. See also Jonathan Culler's comparison of Bloom and Barthes in "Presupposition and Intertextuality," *MLN* 91, no. 6 (December 1976): 1380–97.

38. Ungar, "RB," p. 76.

39. Michael Riffaterre, "*Sade*, or Text as Fantasy," *Diacritics* 2, no. 3 (fall 1972): 2–9.

40. Koch, "Melancholy King of Cats," pp. 33–34.

41. Hartman, "Signs and Symbols," p. 34.

42. Stephen Heath, *Le Vertige du déplacement: Lecture de Barthes* (Paris: Fayard, 1974).

43. See Ungar's discussion of this in "RB," pp. 76–77.

44. Heath, *Le Vertige*, p. 175.

45. "The Third Meaning," in *Image*, pp. 66–67.

46. Koch, "Melancholy King of Cats," p. 34.

47. "The Structuralist Activity," in Barthes, *Critical Essays*, trans. Richard Howard (Evanston: Northwestern Univ. Press, 1972), pp. 214–15. (Hereafter cited as *Essays*.)

48. "Taking Sides," p. 169, and "What Is Criticism?," p. 257, in *Essays*.

49. Barthes, *Elements of Semiology*, trans. Annette Lavers and Colin Smith (Boston: Beacon Press, 1970), pp. 93–94. (Hereafter cited as *Elements*.)

50. *Roland Barthes*, p. 60. Heath's *Le Vertige* discusses these shifts of level.

51. Philip Thody, *Roland Barthes: A Conservative Estimate* (London: The Macmillan Press, 1977), p. 52.

52. See Michael Riffaterre, "French Formalism," in *The Frontiers of Literary Criticism*, ed. David H. Malone, Univ. of Southern California Studies in Comparative Literature, vol. 5 (Los Angeles: Hennessey and Ingalls, 1974), pp. 93–119.

53. Koch, "Melancholy King of Cats," p. 34.

54. Barthes, *S/Z*, trans. Richard Miller (New York: Hill and Wang, 1974), pp. 106–7.

55. "Introduction to the Structural Analysis of Narratives," in *Image*, p. 124.

56. See the "Overture" to Claude Lévi-Strauss, *The Raw and the Cooked*, trans. John Weightman and Doreen Weightman (New York: Harper and Row, 1969).

57. Cf. Jonathan Culler's discussion in *Structuralist Poetics* (London: Routledge & Kegan Paul, 1974).

58. Heath treats this at length in *Le Vertige*.

59. "The Imagination of the Sign," in *Critical Essays*, p. 10.

60. "Literature and Signification," in *Critical Essays*, pp. 268–69, 267.

61. Derrida quoted in Bersani, "Is There A Science of Literature?," p. 552.

62. Lacan's question appears simply as a footnote to "Introduction to the Structural Analysis of Narratives," in *Image*, p. 112.

63. Gregory L. Ulmer, "Fetishism in Roland Barthes's Nietzschean Phase," *Papers in Language and Literature* 14 (summer 1978): 347, 338–39.

64. *Discourse*, p. 202; *Roland Barthes*, p. 166.

65. "Change the Object Itself: Mythology Today," in *Image*, pp. 166–67.

66. Mary Ann Caws, "*Tel Quel*: Text and Revolution," *Diacritics* 3, no. 1 (spring 1973): 2–8.

67. "Lesson in Writing," in *Image*, pp. 173, 175–76.

68. Culler, "The Ever-Moving Finger," p. 934.

69. Ulmer suggest this possibility in "Fetishism in Roland Barthes."

70. Heath, *Le Vertige*, pp. 193–94.

71. "Writers, Intellectuals, Teachers," in *Image*, p. 198.

72. See Ulmer, "Fetishism in Roland Barthes," p. 334.

73. "The Struggle with the Angel," in *Image*, p. 126. See also Heath's translator's note, p. 10.

74. Cf. Heath, *Le Vertige*.

75. "Diderot, Brecht, Eisenstein," in *Image*, pp. 69–70, 76–77.

76. See Ulmer, "Fetishism in Roland Barthes."

77. *On Racine*, trans. Richard Howard (New York: Hill and Wang, 1964), pp. 3–4.

78. Riffaterre, "*Sade*, or Text as Fantasy," pp. 3, 4.

79. Ibid.

80. Ungar, "RB," p. 76.

81. Ulmer, "Fetishism in Roland Barthes," p. 354.

82. Heath, *Le Vertige*, p. 195.

83. Culler, "The Ever-Moving Finger," p. 934.

84. See Ellis's discussion of the unusual nature of Barthes's autobiographical persona in "Barthes and Autobiography."

85. Heath, *Le Vertige*, speaks of Barthes's "ethics of discourse," pp. 180–89.

Afterword

1. "Twenty Writers Select the New Classics," *New York Times Book Review*, 3 June 1979, p. 12.

2. Irvin Ehrenpreis, "Literature in Trouble," *The New York Review of Books*, 28 June 1979, p. 40.

3. Nonetheless, see Gerald Graff's spirited defense of mimesis in *Literature against Itself* (Chicago: Univ. of Chicago Press, 1979).

4. Barbara Johnson, "The Frame of Reference: Poe, Lacan, Derrida," in *Psychoanalysis and the Question of the Text*, ed. Geoffrey Hartman, Selected Papers from the English Institute, 1976–77, n.s.,no. 2 (Baltimore: Johns Hopkins Univ. Press, 1978), p. 170.

5. See, for example, Bloom's own references to Richard Rorty and Thomas Frosch in *Poetry and Repression* (New Haven: Yale Univ. Press, 1976), p. 21, 26–27, as well as the suggestive use made of Bloom in Sandra M. Gilbert and Susan Gubar, *The Madwoman in the Attic* (New Haven: Yale Univ. Press, 1979).

Index

The Johns Hopkins University Press

Bruss: Beautiful Theories

This book was composed in Baskerville text and display type
by Brushwood Graphics from a design by Alan Carter.
It was printed on S. D. Warren's 50-lb. Sebago Eggshell paper
and bound in Holliston Roxite A cloth by Universal
Lithographers.